Henry Wilton & Elizabeth Bond Descendants In America

Compiled & Edited By
Aaron Z. Wilton &
Clyde C. Wilton

Order this book online at www.trafford.com
or email orders@trafford.com

Most Trafford titles are also available at major online book retailers.

© Copyright 2009 Aaron Z. Wilton and co-author Clyde C. Wilton
All rights reserved. No part of this publication may be reproduced, stored in a retrieval system, or transmitted, in any form or by any means, electronic, mechanical, photocopying, recording, or otherwise, without the written prior permission of the author.

Note for Librarians: A cataloguing record for this book is available from Library and Archives Canada at www.collectionscanada.ca/amicus/index-e.html

Printed in Victoria, BC, Canada.

ISBN: 978-1-4269-0459-2 (sc)

Our mission is to efficiently provide the world's finest, most comprehensive book publishing service, enabling every author to experience success. To find out how to publish your book, your way, and have it available worldwide, visit us online at www.trafford.com

Trafford rev. 8/12/2009

 www.trafford.com

North America & international
toll-free: 1 888 232 4444 (USA & Canada)
phone: 250 383 6864 ♦ fax: 812 355 4082

Table Of Contents

Preface	xi
Henry Wilton (1769-1820) 1st generation in America	1-6
Thomas Wilton (2nd generation)	7-12
Charles F. Wilton (3rd generation)	13-18
Thomas Abslum Wilton (4th generation)	19-24
Freedus Ezra Wilton (5th generation)	25-27
Jesse Ruell Wilton (6th generation)	28-31
Bobbye Loine Wilton (7th generation)	32-33
Bama Loine Roberts (8th generation)	34-35
Luther Eppie Wilton (6th generation)	36-37
George Keith Wilton (7th generation)	38-39
Kimberly Faye Wilton (8th generation)	40-41
George Keith Jr. Wilton (8th generation)	42-43
Frank Edward Wilton (7th generation)	44
Eater Virgil Wilton (6th generation)	45-46
Alvin Henry Wilton (5th generation)	47-49
James Everett Wilton (6th generation)	50-53
Everett Waylin Wilton (7th generation)	54-55
Ora Lenora Wilton (7th generation)	56
Karen Larue Shelton (8th generation)	57-58
Melvin Cleo Wilton (6th generation)	59-60
Judy Inez Wilton (7th generation)	61
Ora Izora Wilton (6th generation)	62-63
Linda Lou Dewoody (7th generation)	64-67
David Allan Griffin (8th generation)	68-69
Gregg Randel Griffin (8th generation)	70
Terry Lynn Dewoody (7th generation)	71
Silas Wilton (5th generation)	72-74
Carless Carl Wilton (6th generation)	75-78
Cora Belle Wilton (6th generation)	79
Ruel Calvin Wilton (6th generation)	80-81
Nola E. Wilton (6th generation)	82
Velma Lucile Wilton (6th generation)	83
Cyrus Wilton (5th generation)	84-86
Ira John Wilton (5th generation)	87-90
Lou D. Wilton (6th generation)	91-93
Janice Darlene Wilton (7th generation)	94-97
Dana Darleen Hall (8th generation)	98-99
Norma Dee Hall (8th generation)	100

Twilla Dawn Eaton (8th generation)...101
Ira John Wilton (7th generation)...102
Mary Lucille Wilton (6th generation)..103-105
Gladys Nell Wilton (6th generation)..106-107
Linda Frances Kay (7th generation)...108-109
Paula Nell Kay (7th generation)..110
Bobby Louis Kay (7th generation)...111
Alvin Henry Wilton (6th generation)..112-114
Alva Eulene Wilton (7th generation)..115-116
Helen Ruth Wilton (6th generation)..117
Donnie Jay Brown (7th generation)..118-119
Travis Ray Brown (7th generation)...120
Billie Duane Wilton (6th generation)..121-122
Gerald Ray Wilton (7th generation)..123-124
Ida May Wilton (5th generation)...125-127
Norris Truett Reynolds (6th generation)...128-129
Emma Livona Wilton (5th generation)..130-132
Ollie Belgium McCasland (6th generation)...133-136
Clayton Dee Haskew (7th generation)..137-138
Hettie Jewel McCasland (6th generation)...139-141
Verdia Ellen McCasland (6th generation)...142-144
Carrie Esther McCasland (6th generation)..145-147
Josephine Inge (7th generation)..148-150
Charlotte Gail Criswell (8th generation)...151-152
Dora Elsie McCasland (6th generation)..153-155
Benjamin Harrison Wilton (5th generation)..156-158
Effa Belle Wilton (5th generation)..159-162
Ester Elzada Hannah (6th generation)...163-166
Wanda Joy Stephens (7th generation)...167-168
Janice Darlene Stephens (7th generation)..169
Sherry Jo Stephens (7th generation)...170
Olan Odessa Hannah (6th generation)...171-174
Dolores Lee Hannah (7th generation)...175-176
Jackie Kathleen Hannah (7th generation)..177
Ora Mae Inez Hannah (6th generation)...178-179
Gwendolyn Inez Bevers (7th generation)..180-181
Raymond Derrell Hannah (6th generation)...182-183
Anita Marie Hannah (7th generation)...184-185
James Eldon Hannah (6th generation)..186-188
Eldon Ray Hannah (7th generation)...189-190
Johnie Melvin Wilton (5th generation)...191-194
Melvin Wayman Wilton (6th generation)...195-198

Margie Nell Wilton (7th generation)...199-201
Cecil Don Wilton (7th generation)...202-204
Marlin Don Wilton (8th generation)...205-207
Cory Wayne Wilton (8th generation)..208-209
Lee Anne Wilton (8th generation)..210-211
Lloyd Orville Wilton (6th generation)...212-213
Wilma Fasline Wilton (6th generation)...214-216
David Michael Fry (7th generation)..217-218
Marsha Karen Fry (7th generation)..219-220
Melba Louise Wilton (6th generation)..221
Henry Franklin Wilton (4th generation)..222-226
Elmer Elisha Wilton (5th generation)..227-232
Luther Virgil Wilton (6th generation)..233-237
Luther Virgil Jr. Wilton (7th generation)...238-240
Charles Anthony Wilton (6th generation)...241-245
Connie Charles Wilton (7th generation)...246-247
Treva Daphane Wilton (7th generation)...248-249
Toni Dell Wilton (7th generation)...250-251
Curtis Lee Wilton (7th generation)...252-253
Clyde Chalmer Wilton (6th generation)...254-259
Aaron Zanoah Wilton (7th generation)..260-265
Regina Fawncyne Wilton (7th generation)...266-269
Kathy Ilene Wilton (7th generation)...270-274
Sherah R. Wimpee (8th generation)..275-276
Cynthia Joy Wimpee (8th generation)..277
Stanley Wilton (7th generation)..278-281
Amy Rosalie Wilton (5th generation)...282-285
Hazel Evelyn Parrish (6th generation)...286-290
Martha Laverne Marley (7th generation)..291-292
Patricia Ann Marley (7th generation)..293-294
Thomas Wayne Marley (7th generation)...295-296
Robert Wade Jr. Marley (7th generation)..297
Charles Victor Marley (7th generation)...298
Herbert Charles Parrish (6th generation)...299-301
Byron Newton Parrish (7th generation)..302-303
Norman Wilton Parrish (7th generation)..304
Roberta Jean Parrish (7th generation)...305
Charles Joseph Wilton (5th generation)..306-312
Thomas Vester Wilton (6th generation)...313-317
Emerson Van Wilton (6th generation)..318-322
Charles Vernon Wilton (7th generation)..323-324
Mary Jo Wilton (7th generation)...325-327

Michael A. Jr. Adams (8th generation)..328-329
Melissa Adams (8th generation)..330
Ann Michelle Adams (8th generation)...331
Melanie Adams (8th generation)..332
Matthew Joseph Adams (8th generation)..333-334
Timothy Mitchell Adams (8th generation)...335
Deborah Agnes Wilton (7th generation)..336
Jeremy Wahl Johnson (8th generation)..337-338
David Van Wilton (7th generation)..339
Catherine Elizabeth Wilton (7th generation)...340
Lona Oretha Wilton (6th generation)...341
Nola Oletha Wilton (6th generation)...342-343
Marquite Carol Little (7th generation)..344-345
Verna Faye Wilton (6th generation)..346-348
Carol Ann Crabtree (7th generation)...349-350
Thomas Blair Crabtree (7th generation)..351
Lee O'Norvell Wilton (6th generation)..352-354
Terri Lynn Wilton (7th generation)...355-356
Leland Norvell Wilton (7th generation)...357
Letha Fay Wilton (7th generation)...358
Charles Joseph Jr. Wilton (6th generation)..359
Charlene Lenoy Wilton (6th generation)...360
Sheila Darlene Jackson (7th generation)...361-362
Colleen Rebecca Wilton (6th generation)..363-364
Debra Deann Gary (7th generation)...365
John Alton Gary (7th generation)...366
Sherri Lorraine Gary (7th generation)..367
Mary Alma Wilton (5th generation)...368-372
Marjorie Helen Reynolds (6th generation)..373-379
Terri Lynn Tapp (7th generation)..380-383
Heather Nicole Brown (8th generation)..384-386
Tammy Jo Tapp (7th generation)..387-388
Herman Atwood Reynolds (6th generation).....................................389-390
Debra Jean Reynolds (7th generation)..391-392
Linda Kay Reynolds (7th generation)..393
Monty Duane Reynolds (7th generation)...394
James Weldon Reynolds (6th generation)...395-397
Gary Wayne Reynolds (7th generation)..398-399
Kenneth Wade Reynolds (7th generation)...400-401
David Alan Reynolds (7th generation)...402
Michael Bruce Reynolds (7th generation)...403
Verna Evelyn Reynolds (6th generation)..404-405

Clarence Chalmer Reynolds (6th generation)..406-407
Anne Elizabeth Reynolds (7th generation)...408
Joseph C. Wilton (3rd generation)..409-414
Sarah Frances Wilton (4th generation)..415-416
Harriett Carrie Wilton (4th generation)..417-418
Martha Wilton (4th generation)...419-420
Mary Wilton (4th generation)...421
Nona Wilton (4th generation)...422-423
Wilton English Wiley (5th generation)..424-426
Joseph S. Wilton (4th generation)..427-429
Nona Fay Wilton (5th generation)...430-431
Virgie Vivian Wilton (5th generation)..432
Wanda Vonciel Stubbs (6th generation)..433-434
Truman Kenneth Stubbs (6th generation)...435
Joseph Drexel Wilton (5th generation)..436
Vanzant V. Wilton (5th generation)...437
Rudolph Wilton (3rd generation)..438-440
Bertha Pauline Wilton (4th generation)...441-443
Blanche Mae Wilton (4th generation)..444
Mary Elizabeth Wilton (3rd generation)...445-446
William Franklin Burkett (4th generation)..447-450
Dorothea Edith Burkett (5th generation)..451-452
Elmer Franklin Burkett (5th generation)..453-456
Amos Franklin Burkett (6th generation)...457-458
Mildred Irene Burkett (6th generation)...459
Dorothea Edith Burkett (6th generation)..460
Helen Anna Burkett (6th generation)..461-462
Raymond Isaac Burkett (6th generation)...463
Mary Eileen Burkett (6th generation)...464
Jeroma Lee Burkett (6th generation)..465
Jane Lucille Burkett (6th generation)..466
Ione Maxine Burkett (6th generation)...467
Elmer Leroy Burkett (6th generation)...468
Mary Annise Burkett (4th generation)...469-472
Charles William Humphries (5th generation)...473-476
Vada Fay Humphries (6th generation)..477-479
Ben Humphries (5th generation)...480
James Humphries (5th generation)...481
Otto Franklin Humphries (5th generation)...482-483
Raymond Humphries (5th generation)...484
Ellen Wilton (3rd generation)..485
Charles Wilton (2nd generation)..486-487

ix

Sarah Agnes Wilton (3rd generation)..488-490
Laura Sophia Foster (4th generation)..491-492
Harriet Caroline Wilton (3rd generation)..493
Joseph Franklin Wilton (3rd generation)...494-497
Ida May Wilton (4th generation)..498-499
Ella Mae Scott (5th generation)..500-501
Rolla Walter Scott (5th generation)...502
Joseph H. Scott (5th generation)..503
Charles Glen Scott (5th generation)...504
Lois Scott (5th generation)...505
Floyd Scott (5th generation)..506
Mary Ella Wilton (4th generation)...507-508
Joseph Charles Wilton (4th generation)..509
Nichols Wilton (4th generation)...510-511
Walter W. Wilton (4th generation)...512
Robert Harry Wilton (5th generation)..513-514
Sarah L. Wilton (4th generation)...515
Sophia Wilton (2nd generation)...516
Acknowledgements   518
Index   519-548

Preface to
Henry Wilton Descendants In America

Endeavoring to present a genealogical record of Wilton ancestors in a measured and easily read format, this work is the culmination of many years of interest in the Wilton Family genealogy. My interest was first peaked by my dad, Clyde Wilton, while I was in college in the 1960's, and over the intervening years, we have collaborated in researching the information that has become available to us. It has been more of a hobby for both of us, since most of the time, neither of us has had the resources or time to spend on tracing the necessary details. In later years, as retirement has approached, we have been more able to spend the time necessary to put together the information obtained over the years. This presentation is not intended to be the product that might come from a polished professional genealogist, but rather from a father and son partnership interested in preserving our family heritage for future generations.

Our first Wilton ancestor in America is traced back to one Henry Wilton who came to America in the 1790's. He was the descendant of Wiltons who were farmers living in the town of Stapleford in Cambridgeshire, England. Beginning about 1640, the first Henry Wilton settled in Stapleford, and until about 1769, there were five generations of Wiltons with the firstborn son given the name of Henry. Prior to living in Stapleford, the family line can be traced to the mid-1500's to the Hauxton area of Cambridgeshire.

The records for our first Wilton ancestor in America, Henry Wilton (c.1769-1820), are very sparse for his early years. Henry apparently arrived first in New York City and then settled in the community of Walton, in the county of Delaware, New York. There is some discrepancy about the actual date of arrival, which was sometime between 1793 and 1796. One record is found in "The History of Delaware County, 1797-1880," where there is mention of a "Henry Wilton, in 1793, where Mr. Harby lives." However, another record indicates that Henry's third child, Harry Wilton, was born in 1794 in England. Yet another record of a proceeding to transfer Henry's control of land in England to others, in which he is mentioned as being "present in court," carries a date of 1796.

Family tradition indicates that when Henry came to America, he brought with him his three sons, Henry, Richard and Harry Wilton. The story told is that when the family was preparing in England to leave by ship, Henry's wife, Elizabeth (Knott) Wilton, refused to board the ship. As a result, Elizabeth was left behind, and the rest of the family sailed on to America. Aside from family tradition, there has not been found any solid evidence to support or deny this story. However, since that is all we have to work with, so far, we must give it some credence. There are, however, a couple of problems with these facts. The first one is that if there was a divorce resulting from this separation by Henry and Elizabeth, there is no record yet found. A divorce would have been very uncommon and hard to obtain at that time. A more likely case would be for Elizabeth to return to her parents' home, but there are no records to support that supposition, either.

The tradition further states that after Henry and his three children arrived in New York, Henry remarried a woman with the last name of Bond. While in New York, Henry then had three children by the assumed second marriage, with children by the names of Thomas, Charles, and Sophia Wilton. If there was such a second marriage, it is wondered if that would make our ancestor a bigamist, since there is no record of a divorce from his first wife. It is curious that there is reference to Henry Wilton in "The History of Walton to 1875," which states that "the next farm up the brook, now owned by Joseph Harby, Sr., and son, was owned by Henry Wilton, whose moral character, I am sorry to say, was not well spoken of by the good people of the town." I am wondering if it might have been community knowledge back then that Henry had two wives, one in England and one in New York. At any rate, this branch of the family is where my own ancestry is traced, and hopefully someday information will come to light to clarify this "mystery."

To complete Henry's story, there is evidence that the family intended to leave New York in mid-1811 and to move to Illinois. There was a delay in their departure, due to an accidental death in the family, presumably the death of Henry's second wife. While still in New York, Henry married a third time to Mary Cook, who was a widow Fielden and who also had a daughter by the name of Jennie. Henry and Mary had a son by the name of John, while also still in New York. It was in the fall of 1811 that the family actually made the long trip to Illinois, settling first in the Shawneetown area of Gallatin County, Illinois. Henry and Mary had four other children while living in Illinois, named, William, Laura, Mariah, and Britanna Wilton.

Old Shawneetown, which is where Henry and family first landed in Illinois, is on the Ohio River, which also borders the northwest Kentucky area. At the time of Henry's move, Shawneetown was a bustling river town, which served as a port of entry and trading center for settlers in inland villages. Though there is no direct evidence, it is presumed that Henry must have arrived by boat by the usual route along the Ohio River, which started in Pennsylvania. At least part of Henry's family, his oldest son, Henry, did not make the trip to Illinois but settled in Pennsylvania.

Henry Wilton and family who arrived in Illinois were among those pioneers who braved the inland territory that was mainly wild and unsettled. Beginning from the Gallatin County area, the family branched out into the neighboring counties. The record for Henry ends about 1820 in the Gallatin and Saline counties area, but by 1850, branches of the family were found in the Hancock, Clinton, and Marion counties of Illinois.

There is another family tradition that about 1820, three of the Wilton brothers, probably Thomas, Charles, and William, were settled in Clinton County, where they were farming the land. During their first year, after planting a crop of corn, they had to sleep out in the cornfield at night, for fear that the Indians might burn their cabin.

While there are three separate branches of the Henry Wilton family, corresponding to Henry's three marriages, our emphasis in this book is to concentrate on descendents by the second marriage of Henry Wilton to Elizabeth Bond, which is the branch that we descended from. We had originally hoped to include all three branches, but due to time and resource considerations were forced to limit this work to one branch. Perhaps in a future edition the scope may be expanded.

To explain our treatment of the material of this work, we have recognized Henry Wilton (1769-1820) as the first Wilton ancestor in America and have numbered each successive generation after him. With Henry as the first generation to arrive in America, to this date there have been approximately 8 generations that have followed. The information presented comes in the form of a variety of detail, corresponding to the amount of information we have been able to assemble. In some cases, there is only a brief outline, but in other cases there are pictures and a biographical sketch along with the outline. The most detail comes from our own offshoot of the Henry Wilton/Elizabeth Bond branch of the tree, which is where we have the most familiarity. At times it has been frustrating in getting cooperation from various descendents to contribute information, so that has limited the amount of detail in many cases. In some cases, the descendant branches were largely unfamiliar and there was no direct contact with its members. In other cases the available resources and cooperation has been overwhelmingly positive. It is hoped that if there is a future edition of this work, other family members will see the value of providing information for generations to come.

The information presented here has come from a variety of sources, some of which are recognized in the acknowledgments section of this book. This book has been the result of many years of accumulating information, and it could not have been done alone. Along the way, others of similar genealogical interest have come along, and by sharing resources and data, what began as a brief outline was expanded into a fuller tree. A big help has recently been through the internet. Some resources, such as state and census records, which were once available largely only by making a personal appearance to search records, have been made available by internet search. That has greatly reduced the time necessary to gather and verify information.

It should be realized that just because a "fact" is seen here in print, it does not mean that we are claiming it to be the final word. What is included is the result of the best information currently available, but those "facts" will always be open to change as better information may become available.

In the treatment of genealogical material, the procedure has been to start with our first Wilton ancestor in America, Henry Wilton, and then to take each member of his family with Elizabeth Bond one at a time, following that "branch" as far as information was available. When that branch was exhausted, the next family member of Henry and Elizabeth was taken in succession. The same procedure was followed within each family within a branch. The first child in the family was followed to its conclusion before going back to the next member in like fashion. A table of contents and an index were included to help find individual members quickly. To conserve space, where a pedigree tree applied to multiple members of a family, the tree was included with just one member of the family, usually the first member, with a note indicating that the tree also applied to the rest of the siblings.

A discussion of our own Wilton heritage would not be complete without mentioning the Texas community of Winn Hill, located in Jack County, Texas, where Henry Franklin Wilton, 4th generation from Henry Wilton, and his brother, Thomas A. Wilton, settled in the 1880's. After our first ancestor, Henry Wilton, moved the family from New York to Illinois, our branch of the family eventually settled in Texas, following the Civil War. After living for awhile in Parker County, Texas, the family then moved to Jack County, where they purchased land near the Winn Hill Community and were employed in farming.

The site of the Winn Hill Community was located in Jack County, Texas, about 12 miles northwest of the city of Jacksboro. The community began its growth in the 1870's, largely as the result of its local rural school, a one-room schoolhouse which provided an elementary education. Although there was never a post office, there was a row of mail boxes located adjacent to a cemetery, later known as the Winn Hill Cemetery. In addition to the schoolhouse, the cemetery was a focal point for the community, and it was located across the road from the school. There was a tabernacle at the entrance to the cemetery where revival meetings and funerals for those buried in the cemetery were held.   The cemetery was established in the 1880's, and it was named after William H. Wynne, who was killed by Indians in 1863. In its earliest days, around 1858-1861, the Winn Hill community was located along the route of the Butterfield Stage/Overland Mail Route. The community also included a church, Bethany Baptist Church, which was located across a creek and just east of the schoolhouse.

    Wilton descendant, Clyde Wilton, who grew up in the Winn Hill vicinity between 1919 and 1940, had fond memories of the Winn Hill Community. Whenever he referred to Winn Hill, he thought of it as "the Holy Land," because that was where he had a number of life-changing experiences. Clyde was a Baptist minister, and he was reminded of the account in the Bible of Moses encountering God in the burning bush and the account of the Jews' receiving their "Promised Land," or the Land of Canaan. In like manner, Winn Hill was Clyde's "promised land," because the tabernacle by the cemetery was where he made his profession of faith; and, the Bethany Baptist Church at Winn Hill was where he attended church during his early years, where he preached his first sermon, where he was married, and where he first served as a pastor.

    Having also gone to school at Winn Hill, Clyde remembered the large one-room building that was used for the schoolhouse. The building was divided in the middle with a wall, and only the north half was in use at the time. When Clyde was at the school, there were only about 25 students who attended, and there was only one teacher. He recalled that there were some large blackboards on the north wall, and in one corner there was a large iron wood-burning stove that was used for heating. There was also a cloakroom by the entrance where the students left their coats and their sack lunches. The teacher then was Miss Edna Meyers, who had just finished her school training, and whom the students affectionately call "Miss Edna." After completing an elementary education at Winn Hill, the students usually continued their education at the high school at the nearest town of Jermyn, Texas. It was located about another six miles, northwest of Winn Hill.

Other memories of Winn Hill included the times that Clyde attended the Bethany Baptist Church. His family lived about a mile and a half from the church, and, as a boy, he remembered that the family usually went to church in their Model-T Ford. They attended Sunday School each Sunday morning, but only half the time a preacher was there to conduct the morning worship service. Sometimes a preacher would even come in the afternoon instead of Sunday morning. The preachers who came over the years were described as "fine people," some being unschooled, and some being very educated, but they all loved the Lord and faithfully brought the gospel of Christ to the community. Sundays were also a time to visit with friends, and on special occasions, the congregation brought the church benches out into the yard and had "dinner on the grounds."

While still a boy, Clyde recalled a particularly fond memory of an occasion when the church members were called upon to recite verses at the church. Mr. H.B. Fox was the Sunday School superintendent, and as was his usual custom, he called upon the adults to recite their favorite verse. However, on this occasion, Mr. Fox included the children, and Clyde was given the opportunity to participate. Being the only one he knew, Clyde promptly said his verse when called upon, "I had a little horse, and I fed him hay; it came a whirlwind and blew him away." To his amazement, Clyde was shocked that the people did not seem pleased with his recitation. It wasn't until later that he realized they were expecting a Bible verse.

As already mentioned, the scope of this work covers the descendants of Henry Wilton, the first of our Wilton ancestors to arrive in America from England, and his second wife, Elizabeth Bond. The hope has been that the information provided will enrich current and future generations of Wilton descendants, and to stimulate interest in others to carry on the job of preserving our Wilton heritage.

Henry Wilton (1769-1820)
[1st. Wilton Ancestor From England]

&

Elizabeth Bond (-1811)
& Family

Notes for Henry Wilton

The Henry Wilton family originated from Stapleford in Cambridgeshire, England, north of London. Henry Wilton, our first ancestor to arrive in America, was from a line of 5 generations of Wiltons living in Stapleford, going back to the mid-1600's, all with the eldest, and heir to the estate, named Henry. Prior to living in Stapleford, the family is traced to the surrounding area of Hauxton, Cambridgeshire, England. Our Henry's interest in the Wilton tract of land in Stapleford, England, which was used for farming, was sold about 1797. It is unclear whether Henry was actually present at the court proceeding for the land title sale, since various sources place him in New York between 1793 and 1797.

When Henry Wilton (c.1679-1820) came to America, there is a tradition that as the family, which then consisted of Henry, his wife, Elizabeth (Knot) Wilton and his three children, Harry, Richard, and Henry, prepared to board ship, Elizabeth refused to go aboard. As a result, she was left behind, and the rest of the family proceeded on toward America (information from Lenora Wilton, but original source unknown). The family members who continued on to America arrived first in New York City and then settled in Walton in Delaware County, New York. The available evidence suggests that Henry married a second time after arriving in New York to Elizabeth Bond. By the second marriage there were three other children, named Thomas, Charles, and Sophia Wilton. It is unclear whether Henry obtained a divorce from his first wife in England before marrying a second time.

According to the book, Past and Present Of Montgomery County (Illinois), after settling in Delaware County, New York, Henry purchased a farm, which he successfully cultivated for some time. There is also evidence that Henry may have been involved for a time in selling general merchandise, since there is a Wilton mentioned in the Business Men Of Walton in reference to a store opened by Chase & Chapman that was "very primitive in its stock…

Wilton succeeded him for a time...." There was also a court case in the Delaware County Court of Common Pleas, dated October 1, 1799, in which Henry Wilton made a complaint against one Elijah Goodrich for failure to pay him for "divers goods, wares, and merchandises...the sum of two hundred dollars." That case was later settled in June 1802 after appealing it to the New York Supreme Court. Henry Wilton is also mentioned in the 1800 Federal Census of Walton, Delaware County, New York, and in various land dealings in Delaware County 1802-1808.

In 1811, Henry decided to move to Illinois. About mid-1811, the family was set to leave New York, but they were delayed, when Henry's second wife died due to an accident (no other details known). While still in New York, Henry married a third time to Mary Cook, a widow Fielden, who had a daughter named Jennie. The first child by Henry's third marriage, named John, was also born while the family was still in New York.

By the Fall of 1811, the family was relocated in Shawneetown, Gallatin County, Illinois. Apparently, they traveled on the Ohio River, arriving in Shawneetown by boat. They must have gone through Pennsylvania before reaching the Ohio River, because one of Henry's children by his first marriage, Henry, remained in Pennsylvania instead of proceeding to Illinois. The indication was that Henry originally planned to settle in Kaskaskia, Illinois, but journeyed only as far as the area around Shawneetown.

Old Shawneetown, which is where Henry and family first landed in Illinois, is located on the Ohio River, bordering the northwest Kentucky area. Shawneetown served as a port of entry and trading center for settlers living farther inland. Members of the family settled first in Gallatin County and later branched out to adjacent counties. While in Illinois, Henry and third wife, Mary, had four other children, William, Laura, Mariah, and Britanna Wilton.

According to the Gallatin County Court Records 1813-1820, there were several mentions of Henry Wilton. In December 1814, Henry Wilton was appointed constable for that year in Saline Township. In 1816, there was mention of preparations for a "road from U.S. Saline on the direction to White court house...," in which

Henry Wilton was "appointed supervisor of that part of the said road, from the north fork of the Saline Creek to the county line...." In 1817, Henry was appointed Commissioner to turn in a list of taxable property in the Saline Township for the year 1817, and he was also appointed Constable for Saline Township. In 1819, Henry Wilton was again mentioned in a proceeding, concerning a road in which it was "Ordered that Henry Wilton be and he is hereby appointed Supervisor on that part of Barker's road from the middle of said Swamp to the ferry landing...." At the March 7, 1820 meeting of the Court, it was ordered that Henry Wilton, along with two others be appointed Trustees of the lands reserved for the use of schools in Township No. 10 in Range no. 8. On June 7, 1820, there is another reference to Henry Wilton in which "he is hereby appointed supervisor of Barkers road from the middle of the Swamp between the fords of Eagle Creek to Ensmingers ferry on the Saline...." On September 9, 1820, the Court met and considered the estate of John Herod Deceased and a voucher for settlement was entered by Henry Wilton for 27.09; and later in the meeting the Court ordered payment to the claimants listing "Henry Wilton Recpt. by H. Wilton 27.09...."

    The 1820 Census of Gallatin County, Illinois shows that Henry and his wife were over 45 years of age, and that they had eight children living with them. In various other censuses, the Wilton's are located in Hancock, Clinton, and Marion counties. There is no record of Henry after 1820 in the censuses, however, in the 1840 and 1850 Census of Clinton County, an elderly Mary Wilton is listed with the family of William Wilton.

Family Group Sheet

Husband: Henry Wilton		
	Born: Bef. 24 Dec 1769	in: Stapleford, Cambridgeshire, England
	Married: Abt. 1797	in: New York
	Died: Abt. Sep 1820	in: Illinois
	Father: Henry Wilton	
	Mother: Maria Frogg	
	Other Spouses: Elizabeth Knott, Mary Cook	
Wife: Elizabeth Bond		
	Born: Unknown	in: ?
	Died: 1811	in: New York

CHILDREN

1 M	Name: Thomas Wilton		
	Born: Abt. 1798	in: New York	
	Died: 23 Aug 1866	in: Marion Co., Illinois	
	Married: Bef. 1827	in: Illinois	
	Spouse: Mary Alma Maddux		
2 M	Name: Charles Wilton		
	Born: 1805	in: New York	
	Died: 02 Apr 1866	in: Clinton Co., Illinois	
	Married: 27 Sep 1832	in: Clinton Co., Illinois	
	Spouse: Mary Harbison		
3 F	Name: Sophia Wilton		
	Born: 1808	in: New York	
	Died: 01 Aug 1875	in: Clinton Co., Illinois	

HENRY WILTON Standard Pedigree Tree

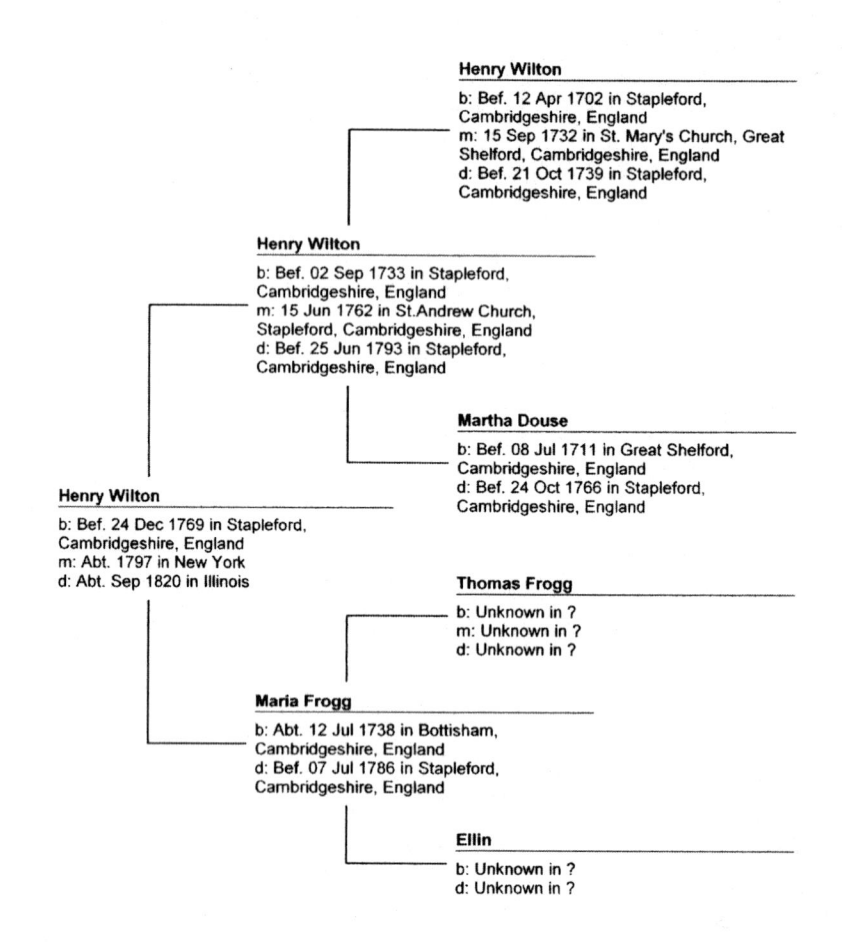

Henry Wilton
b: Bef. 24 Dec 1769 in Stapleford, Cambridgeshire, England
m: Abt. 1797 in New York
d: Abt. Sep 1820 in Illinois

- **Henry Wilton**
  b: Bef. 02 Sep 1733 in Stapleford, Cambridgeshire, England
  m: 15 Jun 1762 in St. Andrew Church, Stapleford, Cambridgeshire, England
  d: Bef. 25 Jun 1793 in Stapleford, Cambridgeshire, England
  - **Henry Wilton**
    b: Bef. 12 Apr 1702 in Stapleford, Cambridgeshire, England
    m: 15 Sep 1732 in St. Mary's Church, Great Shelford, Cambridgeshire, England
    d: Bef. 21 Oct 1739 in Stapleford, Cambridgeshire, England
  - **Martha Douse**
    b: Bef. 08 Jul 1711 in Great Shelford, Cambridgeshire, England
    d: Bef. 24 Oct 1766 in Stapleford, Cambridgeshire, England

- **Maria Frogg**
  b: Abt. 12 Jul 1738 in Bottisham, Cambridgeshire, England
  d: Bef. 07 Jul 1786 in Stapleford, Cambridgeshire, England
  - **Thomas Frogg**
    b: Unknown in ?
    m: Unknown in ?
    d: Unknown in ?
  - **Ellin**
    b: Unknown in ?
    d: Unknown in ?

Thomas Wilton (1798-1866)
[2nd. Generation From Henry Wilton (1769-1820)]

&

Mary Alma Maddux (1805~1881)
& Family

Thomas was the first child by the second marriage of Henry Wilton (c.1769-1820), our first Wilton ancestor from England, and Elizabeth Bond. When Thomas was born c.1798, Henry was then living in Delaware County, New York. Henry had come to America sometime between 1793 and 1797, and since his first wife had not made the trip to the new world, he had married a second time to Elizabeth Bond while in New York. Henry and Elizabeth had two other children while in New York, named Charles and Sophia Wilton.

By 1811, Henry decided to move from New York to Kaskaskia, Illinois. However, they were delayed in moving until the Fall of 1811, because Thomas' mother, Elizabeth, had an untimely death, due to an accident. Before leaving New York, Henry married a third time, to Mary Cook, who was a widow Fielden, having a daughter named Jennie from her previous marriage. Henry and Mary had their first child, John Wilton, before making the trip to Illinois.

In making the trip to Illinois, the family apparently first travelled through Pennsylvania in making a connection to the headwaters of the Ohio River, where they then took the long boat ride for the bulk of their journey. They landed at Old Shawneetown, Illinois, in Gallatin County, located on the Ohio

River and bordering northern Kentucky, in the Fall of 1811. Although the original plan was eventually to travel farther west to Kaskaskia, Henry and family did not get any farther than Shawneetown and surrounding area, settling there, instead. Henry and Mary had four other children while living in Illinois, named William, Laura, Mariah, and Britanna Wilton. After Henry's death in 1820, various members of the family branched out into surrounding counties.

There is a Wilton tradition that three of the Wilton brothers, one of whom was apparently Thomas, settled in Clinton County about 1820. They were farming the land and had put in a corn crop. Tradition has it that they had to sleep out in the cornfield at night the first year, for fear that the Indians might burn down their cabin.

By 1825, Thomas was living in the Carlyle Precinct of Clinton County. He was listed as an "old settler" of the Clement township of Clinton County, Illinois. Thomas apparently married Mary Alma Maddux around that time, because their first child, Charles Freedis Wilton, was born in 1827. There is a Thomas Wilton listed in both the 1830 and 1840 Federal Census for Clinton County, Illinois. Thomas and Mary had five other children, named Franklin, Joseph C., Rudolph, Mary Elizabeth, and Ellen Wilton.

Apparently, the family moved to the adjacent Marion County sometime after 1840, because the family is found in both the 1850 and 1860 Federal Census for Marion County, Illinois. The 1850 census lists Thomas at age 52, with wife, Mary, age 45, and children ranging from 5 to 18 years of age. Charles, his oldest son, is listed with his own family in the same census a short distance away. In the 1860 census, the same family members are found living at home, and Thomas is still listed as a "farmer."

Thomas is also listed in a number of land deals while in Marion County, being the grantor in several transactions between 1850 and 1860. On March 3, 1850, he sold a tract of land in sections twenty-one and twenty-two of range two East of Town four North to William Outhouse for $133.50 (Deed Record Book F, Marion Co., Illinois, p.458); on May 28, 1856, he sold a tract of land in section nine of range two East of Town four North to Garland C.

Shepard for $100.00 (Deed Record Book L, Marion Co., Illinois, p.490); and, on October 8, 1860, he sold a tract of land in section twenty-one of range two East of Town four North to John Bell Chandler for $200.00 (Deed Record Book R, Marion Co., Illinois, p.77).

Thomas died in 1866 at about the age of 68 while living in Marion County, and his wife, Mary, died after 1881 at about the age of 76, also a resident of Marion County. After Thomas' death in 1866, his son, Joseph C. Wilton, became the administrator of the Thomas Wilton estate.

Family Group Sheet

Husband: Thomas Wilton

- Born: Abt. 1798 in: New York
- Married: Bef. 1827 in: Illinois
- Died: 23 Aug 1866 in: Marion Co., Illinois
- Father: Henry Wilton
- Mother: Elizabeth Bond

Wife: Mary Alma Maddux

- Born: Abt. 1805 in: Kentucky
- Died: Aft. 1881 in: Illinois
- Father: Gillis Maddux
- Mother: Eleanor Ellis

CHILDREN

1 M
- Name: Charles Freedis Wilton
- Born: Abt. 1827 in: Marion Co., Illinois
- Died: Aft. 1881 in: Veal Station, Parker Co., Texas
- Married: 12 Jul 1848 in: Marion Co., Illinois
- Spouse: Susanah Cruse
- Married: 15 Mar 1865 in: Clinton Co., Illinois
- Spouse: Mary Ann Richardson

2 M
- Name: Franklin Wilton
- Born: Abt. 1832 in: Illinois
- Died: Bef. Nov 1867 in: ?

3 M
- Name: Joseph C. Wilton
- Born: 16 Aug 1834 in: Illinois
- Died: 09 Nov 1900 in: Tarrant Co., Texas
- Married: 24 Feb 1858 in: Marion Co., Illinois
- Spouse: Mary Annis Prewitt
- Married: 19 Feb 1871 in: Marion Co., Illinois
- Spouse: Sarah Elizabeth Baldwin

4 M
- Name: Rudolph Wilton
- Born: 03 Sep 1839 in: Illinois
- Died: 05 Nov 1928 in: Patoka, Marion Co., Illinois
- Married: Bef. 1862 in: Illinois
- Spouse: Nancy A. Wall
- Married: 20 Nov 1879 in: Marion Co., Illinois
- Spouse: Ellen Jane Pauley

5 F
- Name: Mary Elizabeth Wilton
- Born: Abt. 1842 in: Salem, Marion Co., Illinois
- Died: 13 Aug 1898 in: Poplar Bluff, Butler Co., Missouri
- Married: 07 Aug 1861 in: Edgewood, Effingham Co., Illinois
- Spouse: James Martin Burkett

6 F
- Name: Ellen Wilton
- Born: May 1845 in: Illinois
- Died: 29 Sep 1919 in: Urbana, Champaign Co., Illinois
- Married: 11 Apr 1867 in: Marion Co., Illinois
- Spouse: Felix Monroe Marshall

THOMAS WILTON Standard Pedigree Tree

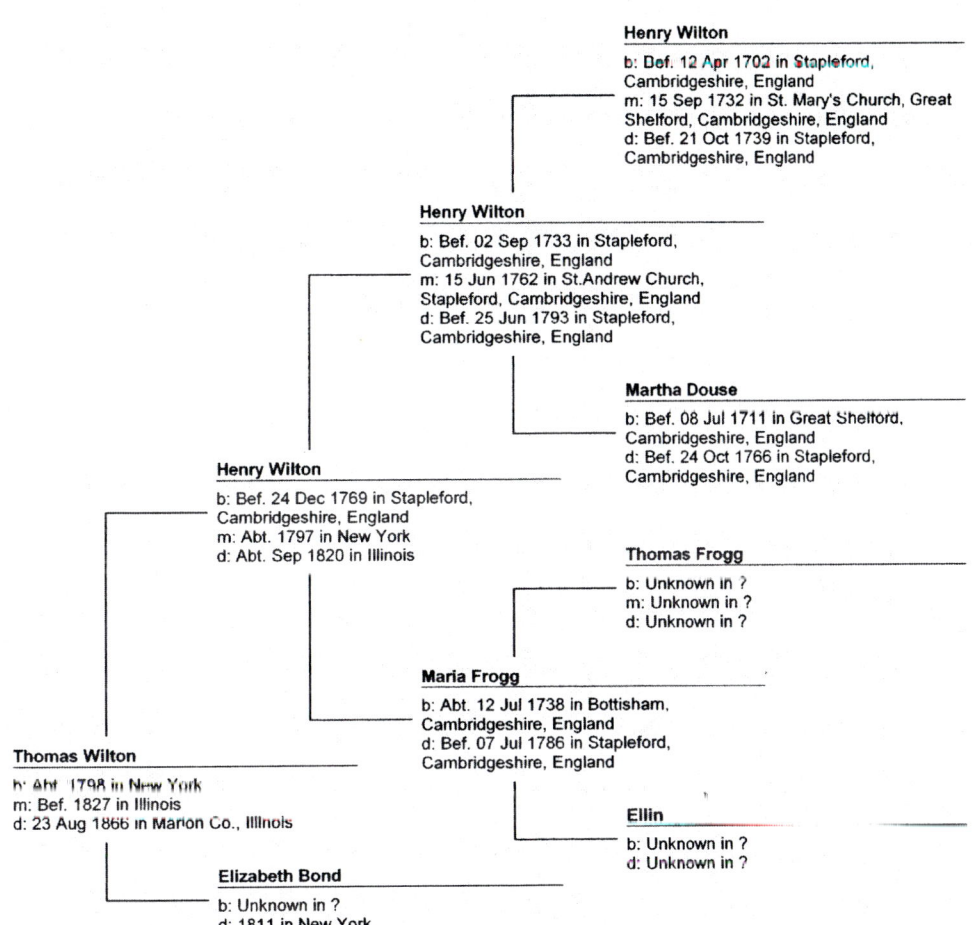

Thomas Wilton
b: Abt. 1798 in New York
m: Bef. 1827 in Illinois
d: 23 Aug 1866 in Marion Co., Illinois

Henry Wilton
b: Bef. 24 Dec 1769 in Stapleford, Cambridgeshire, England
m: Abt. 1797 in New York
d: Abt. Sep 1820 in Illinois

Elizabeth Bond
b: Unknown in ?
d: 1811 in New York

Henry Wilton
b: Bef. 02 Sep 1733 in Stapleford, Cambridgeshire, England
m: 15 Jun 1762 in St. Andrew Church, Stapleford, Cambridgeshire, England
d: Bef. 25 Jun 1793 in Stapleford, Cambridgeshire, England

Maria Frogg
b: Abt. 12 Jul 1738 in Bottisham, Cambridgeshire, England
d: Bef. 07 Jul 1786 in Stapleford, Cambridgeshire, England

Henry Wilton
b: Bef. 12 Apr 1702 in Stapleford, Cambridgeshire, England
m: 15 Sep 1732 in St. Mary's Church, Great Shelford, Cambridgeshire, England
d: Bef. 21 Oct 1739 in Stapleford, Cambridgeshire, England

Martha Douse
b: Bef. 08 Jul 1711 in Great Shelford, Cambridgeshire, England
d: Bef. 24 Oct 1766 in Stapleford, Cambridgeshire, England

Thomas Frogg
b: Unknown in ?
m: Unknown in ?
d: Unknown in ?

Ellin
b: Unknown in ?
d: Unknown in ?

Notes: This Tree also applies to the other children of Henry Wilton & Elizabeth Bond: Charles Wilton & Sophia Wilton.

MARY ALMA MADDUX Standard Pedigree Tree

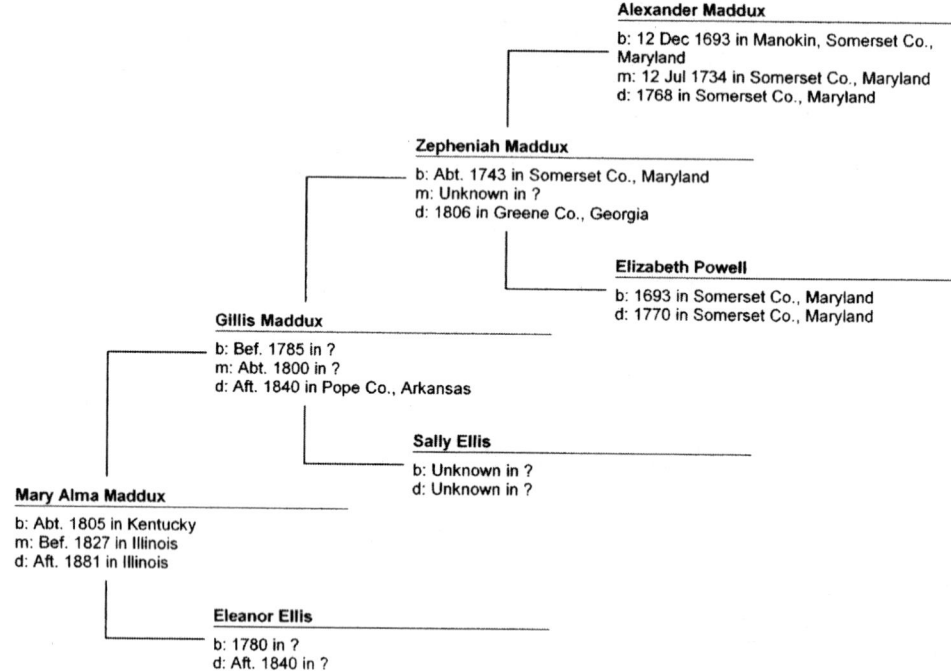

Alexander Maddux
b: 12 Dec 1693 in Manokin, Somerset Co., Maryland
m: 12 Jul 1734 in Somerset Co., Maryland
d: 1768 in Somerset Co., Maryland

Zepheniah Maddux
b: Abt. 1743 in Somerset Co., Maryland
m: Unknown in ?
d: 1806 in Greene Co., Georgia

Elizabeth Powell
b: 1693 in Somerset Co., Maryland
d: 1770 in Somerset Co., Maryland

Gillis Maddux
b: Bef. 1785 in ?
m: Abt. 1800 in ?
d: Aft. 1840 in Pope Co., Arkansas

Sally Ellis
b: Unknown in ?
d: Unknown in ?

Mary Alma Maddux
b: Abt. 1805 in Kentucky
m: Bef. 1827 in Illinois
d: Aft. 1881 in Illinois

Eleanor Ellis
b: 1780 in ?
d: Aft. 1840 in ?

Charles Freedis Wilton (1827-1885)
[3rd. Generation from Henry Wilton (1769-1820)]

&

First Marriage To
Susannah Cruse (1826~1860)
& Family

Second Marriage To
Mary Ann Richardson (1832~1881)
& Family

Charles Freedis Wilton was the oldest son of Thomas & Mary (Maddux) Wilton, born in Marion County, Illinois about 1827. Thomas and family spent some time in Clinton County, Illinois, between 1830 and 1840, and then they settled in the adjacent Marion County.

In July of 1848, Charles married Susannah Cruse, and they began their family in Marion County, Illinois. Their first son, Thomas Abslum Wilton, was born December 1849. In the 1850 Federal Census of Marion County, Charles, age 23, is listed as a farmer with wife, Sarah (Susannah), age 24, and son, Thomas, age 1. The household next door to Charles is the family of Absalom & Rebecca Cruse, the parents of Susannah. Also, not far away in the same census is the family of Thomas & Mary Wilton, the parents of Charles.

While still living in Marion County, in December 1853, Charles & Susannah had one other son, named Henry Franklin Wilton. However, sometime about 1859, Susannah died leaving Charles with their two young children, Thomas, then about 10 years old, and Henry, about 6 years old. About that time, the families of

Absalom Cruse and Charles' brother, Joseph C. Wilton, made a move to Texas, and Charles, with his two sons, traveled along to Texas with the group. They first settled in an area of Texas just north of Fort Worth (where Lake Worth was later located).

When the Civil War broke out in 1861, Charles made the trip back to Illinois with his older son, Thomas, leaving Henry in Texas with his relatives. Charles' residence then became Edgewood in Effingham County, Illinois, which was the location listed on his papers when he enlisted for 3 years' duty in the Civil War in September 1861. Charles became a member of Company E, 11th. Regiment, of the Illinois Infantry, enlisting as a private. His company saw service mainly in Missouri, Tennessee, and Mississippi. He was promoted to Corporal in May 1863, and when his enlistment was ended, he was discharged in Arkansas on September 24, 1864.

Following his service in the Civil War, Charles returned to Marion County, Illinois, where he married Mary A. Richardson, in July 1865. In the meantime, Charles' son, Thomas, also spent time in the war. In 1865, after finishing his service, Thomas returned to Texas, where, in 1870, he married Esther Clark. Charles' younger son, Henry F., who had been in Texas all this time, moved to Illinois in 1874. After marrying Martha Baldwin in 1877, he returned back to Texas.

Between 1865 and 1881 there are a number of references to Charles F. in the available record. One of the first such records is in the Marion County, Illinois, Census Record for 1865. There is found a Charles Wilton (age 30-40) located at "11 North of R4 East," along with a female (age 30-40) and one male (age 10-20).

Beginning in September 1867, there were a number of negotiations regarding a 40 acre section of land that originally was owned by Charle's brother, Rudolph Wilton and his wife, Nancy A. Wilton. After purchasing the land in 1867, Charles and his wife, Mary, used the same section of land in April 1868 as collateral to secure a loan. That mortgage was then paid off in November 1868. Again, the same land was used in May 1878 to secure a Trust Deed, and in July 1881, that Trust Deed was "satisfied." The land was finally sold on July 20, 1881 to a F.J. Arnold.

Charles is also mentioned as an heir to the estate of Thomas Wilton, Charles' father. He was mentioned in a petition dated November 1867, along with other heirs, to sell real estate from the estate of Thomas Wilton, while the will was still in probate.

Charles was also mentioned in the 1870 and 1880 Federal Census' of Marion County, Illinois. In 1870, he was listed as age 42, along with his wife, Mary, age 38. In 1880, he was listed as age 53, along with his wife, Mary, then age 49.

According to family tradition, Charles eventually made one last move to Texas, where he lived near his brother, Joe Wilton, in Parker County, Texas. It was also believed that Charles became part-owner of a grocery store at Veal Station in Parker County, Texas. According to "Handbook of Texas," Veal Station was a townsite in Parker County, located some twelve miles north of Weatherford on the Old Fort Belknap Road. It was one of the oldest settlements of Parker County, first settled in 1852, and originally known as Cream Liel. It may have been that Charles and Mary were preparing to make the move to Texas when they sold their land in Illinois in 1881. Charles died November 9, 1885 and was buried in the Azle Cemetery, located in the adjacent Tarrant County, Texas.

Family Group Sheet

Husband: Charles Freedis Wilton

Born: Abt. 1827 in: Marion Co., Illinois
Married: 12 Jul 1848 in: Marion Co., Illinois
Died: 09 Nov 1885 in: Veal Station, Parker Co., Texas
Father: Thomas Wilton
Mother: Mary Alma Maddux
Other Spouses: Mary Ann Richardson

Wife: Susanah Cruse

Born: 07 Oct 1826 in: Indiana
Died: Bef. 1860 in: Illinois
Father: Absalom B. Cruse
Mother: Rebecca McCoy

CHILDREN

1. M
   Name: Thomas Abslum Wilton
   Born: 01 Dec 1849 in: Marion Co., Illinois
   Died: 19 Jan 1894 in: Jack Co., Texas
   Married: 06 Jan 1870 in: Veal Station, Parker Co., Texas
   Spouse: Easter Britania Clark

2. M
   Name: Henry Franklin Wilton
   Born: 25 Dec 1853 in: Marion Co., Illinois
   Died: 05 Sep 1941 in: Jermyn, Jack Co., Texas
   Married: 15 Feb 1877 in: Home of Mary Jones (Sister of Martha)
   Spouse: Martha Jane Baldwin

Family Group Sheet

Husband: Charles Freedis Wilton

Born: Abt. 1827 in: Marion Co., Illinois
Married: 15 Mar 1865 in: Clinton Co., Illinois
Died: 09 Nov 1885 in: Veal Station, Parker Co., Texas
Father: Thomas Wilton
Mother: Mary Alma Maddux
Other Spouses: Susanah Cruse

Wife: Mary Ann Richardson

Born: Abt. 1832 in: Illinois
Died: Aft. 1881 in: ?

CHARLES FREEDIS WILTON Standard Pedigree Tree

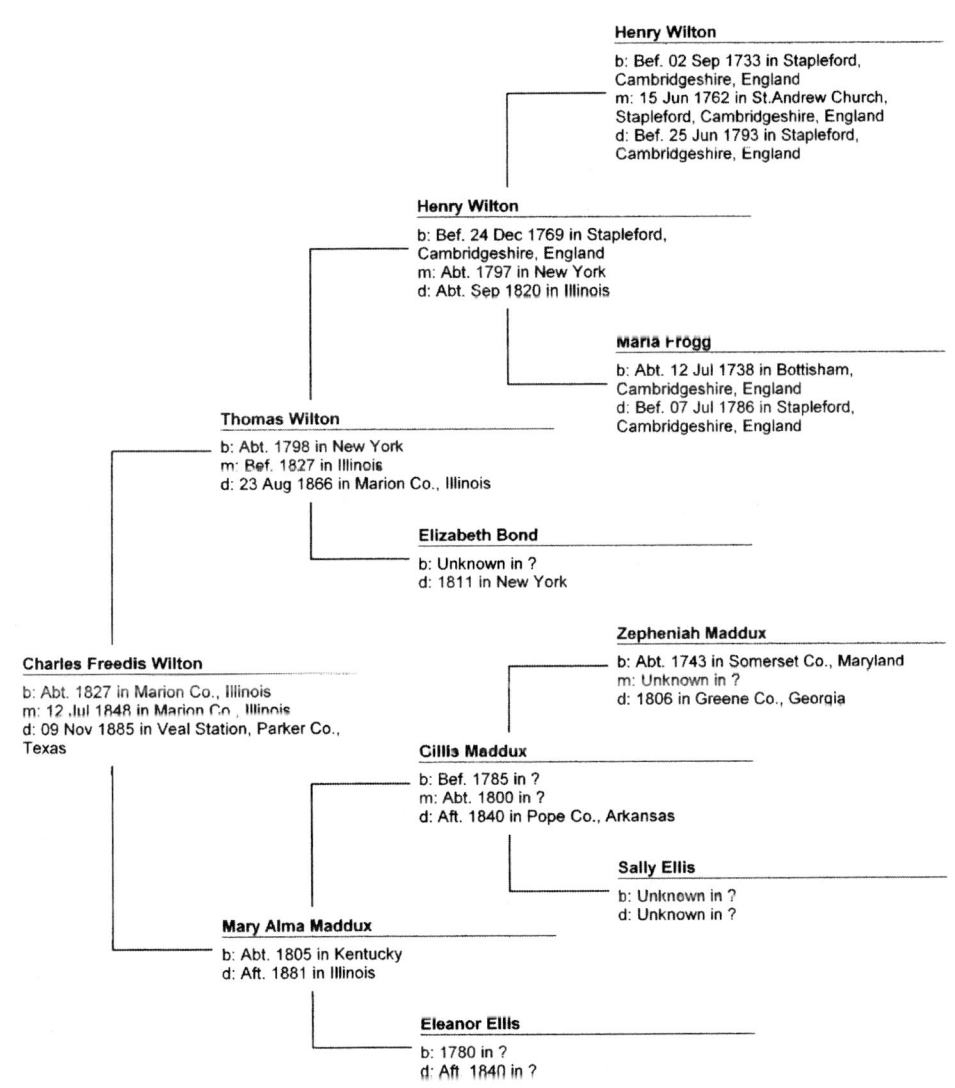

Notes: This Tree also applies to the other children of Thomas Wilton & Mary A. Maddux: Franklin Wilton, Joseph C. Wilton, Rudolph Wilton, Mary Elizabeth Wilton, and Ellen Wilton.

SUSANAH CRUSE Standard Pedigree Tree

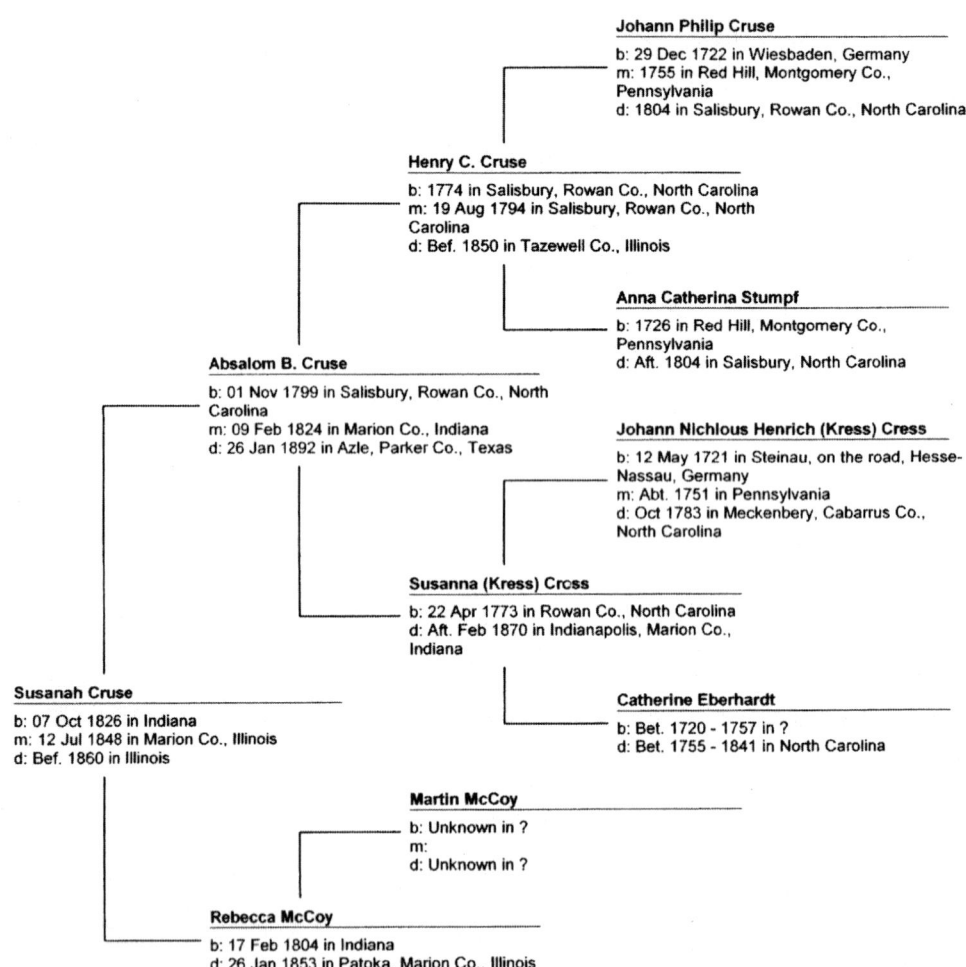

Susanah Cruse
b: 07 Oct 1826 in Indiana
m: 12 Jul 1848 in Marion Co., Illinois
d: Bef. 1860 in Illinois

Absalom B. Cruse
b: 01 Nov 1799 in Salisbury, Rowan Co., North Carolina
m: 09 Feb 1824 in Marion Co., Indiana
d: 26 Jan 1892 in Azle, Parker Co., Texas

Henry C. Cruse
b: 1774 in Salisbury, Rowan Co., North Carolina
m: 19 Aug 1794 in Salisbury, Rowan Co., North Carolina
d: Bef. 1850 in Tazewell Co., Illinois

Johann Philip Cruse
b: 29 Dec 1722 in Wiesbaden, Germany
m: 1755 in Red Hill, Montgomery Co., Pennsylvania
d: 1804 in Salisbury, Rowan Co., North Carolina

Anna Catherina Stumpf
b: 1726 in Red Hill, Montgomery Co., Pennsylvania
d: Aft. 1804 in Salisbury, North Carolina

Susanna (Kress) Cross
b: 22 Apr 1773 in Rowan Co., North Carolina
d: Aft. Feb 1870 in Indianapolis, Marion Co., Indiana

Johann Nichlous Henrich (Kress) Cress
b: 12 May 1721 in Steinau, on the road, Hesse-Nassau, Germany
m: Abt. 1751 in Pennsylvania
d: Oct 1783 in Meckenbery, Cabarrus Co., North Carolina

Catherine Eberhardt
b: Bet. 1720 - 1757 in ?
d: Bet. 1755 - 1841 in North Carolina

Rebecca McCoy
b: 17 Feb 1804 in Indiana
d: 26 Jan 1853 in Patoka, Marion Co., Illinois

Martin McCoy
b: Unknown in ?
m:
d: Unknown in ?

Thomas Abslum Wilton (1849-1894)
[4th. Generation From Henry Wilton (1769-1820)]

&

Easter Britania Clark (1851-1922)
& Family

Thomas was the eldest son of Charles F. Wilton and Susannah Cruse, born December 1848 in Marion County, Illinois. While Thomas was just 10 years old, his mother died, and shortly afterward, he was taken with his father and younger brother to resettle in Texas. The time was about 1861 when the family had reached Texas, and it was also the time of the outbreak of the Civil War. Charles then returned to Illinois, where he enlisted in the Union Army in September 1861, bringing Thomas along with him to Illinois. Charles' address at that time was listed as Edgewood, in Efffingham County, Illinois.

While his dad was still engaged in the war, Thomas also enlisted with the Union Army on May 20, 1864, at the age of 15 years. He actually served two short terms in the war, one from May 1864 through October 1864 with Co. E, 136th. Regiment, of the Illinois Voluntary Infantry, and the other from March 1865 through November 1865 with Co. H of the 7th. Illinois Cavalry. From his enlistment papers, we learn that Thomas had hazel eyes, auburn hair, a sandy complexion, and that he stood 5 feet 5 inches tall. At the time of his first enlistment, Thomas was living in Centralia in Marion County, Illinois, and he stated, incorrectly, that his age was 18 years.

After completing his service in the war, Thomas moved to Texas, where he married Easter Britania Clark. The couple were married at Veal Station in Parker County, Texas, in January 1870. They are also listed in the 1870 Federal Census of Parker County as Thomas Wilton, age 21, occupation farmer, and Brittania Wilton, age 19. Their first child, Freedus E. Wilton, was born in Parker County in November 1870.

About 1878, Thomas moved the family to Jack County, Texas, which was just northwest and adjacent to Parker County. After staying awhile in the Squaw Mountain area, the family moved to the Winn Hill Community, where Thomas settled permanently. In the 1880 Federal Census of Jack County, Thomas is listed with his wife, Easter B., and five children, ranging in age from 2 to 9 years. In all, Thomas and Easter had twelve children, with two dying in infancy. Thomas is credited with donating the land for the Winn Hill Baptist Church, located in the Winn Hill Community just across the creek from the Winn Hill Cemetery. Thomas' younger brother, Henry Franklin Wilton, also lived nearby about three miles away from Thomas.

The indication is that beginning about 1890, Thomas began exhibiting physical problems, because in August 1890 he filed a "Declaration for Invalid Pension," stating that he was unable to earn support by manual labor due to "piles, palpitation of the heart, and disease of the stomach and bowels." Thomas died a few years later, in January 1894. Thomas was buried in the nearby Winn Hill Cemetery.

After the death of Thomas, Easter continued to raise their children in Jack County. She is listed in the 1900, 1910, and 1920 Federal Census for Jack County, Texas. Easter died in December 1922 and was also buried in the Winn Hill Cemetery.

Family Group Sheet

Husband: Thomas Abslum Wilton

Born: 01 Dec 1849 — in: Marion Co., Illinois
Married: 06 Jan 1870 — in: Veal Station, Parker Co., Texas
Died: 19 Jan 1894 — in: Jack Co., Texas
Father: Charles Freedis Wilton
Mother: Susanah Cruse

Wife: Easter Britania Clark

Born: 12 Apr 1851 — in: Washington Co., Arkansas
Died: 15 Dec 1922 — in: Winn Hll, Jack Co., Texas
Father: Ezra Clark
Mother: Livonia Hash

CHILDREN

1. M Name: Freedus Ezra Wilton
Born: 21 Nov 1870 — in: Parker Co., Texas
Died: 06 Jan 1941 — in: Markley, Young Co., Texas
Married: 01 Sep 1895 — in: Parker Co., Texas
Spouse: Amelia Jane Dixon

2. M Name: Alvin Henry Wilton
Born: 12 Jan 1873 — in: Wise Co., Texas
Died: 31 Dec 1939 — in: Jacksboro, Jack Co., Texas
Married: 25 Nov 1906 — in: Texas
Spouse: Leuticia Hannah

3. M Name: Silas Wilton
Born: 16 Dec 1874 — in: Wise Co., Texas
Died: 03 Aug 1935 — in: California
Married: 19 Nov 1898 — in: Texas
Spouse: Mary Elizabeth Underwood

4. M Name: Cyrus Wilton
Born: 01 Mar 1878 — in: Winn Hill, Jack Co., Texas
Died: 17 Dec 1968 — in: Ft. Worth, Tarrant Co., Texas
Married: Abt. 1909 — in: Ft. Worth, Tarrant Co., Texas
Spouse: Ida Bell Admire

5. M Name: Ira John Wilton
Born: 01 Mar 1878 — in: Winn Hill, Jack Co., Texas
Died: 01 Dec 1962 — in: Levelland, Hockley Co., Texas
Married: 21 Feb 1909 — in: Roger Mills Co., Oklahoma
Spouse: Nancy Ann Williams

6. F Name: Ida May Wilton
Born: 03 Aug 1880 — in: Winn Hill, Jack Co., Texas
Died: Abt. 1960 — in: Olney, Young Co., Texas
Married: 18 Aug 1915 — in: Texas
Spouse: William Rufus Reynolds

7. F Name: Emma Livona Wilton
Born: 14 May 1883 — in: Jack Co., Texas
Died: 05 May 1977 — in: Clovis, Curry Co., New Mexico
Married: 13 Dec 1908 — in: Winn Hill, Jack Co., Texas
Spouse: Jefferson Francis Asberry McCasland

8. M Name: Thomas Erastus Wilton
Born: 13 Feb 1886 — in: Jack Co., Texas
Died: 17 Oct 1886 — in: Jack Co., Texas

9. M Name: Marion Grady Wilton
Born: 14 Jan 1888 — in: Winn Hill, Jack Co., Texas
Died: 17 Feb 1888 — in: Winn Hill, Jack Co., Texas

Family Group Sheet

10 M	Name: Benjamin Harrison Wilton Born: 23 May 1889 Died: 08 Mar 1968 Married: Aft. 1930 Spouse: Elzy Florence Gaither		in: Winn Hill, Jack Co., Texas in: Winn Hill, Jack Co., Texas in: Texas
11 F	Name: Effa Belle Wilton Born: 20 Oct 1890 Died: 31 Mar 1981 Married: 07 Jan 1912 Spouse: James Franklin Hannah		in: Jack Co., Texas in: Young Co., Texas in: Texas
12 M	Name: Johnie Melvin Wilton Born: 13 Nov 1892 Died: 15 Sep 1944 Married: 30 Dec 1913 Spouse: Jessie Earl Newman		in: Winn Hill, Jack Co., Texas in: Graham, Young Co., Texas in: Jacksboro, Jack Co., Texas

THOMAS ABSLUM WILTON Standard Pedigree Tree

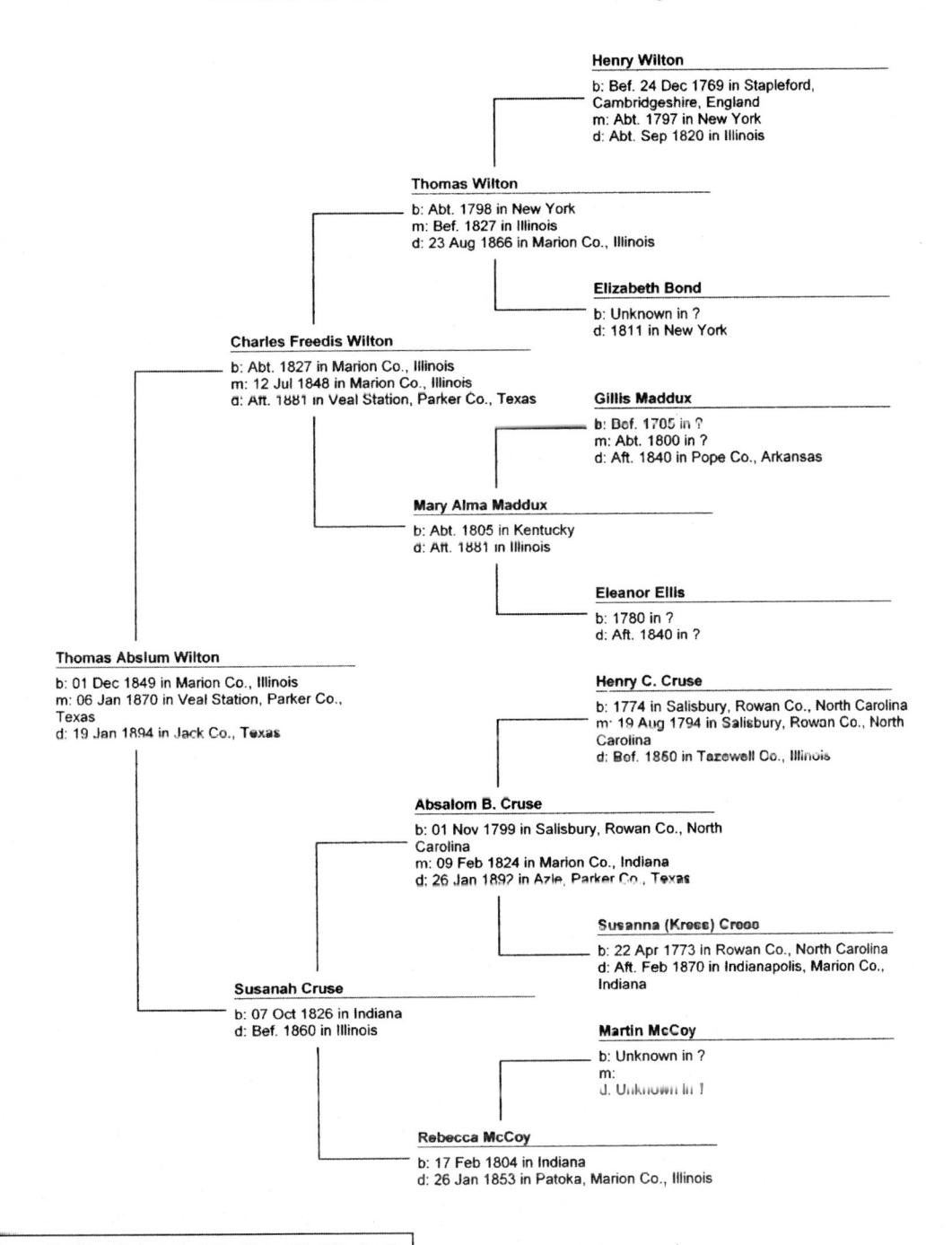

Thomas Abslum Wilton
b: 01 Dec 1849 in Marion Co., Illinois
m: 06 Jan 1870 in Veal Station, Parker Co., Texas
d: 19 Jan 1894 in Jack Co., Texas

- **Charles Freedis Wilton**
  b: Abt. 1827 in Marion Co., Illinois
  m: 12 Jul 1848 in Marion Co., Illinois
  d: Aft. 1881 in Veal Station, Parker Co., Texas

  - **Thomas Wilton**
    b: Abt. 1798 in New York
    m: Bef. 1827 in Illinois
    d: 23 Aug 1866 in Marion Co., Illinois

    - **Henry Wilton**
      b: Bef. 24 Dec 1769 in Stapleford, Cambridgeshire, England
      m: Abt. 1797 in New York
      d: Abt. Sep 1820 in Illinois

    - **Elizabeth Bond**
      b: Unknown in ?
      d: 1811 in New York

  - **Mary Alma Maddux**
    b: Abt. 1805 in Kentucky
    d: Aft. 1881 in Illinois

    - **Gillis Maddux**
      b: Bef. 1705 in ?
      m: Abt. 1800 in ?
      d: Aft. 1840 in Pope Co., Arkansas

    - **Eleanor Ellis**
      b: 1780 in ?
      d: Aft. 1840 in ?

- **Susanah Cruse**
  b: 07 Oct 1826 in Indiana
  d: Bef. 1860 in Illinois

  - **Absalom B. Cruse**
    b: 01 Nov 1799 in Salisbury, Rowan Co., North Carolina
    m: 09 Feb 1824 in Marion Co., Indiana
    d: 26 Jan 1892 in Azle, Parker Co., Texas

    - **Henry C. Cruse**
      b: 1774 in Salisbury, Rowan Co., North Carolina
      m: 19 Aug 1794 in Salisbury, Rowan Co., North Carolina
      d: Bef. 1850 in Tazewell Co., Illinois

    - **Susanna (Kress) Cress**
      b: 22 Apr 1773 in Rowan Co., North Carolina
      d: Aft. Feb 1870 in Indianapolis, Marion Co., Indiana

  - **Rebecca McCoy**
    b: 17 Feb 1804 in Indiana
    d: 26 Jan 1853 in Patoka, Marion Co., Illinois

    - **Martin McCoy**
      b: Unknown in ?
      m:
      d: Unknown in ?

Notes: This Tree also applies to the other child of Charles F. Wilton & Susannah Cruse: Henry Franklin Wilton

EASTER BRITANIA CLARK Standard Pedigree Tree

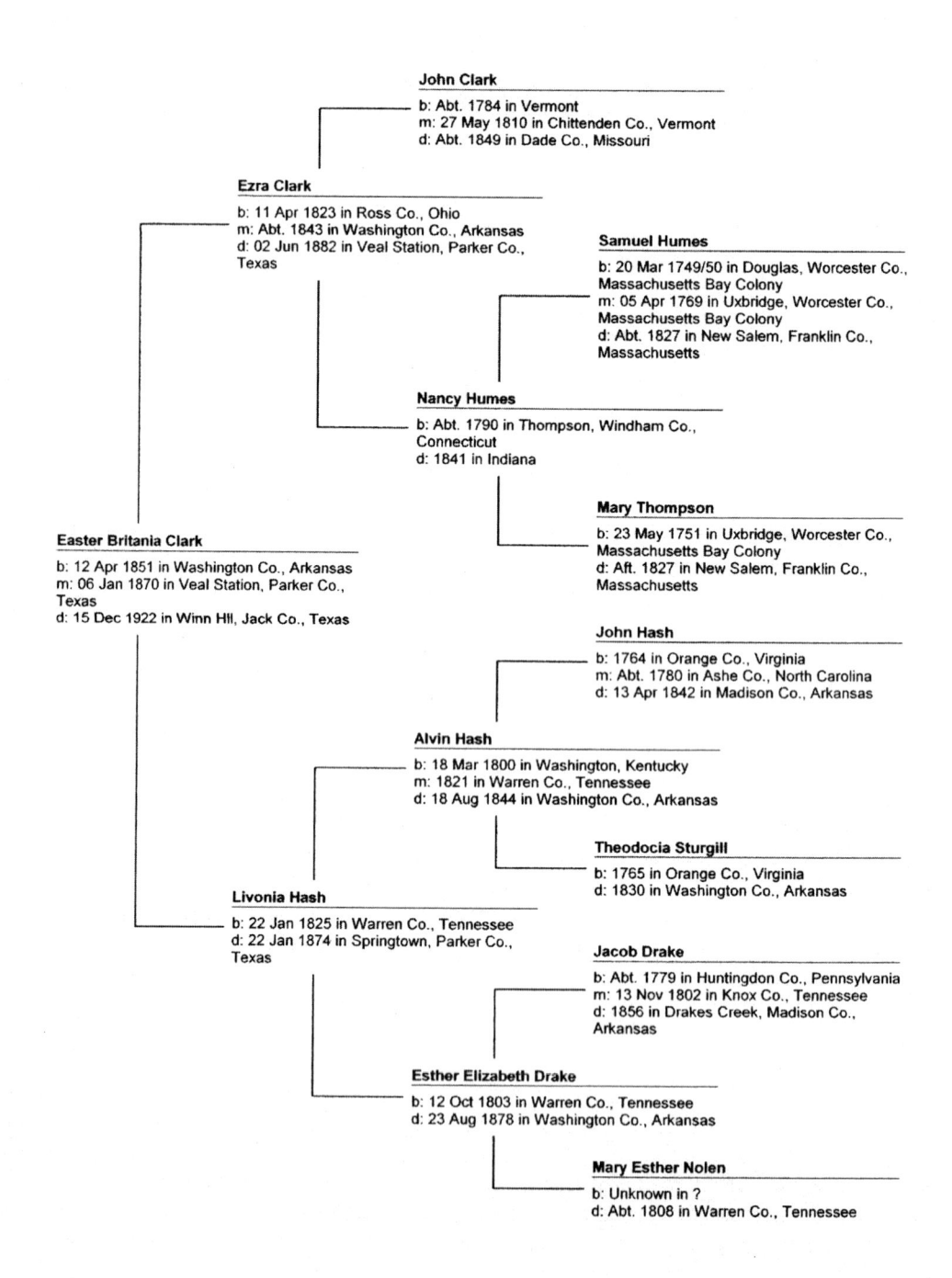

John Clark
b: Abt. 1784 in Vermont
m: 27 May 1810 in Chittenden Co., Vermont
d: Abt. 1849 in Dade Co., Missouri

Ezra Clark
b: 11 Apr 1823 in Ross Co., Ohio
m: Abt. 1843 in Washington Co., Arkansas
d: 02 Jun 1882 in Veal Station, Parker Co., Texas

Samuel Humes
b: 20 Mar 1749/50 in Douglas, Worcester Co., Massachusetts Bay Colony
m: 05 Apr 1769 in Uxbridge, Worcester Co., Massachusetts Bay Colony
d: Abt. 1827 in New Salem, Franklin Co., Massachusetts

Nancy Humes
b: Abt. 1790 in Thompson, Windham Co., Connecticut
d: 1841 in Indiana

Mary Thompson
b: 23 May 1751 in Uxbridge, Worcester Co., Massachusetts Bay Colony
d: Aft. 1827 in New Salem, Franklin Co., Massachusetts

Easter Britania Clark
b: 12 Apr 1851 in Washington Co., Arkansas
m: 06 Jan 1870 in Veal Station, Parker Co., Texas
d: 15 Dec 1922 in Winn Hll, Jack Co., Texas

John Hash
b: 1764 in Orange Co., Virginia
m: Abt. 1780 in Ashe Co., North Carolina
d: 13 Apr 1842 in Madison Co., Arkansas

Alvin Hash
b: 18 Mar 1800 in Washington, Kentucky
m: 1821 in Warren Co., Tennessee
d: 18 Aug 1844 in Washington Co., Arkansas

Theodocia Sturgill
b: 1765 in Orange Co., Virginia
d: 1830 in Washington Co., Arkansas

Livonia Hash
b: 22 Jan 1825 in Warren Co., Tennessee
d: 22 Jan 1874 in Springtown, Parker Co., Texas

Jacob Drake
b: Abt. 1779 in Huntingdon Co., Pennsylvania
m: 13 Nov 1802 in Knox Co., Tennessee
d: 1856 in Drakes Creek, Madison Co., Arkansas

Esther Elizabeth Drake
b: 12 Oct 1803 in Warren Co., Tennessee
d: 23 Aug 1878 in Washington Co., Arkansas

Mary Esther Nolen
b: Unknown in ?
d: Abt. 1808 in Warren Co., Tennessee

Freedus Ezra Wilton (1870-1941)
[5th. Generation From Henry Wilton (1769-1820)]

&

Amelia Jane Dixon (1874-1967)
& Family

Freedus E. was the oldest child of Thomas A. Wilton and Easter B. Clark. He was born in Parker County, Texas, shortly after Thomas returned from serving in the Civil War with the Union Army in Illinois. About 1878, Thomas moved the family to Jack County, Texas, and the first record in the census for Freedus was in the 1880 Federal Census of Jack County. Freedus was listed as age 9 with his parents and four other children, ages 2 thru 7.

In September 1894, Freedus married Amelia Jane Dixon, daughter of E.P. and Elizabeth Dixon, in Parker County, Texas.

By 1910, the family had moved to Young County, Texas, and that is where they settled permanently. For a long time they lived in Markley in Young County. One of the fond memories by Clyde Wilton of when he visited the family in Markley was that the family ate around a big table that had a revolving section on top which made it easier to distribute the food around to family and guests.

Freedus and Amelia had three children, Jesse Ruell, Luther Eppie, and Eater Virgil Wilton, all born in Texas. In the 1910 Federal Census of Young County, Jesse, age 13, and Luther, age 9, were listed with Freedus and Amelia. In the 1920 Federal Census of Young County, all three children were living at home with Freedus and Amelia. In the 1930 Federal Census of Young County, only the youngest child, Virgil E., age 18, was still at home, along with Freedus, Amelia, and E.P. Dixon, Amelia's father.

Both Freedus and Amelia died in Young County, Texas, but they were buried at the Winn Hill Cemetery in Jack County, Texas.

Family Group Sheet

Husband: Freedus Ezra Wilton

Born: 21 Nov 1870	in: Parker Co., Texas
Married: 01 Sep 1895	in: Parker Co., Texas
Died: 06 Jan 1941	in: Markley, Young Co., Texas
Father: Thomas Abslum Wilton	
Mother: Easter Britania Clark	

Wife: Amelia Jane Dixon

Born: 04 Jul 1874	in: Texas
Died: 15 Mar 1967	in: Graham, Young Co., Texas
Father: E. P. Dixon	
Mother: Elizabeth Read	

CHILDREN

1. M
   - Name: Jesse Ruell Wilton
   - Born: 06 Dec 1896 — in: Texas
   - Died: 26 Aug 1965 — in: Wichita Falls, Wichita Co., Texas
   - Married: 14 Apr 1923 — in: Jacksboro, Jack Co., Texas
   - Spouse: Vera Verta Ledbetter

2. M
   - Name: Luther Eppie Wilton
   - Born: 06 Feb 1901 — in: Texas
   - Died: 06 Jul 1959 — in: Texas
   - Married: Abt. 1934 — in: Texas
   - Spouse: Gladys Gertrude Hoak

3. M
   - Name: Eater Virgil Wilton
   - Born: 25 Apr 1911 — in: Texas
   - Died: 25 May 1945 — in: Young Co., Texas
   - Married: 20 Jun 1934 — in: ?
   - Spouse: Edwinona Burch

FREEDUS EZRA WILTON Standard Pedigree Tree

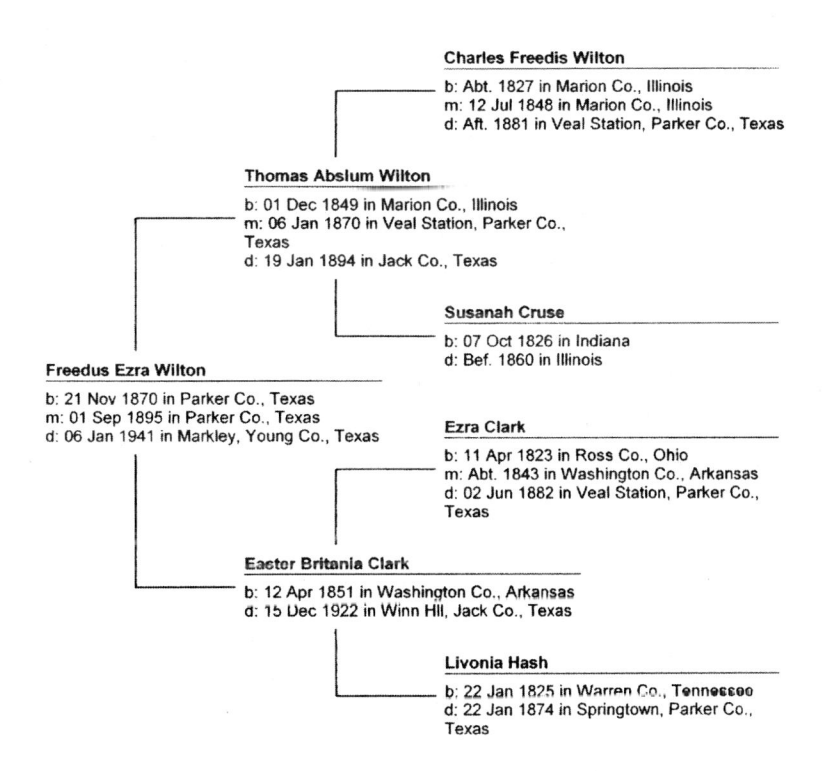

Freedus Ezra Wilton
b: 21 Nov 1870 in Parker Co., Texas
m: 01 Sep 1895 in Parker Co., Texas
d: 06 Jan 1941 in Markley, Young Co., Texas

- **Thomas Abslum Wilton**
  b: 01 Dec 1849 in Marion Co., Illinois
  m: 06 Jan 1870 in Veal Station, Parker Co., Texas
  d: 19 Jan 1894 in Jack Co., Texas
  - **Charles Freedis Wilton**
    b: Abt. 1827 in Marion Co., Illinois
    m: 12 Jul 1848 in Marion Co., Illinois
    d: Aft. 1881 in Veal Station, Parker Co., Texas
  - **Susanah Cruse**
    b: 07 Oct 1826 in Indiana
    d: Bef. 1860 in Illinois

- **Easter Britania Clark**
  b: 12 Apr 1851 in Washington Co., Arkansas
  d: 15 Dec 1922 in Winn Hll, Jack Co., Texas
  - **Ezra Clark**
    b: 11 Apr 1823 in Ross Co., Ohio
    m: Abt. 1843 in Washington Co., Arkansas
    d: 02 Jun 1882 in Veal Station, Parker Co., Texas
  - **Livonia Hash**
    b: 22 Jan 1825 in Warren Co., Tennessee
    d: 22 Jan 1874 in Springtown, Parker Co., Texas

Notes: This Tree also applies to the other children of Thomas A. Wilton & Easter B. Clark: Alvin Henry, Silas, Cyrus, Ira, Ida May, Emma Livona, Thomas Erastus, Marion Grady, Benjamin Harrison, Effa Belle, and Johnie Melvin Wilton.

Jesse Ruell Wilton (1896-1965)
[6th. Generation From Henry Wilton (1769-1820)]

&

Vera Verta Ledbetter (1902-1984)
& Family

Jesse was the oldest of three sons of Freedus E. Wilton and Amelia J. Dixon. He was born in Texas in December 1896, and judging from the 1910 and 1920 Federal Census of Young County, Texas, his early years were spent in Young County.

Jesse married Vera Verta Ledbetter, daughter of William R. & Rose Lee (Sharp) Ledbetter, on April 14, 1923. Vera was born in Texas and was in Throckmorton County, Texas by the 1910 Federal Census. In the 1920 Federal Census of Young County, Texas, both the family of Vera Ledbetter and Jesse Wilton were living in Young County, just three dwellings apart. By the 1930 Federal Census of Young County, Jesse R. Wilton, age 33, occupation merchant (retail grocer) was listed with Vera V. Wilton, wife, age 27, and daughter, Bobbie L. Wilton, age 4/14. Jesse and Vera had only one child, Bobbie L. Wilton, born November 3, 1929 in Graham, Texas in Young County.

Jesse died August 1965 in Wichita County, Texas, and Vera died August 1984 in Wichita County, Texas. Both are buried in the Markley Cemetery in Young County, Texas.

Family Group Sheet

Husband: Jesse Ruell Wilton

Born: 06 Dec 1896	in: Texas
Married: 14 Apr 1923	in: Jacksboro, Jack Co., Texas
Died: 26 Aug 1965	in: Wichita Falls, Wichita Co., Texas
Father: Freedus Ezra Wilton	
Mother: Amelia Jane Dixon	

Wife: Vera Verta Ledbetter

Born: 08 Dec 1902	in: Texas
Died: Aug 1984	in: Wichita Falls, Texas
Father: William Rice Ledbetter	
Mother: Rose Lee Sharp	

CHILDREN

1 F
- Name: Bobbye Loine Wilton
- Born: 03 Nov 1929 in: Graham, Young Co., Texas
- Married: 13 Mar 1950 in: Bryson, Jack Co., Texas
- Spouse: Jimmy Edward Roberts

JESSE RUELL WILTON Standard Pedigree Tree

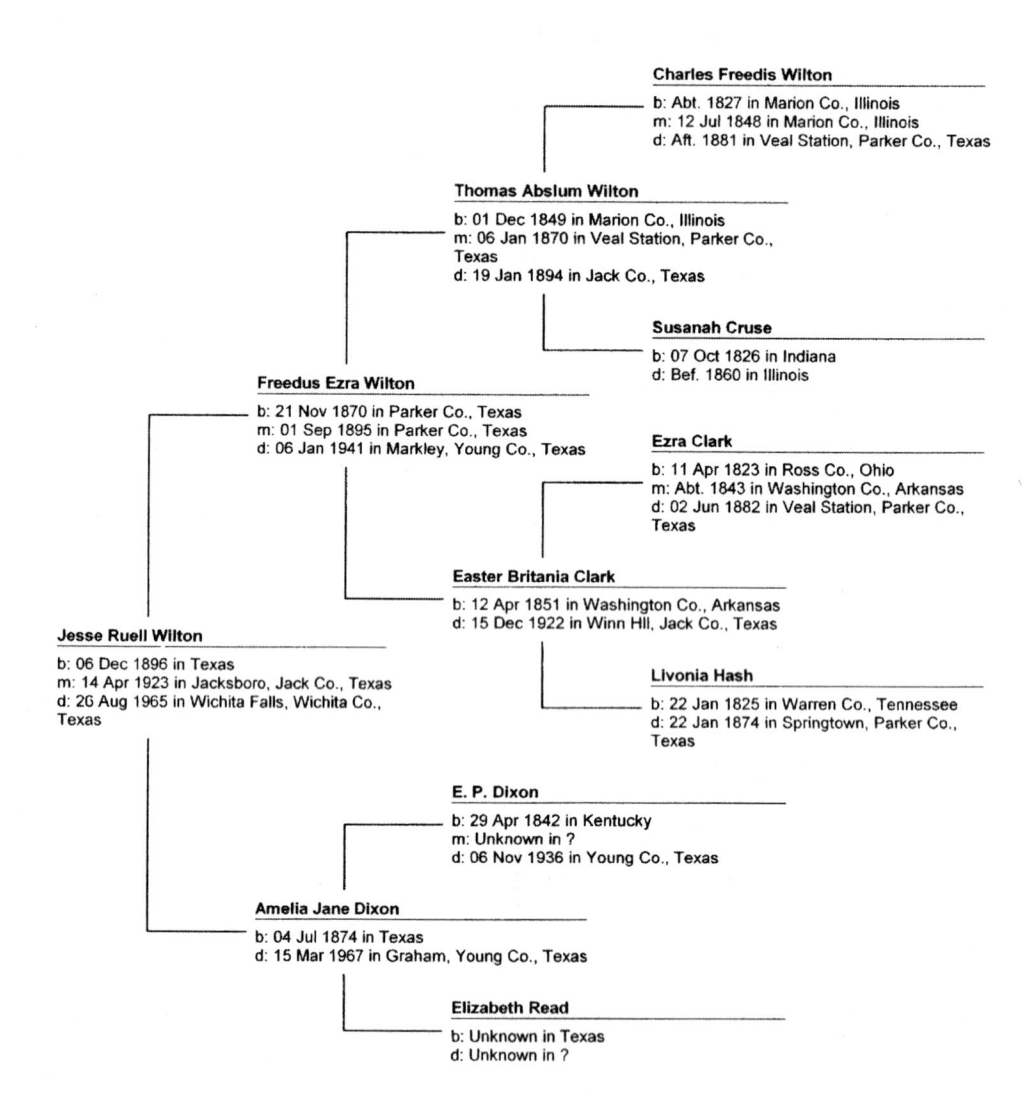

Jesse Ruell Wilton
b: 06 Dec 1896 in Texas
m: 14 Apr 1923 in Jacksboro, Jack Co., Texas
d: 26 Aug 1965 in Wichita Falls, Wichita Co., Texas

- **Freedus Ezra Wilton**
  b: 21 Nov 1870 in Parker Co., Texas
  m: 01 Sep 1895 in Parker Co., Texas
  d: 06 Jan 1941 in Markley, Young Co., Texas

  - **Thomas Abslum Wilton**
    b: 01 Dec 1849 in Marion Co., Illinois
    m: 06 Jan 1870 in Veal Station, Parker Co., Texas
    d: 19 Jan 1894 in Jack Co., Texas

    - **Charles Freedis Wilton**
      b: Abt. 1827 in Marion Co., Illinois
      m: 12 Jul 1848 in Marion Co., Illinois
      d: Aft. 1881 in Veal Station, Parker Co., Texas

    - **Susanah Cruse**
      b: 07 Oct 1826 in Indiana
      d: Bef. 1860 in Illinois

  - **Easter Britania Clark**
    b: 12 Apr 1851 in Washington Co., Arkansas
    d: 15 Dec 1922 in Winn Hll, Jack Co., Texas

    - **Ezra Clark**
      b: 11 Apr 1823 in Ross Co., Ohio
      m: Abt. 1843 in Washington Co., Arkansas
      d: 02 Jun 1882 in Veal Station, Parker Co., Texas

    - **Livonia Hash**
      b: 22 Jan 1825 in Warren Co., Tennessee
      d: 22 Jan 1874 in Springtown, Parker Co., Texas

- **Amelia Jane Dixon**
  b: 04 Jul 1874 in Texas
  d: 15 Mar 1967 in Graham, Young Co., Texas

  - **E. P. Dixon**
    b: 29 Apr 1842 in Kentucky
    m: Unknown in ?
    d: 06 Nov 1936 in Young Co., Texas

  - **Elizabeth Read**
    b: Unknown in Texas
    d: Unknown in ?

Notes: This Tree also applies to the other children of Freedus E. Wilton & Amelia J. Dixon: Luther Eppie Wilton and Eater Virgil Wilton.

VERA VERTA LEDBETTER Standard Pedigree Tree

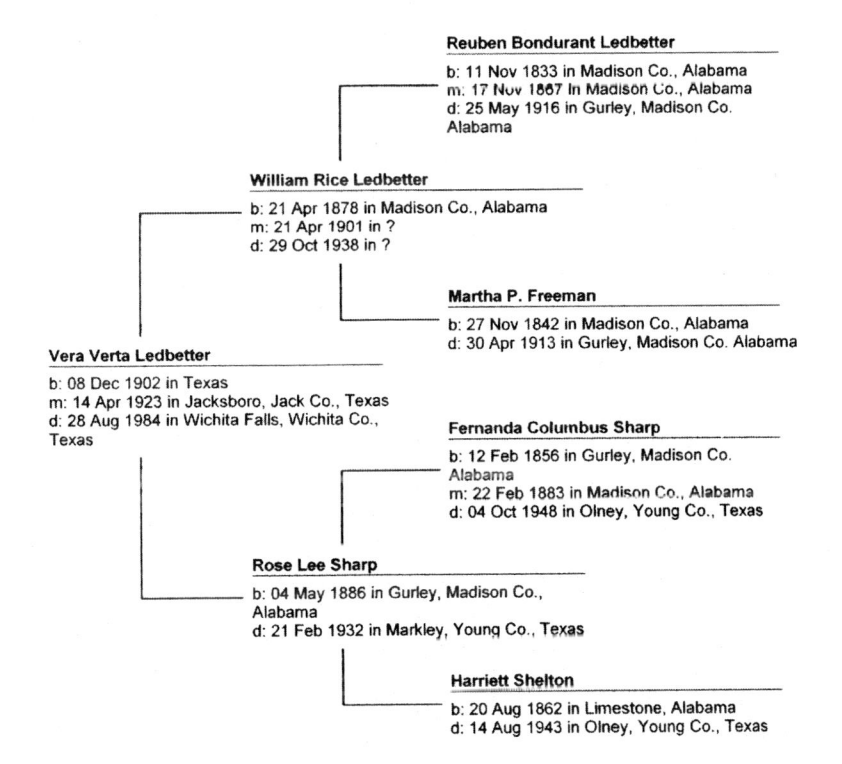

Vera Verta Ledbetter
b: 08 Dec 1902 in Texas
m: 14 Apr 1923 in Jacksboro, Jack Co., Texas
d: 28 Aug 1984 in Wichita Falls, Wichita Co., Texas

- **William Rice Ledbetter**
  b: 21 Apr 1878 in Madison Co., Alabama
  m: 21 Apr 1901 in ?
  d: 29 Oct 1938 in ?
  - **Reuben Bondurant Ledbetter**
    b: 11 Nov 1833 in Madison Co., Alabama
    m: 17 Nov 1867 In Madison Co., Alabama
    d: 25 May 1916 in Gurley, Madison Co. Alabama
  - **Martha P. Freeman**
    b: 27 Nov 1842 in Madison Co., Alabama
    d: 30 Apr 1913 in Gurley, Madison Co. Alabama

- **Rose Lee Sharp**
  b: 04 May 1886 in Gurley, Madison Co., Alabama
  d: 21 Feb 1932 in Markley, Young Co., Texas
  - **Fernanda Columbus Sharp**
    b: 12 Feb 1856 in Gurley, Madison Co. Alabama
    m: 22 Feb 1883 in Madison Co., Alabama
    d: 04 Oct 1948 in Olney, Young Co., Texas
  - **Harriett Shelton**
    b: 20 Aug 1862 in Limestone, Alabama
    d: 14 Aug 1943 in Olney, Young Co., Texas

Bobbye Loine Wilton (1929-   )
[7th. Generation From Henry Wilton (1768-1820)]

&

Jimmy Edward Roberts (1930-   )
& Family

Family Group Sheet

Husband: Jimmy Edward Roberts

Born: 21 Jun 1930	in: Odell, Wilbarger Co., Texas
Married: 13 Mar 1950	in: Bryson, Jack Co., Texas

Wife: Bobbye Loine Wilton

Born: 03 Nov 1929	in: Graham, Young Co., Texas
Father: Jesse Ruell Wilton	
Mother: Vera Verta Ledbetter	

CHILDREN

#		
1 M	Name: Jim Bob Roberts	
	Born: 11 Nov 1950	in: Young Co., Texas
	Died: Jul 1980	in: Snyder, Scurry Co., Texas
	Married: 16 Jun 1973	in: Wichita Co., Texas
	Spouse: Nadine Branscum	
2 M	Name: Terry Edward Roberts	
	Born: 19 Jul 1952	in: Young Co., Texas
	Married: 17 Jun 1972	in: Wichita Co., Texas
	Spouse: Jenny M. Goodson	
3 F	Name: Bama Loine Roberts	
	Born: 30 Jan 1955	in: Young Co., Texas
	Married: 25 May 1970	in: Wichita Co., Texas
	Spouse: Travis Dewayne Anderson	
	Married: 04 Dec 1992	in: Wichita Co., Texas
	Spouse: Richard W. Haskin	
4 F	Name: Trena Nell Roberts	
	Born: 08 Jun 1957	in: Wichita Co., Texas

BOBBYE LOINE WILTON Standard Pedigree Tree

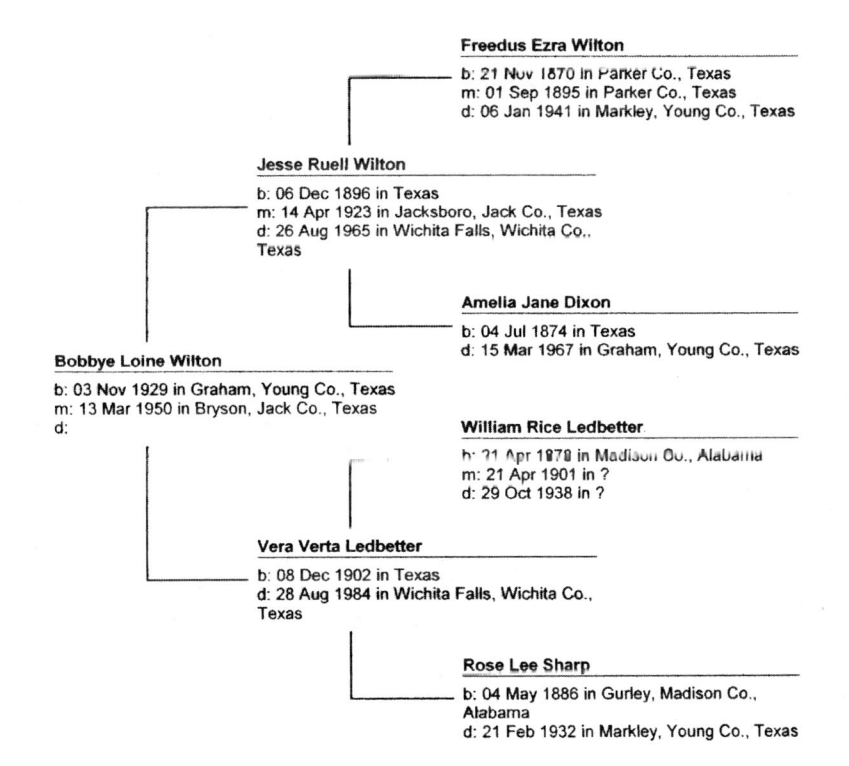

Bobbye Loine Wilton
b: 03 Nov 1929 in Graham, Young Co., Texas
m: 13 Mar 1950 in Bryson, Jack Co., Texas
d:

Jesse Ruell Wilton
b: 06 Dec 1896 in Texas
m: 14 Apr 1923 in Jacksboro, Jack Co., Texas
d: 26 Aug 1965 in Wichita Falls, Wichita Co., Texas

Freedus Ezra Wilton
b: 21 Nov 1870 in Parker Co., Texas
m: 01 Sep 1895 in Parker Co., Texas
d: 06 Jan 1941 in Markley, Young Co., Texas

Amelia Jane Dixon
b: 04 Jul 1874 in Texas
d: 15 Mar 1967 in Graham, Young Co., Texas

Vera Verta Ledbetter
b: 08 Dec 1902 in Texas
d: 28 Aug 1984 in Wichita Falls, Wichita Co., Texas

William Rice Ledbetter
b: 21 Apr 1878 in Madison Co., Alabama
m: 21 Apr 1901 in ?
d: 29 Oct 1938 in ?

Rose Lee Sharp
b: 04 May 1886 in Gurley, Madison Co., Alabama
d: 21 Feb 1932 in Markley, Young Co., Texas

Bama Loine Roberts (1955-   )
[8th. Generation from Henry Wilton (1769-1820)]

&

First Marriage To
Travis Dewayne Anderson (1952-   )
& Family

Second Marriage To
Richard W. Haskin (1937-   )
& Family

Family Group Sheet

Husband: Travis Dewayne Anderson

Born: 01 Dec 1952		in: Wichita Co., Texas
Married 1: 25 May 1970		in: Wichita Co., Texas
Married 2: 19 May 1978		in: Wichita Co., Texas

Wife: Bama Loine Roberts

Born: 30 Jan 1955   in: Young Co., Texas
Father: Jimmy Edward Roberts
Mother: Bobbye Loine Wilton
   Other Spouses: Richard W. Haskin

CHILDREN

1 F	Name: Lisa Christine Anderson Born: 30 Dec 1970	in: Wichita Co., Texas
2 F	Name: Bobbye Gail Anderson Born: 26 Jul 1974	in: Brazos Co., Texas
3 M	Name: Travis Leon Anderson Born: 17 Jul 1976	in: Wichita Co., Texas
4 F	Name: Patsy Jean Anderson Born: 27 Sep 1977	in: Wichita Co., Texas

Family Group Sheet

Husband: Richard W. Haskin

Born: Nov 1937
Married: 04 Dec 1992   in: Wichita Co., Texas

Wife: Bama Loine Roberts

Born: 30 Jan 1955   in: Young Co., Texas
Father: Jimmy Edward Roberts
Mother: Bobbye Loine Wilton
   Other Spouses: Travis Dewayne Anderson

BAMA LOINE ROBERTS Standard Pedigree Tree

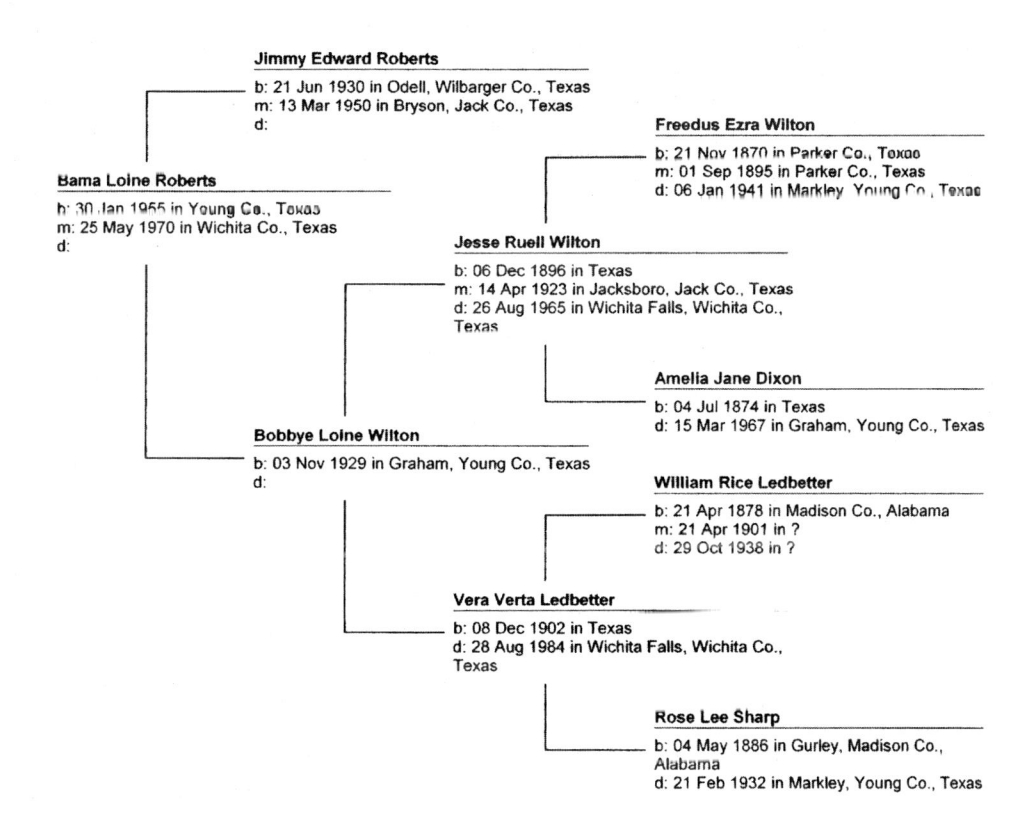

Jimmy Edward Roberts
b: 21 Jun 1930 in Odell, Wilbarger Co., Texas
m: 13 Mar 1950 in Bryson, Jack Co., Texas
d:

Bama Loine Roberts
b: 30 Jan 1955 in Young Co., Texas
m: 25 May 1970 in Wichita Co., Texas
d:

Freedus Ezra Wilton
b: 21 Nov 1870 in Parker Co., Texas
m: 01 Sep 1895 in Parker Co., Texas
d: 06 Jan 1941 in Markley, Young Co., Texas

Jesse Ruell Wilton
b: 06 Dec 1896 in Texas
m: 14 Apr 1923 in Jacksboro, Jack Co., Texas
d: 26 Aug 1965 in Wichita Falls, Wichita Co., Texas

Amelia Jane Dixon
b: 04 Jul 1874 in Texas
d: 15 Mar 1967 in Graham, Young Co., Texas

Bobbye Loine Wilton
b: 03 Nov 1929 in Graham, Young Co., Texas
d:

William Rice Ledbetter
b: 21 Apr 1878 in Madison Co., Alabama
m: 21 Apr 1901 in ?
d: 29 Oct 1938 in ?

Vera Verta Ledbetter
b: 08 Dec 1902 in Texas
d: 28 Aug 1984 in Wichita Falls, Wichita Co., Texas

Rose Lee Sharp
b: 04 May 1886 in Gurley, Madison Co., Alabama
d: 21 Feb 1932 in Markley, Young Co., Texas

Notes: This Tree also applies to the other children of Jimmy Edwards Roberts & Bobbye Loine Wilton: Jim Bob Roberts, Terry Edward Roberts, and Trena Nell Roberts.

Luther Eppie Wilton (1901-1959)
[6th. Generation From Henry Wilton (1769-1820)]

&

Gladys Gertrude Hoak (1908-1975)
& Family

Luther Eppie was the middle son of Freedus E. and Amelia J. Wilton. He was born in Texas in February, 1901. By 1910, the family, which then included Freedus and Amelia and their two sons, Jesse and Luther, had moved to Young County, Texas.

At the time of the 1920 Federal Census of Young County, Texas, Freedus E. and the family were still living in Young County, and they had added one more member to their family, a son named Eater Virgil, who was born in April 1911. Listed in the census were other families nearby that would later become part of the family. Two dwellings away on one side of Freedus was the George William Hoak family, from which George's daughter, Gladys, would marry Luther E. about 1934. In the dwelling next to George on the other side was the family of William Ledbetter, from which another son of Luther E. Wilton, Jesse R. Wilton, would marry William Ledbetter's daughter, Vera V. Ledbetter in 1923.

In the 1930 Federal Census of Young County, Freedus E. was living only one dwelling away from the family of George Hoak. At that time George's daughter, Gladys, was still living at home, but Freedus E. sons, Jesse R. and Luther E., were gone from home. Also at that time, the family of William Ledbetter was three dwellings away on the other side of George Hoak, but daughter, Vera V. Ledbetter, was gone, having married Jesse R. Wilton by this time.

Luther married Gladys Gertrude Hoak about 1934, and they continued to live in Young County, where their two sons, George Keith Wilton and Frank Edward Wilton were born. Luther died in July 1959. Gladys died in 1975 after falling and breaking a hip, an injury from which she never recovered. She lived on the farm where she was born ("old Hoak farm") until the end.

Family Group Sheet

Husband: Luther Eppie Wilton

- Born: 06 Feb 1901 — in: Texas
- Married: Abt. 1934 — in: Texas
- Died: 06 Jul 1959 — in: Texas
- Father: Freedus Ezra Wilton
- Mother: Amelia Jane Dixon

Wife: Gladys Gertrude Hoak

- Born: 04 May 1908 — in: Texas
- Died: 20 Apr 1975 — in: Denton Co., Texas
- Father: George William Hoak
- Mother: Willie Virginia Michael

CHILDREN

1. M — Name: George Keith Wilton
   - Born: 17 May 1935 — in: Young Co., Texas
   - Died: 21 Jun 1997 — in: Wichita Co., Texas
   - Married: Unknown — in: ?
   - Spouse: Vivian Maxine McConnell

2. M — Name: Frank Edward Wilton
   - Born: 22 Mar 1937 — in: Young Co., Texas
   - Married: 24 Aug 1962 — in: ?
   - Spouse: Martha Carolyn Nisle

George Keith Wilton (1935-1997)
[7th. Generation From Henry Wilton (1769-1820)]

&

Vivian Maxine McConnell
& Family

Family Group Sheet

	Husband: George Keith Wilton	
	Born: 17 May 1935	in: Young Co., Texas
	Married: Unknown	in: ?
	Died: 21 Jun 1997	in: Wichita Co., Texas
	Father: Luther Eppie Wilton	
	Mother: Gladys Gertrude Hoak	
	Wife: Vivian Maxine McConnell	
	Born: Unknown	in: ?

	CHILDREN	
1 F	Name: Kimberly Faye Wilton	
	Born: 29 Jan 1959	in: Young Co., Texas
	Married: 11 Jul 1975	in: Young Co., Texas
	Spouse: Neal Fletcher Hearne	
	Married: 19 Aug 1977	in: Young Co., Texas
	Spouse: Dennis Ray Ligon	
2 M	Name: George Keith Jr. Wilton	
	Born: 13 Jul 1961	in: Young Co., Texas
	Married: 15 Feb 1980	in: Young Co., Texas
	Spouse: Leslie C. Dunlap	
	Married: 04 Sep 1982	in: Young Co., Texas
	Spouse: Timi Lyn Boucher	
	Married: 30 Jun 1984	in: Young Co., Texas
	Spouse: Teresa Ann Daniels	
3 F	Name: Mary Ella Wilton	
	Born: 19 Jun 1969	in: Young Co., Texas

GEORGE KEITH WILTON Standard Pedigree Tree

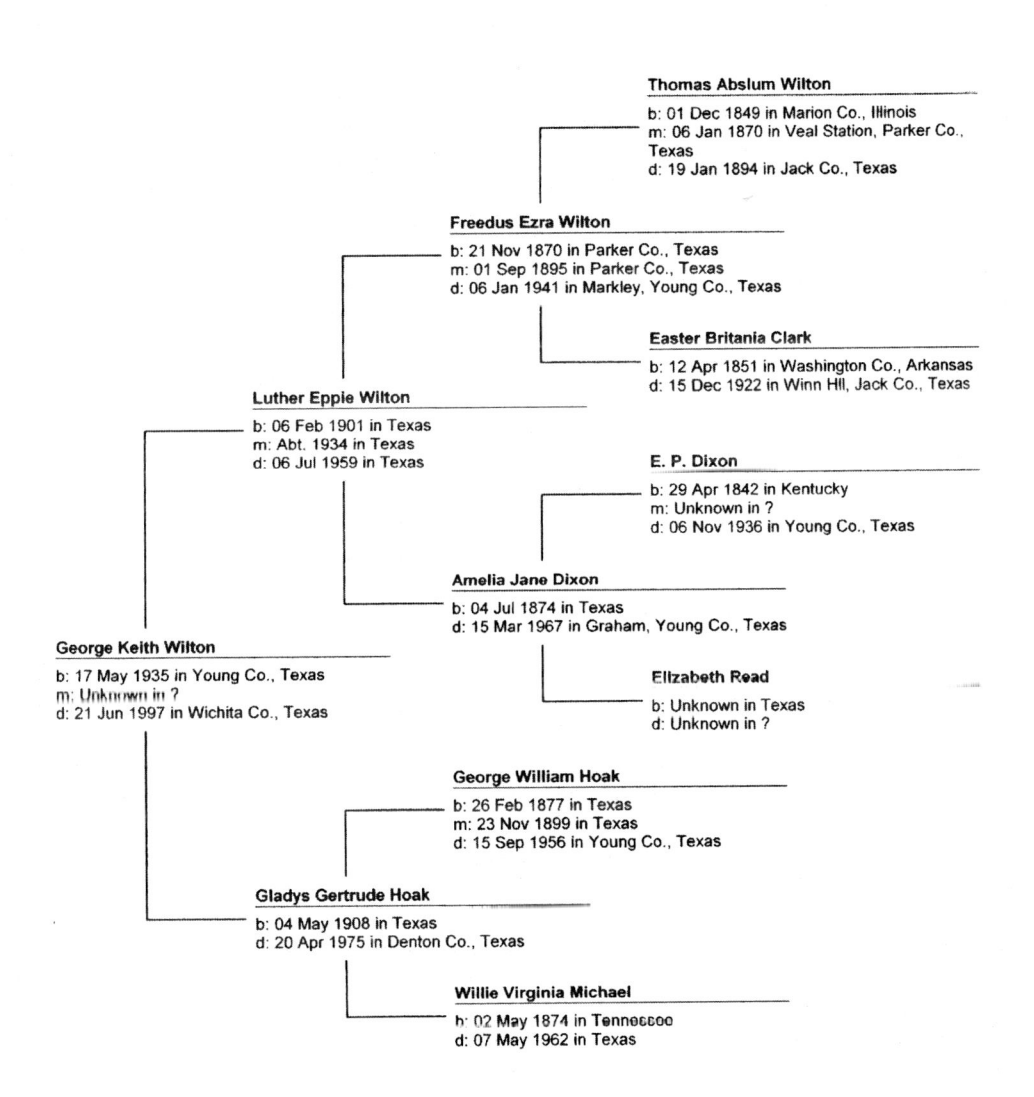

- **George Keith Wilton**
  b: 17 May 1935 in Young Co., Texas
  m: Unknown in ?
  d: 21 Jun 1997 in Wichita Co., Texas
  - **Luther Eppie Wilton**
    b: 06 Feb 1901 in Texas
    m: Abt. 1934 in Texas
    d: 06 Jul 1959 in Texas
    - **Freedus Ezra Wilton**
      b: 21 Nov 1870 in Parker Co., Texas
      m: 01 Sep 1895 in Parker Co., Texas
      d: 06 Jan 1941 in Markley, Young Co., Texas
      - **Thomas Abslum Wilton**
        b: 01 Dec 1849 in Marion Co., Illinois
        m: 06 Jan 1870 in Veal Station, Parker Co., Texas
        d: 19 Jan 1894 in Jack Co., Texas
      - **Easter Britania Clark**
        b: 12 Apr 1851 in Washington Co., Arkansas
        d: 15 Dec 1922 in Winn Hll, Jack Co., Texas
    - **Amelia Jane Dixon**
      b: 04 Jul 1874 in Texas
      d: 15 Mar 1967 in Graham, Young Co., Texas
      - **E. P. Dixon**
        b: 29 Apr 1842 in Kentucky
        m: Unknown in ?
        d: 06 Nov 1936 in Young Co., Texas
      - **Elizabeth Read**
        b: Unknown in Texas
        d: Unknown in ?
  - **Gladys Gertrude Hoak**
    b: 04 May 1908 in Texas
    d: 20 Apr 1975 in Denton Co., Texas
    - **George William Hoak**
      b: 26 Feb 1877 in Texas
      m: 23 Nov 1899 in Texas
      d: 15 Sep 1956 in Young Co., Texas
    - **Willie Virginia Michael**
      b: 02 May 1874 in Tennessee
      d: 07 May 1962 in Texas

Notes: This Tree also applies to the other child of Luther Eppie Wilton & Gladys Gertrude Hoak: Frank Edward Wilton.

Kimberly Faye Wilton (1959-   )
[8th. Generation from Henry Wilton (1769-1820)]

&

First Marriage To
Neal Fletcher Hearne (1959-   )
& Family

Second Marriage To
Dennis Ray Ligon (1954-   )
& Family

Family Group Sheet

Husband: Neal Fletcher Hearne

Born: 11 Jun 1959   in: Young Co., Texas
Married: 11 Jul 1975   in: Young Co., Texas

Wife: Kimberly Faye Wilton

Born: 29 Jan 1959   in: Young Co., Texas
Father: George Keith Wilton
Mother: Vivian Maxine McConnell
Other Spouses: Dennis Ray Ligon

CHILDREN

1 M   Name: Neal Chadwick Hearne
     Born: 10 Apr 1976   in: Young Co., Texas

Family Group Sheet

Husband: Dennis Ray Ligon

Born: 12 Aug 1954   in: Tom Green Co., Texas
Married: 19 Aug 1977   in: Young Co., Texas

Wife: Kimberly Faye Wilton

Born: 29 Jan 1959   in: Young Co., Texas
Father: George Keith Wilton
Mother: Vivian Maxine McConnell
Other Spouses: Neal Fletcher Hearne

CHILDREN

1 M   Name: Adrian Ray Ligon
     Born: 16 Apr 1984   in: Young Co., Texas

2 F   Name: Morgan Brittney Ligon
     Born: 23 Sep 1991   in: Young Co., Texas

KIMBERLY FAYE WILTON Standard Pedigree Tree

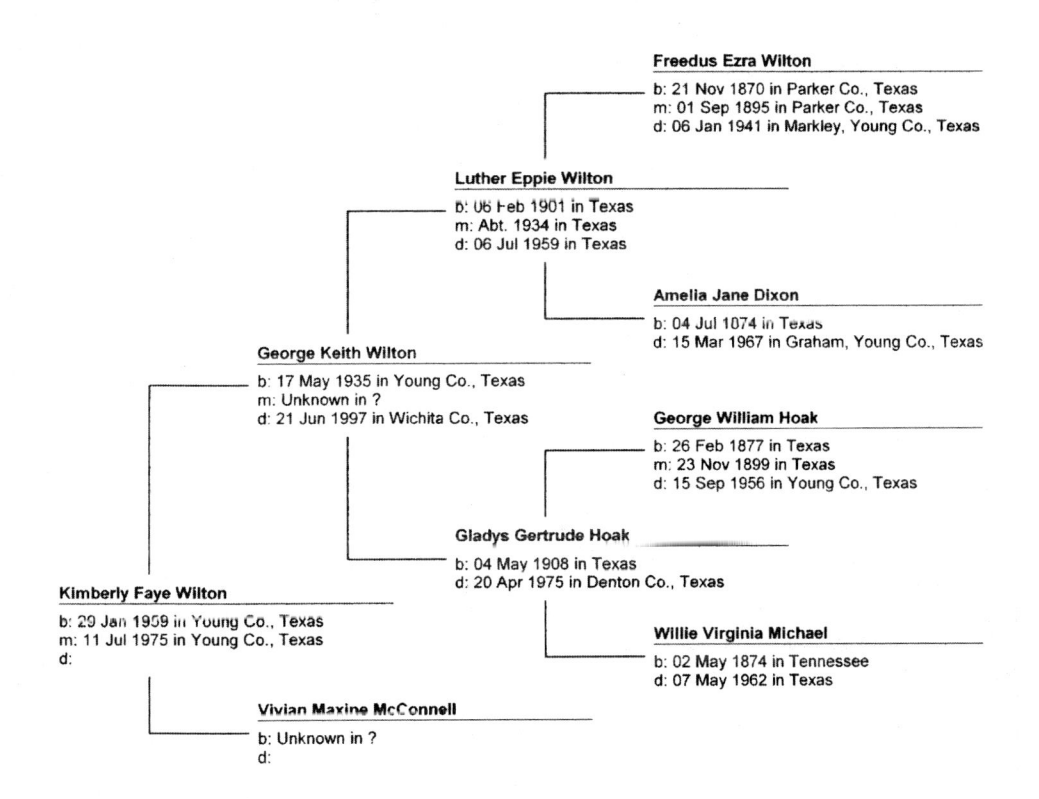

Kimberly Faye Wilton
b: 29 Jan 1959 in Young Co., Texas
m: 11 Jul 1975 in Young Co., Texas
d:

- **George Keith Wilton**
  b: 17 May 1935 in Young Co., Texas
  m: Unknown in ?
  d: 21 Jun 1997 in Wichita Co., Texas

  - **Luther Eppie Wilton**
    b: 06 Feb 1901 in Texas
    m: Abt. 1934 in Texas
    d: 06 Jul 1959 in Texas

    - **Freedus Ezra Wilton**
      b: 21 Nov 1870 in Parker Co., Texas
      m: 01 Sep 1895 in Parker Co., Texas
      d: 06 Jan 1941 in Markley, Young Co., Texas

    - **Amelia Jane Dixon**
      b: 04 Jul 1874 in Texas
      d: 15 Mar 1967 in Graham, Young Co., Texas

  - **Gladys Gertrude Hoak**
    b: 04 May 1908 in Texas
    d: 20 Apr 1975 in Denton Co., Texas

    - **George William Hoak**
      b: 26 Feb 1877 in Texas
      m: 23 Nov 1899 in Texas
      d: 15 Sep 1956 in Young Co., Texas

    - **Willie Virginia Michael**
      b: 02 May 1874 in Tennessee
      d: 07 May 1962 in Texas

- **Vivian Maxine McConnell**
  b: Unknown in ?
  d:

Notes: This Tree also applies to the other children of George Keith Wilton & Vivian Maxine McConnell: George Keith Jr. Wilton and Mary Ella Wilton.

George Keith Jr. Wilton (1961-   )

[8th. Generation from Henry Wilton (1769-1820)]

&

First Marriage To
Leslie C. Dunlap (1962-   )
& Family

Second Marriage To
Timi Lyn Boucher (1965-   )
& Family

Third Marriage To
Theresa Ann Daniels (1966-   )
& Family

Family Group Sheet

Husband: George Keith Jr. Wilton

Born: 13 Jul 1961   in: Young Co., Texas
Married: 15 Feb 1980   in: Young Co., Texas
Father: George Keith Wilton
Mother: Vivian Maxine McConnell
   Other Spouses: Timi Lyn Boucher, Teresa Ann Daniels

Wife: Leslie C. Dunlap

Born: Abt. 1962

Family Group Sheet

Husband: George Keith Jr. Wilton

Born: 13 Jul 1961   in: Young Co., Texas
Married: 04 Sep 1982   in: Young Co., Texas
Father: George Keith Wilton
Mother: Vivian Maxine McConnell
   Other Spouses: Leslie C. Dunlap, Teresa Ann Daniels

Wife: Timi Lyn Boucher

Born: Abt. 1965

CHILDREN

1 F   Name: Jonna Kay Wilton
     Born: 23 Apr 1983   in: Tarrant Co., Texas

Family Group Sheet

Husband: George Keith Jr. Wilton

Born: 13 Jul 1961   in: Young Co., Texas
Married: 30 Jun 1984   in: Young Co., Texas
Father: George Keith Wilton
Mother: Vivian Maxine McConnell
    Other Spouses: Leslie C. Dunlap, Timi Lyn Boucher

Wife: Teresa Ann Daniels

Born: Abt. 1966

CHILDREN

#		
1 F	Name: Michell Lynn Wilton Born: 17 Feb 1985	in: Young Co., Texas
2 M	Name: Larry Mac Wilton Born: 05 Feb 1986	in: Young Co., Texas
3 F	Name: Vanessa Rhae Wilton Born: 03 Feb 1987	in: Young Co., Texas
4 F	Name: Cindy Ranee Wilton Born: 21 Apr 1988	in: Young Co., Texas

Frank Edward Wilton (1937-   )
[7th. Generation From Henry Wilton (1769-1820)]

&

Martha Carolyn Nisle (1943-   )
& Family

Family Group Sheet

Husband: Frank Edward Wilton	
Born: 22 Mar 1937	in: Young Co., Texas
Married: 24 Aug 1962	in: ?
Father: Luther Eppie Wilton	
Mother: Gladys Gertrude Hoak	

Wife: Martha Carolyn Nisle	
Born: 24 Apr 1943	in: Harris Co., Texas

	CHILDREN	
1 M	Name: Mark Edward Wilton	
	Born: 30 Jun 1964	in: Young Co., Texas
	Married: 11 Jul 1998	in: Young Co., Texas
	Spouse: Beverly Diane Archer	
2 M	Name: David Alan Wilton	
	Born: 27 Oct 1967	in: Jefferson Co., Texas

Eater Virgil Wilton (1911-1945)
[6th. Generation From Henry Wilton (1769-1820)]

&

Edwinona Burch
& Family

Eater Virgil was the youngest of three sons of Freedus E. Wilton and Amelia J. Dixon. He was born 1911 in Texas, and his early years were spent in Young County, Texas, which is where his parents made their home.

The first record of Eater V. is found in the 1920 Federal Census of Young County, Texas, where he is listed with his parents and his two older brothers. At the time, he was just 8 years old.

In the 1930 Federal Census of Young County, Eater Virgil is listed with his parents, who were then in their late 50's, and he was then 18 years old. His grandfather, EP Dixon, who was then 85 years old, was also living with the family.

Eater Virgil married Edwinona Burch in June 1934, and at some point made Young County their home. Their third child, Charles Virgil Wilton, was born in Young County in June 1937. Eater V. died in May 1945 in Young County, but he was buried at Winn Hill Cemetery in Jack County, Texas.

Family Group Sheet

Husband: Eater Virgil Wilton		
Born: 25 Apr 1911	in: Texas	
Married: 20 Jun 1934		
Died: 25 May 1945	in: Young Co., Texas	
Father: Freedus Ezra Wilton		
Mother: Amelia Jane Dixon		
Wife: Edwinona Burch		
Born: Unknown		

CHILDREN

1 F	Name: Betty Lou Wilton		
	Born: 03 Jan 1935		
2 M	Name: Warren Wilton		
	Born: Unknown		
3 M	Name: Charles Virgil Wilton		
	Born: 08 Jun 1937	in: Young Co., Texas	
	Died: 01 Mar 1991	in: San Joaquin Co., California	

Alvin Henry Wilton (1873-1939)
[5th. Generation from Henry Wilton (1769-1820)]

&

Leuticia Hannah (1881-1935)
& Family

Alvin Henry Wilton was the second of twelve children of Thomas A. & Easter B. (Clark) Wilton. He was born January 1873 in Wise County, Texas. In the 1880 Federal Census of Jack County, Texas, he was listed with the family as a child of 9 years of age.

For most of his adult life, Alvin was a farmer in Jack County, Texas in the Berwick Community. In the 1900 Federal Census, at the age of 27, he was listed as a boarder and farm laborer with the Loving family (Jermyn, Texas). In addition to being a farmer, family tradition has it that while he was at the Loving Ranch, he also functioned as a cowboy. Located in the same vicinity (Winn Hill, Texas) was his mother, Easter (Clark) Wilton, who was then raising the family that was still home. Alvin's father, Thomas A. Wilton, had died in 1894.

Alvin married Leutica Hannah, the daughter of Francis M. & Mary A. (Hannah) Wilton in November 1906. Leuticia, known as "Tee," was the second of nine children. In the 1910 Federal Census of Jack County, Texas, Alvin & Tee were located just one dwelling away from Tee's parents and family. At the time, Alvin & Tee had one son, named James Everett Wilton, who was born in March 1908.

By 1920, in the Federal Census of Jack County, Alvin & Tee had three children; two sons and one daughter. In addition to James E. Wilton who was born in 1908, Melvin Cleo Wilton was born March 1912, and Ora Izora Wilton was born June 1919.

In the 1930 Federal Census of Jack County, Alvin and Tee were again listed with their three children. At that time, Alvin was age 57, Tee age 48, James E. age 22, Melvin C. age 18, and Ora I. age 11. By this time, Tee's father had died, but Tee's brother, James F. Hannah, along with his wife and six children, was listed just two dwellings away from Alvin & Tee.

Tee died February 1935, and Alvin died December 1939. They were both buried in the Winn Hill Cemetery in Jack County, Texas.

Family Group Sheet

Husband: Alvin Henry Wilton

Born: 12 Jan 1873 in: Wise Co., Texas
Married: 25 Nov 1906 in: Texas
Died: 31 Dec 1939 in: Jacksboro, Jack Co., Texas
Father: Thomas Abslum Wilton
Mother: Easter Britania Clark

Wife: Leuticia Hannah

Born: 08 Sep 1881 in: Corsicana, Navarro Co., Texas
Died: 15 Feb 1935 in: Berwick, Jack Co., Texas
Father: Francis Marion Hannah
Mother: Mary Adeline Melton

CHILDREN

1 M
Name: James Everett Wilton
Born: 30 Mar 1908 in: Jeannette, Jack Co., Texas
Died: 15 Jun 1988 in: Jack Co., Texas
Married: 09 Sep 1931 in: Jack Co, Texas
Spouse: Hazel Ann Dixson

2 M
Name: Melvin Cleo Wilton
Born: 25 Mar 1912 in: Berwick, Jack Co., Texas
Died: 22 Sep 2000 in: Edna, Jackson Co., Texas
Married: Abt. 1938 in: Texas
Spouse: Eula Mae Huskey

3 F
Name: Ora Izora Wilton
Born: 12 Jun 1919 in: Berwick, Jack Co., Texas
Married: 26 Apr 1940 in: Wichita Falls, Wichita Co., Texas
Spouse: Spencer Pinckney Dewoody

LEUTICIA HANNAH Standard Pedigree Tree

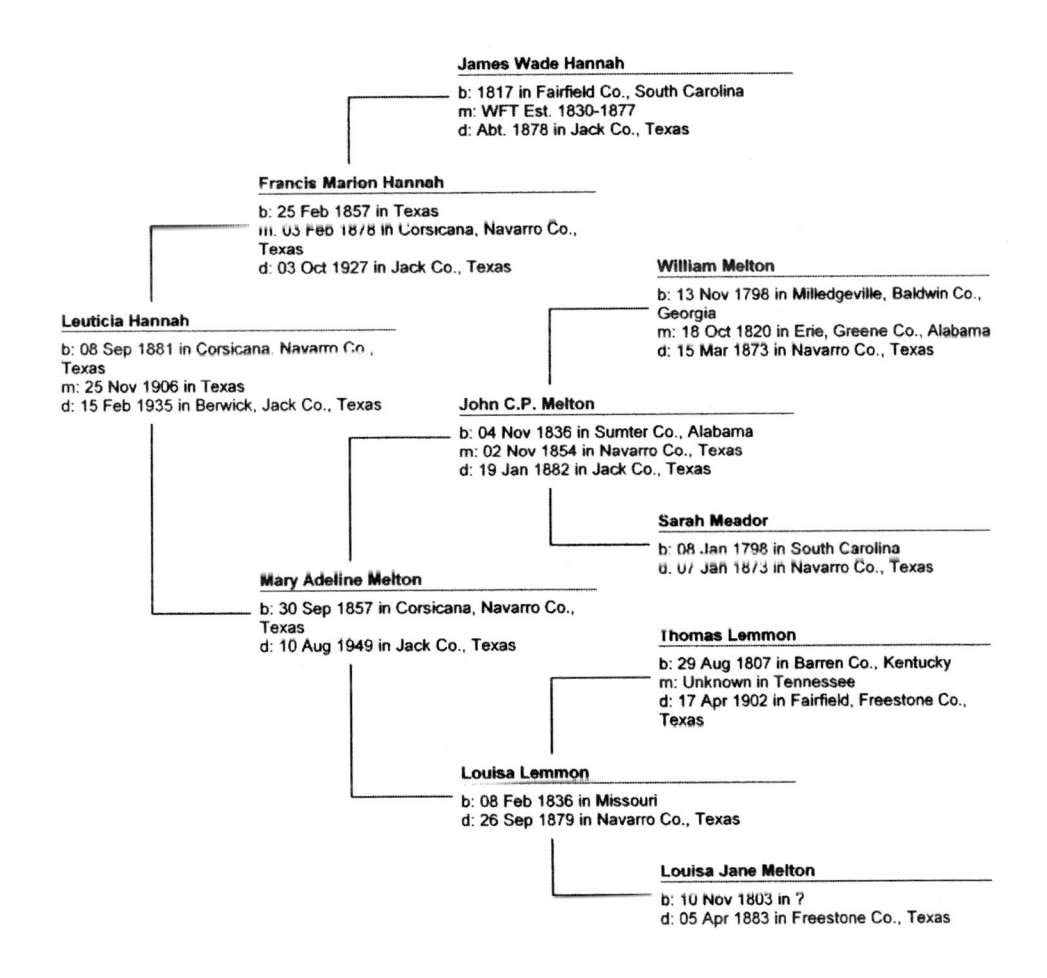

James Wade Hannah
b: 1817 in Fairfield Co., South Carolina
m: WFT Est. 1830-1877
d: Abt. 1878 in Jack Co., Texas

Francis Marion Hannah
b: 25 Feb 1857 in Texas
m: 03 Feb 1878 in Corsicana, Navarro Co., Texas
d: 03 Oct 1927 in Jack Co., Texas

William Melton
b: 13 Nov 1798 in Milledgeville, Baldwin Co., Georgia
m: 18 Oct 1820 in Erie, Greene Co., Alabama
d: 15 Mar 1873 in Navarro Co., Texas

Leuticia Hannah
b: 08 Sep 1881 in Corsicana, Navarro Co., Texas
m: 25 Nov 1906 in Texas
d: 15 Feb 1935 in Berwick, Jack Co., Texas

John C.P. Melton
b: 04 Nov 1836 in Sumter Co., Alabama
m: 02 Nov 1854 in Navarro Co., Texas
d: 19 Jan 1882 in Jack Co., Texas

Sarah Meador
b: 08 Jan 1798 in South Carolina
d: 07 Jan 1873 in Navarro Co., Texas

Mary Adeline Melton
b: 30 Sep 1857 in Corsicana, Navarro Co., Texas
d: 10 Aug 1949 in Jack Co., Texas

Thomas Lemmon
b: 29 Aug 1807 in Barren Co., Kentucky
m: Unknown in Tennessee
d: 17 Apr 1902 in Fairfield, Freestone Co., Texas

Louisa Lemmon
b: 08 Feb 1836 in Missouri
d: 26 Sep 1879 in Navarro Co., Texas

Louisa Jane Melton
b: 10 Nov 1803 in ?
d: 05 Apr 1883 in Freestone Co., Texas

James Everett Wilton (1908-1988)
[6th. Generation from Henry Wilton (1769-1820)]

&

Hazel Ann Dixson (1912-2006)
& Family

James was born March 1908 on the Wilton farm in the Berwick Community, Jack Co., Texas. He was listed at home with his parents and family in the 1910, 1920, and 1930 Federal Census of Jack County, Texas. By 1930, he was listed as age 22, at home as a general farm laborer. He married Hazel Ann Dixson, daughter of Robert Pyles Dixson & Lola Ella Dunn in September 1931.

James and Hazel Ann had two children, named Everett Waylin Wilton, born October 1932, and Ora Lenora Wilton, born January 1940. According to The History of Jack County Texas, Volume #1, James lived in the Berwick Community all of his life, except for a few years while his children were in school. He was a farmer and employee of the County of Jack, where he maintained the county roads. His wife, Hazel Ann, was a homemaker and a retired nurse, and she was one of the first LVN nurses at the Jack County Hospital.

James died June 1988 and was buried in the Winn Hill Cemetery in Jack County. Hazel Ann died July 2006.

Family Group Sheet

Husband: James Everett Wilton

Born: 30 Mar 1908	in: Jeannette, Jack Co., Texas
Married: 09 Sep 1931	in: Jack Co, Texas
Died: 15 Jun 1988	in: Jack Co., Texas
Father: Alvin Henry Wilton	
Mother: Leuticia Hannah	

Wife: Hazel Ann Dixson

Born: 26 Dec 1912	in: Jack Co., Texas
Died: 19 Jul 2006	in: Jacksboro, Jack Co., Texas
Father: Robert Pyles Dixson	
Mother: Lola Ella Dunn	

CHILDREN

1 M
- Name: Everett Waylin Wilton
- Born: 09 Oct 1932 — in: Jacksboro, Jack Co., Texas
- Died: 05 Mar 1986 — in: Palestine, Anderson Co., Texas
- Married: 16 Jul 1958 — in: Texas
- Spouse: Marleen Scott

2 F
- Name: Ora Lenora Wilton
- Born: 08 Jan 1940 — in: Jack Co., Texas
- Married: 23 Jul 1961 — in: Fort Worth, Tarrant Co., Texas
- Spouse: Jimmy Earl Shelton

JAMES EVERETT WILTON Standard Pedigree Tree

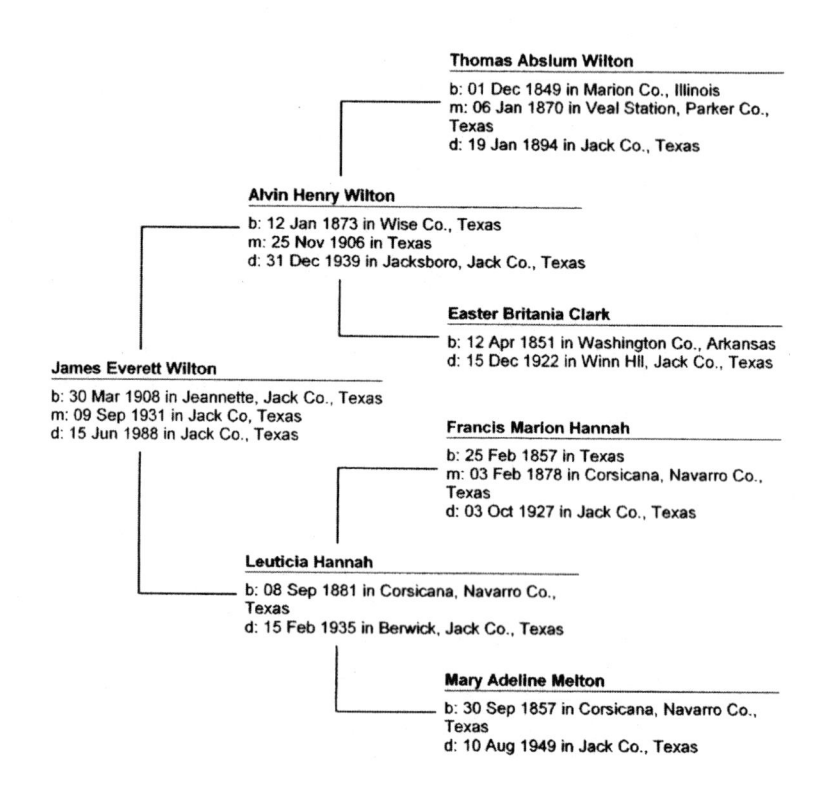

James Everett Wilton
b: 30 Mar 1908 in Jeannette, Jack Co., Texas
m: 09 Sep 1931 in Jack Co, Texas
d: 15 Jun 1988 in Jack Co., Texas

- **Alvin Henry Wilton**
  b: 12 Jan 1873 in Wise Co., Texas
  m: 25 Nov 1906 in Texas
  d: 31 Dec 1939 in Jacksboro, Jack Co., Texas

  - **Thomas Abslum Wilton**
    b: 01 Dec 1849 in Marion Co., Illinois
    m: 06 Jan 1870 in Veal Station, Parker Co., Texas
    d: 19 Jan 1894 in Jack Co., Texas

  - **Easter Britania Clark**
    b: 12 Apr 1851 in Washington Co., Arkansas
    d: 15 Dec 1922 in Winn Hll, Jack Co., Texas

- **Leuticia Hannah**
  b: 08 Sep 1881 in Corsicana, Navarro Co., Texas
  d: 15 Feb 1935 in Berwick, Jack Co., Texas

  - **Francis Marion Hannah**
    b: 25 Feb 1857 in Texas
    m: 03 Feb 1878 in Corsicana, Navarro Co., Texas
    d: 03 Oct 1927 in Jack Co., Texas

  - **Mary Adeline Melton**
    b: 30 Sep 1857 in Corsicana, Navarro Co., Texas
    d: 10 Aug 1949 in Jack Co., Texas

Notes: This Tree also applies to the other children of Alvin Henry Wilton & Leuticia Hannah: Melvin Cleo Wilton and Ora Izora Wilton.

HAZEL ANN DIXSON Standard Pedigree Tree

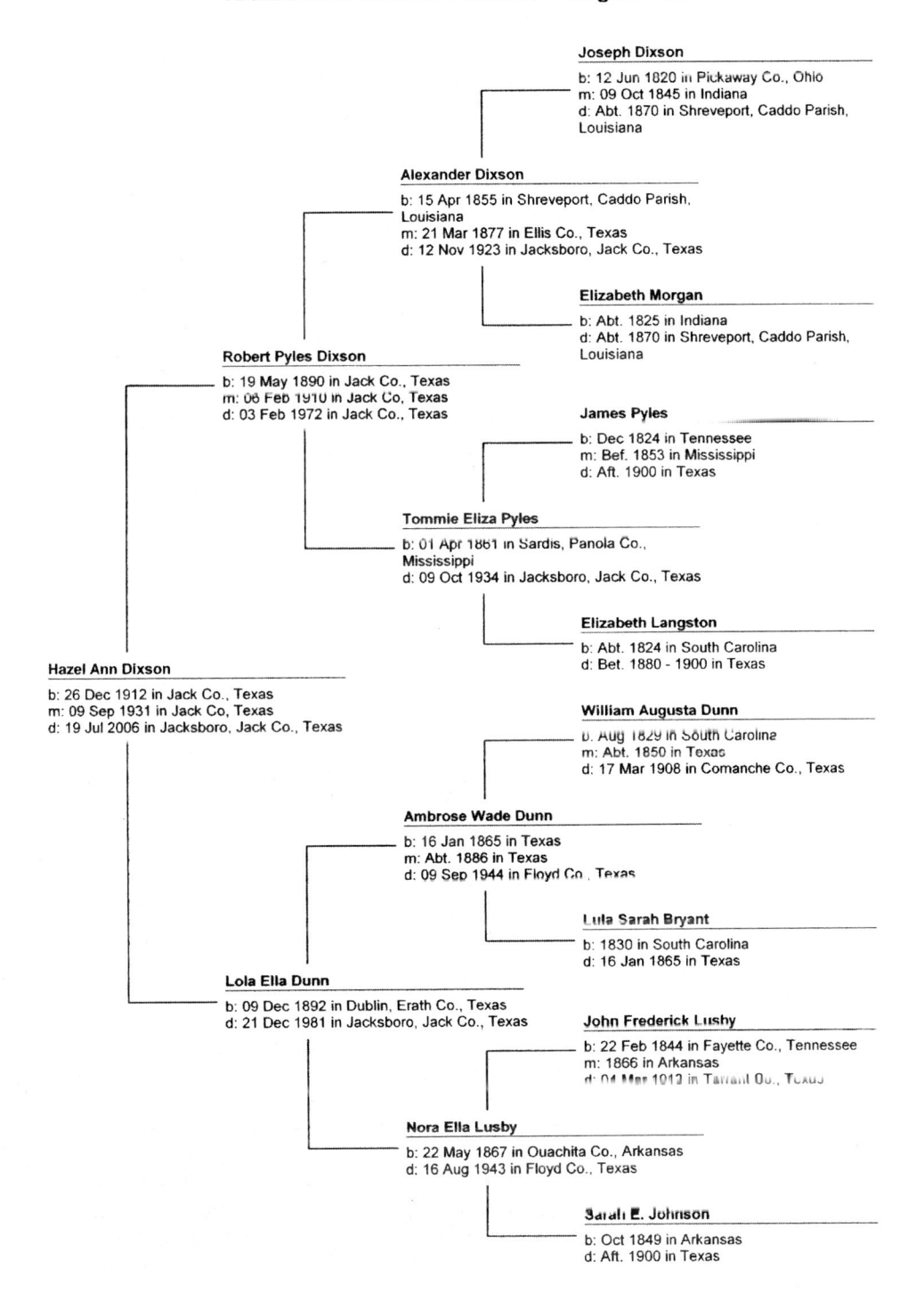

Hazel Ann Dixson
b: 26 Dec 1912 in Jack Co., Texas
m: 09 Sep 1931 in Jack Co, Texas
d: 19 Jul 2006 in Jacksboro, Jack Co., Texas

- **Robert Pyles Dixson**
  b: 19 May 1890 in Jack Co., Texas
  m: 08 Feb 1910 in Jack Co, Texas
  d: 03 Feb 1972 in Jack Co., Texas

  - **Alexander Dixson**
    b: 15 Apr 1855 in Shreveport, Caddo Parish, Louisiana
    m: 21 Mar 1877 in Ellis Co., Texas
    d: 12 Nov 1923 in Jacksboro, Jack Co., Texas

    - **Joseph Dixson**
      b: 12 Jun 1820 in Pickaway Co., Ohio
      m: 09 Oct 1845 in Indiana
      d: Abt. 1870 in Shreveport, Caddo Parish, Louisiana

    - **Elizabeth Morgan**
      b: Abt. 1825 in Indiana
      d: Abt. 1870 in Shreveport, Caddo Parish, Louisiana

  - **Tommie Eliza Pyles**
    b: 01 Apr 1861 in Sardis, Panola Co., Mississippi
    d: 09 Oct 1934 in Jacksboro, Jack Co., Texas

    - **James Pyles**
      b: Dec 1824 in Tennessee
      m: Bef. 1853 in Mississippi
      d: Aft. 1900 in Texas

    - **Elizabeth Langston**
      b: Abt. 1824 in South Carolina
      d: Bet. 1880 - 1900 in Texas

- **Lola Ella Dunn**
  b: 09 Dec 1892 in Dublin, Erath Co., Texas
  d: 21 Dec 1981 in Jacksboro, Jack Co., Texas

  - **Ambrose Wade Dunn**
    b: 16 Jan 1865 in Texas
    m: Abt. 1886 in Texas
    d: 09 Sep 1944 in Floyd Co., Texas

    - **William Augusta Dunn**
      b: Aug 1829 in South Carolina
      m: Abt. 1850 in Texas
      d: 17 Mar 1908 in Comanche Co., Texas

    - **Lula Sarah Bryant**
      b: 1830 in South Carolina
      d: 16 Jan 1865 in Texas

  - **Nora Ella Lusby**
    b: 22 May 1867 in Ouachita Co., Arkansas
    d: 16 Aug 1943 in Floyd Co., Texas

    - **John Frederick Lusby**
      b: 22 Feb 1844 in Fayette Co., Tennessee
      m: 1866 in Arkansas
      d: 04 Mar 1913 in Tarrant Co., Texas

    - **Sarah E. Johnson**
      b: Oct 1849 in Arkansas
      d: Aft. 1900 in Texas

Everett Waylin Wilton (1932-1986)
[7th. Generation from Henry Wilton (1769-1820)]

&

Marleen Scott (1936-   )
& Family

Everett Waylin Wilton was born October 1932, the older of two children by James Everett Wilton and Hazel Ann Dixson. His early years were spent in the Berwick Community of Jack County, Texas, where he grew up on his father's farm.

Everett married Marleen Scott in July 1958, and his work was in the oil field as a Field Supervisor for the Halliburton Oil Field Company. Everett & Marleen had two children, named Neal Dwayne Wilton, born March 1958 in Young County, Texas, and Angela Kay Wilton, born May 1964 in Anderson County, Texas. Everett Waylin died in March 1986 in Palestine in Anderson County, Texas.

Family Group Sheet

Husband: Everett Waylin Wilton

Born: 09 Oct 1932	in: Jacksboro, Jack Co., Texas
Married: 16 Jul 1958	in: Texas
Died: 05 Mar 1986	in: Palestine, Anderson Co., Texas
Father: James Everett Wilton	
Mother: Hazel Ann Dixson	

Wife: Marleen Scott

Born: 10 Dec 1936	in: Postoak, Jack Co., Texas
Father: Burton Scott	
Mother: Lennie Reynolds	

CHILDREN

1 M
- Name: Neal Dwayne Wilton
- Born: 03 Mar 1958 — in: Graham, Young Co., Texas
- Married: 14 Jun 1981 — in: Harris Co., Texas
- Spouse: Darla G. Holley

2 F
- Name: Angela Kay Wilton
- Born: 07 May 1964 — in: Palestine, Anderson Co., Texas
- Married: 14 Apr 1984 — in: Palestine, Anderson Co., Texas
- Spouse: Sandy D. Lowe

EVERETT WAYLIN WILTON Standard Pedigree Tree

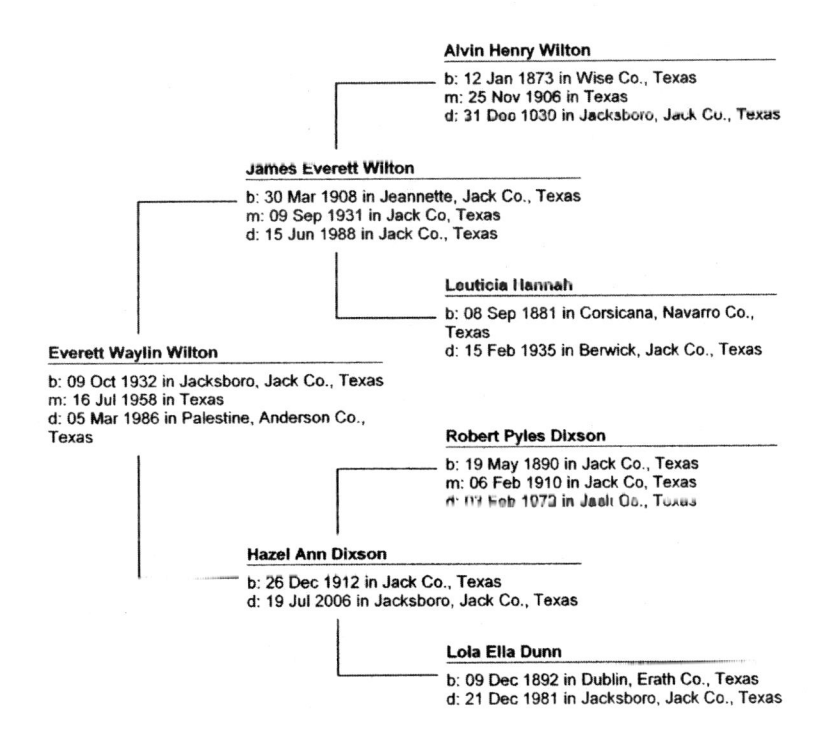

Everett Waylin Wilton
b: 09 Oct 1932 in Jacksboro, Jack Co., Texas
m: 16 Jul 1958 in Texas
d: 05 Mar 1986 in Palestine, Anderson Co., Texas

- **James Everett Wilton**
  b: 30 Mar 1908 in Jeannette, Jack Co., Texas
  m: 09 Sep 1931 in Jack Co, Texas
  d: 15 Jun 1988 in Jack Co., Texas

  - **Alvin Henry Wilton**
    b: 12 Jan 1873 in Wise Co., Texas
    m: 25 Nov 1906 in Texas
    d: 31 Dec 1930 in Jacksboro, Jack Co., Texas

  - **Leuticia Hannah**
    b: 08 Sep 1881 in Corsicana, Navarro Co., Texas
    d: 15 Feb 1935 in Berwick, Jack Co., Texas

- **Hazel Ann Dixson**
  b: 26 Dec 1912 in Jack Co., Texas
  d: 19 Jul 2006 in Jacksboro, Jack Co., Texas

  - **Robert Pyles Dixson**
    b: 19 May 1890 in Jack Co., Texas
    m: 06 Feb 1910 in Jack Co, Texas
    d: 09 Feb 1973 in Jack Co., Texas

  - **Lola Ella Dunn**
    b: 09 Dec 1892 in Dublin, Erath Co., Texas
    d: 21 Dec 1981 in Jacksboro, Jack Co., Texas

Notes: This Tree also applies to the other child of James Everett Wilton & Hazel Ann Dixson: Ora Lenora Wilton.

Ora Lenora Wilton (1940-   )
[7th. Generation from Henry Wilton (1769-1820)]

&

Jimmy Earl Shelton (1937-1976)
& Family

Ora Lenora was the second child of James Everett Wilton & Hazel Ann Dixson. She was born January 1940 in Jack County, Texas, and her early years were spent on her father's farm in the Berwick Community of Jack County.

Oral Lenora married Jimmy Earl Shelton in July 1961. They raised their family of three children in Forth Worth in Tarrant County, Texas.

Family Group Sheet

Husband: Jimmy Earl Shelton

Born: 07 Aug 1937	in: Fort Worth, Tarrant Co., Texas
Married: 23 Jul 1961	in: Fort Worth, Tarrant Co., Texas
Died: 22 Mar 1976	in: Fort Worth, Tarrant Co., Texas
Father: William Maurice Shelton	
Mother: Rosita Tuerecta Thompson	

Wife: Ora Lenora Wilton

Born: 08 Jan 1940	in: Jack Co., Texas
Father: James Everett Wilton	
Mother: Hazel Ann Dixson	

CHILDREN

1 M
- Name: Bruce Glenn Shelton
- Born: 08 Jul 1962 — in: Fort Worth, Tarrant Co., Texas
- Married: 10 Oct 1981 — in: Tarrant Co., Texas
- Spouse: Susan A. Pike

2 F
- Name: Laura Lynn Shelton
- Born: 20 Dec 1965 — in: Fort Worth, Tarrant Co., Texas
- Married: 17 Oct 1980 — in: Tarrant Co., Texas
- Spouse: David Francis Hinz

3 F
- Name: Karen Larue Shelton
- Born: 07 Feb 1972 — in: Fort Worth, Tarrant Co., Texas
- Married: 23 Jan 1988 — in: Tarrant Co., Texas
- Spouse: Robert William Jr. Thomas
- Married: 23 Mar 1996 — in: Johnson Co., Texas
- Spouse: David William Vanderkaay

Karen Larue Shelton (1972-   )
[8th. Generation from Henry Wilton (1769-1820)]

&

First Marriage To
Robert William Jr. Thomas (1967-   )
& Family

Second Marriage To
David William Vanderkaay (1971-   )
& Family

Family Group Sheet

Husband: Robert William Jr. Thomas	
Born: 16 Aug 1967	in: Tarrant Co., Texas
Married: 23 Jan 1988	in: Tarrant Co., Texas

Wife: Karen Larue Shelton	
Born: 07 Feb 1972	in: Fort Worth, Tarrant Co., Texas
Father: Jimmy Earl Shelton	
Mother: Ora Lenora Wilton	
Other Spouses: David William Vanderkaay	

CHILDREN

1 F	Name: Jacinda Lynn Thomas Born: 14 Nov 1986	in: Tarrant Co., Texas
2 M	Name: Rowdy Wayne Thomas Born: 31 Dec 1991	in: Tarrant Co., Texas

---

Family Group Sheet

Husband: David William Vanderkaay	
Born: 14 Jul 1971	in: Hennepin Co., Minnesota
Married: 23 Mar 1996	in: Johnson Co., Texas

Wife: Karen Larue Shelton	
Born: 07 Feb 1972	in: Fort Worth, Tarrant Co., Texas
Father: Jimmy Earl Shelton	
Mother: Ora Lenora Wilton	
Other Spouses: Robert William Jr. Thomas	

CHILDREN

1 F	Name: Shelbi Nicole Vanderkaay Born: 22 Jun 1997	in: Tarrant Co., Texas

KAREN LARUE SHELTON Standard Pedigree Tree

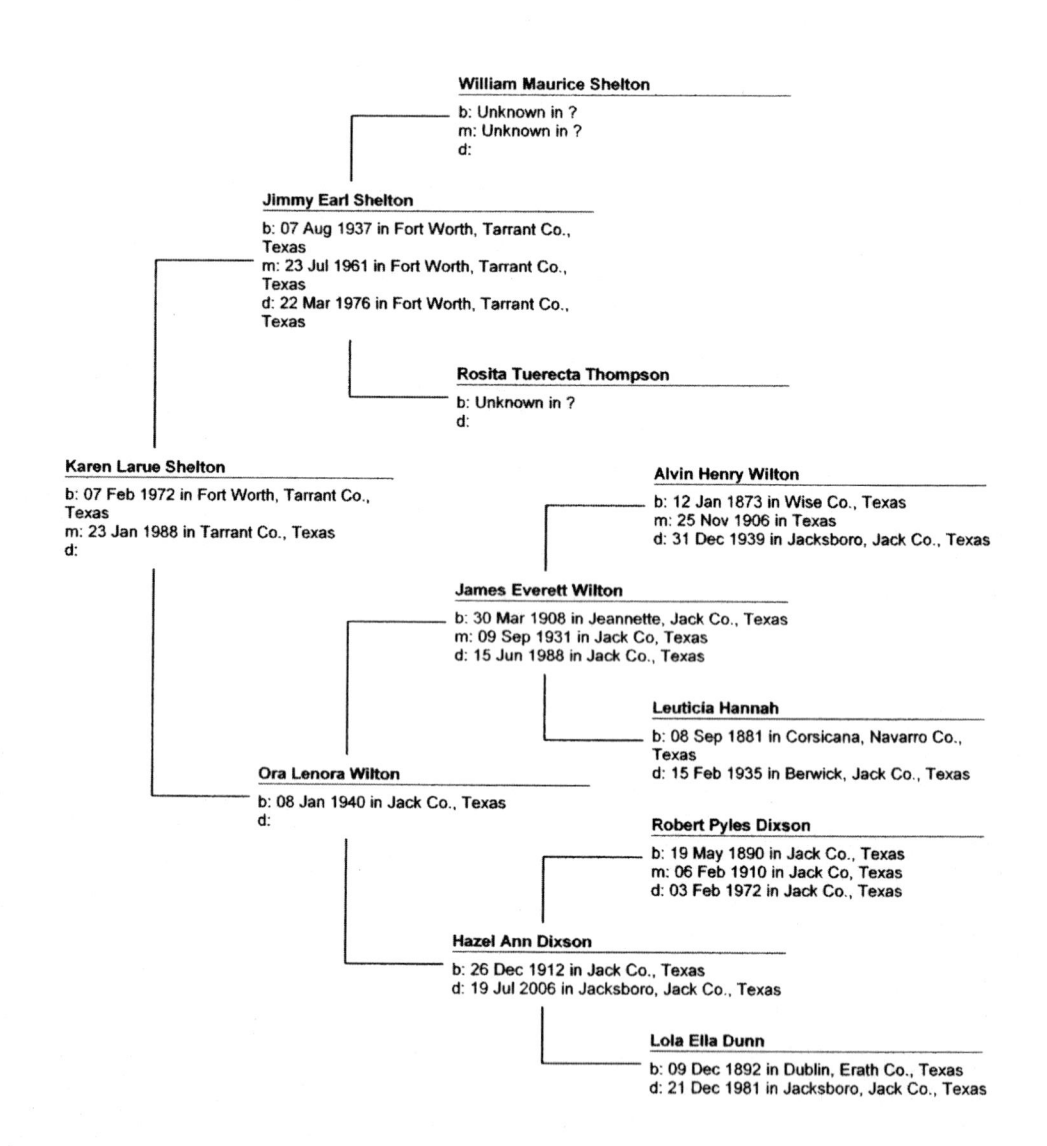

William Maurice Shelton
b: Unknown in ?
m: Unknown in ?
d:

Jimmy Earl Shelton
b: 07 Aug 1937 in Fort Worth, Tarrant Co., Texas
m: 23 Jul 1961 in Fort Worth, Tarrant Co., Texas
d: 22 Mar 1976 in Fort Worth, Tarrant Co., Texas

Rosita Tuerecta Thompson
b: Unknown in ?
d:

Karen Larue Shelton
b: 07 Feb 1972 in Fort Worth, Tarrant Co., Texas
m: 23 Jan 1988 in Tarrant Co., Texas
d:

Alvin Henry Wilton
b: 12 Jan 1873 in Wise Co., Texas
m: 25 Nov 1906 in Texas
d: 31 Dec 1939 in Jacksboro, Jack Co., Texas

James Everett Wilton
b: 30 Mar 1908 in Jeannette, Jack Co., Texas
m: 09 Sep 1931 in Jack Co, Texas
d: 15 Jun 1988 in Jack Co., Texas

Leuticia Hannah
b: 08 Sep 1881 in Corsicana, Navarro Co., Texas
d: 15 Feb 1935 in Berwick, Jack Co., Texas

Ora Lenora Wilton
b: 08 Jan 1940 in Jack Co., Texas
d:

Robert Pyles Dixson
b: 19 May 1890 in Jack Co., Texas
m: 06 Feb 1910 in Jack Co, Texas
d: 03 Feb 1972 in Jack Co., Texas

Hazel Ann Dixson
b: 26 Dec 1912 in Jack Co., Texas
d: 19 Jul 2006 in Jacksboro, Jack Co., Texas

Lola Ella Dunn
b: 09 Dec 1892 in Dublin, Erath Co., Texas
d: 21 Dec 1981 in Jacksboro, Jack Co., Texas

Notes: This Tree also applies to the other children of Jimmy Earl Shelton & Ora Lenora Wilton: Bruce Glenn Shelton and Laura Lynn Shelton.

Melvin Cleo Wilton (1912-2000)
[6th. Generation from Henry Wilton (1769-1820)]

&

Eula Mae Huskey (1917-   )
& Family

Melvin Cleo, born March 1912 in the Berwick Community of Jack County, Texas, was the second child of Alvin Henry Wilton & Leuticia Hannah. His early years were spent on his father's farm in the Berwick Community. He was listed in both the 1920 and 1930 Federal Census of Jack County, living at home with his parents and family. By the 1930 census, Melvin Cleo was age 18 and listed as a general farm laborer.

Melvin Cleo married Eula Mae Huskey about 1938. Eula was the daughter of John R. & Eula L. Huskey, who, beginning about 1920, were from Jefferson County, Oklahoma. Melvin Cleo & Eula Mae had three children. The first child, Judy Inez Wilton, was born August 1939 in Wichita County, Texas; the second, Ronnie Mack Wilton, was born September 1943 in Galveston County, Texas; and the third, Sharon Wilton, was born November 1944 in Galveston County, Texas.

Melvin died September 2000 in Edna in Jackson County, Texas.

Family Group Sheet

Husband: Melvin Cleo Wilton	
Born: 25 Mar 1912	in: Berwick, Jack Co., Texas
Married: Abt. 1938	in: Texas
Died: 22 Sep 2000	in: Edna, Jackson Co., Texas
Father: Alvin Henry Wilton	
Mother: Leuticia Hannah	

Wife: Eula Mae Huskey	
Born: Abt. 1917	in: Oklahoma
Father: John R. Huskey	
Mother: Eula L.	

CHILDREN

1 F	Name: Judy Inez Wilton	
	Born: 30 Aug 1939	in: Wichita Co., Texas
	Married: 09 Aug 1968	in: Harris Co., Texas
	Spouse: Ian Richardson MacIver	
2 M	Name: Ronnie Mack Wilton	
	Born: 19 Sep 1943	in: Galveston Co., Texas
3 F	Name: Sharon Wilton	
	Born: 21 Nov 1944	in: Galveston Co., Texas

Judy Inez Wilton (1939-   )
[7th. Generation from Henry Wilton (1769-1820)]

&

Ian Richardson MacIver (1934-   )
& Family

Family Group Sheet

Husband: Ian Richardson MacIver

Born: Abt. 1934
Married: 09 Aug 1968   in: Harris Co., Texas

Wife: Judy Inez Wilton

Born: 30 Aug 1939   in: Wichita Co., Texas
Father: Melvin Cleo Wilton
Mother: Eula Mae Huskey

CHILDREN

1 F   Name: Alison Ann MacIver
      Born: 23 Jul 1970   in: Harris Co., Texas

Ora Izora Wilton (1919-   )
[6th. Generation from Henry Wilton (1769-1820)]

&

Spencer Pinckney Dewoody (1908-1986)
& Family

Ora Izora Wilton was born June 1919 in Jack County, Texas, the third child of Alvin Henry Wilton & Leuticia Hannah. She grew up on her father's farm in the Berwick Community of Jack County. She was listed in the 1920 and 1930 Federal Census of Jack County, Texas with her parents and family.

Ora married Spencer Pinckney Dewoody on April 26, 1940 in Wichita Falls in Wichita County, Texas. The family settled in Wichita Falls, and Ora and Spencer had two children, which were both born in Wichita Falls. Spencer's occupation was a salesman, and Ora was employed as a beautician. Spencer died in Wichita Falls in November 1986.

Family Group Sheet

Husband: Spencer Pinckney Dewoody

Born: 18 Feb 1908 — in: Aden, Dona Ana Co., New Mexico
Married: 26 Apr 1940 — in: Wichita Falls, Wichita Co., Texas
Died: 12 Nov 1986 — in: Wichita Falls, Wichita Co., Texas
Father: Benjamin Tendol Dewoody
Mother: Essie Lea Neatherlin

Wife: Ora Izora Wilton

Born: 12 Jun 1919 — in: Berwick, Jack Co., Texas
Father: Alvin Henry Wilton
Mother: Leuticia Hannah

CHILDREN

1. F — Name: Linda Lou Dewoody
   Born: 09 Feb 1942 — in: Wichita Falls, Wichita Co., Texas
   Married: 16 Aug 1958 — in: Grandfield, Tillman Co., Oklahoma
   Spouse: Nikki Lynn Griffin

2. F — Name: Terri Lynn Dewoody
   Born: 09 Mar 1954 — in: Wichita Falls, Wichita Co., Texas
   Married: 10 Nov 1973 — in: Wichita Falls, Wichita Co., Texas
   Spouse: Gary Donald Bowen

SPENCER PINCKNEY DEWOODY Standard Pedigree Tree

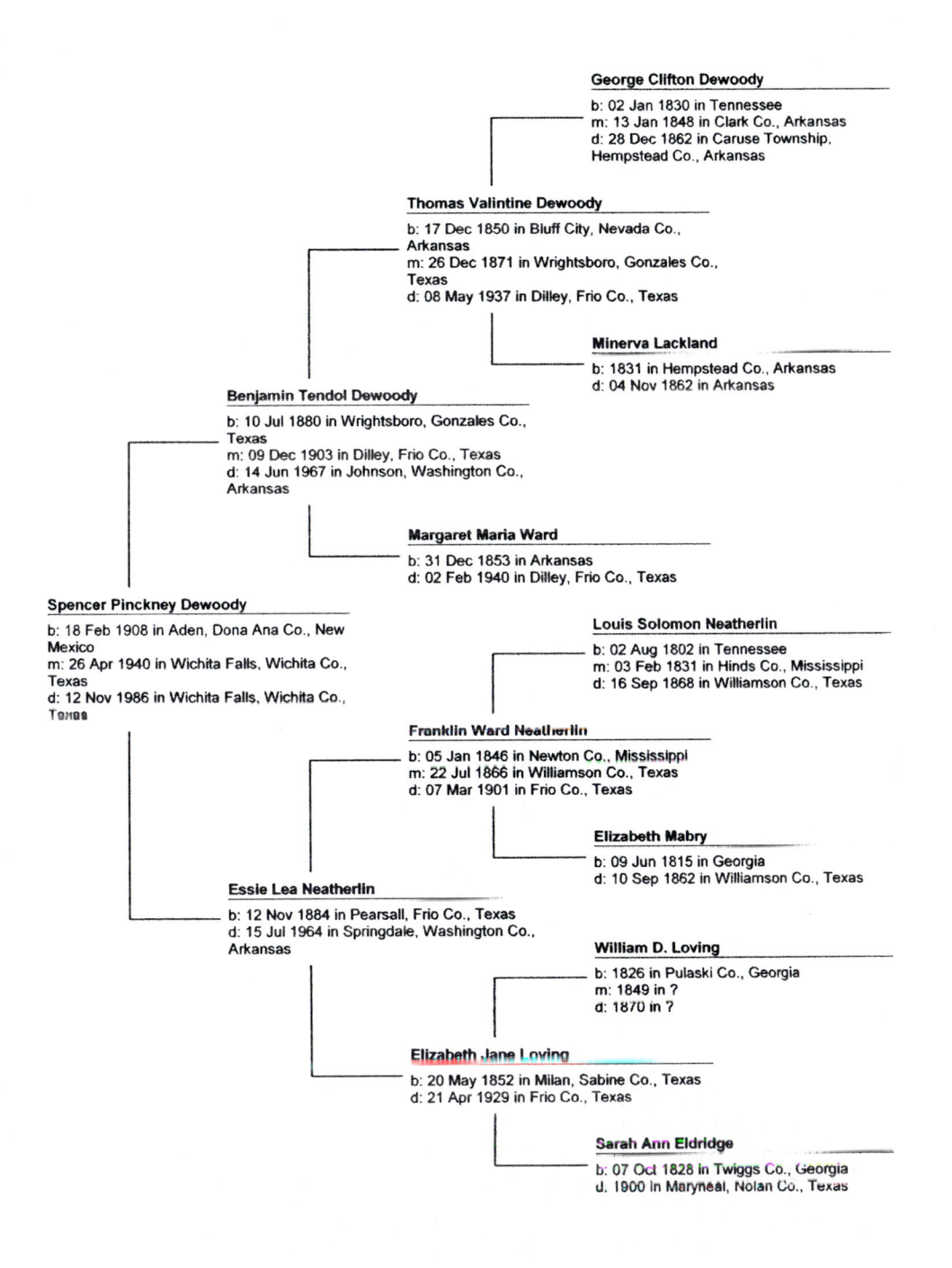

Spencer Pinckney Dewoody
b: 18 Feb 1908 in Aden, Dona Ana Co., New Mexico
m: 26 Apr 1940 in Wichita Falls, Wichita Co., Texas
d: 12 Nov 1986 in Wichita Falls, Wichita Co., Texas

- **Benjamin Tendol Dewoody**
  b: 10 Jul 1880 in Wrightsboro, Gonzales Co., Texas
  m: 09 Dec 1903 in Dilley, Frio Co., Texas
  d: 14 Jun 1967 in Johnson, Washington Co., Arkansas

  - **Thomas Valintine Dewoody**
    b: 17 Dec 1850 in Bluff City, Nevada Co., Arkansas
    m: 26 Dec 1871 in Wrightsboro, Gonzales Co., Texas
    d: 08 May 1937 in Dilley, Frio Co., Texas

    - **George Clifton Dewoody**
      b: 02 Jan 1830 in Tennessee
      m: 13 Jan 1848 in Clark Co., Arkansas
      d: 28 Dec 1862 in Caruse Township, Hempstead Co., Arkansas

    - **Minerva Lackland**
      b: 1831 in Hempstead Co., Arkansas
      d: 04 Nov 1862 in Arkansas

  - **Margaret Maria Ward**
    b: 31 Dec 1853 in Arkansas
    d: 02 Feb 1940 in Dilley, Frio Co., Texas

- **Essie Lea Neatherlin**
  b: 12 Nov 1884 in Pearsall, Frio Co., Texas
  d: 15 Jul 1964 in Springdale, Washington Co., Arkansas

  - **Franklin Ward Neatherlin**
    b: 05 Jan 1846 in Newton Co., Mississippi
    m: 22 Jul 1866 in Williamson Co., Texas
    d: 07 Mar 1901 in Frio Co., Texas

    - **Louis Solomon Neatherlin**
      b: 02 Aug 1802 in Tennessee
      m: 03 Feb 1831 in Hinds Co., Mississippi
      d: 16 Sep 1868 in Williamson Co., Texas

    - **Elizabeth Mabry**
      b: 09 Jun 1815 in Georgia
      d: 10 Sep 1862 in Williamson Co., Texas

  - **Elizabeth Jane Loving**
    b: 20 May 1852 in Milan, Sabine Co., Texas
    d: 21 Apr 1929 in Frio Co., Texas

    - **William D. Loving**
      b: 1826 in Pulaski Co., Georgia
      m: 1849 in ?
      d: 1870 in ?

    - **Sarah Ann Eldridge**
      b: 07 Oct 1828 in Twiggs Co., Georgia
      d: 1900 in Maryneal, Nolan Co., Texas

Linda Lou Dewoody (1942-)
[7th. Generation from Henry Wilton (1769-1820)]

&

Nikki Lynn Griffin (1940-)
& Family

Linda Lou Dewoody was the older of two children of Ora Izora Wilton & Spencer Pinckney Dewoody. Linda was born February 1942 and spent her early years in Wichita Falls, Texas, where her parents and family were settled.

In August 1958, Linda married Nikki Lynn Griffin in Tillman County, Oklahoma. Both Linda and Nikki were born in Wichita Falls in Wichita County, Texas, and that is where they started their family. They had two sons, the older, David Allan Griffin, born March 1959, and the younger, Gregg Randel Griffin, born November 1960, both born in Wichita Falls, Texas.

Beginning July 15, 1976, Nikki, Linda and their sons moved to Ruidoso, New Mexico, where they worked together in a family-owned retail business.

Family Group Sheet

Husband: Nikki Lynn Griffin	
Born: 07 Apr 1940	in: Wichita Falls, Wichita Co., Texas
Married: 16 Aug 1958	in: Grandfield, Tillman Co., Oklahoma
Father: Warren Lee Griffin	
Mother: Rosa Lee Walsh	

Wife: Linda Lou Dewoody	
Born: 09 Feb 1942	in: Wichita Falls, Wichita Co., Texas
Father: Spencer Pinckney Dewoody	
Mother: Ora Izora Wilton	

CHILDREN

1 M
- Name: David Allan Griffin
- Born: 25 Mar 1959 in: Wichita Falls, Wichita Co., Texas
- Married: 25 Sep 1982 in: San Angelo, Tom Green Co., Texas
- Spouse: Lori Ann Burrage

2 M
- Name: Gregg Randel Griffin
- Born: 11 Nov 1960 in: Wichita Falls, Wichita Co., Texas
- Married: 05 May 1984 in: Ruidoso, Lincoln Co., New Mexico
- Spouse: Tana Lynn Bales
- Married: 24 Oct 1998 in: Alamogordo, NM
- Spouse: Lavonne Reid

LINDA LOU DEWOODY Standard Pedigree Tree

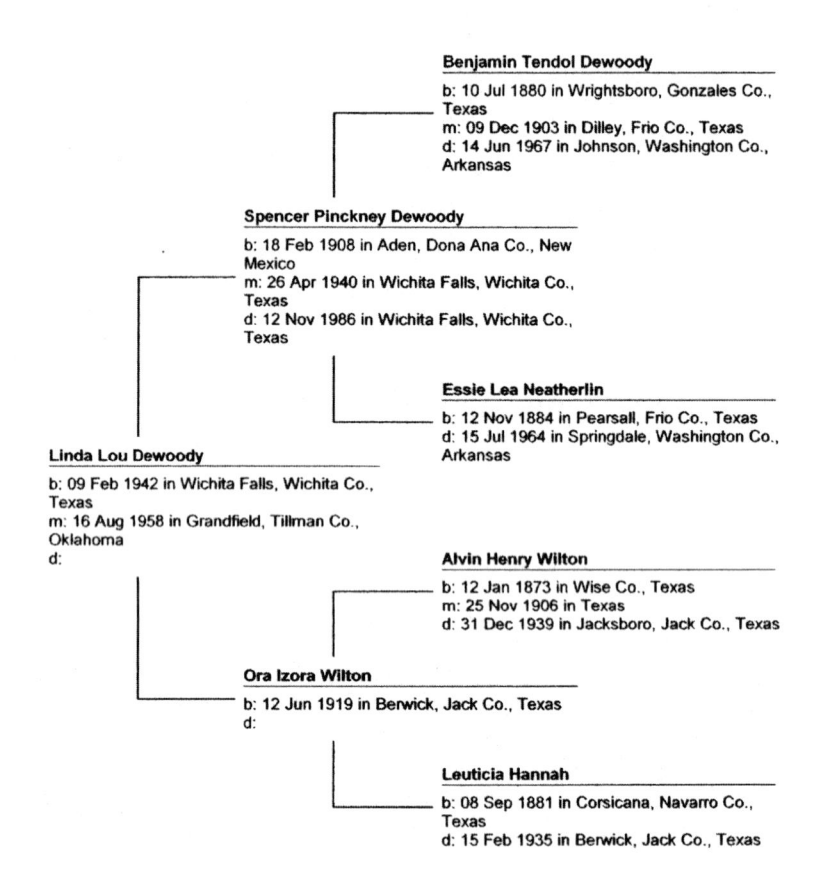

Benjamin Tendol Dewoody
b: 10 Jul 1880 in Wrightsboro, Gonzales Co., Texas
m: 09 Dec 1903 in Dilley, Frio Co., Texas
d: 14 Jun 1967 in Johnson, Washington Co., Arkansas

Spencer Pinckney Dewoody
b: 18 Feb 1908 in Aden, Dona Ana Co., New Mexico
m: 26 Apr 1940 in Wichita Falls, Wichita Co., Texas
d: 12 Nov 1986 in Wichita Falls, Wichita Co., Texas

Essie Lea Neatherlin
b: 12 Nov 1884 in Pearsall, Frio Co., Texas
d: 15 Jul 1964 in Springdale, Washington Co., Arkansas

Linda Lou Dewoody
b: 09 Feb 1942 in Wichita Falls, Wichita Co., Texas
m: 16 Aug 1958 in Grandfield, Tillman Co., Oklahoma
d:

Alvin Henry Wilton
b: 12 Jan 1873 in Wise Co., Texas
m: 25 Nov 1906 in Texas
d: 31 Dec 1939 in Jacksboro, Jack Co., Texas

Ora Izora Wilton
b: 12 Jun 1919 in Berwick, Jack Co., Texas
d:

Leuticia Hannah
b: 08 Sep 1881 in Corsicana, Navarro Co., Texas
d: 15 Feb 1935 in Berwick, Jack Co., Texas

Notes: This Tree also applies to the other child of Spencer Pinckney Dewoody & Ora Izora Wilton: Terri Lynn Dewoody.

NIKKI LYNN GRIFFIN Standard Pedigree Tree

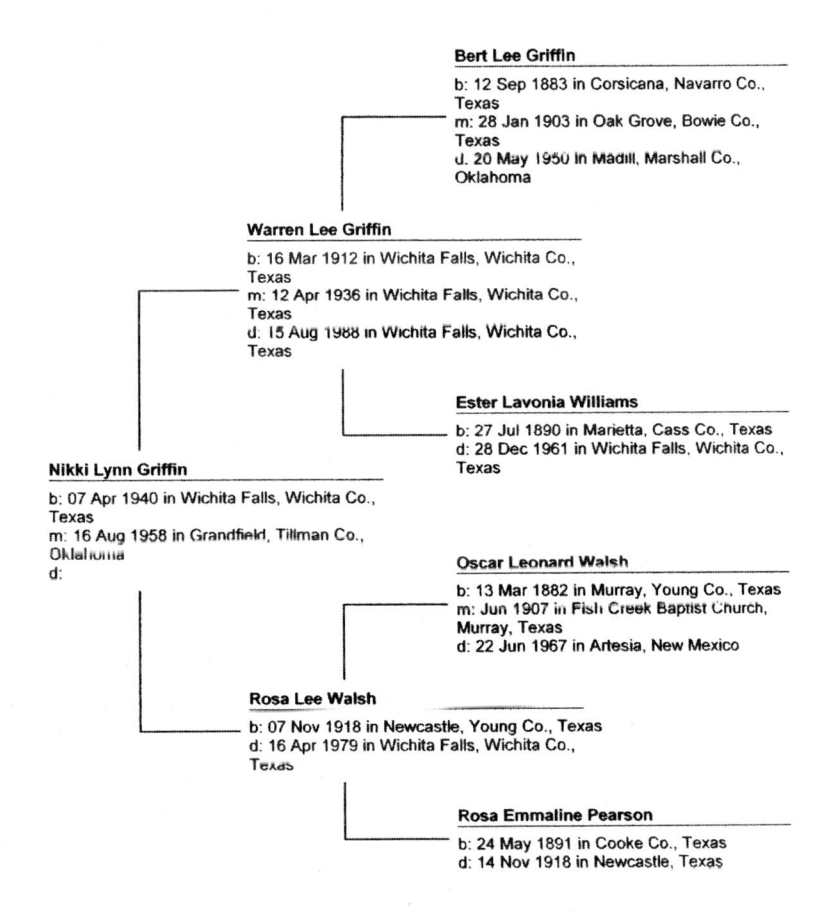

Nikki Lynn Griffin
b: 07 Apr 1940 in Wichita Falls, Wichita Co., Texas
m: 16 Aug 1958 in Grandfield, Tillman Co., Oklahoma
d:

- **Warren Lee Griffin**
  b: 16 Mar 1912 in Wichita Falls, Wichita Co., Texas
  m: 12 Apr 1936 in Wichita Falls, Wichita Co., Texas
  d: 15 Aug 1988 in Wichita Falls, Wichita Co., Texas

  - **Bert Lee Griffin**
    b: 12 Sep 1883 in Corsicana, Navarro Co., Texas
    m: 28 Jan 1903 in Oak Grove, Bowie Co., Texas
    d: 20 May 1950 in Madill, Marshall Co., Oklahoma

  - **Ester Lavonia Williams**
    b: 27 Jul 1890 in Marietta, Cass Co., Texas
    d: 28 Dec 1961 in Wichita Falls, Wichita Co., Texas

- **Rosa Lee Walsh**
  b: 07 Nov 1918 in Newcastle, Young Co., Texas
  d: 16 Apr 1979 in Wichita Falls, Wichita Co., Texas

  - **Oscar Leonard Walsh**
    b: 13 Mar 1882 in Murray, Young Co., Texas
    m: Jun 1907 in Fish Creek Baptist Church, Murray, Texas
    d: 22 Jun 1967 in Artesia, New Mexico

  - **Rosa Emmaline Pearson**
    b: 24 May 1891 in Cooke Co., Texas
    d: 14 Nov 1918 in Newcastle, Texas

David Allan Griffin (1959-   )
[8th. Generation from Henry Wilton (1769-1820)]

&

Lori Ann Burrage (1963-   )
& Family

Family Group Sheet

Husband: David Allan Griffin	
Born: 25 Mar 1959	in: Wichita Falls, Wichita Co., Texas
Married: 25 Sep 1982	in: San Angelo, Tom Green Co., Texas
Father: Nikki Lynn Griffin	
Mother: Linda Lou Dewoody	

Wife: Lori Ann Burrage	
Born: 18 Jun 1963	in: San Angelo, Tom Green Co., Texas

CHILDREN

1 M	Name: Garrett Allan Griffin	
	Born: 06 Sep 1989	in: Ruidoso, Lincoln Co., New Mexico
2 F	Name: Haley Ann Griffin	
	Born: 27 Apr 1993	in: Ruidoso, Lincoln Co., New Mexico

DAVID ALLAN GRIFFIN Standard Pedigree Tree

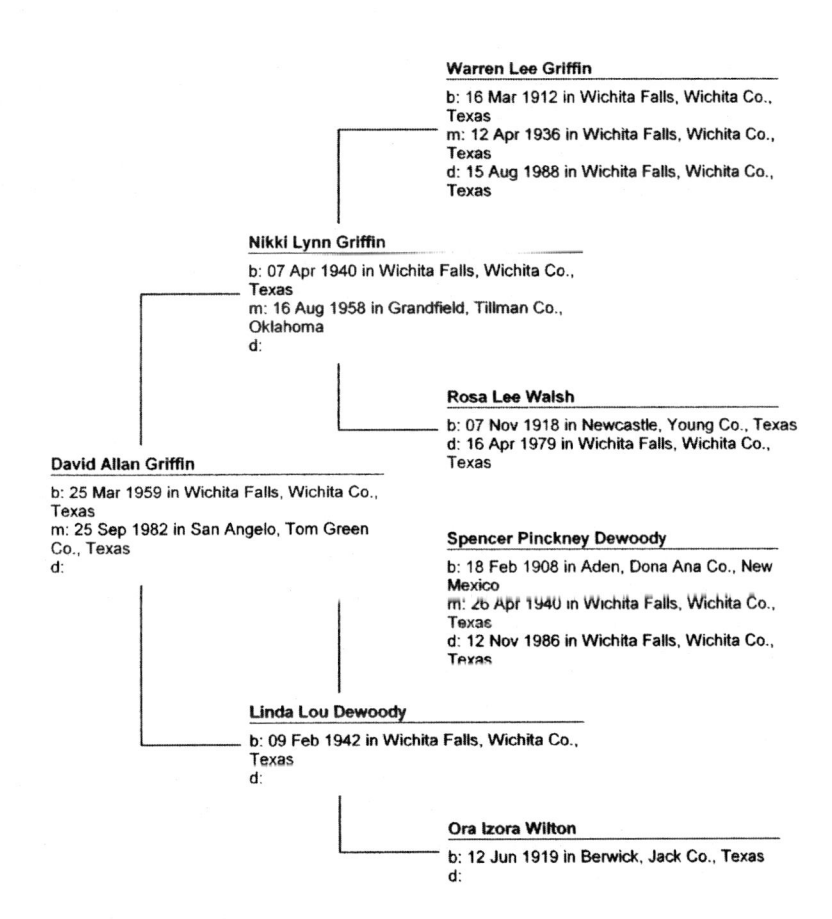

Warren Lee Griffin
b: 16 Mar 1912 in Wichita Falls, Wichita Co., Texas
m: 12 Apr 1936 in Wichita Falls, Wichita Co., Texas
d: 15 Aug 1988 in Wichita Falls, Wichita Co., Texas

Nikki Lynn Griffin
b: 07 Apr 1940 in Wichita Falls, Wichita Co., Texas
m: 16 Aug 1958 in Grandfield, Tillman Co., Oklahoma
d:

Rosa Lee Walsh
b: 07 Nov 1918 in Newcastle, Young Co., Texas
d: 16 Apr 1979 in Wichita Falls, Wichita Co., Texas

David Allan Griffin
b: 25 Mar 1959 in Wichita Falls, Wichita Co., Texas
m: 25 Sep 1982 in San Angelo, Tom Green Co., Texas
d:

Spencer Pinckney Dewoody
b: 18 Feb 1908 in Aden, Dona Ana Co., New Mexico
m: 26 Apr 1940 in Wichita Falls, Wichita Co., Texas
d: 12 Nov 1986 in Wichita Falls, Wichita Co., Texas

Linda Lou Dewoody
b: 09 Feb 1942 in Wichita Falls, Wichita Co., Texas
d:

Ora Izora Wilton
b: 12 Jun 1919 in Berwick, Jack Co., Texas
d:

Notes: This Tree also applies to the other child of Nikki Lynn Griffin & Linda Lou Dewoody: Gregg Randel Griffin.

Gregg Randel Griffin (1960-   )
[8th. Generation from Henry Wilton (1769-1820)]

&

First Marriage To
Tana Lynn Bales
& Family

Second Marriage To
Lavonne Reid (1963-   )
& Family

Family Group Sheet

Husband: Gregg Randel Griffin

Born: 11 Nov 1960   in: Wichita Falls, Wichita Co., Texas
Married: 05 May 1984   in: Ruidoso, Lincoln Co., New Mexico
Father: Nikki Lynn Griffin
Mother: Linda Lou Dewoody
     Other Spouses: Lavonne Reid

Wife: Tana Lynn Bales

Born: Private

CHILDREN

1 F   Name: Casey Lynn Griffin
      Born: 25 Jan 1986   in: Ruidoso, Lincoln Co., New Mexico

2 M   Name: Clay Randal Griffin
      Born: 27 Apr 1989   in: Ruidoso, Lincoln Co., New Mexico

Family Group Sheet

Husband: Gregg Randel Griffin

Born: 11 Nov 1960   in: Wichita Falls, Wichita Co., Texas
Married: 24 Oct 1998   in: Alamogordo, Otero Co., New Mexico
Father: Nikki Lynn Griffin
Mother: Linda Lou Dewoody
     Other Spouses: Tana Lynn Bales

Wife: Lavonne Reid

Born: 04 Oct 1963

Terri Lynn Dewoody (1954-   )
[7th. Generation from Henry Wilton (1769-1820)]

&

Gary Donald Bowen (1951-   )
& Family

Family Group Sheet

Husband: Gary Donald Bowen

Born: 14 Oct 1951 — in: Wichita Falls, Wichita Co., Texas
Married: 10 Nov 1973 — in: Wichita Falls, Wichita Co., Texas
Father: Donald Edwin Bowen
Mother: Bessie Pearl Green

Wife: Terri Lynn Dewoody

Born: 09 Mar 1954 — in: Wichita Falls, Wichita Co., Texas
Father: Spencer Pinckney Dewoody
Mother: Ora Izora Wilton

CHILDREN

1 M — Name: Jeffery Heath Bowen
Born: 15 Nov 1975 — in: Wichita Co., Texas

2 F — Name: Cori Denise Bowen
Born: 11 Jan 1981 — in: Wichita Co., Texas

Silas Wilton (1874-1935)
[5th. Generation from Henry Wilton (1769-1820)]

&

Mary Elizabeth Underwood (1877-1945)
& Family

Silas was born December 1874 in Wise County, Texas, the third child of Thomas A. Wilton & Easter B. Clark. His early years were spent in the Winn Hill Community of Jack County, Texas, where his father and family settled about 1878. The first record of Silas is found in the 1880 Federal Census of Jack County, where he is listed at the age of 2 with his parents and four other brothers.

According to family tradition, Silas left home at the age of 17 and moved to California. However, from census and family records, it appears that Silas spent some time in Oklahoma and Texas before moving to California. In November 1898, Silas married Mary Elizabeth Underwood in Texas and then moved to Oklahoma. According to the 1900 Federal Census of Greer County, Oklahoma, enumerated in June 1900, Silas, occupation farmer, and wife, Betty, had been married for two years and at that time had no children. Their first child, Carless Carl Wilton, was born August 24, 1900 in Oklahoma.

In the 1910 and 1920 Federal Census of Uvalde County, Texas, we find the family of Silas and Mary still in Texas. In the 1910 Federal Census of Uvalde County, Silas, occupation general farmer, and Mary were listed with four children at that time. It is curious that their second and third children, Cora Belle Wilton, born March 1901, and Ruel Calvin Wilton, born July 1905, were listed as being born in Mexico. Later information suggests that the location may have been in Tamaulipas, Mexico. The fourth child, Nola E. Wilton, was born February 1908 in Texas. Silas and Mary had two more children while still in Texas, Sylvia Leora Wilton, born 1911, and Velma Lucile Wilton, born September 1913. Sylvia Leora died prematurely in May 1912 in Uvalde County, Texas. In the 1920 Federal Census of Uvalde County, Texas, Silas, occupation laborer, and Mary were listed with four of their six children.

In the mid-1920's, most of the family moved to California, settling in Orange County. In the 1930 Federal Census of Orange County, California, Silas and Mary are listed with two of their children, Ruel C. Wilton, age 24, and Velma Wilton, age 16. At that time, three of their children had their own families also living in California.

Silas died in August 1935 in California, and Mary died 1945 in Orange County, California. Except for Sylvia Leora, who died at an early age in Texas, all the rest of the family died in California.

Family Group Sheet

Husband: Silas Wilton

Born: 16 Dec 1874	in: Wise Co., Texas
Married: 19 Nov 1898	in: Texas
Died: 03 Aug 1935	in: California
Father: Thomas Abslum Wilton	
Mother: Easter Britania Clark	

Wife: Mary Elizabeth Underwood

Born: May 1877	in: Alabama
Died: 1945	in: Orange Co., California

CHILDREN

#		
1 M	Name: Carless Carl Wilton Born: 24 Aug 1900 Died: 17 Jun 1963 Married: 1922 Spouse: Bertha Lee Welty	in: Oklahoma in: Orange Co., California in: Texas
2 F	Name: Cora Belle Wilton Born: 20 Mar 1903 Died: 26 Jul 1981 Married: 1924 Spouse: Leo Gilbert Opsomer	in: Tamaulipas, Mexico in: Orange Co., California in: California
3 M	Name: Ruel Calvin Wilton Born: 17 Jul 1905 Died: 17 Oct 1981 Married: 1933 Spouse: Florence Martha Scholfield	in: Tamaulipas, Mexico in: Orange Co., California in: California
4 F	Name: Nola E. Wilton Born: 11 Feb 1908 Died: 17 Jan 1953 Married: Abt. 1924 Spouse: Dorsey Marion Campbell	in: Texas in: Los Angeles Co., California in: California
5 F	Name: Sylvia Leora Wilton Born: 1911 Died: 22 May 1912	in: Texas in: Uvalde Co., Texas
6 F	Name: Velma Lucile Wilton Born: 11 Sep 1913 Died: 26 Dec 1977 Married: 1931 Spouse: Russell Bailey	in: Uvalde Co., Texas in: Orange Co., California

Carless Carl Wilton (1900-1963)
[6th. Generation from Henry Wilton (1769-1820)]

&

Bertha Welty (1903-   )
& Family

Carl was the oldest child of Silas Wilton and Mary Elizabeth Underwood, born August 1900 in Oklahoma. The family eventually settled in California in the mid-1920's, but first spent time in Oklahoma and Texas. Before moving to California, Carl married Bertha Welty in 1922 in Texas. Their daughter, Ida Mae Wilton, was also born in Texas in June 1923.

In the 1930 Federal Census of Orange County, California, Carl C., occupation municipal surveyor, was listed with wife, Bertha, and daughter, Ida, age 6. They were living only one dwelling away from Carl's father and family, then consisting of parents and two children.

Both Carl and Bertha died in California, Carl in June 1963, and Bertha in September 1978.

Family Group Sheet

Husband: Carless Carl Wilton		
Born: 24 Aug 1900	in: Oklahoma	
Married: 1922	in: Texas	
Died: 17 Jun 1963	in: Orange Co., California	
Father: Silas Wilton		
Mother: Mary Elizabeth Underwood		
Wife: Bertha Lee Welty		
Born: 29 Mar 1902	in: New Mexico	
Died: 14 Sep 1978	in: Riverside Co., California	
Father: John Henry Welty		
Mother: Hattie Alma Ward		

CHILDREN

1 F
- Name: Ida Mae Wilton
- Born: 14 Jun 1923 in: Texas
- Died: 29 Dec 1992 in: Riverside Co., California

CARLESS CARL WILTON Standard Pedigree Tree

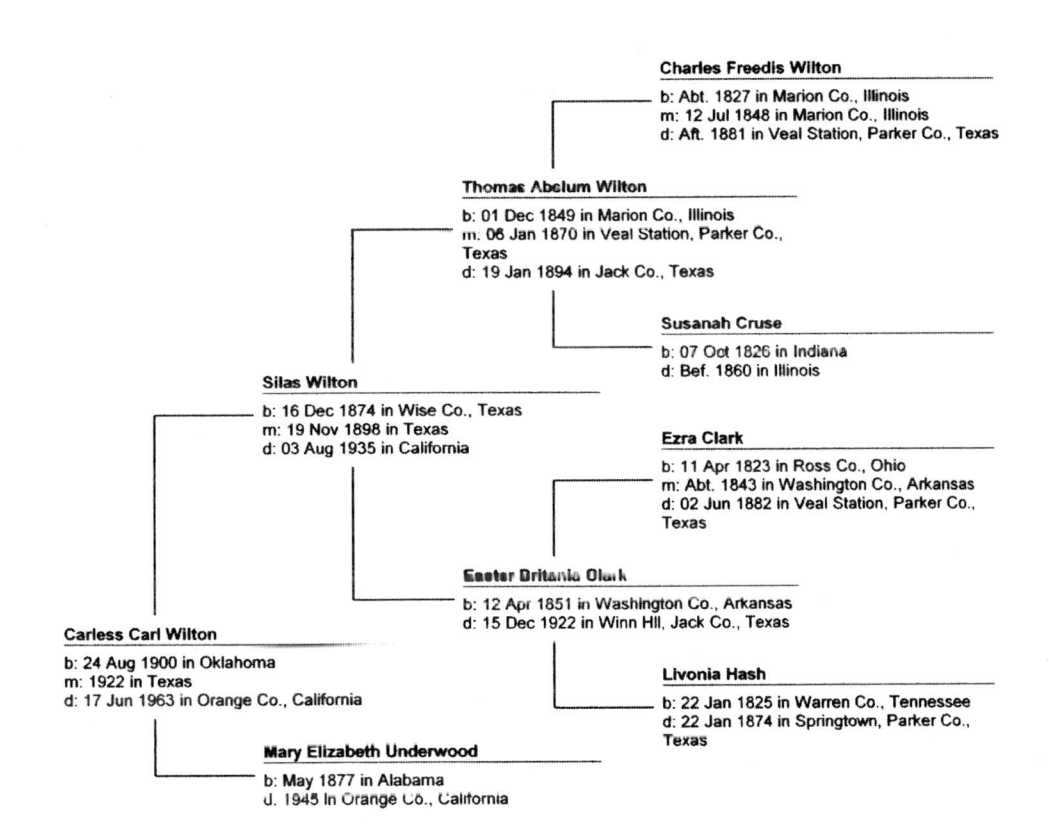

Charles Freedis Wilton
b: Abt. 1827 in Marion Co., Illinois
m: 12 Jul 1848 in Marion Co., Illinois
d: Aft. 1881 in Veal Station, Parker Co., Texas

Thomas Abelum Wilton
b: 01 Dec 1849 in Marion Co., Illinois
m: 06 Jan 1870 in Veal Station, Parker Co., Texas
d: 19 Jan 1894 in Jack Co., Texas

Susanah Cruse
b: 07 Oct 1826 in Indiana
d: Bef. 1860 in Illinois

Silas Wilton
b: 16 Dec 1874 in Wise Co., Texas
m: 19 Nov 1898 in Texas
d: 03 Aug 1935 in California

Ezra Clark
b: 11 Apr 1823 in Ross Co., Ohio
m: Abt. 1843 in Washington Co., Arkansas
d: 02 Jun 1882 in Veal Station, Parker Co., Texas

Easter Britania Clark
b: 12 Apr 1851 in Washington Co., Arkansas
d: 15 Dec 1922 in Winn Hll, Jack Co., Texas

Carless Carl Wilton
b: 24 Aug 1900 in Oklahoma
m: 1922 in Texas
d: 17 Jun 1963 in Orange Co., California

Livonia Hash
b: 22 Jan 1825 in Warren Co., Tennessee
d: 22 Jan 1874 in Springtown, Parker Co., Texas

Mary Elizabeth Underwood
b: May 1877 in Alabama
d: 1945 in Orange Co., California

Notes: This Tree also applies to the other children of Silas Wilton & Mary Elizabeth Underwood: Cora Belle Wilton, Ruel Calvin Wilton, Nola E. Wilton, Sylvia Leora Wilton, and Velma Lucile Wilton.

BERTHA LEE WELTY Standard Pedigree Tree

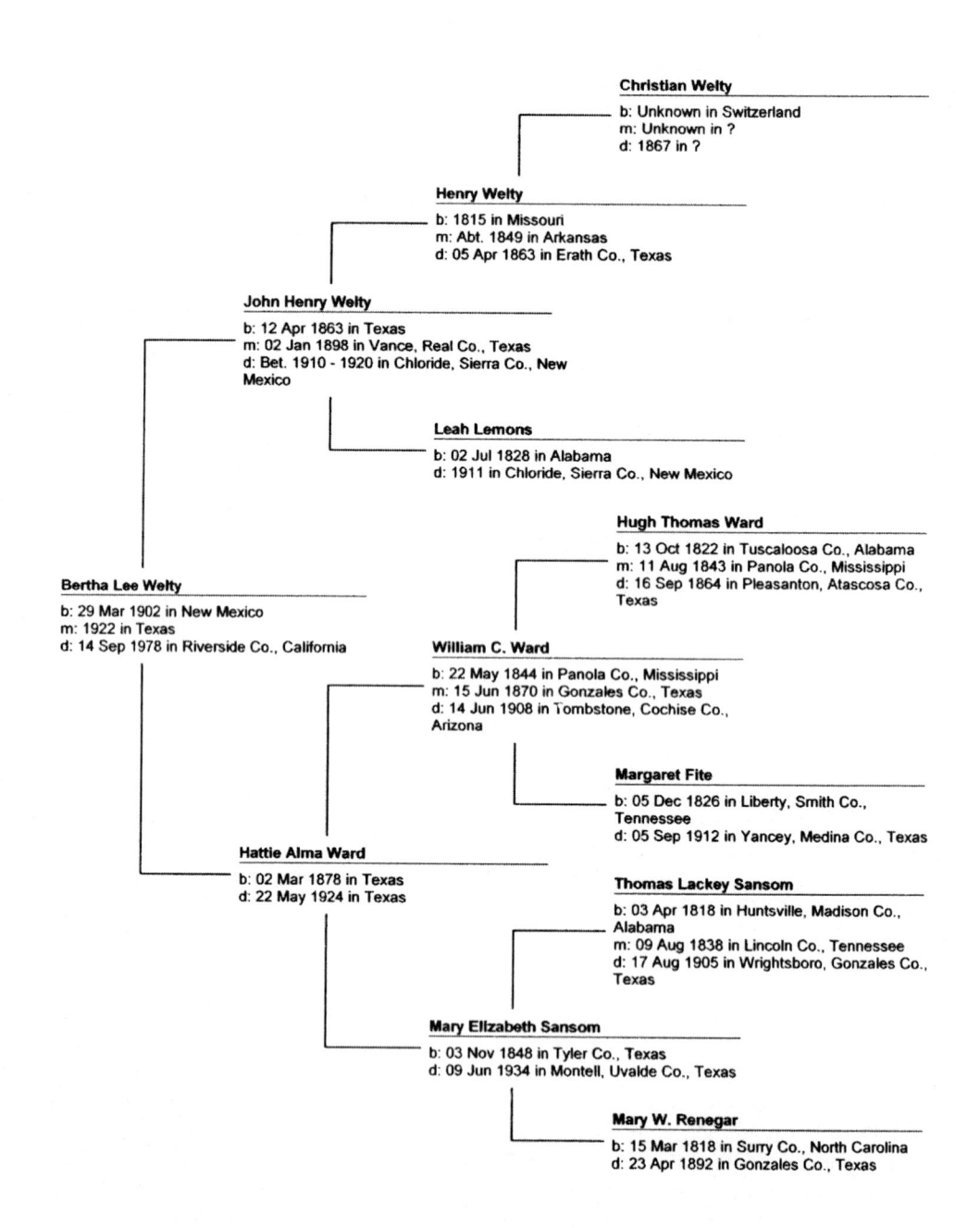

Bertha Lee Welty
b: 29 Mar 1902 in New Mexico
m: 1922 in Texas
d: 14 Sep 1978 in Riverside Co., California

- **John Henry Welty**
  b: 12 Apr 1863 in Texas
  m: 02 Jan 1898 in Vance, Real Co., Texas
  d: Bet. 1910 - 1920 in Chloride, Sierra Co., New Mexico

  - **Henry Welty**
    b: 1815 in Missouri
    m: Abt. 1849 in Arkansas
    d: 05 Apr 1863 in Erath Co., Texas

    - **Christian Welty**
      b: Unknown in Switzerland
      m: Unknown in ?
      d: 1867 in ?

  - **Leah Lemons**
    b: 02 Jul 1828 in Alabama
    d: 1911 in Chloride, Sierra Co., New Mexico

- **Hattie Alma Ward**
  b: 02 Mar 1878 in Texas
  d: 22 May 1924 in Texas

  - **William C. Ward**
    b: 22 May 1844 in Panola Co., Mississippi
    m: 15 Jun 1870 in Gonzales Co., Texas
    d: 14 Jun 1908 in Tombstone, Cochise Co., Arizona

    - **Hugh Thomas Ward**
      b: 13 Oct 1822 in Tuscaloosa Co., Alabama
      m: 11 Aug 1843 in Panola Co., Mississippi
      d: 16 Sep 1864 in Pleasanton, Atascosa Co., Texas

    - **Margaret Fite**
      b: 05 Dec 1826 in Liberty, Smith Co., Tennessee
      d: 05 Sep 1912 in Yancey, Medina Co., Texas

  - **Mary Elizabeth Sansom**
    b: 03 Nov 1848 in Tyler Co., Texas
    d: 09 Jun 1934 in Montell, Uvalde Co., Texas

    - **Thomas Lackey Sansom**
      b: 03 Apr 1818 in Huntsville, Madison Co., Alabama
      m: 09 Aug 1838 in Lincoln Co., Tennessee
      d: 17 Aug 1905 in Wrightsboro, Gonzales Co., Texas

    - **Mary W. Renegar**
      b: 15 Mar 1818 in Surry Co., North Carolina
      d: 23 Apr 1892 in Gonzales Co., Texas

Cora Belle Wilton (1903-1981)
[6th. Generation from Henry Wilton (1769-1820)]

&

Leo Gilbert Opsomer (1897-1969)
& Family

Cora Belle, born March 1901, was the second child of Silas Wilton & Mary E. Underwood. There is conflicting information about where she was born, suggesting either Mexico or Texas. However, it is clear that Cora's parents did spend time in Oklahoma and Texas between 1900 and 1920. In the mid-1920's, Cora, along with the family, moved to California, settling in Orange County.

In 1924, Cora married Leo Gilbert Opsomer, then living in California. Leo died May 1969, with a last address listed as San Ysidro in San Diego County, California. Cora died in July 1981, with a last address listed as Huntington Beach, located in Orange County, California.

Family Group Sheet

Husband: Leo Gilbert Opsomer

Born: 20 Apr 1897	in: West Bay City, Bay Co., Michigan
Married: 1924	in: California
Died: 05 May 1969	in: San Diego Co., California
Father: Leonard Opsomer	
Mother: Lisa Jeauveneaux	

Wife: Cora Belle Wilton

Born: 20 Mar 1903	in: Tamaulipas, Mexico
Died: 26 Jul 1981	in: Orange Co., California
Father: Silas Wilton	
Mother: Mary Elizabeth Underwood	

Ruel Calvin Wilton (1905-1981)
[6th. Generation from Henry Wilton (1769-1820)]

&

Florence Martha Scholfield (1906-1966)
& Family

Ruel Calvin Wilton was born July 1905, the third child of Silas Wilton & Mary Elizabeth Underwood. There is conflicting information about where he was born. The 1910 Federal Census indicates that he was born in Mexico, and the 1920 Federal Census first indicated Tamaulipas (Mexico) with a correction reading "American Citizen." After living in Texas a number of years, the family moved in mid-1920 to California, settling in Orange County.

It was in California, in 1933, that Ruel married Florence Martha Scholfield. Ruel also went by the name of "Roy," and they also settled in Orange County, California. Ruel and Florence both died in Orange County, Ruel in 1981, and Florence in 1966.

Family Group Sheet

Husband: Ruel Calvin Wilton

Born: 17 Jul 1905 in: Tamaulipas, Mexico
Married: 1933 in: California
Died: 17 Oct 1981 in: Orange Co., California
Father: Silas Wilton
Mother: Mary Elizabeth Underwood

Wife: Florence Martha Scholfield

Born: 05 May 1906 in: Girard, Crawford Co., Kansas
Died: 20 Dec 1966 in: Huntington Beach, Orange Co., California
Father: Frank Edgar Scholfield
Mother: Elizabeth Irene Hemphill

FLORENCE MARTHA SCHOLFIELD Standard Pedigree Tree

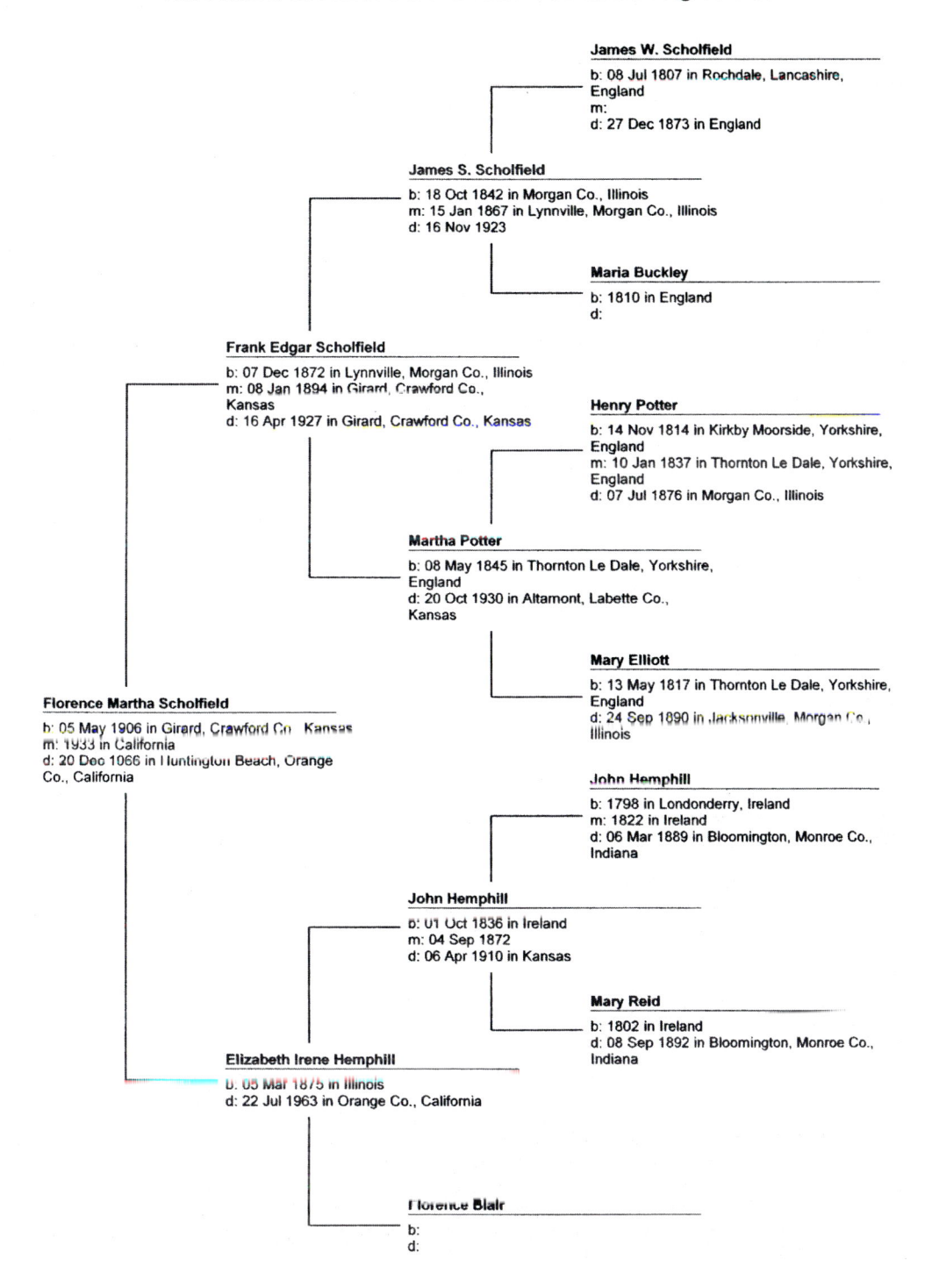

- **James S. Scholfield**
  - b: 18 Oct 1842 in Morgan Co., Illinois
  - m: 15 Jan 1867 in Lynnville, Morgan Co., Illinois
  - d: 16 Nov 1923
  - Father: **James W. Scholfield**
    - b: 08 Jul 1807 in Rochdale, Lancashire, England
    - m:
    - d: 27 Dec 1873 in England
  - Mother: **Maria Buckley**
    - b: 1810 in England
    - d:

- **Frank Edgar Scholfield**
  - b: 07 Dec 1872 in Lynnville, Morgan Co., Illinois
  - m: 08 Jan 1894 in Girard, Crawford Co., Kansas
  - d: 16 Apr 1927 in Girard, Crawford Co., Kansas

- **Martha Potter**
  - b: 08 May 1845 in Thornton Le Dale, Yorkshire, England
  - d: 20 Oct 1930 in Altamont, Labette Co., Kansas
  - Father: **Henry Potter**
    - b: 14 Nov 1814 in Kirkby Moorside, Yorkshire, England
    - m: 10 Jan 1837 in Thornton Le Dale, Yorkshire, England
    - d: 07 Jul 1876 in Morgan Co., Illinois
  - Mother: **Mary Elliott**
    - b: 13 May 1817 in Thornton Le Dale, Yorkshire, England
    - d: 24 Sep 1890 in Jacksonville, Morgan Co., Illinois

- **Florence Martha Scholfield**
  - b: 05 May 1906 in Girard, Crawford Co., Kansas
  - m: 1933 in California
  - d: 20 Dec 1966 in Huntington Beach, Orange Co., California

- **John Hemphill**
  - b: 01 Oct 1836 in Ireland
  - m: 04 Sep 1872
  - d: 06 Apr 1910 in Kansas
  - Father: **John Hemphill**
    - b: 1798 in Londonderry, Ireland
    - m: 1822 in Ireland
    - d: 06 Mar 1889 in Bloomington, Monroe Co., Indiana
  - Mother: **Mary Reid**
    - b: 1802 in Ireland
    - d: 08 Sep 1892 in Bloomington, Monroe Co., Indiana

- **Elizabeth Irene Hemphill**
  - b: 05 Mar 1875 in Illinois
  - d: 22 Jul 1963 in Orange Co., California

- **Florence Blair**
  - b:
  - d:

Nola E. Wilton (1908-1953)
[6th. Generation from Henry Wilton (1769-1820)]

&

Dorsey Marion Campbell (1897-1969)
& Family

Nola E. Wilton was born February 1908 in Texas, the fourth child of Silas Wilton & Mary Elizabeth Underwood. After living in Uvalde County, Texas, beginning sometime after 1900, the family resettled in Orange County, California in the mid-1920's.

About 1924, Nola married Dorsey Marion Campbell in California. Dorsey was the son of Marion and Cora Campbell, originally from Pennsylvania. The Campbell's settled in Fresno County, California sometime after 1900.

In the 1930 Federal Census of Orange County, California, Dorsey Campbell, occupation fisherman, age 32, is listed with Nola E. Campbell, wife, age 22. At that time, they had been married for six years.

Nola died in January 1953 in Los Angeles County, California; Dorsey died May 1969 in Monterey County, California.

Family Group Sheet

Husband: Dorsey Marion Campbell	
Born: 13 Nov 1897	in: Pennsylvania
Married: Abt. 1924	in: California
Died: May 1969	in: Monterey Co., California

Wife: Nola E. Wilton	
Born: 11 Feb 1908	in: Texas
Died: 17 Jan 1953	in: Los Angeles Co., California
Father: Silas Wilton	
Mother: Mary Elizabeth Underwood	

Velma Lucile Wilton (1913-1977)
[6th. Generation from Henry Wilton (1769-1820)]

&

Russell Bailey
& Family

Velma Lucile Wilton, born September 1913 in Uvalde County, Texas, was the sixth, and last, child of Silas Wilton & Mary Elizabeth Underwood. After living in Uvalde County from about 1910 to the mid-1920's, the family resettled in Orange County, California.

Velma married Russell Bailey in 1931 and they started their own family in Orange County. Their two children, Dorothy Jean Bailey, born December 1935, and Russell Nolan Bailey, born December 1938, were both born in Orange County, California.

Velma Lucile died December 26, 1977 in Orange County, California.

Family Group Sheet

Husband: Russell Bailey

Born: Unknown
Married: 1931

Wife: Velma Lucile Wilton

Born: 11 Sep 1913 — in: Uvalde Co., Texas
Died: 26 Dec 1977 — in: Orange Co., California
Father: Silas Wilton
Mother: Mary Elizabeth Underwood

CHILDREN

1 F
Name: Dorothey Jean Bailey
Born: 26 Dec 1935 — in: Orange Co., California
Married: Unknown
Spouse: Ralph Luna

2 M
Name: Russell Nolan Bailey
Born: 14 Dec 1938 — in: Orange Co., California
Died: 1969

Cyrus Wilton (1878-1968)
[5th. Generation from Henry Wilton (1769-1820)]

&

Ida Bell Admire (1894-1984)
& Family

Cyrus Wilton and his twin brother, Ira Wilton, were born March 1, 1878 at Winn Hill in Jack County, Texas. Cyrus' parents Thomas A. Wilton & Easter B. Clark had recently resettled permanently in the Winn Hill Community in Jack County. Cyrus and Ira, at the age of 2 years, were listed in the 1880 Federal Census of Jack County, along with their three older brothers and parents.

By the 1900 Federal Census, Cyrus had moved to Tarrant County, Texas with his (great) uncle, Joseph Wilton, where he was employed as a farm laborer. In the 1900 Federal Census of Tarrant County, he is listed at age 22, along with the family of Joseph Wilton, his wife, Sarah, and five of their children.

About 1909, Cyrus married Ida Bell Admire in Tarrant County, Texas and they began their own family. In the 1910 Federal Census of Tarrant County, Cyrus, occupation farm laborer, and wife, Ida, were living in the dwelling next to the family of Sarah Wilton and two of her sons. Sarah's husband, Joseph Wilton, had died by that time.

In the 1920 Federal Census of Tarrant County, Texas, Cyrus was listed as a general farmer with his wife, Ida, and their two daughters, Margie Wilton, age 9, and Lois Wilton, age 6. Just eight dwellings away, the son of Joseph and Sarah Wilton, Jodie (Joseph) S.Wilton, was living with his wife, Bessie, two of their children, and Sarah, his mother.

Cyrus and Ida were also listed in the 1930 Federal Census of Tarrant County, Texas. In this census, Cyrus was listed with an occupation of public works truck driver, at age 53. Also included were Ida and their four children. By the time of this census, their two younger children, Cy Jr. Wilton, age 8, and Samuel H. Wilton, age 1, were included. Their oldest daughter, Margie, who was age 19 at the time, was still living at home and employed as a department store saleslady. The family of Jodie S. and Bessie Wilton, four of their children, and Sarah, Jodie's mother, were also found in the 1930 census, but by that time they were about 103 dwellings away from Cyrus and family.

Cyrus and Ida both died in Tarrant County, Texas, Cyrus in December 1968, and Ida in February 1984.

Family Group Sheet

Husband: Cyrus Wilton

Born: 01 Mar 1878	in: Winn Hill, Jack Co., Texas
Married: Abt. 1909	in: Ft. Worth, Tarrant Co., Texas
Died: 17 Dec 1968	in: Ft. Worth, Tarrant Co., Texas
Father: Thomas Abelum Wilton	
Mother: Easter Britania Clark	

Wife: Ida Bell Admire

Born: 04 Feb 1894	in: Benton Co., Arkansas
Died: 29 Feb 1984	in: Ft. Worth, Tarrant Co., Texas
Father: Livey Leslie Admire	
Mother: Martha Ann Wilson	

CHILDREN

#			
1 F	Name: Margie Wilton		
	Born: 1911	in: Texas	
2 F	Name: Lois Wilton		
	Born: 1914	in: Texas	
3 M	Name: Cyrus Wilton		
	Born: 1922	in: Texas	
4 M	Name: Samuel Harris Wilton		
	Born: 26 Dec 1928	in: Tarrant Co., Texas	

IDA BELL ADMIRE Standard Pedigree Tree

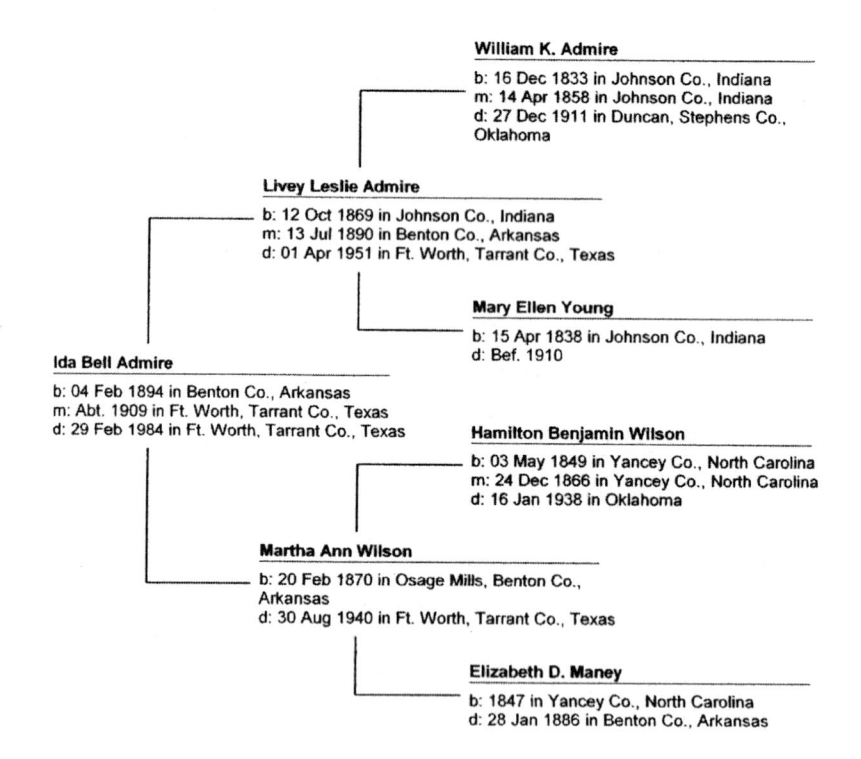

Ida Bell Admire
b: 04 Feb 1894 in Benton Co., Arkansas
m: Abt. 1909 in Ft. Worth, Tarrant Co., Texas
d: 29 Feb 1984 in Ft. Worth, Tarrant Co., Texas

Livey Leslie Admire
b: 12 Oct 1869 in Johnson Co., Indiana
m: 13 Jul 1890 in Benton Co., Arkansas
d: 01 Apr 1951 in Ft. Worth, Tarrant Co., Texas

William K. Admire
b: 16 Dec 1833 in Johnson Co., Indiana
m: 14 Apr 1858 in Johnson Co., Indiana
d: 27 Dec 1911 in Duncan, Stephens Co., Oklahoma

Mary Ellen Young
b: 15 Apr 1838 in Johnson Co., Indiana
d: Bef. 1910

Martha Ann Wilson
b: 20 Feb 1870 in Osage Mills, Benton Co., Arkansas
d: 30 Aug 1940 in Ft. Worth, Tarrant Co., Texas

Hamilton Benjamin Wilson
b: 03 May 1849 in Yancey Co., North Carolina
m: 24 Dec 1866 in Yancey Co., North Carolina
d: 16 Jan 1938 in Oklahoma

Elizabeth D. Maney
b: 1847 in Yancey Co., North Carolina
d: 28 Jan 1886 in Benton Co., Arkansas

Ira John Wilton (1878-1962)
[5th. Generation from Henry Wilton (1769-1820)]

&

Nancy Ann Williams (1884-1977)
& Family

Ira Wilton and his twin brother, Cyrus Wilton, were born March 1, 1878 at Winn Hill in Jack County, Texas. They were the fourth and fifth sons of Thomas A. Wilton & Easter B. Clark. The family had recently resettled in Jack County after first living in Parker County when the couple were married in 1870. After moving to the Winn Hill Community, that became the permanent home for Thomas and Easter.

After Ira's father, Thomas A. Wilton, died in 1894, Ira apparently spent some time in Oklahoma, because it was on February 21 1909 in Roger Mills County, Oklahoma, that he married Nancy Ann Williams. Nancy was the daughter of Joseph S. Williams & Mary Ann Weir, who had made Oklahoma their home since before 1900.

By 1910, Ira and Nancy had moved to West Texas. In the 1910 Federal Census of Swisher County, Texas, Ira is listed at age 31 with an occupation of odd job laborer. With him were his wife, Nancy A., age 25, and a son, L.D., age one month, having been born in Texas. Apparently, Nancy's father, Joseph S. Williams, and family accompanied Ira and Nancy to Swisher County, because they were also listed in the 1910 Federal Census of Swisher County, Texas, but they were separated by about 40 dwellings.

In 1918, Ira was located in Crystal Falls in Stephens County, Texas. That was the address given when he registered for the WWI draft in September 1918. He was also listed with an occupation of laborer, and his nearest relative as Nannie Wilton, with the same address.

By 1920, Ira and Nancy had made another move, this time to Lockney in Floyd County, Texas, which was adjacent to Swisher County. In the 1920 Federal Census of Floyd County, Texas, Ira, occupation teamster, age 41, is listed with his wife, "Nanie," age 33, and four children. Apparently, the family spent some time in New Mexico between 1910 and 1920, since the second child of Ira and Nancy, Mary Lucille Wilton, was born in New Mexico in 1912. The two younger children at the time, Gladys Nell Wilton, and Alvin Henry Wilton, were born in Texas, Gladys in 1914, and Alvin in 1916. It appears that Nancy's father and family again accompanied Ira and Nancy to Floyd County, Texas, because they were also listed in the 1920 Federal Census for Lockney in Floyd County.

By the census of 1930, Ira and Nancy were located in Dawson County, Texas, which was several counties southwest of Floyd County. In the 1930 Federal Census of Dawson County, Ira is listed as a general farmer, age 52, with his wife, "Nannie," age 45, and all of his six children. The last children were Helen Ruth Wilton, born February 1921, and Billie Duane Wilton, born March 1929, both born in Lockney in Floyd County, Texas.

Ira died December 1962 in Hockley County, Texas, and Nancy died in the adjacent Lubbock County in August 1977.

Family Group Sheet

Husband: Ira John Wilton

Born: 01 Mar 1878 in: Winn Hill, Jack Co., Texas
Married: 21 Feb 1909 in: Roger Mills Co., Oklahoma
Died: 01 Dec 1962 in: Levelland, Hockley Co., Texas
Father: Thomas Abslum Wilton
Mother: Easter Britania Clark

Wife: Nancy Ann Williams

Born: 19 Sep 1884 in: Wooster, Faulker Co., Arkansas
Died: 09 Aug 1977 in: Lubbock, Lubbock Co., Texas
Father: Joseph Soloman Williams
Mother: Mary Ann Wear

CHILDREN

1 M
Name: Lou D. Wilton
Born: 14 Mar 1910 in: Happy, Swisher Co., Texas
Died: 20 Dec 1966 in: Levelland, Hockley Co., Texas
Married: 14 Feb 1935 in: Texas
Spouse: Carmen Roela Howlett

2 F
Name: Mary Lucille Wilton
Born: 27 Feb 1912 in: Tucumcari, Quay Co., New Mexico
Died: 19 Jan 2003 in: Gilbert, Maricopa Co., Arizona
Married: 05 Oct 1934 in: Crystal City, Zavala Co., Texas
Spouse: Thomas Jefferson Nigh

3 F
Name: Gladys Nell Wilton
Born: 04 Apr 1914 in: Mobeetie, Wheeler Co., Texas
Died: 15 Apr 1995 in: Lubbock, Lubbock Co., Texas
Married: 03 Sep 1941 in: Pixley, Tulare Co., California
Spouse: Robert Leonard Kay

4 M
Name: Alvin Henry Wilton
Born: 28 Oct 1916 in: Lockney, Floyd Co., Texas
Died: 31 Mar 1987 in: Muskogee, Muskogee Co., Oklahoma
Married: 09 Dec 1941 in: Levelland, Hockley Co., Texas
Spouse: Mary Lucille Hoffman

5 F
Name: Helen Ruth Wilton
Born: 23 Feb 1921 in: Lockney, Floyd Co., Texas
Married: Unknown
Spouse: John William Brown

6 M
Name: Billie Duane Wilton
Born: 18 Mar 1929 in: Lockney, Floyd Co., Texas
Died: 20 Apr 1995 in: El Paso, El Paso Co., Texas
Married: Unknown in: Germany
Spouse: Katharina Nixdorf

NANCY ANN WILLIAMS Standard Pedigree Tree

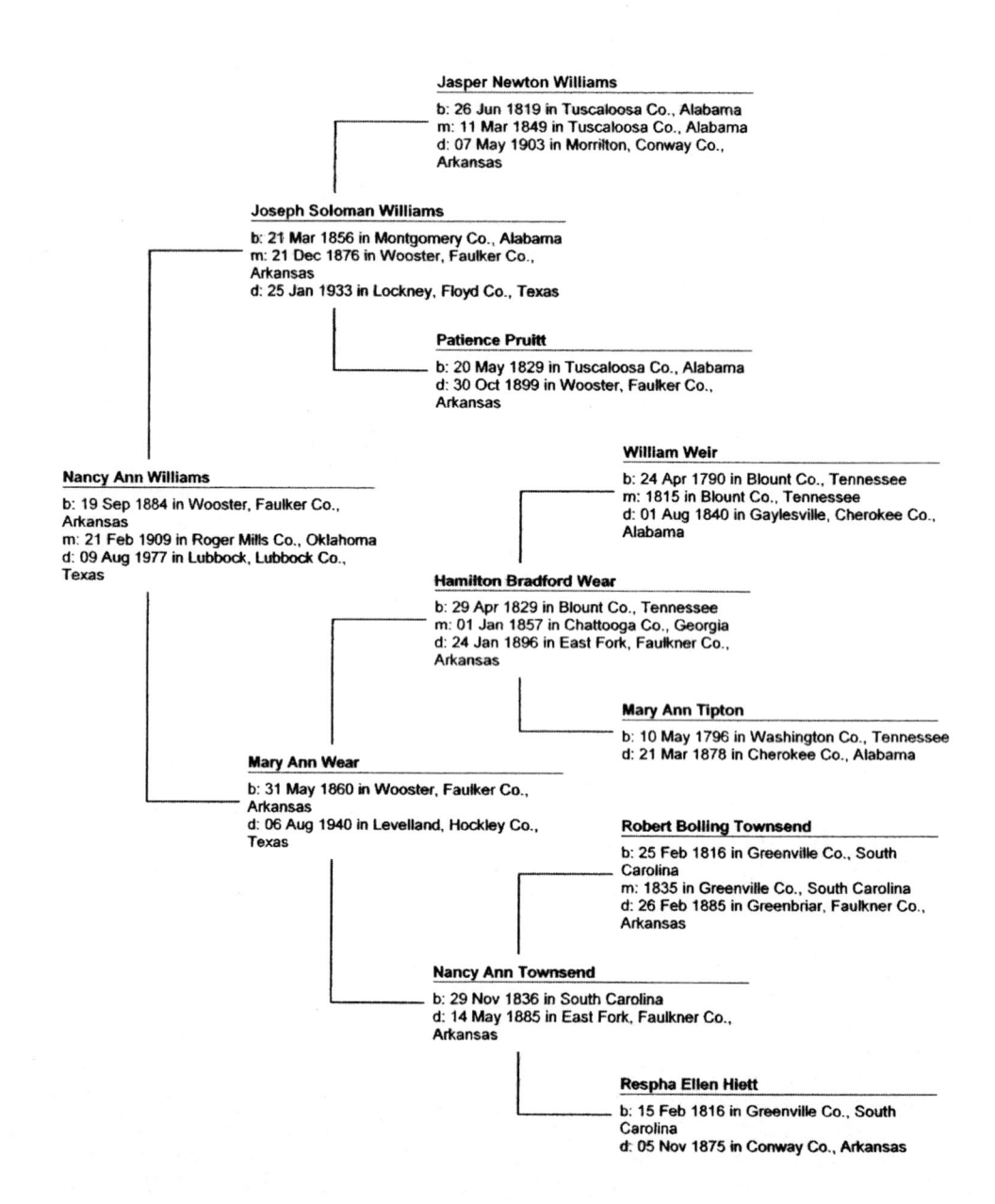

Nancy Ann Williams
b: 19 Sep 1884 in Wooster, Faulker Co., Arkansas
m: 21 Feb 1909 in Roger Mills Co., Oklahoma
d: 09 Aug 1977 in Lubbock, Lubbock Co., Texas

- **Joseph Soloman Williams**
  b: 21 Mar 1856 in Montgomery Co., Alabama
  m: 21 Dec 1876 in Wooster, Faulker Co., Arkansas
  d: 25 Jan 1933 in Lockney, Floyd Co., Texas

  - **Jasper Newton Williams**
    b: 26 Jun 1819 in Tuscaloosa Co., Alabama
    m: 11 Mar 1849 in Tuscaloosa Co., Alabama
    d: 07 May 1903 in Morrilton, Conway Co., Arkansas

  - **Patience Pruitt**
    b: 20 May 1829 in Tuscaloosa Co., Alabama
    d: 30 Oct 1899 in Wooster, Faulker Co., Arkansas

- **Mary Ann Wear**
  b: 31 May 1860 in Wooster, Faulker Co., Arkansas
  d: 06 Aug 1940 in Levelland, Hockley Co., Texas

  - **Hamilton Bradford Wear**
    b: 29 Apr 1829 in Blount Co., Tennessee
    m: 01 Jan 1857 in Chattooga Co., Georgia
    d: 24 Jan 1896 in East Fork, Faulkner Co., Arkansas

    - **William Weir**
      b: 24 Apr 1790 in Blount Co., Tennessee
      m: 1815 in Blount Co., Tennessee
      d: 01 Aug 1840 in Gaylesville, Cherokee Co., Alabama

    - **Mary Ann Tipton**
      b: 10 May 1796 in Washington Co., Tennessee
      d: 21 Mar 1878 in Cherokee Co., Alabama

  - **Nancy Ann Townsend**
    b: 29 Nov 1836 in South Carolina
    d: 14 May 1885 in East Fork, Faulkner Co., Arkansas

    - **Robert Bolling Townsend**
      b: 25 Feb 1816 in Greenville Co., South Carolina
      m: 1835 in Greenville Co., South Carolina
      d: 26 Feb 1885 in Greenbriar, Faulkner Co., Arkansas

    - **Respha Ellen Hiett**
      b: 15 Feb 1816 in Greenville Co., South Carolina
      d: 05 Nov 1875 in Conway Co., Arkansas

Lou D. Wilton (1910-1966)
[6th. Generation from Henry Wilton (1769-1820)]

&

Carmen Roela Howlett (1915-   )
& Family

Lou D., also known as L.D., was the first child of Ira Wilton & Nancy A. Williams. L.D. was born March 1910 in the town of Happy in Swisher County, Texas, shortly after Ira and Nancy moved to West Texas from Oklahoma. At the time of the 1910 Federal Census of Swisher County, L.D. was just one month old.

For his early years, L.D. lived in West Texas, living for awhile in Floyd County and then in Dawson County, Texas. In the 1920 Federal Census of Floyd County, Texas, L.D. was listed at age 9 years, living with his parents and two sisters and a brother. The family probably lived in Floyd County up until 1929, since L.D.'s youngest brother, Billie D. Wilton, was born March 1929 in Floyd County. By the 1930 Federal Census of Dawson County, Texas, L.D. was listed at age 20, living with his parents and family, which then included a total of six children. The occupation listed for L.D. was general laborer.

L.D. apparently made West Texas his home, at least until the late 1930's, because after he married Carmen Roela Howlett in 1935, their first child, Janice Darlene Wilton, was born March 1938 in Hockley County, Texas. They had one other child, Ira John Wilton, born March 1942. L.D. died in Hockley County in December 1966.

Family Group Sheet

Husband: Lou D. Wilton

Born: 14 Mar 1910 in: Happy, Swisher Co., Texas
Married: 14 Feb 1935 in: Texas
Died: 20 Dec 1966 in: Levelland, Hockley Co., Texas
Father: Ira John Wilton
Mother: Nancy Ann Williams

Wife: Carmen Roela Howlett

Born: 17 Sep 1915 in: Hansford Co., Texas
Father: John L. Howlett
Mother: Clara Cleo Goucher

CHILDREN

1 F
Name: Janice Darlene Wilton
Born: 15 Mar 1938 in: Levelland, Hockley Co., Texas
Died: 04 Jun 2007 in: Farmington, San Juan Co., New Mexico
Married: Unknown
Spouse: Norman Russell Hall
Married: Unknown
Spouse: Gary Leroy Payson

2 M
Name: Ira John Wilton
Born: 01 Mar 1942
Married: Unknown
Spouse: Nanalee Vondell

LOU D. WILTON Standard Pedigree Tree

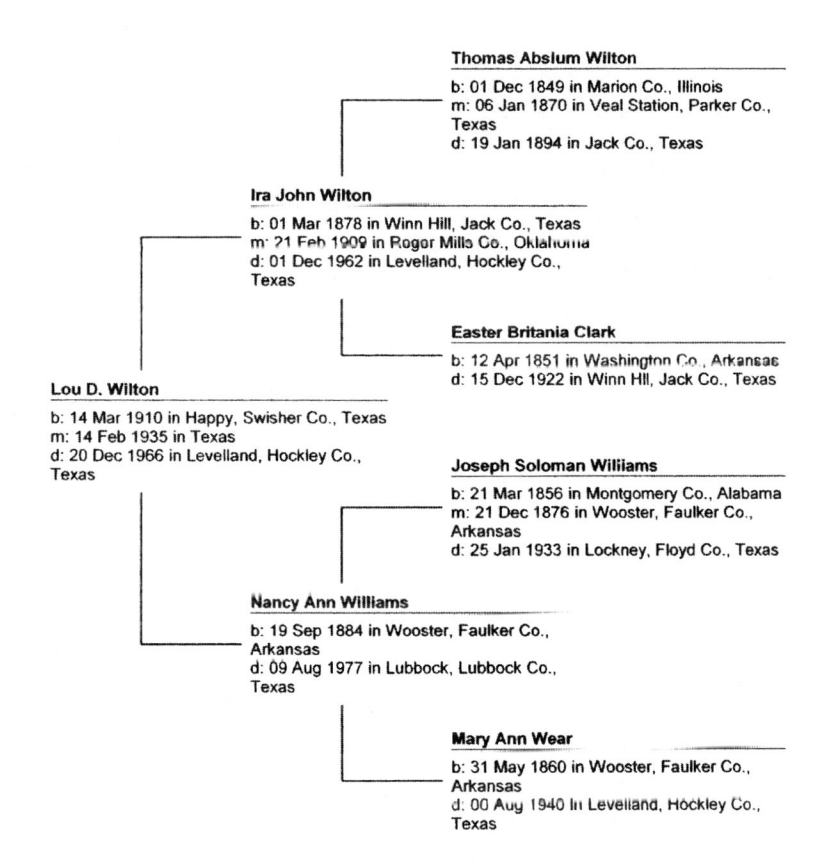

Lou D. Wilton
b: 14 Mar 1910 in Happy, Swisher Co., Texas
m: 14 Feb 1935 in Texas
d: 20 Dec 1966 in Levelland, Hockley Co., Texas

- **Ira John Wilton**
  b: 01 Mar 1878 in Winn Hill, Jack Co., Texas
  m: 21 Feb 1909 in Roger Mills Co., Oklahoma
  d: 01 Dec 1962 in Levelland, Hockley Co., Texas
  - **Thomas Abslum Wilton**
    b: 01 Dec 1849 in Marion Co., Illinois
    m: 06 Jan 1870 in Veal Station, Parker Co., Texas
    d: 19 Jan 1894 in Jack Co., Texas
  - **Easter Britania Clark**
    b: 12 Apr 1851 in Washington Co., Arkansas
    d: 15 Dec 1922 in Winn Hll, Jack Co., Texas

- **Nancy Ann Williams**
  b: 19 Sep 1884 in Wooster, Faulker Co., Arkansas
  d: 09 Aug 1977 in Lubbock, Lubbock Co., Texas
  - **Joseph Soloman Wiliams**
    b: 21 Mar 1856 in Montgomery Co., Alabama
    m: 21 Dec 1876 in Wooster, Faulker Co., Arkansas
    d: 25 Jan 1933 in Lockney, Floyd Co., Texas
  - **Mary Ann Wear**
    b: 31 May 1860 in Wooster, Faulker Co., Arkansas
    d: 00 Aug 1940 in Levelland, Hockley Co., Texas

Notes: This Tree also applies to the other children of Ira John Wilton & Nancy Ann Williams: Mary Lucille Wilton, Gladys Nell Wilton, Alvin Henry Wilton, Helen Ruth Wilton, and Billie Duane Wilton.

Janice Darlene Wilton (1938-2007)
[7th. Generation from Henry Wilton (1769-1820)]

&
Norman Russell Hall (1934-2004)
& Family

&
Gary Leroy Payson (1931-1998)
& Family

Janice Darlene Wilton, the first child of Lou D. Wilton & Carmen Howlett, was born March 1938 in Levelland in Hockley County, Texas.

Janice spent her early years in West Texas, but at some point she moved to New Mexico. Her first husband, Norman Russell Hall, worked for El Paso Natural Gas for 23 years and served in the Armed Forces. He then resided in Lindrith in Rio Aribba County, New Mexico, for the 36 years prior to his death in May 2004. Norman & Janice had two children, Dana Darleen Hall and Norma Dee Hall, who were born in New Mexico. Janice also had a third child, Twilla Dawn Eaton, also born in New Mexico, whose father was Vic Eaton.

After a divorce from her first husband, Janice married Gary Leroy Payson, and they made their home in Bloomfield in San Juan County, New Mexico. Her second husband died June 1998 in Bloomfield, and at some point she moved to Aztec, also located in San Juan County. Janice died June 2007 in San Juan County, New Mexico.

Family Group Sheet

Husband: Norman Russell Hall

Born: 23 Feb 1934 in: Alamogordo, Otero Co., New Mexico
Married: Unknown
Died: 16 May 2004 in: Aztec, San Juan Co., New Mexico
Father: Roy Wells Hall
Mother: Georgia Mabel Brown

Wife: Janice Darlene Wilton

Born: 15 Mar 1938 in: Levelland, Hockley Co., Texas
Died: 04 Jun 2007 in: Farmington, San Juan Co., New Mexico
Father: Lou D. Wilton
Mother: Carmen Roela Howlett
Other Spouses: Gary Leroy Payson

CHILDREN

1. F
   Name: Dana Darleen Hall
   Born: Unknown in: New Mexico
   Married: Unknown
   Spouse: Troy Duane Hamilton

2. F
   Name: Norma Dee Hall
   Born: Unknown in: New Mexico
   Married: Unknown
   Spouse: Michael A. Gonzalez

3. F
   Name: Twilla Dawn Eaton
   Born: Unknown in: New Mexico
   Married: Unknown
   Spouse: Rodolpho David Sanchez

Family Group Sheet

Husband: Gary Leroy Payson

Born: 02 Jan 1931 in: Colorado
Married: Unknown
Died: 15 Jun 1998 in: Bloomfield, San Juan Co., New Mexico
Father: Norman Stephen Payson
Mother: Sophie E. Coon

Wife: Janice Darlene Wilton

Born: 15 Mar 1938 in: Levelland, Hockley Co., Texas
Died: 04 Jun 2007 in: Farmington, San Juan Co., New Mexico
Father: Lou D. Wilton
Mother: Carmen Roela Howlett
Other Spouses: Norman Russell Hall

JANICE DARLENE WILTON Standard Pedigree Tree

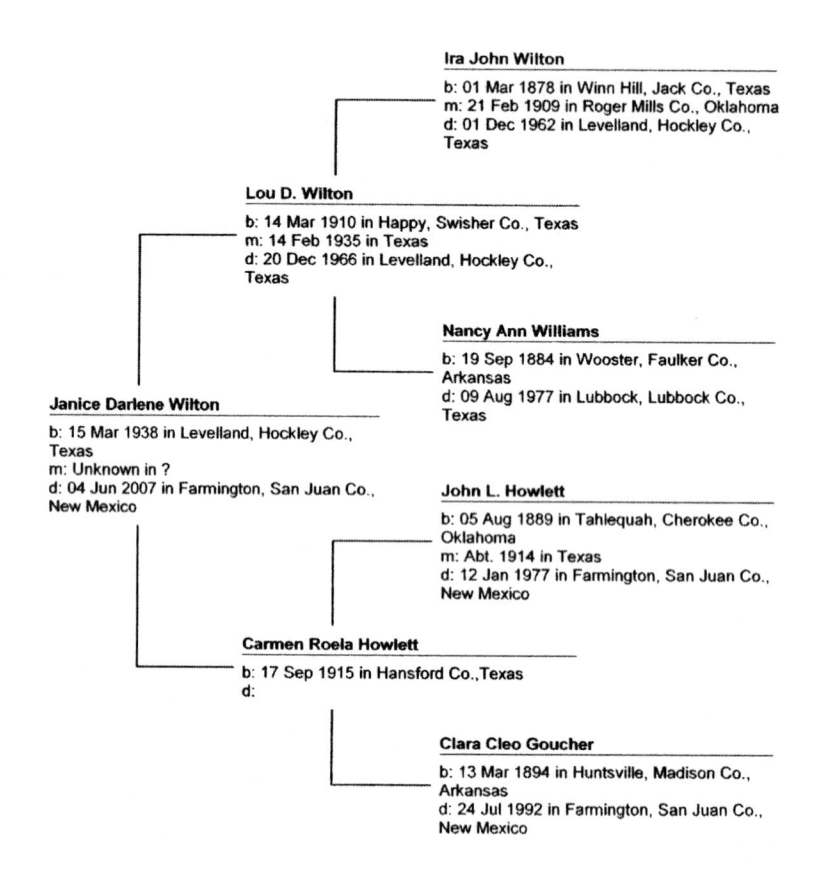

Janice Darlene Wilton
b: 15 Mar 1938 in Levelland, Hockley Co., Texas
m: Unknown in ?
d: 04 Jun 2007 in Farmington, San Juan Co., New Mexico

- **Lou D. Wilton**
  b: 14 Mar 1910 in Happy, Swisher Co., Texas
  m: 14 Feb 1935 in Texas
  d: 20 Dec 1966 in Levelland, Hockley Co., Texas
  - **Ira John Wilton**
    b: 01 Mar 1878 in Winn Hill, Jack Co., Texas
    m: 21 Feb 1909 in Roger Mills Co., Oklahoma
    d: 01 Dec 1962 in Levelland, Hockley Co., Texas
  - **Nancy Ann Williams**
    b: 19 Sep 1884 in Wooster, Faulker Co., Arkansas
    d: 09 Aug 1977 in Lubbock, Lubbock Co., Texas

- **Carmen Roela Howlett**
  b: 17 Sep 1915 in Hansford Co., Texas
  d:
  - **John L. Howlett**
    b: 05 Aug 1889 in Tahlequah, Cherokee Co., Oklahoma
    m: Abt. 1914 in Texas
    d: 12 Jan 1977 in Farmington, San Juan Co., New Mexico
  - **Clara Cleo Goucher**
    b: 13 Mar 1894 in Huntsville, Madison Co., Arkansas
    d: 24 Jul 1992 in Farmington, San Juan Co., New Mexico

Notes: This Tree also applies to the other child of Lou D. Wilton & Carmen Howlett: Ira John Wilton.

NORMAN RUSSELL HALL Standard Pedigree Tree

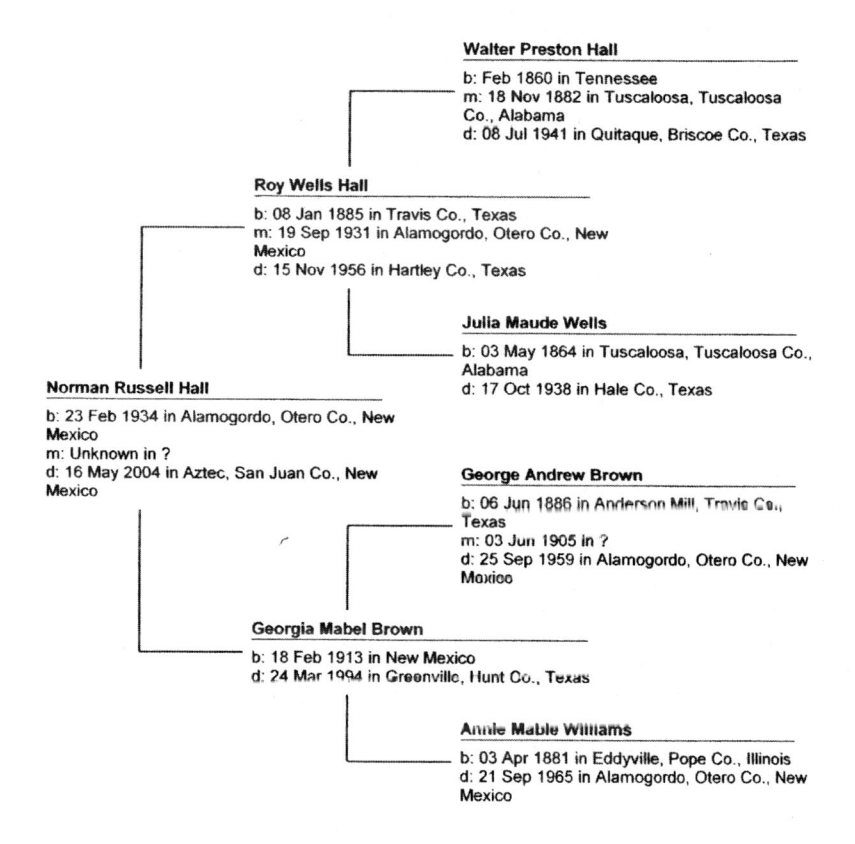

Walter Preston Hall
b: Feb 1860 in Tennessee
m: 18 Nov 1882 in Tuscaloosa, Tuscaloosa Co., Alabama
d: 08 Jul 1941 in Quitaque, Briscoe Co., Texas

Roy Wells Hall
b: 08 Jan 1885 in Travis Co., Texas
m: 19 Sep 1931 in Alamogordo, Otero Co., New Mexico
d: 15 Nov 1956 in Hartley Co., Texas

Julia Maude Wells
b: 03 May 1864 in Tuscaloosa, Tuscaloosa Co., Alabama
d: 17 Oct 1938 in Hale Co., Texas

Norman Russell Hall
b: 23 Feb 1934 in Alamogordo, Otero Co., New Mexico
m: Unknown in ?
d: 16 May 2004 in Aztec, San Juan Co., New Mexico

George Andrew Brown
b: 06 Jun 1886 in Anderson Mill, Travis Co., Texas
m: 03 Jun 1905 in ?
d: 25 Sep 1959 in Alamogordo, Otero Co., New Mexico

Georgia Mabel Brown
b: 18 Feb 1913 in New Mexico
d: 24 Mar 1994 in Greenville, Hunt Co., Texas

Annie Mable Williams
b: 03 Apr 1881 in Eddyville, Pope Co., Illinois
d: 21 Sep 1965 in Alamogordo, Otero Co., New Mexico

Dana Darleen Hall
[8th. Generation from Henry Wilton (1769-1820)]

&

Troy Duane Hamilton
& Family

Family Group Sheet

Husband: Troy Duane Hamilton

    Born: Unknown
    Married: Unknown

Wife: Dana Darleen Hall

    Born: Unknown   in: New Mexico
    Father: Norman Russell Hall
    Mother: Janice Darlene Wilton

CHILDREN

1 M   Name: Timothy Russell Hamilton
       Born: Unknown   in: Farmington, San Juan Co., New Mexico

2 M   Name: Samuel Troy Hamilton
       Born: 07 Jun 1986   in: Farmington, San Juan Co., New Mexico
       Died: 12 Sep 1991   in: Farmington, San Juan Co., New Mexico

DANA DARLEEN HALL Standard Pedigree Tree

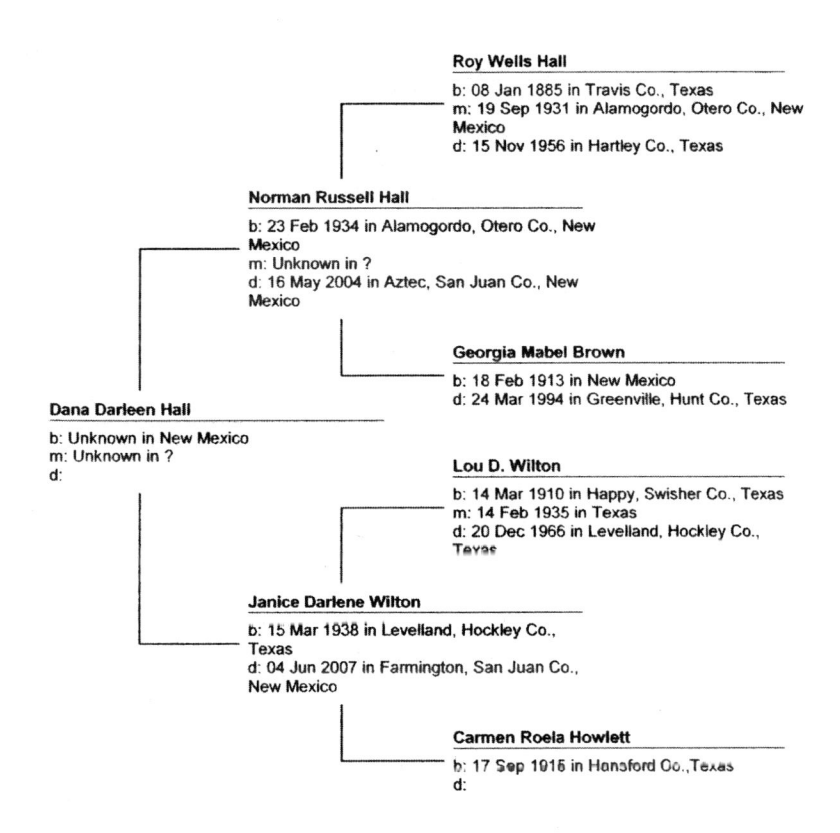

Dana Darleen Hall
b: Unknown in New Mexico
m: Unknown in ?
d:

- **Norman Russell Hall**
  b: 23 Feb 1934 in Alamogordo, Otero Co., New Mexico
  m: Unknown in ?
  d: 16 May 2004 in Aztec, San Juan Co., New Mexico

  - **Roy Wells Hall**
    b: 08 Jan 1885 in Travis Co., Texas
    m: 19 Sep 1931 in Alamogordo, Otero Co., New Mexico
    d: 15 Nov 1956 in Hartley Co., Texas

  - **Georgia Mabel Brown**
    b: 18 Feb 1913 in New Mexico
    d: 24 Mar 1994 in Greenville, Hunt Co., Texas

- **Janice Darlene Wilton**
  b: 15 Mar 1938 in Levelland, Hockley Co., Texas
  d: 04 Jun 2007 in Farmington, San Juan Co., New Mexico

  - **Lou D. Wilton**
    b: 14 Mar 1910 in Happy, Swisher Co., Texas
    m: 14 Feb 1935 in Texas
    d: 20 Dec 1966 in Levelland, Hockley Co., Texas

  - **Carmen Roela Howlett**
    b: 17 Sep 1916 in Hansford Co., Texas
    d:

Notes: This Tree also applies to the other children of Janice Darlene Wilton: Norma Dee Hall & Twilla Dawn Eaton.

Norma Dee Hall
[8th. Generation from Henry Wilton (1769-1820)]

&

Michael A. Gonzalez
& Family

Family Group Sheet

Husband: Michael A. Gonzalez
Born: Unknown
Married: Unknown

Wife: Norma Dee Hall	
Born: Unknown	in: New Mexico
Father: Norman Russell Hall	
Mother: Janice Darlene Wilton	

	CHILDREN
1 F	Name: Christy Darleen Gonzalez Born: Unknown
2 F	Name: Carmen Denise Hall Born: Unknown Married: Unknown Spouse: Radouane Ghrighez

Twilla Dawn Eaton
[8th. Generation from Henry Wilton (1769-1820)]

&

Rodolpho David Sanchez
& Family

Family Group Sheet

Husband: Rodolpho David Sanchez

Born: Unknown
Married: Unknown

Wife: Twilla Dawn Eaton

Born: Unknown in: New Mexico
Father: Norman Russell Hall
Mother: Janice Darlene Wilton

CHILDREN

1 F	Name: Brandy Dawn Sanchez Born: Unknown

Ira John Wilton (1942-   )
[7th. Generation from Henry Wilton (1769-1820)]

&

Nanalee Vondell
& Family

Family Group Sheet

Husband: Ira John Wilton	
Born: 01 Mar 1942	
Married: Unknown	
Father: Lou D. Wilton	
Mother: Carmen Roela Howlett	

Wife: Nanalee Vondell	
Born: Unknown	

	CHILDREN	
1 M	Name: Roland Wayne Wilton	
	Born: 01 May 1959	in: Alamogordo, Otero Co., New Mexico
	Died: 12 May 1979	in: Truth or Consequences, Sierra Co., New Mexico
2 M	Name: Monty Eugene Wilton	
	Born: 15 Jul 1961	in: Albuquerque, Bernalillo Co., New Mexico
	Died: 12 May 1979	in: Truth or Consequences, Sierra Co., New Mexico
3 M	Name: Timmy Wilton	
	Born: 05 May 1963	in: Alamogordo, Otero Co., New Mexico
	Died: Unknown	in: New Mexico

Mary Lucille Wilton (1912-2003)
[6th. Generation from Henry Wilton (1769-1820)]

&

Thomas Jefferson Nigh (1906-1978)
& Family

Mary Lucille Wilton, born February 1912 in Quay County, New Mexico, was the second child of Ira Wilton & Nancy Ann Williams. Ira and Nancy started their family in Oklahoma, where they were married in 1909, but shortly afterwards moved to West Texas, where they spent most of their lives. Except for Mary Lucille, all of their other children were born in West Texas.

Mary married Thomas Jefferson Nigh, son of Marion Franklin Nigh & Lana Ellen Miller, in October 1934 in Zavala County, Texas. Their first child, Wanda Lucille Nigh, was born May 1936 in nearby Dimmit County, Texas in South Texas. By 1940, the family had moved to West Texas in Hockley County, because that is where their second child, Martha Sue Nigh, was born in January 1940. Their remaining three children, Iris Ann Nigh, Tommy Wayne Nigh, and Faye Beth Night, were also born in Hockley County, Texas.

Sometime after 1950, Mary and Thomas moved to Maricopa County, Arizona near Phoenix. Thomas died October 1978 in Chandler, Arizona, and Mary died January 2003 in Gilbert, Arizona.

Family Group Sheet

Husband: Thomas Jefferson Nigh

Born: 02 Feb 1906 in: Montague Co., Texas
Married: 05 Oct 1934 in: Crystal City, Zavala Co., Texas
Died: 25 Oct 1978 in: Chandler, Maricopa Co., Arizona
Father: Marion Franklin Nigh
Mother: Lana Ellen Miller

Wife: Mary Lucille Wilton

Born: 27 Feb 1912 in: Tucumcari, Quay Co., New Mexico
Died: 19 Jan 2003 in: Gilbert, Maricopa Co., Arizona
Father: Ira John Wilton
Mother: Nancy Ann Williams

CHILDREN

#		
1 F	Name: Wanda Lucille Nigh Born: 04 May 1936	in: Dimmit Co., Texas
2 F	Name: Martha Sue Nigh Born: 24 Jan 1940	in: Hockley Co., Texas
3 F	Name: Iris Ann Nigh Born: 06 Apr 1942	in: Hockley Co., Texas
4 M	Name: Tommy Wayne Nigh Born: 11 Nov 1948	in: Hockley Co., Texas
5 F	Name: Faye Beth Nigh Born: 12 Oct 1950	in: Hockley Co., Texas

THOMAS JEFFERSON NIGH Standard Pedigree Tree

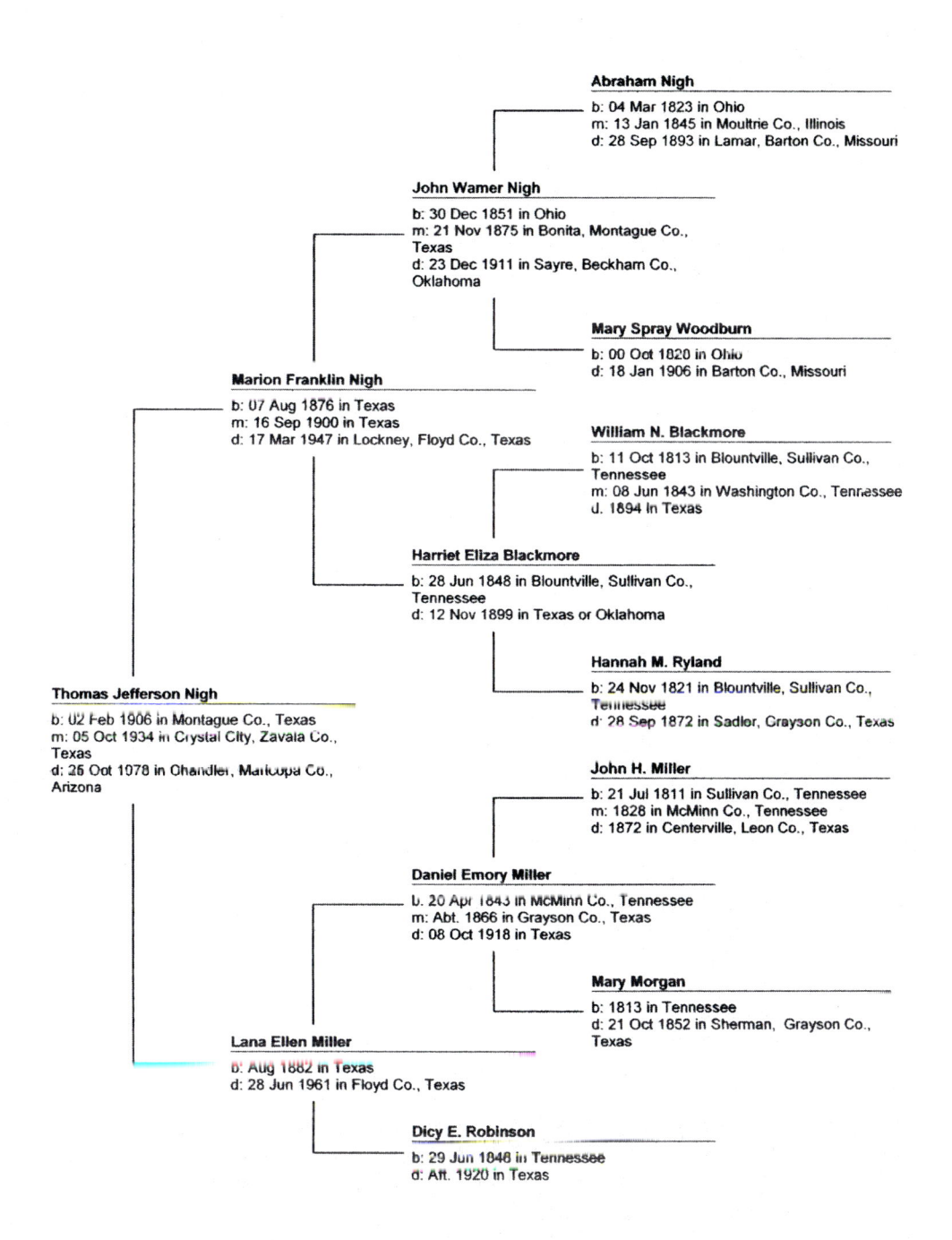

Thomas Jefferson Nigh
b: 02 Feb 1906 in Montague Co., Texas
m: 05 Oct 1934 in Crystal City, Zavala Co., Texas
d: 26 Oct 1978 in Chandler, Maricopa Co., Arizona

Marion Franklin Nigh
b: 07 Aug 1876 in Texas
m: 16 Sep 1900 in Texas
d: 17 Mar 1947 in Lockney, Floyd Co., Texas

John Warner Nigh
b: 30 Dec 1851 in Ohio
m: 21 Nov 1875 in Bonita, Montague Co., Texas
d: 23 Dec 1911 in Sayre, Beckham Co., Oklahoma

Abraham Nigh
b: 04 Mar 1823 in Ohio
m: 13 Jan 1845 in Moultrie Co., Illinois
d: 28 Sep 1893 in Lamar, Barton Co., Missouri

Mary Spray Woodburn
b: 00 Oct 1820 in Ohio
d: 18 Jan 1906 in Barton Co., Missouri

Harriet Eliza Blackmore
b: 28 Jun 1848 in Blountville, Sullivan Co., Tennessee
d: 12 Nov 1899 in Texas or Oklahoma

William N. Blackmore
b: 11 Oct 1813 in Blountville, Sullivan Co., Tennessee
m: 08 Jun 1843 in Washington Co., Tennessee
d: 1894 in Texas

Hannah M. Ryland
b: 24 Nov 1821 in Blountville, Sullivan Co., Tennessee
d: 28 Sep 1872 in Sadler, Grayson Co., Texas

Lana Ellen Miller
b: Aug 1882 in Texas
d: 28 Jun 1961 in Floyd Co., Texas

Daniel Emory Miller
b: 20 Apr 1843 in McMinn Co., Tennessee
m: Abt. 1866 in Grayson Co., Texas
d: 08 Oct 1918 in Texas

John H. Miller
b: 21 Jul 1811 in Sullivan Co., Tennessee
m: 1828 in McMinn Co., Tennessee
d: 1872 in Centerville, Leon Co., Texas

Mary Morgan
b: 1813 in Tennessee
d: 21 Oct 1852 in Sherman, Grayson Co., Texas

Dicy E. Robinson
b: 29 Jun 1846 in Tennessee
d: Aft. 1920 in Texas

Gladys Nell Wilton (1914-1995)
[6th. Generation from Henry Wilton (1769-1820)]

&

Robert Leonard Kay (1905-1976)
& Family

Gladys Nell Wilton, the third child of Ira Wilton & Nancy Ann Williams, was born April 1914 in Wheeler County, Texas. The family had just settled permanently in West Texas about that time.

Gladys married Robert Leonard Kay on September 3, 1941 in Tulare County, California. It appears that from WWII Army Enlistment Records, Robert L. Kay, was a resident in Hockley County, Texas, soon afterwards. He enlisted in the Air Corps on November 1, 1942 from Lubbock, Texas. His occupation was listed as geographer.

Gladys and Robert lived for sometime in Hockley County, Texas. Their first three children were born in Hockley County. Their first daughter, Linda Frances Kay, was born July 1943; their second daughter, Betty Jo Kay, was born in September 1946; and their third daughter, Paula Nell Kay, was born in March 1948. They also had one son, Bobby Louis Kay, who was born February 1953.

Robert and Gladys both died in Lubbock, Texas, Robert in February 1976, and Gladys in April 1995.

Family Group Sheet

Husband: Robert Leonard Kay

Born: 03 Sep 1905 — in: Oklahoma
Married: 03 Sep 1941 — in: Pixley, Tulare Co., California
Died: 26 Feb 1976 — in: Lubbock, Lubbock Co., Texas

Wife: Gladys Nell Wilton

Born: 04 Apr 1914 — in: Mobeetie, Wheeler Co., Texas
Died: 15 Apr 1995 — in: Lubbock, Lubbock Co., Texas
Father: Ira John Wilton
Mother: Nancy Ann Williams

CHILDREN

1 F
Name: Linda Frances Kay
Born: 07 Jul 1943 — in: Hockley Co., Texas
Married: Unknown
Spouse: Floyd Eugene Townsend

2 F
Name: Betty Jo Kay
Born: 16 Sep 1946 — in: Hockley Co., Texas

3 F
Name: Paula Nell Kay
Born: 23 Mar 1948 — in: Hockley Co., Texas
Married: 23 Jun 1967
Spouse: Curtis Eugene Crosier
Married: Unknown
Spouse: John Ted King

4 M
Name: Bobby Louis Kay
Born: 24 Feb 1953
Married: 27 Mar 1980 — in: Lubbock Co., Texas
Spouse: Cathy Lynn Vawter

Linda Frances Kay (1943-   )
[7th. Generation from Henry Wilton (1769-1820)]

&

Floyd Eugene Townsend
& Family

Family Group Sheet

Husband: Floyd Eugene Townsend		
Born: 02 Mar 1942	in: Lubbock Co., Texas	
Married: Unknown		
Wife: Linda Frances Kay		
Born: 07 Jul 1943	in: Hockley Co., Texas	
Father: Robert Leonard Kay		
Mother: Gladys Nell Wilton		
CHILDREN		
1 F	Name: Shelly Lynn Townsend	
	Born: 28 Mar 1966	in: Lubbock Co., Texas

LINDA FRANCES KAY Standard Pedigree Tree

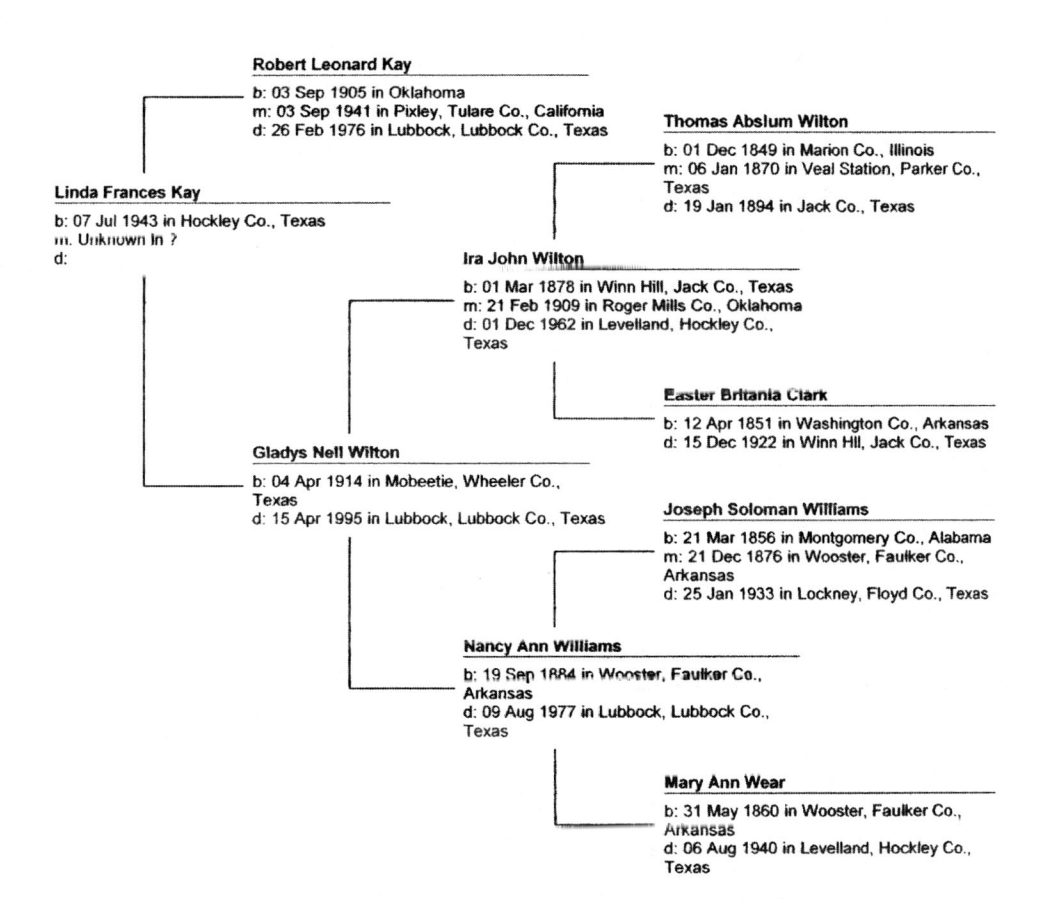

Linda Frances Kay
b: 07 Jul 1943 in Hockley Co., Texas
m: Unknown in ?
d:

- **Robert Leonard Kay**
  b: 03 Sep 1905 in Oklahoma
  m: 03 Sep 1941 in Pixley, Tulare Co., California
  d: 26 Feb 1976 in Lubbock, Lubbock Co., Texas

- **Gladys Nell Wilton**
  b: 04 Apr 1914 in Mobeetie, Wheeler Co., Texas
  d: 15 Apr 1995 in Lubbock, Lubbock Co., Texas

  - **Ira John Wilton**
    b: 01 Mar 1878 in Winn Hill, Jack Co., Texas
    m: 21 Feb 1909 in Roger Mills Co., Oklahoma
    d: 01 Dec 1962 in Levelland, Hockley Co., Texas

    - **Thomas Abslum Wilton**
      b: 01 Dec 1849 in Marion Co., Illinois
      m: 06 Jan 1870 in Veal Station, Parker Co., Texas
      d: 19 Jan 1894 in Jack Co., Texas

    - **Easter Britania Clark**
      b: 12 Apr 1851 in Washington Co., Arkansas
      d: 15 Dec 1922 in Winn Hill, Jack Co., Texas

  - **Nancy Ann Williams**
    b: 19 Sep 1884 in Wooster, Faulker Co., Arkansas
    d: 09 Aug 1977 in Lubbock, Lubbock Co., Texas

    - **Joseph Soloman Williams**
      b: 21 Mar 1856 in Montgomery Co., Alabama
      m: 21 Dec 1876 in Wooster, Faulker Co., Arkansas
      d: 25 Jan 1933 in Lockney, Floyd Co., Texas

    - **Mary Ann Wear**
      b: 31 May 1860 in Wooster, Faulker Co., Arkansas
      d: 06 Aug 1940 in Levelland, Hockley Co., Texas

Notes: This Tree also applies to the other children of Robert Leonard Kay & Gladys Nell Wilton: Betty Jo Kay, Paula Nell Kay, and Bobby Louis Kay.

Paula Nell Kay (1948-   )
[7th. Generation from Henry Wilton (1769-1820)]

&
Curtis Eugene Crosier (1944-   )
& Family

&
John Ted King (1946-1982)
& Family

Family Group Sheet

Husband: Curtis Eugene Crosier

Born: 31 Aug 1944   in: Hemphill Co., Texas
Married: 23 Jun 1967

Wife: Paula Nell Kay

Born: 23 Mar 1948   in: Hockley Co., Texas
Father: Robert Leonard Kay
Mother: Gladys Nell Wilton
    Other Spouses: John Ted King

CHILDREN

1 M   Name: Jason Todd Crosier
    Born: 31 Dec 1972   in: Lubbock Co., Texas

Family Group Sheet

Husband: John Ted King

Born: 01 Aug 1946   in: Sayre, Beckham Co., Oklahoma
Married: Unknown
Died: 19 Jun 1982   in: Arkadelphia, Clark Co., Arkansas

Wife: Paula Nell Kay

Born: 23 Mar 1948   in: Hockley Co., Texas
Father: Robert Leonard Kay
Mother: Gladys Nell Wilton
    Other Spouses: Curtis Eugene Crosier

CHILDREN

1 M   Name: Joshua Tanner King
    Born: Unknown

Bobby Louis Kay (1953-   )
[7th. Generation from Henry Wilton (1769-1820)]

&

Cathy Lynn Vawter (1956-   )
& Family

Family Group Sheet

Husband: Bobby Louis Kay	
Born: 24 Feb 1953	
Married: 27 Mar 1980	in: Lubbock Co., Texas
Father: Robert Leonard Kay	
Mother: Gladys Nell Wilton	

Wife: Cathy Lynn Vawter	
Born: 08 Feb 1956	in: Fresno Co., California

CHILDREN

1 M	Name: Zachary Adam Kay	
	Born: 31 May 1982	in: Lubbock, Lubbock Co., Texas
2 M	Name: Nicholas Jordan Kay	
	Born: 19 Jul 1985	in: Lubbock, Lubbock Co., Texas

Alvin Henry Wilton (1916-1987)
[6th. Generation from Henry Wilton (1769-1820)]

&

Mary Lucille Hoffman (1924-2002)
& Family

Alvin Henry Wilton, the fourth child of Ira Wilton & Nancy Ann Williams, was born October 1916 in Floyd County, Texas. Ira and Nancy had recently settled the family in West Texas, and that is where Alvin spent most of his early years.

At the age of 25, Alvin married Mary Lucille Hoffman in December 1941 in Hockley County, Texas. Mary Lucille was the daughter of Ulie Albert Hoffman and Winifred Pearl Strahan, who had settled in Childress County, Texas. Mary was born in Beckham County, Oklahoma, which was on the border with Texas and north of Childress County, Texas. Mary's mother, Winifred Pearl Strahan, was born in the Chickasaw Indian Territory of Oklahoma.

For a number of years, Alvin and Mary settled their family in Hockley County, and the adjacent Cochran County, which was on the New Mexico border. Alvin's first two children, Alva Eulene Wilton and Ira Gayle Wilton, were born in Hockley County. The third and last child, Jimmy Dale Wilton, was born July 1950 in Cochran County, Texas.

At some point Alvin and Mary moved to Oklahoma, because that is where they both died. Alvin Henry died March 1987 in Muskogee County, Oklahoma. Mary Lucille died April 2002 in Tulsa County, Oklahoma.

Family Group Sheet

Husband: Alvin Henry Wilton

Born: 28 Oct 1916 in: Lockney, Floyd Co., Texas
Married: 09 Dec 1941 in: Levelland, Hockley Co., Texas
Died: 31 Mar 1987 in: Muskogee, Muskogee Co., Oklahoma
Father: Ira John Wilton
Mother: Nancy Ann Williams

Wife: Mary Lucille Hoffman

Born: 22 Jun 1924 in: Sayre, Beckham Co, Delhi Settlement, Oklahoma
Died: 08 Apr 2002 in: Tulsa, Tulsa Co., Oklahoma
Father: Ulie Albert Hoffman
Mother: Winifred Pearl Strahan

CHILDREN

1 F
Name: Alva Eulene Wilton
Born: 28 Jan 1943 in: Hockley Co., Texas
Married: 21 Aug 1960 in: Oklahoma
Spouse: Kenneth Ray Carroll

2 M
Name: Ira Gayle Wilton
Born: 16 Jan 1947 in: Levelland, Hockley Co., Texas
Married: Unknown in: Oklahoma
Spouse: Janice

3 M
Name: Jimmy Dale Wilton
Born: 11 Jul 1950 in: Cochran Co., Texas
Married: Unknown in: Oklahoma
Spouse: Shirley Perryman

MARY LUCILLE HOFFMAN Standard Pedigree Tree

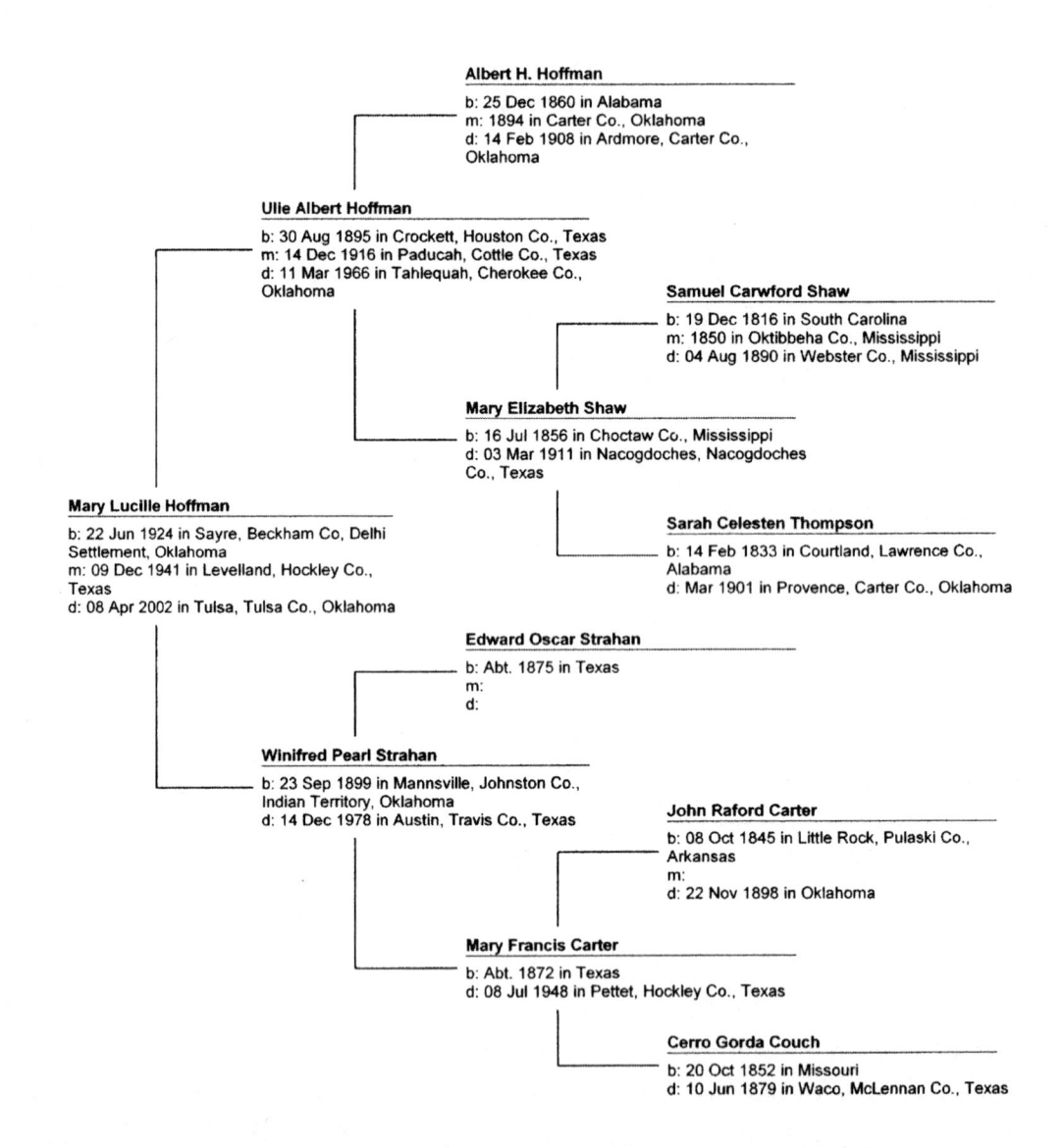

Albert H. Hoffman
b: 25 Dec 1860 in Alabama
m: 1894 in Carter Co., Oklahoma
d: 14 Feb 1908 in Ardmore, Carter Co., Oklahoma

Ulie Albert Hoffman
b: 30 Aug 1895 in Crockett, Houston Co., Texas
m: 14 Dec 1916 in Paducah, Cottle Co., Texas
d: 11 Mar 1966 in Tahlequah, Cherokee Co., Oklahoma

Samuel Carwford Shaw
b: 19 Dec 1816 in South Carolina
m: 1850 in Oktibbeha Co., Mississippi
d: 04 Aug 1890 in Webster Co., Mississippi

Mary Elizabeth Shaw
b: 16 Jul 1856 in Choctaw Co., Mississippi
d: 03 Mar 1911 in Nacogdoches, Nacogdoches Co., Texas

Sarah Celesten Thompson
b: 14 Feb 1833 in Courtland, Lawrence Co., Alabama
d: Mar 1901 in Provence, Carter Co., Oklahoma

Mary Lucille Hoffman
b: 22 Jun 1924 in Sayre, Beckham Co, Delhi Settlement, Oklahoma
m: 09 Dec 1941 in Levelland, Hockley Co., Texas
d: 08 Apr 2002 in Tulsa, Tulsa Co., Oklahoma

Edward Oscar Strahan
b: Abt. 1875 in Texas
m:
d:

Winifred Pearl Strahan
b: 23 Sep 1899 in Mannsville, Johnston Co., Indian Territory, Oklahoma
d: 14 Dec 1978 in Austin, Travis Co., Texas

John Raford Carter
b: 08 Oct 1845 in Little Rock, Pulaski Co., Arkansas
m:
d: 22 Nov 1898 in Oklahoma

Mary Francis Carter
b: Abt. 1872 in Texas
d: 08 Jul 1948 in Pettet, Hockley Co., Texas

Cerro Gorda Couch
b: 20 Oct 1852 in Missouri
d: 10 Jun 1879 in Waco, McLennan Co., Texas

Alva Eulene Wilton (1943-)
[7th. Generation from Henry Wilton (1769-1820)]

&

Kenneth Ray Carroll (1941-1987)
& Family

Family Group Sheet

Husband: Kenneth Ray Carroll	
Born: 27 Jun 1941	in: Orr, Love Co., Oklahoma
Married: 21 Aug 1960	in: Oklahoma
Died: 24 Jun 1987	in: Healdton, Carter Co., Oklahoma
Wife: Alva Eulene Wilton	
Born: 28 Jan 1943	in: Hockley Co., Texas
Father: Alvin Henry Wilton	
Mother: Mary Lucille Hoffman	

	CHILDREN	
1 F	Name: Nancy Lynn Carroll	
	Born: Apr 1966	in: Oklahoma
	Married: Unknown	in: Oklahoma
	Spouse: Aaron S. Deerinwater	
2 F	Name: Kennie Sue Carroll	
	Born: Unknown	in: Oklahoma
	Married: Unknown	
	Spouse: Joe Mitchell	

ALVA EULENE WILTON Standard Pedigree Tree

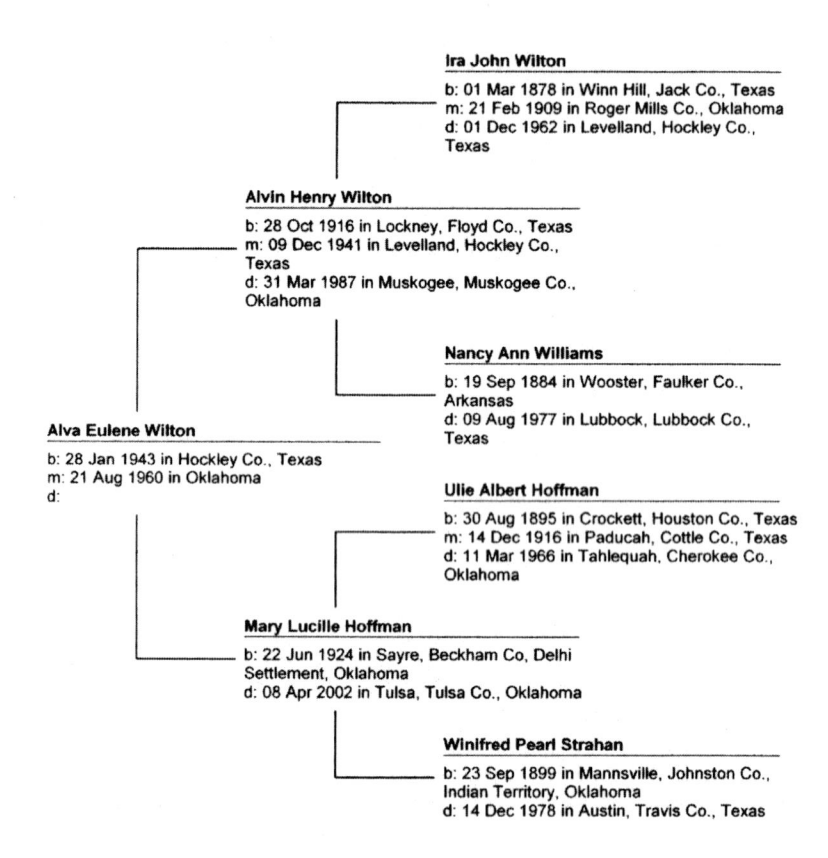

Alva Eulene Wilton
b: 28 Jan 1943 in Hockley Co., Texas
m: 21 Aug 1960 in Oklahoma
d:

- **Alvin Henry Wilton**
  b: 28 Oct 1916 in Lockney, Floyd Co., Texas
  m: 09 Dec 1941 in Levelland, Hockley Co., Texas
  d: 31 Mar 1987 in Muskogee, Muskogee Co., Oklahoma
  - **Ira John Wilton**
    b: 01 Mar 1878 in Winn Hill, Jack Co., Texas
    m: 21 Feb 1909 in Roger Mills Co., Oklahoma
    d: 01 Dec 1962 in Levelland, Hockley Co., Texas
  - **Nancy Ann Williams**
    b: 19 Sep 1884 in Wooster, Faulker Co., Arkansas
    d: 09 Aug 1977 in Lubbock, Lubbock Co., Texas

- **Mary Lucille Hoffman**
  b: 22 Jun 1924 in Sayre, Beckham Co, Delhi Settlement, Oklahoma
  d: 08 Apr 2002 in Tulsa, Tulsa Co., Oklahoma
  - **Ulie Albert Hoffman**
    b: 30 Aug 1895 in Crockett, Houston Co., Texas
    m: 14 Dec 1916 in Paducah, Cottle Co., Texas
    d: 11 Mar 1966 in Tahlequah, Cherokee Co., Oklahoma
  - **Winifred Pearl Strahan**
    b: 23 Sep 1899 in Mannsville, Johnston Co., Indian Territory, Oklahoma
    d: 14 Dec 1978 in Austin, Travis Co., Texas

Notes: This Tree also applies to the other children of Alvin Henry Wilton & Mary Lucille Hoffman: Ira Gayle Wilton and Jimmy Dale Wilton.

Helen Ruth Wilton (1921-   )
[6th. Generation from Henry Wilton (1769-1820)]

&

John William Brown
& Family

Helen Ruth Wilton, born February 1921 in Floyd County, Texas, was the fifth child of Ira Wilton & Nancy Ann Wilton. Beginning about 1910, Ira and Nancy had made their home in the Panhandle area around Lubbock, Texas. That is where Helen Ruth spent her early years, in Floyd County and Dawson County, Texas.

Helen Ruth married John William Brown about 1944, and they also began their family in the West Texas area. Their first child, Donnie Jay Brown, was born January 1945 in Levelland in Hockley County, Texas. Their second child, Travis Ray Brown, was also born in Hockley County, Texas in September 1950.

Family Group Sheet

Husband: John William Brown		
	Born: Unknown	
	Married: Unknown	
Wife: Helen Ruth Wilton		
	Born: 23 Feb 1921	in: Lockney, Floyd Co., Texas
	Father: Ira John Wilton	
	Mother: Nancy Ann Williams	
CHILDREN		
1 M	Name: Donnie Jay Brown	
	Born: 05 Jan 1945	in: Levelland, Hockley Co., Texas
	Died: May 1989	in: Las Cruces, Doña Ana Co., New Mexico
	Married: 20 May 1974	in: El Paso Co., Texas
	Spouse: Zulema Martinez	
	Married: Unknown	
	Spouse: Gayle Webster	
2 M	Name: Travis Ray Brown	
	Born: 17 Sep 1950	in: Hockley Co., Texas
	Married: Unknown	
	Spouse: Patricia Lee Deroy	

Donnie Jay Brown (1945-1989)
[7th. Generation from Henry Wilton (1769-1820)]

&
Zulema Martinez (1951-   )
& Family

&
Gayle Webster
& Family

Family Group Sheet

Husband: Donnie Jay Brown

    Born: 05 Jan 1945   in: Levelland, Hockley Co., Texas
  Married: 20 May 1974   in: El Paso Co., Texas
    Died: May 1989   in: Las Cruces, Dona Ana Co., New Mexico
  Father: John William Brown
  Mother: Helen Ruth Wilton
    Other Spouses: Gayle Webster

Wife: Zulema Martinez

  Born: Abt. 1951

CHILDREN

1 M   Name: Israel Brown
    Born: Unknown

2 M   Name: Eric Joseph Brown
    Born: Unknown

Family Group Sheet

Husband: Donnie Jay Brown

    Born: 05 Jan 1945   in: Levelland, Hockley Co., Texas
  Married: Unknown
    Died: May 1989   in: Las Cruces, Dona Ana Co., New Mexico
  Father: John William Brown
  Mother: Helen Ruth Wilton
    Other Spouses: Zulema Martinez

Wife: Gayle Webster

  Born: Unknown

CHILDREN

1 M   Name: Gregory John Brown
    Born: Unknown

DONNIE JAY BROWN Standard Pedigree Tree

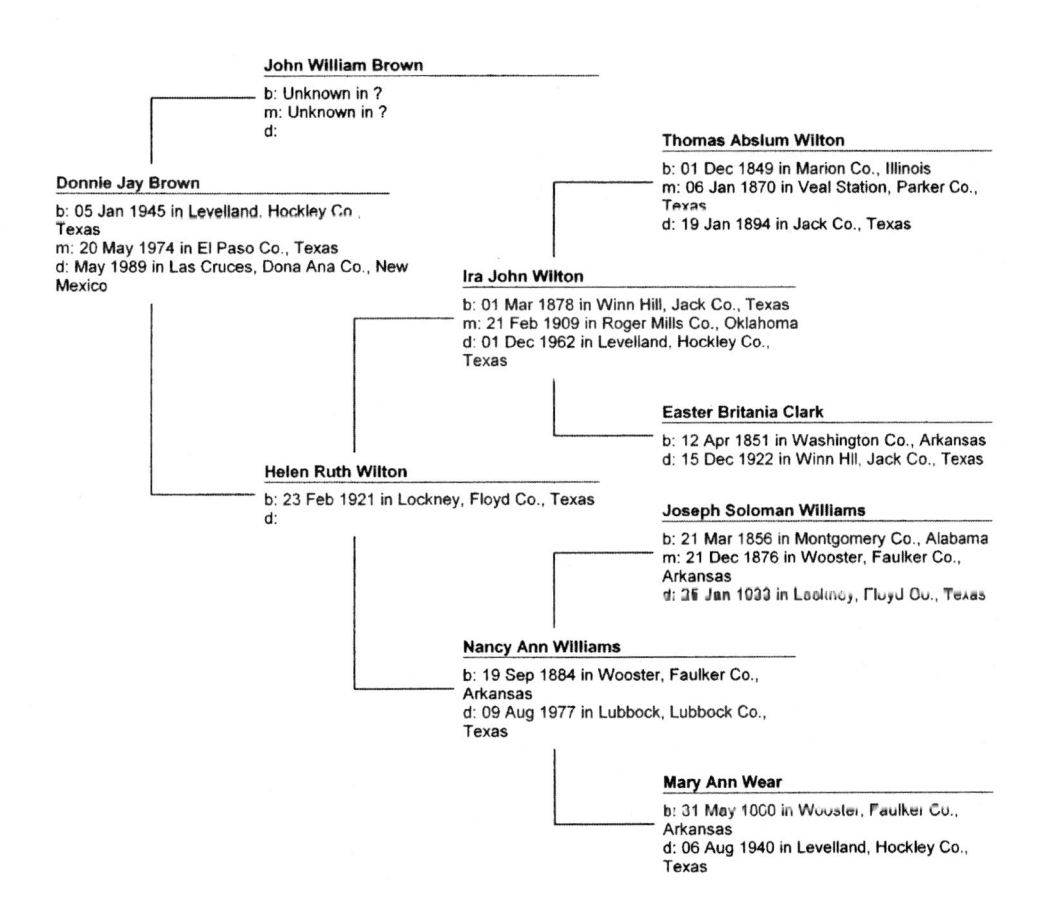

John William Brown
- b: Unknown in ?
- m: Unknown in ?
- d:

Donnie Jay Brown
- b: 05 Jan 1945 in Levelland, Hockley Co., Texas
- m: 20 May 1974 in El Paso Co., Texas
- d: May 1989 in Las Cruces, Dona Ana Co., New Mexico

Thomas Abslum Wilton
- b: 01 Dec 1849 in Marion Co., Illinois
- m: 06 Jan 1870 in Veal Station, Parker Co., Texas
- d: 19 Jan 1894 in Jack Co., Texas

Ira John Wilton
- b: 01 Mar 1878 in Winn Hill, Jack Co., Texas
- m: 21 Feb 1909 in Roger Mills Co., Oklahoma
- d: 01 Dec 1962 in Levelland, Hockley Co., Texas

Easter Britania Clark
- b: 12 Apr 1851 in Washington Co., Arkansas
- d: 15 Dec 1922 in Winn Hill, Jack Co., Texas

Helen Ruth Wilton
- b: 23 Feb 1921 in Lockney, Floyd Co., Texas
- d:

Joseph Soloman Williams
- b: 21 Mar 1856 in Montgomery Co., Alabama
- m: 21 Dec 1876 in Wooster, Faulker Co., Arkansas
- d: 26 Jan 1933 in Lockney, Floyd Co., Texas

Nancy Ann Williams
- b: 19 Sep 1884 in Wooster, Faulker Co., Arkansas
- d: 09 Aug 1977 in Lubbock, Lubbock Co., Texas

Mary Ann Wear
- b: 31 May 1860 in Wooster, Faulker Co., Arkansas
- d: 06 Aug 1940 in Levelland, Hockley Co., Texas

Notes: This Tree also applies to the other child of John William Brown & Helen Ruth Wilton: Travis Ray Brown.

Travis Ray Brown (1950-)
[7th. Generation from Henry Wilton (1769-1820)]

&

Patricia Lee Deroy
& Family

Family Group Sheet

Husband: Travis Ray Brown	
Born: 17 Sep 1950	in: Hockley Co., Texas
Married: Unknown	
Father: John William Brown	
Mother: Helen Ruth Wilton	
Wife: Patricia Lee Deroy	
Born: Unknown	
CHILDREN	
1 F	Name: Rhonda Ellen Brown Born: Unknown
2 M	Name: Nathan Leland Brown Born: Unknown
3 M	Name: Brian Jeffrey Brown Born: Unknown

Billie Duane Wilton (1929-1995)
[6th. Generation from Henry Wilton (1769-1820)]

&

Katharina Nixdorf (1927-   )
& Family

Billie Duane Wilton, born March 1929 in Floyd County, Texas, was the sixth and last child of Ira Wilton & Nancy Ann Wilton. By the time Billie was born, Ira and Nancy had settled in Floyd County, located in the Panhandle of West Texas. Billie's early years were also spent in West Texas, the family having moved about 1930 to Dawson County, Texas, located south of the Lubbock, Texas area.

Available records indicate that about April 1946, Billie was in the U.S. Army. He must have spent time in Germany, because he married Katharina Nixdorf of Germany, prior to March 1950. According to the passenger manifest of the USNS "Henry Gibbins," arriving in New York from Bremerhaven, Germany in March 1950, there is a "Katharine" Wilton with a destination of 702 9th. St. in Lovelland, Texas. The ship was a military transport that was apparently transporting military dependents from Germany to the U.S. The ship manifest also lists "Katharine" Wilton as age 23, married, with a nationality of German.

Billie and Katharina must have spent some time in Oklahoma, because that is where their son, Gerald Ray Wilton, was born in November 1951. At some point, the family moved to El Paso, Texas, because that is where Billie died in April 1995.

Family Group Sheet

Husband: Billie Duane Wilton	
Born: 18 Mar 1929	in: Lockney, Floyd Co., Texas
Married: Unknown	in: Germany
Died: 20 Apr 1995	in: El Paso, El Paso Co., Texas
Father: Ira John Wilton	
Mother: Nancy Ann Williams	

Wife: Katharina Nixdorf	
Born: 1927	in: Germany

CHILDREN

1. M
   - Name: Gerald Ray Wilton
   - Born: 23 Nov 1951 in: Oklahoma
   - Married: 08 Jun 1976 in: El Paso Co., Texas
   - Spouse: Vicki Cheryl Fritz

Gerald Ray Wilton (1951-   )
[7th. Generation from Henry Wilton (1769-1820)]

&

Vicki Cheryl Fritz (1955-   )
& Family

Family Group Sheet

Husband: Gerald Ray Wilton

Born: 23 Nov 1951	in: Oklahoma
Married: 08 Jun 1976	in: El Paso Co., Texas
Father: Billie Duane Wilton	
Mother: Katharina Nixdorf	

Wife: Vicki Cheryl Fritz

Born: Abt. 1955

CHILDREN

1 M	Name: Gerald Ray Jr. Wilton		
	Born: 24 Jan 1977	in: El Paso Co., Texas	
2 M	Name: Jeffrey Scott Wilton		
	Born: 26 Jan 1979	in: El Paso Co., Texas	

GERALD RAY WILTON Standard Pedigree Tree

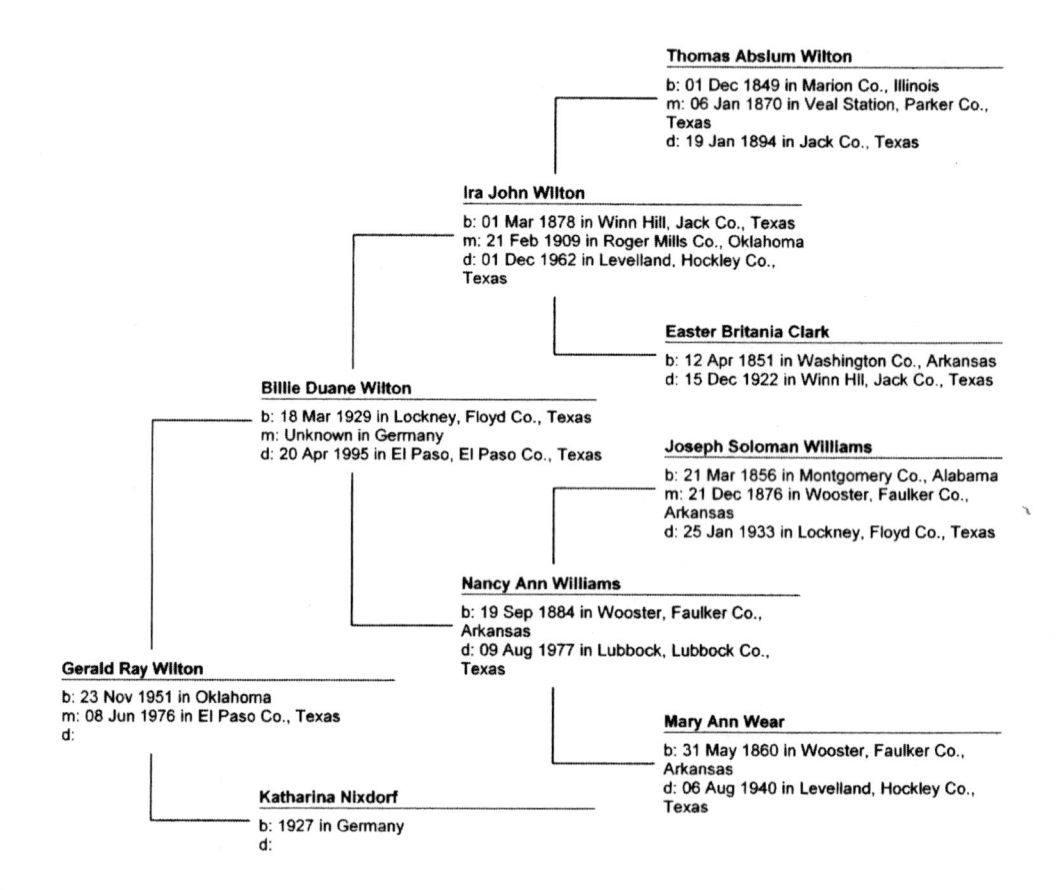

Thomas Abslum Wilton
b: 01 Dec 1849 in Marion Co., Illinois
m: 06 Jan 1870 in Veal Station, Parker Co., Texas
d: 19 Jan 1894 in Jack Co., Texas

Ira John Wilton
b: 01 Mar 1878 in Winn Hill, Jack Co., Texas
m: 21 Feb 1909 in Roger Mills Co., Oklahoma
d: 01 Dec 1962 in Levelland, Hockley Co., Texas

Easter Britania Clark
b: 12 Apr 1851 in Washington Co., Arkansas
d: 15 Dec 1922 in Winn Hll, Jack Co., Texas

Billie Duane Wilton
b: 18 Mar 1929 in Lockney, Floyd Co., Texas
m: Unknown in Germany
d: 20 Apr 1995 in El Paso, El Paso Co., Texas

Joseph Soloman Williams
b: 21 Mar 1856 in Montgomery Co., Alabama
m: 21 Dec 1876 in Wooster, Faulker Co., Arkansas
d: 25 Jan 1933 in Lockney, Floyd Co., Texas

Nancy Ann Williams
b: 19 Sep 1884 in Wooster, Faulker Co., Arkansas
d: 09 Aug 1977 in Lubbock, Lubbock Co., Texas

Gerald Ray Wilton
b: 23 Nov 1951 in Oklahoma
m: 08 Jun 1976 in El Paso Co., Texas
d:

Mary Ann Wear
b: 31 May 1860 in Wooster, Faulker Co., Arkansas
d: 06 Aug 1940 in Levelland, Hockley Co., Texas

Katharina Nixdorf
b: 1927 in Germany
d:

Ida May Wilton (1880~1960)
[5th. Generation from Henry Wilton (1769-1820)]

&

William Rufus Reynolds (1868-1949)
& Family

Ida May Wilton, born August 1880 at Winn Hill in Jack County, Texas, was the sixth child of Thomas A. Wilton & Easter B. Clark. About 1878, Thomas and Easter had settled permanently in the Winn Hill Community of Jack County, and that is where Ida May spent her formative years.

Ida May is listed in both the 1900 and 1910 Federal Census of Jack County, Texas. By this time, her father, Thomas A. Wilton, had died, and she was living at home with her mother, Easter B. Wilton, and her younger brothers and sisters. In the 1900 Federal Census of Jack County, Ida M. is listed at age 19, along with her mother and two brothers and two sisters. In the 1910 Federal Census of Jack County, Ida M. is listed at age 28, with her mother and two brothers and one sister.

In August 1915, Ida married William Rufus Reynolds, son of John Andrew Reynolds and Lara Ann Jones. William Rufus was born in Alabama, and that is where he spent his early years. He was about 12 years older than Ida, and this was his second marriage. There was an additional connection with the Wilton family, because one of his children, James Roscoe Reynolds, by his first marriage to Alma Lena Meadows, married Mary Alma Wilton, the daughter of Henry Franklin Wilton & Martha Jane Baldwin, and cousin to Ida May.

Prior to his marriage to Ida May, William Rufus was listed in the 1900 and 1910 Federal Census of Talladega County, Alabama. From his first marriage to Alma Lena Meadows, there were eight children, all born in Alabama. His first wife died in October 1910 in Talladaga County, Alabama.

Ida May and William Rufus had one child together, named Norris Truett Reynolds, born November 1919 in Texas. Beginning with the 1920 Federal Census, William Rufus was listed with Ida May in the Federal Census of Parker County, Texas. In 1920, William Rufus was listed as a farmer, age 52, with his wife, May I., age 39, three children by his first marriage, and their one child together, Norris T. Reynolds, age seven months.

Sometime between 1920 and 1930, Ida and Rufus moved the family to Archer County, Texas, near the border with Oklahoma. In the 1930 Federal Census of Archer County, Texas, Rufus was listed at age 62 with an occupation of country store merchant, along with his wife, "Mae," age 49, and son, Norris, age 10. In the same census, living only three dwellings away from Ida and Rufus, was Roger W. Reynolds, the sixth child of Rufus' first marriage, and his family.

Sometime after 1930, Ida and Rufus must have moved to the adjacent Young County, Texas, because that is where they both died, Rufus in 1949, and Ida about 1960.

Family Group Sheet

Husband: William Rufus Reynolds

Born: 17 Jul 1868	in: Roanoke, Randolph Co., Alabama
Married: 18 Aug 1915	in: Texas
Died: 06 Sep 1949	in: Olney, Young Co., Texas
Father: John Andrew Reynolds	
Mother: Lara Ann Jones	
Other Spouses: Alma Lena Meadows	

Wife: Ida May Wilton

Born: 03 Aug 1880	in: Winn Hill, Jack Co., Texas
Died: Abt. 1960	in: Olney, Young Co., Texas
Father: Thomas Abslum Wilton	
Mother: Easter Britania Clark	

CHILDREN

1 M	Name: Norris Truett Reynolds		
	Born: 24 Nov 1919	in: Texas	
	Died: 03 Nov 1981	in: Harris Co., Texas	

WILLIAM RUFUS REYNOLDS Standard Pedigree Tree

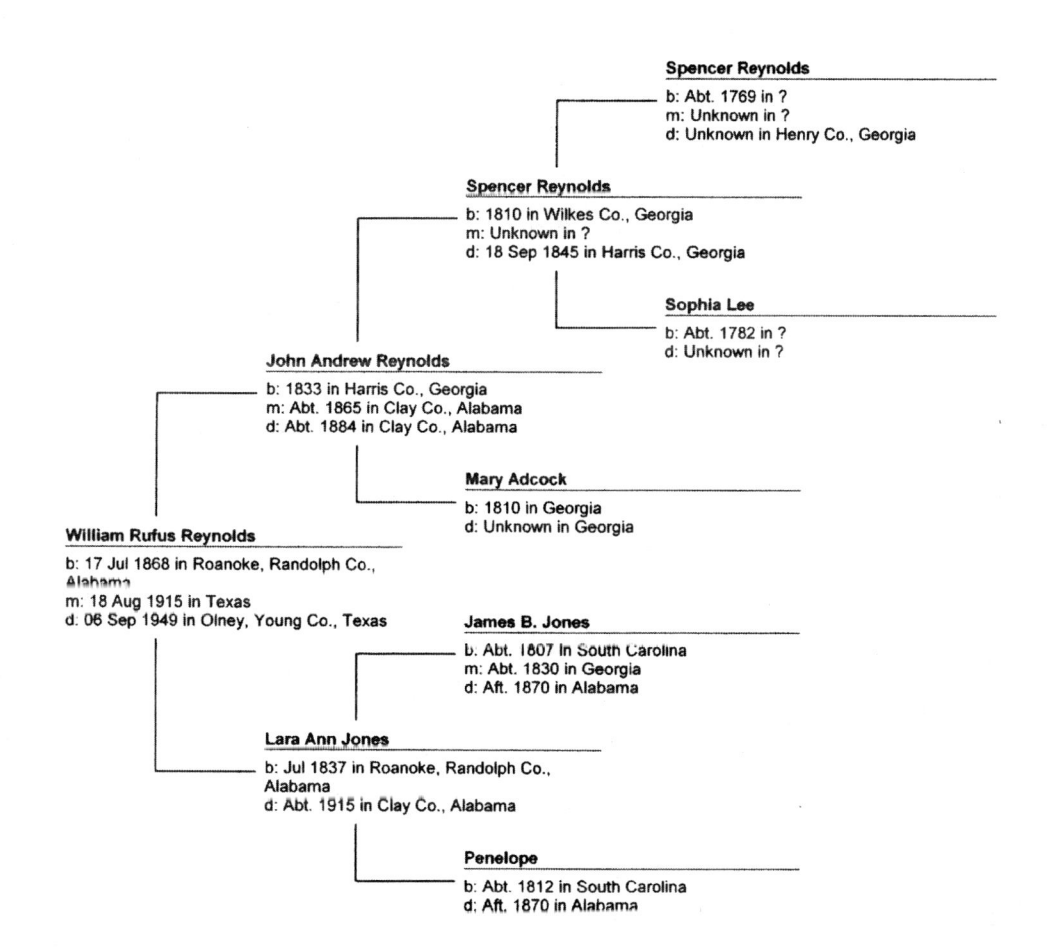

Spencer Reynolds
- b: Abt. 1769 in ?
- m: Unknown in ?
- d: Unknown in Henry Co., Georgia

Spencer Reynolds
- b: 1810 in Wilkes Co., Georgia
- m: Unknown in ?
- d: 18 Sep 1845 in Harris Co., Georgia

Sophia Lee
- b: Abt. 1782 in ?
- d: Unknown in ?

John Andrew Reynolds
- b: 1833 in Harris Co., Georgia
- m: Abt. 1865 in Clay Co., Alabama
- d: Abt. 1884 in Clay Co., Alabama

Mary Adcock
- b: 1810 in Georgia
- d: Unknown in Georgia

William Rufus Reynolds
- b: 17 Jul 1868 in Roanoke, Randolph Co., Alabama
- m: 18 Aug 1915 in Texas
- d: 06 Sep 1949 in Olney, Young Co., Texas

James B. Jones
- b: Abt. 1807 in South Carolina
- m: Abt. 1830 in Georgia
- d: Aft. 1870 in Alabama

Lara Ann Jones
- b: Jul 1837 in Roanoke, Randolph Co., Alabama
- d: Abt. 1915 in Clay Co., Alabama

Penelope
- b: Abt. 1812 in South Carolina
- d: Aft. 1870 in Alabama

Norris Truett Reynolds (1919-1981)
[6th. Generation from Henry Wilton (1769-1820)]

&

Swanwick
& Family

&

Alpha M.
& Family

Norris Truett Reynolds, born November 1919 in Texas, was the son of William Rufus and his second wife, Ida May Wilton. After first starting his family in Alabama, William Rufus moved to Texas about 1910 after the death of his first wife, Alma Lena Meadows. Norris Truett spent his early years in Texas in Parker County and the area around Archer County.

The rest of the information about Norris is fragmentary. At one point, he went to Australia, where, sometime around 1941, he married a girl with the last name of Swanwick. They had one child.

Norris Truett was also a Staff Sergeant in the U.S. Army during World War II, enlisting as part of the Texas National Guard from Jack County, Texas. He eventually saw action in Germany in 1944, and was part of "The Lost Battalion" of WWII. As a result of that conflict, he became a prisoner of war, and his last report date was March 18, 1946.

In April of 1965, Norris Truett married a second time, to a girl with the given name of Alpha M. That marriage ended in divorce in September 1974 in Lubbock County, Texas, with no children.

Norris died in November 1981 in Harris County, Texas, and he was buried as a military veteran in the Houston National Cemetery.

NORRIS TRUETT REYNOLDS Standard Pedigree Tree

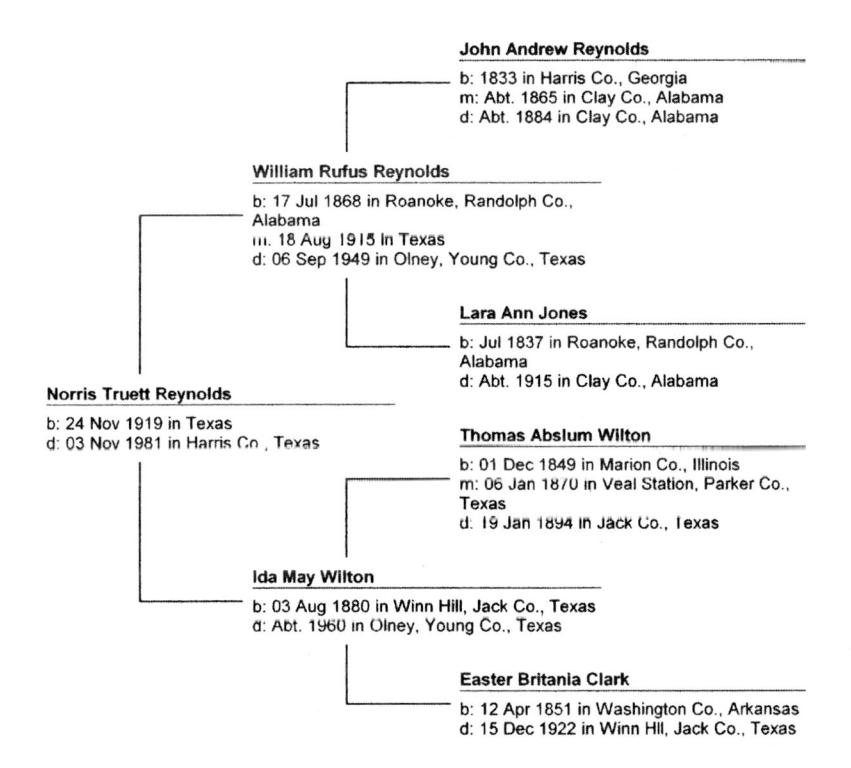

Norris Truett Reynolds
b: 24 Nov 1919 in Texas
d: 03 Nov 1981 in Harris Co., Texas

William Rufus Reynolds
b: 17 Jul 1868 in Roanoke, Randolph Co., Alabama
m: 18 Aug 1915 in Texas
d: 06 Sep 1949 in Olney, Young Co., Texas

John Andrew Reynolds
b: 1833 in Harris Co., Georgia
m: Abt. 1865 in Clay Co., Alabama
d: Abt. 1884 in Clay Co., Alabama

Lara Ann Jones
b: Jul 1837 in Roanoke, Randolph Co., Alabama
d: Abt. 1915 in Clay Co., Alabama

Ida May Wilton
b: 03 Aug 1880 in Winn Hill, Jack Co., Texas
d: Abt. 1960 in Olney, Young Co., Texas

Thomas Abslum Wilton
b: 01 Dec 1849 in Marion Co., Illinois
m: 06 Jan 1870 in Veal Station, Parker Co., Texas
d: 19 Jan 1894 in Jack Co., Texas

Easter Britania Clark
b: 12 Apr 1851 in Washington Co., Arkansas
d: 15 Dec 1922 in Winn Hll, Jack Co., Texas

Emma Livona Wilton (1883-1977)
[5th. Generation from Henry Wilton (1769-1820)]

&

Jefferson Francis Asberry McCasland (1874-1949)
& Family

Emma Livona Wilton, also known as "Vonie," was born May 1883 in Jack County, Texas, the seventh child of Thomas A. Wilton and Easter B. Clark. Her formative years were spent in the Winn Hill Community of Jack County, Texas, where the family permanently settled, beginning about 1878.

In the 1900 Federal Census of Jack County, Texas, Emma was listed at home at the age of 17, with her mother, Easter B. Wilton, age 42, and two brothers and two sisters. Her father, Thomas A. Wilton, died in January 1894, and her mother had taken over the task of raising the family.

Emma married Jefferson Francis McCasland, son of James Alexander McCasland & Ura Kanutsen, in December 1908 at Winn Hill in Jack County, Texas. Together they had five daughters, four of whom were born in Jack County, Texas between 1910 and 1917. The youngest daughter, Elsie McCasland, was also born in Texas in February 1920.

By 1920, the family had moved to Baylor County, Texas, which was just two counties to the west of Jack County, Texas. In the 1920 Federal Census of Baylor County, Texas, J.F. McCasland was listed at age 45 with an occupation of teamster, along with his wife, Emma L., age 36, and four of their daughters. The enumeration for the census was January 1920, and their youngest daughter, Elsie, had not yet been born.

Sometime between 1920 and 1930, Jefferson and Emma moved the family to New Mexico, because by the 1930 Federal Census, they were listed in the census of Roosevelt County, New Mexico. In the 1930 census, Jeff F. McCasland was listed at age 55 with an occupation of farmer, along with his wife, Vonie E., age 47, and three of their children, Verdia E., Carrie E., and Elsie D. McCasland.

Jefferson Frances McCasland died January 1949 in Roosevelt County, New Mexico, and Emma Livona died May 1977 in Curry County, New Mexico.

Family Group Sheet

Husband: Jefferson Francis Asberry McCasland

Born: 24 Sep 1874	in: Royse City, Rockwall Co., Texas
Married: 13 Dec 1908	in: Winn Hill, Jack Co., Texas
Died: 16 Jan 1949	in: Portales, Roosevelt Co., New Mexico
Father: James Alexander McCasland	
Mother: Ura Kanutsen	

Wife: Emma Livona Wilton

Born: 14 May 1883	in: Jack Co., Texas
Died: 05 May 1977	in: Clovis, Curry Co., New Mexico
Father: Thomas Abslum Wilton	
Mother: Easter Britania Clark	

CHILDREN

1. F
   - Name: Ollie Belgium McCasland
   - Born: 23 Feb 1910 — in: Jack Co., Texas
   - Died: 13 Feb 1939 — in: Arch, Roosevelt Co., New Mexico
   - Married: 12 Jun 1927 — in: Portales, Roosevelt Co., New Mexico
   - Spouse: Clarence Darkin Haskew

2. F
   - Name: Hettie Jewel McCasland
   - Born: 01 Jan 1912 — in: Jack Co., Texas
   - Died: 23 Oct 1995 — in: Mesquite, Dallas Co., Texas
   - Married: Abt. 1929 — in: Texas
   - Spouse: Byno Lou Roberson

3. F
   - Name: Verdia Ellen McCasland
   - Born: 30 Aug 1914 — in: Jack Co., Texas
   - Married: Unknown — in: New Mexico
   - Spouse: Maurice Errol Roberson

4. F
   - Name: Carrie Esther McCasland
   - Born: 10 Mar 1917 — in: Jack Co., Texas
   - Died: 12 Jan 1991 — in: Portales, Roosevelt Co., New Mexico
   - Married: 22 Apr 1934 — in: Arch, Roosevelt Co., New Mexico
   - Spouse: Everett James Inge

5. F
   - Name: Dora Elsie McCasland
   - Born: 29 Feb 1920 — in: Texas
   - Died: Jul 1987 — in: Portales, Roosevelt Co., New Mexico
   - Married: Abt. 1939 — in: Texas
   - Spouse: Orvil Wade Gray

JEFFERSON FRANCIS ASBERRY MCCASLAND Standard Pedigree Tree

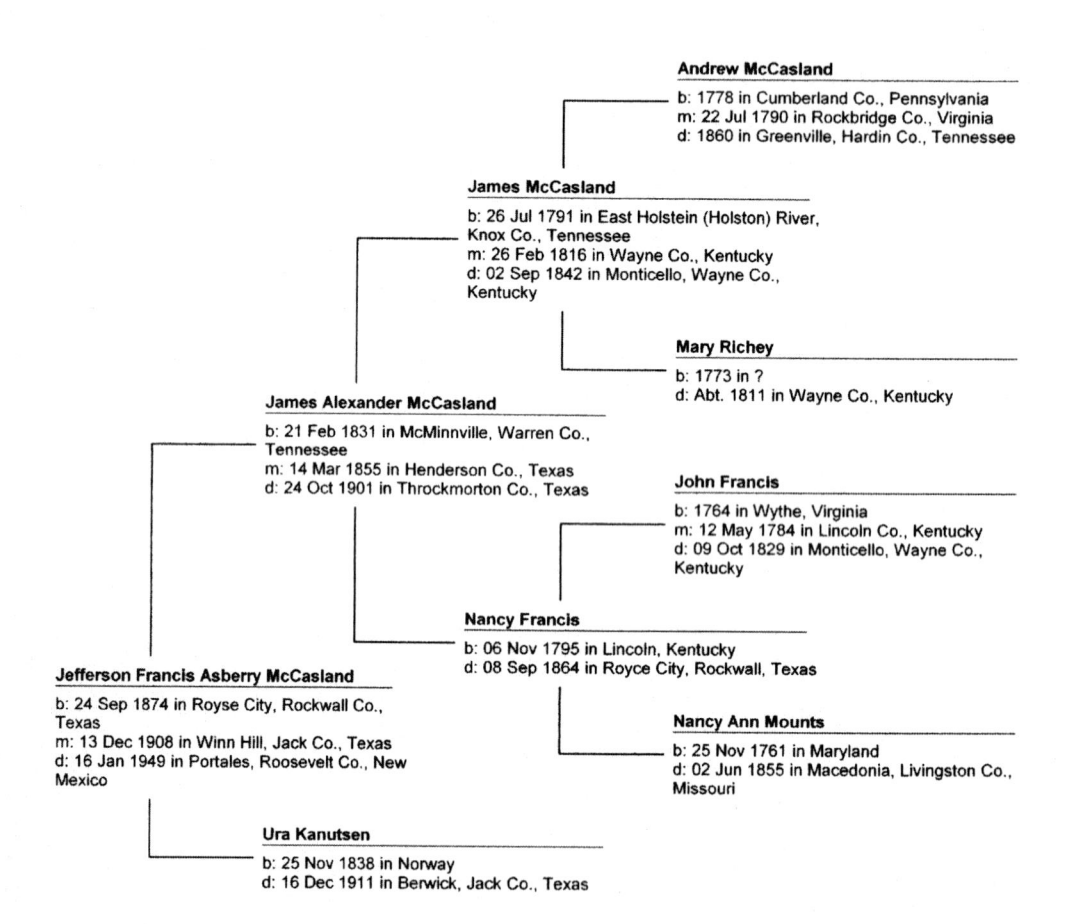

Jefferson Francis Asberry McCasland
b: 24 Sep 1874 in Royse City, Rockwall Co., Texas
m: 13 Dec 1908 in Winn Hill, Jack Co., Texas
d: 16 Jan 1949 in Portales, Roosevelt Co., New Mexico

- **James Alexander McCasland**
  b: 21 Feb 1831 in McMinnville, Warren Co., Tennessee
  m: 14 Mar 1855 in Henderson Co., Texas
  d: 24 Oct 1901 in Throckmorton Co., Texas

  - **James McCasland**
    b: 26 Jul 1791 in East Holstein (Holston) River, Knox Co., Tennessee
    m: 26 Feb 1816 in Wayne Co., Kentucky
    d: 02 Sep 1842 in Monticello, Wayne Co., Kentucky

    - **Andrew McCasland**
      b: 1778 in Cumberland Co., Pennsylvania
      m: 22 Jul 1790 in Rockbridge Co., Virginia
      d: 1860 in Greenville, Hardin Co., Tennessee

    - **Mary Richey**
      b: 1773 in ?
      d: Abt. 1811 in Wayne Co., Kentucky

  - **Nancy Francis**
    b: 06 Nov 1795 in Lincoln, Kentucky
    d: 08 Sep 1864 in Royce City, Rockwall, Texas

    - **John Francis**
      b: 1764 in Wythe, Virginia
      m: 12 May 1784 in Lincoln Co., Kentucky
      d: 09 Oct 1829 in Monticello, Wayne Co., Kentucky

    - **Nancy Ann Mounts**
      b: 25 Nov 1761 in Maryland
      d: 02 Jun 1855 in Macedonia, Livingston Co., Missouri

- **Ura Kanutsen**
  b: 25 Nov 1838 in Norway
  d: 16 Dec 1911 in Berwick, Jack Co., Texas

Ollie Belgium McCasland (1910-1939)
[6th. Generation from Henry Wilton (1769-1820)]

&

Clarence Darkin Haskew (1898-1968)
& Family

Ollie Belgium (Bell) McCasland was the first child of Emma Livona Wilton and Jefferson Francis McCasland. Ollie was born February 23, 1910, in Jack County, Texas. By 1920, the family had moved to Baylor County, Texas, located two counties to the west of Jack County. Between 1920 and 1930, the family moved again to Roosevelt County, New Mexico, where Ollie's parents, Emma and Jeff, settled permanently.

Ollie Bell married Clarence D. Haskew, son of Samuel B. Haskew & Winney Josephine Post, on June 12, 1927, in Portales in Roosevelt Co., New Mexico. The Haskew family had an additional connection with the McCasland's, in that Ollie's two younger sisters, Hettie Jewel and Verdia Ellen, married Roberson brothers in the family of James L. Roberson and Sally McElroy. James L. Roberson's father, Hezekiah Roberson, had a sister, named Mary Rebecca Roberson, who married Joseph Birdwell Haskew, who was also the grandfather of Ollie's husband, Clarence D. Haskew.

By the 1930 Federal Census of Roosevelt County, New Mexico, Clarence D. Haskew was listed at age 29, with an occupation of farmer, along with his wife, Ollie B. Haskew, age 20, and their first child, Clayton D. Haskew, age 2 years and two months.

Apparently, the family remained in the Roosevelt County area of New Mexico until the death of Ollie Bell in February 1939. The couple had six children, with one child, Clinton Haskew, dying at birth in August 1937. Three of their children eventually settled in other states. Roberta Haskew moved to Oklahoma; Josephine Haskew moved to Texas; and, Bill Haskew moved to Missouri. Clarence D. Haskew died in January 1968 in Bailey County, Texas.

Family Group Sheet

Husband: Clarence Darkin Haskew	
Born: 18 Dec 1898	in: Haskell, Haskell Co., Texas
Married: 12 Jun 1927	in: Portales, Roosevelt Co., New Mexico
Died: 04 Jan 1968	in: Muleshoe, Bailey Co., Texas
Father: Samuel Brown Haskew	
Mother: Winney Josephine Post	

Wife: Ollie Belgium McCasland	
Born: 23 Feb 1910	in: Jack Co., Texas
Died: 13 Feb 1939	in: Arch, Roosevelt Co., New Mexico
Father: Jefferson Francis Asberry McCasland	
Mother: Emma Livona Wilton	

CHILDREN

#		
1 M	Name: Clayton Dee Haskew Born: 14 Mar 1928 Died: 29 Nov 2005 Married: Unknown Spouse: Esther Martinez	in: Arch, Roosevelt Co., New Mexico in: Belen, Valencia Co., New Mexico
2 M	Name: Connie Joe Haskew Born: 12 May 1935 Died: 28 Oct 1993 Married: Abt. 1957 Spouse: Mary Ann Franklin	in: Arch, Roosevelt Co., New Mexico in: Clovis, Curry Co., New Mexico
3 M	Name: Clinton Haskew Born: 15 Aug 1937 Died: 15 Aug 1937	in: Arch, Roosevelt Co., New Mexico in: Arch, Roosevelt Co., New Mexico
4 F	Name: Sylvia Roberta Haskew Born: Abt. 1938	in: New Mexico
5 F	Name: Josephine Haskew Born: Abt. 1939	in: New Mexico
6 M	Name: Billy Clay Haskew Born: Unknown	in: New Mexico

OLLIE BELGIUM MCCASLAND Standard Pedigree Tree

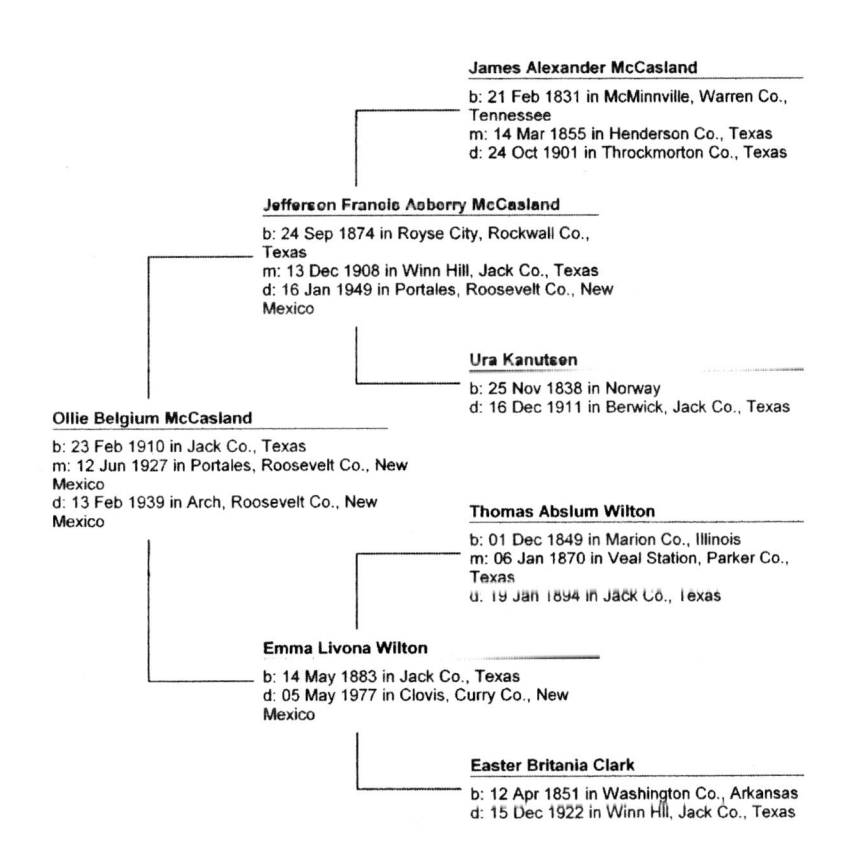

Ollie Belgium McCasland
b: 23 Feb 1910 in Jack Co., Texas
m: 12 Jun 1927 in Portales, Roosevelt Co., New Mexico
d: 13 Feb 1939 in Arch, Roosevelt Co., New Mexico

- **Jefferson Francis Asberry McCasland**
  b: 24 Sep 1874 in Royse City, Rockwall Co., Texas
  m: 13 Dec 1908 in Winn Hill, Jack Co., Texas
  d: 16 Jan 1949 in Portales, Roosevelt Co., New Mexico

  - **James Alexander McCasland**
    b: 21 Feb 1831 in McMinnville, Warren Co., Tennessee
    m: 14 Mar 1855 in Henderson Co., Texas
    d: 24 Oct 1901 in Throckmorton Co., Texas

  - **Ura Kanutsen**
    b: 25 Nov 1838 in Norway
    d: 16 Dec 1911 in Berwick, Jack Co., Texas

- **Emma Livona Wilton**
  b: 14 May 1883 in Jack Co., Texas
  d: 05 May 1977 in Clovis, Curry Co., New Mexico

  - **Thomas Abslum Wilton**
    b: 01 Dec 1849 in Marion Co., Illinois
    m: 06 Jan 1870 in Veal Station, Parker Co., Texas
    d: 19 Jan 1894 in Jack Co., Texas

  - **Easter Britania Clark**
    b: 12 Apr 1851 in Washington Co., Arkansas
    d: 15 Dec 1922 in Winn Hll, Jack Co., Texas

Notes: This Tree also applies to the other children of Jefferson Francis McCasland & Emma Livona Wilton: Hettie Jewel McCasland, Verdia Ellen McCasland, Carrie Esther McCasland, and Dora Elsie McCasland.

CLARENCE DARKIN HASKEW Standard Pedigree Tree

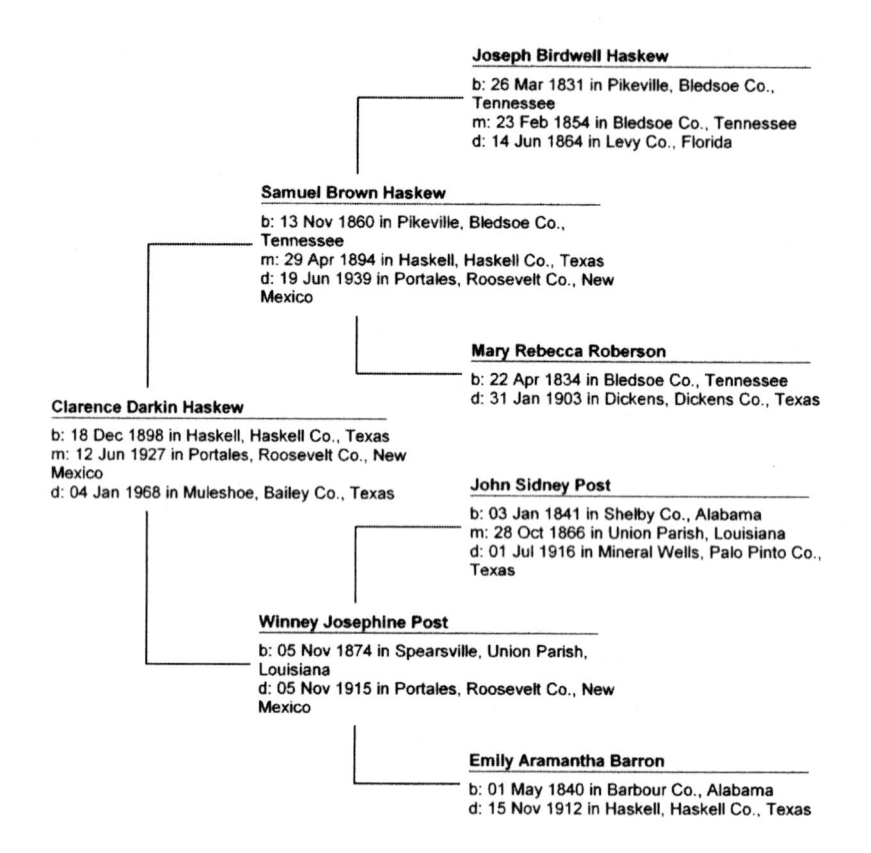

Clarence Darkin Haskew
b: 18 Dec 1898 in Haskell, Haskell Co., Texas
m: 12 Jun 1927 in Portales, Roosevelt Co., New Mexico
d: 04 Jan 1968 in Muleshoe, Bailey Co., Texas

- **Samuel Brown Haskew**
  b: 13 Nov 1860 in Pikeville, Bledsoe Co., Tennessee
  m: 29 Apr 1894 in Haskell, Haskell Co., Texas
  d: 19 Jun 1939 in Portales, Roosevelt Co., New Mexico
  - **Joseph Birdwell Haskew**
    b: 26 Mar 1831 in Pikeville, Bledsoe Co., Tennessee
    m: 23 Feb 1854 in Bledsoe Co., Tennessee
    d: 14 Jun 1864 in Levy Co., Florida
  - **Mary Rebecca Roberson**
    b: 22 Apr 1834 in Bledsoe Co., Tennessee
    d: 31 Jan 1903 in Dickens, Dickens Co., Texas

- **Winney Josephine Post**
  b: 05 Nov 1874 in Spearsville, Union Parish, Louisiana
  d: 05 Nov 1915 in Portales, Roosevelt Co., New Mexico
  - **John Sidney Post**
    b: 03 Jan 1841 in Shelby Co., Alabama
    m: 28 Oct 1866 in Union Parish, Louisiana
    d: 01 Jul 1916 in Mineral Wells, Palo Pinto Co., Texas
  - **Emily Aramantha Barron**
    b: 01 May 1840 in Barbour Co., Alabama
    d: 15 Nov 1912 in Haskell, Haskell Co., Texas

Clayton Dee Haskew (1929-2005)
[7th. Generation from Henry Wilton (1769-1820)]

&

Esther Martinez
& Family

Family Group Sheet

Husband: Clayton Dee Haskew

Born: 14 Mar 1928 in: Arch, Roosevelt Co., New Mexico
Married: Unknown
Died: 29 Nov 2005 in: Belen, Valencia Co., New Mexico
Father: Clarence Darkin Haskew
Mother: Ollie Belgium McCasland

Wife: Esther Martinez

Born: Unknown

CHILDREN

1 F	Name: Helen Haskew Born: Apr 1957	in: New Mexico	
2 F	Name: Nancy Haskew Born: Unknown	in: New Mexico	
3 M	Name: Clayton D. Jr. Haskew Born: Abt. 1960 Married: 07 May 1980 Spouse: Peggy L. Lewing	in: New Mexico in: Parker Co., Texas	
4 F	Name: Ollie Bell Haskew Born: Unknown	in: New Mexico	
5 M	Name: Billy Joe Haskew Born: Unknown	in: New Mexico	
6 F	Name: Connie Haskew Born: Unknown	in: New Mexico	

CLAYTON DEE HASKEW Standard Pedigree Tree

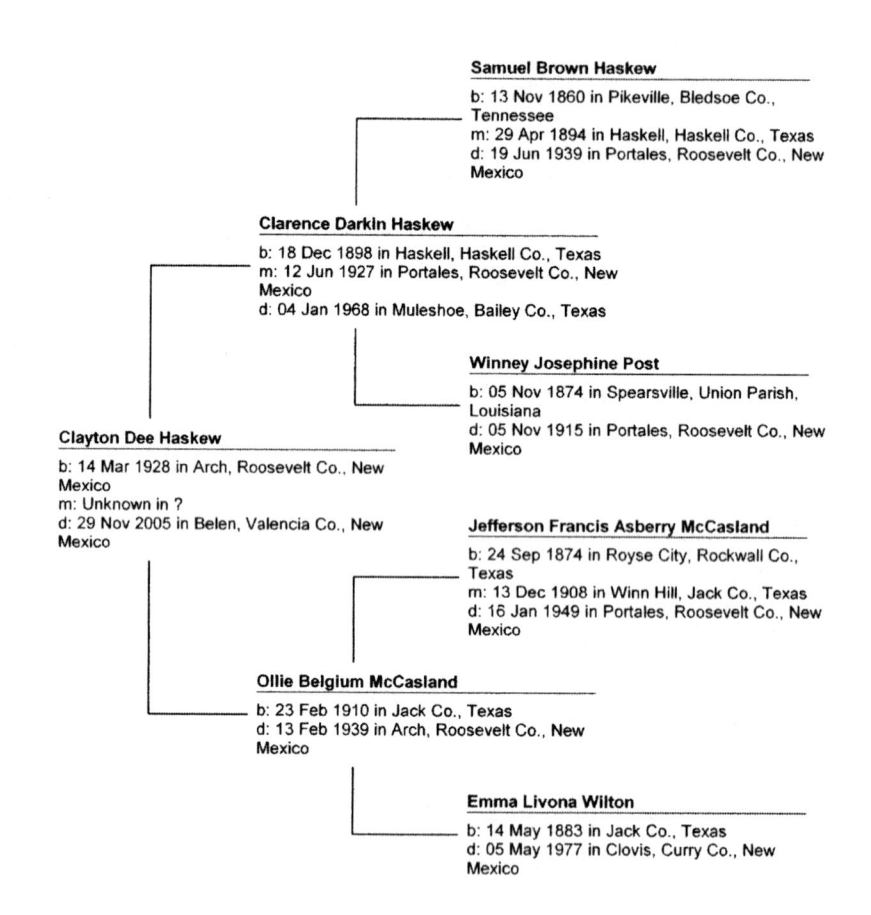

Clayton Dee Haskew
b: 14 Mar 1928 in Arch, Roosevelt Co., New Mexico
m: Unknown in ?
d: 29 Nov 2005 in Belen, Valencia Co., New Mexico

- **Clarence Darkin Haskew**
  b: 18 Dec 1898 in Haskell, Haskell Co., Texas
  m: 12 Jun 1927 in Portales, Roosevelt Co., New Mexico
  d: 04 Jan 1968 in Muleshoe, Bailey Co., Texas

  - **Samuel Brown Haskew**
    b: 13 Nov 1860 in Pikeville, Bledsoe Co., Tennessee
    m: 29 Apr 1894 in Haskell, Haskell Co., Texas
    d: 19 Jun 1939 in Portales, Roosevelt Co., New Mexico

  - **Winney Josephine Post**
    b: 05 Nov 1874 in Spearsville, Union Parish, Louisiana
    d: 05 Nov 1915 in Portales, Roosevelt Co., New Mexico

- **Ollie Belgium McCasland**
  b: 23 Feb 1910 in Jack Co., Texas
  d: 13 Feb 1939 in Arch, Roosevelt Co., New Mexico

  - **Jefferson Francis Asberry McCasland**
    b: 24 Sep 1874 in Royse City, Rockwall Co., Texas
    m: 13 Dec 1908 in Winn Hill, Jack Co., Texas
    d: 16 Jan 1949 in Portales, Roosevelt Co., New Mexico

  - **Emma Livona Wilton**
    b: 14 May 1883 in Jack Co., Texas
    d: 05 May 1977 in Clovis, Curry Co., New Mexico

Notes: This Tree also applies to the other children of Clarence D. Haskew & Ollie B. McCasland: Clinton Haskew, Josephine Haskew, Sylvia Roberta Haskew, Connie Joe Haskew, and Billy Clay Haskew.

Hettie Jewel McCasland (1912-1995)
[6th. Generation from Henry Wilton (1769-1820)]

&

Byno Lou Roberson (1905-1981)
& Family

Hettie Jewel McCasland, born January 1912 in Jack County, Texas, was the second child of Jefferson Francis McCasland and Emma Livona Wilton. From their marriage in 1908 until after 1917, Hettie's parents made their home in Jack County, Texas, but about 1920 they moved the family to Baylor County, Texas. Sometime between 1920 and 1930, they made one more move to Roosevelt County, New Mexico, where they settled permanently.

Hettie married Byno Lou Roberson, son of James L. Roberson and Sally L. McElroy, about 1929. At the time of the 1920 Federal Census, James L. and Sally were located with their family in Roosevelt County, New Mexico. It is not certain whether Hettie made the trip with her family to New Mexico, because by the 1930 Federal Census, Hettie and Byno were located in Deaf Smith County, Texas, located on the border with New Mexico.

There are additional connections of the Roberson family with the McCasland family. Byno's brother, Maurice E. Roberson, married Hettie's younger sister, Verdia Ellen McCasland. Also, farther back in the family tree, Byno's grandfather, Hezekiah Roberson, had a sister named Mary Rebecca Roberson, who married Joseph Birdwell Haskew. The grandson of Joseph Birdwell Haskew, Clarence D. Haskew, married Hettie's older sister, Ollie Bell McCasland.

In the 1930 Federal Census of Deaf Smith County, Texas, Byno (Jack) was listed at age 24, with an occupation of railroad section laborer, and Hettie J. was listed at age 18, having been married only about one year. Their first child, Doris Dean Roberson, was born June 18, 1930 in Deaf Smith County, Texas.

Byno and Hettie had two other children, Myrtle Marie Roberson, and Walter Gene Roberson, but it is uncertain where or when.

Byno and Hettie both died in Dallas County, Texas, Byno in December 1981, and Hettie in October 1995.

Family Group Sheet

Husband: Byno Lou Roberson

Born: 09 Oct 1905 in: Texas
Married: Abt. 1929 in: Texas
Died: 06 Dec 1981 in: Dallas Co., Texas
Father: James Lafayette Roberson
Mother: Sally Lucinda McElroy

Wife: Hettie Jewel McCasland

Born: 01 Jan 1912 in: Jack Co., Texas
Died: 23 Oct 1995 in: Mesquite, Dallas Co., Texas
Father: Jefferson Francis Asberry McCasland
Mother: Emma Livona Wilton

CHILDREN

1 F Name: Doris Dean Roberson
     Born: 18 Jun 1930   in: Deaf Smith Co., Texas

2 F Name: Myrtle Marie Roberson
     Born: Unknown

3 M Name: Walter Gene Roberson
     Born: Unknown

BYNO LOU ROBERSON Standard Pedigree Tree

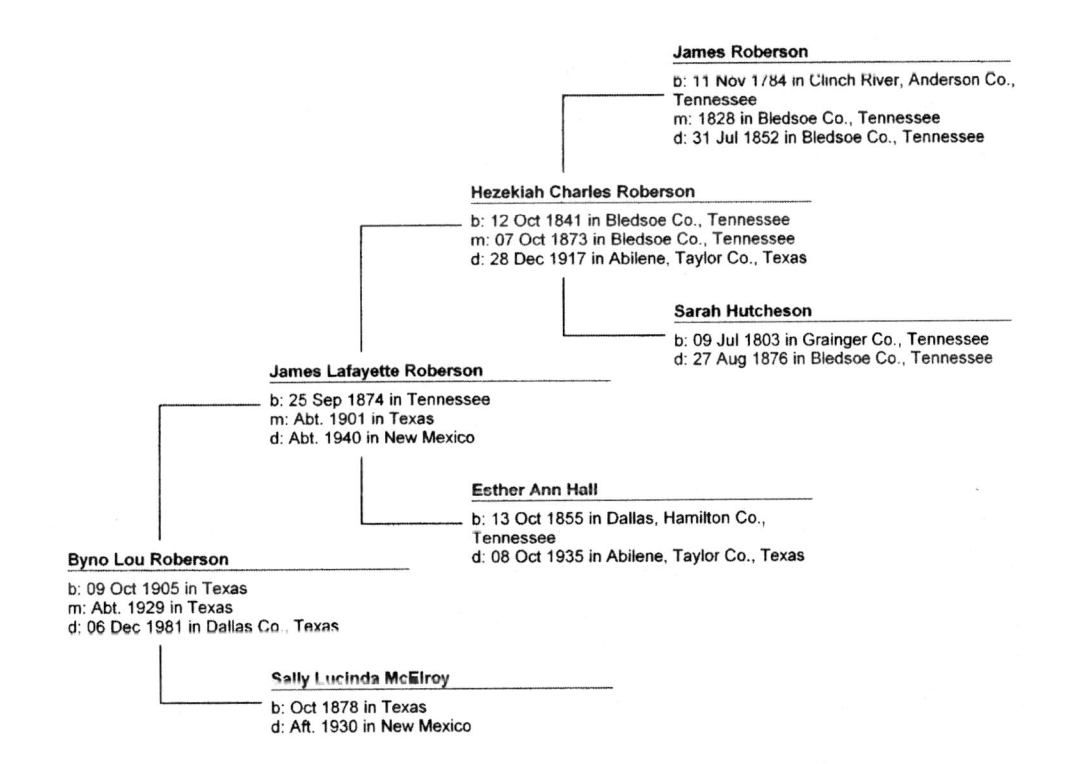

- **Byno Lou Roberson**
  b: 09 Oct 1905 in Texas
  m: Abt. 1929 in Texas
  d: 06 Dec 1981 in Dallas Co., Texas

  - **James Lafayette Roberson**
    b: 25 Sep 1874 in Tennessee
    m: Abt. 1901 in Texas
    d: Abt. 1940 in New Mexico

    - **Hezekiah Charles Roberson**
      b: 12 Oct 1841 in Bledsoe Co., Tennessee
      m: 07 Oct 1873 in Bledsoe Co., Tennessee
      d: 28 Dec 1917 in Abilene, Taylor Co., Texas

      - **James Roberson**
        b: 11 Nov 1784 in Clinch River, Anderson Co., Tennessee
        m: 1828 in Bledsoe Co., Tennessee
        d: 31 Jul 1852 in Bledsoe Co., Tennessee

      - **Sarah Hutcheson**
        b: 09 Jul 1803 in Grainger Co., Tennessee
        d: 27 Aug 1876 in Bledsoe Co., Tennessee

    - **Esther Ann Hall**
      b: 13 Oct 1855 in Dallas, Hamilton Co., Tennessee
      d: 08 Oct 1935 in Abilene, Taylor Co., Texas

  - **Sally Lucinda McElroy**
    b: Oct 1878 in Texas
    d: Aft. 1930 in New Mexico

Verdia Ellen McCasland (1914-   )
[6th. Generation from Henry Wilton (1769-1820)]

&

Maurice Errol Roberson (1911-   )
& Family

Verdia Ellen McCasland, born August 1914 in Jack County, Texas, was the third daughter of Jefferson Francis McCasland & Emma Livona Wilton. At the time of Verdia's birth, the family had made Jack County their home for about 6 years. About 1920, the family moved to Baylor County, Texas, just two counties to the west of Jack County; and, between 1920 and 1930, the family moved permanently to Roosevelt County, New Mexico.

At the time of the 1930 Federal Census of Roosevelt County, New Mexico, Verdia was listed at age 15, along with her parents and two younger sisters, Carrie E. McCasland, age 13, and Elsie D. McCasland, age 10. Her two older sisters were already married and starting their own families.

Sometime after 1930, Verdia Ellen married Maurice Errol Roberson, the youngest son of James L. Roberson & Sally McElroy. About that time, both Verdia and Maurice were living in Roosevelt County, New Mexico. Maurice was born in Texas in 1911, but he was listed in both the 1920 and 1930 Federal Census of Roosevelt County, New Mexico, along with his parents and family.

There were additional connections of the McCasland and Roberson family, in that Verdia's older sister, Hettie J. McCasland, married an older brother of Maurice Roberson, Byno L. Roberson; and, Verdia's oldest sister, Ollie Bell McCasland, married Clarence D. Haskew, a descendant of Mary Rebecca Roberson, the sister of Maurice Roberson's grandfather.

Although sketchy, the available evidence suggests that Verdia & Maurice settled in New Mexico and had a family of at least five children.

Family Group Sheet

Husband: Maurice Errol Roberson

Born: 1911 in: Texas
Married: Unknown in: New Mexico
Father: James Lafayette Roberson
Mother: Sally Lucinda McElroy

Wife: Verdia Ellen McCasland

Born: 30 Aug 1914 in: Jack Co., Texas
Father: Jefferson Francis Asberry McCasland
Mother: Emma Livona Wilton

CHILDREN

1 M — Name: Donald Ralph Roberson
Born: Unknown in: New Mexico

2 M — Name: Herold Wade Roberson
Born: Unknown in: New Mexico

3 M — Name: Jackie Junior Roberson
Born: Unknown in: New Mexico

4 F — Name: Loretta Faye Roberson
Born: Unknown in: New Mexico

5 M — Name: Maurice Ray Roberson
Born: Unknown in: New Mexico

MAURICE ERROL ROBERSON Standard Pedigree Tree

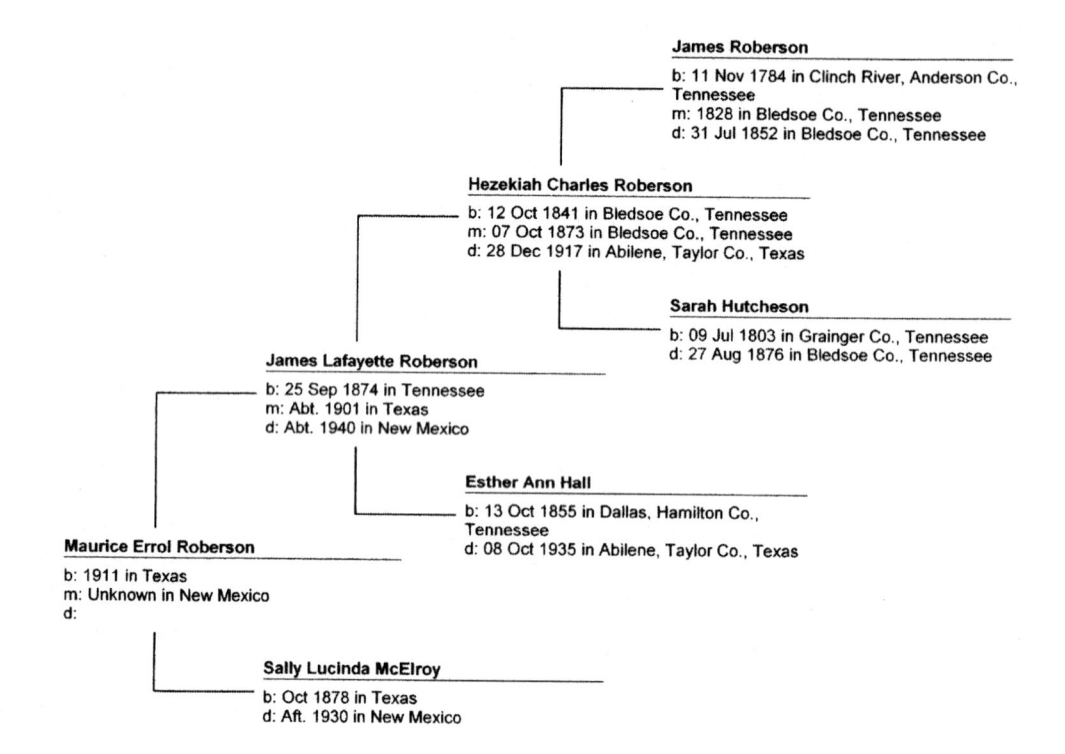

James Roberson
b: 11 Nov 1784 in Clinch River, Anderson Co., Tennessee
m: 1828 in Bledsoe Co., Tennessee
d: 31 Jul 1852 in Bledsoe Co., Tennessee

Hezekiah Charles Roberson
b: 12 Oct 1841 in Bledsoe Co., Tennessee
m: 07 Oct 1873 in Bledsoe Co., Tennessee
d: 28 Dec 1917 in Abilene, Taylor Co., Texas

Sarah Hutcheson
b: 09 Jul 1803 in Grainger Co., Tennessee
d: 27 Aug 1876 in Bledsoe Co., Tennessee

James Lafayette Roberson
b: 25 Sep 1874 in Tennessee
m: Abt. 1901 in Texas
d: Abt. 1940 in New Mexico

Esther Ann Hall
b: 13 Oct 1855 in Dallas, Hamilton Co., Tennessee
d: 08 Oct 1935 in Abilene, Taylor Co., Texas

Maurice Errol Roberson
b: 1911 in Texas
m: Unknown in New Mexico
d:

Sally Lucinda McElroy
b: Oct 1878 in Texas
d: Aft. 1930 in New Mexico

Carrie Esther McCasland (1917-1991)
[6th. Generation from Henry Wilton (1769-1820)]

&

Everett James Inge (1910-1987)
& Family

Carrie Esther McCasland, born March 1917 in Jack County, Texas, was the fourth child of Jefferson Francis McCasland & Emma Livona Wilton. Between 1920 and 1930, after first making Texas their home for a numbers of years, Carrie's parents moved the family from Texas to Roosevelt County, New Mexico. In the 1930 Federal Census of Roosevelt County, New Mexico, Carrie was listed at age 13, along with two of her sisters and her parents.

On April 22, 1934, in Arch in Roosevelt County, New Mexico, Carrie Esther married Everett James Inge. Everett James, a son of Richard Inge & Nancy Rebecca Lauton, was born in Texas in 1910, but by 1930, his family was also living in Roosevelt County, New Mexico.

Carrie Esther and Everett James settled in Roosevelt County, New Mexico, where two of their children were born. Bobby Wayne Inge was born December 1934, and Josephine Inge was born November 1938.

Both Everett James and Carrie Esther died in Portales in Roosevelt County, New Mexico. Everett James died on December 29, 1987, and Carrie Esther died on January 12, 1991.

Family Group Sheet

Husband: Everett James Inge

Born: 23 Jan 1910 in: Jacksonville, Cherokee Co., Texas
Married: 22 Apr 1934 in: Arch, Roosevelt Co., New Mexico
Died: 29 Dec 1987 in: Portales, Roosevelt Co., New Mexico
Father: Richard Inge
Mother: Nancy Rebecca Lauton

Wife: Carrie Esther McCasland

Born: 10 Mar 1917 in: Jack Co., Texas
Died: 12 Jan 1991 in: Portales, Roosevelt Co., New Mexico
Father: Jefferson Francis Asberry McCasland
Mother: Emma Livona Wilton

CHILDREN

1 M
Name: Bobby Wayne Inge
Born: 11 Dec 1934 in: Arch, Roosevelt Co., New Mexico

2 F
Name: Josephine Inge
Born: 17 Nov 1938 in: Arch, Roosevelt Co., New Mexico
Married: 14 Jan 1954
Spouse: William Mertan Criswell

EVERETT JAMES INGE Standard Pedigree Tree

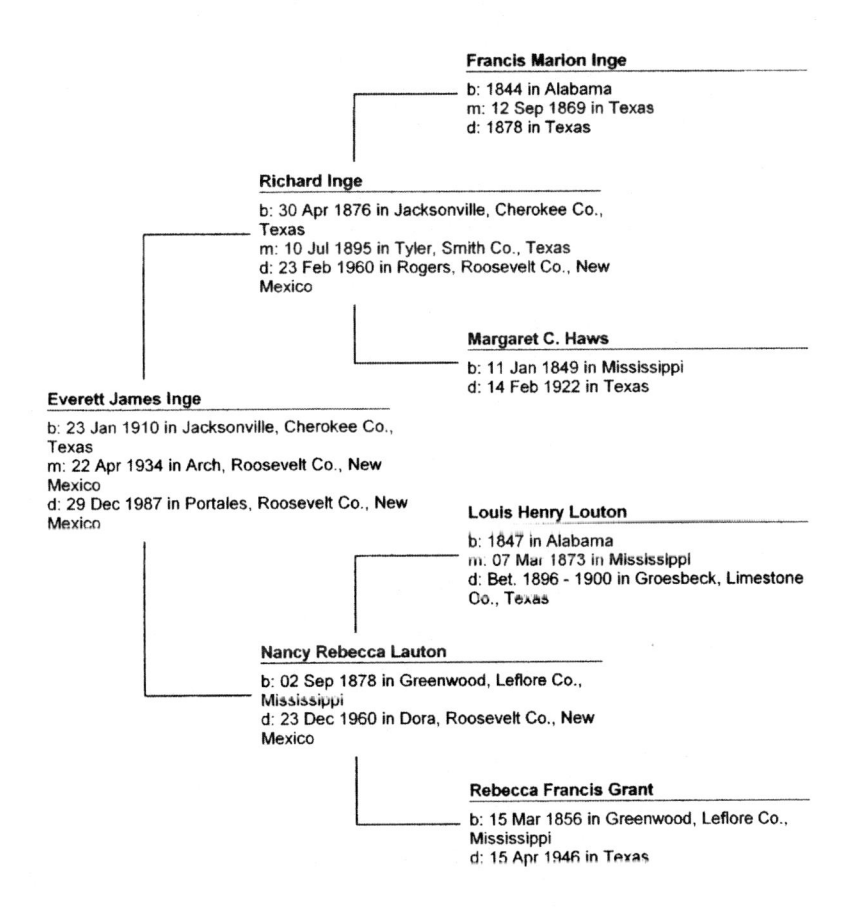

Everett James Inge
b: 23 Jan 1910 in Jacksonville, Cherokee Co., Texas
m: 22 Apr 1934 in Arch, Roosevelt Co., New Mexico
d: 29 Dec 1987 in Portales, Roosevelt Co., New Mexico

- **Richard Inge**
  b: 30 Apr 1876 in Jacksonville, Cherokee Co., Texas
  m: 10 Jul 1895 in Tyler, Smith Co., Texas
  d: 23 Feb 1960 in Rogers, Roosevelt Co., New Mexico

  - **Francis Marion Inge**
    b: 1844 in Alabama
    m: 12 Sep 1869 in Texas
    d: 1878 in Texas

  - **Margaret C. Haws**
    b: 11 Jan 1849 in Mississippi
    d: 14 Feb 1922 in Texas

- **Nancy Rebecca Lauton**
  b: 02 Sep 1878 in Greenwood, Leflore Co., Mississippi
  d: 23 Dec 1960 in Dora, Roosevelt Co., New Mexico

  - **Louis Henry Louton**
    b: 1847 in Alabama
    m: 07 Mar 1873 in Mississippi
    d: Bet. 1896 - 1900 in Groesbeck, Limestone Co., Texas

  - **Rebecca Francis Grant**
    b: 15 Mar 1856 in Greenwood, Leflore Co., Mississippi
    d: 15 Apr 1946 in Texas

Josephine Inge (1938-)
[7th. Generation from Henry Wilton (1769-1820)]

&

William Merton Criswell (1930-2004)
& Family

Family Group Sheet

Husband: William Merton Criswell		
Born: 27 Feb 1930	in: Fort Stockton, Pecos Co., Texas	
Married: 14 Jan 1954	in: New Mexico	
Died: 17 Mar 2004	in: Parker Co., Texas	
Father: Charles Edger Criswell		
Mother: Ada Pearl Fulcher		
Wife: Josephine Inge		
Born: 17 Nov 1938	in: Arch, Roosevelt Co., New Mexico	
Father: Everett James Inge		
Mother: Carrie Esther McCasland		

CHILDREN

1 F
- Name: Charlotte Gail Criswell
- Born: 14 Jul 1955 — in: Portales, Roosevelt Co., New Mexico
- Married: 30 May 1970 — in: Ward Co., Texas
- Spouse: Harve Mark Rainwater
- Married: 01 Jan 1974 — in: Ward Co., Texas
- Spouse: Riley Eugene Foshee

2 M
- Name: Everett Lynn Criswell
- Born: 21 Jun 1956 — in: Portales, Roosevelt Co., New Mexico
- Died: 23 Aug 1956 — in: Portales, Roosevelt Co., New Mexico

JOSEPHINE INGE Standard Pedigree Tree

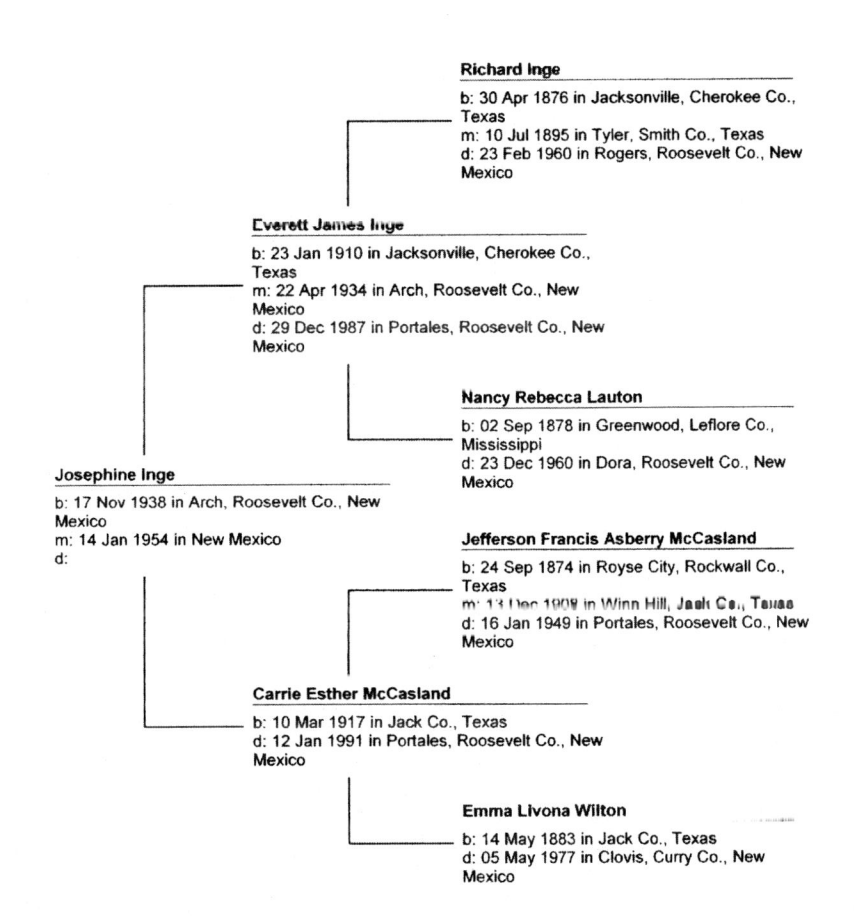

Josephine Inge
b: 17 Nov 1938 in Arch, Roosevelt Co., New Mexico
m: 14 Jan 1954 in New Mexico
d:

- **Everett James Inge**
  b: 23 Jan 1910 in Jacksonville, Cherokee Co., Texas
  m: 22 Apr 1934 in Arch, Roosevelt Co., New Mexico
  d: 29 Dec 1987 in Portales, Roosevelt Co., New Mexico

  - **Richard Inge**
    b: 30 Apr 1876 in Jacksonville, Cherokee Co., Texas
    m: 10 Jul 1895 in Tyler, Smith Co., Texas
    d: 23 Feb 1960 in Rogers, Roosevelt Co., New Mexico

  - **Nancy Rebecca Lauton**
    b: 02 Sep 1878 in Greenwood, Leflore Co., Mississippi
    d: 23 Dec 1960 in Dora, Roosevelt Co., New Mexico

- **Carrie Esther McCasland**
  b: 10 Mar 1917 in Jack Co., Texas
  d: 12 Jan 1991 in Portales, Roosevelt Co., New Mexico

  - **Jefferson Francis Asberry McCasland**
    b: 24 Sep 1874 in Royse City, Rockwall Co., Texas
    m: 13 Dec 1908 in Winn Hill, Jack Co., Texas
    d: 16 Jan 1949 in Portales, Roosevelt Co., New Mexico

  - **Emma Livona Wilton**
    b: 14 May 1883 in Jack Co., Texas
    d: 05 May 1977 in Clovis, Curry Co., New Mexico

Notes: This Tree also applies to the other child of Everett James Inge & Carrie Esther McCasland: Bobby Wayne Inge.

WILLIAM MERTON CRISWELL Standard Pedigree Tree

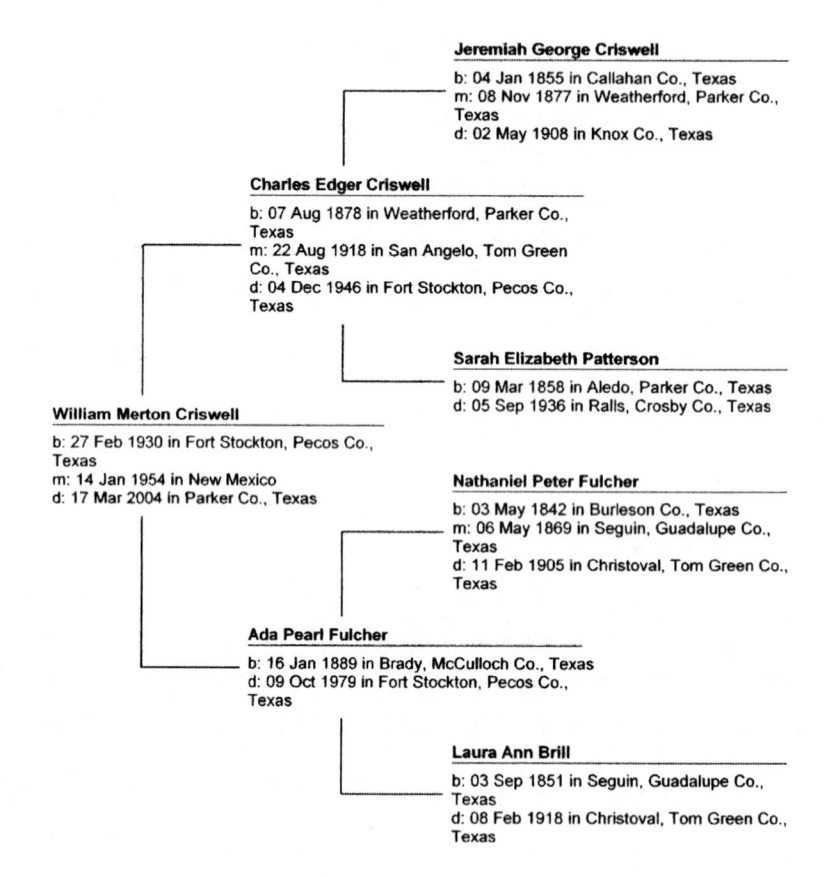

Jeremiah George Criswell
b: 04 Jan 1855 in Callahan Co., Texas
m: 08 Nov 1877 in Weatherford, Parker Co., Texas
d: 02 May 1908 in Knox Co., Texas

Charles Edger Criswell
b: 07 Aug 1878 in Weatherford, Parker Co., Texas
m: 22 Aug 1918 in San Angelo, Tom Green Co., Texas
d: 04 Dec 1946 in Fort Stockton, Pecos Co., Texas

Sarah Elizabeth Patterson
b: 09 Mar 1858 in Aledo, Parker Co., Texas
d: 05 Sep 1936 in Ralls, Crosby Co., Texas

William Merton Criswell
b: 27 Feb 1930 in Fort Stockton, Pecos Co., Texas
m: 14 Jan 1954 in New Mexico
d: 17 Mar 2004 in Parker Co., Texas

Nathaniel Peter Fulcher
b: 03 May 1842 in Burleson Co., Texas
m: 06 May 1869 in Seguin, Guadalupe Co., Texas
d: 11 Feb 1905 in Christoval, Tom Green Co., Texas

Ada Pearl Fulcher
b: 16 Jan 1889 in Brady, McCulloch Co., Texas
d: 09 Oct 1979 in Fort Stockton, Pecos Co., Texas

Laura Ann Brill
b: 03 Sep 1851 in Seguin, Guadalupe Co., Texas
d: 08 Feb 1918 in Christoval, Tom Green Co., Texas

Charlotte Gail Criswell (1955-   )
[8th. Generation from Henry Wilton (1769-1820)]

&
Harve Mark Rainwater (1949-   )
& Family

&
Riley Eugene Foshee (1954-   )
& Family

Family Group Sheet

Husband: Harve Mark Rainwater	
Born: 16 Oct 1949	in: Jones Co., Texas
Married: 30 May 1970	in: Ward Co., Texas

Wife: Charlotte Gail Criswell	
Born: 14 Jul 1955	in: Portales, Roosevelt Co., New Mexico
Father: William Merton Criswell	
Mother: Josephine Inge	
Other Spouses: Riley Eugene Foshee	

CHILDREN

1 F	Name: Darla Denise Rainwater	
	Born: 10 Dec 1970	in: Winkler Co., Texas

Family Group Sheet

Husband: Riley Eugene Foshee	
Born: Abt. 1954	
Married: 01 Jan 1974	in: Ward Co., Texas

Wife: Charlotte Gail Criswell	
Born: 14 Jul 1955	in: Portales, Roosevelt Co., New Mexico
Father: William Merton Criswell	
Mother: Josephine Inge	
Other Spouses: Harve Mark Rainwater	

CHILDREN

1 F	Name: Cristal Dawn Foshee	
	Born: 03 Nov 1974	in: Ector Co., Texas

CHARLOTTE GAIL CRISWELL Standard Pedigree Tree

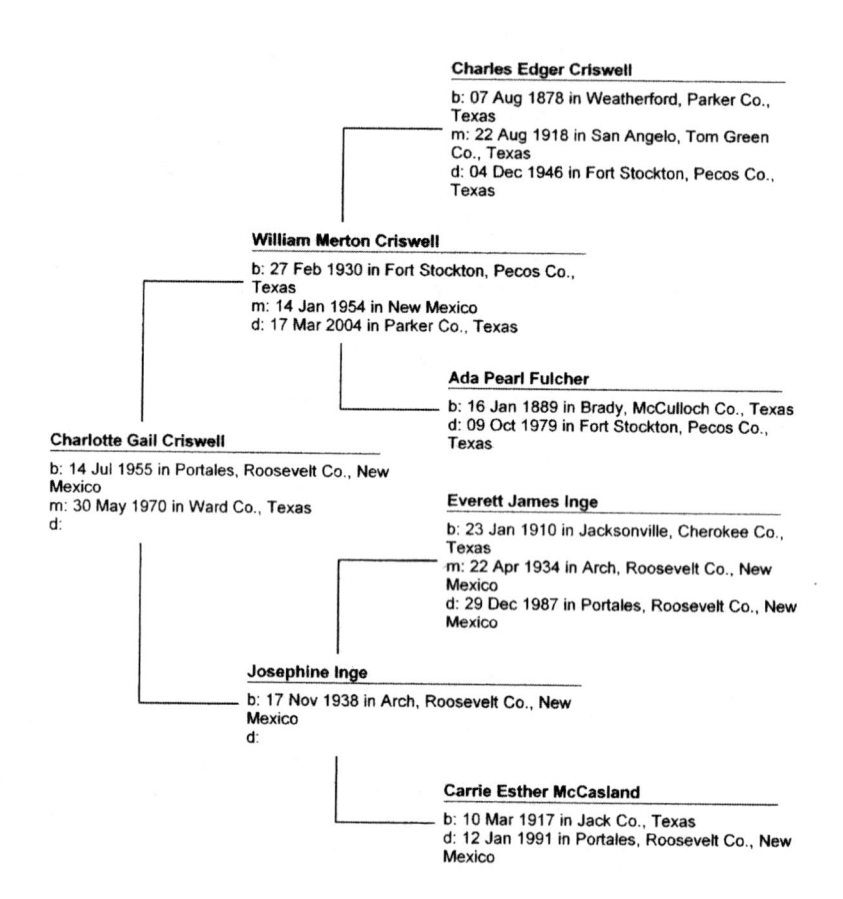

Charles Edger Criswell
b: 07 Aug 1878 in Weatherford, Parker Co., Texas
m: 22 Aug 1918 in San Angelo, Tom Green Co., Texas
d: 04 Dec 1946 in Fort Stockton, Pecos Co., Texas

William Merton Criswell
b: 27 Feb 1930 in Fort Stockton, Pecos Co., Texas
m: 14 Jan 1954 in New Mexico
d: 17 Mar 2004 in Parker Co., Texas

Ada Pearl Fulcher
b: 16 Jan 1889 in Brady, McCulloch Co., Texas
d: 09 Oct 1979 in Fort Stockton, Pecos Co., Texas

Charlotte Gail Criswell
b: 14 Jul 1955 in Portales, Roosevelt Co., New Mexico
m: 30 May 1970 in Ward Co., Texas
d:

Everett James Inge
b: 23 Jan 1910 in Jacksonville, Cherokee Co., Texas
m: 22 Apr 1934 in Arch, Roosevelt Co., New Mexico
d: 29 Dec 1987 in Portales, Roosevelt Co., New Mexico

Josephine Inge
b: 17 Nov 1938 in Arch, Roosevelt Co., New Mexico
d:

Carrie Esther McCasland
b: 10 Mar 1917 in Jack Co., Texas
d: 12 Jan 1991 in Portales, Roosevelt Co., New Mexico

Notes: This Tree also applies to the other child of William Merton Criswell & Josephine Inge: Everett Lynn Criswell.

Dora Elsie McCasland (1920-   )
[6th. Generation from Henry Wilton (1769-1820)]

&

Orvil Wade Gray (1912-   )
& Family

Dora Elsie McCasland, born February 1920 in Texas, was the fifth, and last child of Jefferson Francis McCasland & Emma Livona Wilton. Shortly after Dora Elsie was born, the family moved from Texas to Roosevelt County, New Mexico. In the 1930 Federal Census of Roosevelt County, New Mexico, Elsie D. was listed at age 10, along with her parents and two of her sisters.

Elsie resettled in Texas about 1939, when she married Orvil Wade Gray, a son of George Edwin Gray & Nina G. Frost. Orvil Wade was listed with George Wade & Nina G. in both the 1920 and 1930 Federal Census of Jack County, Texas. The first child of Elsie and Orvil Wade Gray, Harlan Roy Gray, was also born in Jack County, Texas on July 21, 1940. They had one other child, Douglas Edward Gray, who was born July 30, 1942, in Grayson County, Texas.

Available evidence is sketchy, but it appears that Orvil and Elsie may have divorced sometime before 1949. Elsie may have moved back to New Mexico and remarried. She died in Portales, Roosevelt County, New Mexico.

Family Group Sheet

Husband: Orvil Wade Gray

Born: Abt. 1912 in: Texas
Married: Abt. 1939 in: Texas
Father: George Edwin Gray
Mother: Nina G. Frost

Wife: Dora Elsie McCasland

Born: 29 Feb 1920 in: Texas
Died: Jul 1987 in: Portales, Roosevelt Co., New Mexico
Father: Jefferson Francis Asberry McCasland
Mother: Emma Livona Wilton

CHILDREN

1 M	Name: Harlan Roy Gray Born: 21 Jul 1940	in: Jack Co., Texas
2 M	Name: Douglas Edward Gray Born: 30 Jul 1942	in: Grayson Co., Texas

ORVIL WADE GRAY Standard Pedigree Tree

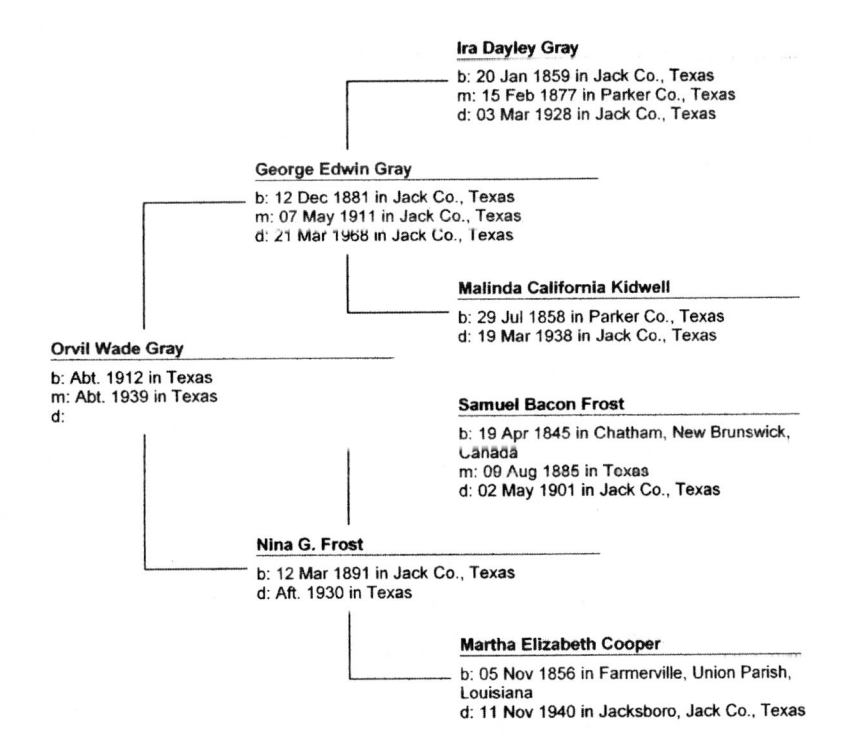

Orvil Wade Gray
b: Abt. 1912 in Texas
m: Abt. 1939 in Texas
d:

- **George Edwin Gray**
  b: 12 Dec 1881 in Jack Co., Texas
  m: 07 May 1911 in Jack Co., Texas
  d: 21 Mar 1968 in Jack Co., Texas
  - **Ira Dayley Gray**
    b: 20 Jan 1859 in Jack Co., Texas
    m: 15 Feb 1877 in Parker Co., Texas
    d: 03 Mar 1928 in Jack Co., Texas
  - **Malinda California Kidwell**
    b: 29 Jul 1858 in Parker Co., Texas
    d: 19 Mar 1938 in Jack Co., Texas

- **Nina G. Frost**
  b: 12 Mar 1891 in Jack Co., Texas
  d: Aft. 1930 in Texas
  - **Samuel Bacon Frost**
    b: 19 Apr 1845 in Chatham, New Brunswick, Canada
    m: 09 Aug 1885 in Texas
    d: 02 May 1901 in Jack Co., Texas
  - **Martha Elizabeth Cooper**
    b: 05 Nov 1856 in Farmerville, Union Parish, Louisiana
    d: 11 Nov 1940 in Jacksboro, Jack Co., Texas

Benjamin Harrison Wilton (1889-1968)
[5th. Generation from Henry Wilton (1769-1820)]

&
Elzy Florence Gaither (1883-1955)
& Family

&
Sarah Francis Gaither (1892-1973)
& Family

Benjamin Harrison Wilton was the tenth child of Thomas A. Wilton and Easter B. Clark. He was born May 23, 1889 at Winn Hill in Jack County, Texas. The family had made the Winn Hill Community their permanent home since shortly after 1878. A younger cousin of Ben by the name of Clyde Wilton remembers that Ben was always friendly and good-natured, with a friendly laugh.

In the 1900 Federal Census of Jack County, Benjamin was listed at age 11 with his mother, Easter B. (Clark) Wilton, and three sisters and one brother. By 1900, Benjamin's father, Thomas A. Wilton, had died, and his mother was the head of the household.

In the 1910 Federal Census of Jack County, Benjamin was listed at age 20, with an occupation of farmer. One brother, John M. Wilton, was also still at home, listed at age 17, and also with an occupation of farmer. At the time, Benjamin's mother and two sisters were still living together.

At least by 1917, Benjamin was the primary caregiver for his mother, because on his World War I Draft Registration of 1917, he claimed an exemption due to his "blind dependent mother." In the 1920 Federal Census of Jack County, Benjamin was again listed, at age 31, along with his mother, who was then age 72.

Benjamin's mother, Easter B. (Clark) Wilton, died at Winn Hill on December 15, 1922. In the 1930 Federal Census of Jack

County, Ben was listed at age 40, as single, with an occupation of farmer.

Available information indicates that Benjamin first married Elzy Florence Gaither. The date of December 13, 1908 was given by her Van Hoose relatives, but there has been no independent verification of the date. She was not listed along with her husband in any of the available census data. Elzy Florence was the daughter of Joseph Gaither & Sarah E. Wilton. After Elzy died in 1955, Benjamin married her sister, Sarah Francis Gaither, who was the widow of James MacDonald Van Hoose. Sarah's first husband died May 1953, leaving a number of children by their marriage, but Benjamin apparently did not have any children of his own.

Benjamin and both of his wives died in Jack County, Texas. Benjamin died in March 1968; Elzy Florence (Gaither) Wilton died June 1955; and, Sarah Francis (Gaither) Wilton died March 1973.

Family Group Sheet

Husband: Benjamin Harrison Wilton

Born: 23 May 1889 in: Winn Hill, Jack Co., Texas
Married: 13 Dec 1908 in: Texas
Died: 08 Mar 1968 in: Winn Hill, Jack Co., Texas
Father: Thomas Abslum Wilton
Mother: Easter Britania Clark
Other Spouses: Sarah Francis Gaither

Wife: Elzy Florence Gaither

Born: 19 Mar 1883 in: Woodbury, Cannon Co., Tennessee
Died: 07 Jun 1955 in: Jack Co., Texas
Father: Joseph R. Gaither
Mother: Sarah Elizabeth Wilson

Family Group Sheet

Husband: Benjamin Harrison Wilton

Born: 23 May 1889 in: Winn Hill, Jack Co., Texas
Married: Aft. 1955 in: Texas
Died: 08 Mar 1968 in: Winn Hill, Jack Co., Texas
Father: Thomas Abslum Wilton
Mother: Easter Britania Clark
Other Spouses: Elzy Florence Gaither

Wife: Sarah Francis Gaither

Born: 04 Sep 1892 in: Woodbury, Cannon Co., Tennessee
Died: 17 Mar 1973 in: Jacksboro, Jack Co., Texas
Father: Joseph R. Gaither
Mother: Sarah Elizabeth Wilson
Other Spouses: James MacDonald Van Hoose

ELZY FLORENCE GAITHER Standard Pedigree Tree

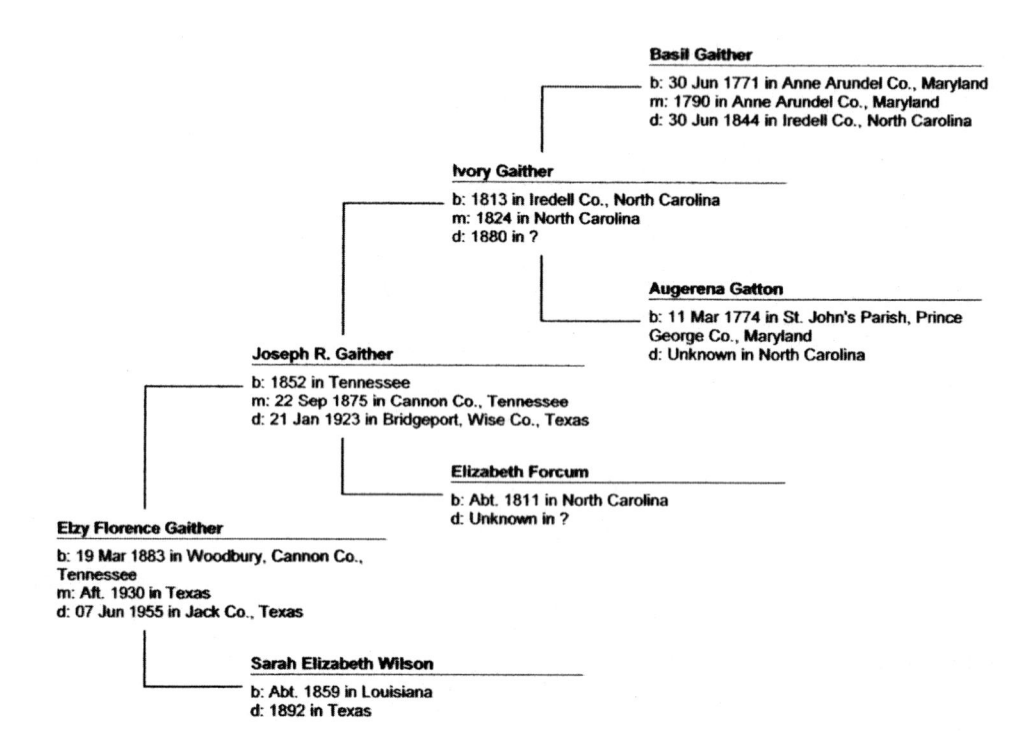

Basil Gaither
b: 30 Jun 1771 in Anne Arundel Co., Maryland
m: 1790 in Anne Arundel Co., Maryland
d: 30 Jun 1844 in Iredell Co., North Carolina

Ivory Gaither
b: 1813 in Iredell Co., North Carolina
m: 1824 in North Carolina
d: 1880 in ?

Augerena Gatton
b: 11 Mar 1774 in St. John's Parish, Prince George Co., Maryland
d: Unknown in North Carolina

Joseph R. Gaither
b: 1852 in Tennessee
m: 22 Sep 1875 in Cannon Co., Tennessee
d: 21 Jan 1923 in Bridgeport, Wise Co., Texas

Elizabeth Forcum
b: Abt. 1811 in North Carolina
d: Unknown in ?

Elzy Florence Gaither
b: 19 Mar 1883 in Woodbury, Cannon Co., Tennessee
m: Aft. 1930 in Texas
d: 07 Jun 1955 in Jack Co., Texas

Sarah Elizabeth Wilson
b: Abt. 1859 in Louisiana
d: 1892 in Texas

Notes: This Tree also applies to the sister of Elzy Florence Gaither: Sarah Francis Gaither.

Effa Belle Wilton (1890-1981)
[5th. Generation from Henry Wilton (1769-1820)]

&

James Franklin Hannah (1884-1967)
& Family

Effa (Effie) Belle Wilton, born October 1890 in Jack County, Texas, was the eleventh child of Thomas A. Wilton & Easter B. Clark. The family was living in the Winn Hill Community of Jack County at that time, which had been their permanent home since about 1878.

Effie's father, Thomas A. Wilton, died in 1894, and her mother, Easter B. (Clark) Wilton, became the head of the household. In the 1900 Federal Census of Jack County, Texas, Effie was listed at age 9, along with her mother, two brothers, and two sisters. In the 1910 Federal Census of Jack County, Texas, Effie was listed at age 19, along with her mother, two brothers, and one sister.

In January 1912, Effie married James Franklin Hannah, son of Francis Marion Hannah & Mary Adeline Melton. James Hannah was a longtime resident of Berwick, also located in Jack County, Texas. Effie and James first established their family in the Winn Hill Community near her childhood home. In the 1920 Federal Census of Jack County, Texas, J.F. (James Franklin) Hannah was listed at age 38 with an occupation of farmer, along with Effie Hannah, age 30, and their first three children. In the same 1920 census, Effie's mother, along with an older brother, Ben Wilton, where listed just twelve dwellings away.

Sometime in 1920, after their first three children were born, Effie and James moved, by covered wagon, to Benjamin in Knox County, Texas, where James worked on the railroad. They moved again in 1923 to Follie in Motley County, Texas, where James farmed and was a deputy sheriff.

In 1928, James' father died, and he moved the family back to Jack County, Texas to be near his mother, traveling by train and Model-T Ford. Two years later, they moved back to the Winn Hill Community. In the 1930 Federal Census of Jack County, Texas, James F. Hannah was listed at age 46 with an occupation of farmer, along with Effie B., age 39, and all of their six children, which were four daughters and two sons, ranging in age from 8 months to 15 years.

James moved the family again in 1931 to Berwick, Texas, to occupy his share of the Frank Hannah estate. Finally, in 1948, the family moved to Graham in Young County, Texas, where they remained until James died in October 1967. In his later years, James worked as a carpenter.

Effie died in March 1981 in Young County, Texas. James Hannah, Effie (Wilton) Hannah, and children, Mary Lois Hannah and James Eldon Hannah, were all buried in the Pioneer Cemetery at Graham in Young County, Texas.

Family Group Sheet

Husband: James Franklin Hannah

Born: 30 Jan 1884 in: Navarro Co., Texas
Married: 07 Jan 1912 in: Texas
Died: 11 Oct 1967 in: Graham, Young Co., Texas
Father: Francis Marion Hannah
Mother: Mary Adeline Melton

Wife: Effa Belle Wilton

Born: 20 Oct 1890 in: Jack Co., Texas
Died: 31 Mar 1981 in: Young Co., Texas
Father: Thomas Abslum Wilton
Mother: Easter Britania Clark

CHILDREN

1 F
Name: Ester Elzada Hannah
Born: 29 Dec 1914 in: Winn Hill, Jack Co., Texas
Died: 22 Jan 1999 in: Graham, Young Co., Texas
Married: 12 Jul 1934 in: Texas
Spouse: Wilburn Elton Stephens

2 F
Name: Mary Lois Hannah
Born: 13 Mar 1917 in: Winn Hill, Jack Co., Texas
Died: 15 Mar 1955 in: Young Co., Texas

3 F
Name: Olan Odessa Hannah
Born: 18 Jul 1918 in: Winn Hill, Jack Co., Texas
Married: Abt. 1935 in: Texas
Spouse: Prince Collins Helvey
Married: 09 Jan 1940 in: Texas
Spouse: Leonard Key Hannah

4 F
Name: Ora Mae Inez Hannah
Born: 05 Mar 1922 in: Benjamin, Knox Co., Texas
Died: 04 Aug 1991 in: Wichita Co., Texas
Married: Bef 1943 in: Texas
Spouse: Leroy Bevers

5 M
Name: Raymond Derrell Hannah
Born: 14 Dec 1927 in: Motley Co., Texas
Married: 17 Sep 1948 in: Texas
Spouse: Lena Marie Walker

6 M
Name: James Eldon Hannah
Born: 28 Feb 1930 in: Berwick, Jack Co., Texas
Died: 02 Aug 1984 in: Graham, Young Co., Texas
Married: 03 May 1949 in: Texas
Spouse: Jo Evelyn Cumpton

JAMES FRANKLIN HANNAH Standard Pedigree Tree

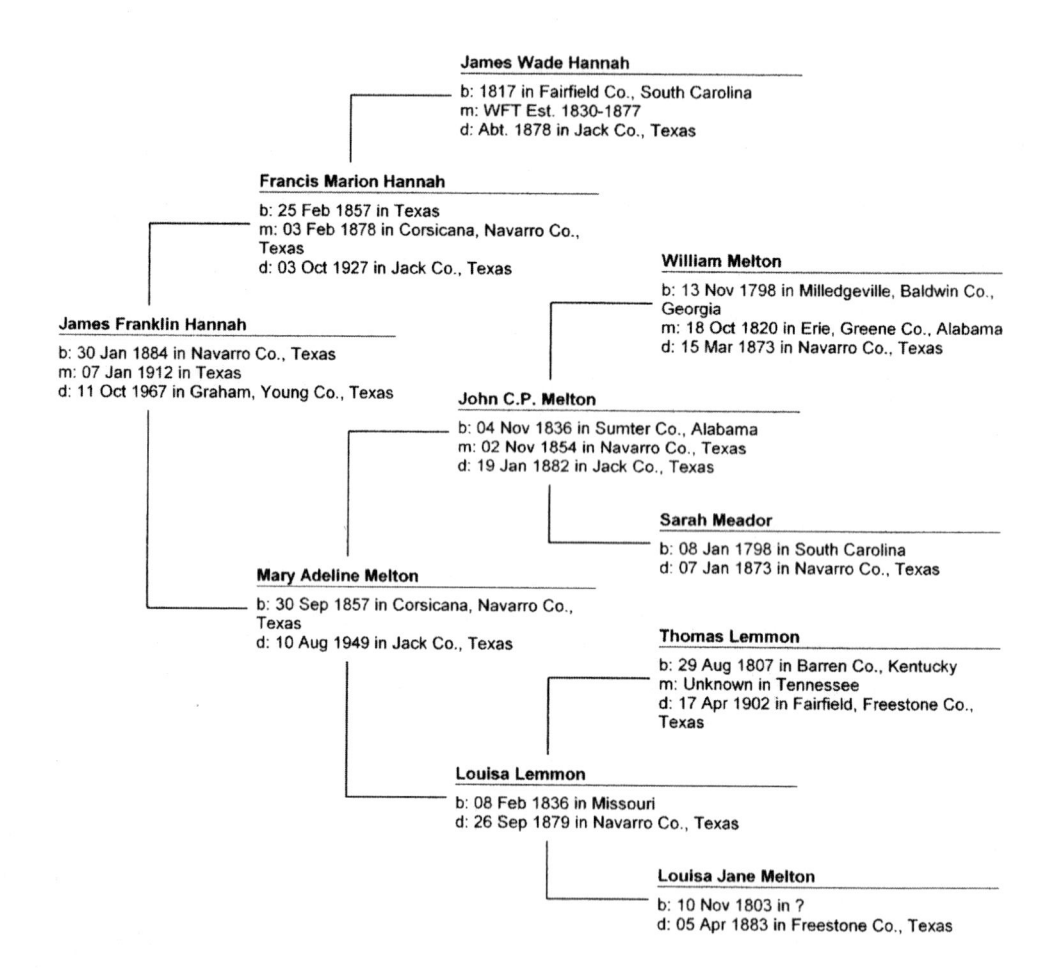

James Franklin Hannah
b: 30 Jan 1884 in Navarro Co., Texas
m: 07 Jan 1912 in Texas
d: 11 Oct 1967 in Graham, Young Co., Texas

Francis Marion Hannah
b: 25 Feb 1857 in Texas
m: 03 Feb 1878 in Corsicana, Navarro Co., Texas
d: 03 Oct 1927 in Jack Co., Texas

James Wade Hannah
b: 1817 in Fairfield Co., South Carolina
m: WFT Est. 1830-1877
d: Abt. 1878 in Jack Co., Texas

Mary Adeline Melton
b: 30 Sep 1857 in Corsicana, Navarro Co., Texas
d: 10 Aug 1949 in Jack Co., Texas

John C.P. Melton
b: 04 Nov 1836 in Sumter Co., Alabama
m: 02 Nov 1854 in Navarro Co., Texas
d: 19 Jan 1882 in Jack Co., Texas

William Melton
b: 13 Nov 1798 in Milledgeville, Baldwin Co., Georgia
m: 18 Oct 1820 in Erie, Greene Co., Alabama
d: 15 Mar 1873 in Navarro Co., Texas

Sarah Meador
b: 08 Jan 1798 in South Carolina
d: 07 Jan 1873 in Navarro Co., Texas

Louisa Lemmon
b: 08 Feb 1836 in Missouri
d: 26 Sep 1879 in Navarro Co., Texas

Thomas Lemmon
b: 29 Aug 1807 in Barren Co., Kentucky
m: Unknown in Tennessee
d: 17 Apr 1902 in Fairfield, Freestone Co., Texas

Louisa Jane Melton
b: 10 Nov 1803 in ?
d: 05 Apr 1883 in Freestone Co., Texas

Family Group Sheet

Husband: James Franklin Hannah

Born: 30 Jan 1884 in: Navarro Co., Texas
Married: 07 Jan 1912 in: Texas
Died: 11 Oct 1967 in: Graham, Young Co., Texas
Father: Francis Marion Hannah
Mother: Mary Adeline Melton

Wife: Effa Belle Wilton

Born: 20 Oct 1890 in: Jack Co., Texas
Died: 31 Mar 1981 in: Young Co., Texas
Father: Thomas Abslum Wilton
Mother: Easter Britania Clark

CHILDREN

1 F
Name: Ester Elzada Hannah
Born: 29 Dec 1914 in: Winn Hill, Jack Co., Texas
Died: 22 Jan 1999 in: Graham, Young Co., Texas
Married: 12 Jul 1934 in: Texas
Spouse: Wilburn Elton Stephens

2 F
Name: Mary Lois Hannah
Born: 13 Mar 1917 in: Winn Hill, Jack Co., Texas
Died: 15 Mar 1955 in: Young Co., Texas

3 F
Name: Olan Odessa Hannah
Born: 18 Jul 1918 in: Winn Hill, Jack Co., Texas
Married: Abt. 1935 in: Texas
Spouse: Prince Collins Helvey
Married: 09 Jan 1940 in: Texas
Spouse: Leonard Key Hannah

4 F
Name: Ora Mae Inez Hannah
Born: 05 Mar 1922 in: Benjamin, Knox Co., Texas
Died: 04 Aug 1991 in: Wichita Co., Texas
Married: Bef. 1943 in: Texas
Spouse: Leroy Bevers

5 M
Name: Raymond Derrell Hannah
Born: 14 Dec 1927 in: Motley Co., Texas
Married: 17 Sep 1948 in: Texas
Spouse: Lena Marie Walker

6 M
Name: James Eldon Hannah
Born: 28 Feb 1930 in: Berwick, Jack Co., Texas
Died: 02 Aug 1984 in: Graham, Young Co., Texas
Married: 03 May 1949 in: Texas
Spouse: Jo Evelyn Cumpton

JAMES FRANKLIN HANNAH Standard Pedigree Tree

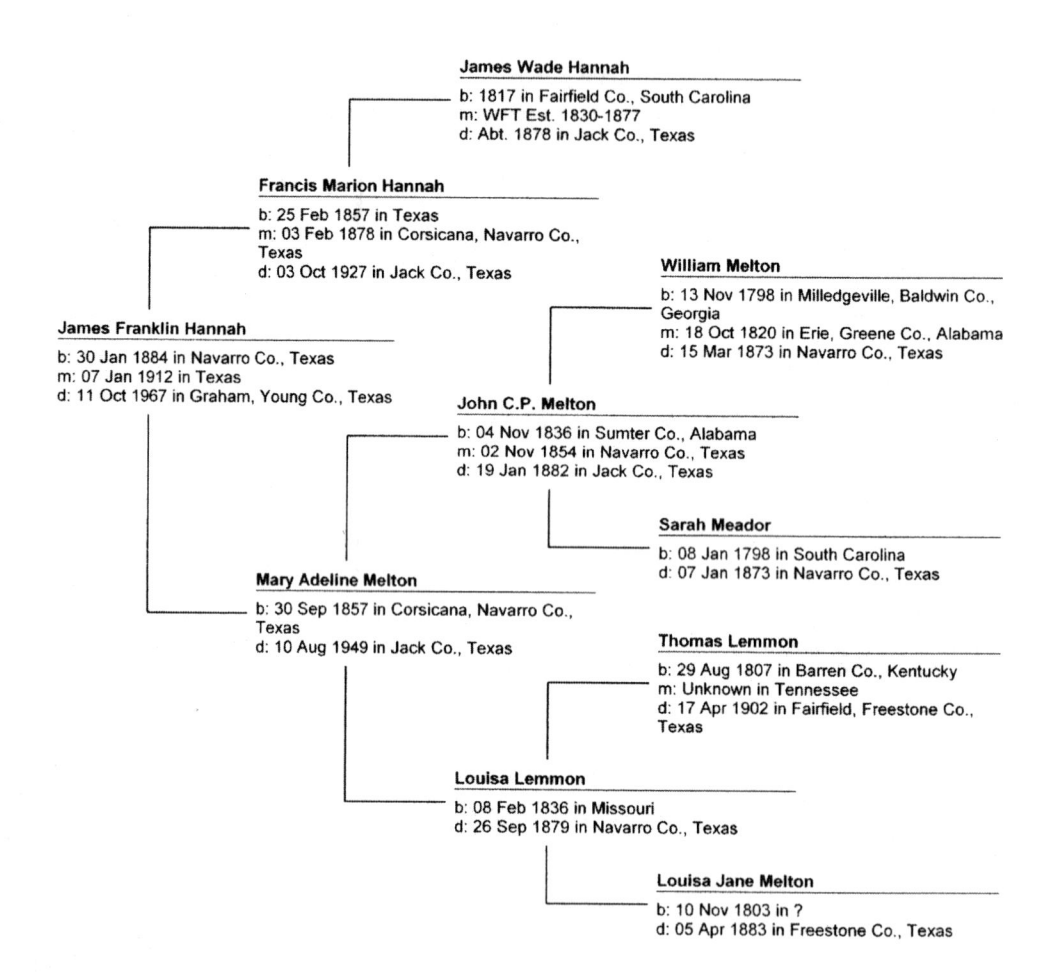

James Franklin Hannah
b: 30 Jan 1884 in Navarro Co., Texas
m: 07 Jan 1912 in Texas
d: 11 Oct 1967 in Graham, Young Co., Texas

- **Francis Marion Hannah**
  b: 25 Feb 1857 in Texas
  m: 03 Feb 1878 in Corsicana, Navarro Co., Texas
  d: 03 Oct 1927 in Jack Co., Texas
  - **James Wade Hannah**
    b: 1817 in Fairfield Co., South Carolina
    m: WFT Est. 1830-1877
    d: Abt. 1878 in Jack Co., Texas

- **Mary Adeline Melton**
  b: 30 Sep 1857 in Corsicana, Navarro Co., Texas
  d: 10 Aug 1949 in Jack Co., Texas
  - **John C.P. Melton**
    b: 04 Nov 1836 in Sumter Co., Alabama
    m: 02 Nov 1854 in Navarro Co., Texas
    d: 19 Jan 1882 in Jack Co., Texas
    - **William Melton**
      b: 13 Nov 1798 in Milledgeville, Baldwin Co., Georgia
      m: 18 Oct 1820 in Erie, Greene Co., Alabama
      d: 15 Mar 1873 in Navarro Co., Texas
    - **Sarah Meador**
      b: 08 Jan 1798 in South Carolina
      d: 07 Jan 1873 in Navarro Co., Texas
  - **Louisa Lemmon**
    b: 08 Feb 1836 in Missouri
    d: 26 Sep 1879 in Navarro Co., Texas
    - **Thomas Lemmon**
      b: 29 Aug 1807 in Barren Co., Kentucky
      m: Unknown in Tennessee
      d: 17 Apr 1902 in Fairfield, Freestone Co., Texas
    - **Louisa Jane Melton**
      b: 10 Nov 1803 in ?
      d: 05 Apr 1883 in Freestone Co., Texas

Ester Elzada Hannah (1914-1999)
[6th. Generation from Henry Wilton (1769-1820)]

&

Wilburn Elton Stephens (1915-1997)
& Family

Ester Elzada Hannah, born December 1914 at Winn Hill in Jack County, Texas, was the oldest child of Effa (Effie) Belle Wilton & James Franklin Hannah. Effie & James had started their home in the Winn Hill Community shortly after their marriage in March 1912. In the 1920 Federal Census of Jack County, Elzada was listed at age 5, with her parents and two younger sisters, Mary Lois Hannah and Olan Odessa Hannah.

After spending several years in Knox County, Texas and Motley County, Texas, between 1920 and 1928, which were associated with James Hannah's employment, the family returned again to the Winn Hill Community in Jack County, Texas. In the 1930 Federal Census of Jack County, Elzada was listed at age 15, with her parents, along with three sisters and two brothers.

Elzada married Wilburn Elton Stephens, a son of Wiley Emmanuel Stephens & Elizabeth Frances Spradlin, on July 12, 1934. By the 1930 Federal Census, the family of Wiley & Elizabeth (Bettie) Stephens had also made their home in Jack County, Texas.

Sometime after their marriage in 1934, Elzada and Wilburn Elton made their home in Young County, Texas. That is where their first daughter, Wanda Joy Stephens, was born in March 1938 in Graham in Young County, Texas. They had two other daughters, Janice Darlene Stephens, who was born June 1941, in adjacent Palo Pinto County, and Sherry Jo Stephens, who was born January 1947 in Graham in Young County, Texas.

Wilburn Elton Stephens served in the Navy during WWII. He died April 7, 1997 in Graham, Texas and was buried at the Oak Grove Cemetery in Graham, Texas. Elzada also died in Graham in Young County, Texas, on January 22, 1999.

Family Group Sheet

Husband: Wilburn Elton Stephens

Born: 21 Nov 1915   in: Texas
Married: 12 Jul 1934   in: Texas
Died: 07 Apr 1997   in: Graham, Young Co., Texas
Father: Wiley Emmanuel Stephens
Mother: Elizabeth Frances Spradlin

Wife: Ester Elzada Hannah

Born: 29 Dec 1914   in: Winn Hill, Jack Co., Texas
Died: 22 Jan 1999   in: Graham, Young Co., Texas
Father: James Franklin Hannah
Mother: Effa Belle Wilton

CHILDREN

1 F
Name: Wanda Joy Stephens
Born: 11 Mar 1938   in: Graham, Young Co., Texas
Married: Unknown
Spouse: James Cecil Perry

2 F
Name: Janice Darlene Stephens
Born: 10 Jun 1941   in: Mineral Wells, Palo Pinto Co., Texas
Married: 30 Aug 1966   in: Young Co., Texas
Spouse: Don Bruce Lybrand

3 F
Name: Sherry Jo Stephens
Born: 17 Jan 1947   in: Graham, Young Co., Texas
Married: Unknown
Spouse: John Bryan

ESTER ELZADA HANNAH Standard Pedigree Tree

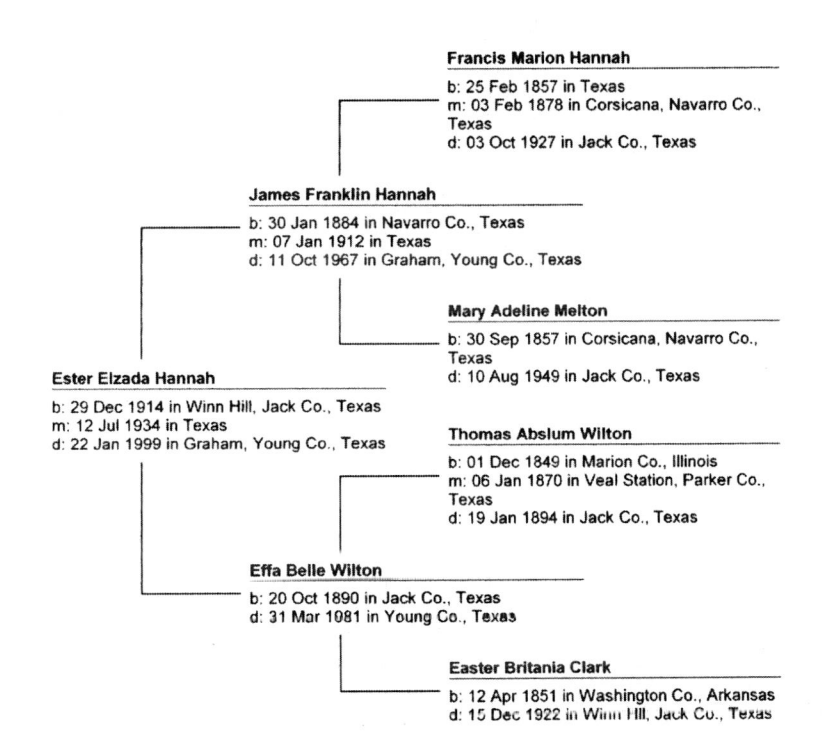

Francis Marion Hannah
b: 25 Feb 1857 in Texas
m: 03 Feb 1878 in Corsicana, Navarro Co., Texas
d: 03 Oct 1927 in Jack Co., Texas

James Franklin Hannah
b: 30 Jan 1884 in Navarro Co., Texas
m: 07 Jan 1912 in Texas
d: 11 Oct 1967 in Graham, Young Co., Texas

Mary Adeline Melton
b: 30 Sep 1857 in Corsicana, Navarro Co., Texas
d: 10 Aug 1949 in Jack Co., Texas

Ester Elzada Hannah
b: 29 Dec 1914 in Winn Hill, Jack Co., Texas
m: 12 Jul 1934 in Texas
d: 22 Jan 1999 in Graham, Young Co., Texas

Thomas Abslum Wilton
b: 01 Dec 1849 in Marion Co., Illinois
m: 06 Jan 1870 in Veal Station, Parker Co., Texas
d: 19 Jan 1894 in Jack Co., Texas

Effa Belle Wilton
b: 20 Oct 1890 in Jack Co., Texas
d: 31 Mar 1981 in Young Co., Texas

Easter Britania Clark
b: 12 Apr 1851 in Washington Co., Arkansas
d: 15 Dec 1922 in Winn Hill, Jack Co., Texas

Notes: This Tree also applies to the other children of James Franklin Hannah & Effa Belle Wilton: Mary Lois Hannah, Olan Odessa Hannah, Ora Mae Inez Hannah, Raymond Derrell Hannah, and James Eldon Hannah.

WILBURN ELTON STEPHENS Standard Pedigree Tree

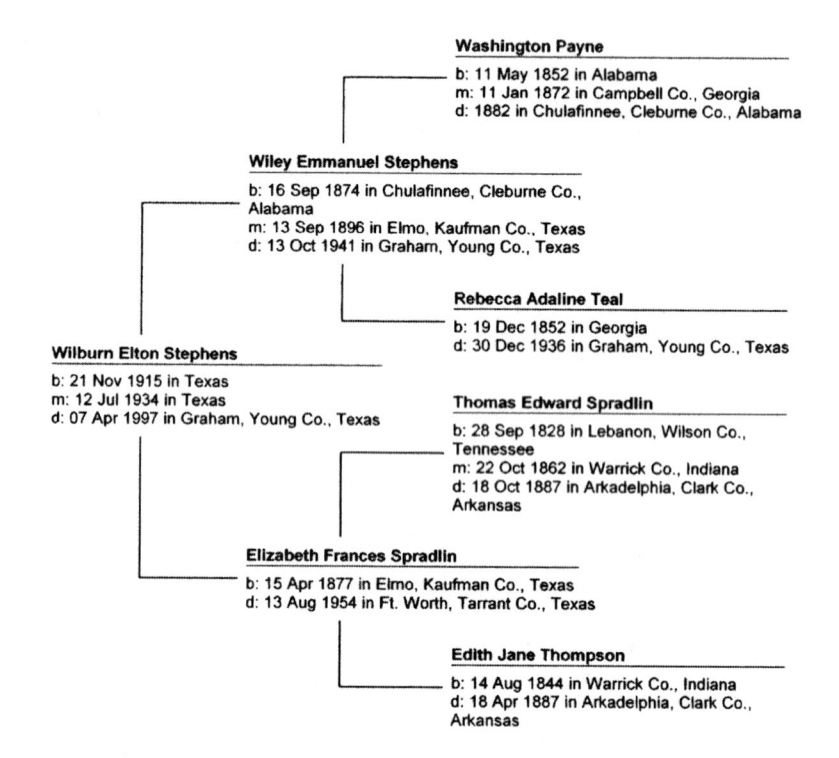

Wilburn Elton Stephens
b: 21 Nov 1915 in Texas
m: 12 Jul 1934 in Texas
d: 07 Apr 1997 in Graham, Young Co., Texas

- **Wiley Emmanuel Stephens**
  b: 16 Sep 1874 in Chulafinnee, Cleburne Co., Alabama
  m: 13 Sep 1896 in Elmo, Kaufman Co., Texas
  d: 13 Oct 1941 in Graham, Young Co., Texas
  - **Washington Payne**
    b: 11 May 1852 in Alabama
    m: 11 Jan 1872 in Campbell Co., Georgia
    d: 1882 in Chulafinnee, Cleburne Co., Alabama
  - **Rebecca Adaline Teal**
    b: 19 Dec 1852 in Georgia
    d: 30 Dec 1936 in Graham, Young Co., Texas

- **Elizabeth Frances Spradlin**
  b: 15 Apr 1877 in Elmo, Kaufman Co., Texas
  d: 13 Aug 1954 in Ft. Worth, Tarrant Co., Texas
  - **Thomas Edward Spradlin**
    b: 28 Sep 1828 in Lebanon, Wilson Co., Tennessee
    m: 22 Oct 1862 in Warrick Co., Indiana
    d: 18 Oct 1887 in Arkadelphia, Clark Co., Arkansas
  - **Edith Jane Thompson**
    b: 14 Aug 1844 in Warrick Co., Indiana
    d: 18 Apr 1887 in Arkadelphia, Clark Co., Arkansas

Wanda Joy Stephens (1938-   )
[7th. Generation from Henry Wilton (1769-1820)]

&

James Cecil Perry
& Family

Family Group Sheet

Husband: James Cecil Perry

Born: Unknown
Married: Unknown

Wife: Wanda Joy Stephens

Born: 11 Mar 1938   in: Graham, Young Co., Texas
Father: Wilburn Elton Stephens
Mother: Ester Elzada Hannah

CHILDREN

1 M	Name: James Travis Perry Born: 18 Aug 1957	in: Tarrant Co., Texas
2 M	Name: Keith Allen Perry Born: 12 May 1961	in: Young Co., Texas
3 M	Name: Mike W. Perry Born: Unknown	
4 M	Name: Ronny Perry Born: Unknown	

WANDA JOY STEPHENS Standard Pedigree Tree

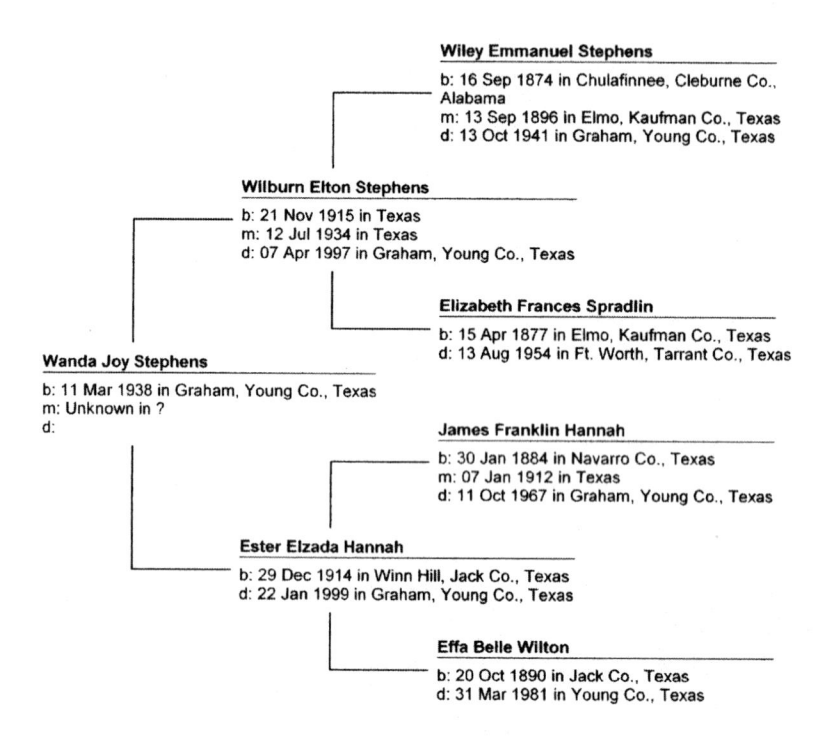

Wiley Emmanuel Stephens
b: 16 Sep 1874 in Chulafinnee, Cleburne Co., Alabama
m: 13 Sep 1896 in Elmo, Kaufman Co., Texas
d: 13 Oct 1941 in Graham, Young Co., Texas

Wilburn Elton Stephens
b: 21 Nov 1915 in Texas
m: 12 Jul 1934 in Texas
d: 07 Apr 1997 in Graham, Young Co., Texas

Elizabeth Frances Spradlin
b: 15 Apr 1877 in Elmo, Kaufman Co., Texas
d: 13 Aug 1954 in Ft. Worth, Tarrant Co., Texas

Wanda Joy Stephens
b: 11 Mar 1938 in Graham, Young Co., Texas
m: Unknown in ?
d:

James Franklin Hannah
b: 30 Jan 1884 in Navarro Co., Texas
m: 07 Jan 1912 in Texas
d: 11 Oct 1967 in Graham, Young Co., Texas

Ester Elzada Hannah
b: 29 Dec 1914 in Winn Hill, Jack Co., Texas
d: 22 Jan 1999 in Graham, Young Co., Texas

Effa Belle Wilton
b: 20 Oct 1890 in Jack Co., Texas
d: 31 Mar 1981 in Young Co., Texas

Notes: This Tree also applies to the other children of Wilburn Elton Stephens & Ester Elzada Hannah: Janice Darlene Stephens and Sherry Jo Stephens.

Janice Darlene Stephens (1941-   )
[7th. Generation from Henry Wilton (1769-1820)]

&

Don Bruce Lybrand (1940-1984)
& Family

Family Group Sheet

Husband: Don Bruce Lybrand		
Born: 02 Jan 1940		
Married: 30 Aug 1966	in: Young Co., Texas	
Died: 27 Jan 1984	in: Dallas Co., Texas	
Wife: Janice Darlene Stephens		
Born: 10 Jun 1941	in: Mineral Wells, Palo Pinto Co., Texas	
Father: Wilburn Elton Stephens		
Mother: Ester Elzada Hannah		

	CHILDREN	
1 M	Name: Richard Don Lybrand Born: 09 May 1967	in: Young Co., Texas
2 F	Name: Vickie Renae Lybrand Born: 27 Sep 1961	in: Young Co., Texas

Sherry Jo Stephens (1947-   )
[7th. Generation from Henry Wilton (1769-1820)]

&

John Bryan
& Family

Family Group Sheet

Husband: John Bryan
Born: Unknown Married: Unknown

Wife: Sherry Jo Stephens
Born: 17 Jan 1947   in: Graham, Young Co., Texas Father: Wilburn Elton Stephens Mother: Ester Elzada Hannah

	CHILDREN
1 M	Name: Charles C. Bryan Born: Unknown
2 M	Name: Phillip Hale Bryan Born: Unknown

Olan Odessa Hannah (1918-   )
[6th. Generation from Henry Wilton (1769-1820)]

&
Prince Collins Helvey (1915-1979)
& Family

&
Leonard Key Hannah (1916-1998)
& Family

Olan Odessa Hannah, born July 1918 at Winn Hill in Jack County, Texas, was the third child of Effa (Effie) Belle Wilton & James Franklin Hannah. In the 1920 Federal Census of Jack County, Texas, Olan Odessa (Odesie) was listed at age 2 years, along with her parents and two older sisters, Elzada Hannah and Mary L. Hannah.

In 1920, Effie and James Hannah moved the family to Knox County, Texas, where James worked on the railroad. The family moved again in 1923 to Motley County, Texas, where James farmed and acted as a deputy sheriff. In 1928, after the death of James' father, Francis Marion Hannah, James moved the family back to Jack County, Texas, to be near his mother, Mary (Melton) Hannah. About 1930, the family was again living in the Winn Hill Community in Jack County, Texas. In the 1930 Federal Census of Jack County, Texas, Odessa was listed at age 11, along with her parents and the rest of the family of six children. Moving again in 1931, the family settled for awhile in Berwick in Jack County, where James occupied his share of the Frank Hannah Estate.

Sometime about 1935, Olan Odessa married Prince C. Helvey, who was also a resident of Jack County. They had one child together, Betty Imogene Helvey, born February 13, 1936, in Jack County, Texas.

Olan Odesssa married a second time on January 9, 1940, to Leonard Key Hannah, son of John Wade Hannah & Asalee Brock. Olan Odessa Hannah and Leonard Key Hannah were related through a common ancestor, named James Wade Hannah (1817-1878). James Wade Hannah was a great-grandfather of Olan Odessa Hannah and a grandfather of Leonard Key Hannah.

Olan and Leonard remained in Texas, but only their first child, Dolores Lee Hannah, was born in Jack County, Texas. Their second child, Jackie Kathleen Hannah, was born 1948 in Galveston County, Texas. Leonard Key Hannah died January 26, 1998 in Harris County, Texas.

Family Group Sheet

Husband: Prince Collins Helvey

Born: 29 Jul 1915 in: Texas
Married: Abt. 1935 in: Texas
Died: 31 Jan 1979 in: Montague Co., Texas
Other Spouses: Ollie Louise Conway

Wife: Olan Odessa Hannah

Born: 18 Jul 1918 in: Winn Hill, Jack Co., Texas
Father: James Franklin Hannah
Mother: Effa Belle Wilton
Other Spouses: Leonard Key Hannah

CHILDREN

1 F
Name: Betty Imogene Helvey
Born: 13 Feb 1936 in: Jack Co., Texas
Married: Unknown
Spouse: Darrel Ray Vanderford

Family Group Sheet

Husband: Leonard Key Hannah

Born: 06 Feb 1916 in: Jack Co., Texas
Married: 09 Jan 1940 in: Texas
Died: 26 Jan 1998 in: Harris Co., Texas
Father: John Wade Hannah
Mother: Asalee Brock

Wife: Olan Odessa Hannah

Born: 18 Jul 1918 in: Winn Hill, Jack Co., Texas
Father: James Franklin Hannah
Mother: Effa Belle Wilton
Other Spouses: Prince Collins Helvey

CHILDREN

1 F
Name: Dolores Lee Hannah
Born: 02 Jan 1942 in: Jack Co., Texas
Married: Unknown
Spouse: John Morgan Hoot

2 F
Name: Jackie Kathleen Hannah
Born: 29 Apr 1948 in: Galveston Co., Texas
Married: 09 Mar 1968 in: Galveston Co., Texas
Spouse: Joseph Anthony Matranga

LEONARD KEY HANNAH Standard Pedigree Tree

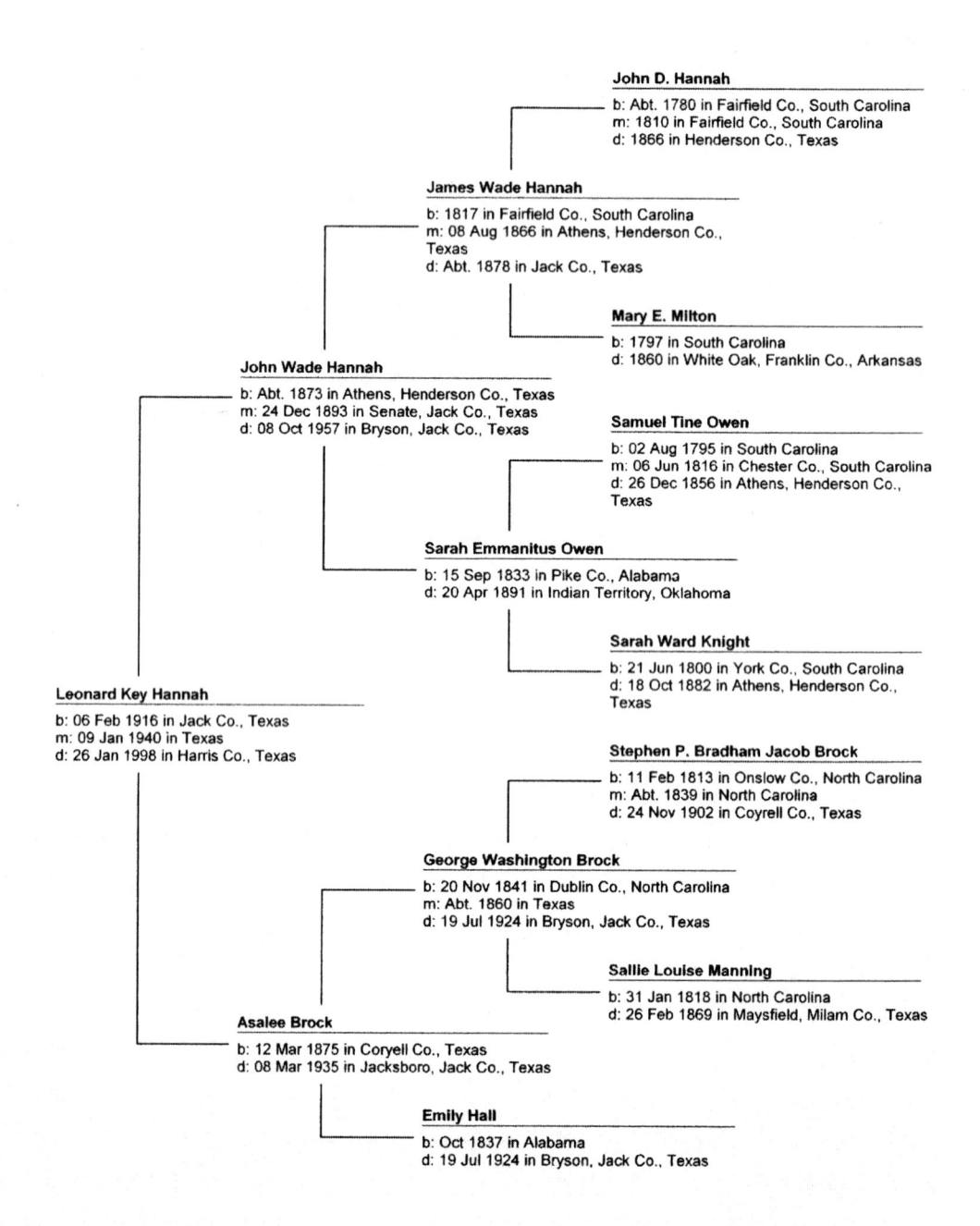

John D. Hannah
b: Abt. 1780 in Fairfield Co., South Carolina
m: 1810 in Fairfield Co., South Carolina
d: 1866 in Henderson Co., Texas

James Wade Hannah
b: 1817 in Fairfield Co., South Carolina
m: 08 Aug 1866 in Athens, Henderson Co., Texas
d: Abt. 1878 in Jack Co., Texas

Mary E. Milton
b: 1797 in South Carolina
d: 1860 in White Oak, Franklin Co., Arkansas

John Wade Hannah
b: Abt. 1873 in Athens, Henderson Co., Texas
m: 24 Dec 1893 in Senate, Jack Co., Texas
d: 08 Oct 1957 in Bryson, Jack Co., Texas

Samuel Tine Owen
b: 02 Aug 1795 in South Carolina
m: 06 Jun 1816 in Chester Co., South Carolina
d: 26 Dec 1856 in Athens, Henderson Co., Texas

Sarah Emmanitus Owen
b: 15 Sep 1833 in Pike Co., Alabama
d: 20 Apr 1891 in Indian Territory, Oklahoma

Sarah Ward Knight
b: 21 Jun 1800 in York Co., South Carolina
d: 18 Oct 1882 in Athens, Henderson Co., Texas

Leonard Key Hannah
b: 06 Feb 1916 in Jack Co., Texas
m: 09 Jan 1940 in Texas
d: 26 Jan 1998 in Harris Co., Texas

Stephen P. Bradham Jacob Brock
b: 11 Feb 1813 in Onslow Co., North Carolina
m: Abt. 1839 in North Carolina
d: 24 Nov 1902 in Coyrell Co., Texas

George Washington Brock
b: 20 Nov 1841 in Dublin Co., North Carolina
m: Abt. 1860 in Texas
d: 19 Jul 1924 in Bryson, Jack Co., Texas

Sallie Louise Manning
b: 31 Jan 1818 in North Carolina
d: 26 Feb 1869 in Maysfield, Milam Co., Texas

Asalee Brock
b: 12 Mar 1875 in Coryell Co., Texas
d: 08 Mar 1935 in Jacksboro, Jack Co., Texas

Emily Hall
b: Oct 1837 in Alabama
d: 19 Jul 1924 in Bryson, Jack Co., Texas

Dolores Lee Hannah (1942-   )
[7th. Generation from Henry Wilton (1769-1820)]

&

John Morgan Hoot
& Family

Family Group Sheet

Husband: John Morgan Hoot	
Born: Unknown	
Married: Unknown	

Wife: Dolores Lee Hannah	
Born: 02 Jan 1942	in: Jack Co., Texas
Father: Leonard Key Hannah	
Mother: Olan Odessa Hannah	

CHILDREN

1 M	Name: John Kevin Hoot Born: 26 Jul 1969	in: Galveston Co., Texas
2 M	Name: Christopher Key Hoot Born: 26 Mar 1972	in: Galveston Co., Texas

DOLORES LEE HANNAH Standard Pedigree Tree

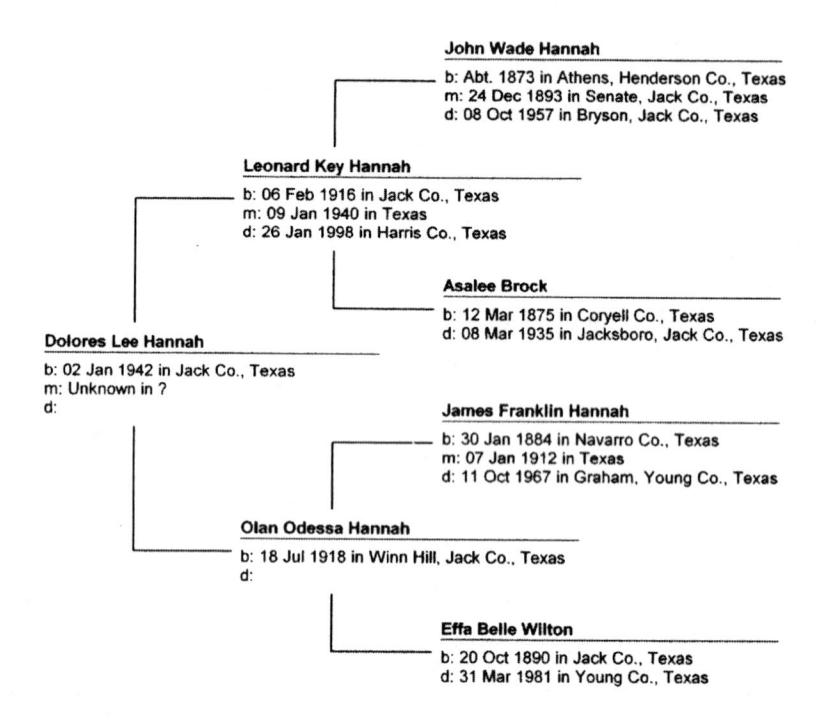

Dolores Lee Hannah
b: 02 Jan 1942 in Jack Co., Texas
m: Unknown in ?
d:

- **Leonard Key Hannah**
  b: 06 Feb 1916 in Jack Co., Texas
  m: 09 Jan 1940 in Texas
  d: 26 Jan 1998 in Harris Co., Texas
  - **John Wade Hannah**
    b: Abt. 1873 in Athens, Henderson Co., Texas
    m: 24 Dec 1893 in Senate, Jack Co., Texas
    d: 08 Oct 1957 in Bryson, Jack Co., Texas
  - **Asalee Brock**
    b: 12 Mar 1875 in Coryell Co., Texas
    d: 08 Mar 1935 in Jacksboro, Jack Co., Texas

- **Olan Odessa Hannah**
  b: 18 Jul 1918 in Winn Hill, Jack Co., Texas
  d:
  - **James Franklin Hannah**
    b: 30 Jan 1884 in Navarro Co., Texas
    m: 07 Jan 1912 in Texas
    d: 11 Oct 1967 in Graham, Young Co., Texas
  - **Effa Belle Wilton**
    b: 20 Oct 1890 in Jack Co., Texas
    d: 31 Mar 1981 in Young Co., Texas

Notes: This Tree also applies to the other child of Leonard Key Hannah & Olan Odessa Hannah: Jackie Kathleen Hannah.

Jackie Kathleen Hannah (1948-   )
[7th. Generation from Henry Wilton (1769-1820)]

&

Joseph Anthony Matranga (1945-1968)
& Family

Family Group Sheet

Husband: Joseph Anthony Matranga	
Born: 09 Sep 1945	in: Galveston Co., Texas
Married: 09 Mar 1968	in: Galveston Co., Texas

Wife: Jackie Kathleen Hannah	
Born: 29 Apr 1948	in: Galveston Co., Texas
Father: Leonard Key Hannah	
Mother: Olan Odessa Hannah	

	CHILDREN	
1 F	Name: Lisa Deann Matranga	
	Born: 26 Jan 1973	in: Galveston Co., Texas
2 M	Name: Michael Anthony Matranga	
	Born: 21 Aug 1977	in: Galveston Co., Texas

Ora Mae Inez Hannah (1922-1991)
[6th. Generation from Henry Wilton (1769-1820)]

&

Lee Roy Bevers (1920-1986)
& Family

Ora Mae Inez Hannah, born March 1922 in Knox County, Texas, was the fourth child of Effa (Effie) Belle Wilton & James Franklin Hannah. At the time of her birth, the family had moved from Jack County, Texas to Knox County, where her father was then working on the railroad. The family made moves to Motley County, Texas, in 1923, where James Hannah farmed and acted as a deputy sheriff, and back to Jack County in 1928, when his father died, so James could be near his mother, Effie Belle (Wilton) Hannah.

In the 1930 Federal Census of Jack County, Texas, Ora Mae was listed at age 8, along with her parents and family of six children. A short time later, in 1931, the family moved to Berwick in Jack County, Texas, where James Hannah occupied his share of the Frank Hannah estate.

Ora Mae married Lee Roy (Leroy) Bevers about 1943. The family settled in Palo Pinto County, Texas, which was where Leroy's family was located and where he spent his early years. The couple's two living children, Gwendolyn Inez Bevers, and Roy Duane Bevers, were both born in Palo Pinto County, Texas, during the 1940's.

Leroy died February 1986 in Young County, Texas, and Ora Mae died August 1991 in Wichita County, Texas.

Family Group Sheet

Husband: Lee Roy Bevers

Born: 09 Jul 1920 in: Texas
Married: Bef. 1943 in: Texas
Died: Feb 1986 in: Young Co., Texas
Father: Lee Roy Bevers
Mother: Lonnie Harris

Wife: Ora Mae Inez Hannah

Born: 05 Mar 1922 in: Benjamin, Knox Co., Texas
Died: 04 Aug 1991 in: Wichita Co., Texas
Father: James Franklin Hannah
Mother: Effa Belle Wilton

CHILDREN

1 F
Name: Gwendolyn Inez Bevers
Born: 12 Feb 1943 in: Palo Pinto Co., Texas
Married: Bef. 1966
Spouse: Johnny Augustus Gooch

2 M
Name: Roy Duane Bevers
Born: 01 Mar 1947 in: Palo Pinto Co., Texas
Married: 20 Mar 1968 in: Young Co., Texas
Spouse: Bobbie June Smith

3 F
Name: Brenda Bevers
Born: Unknown in: died at birth

Gwendolyn Inez Bevers (1943-   )
[7th. Generation from Henry Wilton (1769-1820)]

&

Johnny Augustus Gooch
& Family

Family Group Sheet

Husband: Johnny Augustus Gooch	
Born: Unknown	
Married: Bef. 1966	

Wife: Gwendolyn Inez Bevers	
Born: 12 Feb 1943	in: Palo Pinto Co., Texas
Father: Lee Roy Bevers	
Mother: Ora Mae Inez Hannah	

	CHILDREN	
1 F	Name: Kimberly Dawnette Gooch	
	Born: 10 Dec 1966	in: Young Co., Texas
2 M	Name: Johnny Wade Gooch	
	Born: 21 Oct 1970	in: Young Co., Texas

GWENDOLYN INEZ BEVERS Standard Pedigree Tree

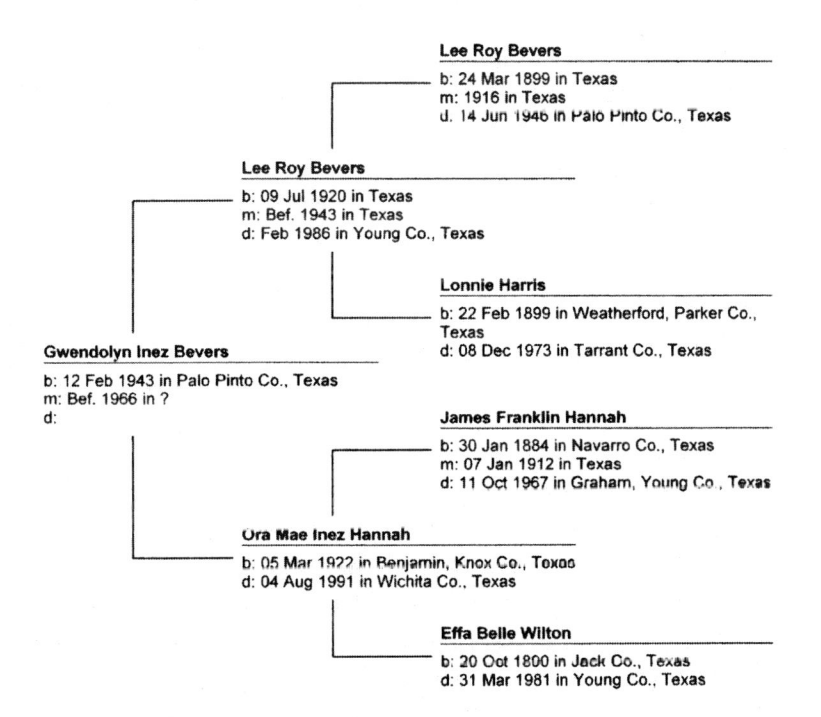

Gwendolyn Inez Bevers
b: 12 Feb 1943 in Palo Pinto Co., Texas
m: Bef. 1966 in ?
d:

- **Lee Roy Bevers**
  b: 09 Jul 1920 in Texas
  m: Bef. 1943 in Texas
  d: Feb 1986 in Young Co., Texas

  - **Lee Roy Bevers**
    b: 24 Mar 1899 in Texas
    m: 1916 in Texas
    d: 14 Jun 1946 in Palo Pinto Co., Texas

  - **Lonnie Harris**
    b: 22 Feb 1899 in Weatherford, Parker Co., Texas
    d: 08 Dec 1973 in Tarrant Co., Texas

- **Ora Mae Inez Hannah**
  b: 05 Mar 1922 in Benjamin, Knox Co., Texas
  d: 04 Aug 1991 in Wichita Co., Texas

  - **James Franklin Hannah**
    b: 30 Jan 1884 in Navarro Co., Texas
    m: 07 Jan 1912 in Texas
    d: 11 Oct 1967 in Graham, Young Co., Texas

  - **Effa Belle Wilton**
    b: 20 Oct 1890 in Jack Co., Texas
    d: 31 Mar 1981 in Young Co., Texas

Notes: This Tree also applies to the other child of Lee Roy Bevers & Ora Mae Inez Hannah: Roy Duane Bevers.

Raymond Derrell Hannah (1927-   )
[6th. Generation from Henry Wilton (1769-1820)]

&

Lena Marie Walker (1933-   )
& Family

Raymond Derrell Hannah, born December 1927 in Motley County, Texas, was the fifth child of Effa (Effie) Belle Wilton and James Franklin Hannah. The family originally settled at the Winn Hill Community in Jack County, Texas, after Effie and James were married in 1912. Beginning about 1920, the family began several moves that corresponded with James' employment. For awhile the family lived in Benjamin in Knox County, Texas, where James worked for the railroad. In 1923, they moved to Follie in Motley County, Texas, where James farmed and was a deputy sheriff. Raymond Derrell Hannah was born while the family was living in Motley County.

When James' father, Francis Marion Hannah, died in 1928, the family moved back to Jack County, Texas, and by 1930, the family was again living in the Winn Hill Community of Jack County. In the 1930 Federal Census of Jack County, Raymond D. Hannah was listed at age 2 years, along with James and Effie Hannah and the rest of the family of six children.

After another move in 1931 to Berwick, Texas, where James occupied his share of the Frank Hannah estate, the family finally settled permanently, in 1948, at Graham in Young County, Texas. In September 1948, Raymond Derrell married Lena Marie Walker, daughter of James Fred Walker and Rosa Lena McGehee, who were also residents of Young County.

Raymond Derrell and Lena Marie had three children, born between 1954 and 1959, who were all born in Young County, Texas.

Family Group Sheet

Husband: Raymond Derrell Hannah		
Born: 14 Dec 1927	in: Motley Co., Texas	
Married: 17 Sep 1948	in: Texas	
Father: James Franklin Hannah		
Mother: Effa Belle Wilton		

Wife: Lena Marie Walker	
Born: 16 Jan 1933	in: Young Co., Texas
Father: James Fred Walker	
Mother: Rosa Lena McGehee	

CHILDREN

#		
1 F	Name: Anita Marie Hannah	
	Born: 18 Aug 1954	in: Graham, Young Co., Texas
	Married: 10 Sep 1976	in: Clark Co., Nevada
	Spouse: Ronald Dewayne Epperson	
2 M	Name: Derrrell Lynn Hannah	
	Born: 18 Apr 1956	in: Graham, Young Co., Texas
3 M	Name: Leslie Jean Hannah	
	Born: 29 Apr 1959	in: Graham, Young Co., Texas

Anita Marie Hannah (1954-   )
[7th. Generation from Henry Wilton (1769-1820)]

&

Ronald Dewayne Epperson (1952-   )
& Family

Family Group Sheet

Husband: Ronald Dewayne Epperson	
Born: 01 Aug 1952	in: Jack Co., Texas
Married: 10 Sep 1976	in: Clark Co., Nevada
Wife: Anita Marie Hannah	
Born: 18 Aug 1954	in: Graham, Young Co., Texas
Father: Raymond Derrell Hannah	
Mother: Lena Marie Walker	

CHILDREN

1 F
Name: Meredith Rachelle Epperson
Born: 23 Sep 1978   in: Young Co., Texas

ANITA MARIE HANNAH Standard Pedigree Tree

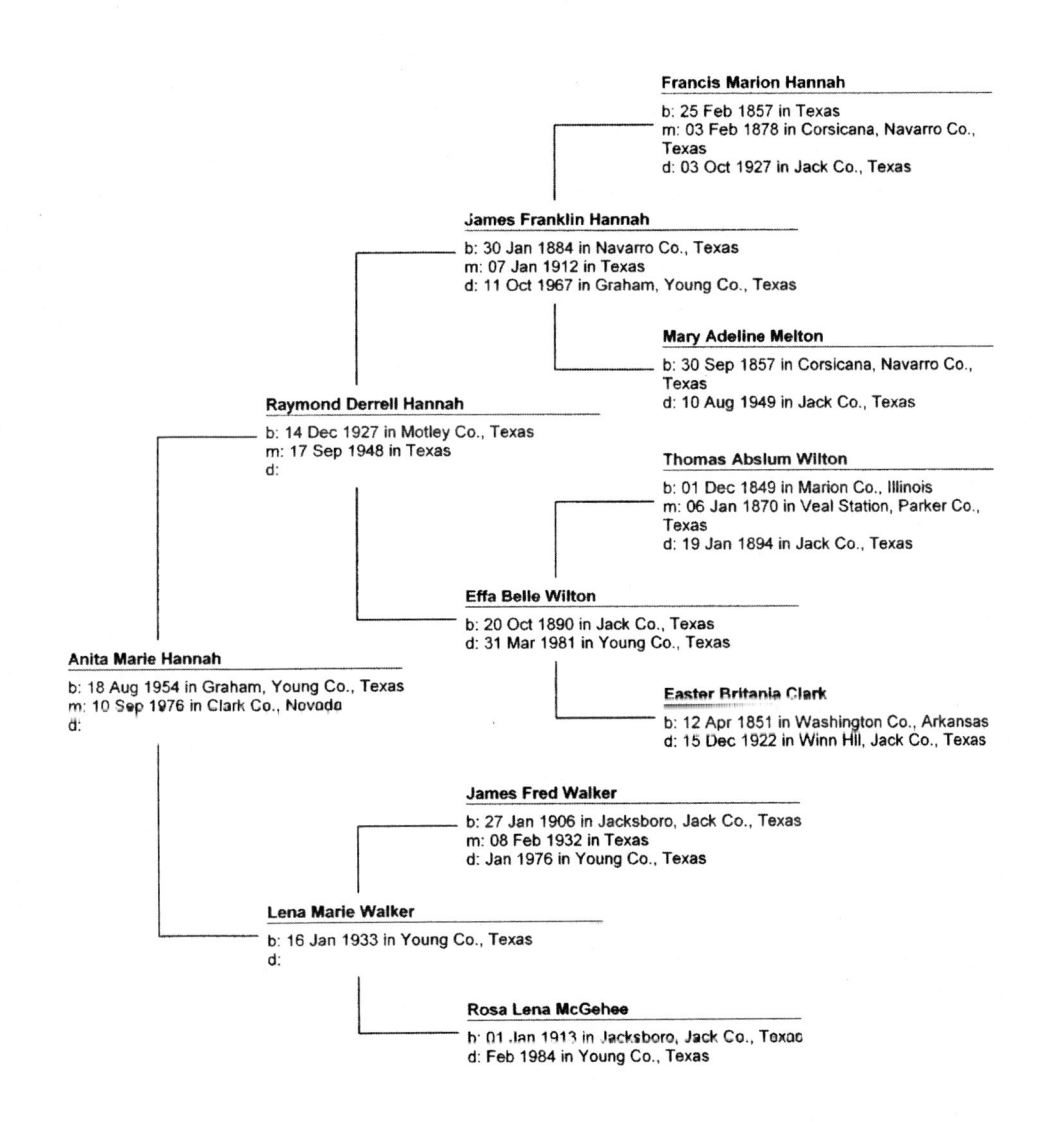

Anita Marie Hannah
b: 18 Aug 1954 in Graham, Young Co., Texas
m: 10 Sep 1976 in Clark Co., Nevada
d:

- **Raymond Derrell Hannah**
  b: 14 Dec 1927 in Motley Co., Texas
  m: 17 Sep 1948 in Texas
  d:

  - **James Franklin Hannah**
    b: 30 Jan 1884 in Navarro Co., Texas
    m: 07 Jan 1912 in Texas
    d: 11 Oct 1967 in Graham, Young Co., Texas

    - **Francis Marion Hannah**
      b: 25 Feb 1857 in Texas
      m: 03 Feb 1878 in Corsicana, Navarro Co., Texas
      d: 03 Oct 1927 in Jack Co., Texas

    - **Mary Adeline Melton**
      b: 30 Sep 1857 in Corsicana, Navarro Co., Texas
      d: 10 Aug 1949 in Jack Co., Texas

  - **Effa Belle Wilton**
    b: 20 Oct 1890 in Jack Co., Texas
    d: 31 Mar 1981 in Young Co., Texas

    - **Thomas Abslum Wilton**
      b: 01 Dec 1849 in Marion Co., Illinois
      m: 06 Jan 1870 in Veal Station, Parker Co., Texas
      d: 19 Jan 1894 in Jack Co., Texas

    - **Easter Britania Clark**
      b: 12 Apr 1851 in Washington Co., Arkansas
      d: 15 Dec 1922 in Winn Hil, Jack Co., Texas

- **Lena Marie Walker**
  b: 16 Jan 1933 in Young Co., Texas
  d:

  - **James Fred Walker**
    b: 27 Jan 1906 in Jacksboro, Jack Co., Texas
    m: 08 Feb 1932 in Texas
    d: Jan 1976 in Young Co., Texas

  - **Rosa Lena McGehee**
    b: 01 Jan 1913 in Jacksboro, Jack Co., Texas
    d: Feb 1984 in Young Co., Texas

Notes: This Tree also applies to the other children of Raymond Derrell Hannah & Lena Marie Walker: Derrell Lynn Hannah & Leslie Jean Hannah

James Eldon Hannah (1930-1984)
[6th. Generation from Henry Wilton (1769-1820)]

&

Jo Evelyn Cumpton (1929-   )
& Family

James Eldon Hannah, born February 1930 in Berwick, Texas, was the sixth child of Effa (Effie) Belle Wilton and James Franklin Hannah. Shortly after their marriage in 1912, Effie Belle and James Franklin settled their family in the Winn Hill Community of Jack County, Texas. After moves to Knox County in 1920 and Motley County in 1923, the family resettled back in Jack County, Texas, by 1928. James Eldon was born in Berwick in Jack County, Texas in 1930, and by 1931 the family began living in Berwick, where James Franklin occupied his share of his late father's estate. Later, in 1948, the family resettled permanently in Graham in Young County, Texas.

James Eldon married Jo Evelyn Cumpton, daughter of Joseph Herman Cumpton and Bertha Evelyn Dodson, who were also residents of Young County, on May 3, 1949. James and Jo Evelyn made their home in Graham in Young County, where James was employed as a building contractor. His other interests included tending cattle and horses, hunting and trout fishing in Colorado, and spending time with the grandchildren.

James and Jo Evelyn had one child, a son named Eldon Ray Hannah, born March 13, 1952. James Eldon died August 1984 from cancer and was buried in the Pioneer Cemetery of Graham, Texas.

Family Group Sheet

Husband: James Eldon Hannah	
Born: 28 Feb 1930	in: Berwick, Jack Co., Texas
Married: 03 May 1949	in: Texas
Died: 02 Aug 1984	in: Graham, Young Co., Texas
Father: James Franklin Hannah	
Mother: Effa Belle Wilton	

Wife: Jo Evelyn Cumpton	
Born: 14 Sep 1929	in: Jean, Young Co., Texas
Father: Joseph Herman Cumpton	
Mother: Bertha Evelyn Dodson	

CHILDREN

1 M
- Name: Eldon Ray Hannah
- Born: 13 Mar 1952 — in: Young Co., Texas
- Married: 01 Dec 1973 — in: Young Co., Texas
- Spouse: Judy Marie Whitson

JO EVELYN CUMPTON Standard Pedigree Tree

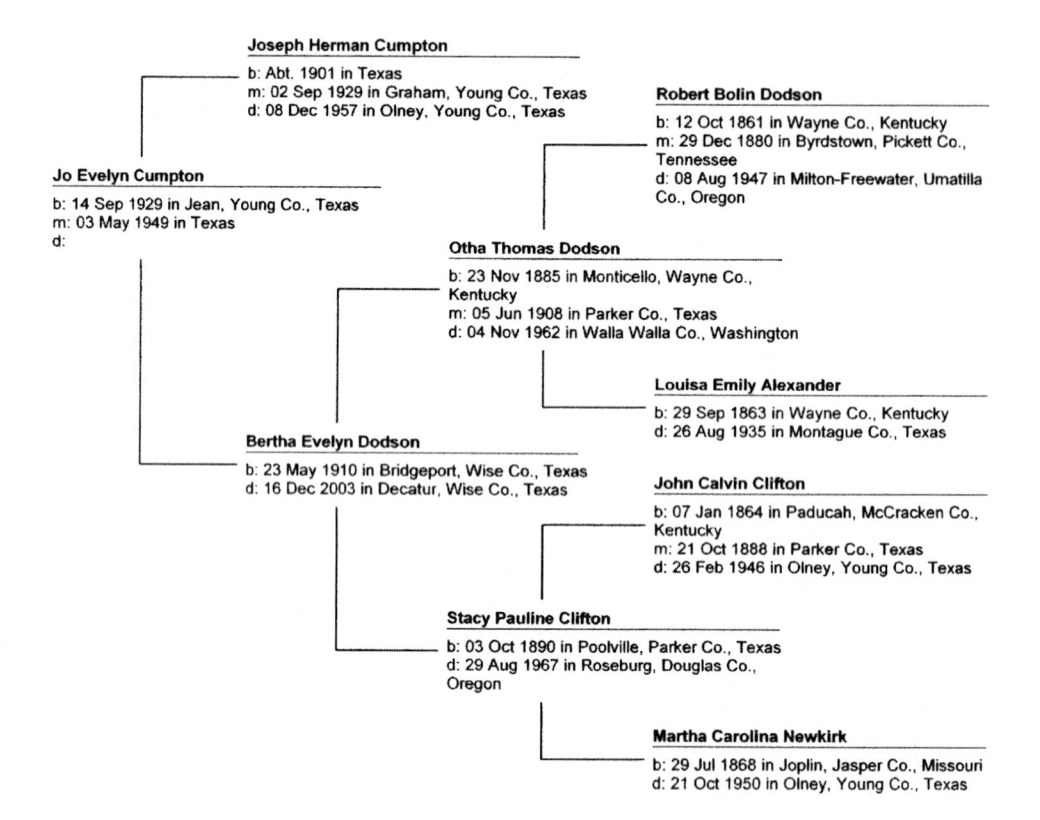

Jo Evelyn Cumpton
b: 14 Sep 1929 in Jean, Young Co., Texas
m: 03 May 1949 in Texas
d:

Joseph Herman Cumpton
b: Abt. 1901 in Texas
m: 02 Sep 1929 in Graham, Young Co., Texas
d: 08 Dec 1957 in Olney, Young Co., Texas

Bertha Evelyn Dodson
b: 23 May 1910 in Bridgeport, Wise Co., Texas
d: 16 Dec 2003 in Decatur, Wise Co., Texas

Otha Thomas Dodson
b: 23 Nov 1885 in Monticello, Wayne Co., Kentucky
m: 05 Jun 1908 in Parker Co., Texas
d: 04 Nov 1962 in Walla Walla Co., Washington

Stacy Pauline Clifton
b: 03 Oct 1890 in Poolville, Parker Co., Texas
d: 29 Aug 1967 in Roseburg, Douglas Co., Oregon

Robert Bolin Dodson
b: 12 Oct 1861 in Wayne Co., Kentucky
m: 29 Dec 1880 in Byrdstown, Pickett Co., Tennessee
d: 08 Aug 1947 in Milton-Freewater, Umatilla Co., Oregon

Louisa Emily Alexander
b: 29 Sep 1863 in Wayne Co., Kentucky
d: 26 Aug 1935 in Montague Co., Texas

John Calvin Clifton
b: 07 Jan 1864 in Paducah, McCracken Co., Kentucky
m: 21 Oct 1888 in Parker Co., Texas
d: 26 Feb 1946 in Olney, Young Co., Texas

Martha Carolina Newkirk
b: 29 Jul 1868 in Joplin, Jasper Co., Missouri
d: 21 Oct 1950 in Olney, Young Co., Texas

Eldon Ray Hannah (1952-   )
[7th. Generation from Henry Wilton (1769-1820)]

&

Judy Marie Whitson (1955-   )
& Family

Family Group Sheet

Husband: Eldon Ray Hannah

Born: 13 Mar 1952 — in: Young Co., Texas
Married: 01 Dec 1973 — in: Young Co., Texas
Father: James Eldon Hannah
Mother: Jo Evelyn Cumpton

Wife: Judy Marie Whitson

Born: 21 Jun 1955 — in: Wichita Co., Texas
Father: Horace Edwin Whitson
Mother: Edna Lorene Dipprey

CHILDREN

1 F — Name: Crystal Lynn Hannah
Born: 28 Jun 1978 — in: Wichita Co., Texas

2 F — Name: Ashley Renee Hannah
Born: 17 Mar 1983 — in: Young Co., Texas

3 M — Name: Brian Kurt Hannah
Born: 01 Apr 1985 — in: Wichita Co., Texas

JUDY MARIE WHITSON Standard Pedigree Tree

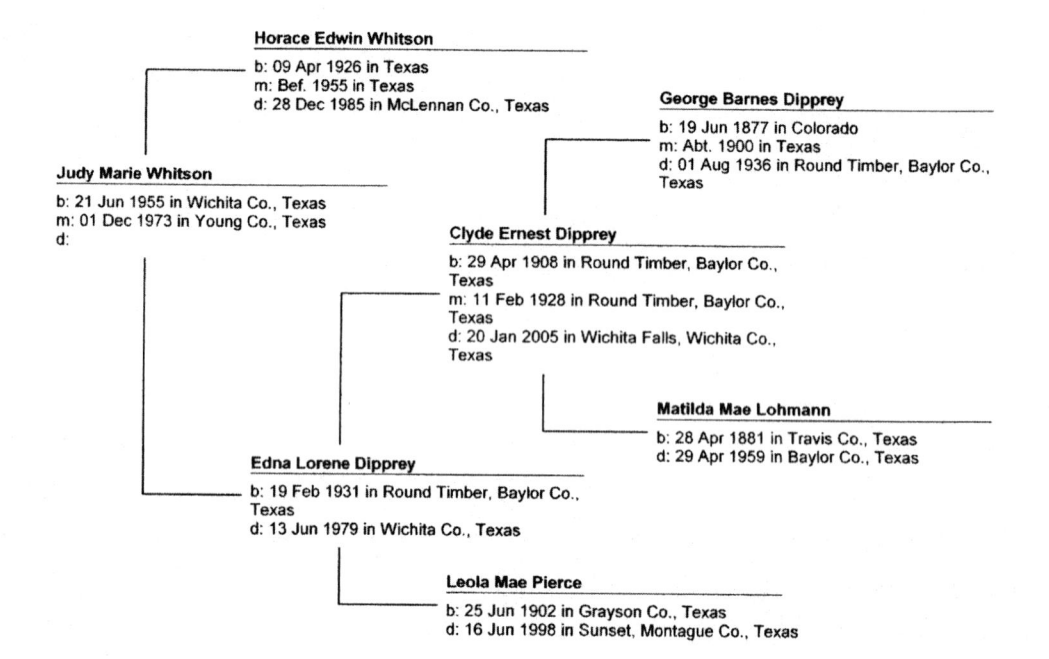

Horace Edwin Whitson
b: 09 Apr 1926 in Texas
m: Bef. 1955 in Texas
d: 28 Dec 1985 in McLennan Co., Texas

George Barnes Dipprey
b: 19 Jun 1877 in Colorado
m: Abt. 1900 in Texas
d: 01 Aug 1936 in Round Timber, Baylor Co., Texas

Judy Marie Whitson
b: 21 Jun 1955 in Wichita Co., Texas
m: 01 Dec 1973 in Young Co., Texas
d:

Clyde Ernest Dipprey
b: 29 Apr 1908 in Round Timber, Baylor Co., Texas
m: 11 Feb 1928 in Round Timber, Baylor Co., Texas
d: 20 Jan 2005 in Wichita Falls, Wichita Co., Texas

Matilda Mae Lohmann
b: 28 Apr 1881 in Travis Co., Texas
d: 29 Apr 1959 in Baylor Co., Texas

Edna Lorene Dipprey
b: 19 Feb 1931 in Round Timber, Baylor Co., Texas
d: 13 Jun 1979 in Wichita Co., Texas

Leola Mae Pierce
b: 25 Jun 1902 in Grayson Co., Texas
d: 16 Jun 1998 in Sunset, Montague Co., Texas

Johnie Melvin Wilton (1892-1944)
[5th. Generation from Henry Wilton (1769-1820)]

&

Jessie Earl Newman (1889-1973)
& Family

Johnie Melvin Wilton, born November 13, 1892 at Winn Hill in Jack County, Texas, was the twelfth, and last, child of Thomas Abslum Wilton & Easter Britania Clark. The family had settled permanently in the Winn Hill Community since about 1880.

In 1894, Johnie's father, Thomas Abslum Wilton, died, and his mother, Easter Britania (Clark) Wilton, took on the responsibility of raising the family that was still at home. In the 1900 Federal Census of Jack County, Texas, John (Johnie) M. was listed at age 7, along with his mother, one brother, and three of his sisters. In the 1910 Federal Census of Jack County, John M. was listed at age 17, along with his mother, one brother, and two of his sisters. By 1910, both Johnie and his brother, Benjamin Harrison Wilton, were still at home and involved in farming.

In December 1913, Johnie married Jessie Earl Newman, daughter of Sam Newman & Mary Hannah, who were also residents of Jack County. Shortly after their marriage, Johnie and Jessie Earl moved from Winn Hill to the vicinity of Jermyn, Texas, where Johnie worked at the G.T. & W. Railroad roundhouse located at Jermyn. At the time of his registration for the WWI draft in June 1917, Johnie listed his occupation as a "car repairer" for the railroad.

In the 1920 Federal Census of Jack County, Johnie was listed at age 26 with an occupation of railroad carpenter, along with his wife and two children, Melvin, age 4, and Cecil, age 3. While living in Jermyn in Jack County, Texas, Johnie and Jessie Earl had most of their seven children, and in the 1930 Federal Census of Jack County,

John was listed at age 37 with the same occupation of railroad shop carpenter, along with his wife and four children. One childen, Elbert Claud Wilton, died in infancy in 1923. Johnie & Jessie Earl also had a set of twins, Melba Louis Wilton and John M. Wilton, born October 31, 1930 in Jacksboro, Texas. One of the twins, John M. Wilton, died in infancy.

Johnie Melvin died September 1944 in Young County, Texas, and Jessie Earl died November 1973 in Jack County, Texas. They were both buried at the Winn Hill Cemetery.

Family Group Sheet

Husband: Johnie Melvin Wilton

Born: 13 Nov 1892 in: Winn Hill, Jack Co., Texas
Married: 30 Dec 1913 in: Jacksboro, Jack Co., Texas
Died: 15 Sep 1944 in: Graham, Young Co., Texas
Father: Thomas Abslum Wilton
Mother: Easter Britania Clark

Wife: Jessie Earl Newman

Born: 22 Jul 1889 in: Kerens, Navarro Co., Texas
Died: 14 Nov 1973 in: Jacksboro, Jack Co., Texas
Father: Sam Sr. Newman
Mother: Mary Hannah

CHILDREN

1 M
Name: Melvin Wayman Wilton
Born: 04 Jan 1915 in: Winn Hill, Jack Co., Texas
Died: 03 Mar 1985 in: Olney, Young Co., Texas
Married: 30 Nov 1933 in: Bridgeport, Wise Co., Texas
Spouse: Thelma Mae Sheppard

2 M
Name: Cecil Winfred Wilton
Born: 09 Jun 1916 in: Jermyn, Jack Co., Texas
Died: 30 Jul 1986 in: Aztec, San Juan Co., New Mexico
Married: 1951
Spouse: Mary Hoskins

3 M
Name: Elbert Claud Wilton
Born: 14 Feb 1922 in: Jermyn, Jack Co., Texas
Died: 22 Feb 1923 in: Jermyn, Jack Co., Texas

4 M
Name: Lloyd Orville Wilton
Born: 10 Apr 1924 in: Jermyn, Jack Co., Texas
Died: 25 Jul 1980 in: Ft. Worth, Tarrant Co., Texas
Married: 1951 in: Texas
Spouse: Iris Wynona Hall

5 F
Name: Wilma Fostine Wilton
Born: 22 Nov 1925 in: Jermyn, Jack Co., Texas
Died: 30 Dec 2008 in: Wichita Falls, Wichita Co., Texas
Married: 03 Jul 1947 in: Jermyn, Jack Co., Texas
Spouse: Jack Franklin Fry

6 F
Name: Melba Louise Wilton
Born: 31 Oct 1930 in: Jacksboro, Jack Co., Texas
Married: 1949
Spouse: Leland Stanford Cole
Married: 1963 in: Texas
Spouse: Jesse T. Lebow

7 M
Name: John M. Wilton
Born: 31 Oct 1930 in: Jacksboro, Jack Co., Texas
Died: 1930 in: Jack Co., Texas

JESSIE EARL NEWMAN Standard Pedigree Tree

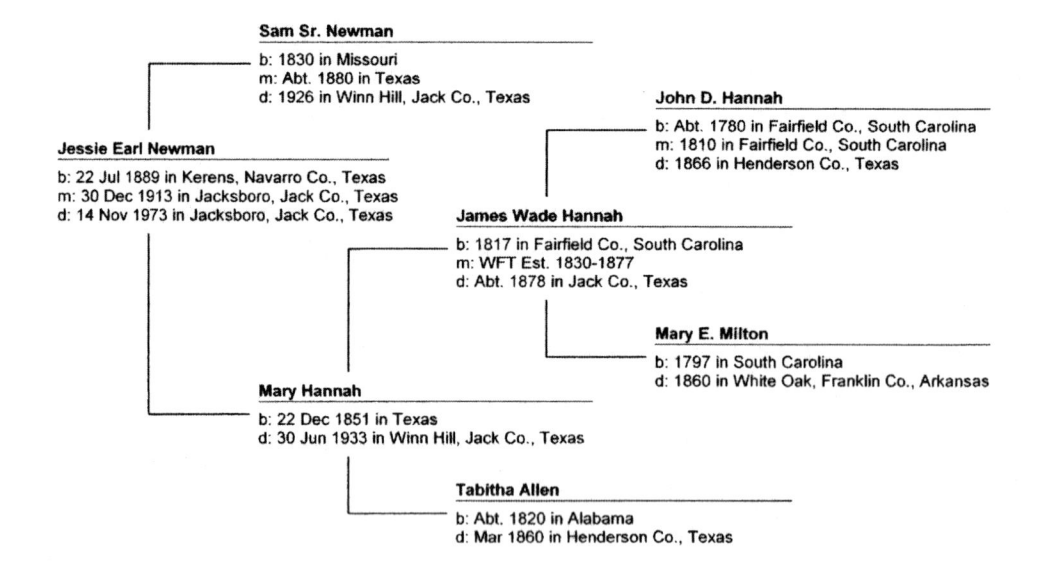

Sam Sr. Newman
b: 1830 in Missouri
m: Abt. 1880 in Texas
d: 1926 in Winn Hill, Jack Co., Texas

Jessie Earl Newman
b: 22 Jul 1889 in Kerens, Navarro Co., Texas
m: 30 Dec 1913 in Jacksboro, Jack Co., Texas
d: 14 Nov 1973 in Jacksboro, Jack Co., Texas

John D. Hannah
b: Abt. 1780 in Fairfield Co., South Carolina
m: 1810 in Fairfield Co., South Carolina
d: 1866 in Henderson Co., Texas

James Wade Hannah
b: 1817 in Fairfield Co., South Carolina
m: WFT Est. 1830-1877
d: Abt. 1878 in Jack Co., Texas

Mary E. Milton
b: 1797 in South Carolina
d: 1860 in White Oak, Franklin Co., Arkansas

Mary Hannah
b: 22 Dec 1851 in Texas
d: 30 Jun 1933 in Winn Hill, Jack Co., Texas

Tabitha Allen
b: Abt. 1820 in Alabama
d: Mar 1860 in Henderson Co., Texas

Melvin Wayman Wilton (1915-1985)
[6th. Generation from Henry Wilton (1769-1820)]

&

Thelma Mae Sheppard (1914-1997)
& Family

Melvin Wayman (Ted) Wilton, the oldest child of Johnie Melvin Wilton and Jessie Earl Newman, was born January 4, 1915 at Winn Hill in Jack County, Texas. Sometime shortly after Johnie Melvin and Jessie Earl were married in 1913, the family settled on a farm north of Jermyn in Jack County, Texas. Johnie's main reason for the move was to be near the G.T. & W. Railroad roundhouse in Jermyn, where he was employed as a carpenter.

Melvin Wayman spent most of his life in Jermyn, Texas. In his earlier years, he regularly walked the nearly two miles from his home to attend the school at Jermyn. In November 1933, he married Thelma Mae Sheppard, daughter of Orzo Sheppard and Daisy Retta Allen. Thelma was born and raised at Willow Point in Wise County, the adjacent county to the east of Jack County. After Melvin and Thelma were married at Bridgeport in Wise County, they moved to Jermyn and settled permanently on their own farm.

When the G.T. & W. Railroad ceased operations in Jermyn in 1939, Melvin worked for awhile as a farmer, but shortly thereafter, changed jobs to an oil field worker. That remained his occupation until he retired in the mid-1970's. Although retired, Melvin still worked part-time pumping a couple of oil wells regularly, and he loved working in his garden. Thelma was a stay-at-home mom.

Melvin and Thelma raised two children while living at Jermyn. The older daughter, Margie Nell Wilton, was born October 1936; and the younger son, Cecil Don Wilton, was born September

1940. Melvin and Thelma enjoyed over fifty years of married life at Jermyn, celebrating their 50th wedding anniversary in October 1983. Melvin died March 1985, while Thelma died March 1997 from injuries resulting from a car accident. They were both buried at the Graceland Cemetery in Jermyn, Texas.

Family Group Sheet

Husband: Melvin Wayman Wilton

Born: 04 Jan 1915 in: Winn Hill, Jack Co., Texas
Married: 30 Nov 1933 in: Bridgeport, Wise Co., Texas
Died: 03 Mar 1985 in: Olney, Young Co., Texas
Father: Johnie Melvin Wilton
Mother: Jessie Earl Newman

Wife: Thelma Mae Sheppard

Born: 05 Feb 1914 in: Willow Point, Wise Co., Texas
Died: 24 Mar 1997 in: Wichita Falls, Texas
Father: Ozro Sr. Sheppard
Mother: Daisy Retta Allen

CHILDREN

1 F
Name: Margie Nell Wilton
Born: 05 Oct 1936 in: Jermyn, Jack Co., Texas
Married: 26 Jul 1968 in: Wichita Falls, Wichita Co., Texas
Spouse: Ronald Dale Harbour

2 M
Name: Cecil Don Wilton
Born: 11 Sep 1940 in: Jacksboro, Jack Co., Texas
Married: 21 Nov 1959 in: Graham, Young Co., Texas
Spouse: Barbara Lynn Souther

MELVIN WAYMAN WILTON Standard Pedigree Tree

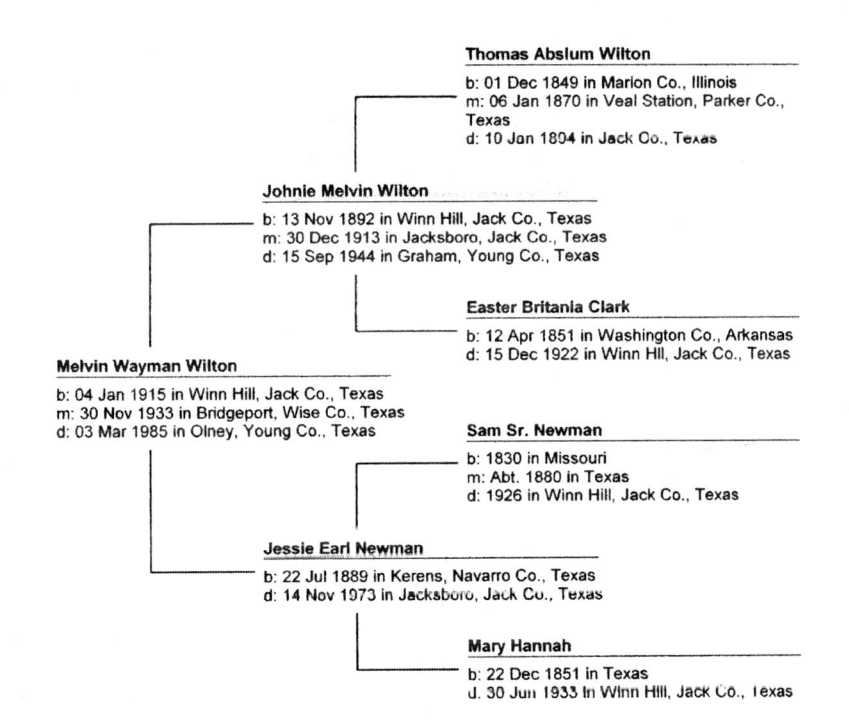

Thomas Abslum Wilton
b: 01 Dec 1849 in Marion Co., Illinois
m: 06 Jan 1870 in Veal Station, Parker Co., Texas
d: 10 Jan 1804 in Jack Co., Texas

Johnie Melvin Wilton
b: 13 Nov 1892 in Winn Hill, Jack Co., Texas
m: 30 Dec 1913 in Jacksboro, Jack Co., Texas
d: 15 Sep 1944 in Graham, Young Co., Texas

Easter Britania Clark
b: 12 Apr 1851 in Washington Co., Arkansas
d: 15 Dec 1922 in Winn Hill, Jack Co., Texas

Melvin Wayman Wilton
b: 04 Jan 1915 in Winn Hill, Jack Co., Texas
m: 30 Nov 1933 in Bridgeport, Wise Co., Texas
d: 03 Mar 1985 in Olney, Young Co., Texas

Sam Sr. Newman
b: 1830 in Missouri
m: Abt. 1880 in Texas
d: 1926 in Winn Hill, Jack Co., Texas

Jessie Earl Newman
b: 22 Jul 1889 in Kerens, Navarro Co., Texas
d: 14 Nov 1973 in Jacksboro, Jack Co., Texas

Mary Hannah
b: 22 Dec 1851 in Texas
d: 30 Jun 1933 in Winn Hill, Jack Co., Texas

Notes: This Tree also applies to the other children of Johnie Melvin Wilton & Jessie Earl Newman: Cecil Winfred Wilton, Elbert Claud Wilton, Lloyd Orville Wilton, Wilma Fasline Wilton, Melba Louise Wilton, and John M. Wilton.

THELMA MAE SHEPPARD Standard Pedigree Tree

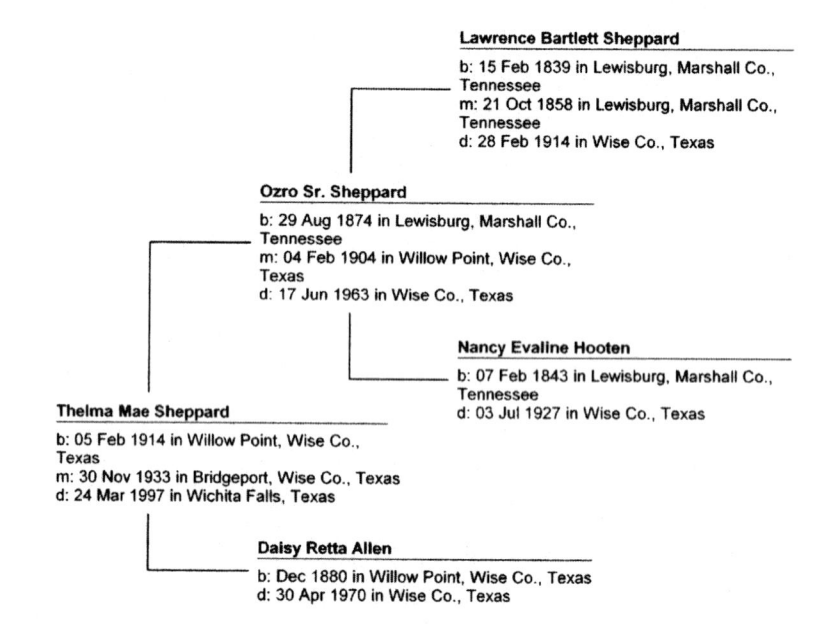

Lawrence Bartlett Sheppard
b: 15 Feb 1839 in Lewisburg, Marshall Co., Tennessee
m: 21 Oct 1858 in Lewisburg, Marshall Co., Tennessee
d: 28 Feb 1914 in Wise Co., Texas

Ozro Sr. Sheppard
b: 29 Aug 1874 in Lewisburg, Marshall Co., Tennessee
m: 04 Feb 1904 in Willow Point, Wise Co., Texas
d: 17 Jun 1963 in Wise Co., Texas

Nancy Evaline Hooten
b: 07 Feb 1843 in Lewisburg, Marshall Co., Tennessee
d: 03 Jul 1927 in Wise Co., Texas

Thelma Mae Sheppard
b: 05 Feb 1914 in Willow Point, Wise Co., Texas
m: 30 Nov 1933 in Bridgeport, Wise Co., Texas
d: 24 Mar 1997 in Wichita Falls, Texas

Daisy Retta Allen
b: Dec 1880 in Willow Point, Wise Co., Texas
d: 30 Apr 1970 in Wise Co., Texas

Margie Nell Wilton (1936-   )
[7th. Generation from Henry Wilton (1769-1820)]

&

Ronald Dale Harbour (1938-1979)
& Family

Margie Nell Wilton, born October 1936 in Jermyn, Texas, was the older child of Melvin Wayman (Ted) Wilton & Thelma Mae Sheppard. Ted had spent most of his early years in Jermyn, located in Jack County, Texas, and when he and Thelma were married in 1933, they also made Jermyn their permanent home. As a result, Margie also spent her early years in Jermyn, where she began her education at the Jermyn school. Margie remembered her years at the Jermyn school fondly, where she was taught values and skills that served her well for the rest of her life.

When the G.T.& W. Railroad closed its operation in Jermyn in 1939, the Jermyn school began a process of consolidating with the Bryson school. After completing grades one thru six at Jermyn, Margie was then bussed to the Bryson school for grades 7 thru high school. The adjustment to the larger school at Bryson was difficult, but she worked hard through high school and was the valedictorian of her senior class. She also received a four-year tuition scholarship to Midwestern University in Wichita Falls, Texas to continue her education.

After earning a B.S. and Masters degrees at Midwestern, Margie did further graduate work at Abilene Christian University, Texas Christian University, and Texas Tech University, in Texas, and Claremont Graduate School, in California. While at Midwestern University, she was a member of Alpha Chi and was chosen for "Who's Who in American Universities and Colleges."

After completing her formal education, Margie earned a teaching certificate in history and government, and she began a teaching career. She taught in public school in Stamford, Burkburnett, Windthorst, and Wichita Falls, Texas. Then, for a number of years she taught at the Academy of Mary Immaculate and Notre Dame High School in Wichita Falls. At the college level she also taught history and government at Midwestern State University, Cisco Junior College in Cisco, Texas, and Ranger College in Graham, Texas.

On July 26, 1968, Margie married Ronald Dale Harbour, son of Clarence Harbour and Nora Proctor, and they made Wichita Falls, Texas, their home. Together, they had one son, Lomand Britt Harbour, who was born September 1970 in Wichita Falls, Texas. Tragically, her husband died in April 1979 as a result of a tornado that struck Wichita Falls. Margie retired from teaching in 1998 but continued to live in Wichita Falls, where she was active in her church, acted as a tutor at two elementary schools, and spent time ministering to the sick, bereaved, and needy.

Family Group Sheet

Husband: Ronald Dale Harbour

Born: 20 Nov 1938 — in: Ringling, Jefferson Co., Oklahoma
Married: 26 Jul 1968 — in: Wichita Falls, Wichita Co., Texas
Died: 10 Apr 1979 — in: Wichita Falls, Wichita Co., Texas
Father: Clarence A. Harbour
Mother: Nora Proctor

Wife: Margie Nell Wilton

Born: 05 Oct 1936 — in: Jermyn, Jack Co., Texas
Father: Melvin Wayman Wilton
Mother: Thelma Mae Sheppard

CHILDREN

1 M — Name: Lomand Britt Harbour
Born: 17 Sep 1970 — in: Wichita Falls, Wichita Co., Texas

MARGIE NELL WILTON Standard Pedigree Tree

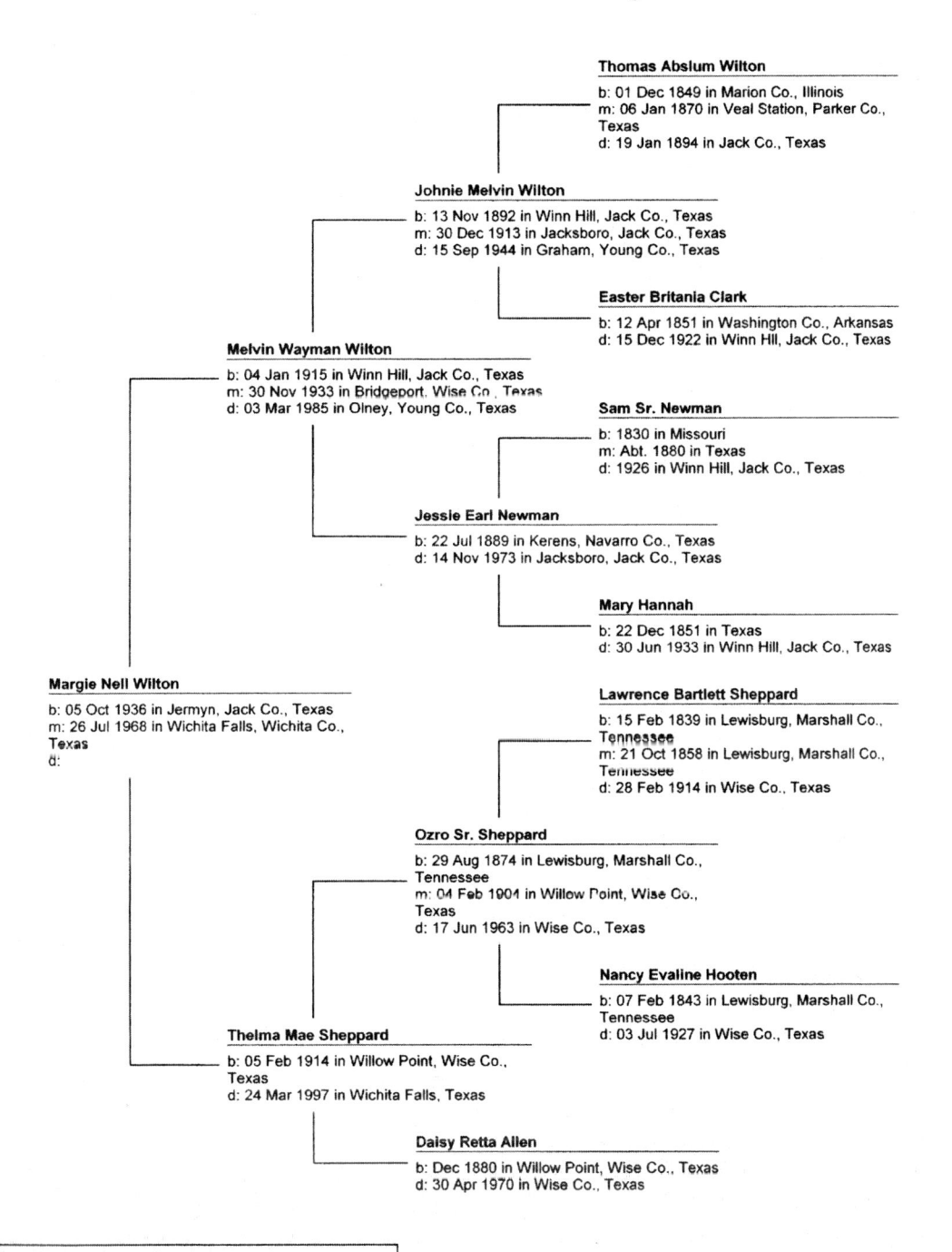

Margie Nell Wilton
b: 05 Oct 1936 in Jermyn, Jack Co., Texas
m: 26 Jul 1968 in Wichita Falls, Wichita Co., Texas
d:

Paternal Line

Melvin Wayman Wilton
b: 04 Jan 1915 in Winn Hill, Jack Co., Texas
m: 30 Nov 1933 in Bridgeport, Wise Co., Texas
d: 03 Mar 1985 in Olney, Young Co., Texas

Johnie Melvin Wilton
b: 13 Nov 1892 in Winn Hill, Jack Co., Texas
m: 30 Dec 1913 in Jacksboro, Jack Co., Texas
d: 15 Sep 1944 in Graham, Young Co., Texas

Thomas Abslum Wilton
b: 01 Dec 1849 in Marion Co., Illinois
m: 06 Jan 1870 in Veal Station, Parker Co., Texas
d: 19 Jan 1894 in Jack Co., Texas

Easter Britania Clark
b: 12 Apr 1851 in Washington Co., Arkansas
d: 15 Dec 1922 in Winn Hill, Jack Co., Texas

Jessie Earl Newman
b: 22 Jul 1889 in Kerens, Navarro Co., Texas
d: 14 Nov 1973 in Jacksboro, Jack Co., Texas

Sam Sr. Newman
b: 1830 in Missouri
m: Abt. 1880 in Texas
d: 1926 in Winn Hill, Jack Co., Texas

Mary Hannah
b: 22 Dec 1851 in Texas
d: 30 Jun 1933 in Winn Hill, Jack Co., Texas

Maternal Line

Thelma Mae Sheppard
b: 05 Feb 1914 in Willow Point, Wise Co., Texas
d: 24 Mar 1997 in Wichita Falls, Texas

Ozro Sr. Sheppard
b: 29 Aug 1874 in Lewisburg, Marshall Co., Tennessee
m: 04 Feb 1904 in Willow Point, Wise Co., Texas
d: 17 Jun 1963 in Wise Co., Texas

Lawrence Bartlett Sheppard
b: 15 Feb 1839 in Lewisburg, Marshall Co., Tennessee
m: 21 Oct 1858 in Lewisburg, Marshall Co., Tennessee
d: 28 Feb 1914 in Wise Co., Texas

Nancy Evaline Hooten
b: 07 Feb 1843 in Lewisburg, Marshall Co., Tennessee
d: 03 Jul 1927 in Wise Co., Texas

Daisy Retta Allen
b: Dec 1880 in Willow Point, Wise Co., Texas
d: 30 Apr 1970 in Wise Co., Texas

Notes: This Tree also applies to the other child of Melvin Wayman Wilton & Thelma Mae Sheppard: Cecil Don Wilton.

Cecil Don Wilton (1940-   )
[7th. Generation from Henry Wilton (1769-1820)]

&

Barbara Lynn Souther (1942-2002)
& Family

Cecil Don Wilton, born September 1940 in Jacksboro in Jack County, Texas, was the younger child of Melvin Wayman (Ted) Wilton & Thelma Mae Sheppard. Cecil Don spent most of his early years in Jermyn in Jack County, Texas, where Ted and Thelma had permanently established their home. Cecil recalled that during his first fifteen years of life, the family lived in a three-room house, and it wasn't until he was a freshman in high school that his dad could afford a better home. Their new house was built just to the west side of the original house, and it was a very special time for the family when they moved into their new home.

After attending his first three grades at the Jermyn school, Cecil began his fourth grade at the Bryson school. The Jermyn school had begun consolidating with the Bryson school after the closing of the G.T. & W. Railroad operations in 1939. Cecil graduated from the Bryson school in May 1959, and then he began working in the oil and gas industry, following the same career path that his father had taken.

In November 1959, Cecil married Barbara Lynn Souther, daughter of Melvin Herman Souther and Bernice Evelyn Boyd. Cecil and Barbara then moved to Wichita Falls, Texas, where Cecil was employed by Dowell, a division of the Dow Chemical Company. While living in Wichita Falls, the couple had their first two children, Marlin Don Wilton, born September 4, 1962, and Cory Wayne Wilton, born November 18, 1965.

Beginning in 1969, the family made a number of moves associated with Don's work. After first being transferred in 1969 to Enid, Oklahoma, Don was again transferred in 1971 to Eureka, Kansas. While in Kansas, Don and Barbara had their third child, a girl, named Lee Ann Wilton, born February 21, 1972. In the same year, 1972, Don was again transferred back to Enid, Oklahoma.

In November 1977, Don left employment with the Dowell Company and took a job with the Bogert Oil & Gas Company, an independent oil and gas operator in Oklahoma. When the Bogert company sold its operations to the Louis Dreyfus Natural Gas Corporation in 1990, Don stayed with the new company and became its operations manager for their Northern Mid-Continent District.

Don's three children, Marlin Don, Cory Wayne, and Lee Ann, all graduated from the Pioneer-Pleasant Vale High School in Enid, Oklahoma, in the years 1981, 1984, and 1990, respectively. After the third child graduated in 1990, Don and Barbara moved the family to Edmond, Oklahoma.

Over the years while Don worked in the oil field, Barbara was a stay-at-home mom. However, she did enjoy taking part-time jobs, which included babysitting, selling jewelry, instructing aerobic dance classes, and training aerobic instructors. Her other interests included cooking, flower arranging, decorating, and her grandchildren. Barbara died April 2002 in Edmond, Oklahoma.

Family Group Sheet

Husband: Cecil Don Wilton

Born: 11 Sep 1940	in: Jacksboro, Jack Co., Texas
Married: 21 Nov 1959	in: Graham, Young Co., Texas
Father: Melvin Wayman Wilton	
Mother: Thelma Mae Sheppard	

Wife: Barbara Lynn Souther

Born: 08 Jan 1942	in: Graham, Young Co., Texas
Died: 24 Apr 2002	in: Edmond, Oklahoma
Father: Melvin Herman Souther	
Mother: Bernice Evelyn Boyd	

CHILDREN

1 M
- Name: Marlin Don Wilton
- Born: 04 Sep 1962 — in: Wichita Falls, Wichita Co., Texas
- Married: 26 May 1984 — in: Greenfield, Blaine Co., Oklahoma
- Spouse: Rose Ann Rhodes

2 M
- Name: Cory Wayne Wilton
- Born: 18 Nov 1965 — in: Wichita Falls, Wichita Co., Texas
- Married: 1989 — in: Oklahoma
- Spouse: Linda May Williamson

3 F
- Name: Lee Ann Wilton
- Born: 21 Feb 1972 — in: Eureka, Greenwood Co., Kansas
- Married: 1992 — in: Oklahoma
- Spouse: Jody Anson Potter

Marlin Don Wilton (1962-   )
[8th. Generation from Henry Wilton (1769-1820)]

&

Rose Ann Rhodes (1962-   )
& Family

Marlin Don Wilton was the oldest child of Cecil Don Wilton and Barbara Lynn Souther, born September 1962 in Wichita Falls, Texas, in Wichita County. Cecil Don and Barbara started their family in Wichita Falls when they were married in 1959, and that was where their first two children were born. Beginning in 1969, the family moved to Oklahoma, where Cecil Don was transferred by his employer.

Marlin Don spent most of his early years in Enid, Oklahoma, and he graduated from the Pioneer-Pleasant Vale High School in Enid in 1981. Following high school, Marlin Don attended the Oklahoma State University (OSU) in Stillwater, Oklahoma, and he graduated in 1985 with a B.S. degree in Petroleum Engineering Technology. He was then employed with the Range Resources Corporation in Oklahoma in Oklahoma City, where he became a Senior Reservoir Engineer.

In May 1984, Marlin Don married Rose Ann Rhodes, making their home in Edmond, Oklahoma. Rose Ann graduated from the Greenfield High School in Greenfield, Oklahoma, in 1980, and she attended Southwestern Oklahoma State University in Weatherford, Oklahoma, where she graduated in 1983 with a B.A. degree in English Education. Later, she worked as a graphic designer and operated her own publishing business.

Residing in Edmond, Oklahoma, Marlin Don and Rose Ann had two children, Jessica Lynn Wilton, born 1990, and Michael Don Wilton, born 1996.

Family Group Sheet

Husband: Marlin Don Wilton

Born: 04 Sep 1962 in: Wichita Falls, Wichita Co., Texas
Married: 26 May 1984 in: Greenfield, Blaine Co., Oklahoma
Father: Cecil Don Wilton
Mother: Barbara Lynn Souther

Wife: Rose Ann Rhodes

Born: Abt. 1962 in: Oklahoma

CHILDREN

1 F — Name: Jessica Lynn Wilton
Born: 1990 in: Oklahoma

2 M — Name: Michael Don Wilton
Born: 1996 in: Oklahoma

MARLIN DON WILTON Standard Pedigree Tree

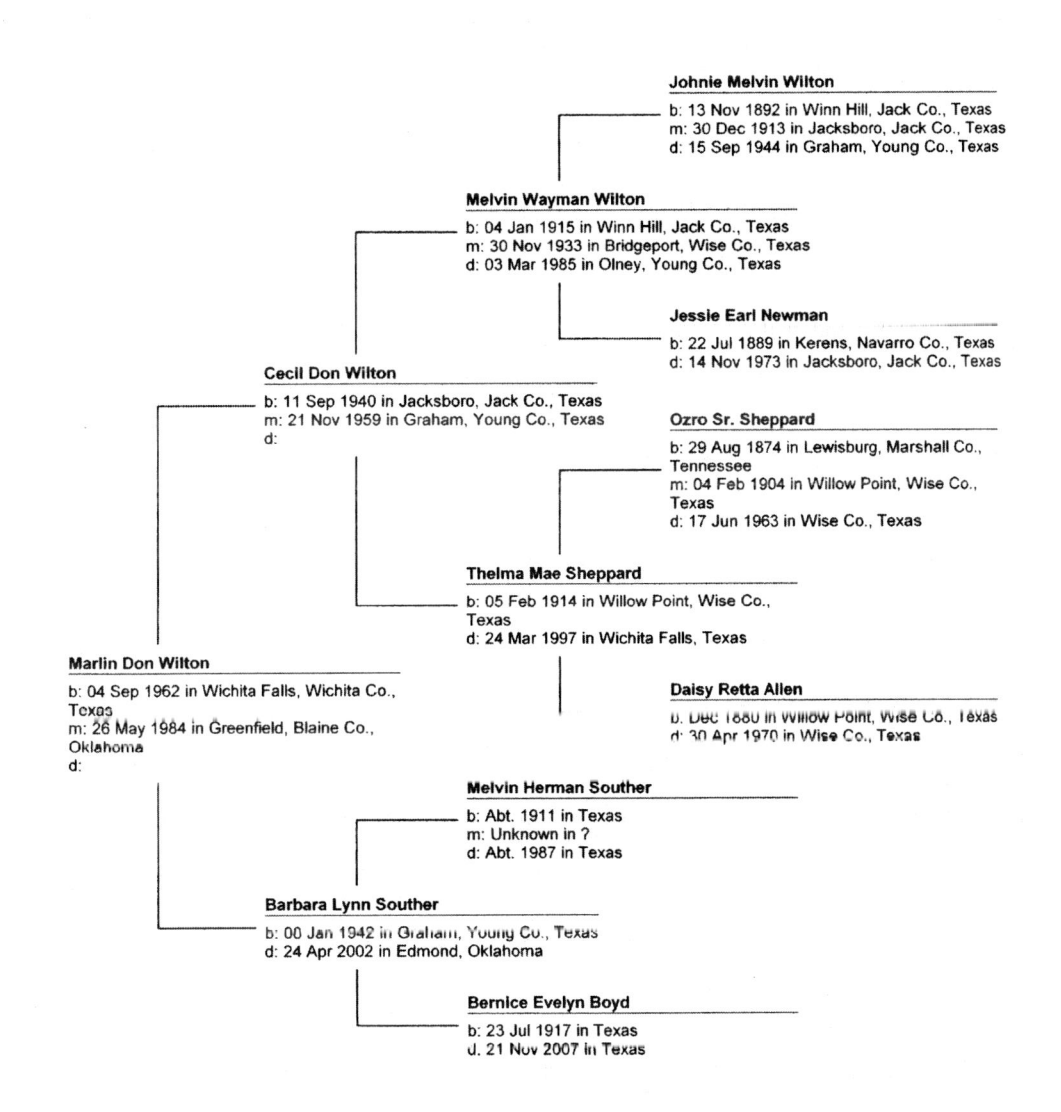

Marlin Don Wilton
b: 04 Sep 1962 in Wichita Falls, Wichita Co., Texas
m: 26 May 1984 in Greenfield, Blaine Co., Oklahoma
d:

- **Cecil Don Wilton**
  b: 11 Sep 1940 in Jacksboro, Jack Co., Texas
  m: 21 Nov 1959 in Graham, Young Co., Texas
  d:

  - **Melvin Wayman Wilton**
    b: 04 Jan 1915 in Winn Hill, Jack Co., Texas
    m: 30 Nov 1933 in Bridgeport, Wise Co., Texas
    d: 03 Mar 1985 in Olney, Young Co., Texas

    - **Johnie Melvin Wilton**
      b: 13 Nov 1892 in Winn Hill, Jack Co., Texas
      m: 30 Dec 1913 in Jacksboro, Jack Co., Texas
      d: 15 Sep 1944 in Graham, Young Co., Texas

    - **Jessie Earl Newman**
      b: 22 Jul 1889 in Kerens, Navarro Co., Texas
      d: 14 Nov 1973 in Jacksboro, Jack Co., Texas

  - **Thelma Mae Sheppard**
    b: 05 Feb 1914 in Willow Point, Wise Co., Texas
    d: 24 Mar 1997 in Wichita Falls, Texas

    - **Ozro Sr. Sheppard**
      b: 29 Aug 1874 in Lewisburg, Marshall Co., Tennessee
      m: 04 Feb 1904 in Willow Point, Wise Co., Texas
      d: 17 Jun 1963 in Wise Co., Texas

    - **Daisy Retta Allen**
      b: Dec 1880 in Willow Point, Wise Co., Texas
      d: 30 Apr 1970 in Wise Co., Texas

- **Barbara Lynn Souther**
  b: 00 Jan 1942 in Graham, Young Co., Texas
  d: 24 Apr 2002 in Edmond, Oklahoma

  - **Melvin Herman Souther**
    b: Abt. 1911 in Texas
    m: Unknown in ?
    d: Abt. 1987 in Texas

  - **Bernice Evelyn Boyd**
    b: 23 Jul 1917 in Texas
    d: 21 Nov 2007 in Texas

Notes: This Tree also applies to the other children of Cecil Don Wilton & Barbara Lynn Souther: Cory Wayne Wilton & Lee Ann Wilton.

Cory Wayne Wilton (1965-   )
[8th. Generation from Henry Wilton (1769-1820)]

&

Linda May Williamson (1966-   )
& Family

Cory Wayne Wilton, the second child of Cecil Don Wilton & Barbara Lynn Souther, was born November 1965 in Wichita Falls, Texas. The family had made Wichita Falls, in Wichita County, Texas, their home since shortly after Cecil Don and Barbara were married in 1959. In 1969, they moved to Oklahoma, where Cecil Don was transferred by his employer.

Spending most of his early years in Enid, Oklahoma, Cory Wayne graduated in 1984, as valedictorian, from the Pioneer-Pleasant Vale High School in Enid. Following high school, he attended the Oklahoma State University (OSU) in Stillwater, Oklahoma, where he served on the President's Leadership Council and was the Vice president of the Kappa Sigma Fraternity. Cory Wayne then attended the Southwestern Oklahoma State University in Weatherford, Oklahoma, where, in 1990, he graduated with a B.S. degree in Pharmacy. Holding the title of Clinical Pharmacy Specialist in Antilipidemia and Anticoagulation, Cory Wayne was employed as a Senior Pharmacist at the Claremore Indian Hospital in Claremore, Oklahoma, where he was also the founder and manager of the Cardiovascular Risk Reduction Clinic.

In 1989, Cory Wayne married Linda May Williamson. Linda graduated from the Claremore High School in Claremore, Oklahoma, in 1984, and then she attended OSU, where she graduated with a B.S. degree in Political Science, in 1988. She then attended Langston University in Langston, Oklahoma, where, in 1992, she received a B.S. degree in Psychology.

Cory and Linda settled in Claremore, Oklahoma with their three children, Brady Don Wilton, born 1992, Bailey May Wilton, born 1995, and Blake Joseph Wilton, born 1997.

Family Group Sheet

Husband: Cory Wayne Wilton	
Born: 18 Nov 1965	in: Wichita Falls, Wichita Co., Texas
Married: 1989	in: Oklahoma
Father: Cecil Don Wilton	
Mother: Barbara Lynn Souther	

Wife: Linda May Williamson	
Born: 1966	in: Oklahoma

CHILDREN

1 M	Name: Brady Don Wilton	
	Born: 1992	in: Oklahoma
2 F	Name: Baily May Wilton	
	Born: 1994	in: Oklahoma
3 M	Name: Blake Joseph Wilton	
	Born: 1997	in: Oklahoma

Lee Anne Wilton (1972-   )
[8th. Generation from Henry Wilton (1769-1820)]

&

Jody Anson Potter (1967-   )
& Family

Lee Ann Wilton, born 1972 in Eureka, Kansas, was the third child of Cecil Don Wilton & Barbara Lynn Souther. The family had first moved from Texas to Enid, Oklahoma, in 1969, where Cecil Don was transferred by his employer. The company then transferred Cecil briefly to Kansas in 1971-1972. While in Kansas, Lee Ann was born, and then the family was transferred back to Enid, Oklahoma, where Lee Ann spent most of her early years.

Lee Ann graduated from the Pioneer-Pleasant Vale High School in Enid, Oklahoma, in 1990. After high school, she first attended the University of Central Oklahoma in Edmond, Oklahoma; and, then she attended the Southwestern Oklahoma State University in Weatherford, Oklahoma, where, in 1977, she graduated with a B.S. degree in Pharmacy. Lee Ann was employed as a pharmacist in Oklahoma City at the St. Anthony's Hospital and the Spectrum Pharmacy.

In 1992, Lee Anne married Jody Anson Potter. Jody graduated from the Newkirk High School in Newkirk, Oklahoma, in 1985; and, then he attended the Central State University in Edmond, Oklahoma, where he received a B.S. degree in Computer Science, in 1990. He was employed by the Database Consultants, Inc. in Oklahoma City, and was an Oracle Database Administrator.

Lee Anne and Jody settled in Edmond, Oklahoma with their daughter, Emily Anne Potter, who was born 2002.

Family Group Sheet

	Husband: Jody Anson Potter	
	Born: May 1967	in: Oklahoma
	Married: 1992	in: Oklahoma

	Wife: Lee Anne Wilton	
	Born: 21 Feb 1972	in: Eureka, Greenwood Co., Kansas
	Father: Cecil Don Wilton	
	Mother: Barbara Lynn Souther	

CHILDREN

1 F	Name: Emily Anne Potter	
	Born: 2002	in: Oklahoma

Lloyd Orville Wilton (1924-1980)
[6th. Generation from Henry Wilton (1769-1820)]

&

Iris Wynona Hall (1929-   )
& Family

Lloyd Orville Wilton, born April 1924 in Jermyn, Texas, was the fourth child of Johnie Melvin Wilton and Jessie Earl Newman. The family had settled in Jermyn in Jack County, Texas shortly after Johnie Melvin and Jessie Earl were married in 1913. At the time of the 1930 Federal Census of Jack County, Lloyd was listed at age 6, along with his parents, two older brothers, Melvin W. Wilton and Cecil W. Wilton, and a younger sister, Wilma F. Wilton.

Lloyd Orvile married Iris Wynona Hall, daughter of Guy Kay Hall and Rebecca May Ice, in 1951, and they settled for some time in Young County, Texas. Lloyd adopted Iris's daughter, born October 1950 in Jacksboro, Texas, naming her Loretta Lynn Wilton. Lloyd Orville and Iris Wynona also had a child together, John Richard Wilton, born June 23, 1954 in Young County, Texas.

Lloyd died July 1980 in Tarrant County, Texas, and he was buried at the Winn Hill Cemetery in Jack County.

Family Group Sheet

Husband: Lloyd Orville Wilton	
Born: 10 Apr 1924	in: Jermyn, Jack Co., Texas
Married: 1951	in: Texas
Died: 25 Jul 1980	in: Ft. Worth, Tarrant Co., Texas
Father: Johnie Melvin Wilton	
Mother: Jessie Earl Newman	

Wife: Iris Wynona Hall	
Born: 23 Jan 1929	in: Wink, Winkler Co., Texas
Father: Guy Kay Hall	
Mother: Rebecca May Ice	

CHILDREN

1. F
   - Name: Loretta Lynn Wilton
   - Born: 30 Oct 1950 — in: Jacksboro, Jack Co., Texas
   - Married: 26 May 1974 — in: Young Co., Texas
   - Spouse: Michael Wayne Pitts
   - Married: 16 Sep 1977 — in: Young Co., Texas
   - Spouse: Larry Dean Henderson

2. M
   - Name: John Richard Wilton
   - Born: 23 Jun 1954 — in: Young Co., Texas
   - Married: 06 Sep 1980 — in: Young Co., Texas
   - Spouse: Jeffie Suzanne Harris

Wilma Fostine Wilton (1925-2008)
[6th. Generation from Henry Wilton (1769-1820)]

&

Jack Franklin Fry (1924-1976)
& Family

Wilma Fostine Wilton was the fifth child of Johnie Melvin Wilton and Jessie Earl Newman, born November 1925 in Jermyn, Texas. The family had made Jermyn in Jack County, Texas their home since about 1913, when Johnie and Jessie were married. In the 1930 Federal Census of Jack County, Wilma F. was listed at age 4, along with her parents and three of her older brothers, Melvin, Cecil, and Lloyd.

Wilma married Jack Franklin Fry, son of David Fry and Betha Spears, on July 3, 1947 in Jermyn, Texas. Wilma and Jack had four children. The first child, David Michael Fry, was born April 10, 1948 in Young County, Texas. Their three daughters, Marsha Karen Fry, Mary Helen Fry, and Molly Daire Fry, born July 1953, February 1956, and February 1958, respectively, were all born in Wichita Falls in Wichita County, Texas. In addition to being a mom, Wilma was also a teacher. Jack's occupation was a mortician. Wilma died December 30, 2008 in Wichita Falls, Texas.

Family Group Sheet

Husband: Jack Franklin Fry

- Born: 30 Jul 1924 in: Shannon, Clay Co., Texas
- Married: 03 Jul 1947 in: Jermyn, Jack Co., Texas
- Died: 01 Jul 1976 in: Scotland, Archer Co., Texas
- Father: David Evander Fry
- Mother: Betha Mahala Spears

Wife: Wilma Fostine Wilton

- Born: 22 Nov 1925 in: Jermyn, Jack Co., Texas
- Died: 30 Dec 2008 in: Wichita Falls, Wichita Co., Texas
- Father: Johnie Melvin Wilton
- Mother: Jessie Earl Newman

CHILDREN

1. M
- Name: David Michael Fry
- Born: 10 Apr 1948 in: Graham, Young Co., Texas
- Married: 20 Jun 1972 in: Wichita Falls, Wichita Co., Texas
- Spouse: Donna Jo Spangler
- Married: 20 Nov 1986 in: Wichita Falls, Wichita Co., Texas
- Spouse: Sherry Annette Shewmake

2. F
- Name: Marsha Karen Fry
- Born: 18 Jul 1953 in: Wichita Falls, Wichita Co., Texas
- Married: 20 Jan 1970
- Spouse: Randall Lee Garner
- Married: 12 Aug 1977 in: Dallas Co., Texas
- Spouse: Gary Lynn Allen
- Married: 10 Aug 1988 in: Tarrant Co., Texas
- Spouse: Vincent Paul Redder

3. F
- Name: Mary Helen Fry
- Born: 23 Feb 1956 in: Wichita Falls, Wichita Co., Texas
- Married: 22 Sep 1973
- Spouse: Johnny Jr. Ojeda
- Married: 13 Jan 1983 in: Wichita Co., Texas
- Spouse: Benjamin Sheppard IV Ferguson

4. F
- Name: Molly Daire Fry
- Born: 14 Feb 1958 in: Wichita Falls, Wichita Co., Texas
- Married: 16 Jan 1982 in: Wichita Co., Texas
- Spouse: Del Duane Britton

JACK FRANKLIN FRY Standard Pedigree Tree

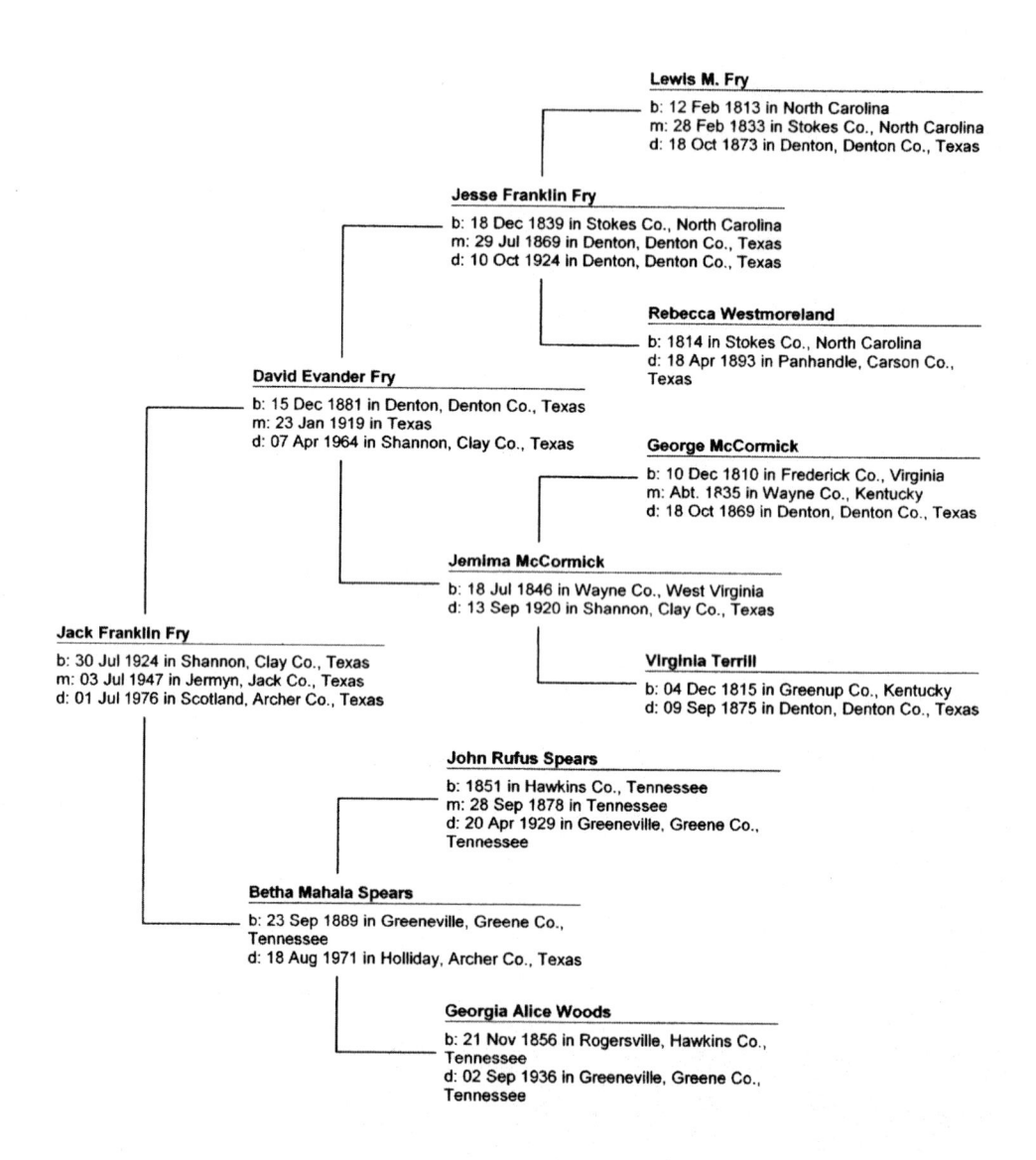

Jack Franklin Fry
b: 30 Jul 1924 in Shannon, Clay Co., Texas
m: 03 Jul 1947 in Jermyn, Jack Co., Texas
d: 01 Jul 1976 in Scotland, Archer Co., Texas

- **David Evander Fry**
  b: 15 Dec 1881 in Denton, Denton Co., Texas
  m: 23 Jan 1919 in Texas
  d: 07 Apr 1964 in Shannon, Clay Co., Texas

  - **Jesse Franklin Fry**
    b: 18 Dec 1839 in Stokes Co., North Carolina
    m: 29 Jul 1869 in Denton, Denton Co., Texas
    d: 10 Oct 1924 in Denton, Denton Co., Texas

    - **Lewis M. Fry**
      b: 12 Feb 1813 in North Carolina
      m: 28 Feb 1833 in Stokes Co., North Carolina
      d: 18 Oct 1873 in Denton, Denton Co., Texas

    - **Rebecca Westmoreland**
      b: 1814 in Stokes Co., North Carolina
      d: 18 Apr 1893 in Panhandle, Carson Co., Texas

  - **Jemima McCormick**
    b: 18 Jul 1846 in Wayne Co., West Virginia
    d: 13 Sep 1920 in Shannon, Clay Co., Texas

    - **George McCormick**
      b: 10 Dec 1810 in Frederick Co., Virginia
      m: Abt. 1835 in Wayne Co., Kentucky
      d: 18 Oct 1869 in Denton, Denton Co., Texas

    - **Virginia Terrill**
      b: 04 Dec 1815 in Greenup Co., Kentucky
      d: 09 Sep 1875 in Denton, Denton Co., Texas

- **Betha Mahala Spears**
  b: 23 Sep 1889 in Greeneville, Greene Co., Tennessee
  d: 18 Aug 1971 in Holliday, Archer Co., Texas

  - **John Rufus Spears**
    b: 1851 in Hawkins Co., Tennessee
    m: 28 Sep 1878 in Tennessee
    d: 20 Apr 1929 in Greeneville, Greene Co., Tennessee

  - **Georgia Alice Woods**
    b: 21 Nov 1856 in Rogersville, Hawkins Co., Tennessee
    d: 02 Sep 1936 in Greeneville, Greene Co., Tennessee

David Michael Fry (1948-   )
[7th. Generation from Henry Wilton (1769-1820)]

&
Donna Jo Spangler (1950-   )
& Family

&
Sherry Annette Shewmake (1946-   )
& Family

Family Group Sheet

Husband: David Michael Fry

Born: 10 Apr 1948   in: Graham, Young Co., Texas
Married: 20 Jun 1972   in: Wichita Falls, Wichita Co., Texas
Father: Jack Franklin Fry
Mother: Wilma Fostine Wilton
Other Spouses: Sherry Annette Shewmake

Wife: Donna Jo Spangler

Born: 12 Jul 1950   in: Wichita Falls, Wichita Co., Texas

CHILDREN

1 F
Name: Calyn Grace Fry
Born: 12 Jan 1976   in: Houston, Harris Co., Texas

2 F
Name: Kathryn Michelle Fry
Born: 26 Jun 1978   in: Houston, Harris Co., Texas

Family Group Sheet

Husband: David Michael Fry

Born: 10 Apr 1948   in: Graham, Young Co., Texas
Married: 20 Nov 1986   in: Wichita Falls, Wichita Co., Texas
Father: Jack Franklin Fry
Mother: Wilma Fostine Wilton
Other Spouses: Donna Jo Spangler

Wife: Sherry Annette Shewmake

Born: 31 Jul 1946   in: Fort Worth, Tarrant Co., Texas
Father: Buster Shewmake
Mother: Dorothy Sherry Crowley

DAVID MICHAEL FRY Standard Pedigree Tree

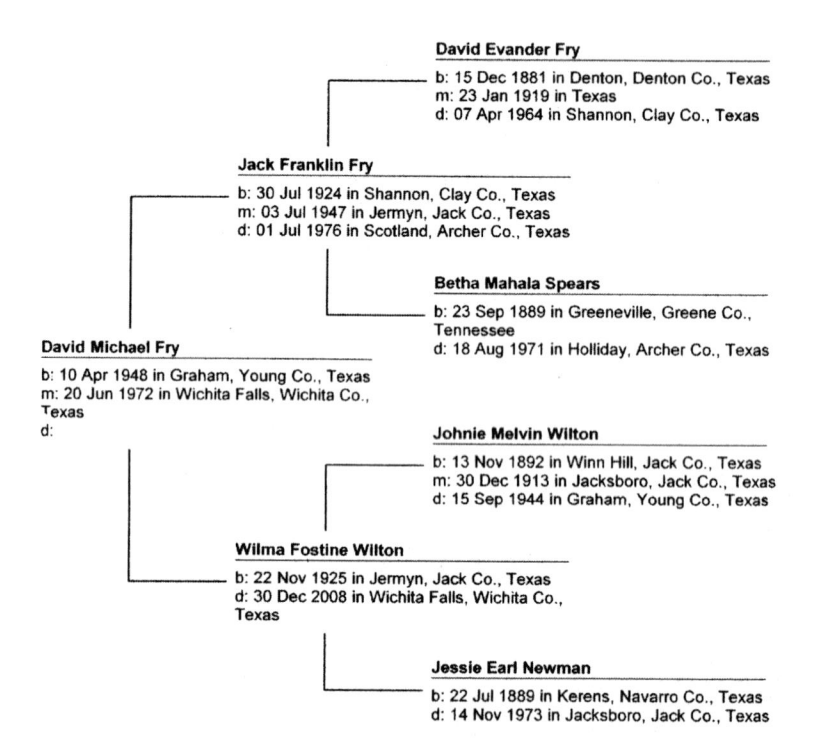

David Michael Fry
b: 10 Apr 1948 in Graham, Young Co., Texas
m: 20 Jun 1972 in Wichita Falls, Wichita Co., Texas
d:

- **Jack Franklin Fry**
  b: 30 Jul 1924 in Shannon, Clay Co., Texas
  m: 03 Jul 1947 in Jermyn, Jack Co., Texas
  d: 01 Jul 1976 in Scotland, Archer Co., Texas
  - **David Evander Fry**
    b: 15 Dec 1881 in Denton, Denton Co., Texas
    m: 23 Jan 1919 in Texas
    d: 07 Apr 1964 in Shannon, Clay Co., Texas
  - **Betha Mahala Spears**
    b: 23 Sep 1889 in Greeneville, Greene Co., Tennessee
    d: 18 Aug 1971 in Holliday, Archer Co., Texas

- **Wilma Fostine Wilton**
  b: 22 Nov 1925 in Jermyn, Jack Co., Texas
  d: 30 Dec 2008 in Wichita Falls, Wichita Co., Texas
  - **Johnie Melvin Wilton**
    b: 13 Nov 1892 in Winn Hill, Jack Co., Texas
    m: 30 Dec 1913 in Jacksboro, Jack Co., Texas
    d: 15 Sep 1944 in Graham, Young Co., Texas
  - **Jessie Earl Newman**
    b: 22 Jul 1889 in Kerens, Navarro Co., Texas
    d: 14 Nov 1973 in Jacksboro, Jack Co., Texas

Notes: This Tree also applies to the other children of Jack Franklin Fry & Wilma Fostine Wilton: Marsha Karen Fry, Mary Helen Fry, and Molly Daire Fry.

Marsha Karen Fry (1953-   )
[7th. Generation from Henry Wilton (1769-1820)]

&
Randall Lee Garner (1948-   )
& Family

&
Gary Lynn Allen (1953-   )
& Family

&
Vincent Paul Redder (1957-   )
& Family

Family Group Sheet

Husband: Randall Lee Garner
Born: Abt. 1948
Married: 20 Jan 1970

Wife: Marsha Karen Fry
Born: 18 Jul 1953   in: Wichita Falls, Wichita Co., Texas
Father: Jack Franklin Fry
Mother: Wilma Fostine Wilton
Other Spouses: Gary Lynn Allen, Vincent Paul Redder

	CHILDREN	
1 F	Name: Holly Karen Garner	
	Born: 01 May 1973	in: Tarrant Co., Texas
2 M	Name: Zachery Franklin Garner	
	Born: 12 Mar 1979	in: Wichita Co., Texas

Family Group Sheet

Husband: Gary Lynn Allen

Born: Abt. 1953
Married: 12 Aug 1977 in: Dallas Co., Texas

Wife: Marsha Karen Fry

Born: 18 Jul 1953 in: Wichita Falls, Wichita Co., Texas
Father: Jack Franklin Fry
Mother: Wilma Fostine Wilton
Other Spouses: Randall Lee Garner, Vincent Paul Redder

Family Group Sheet

Husband: Vincent Paul Redder

Born: 04 Jul 1957 in: Tarrant Co., Texas
Married: 10 Aug 1988 in: Tarrant Co., Texas

Wife: Marsha Karen Fry

Born: 18 Jul 1953 in: Wichita Falls, Wichita Co., Texas
Father: Jack Franklin Fry
Mother: Wilma Fostine Wilton
Other Spouses: Randall Lee Garner, Gary Lynn Allen

CHILDREN

1 F	Name: Hannah Elizabeth Redder Born: 26 May 1993	in: Wichita Co., Texas
2 M	Name: Joseph Albert Redder Born: 15 Oct 1997	in: Wichita Co., Texas

Melba Louise Wilton (1930-   )
[6th. Generation from Henry Wilton (1769-1820)]

&
Leland Stanford Cole (1929-   )
& Family

&
Jesse T. Lebow (1918-   )
& Family

Family Group Sheet

Husband: Leland Stanford Cole

Born: 1929
Married: 1949

Wife: Melba Louise Wilton

Born: 31 Oct 1930   in: Jacksboro, Jack Co., Texas
Father: Johnie Melvin Wilton
Mother: Jessie Earl Newman
    Other Spouses: Jesse T. Lebow

CHILDREN

1 M	Name: David Stanford Cole Born: 26 Dec 1950 in: Wichita Co., Texas Married: 1982 Spouse: Beverly Jean Bruce

Family Group Sheet

Husband: Jesse T. Lebow

Born: May 1918   in: Texas
Married: 1963   in: Texas

Wife: Melba Louise Wilton

Born: 31 Oct 1930   in: Jacksboro, Jack Co., Texas
Father: Johnie Melvin Wilton
Mother: Jessie Earl Newman
    Other Spouses: Leland Stanford Cole

Henry Franklin Wilton (1853-1941)
[4th. Generation From Henry Wilton (1769-1820)]

&

Martha Jane Baldwin (1856-1946)
& Family

Henry Franklin Wilton, born December 1853 in Marion County, Illinois, was the younger of two sons of Charles Freedis Wilton & Susanah Cruse. Charles and Susanah had made their home in Marion County after their marriage in July 1848. Susanah died about 1859, leaving Charles with their two young sons, Thomas A.Wilton, age 10, and Henry Franklin Wilton, only about 6 years old.

Shortly after Susanah (Cruse) Wilton died, about 1859, Charles and his two sons moved to Texas with a larger group, consisting of Charles' brother, Joseph C. Wilton and family, and the family of Absalom Cruse, the father of Susanah (Cruse) Wilton. The group first settled in an area just north of Forth Worth in Tarrant County, Texas, which later became where Lake Worth is located. When the Civil War broke out in 1861, Charles travelled back to Illinois with his older son, Thomas A., to enlist in the war, but he left Henry Franklin in Texas with his relatives.

After spending his formative years in Texas, in 1874, at the age of 21, Henry Franklin went back to Illinois to visit with his Illinois relatives. While in Illinois, he met Martha Jane Baldwin, daughter of Thomas Holland Baldwin & Harriet Tite, who was reported to have said to a friend when she first saw Henry, "That young man is going to be my future husband." Henry Franklin and Martha Jane were married February 15, 1877 in Marion County, Illinois at the home of Martha's sister, Mary (Baldwin) Jones.

Shortly after their marriage, traveling by train, Henry Franklin and Martha Jane moved back to Texas. They first settled for a few years at Veal Station in Parker County, Texas. In the 1880 Federal Census of Parker County, Texas, H.F. (Henry Franklin) Wilton was listed at age 25, along with M.J. (Martha Jane) Wilton and one son, E.V. (Virgil) Wilton, age 1. While living in Parker County, Henry Franklin and Martha Jane had three children, Virgil Wilton, born February 1879, Elmer Elisha Wilton, born December 1881, and Amy Rosalie Wilton, born September 1885.

About 1886, the family moved to the Bumble Bee Prairie Community of Jack County, Texas, where they lived for about three years. Then about 1889, they settled permanently near the Winn Hill Community in Jack County. The remaining three of the family of six children were born between 1889 and 1895. Holland Wilton, the fourth child, born January 1889, died in infancy. The remaining two children were Charles Joseph Wilton, born March 1891, and Mary Alma Wilton, born November 1895. In the 1900 Federal Census of Jack County, Henry (F.) Wilton was listed at age 46, occupation farmer, along with his wife and five of their six children. What came to be known as "the Wilton homeplace" was built on North Creek in 1904 on the Wilton's 380 acre farm and ranch, located about 3 &1/2 miles from Jermyn, Texas and about 12 miles from Jacksboro, Texas. The old Butterfield Trail and Stagecoach route came through their property. The oldest son, Virgil Wilton, died in June 1906 after being kicked by a mule.

Thomas A. Wilton, Henry Franklin's older brother, also settled in the Winn Hill Community, living just three miles away. The next closest Wilton relatives, the family of Joseph C. Wilton, lived in Parker and Tarrant counties, and the families periodically travelled the long distance for visits. Henry Franklin had an especially close connection with Joseph C., a younger brother of

Henry's father, Charles F. Wilton, since their wives were sisters. Sarah Elizabeth (Baldwin) Wilton, wife of Joseph C. Wilton, was an older sister of Martha Jane (Baldwin) Wilton.

In the 1910 Federal Census of Jack County, Henry F. Wilton was listed at age 56, along with his wife and four children. In 1911, Henry's son, Elmer Elisha Wilton, married Eula Mae Rhoades, and Henry sold part of his land to his son, with the two families living in nearby dwellings. In the 1920 Federal Census of Jack County, Henry F. Wilton was listed at age 66, along with his wife and one child, Mary, the youngest. (Elmer) Elisha Wilton was listed in the next dwelling with his wife and family of three children. In the 1930 Federal Census of Jack County, Henry F. Wilton was listed at age 76, along with his wife, Martha J. Wilton, age 73. Again, in the next dwelling was Elmer Wilton, age 45, along with his wife and three children.

Henry Franklin Wilton was described as "a fine man, honest, honorable and...the very best kind of a neighbor." Both Henry and Martha were hard workers and learned how to get along with limited resources. Henry was very inventive, able to make things out of almost nothing. Possibly, he could have been a great inventor if he had the education and financial means. He had very little schooling, and Martha taught him to read after they were married. In his later years, Henry was an avid reader, reading every newspaper, magazine and book he could get his hands on, and he read the Bible through several times. Martha was a good cook and also very resourceful, able to make a good meal out of whatever was on hand. They always had a good garden, and they raised chickens, guineas, turkeys, and hogs. There were also pecan trees along the creek.

Once each year, in the fall, Henry along with several neighbor families, traveled by covered wagon to Weatherford in Parker

County, Texas, to buy their supplies for the next year. This trip took several days, and they ate by the campfire and slept in wagons along the way. They would buy material by the bolt to make shirts for the men and dresses for the women. They also bought provisions, such as sugar, which they could not grow on the farm.

The family belonged to the Methodist Church, and Henry was a member of the Masonic Lodge. He remained on his land, where he raised stock and farmed, until his death, September 4, 1941. Martha Jane died November 9, 1946. They were both buried at the Winn Hill Cemetery in Jack County, Texas.

Family Group Sheet

Husband: Henry Franklin Wilton

Born: 25 Dec 1853	in: Marion Co., Illinois
Married: 15 Feb 1877	in: Home of Mary Jones (Sister of Martha), Marion Co., Illinois
Died: 04 Sep 1941	in: Jermyn, Jack Co., Texas
Father: Charles Freedis Wilton	
Mother: Susanah Cruse	

Wife: Martha Jane Baldwin

Born: 19 Jul 1856	in: Marion Co., Illinois
Died: 09 Nov 1946	in: Jermyn, Jack Co., Texas
Father: Thomas Holland Baldwin	
Mother: Harriet Tite	

CHILDREN

1. M — Name: Virgil Wilton
   - Born: 11 Feb 1879 — in: Parker Co., Texas
   - Died: 13 Jun 1906 — in: Benjamin, Knox Co., Texas

2. M — Name: Elmer Elisha Wilton
   - Born: 17 Dec 1881 — in: Parker Co., Texas
   - Died: 12 Jan 1945 — in: Jacksboro, Jack Co., Texas
   - Married: 26 Feb 1911 — in: Jermyn, Jack Co., Texas
   - Spouse: Eula May Rhoades

3. F — Name: Amy Rosalie Wilton
   - Born: 12 Sep 1884 — in: Springtown, Parker Co., Texas
   - Died: 06 Jun 1958 — in: Jacksboro, Jack Co., Texas
   - Married: 26 Feb 1911 — in: Jermyn, Jack Co., Texas
   - Spouse: Jacob Newton Parrish

4. M — Name: Holland Wilton
   - Born: 25 Jan 1889 — in: Jack Co., Texas
   - Died: 03 Apr 1890 — in: Jack Co., Texas

5. M — Name: Charles Joseph Wilton
   - Born: 12 Mar 1891 — in: Bryson, Jack Co., Texas
   - Died: 28 Sep 1967 — in: Jacksboro, Jack Co., Texas
   - Married: 17 Sep 1913 — in: Jack Co., Texas
   - Spouse: Lona Blanche Parrish
   - Married: 1935 — in: Waurika, Jefferson Co., Oklahoma
   - Spouse: Lydia Ann Evans

6. F — Name: Mary Alma Wilton
   - Born: 23 Nov 1895 — in: Jermyn, Jack Co., Texas
   - Died: 04 Sep 1979 — in: Henderson, Henderson Co., Kentucky
   - Married: 09 Aug 1924 — in: Bryson, Jack Co., Texas
   - Spouse: James Roscoe Reynolds

MARTHA JANE BALDWIN Standard Pedigree Tree

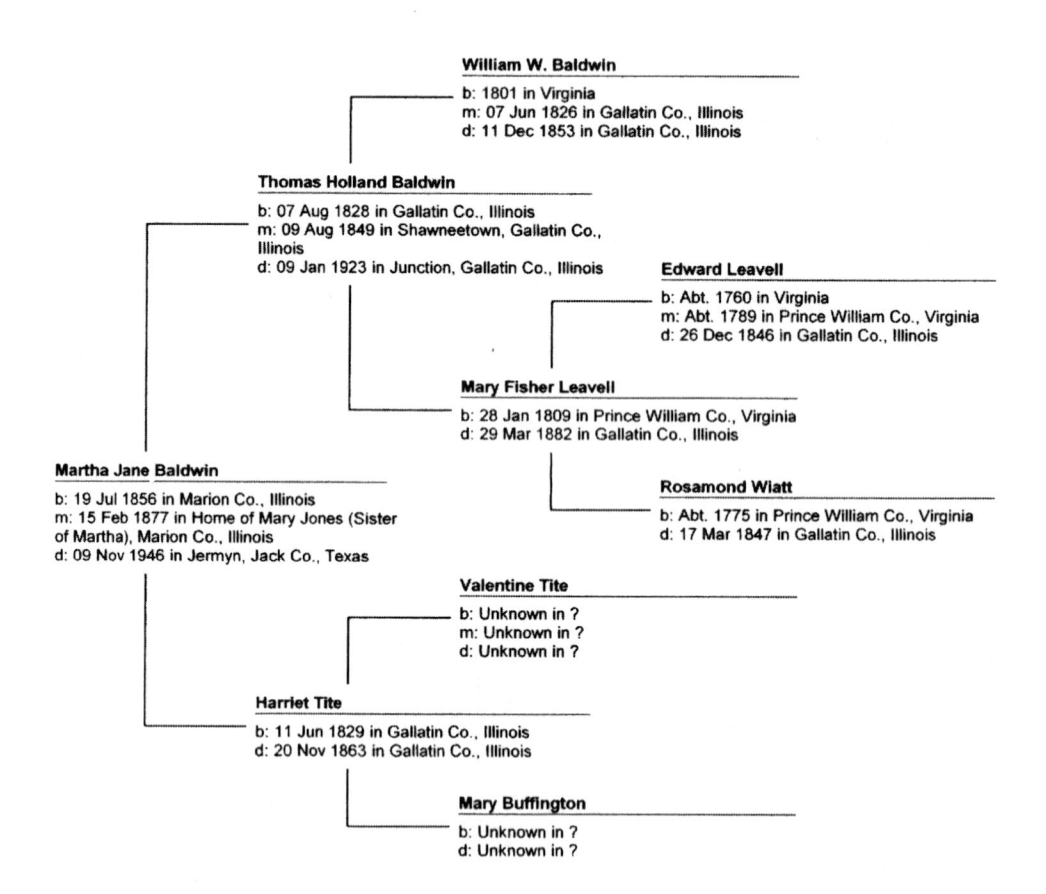

William W. Baldwin
- b: 1801 in Virginia
- m: 07 Jun 1826 in Gallatin Co., Illinois
- d: 11 Dec 1853 in Gallatin Co., Illinois

Thomas Holland Baldwin
- b: 07 Aug 1828 in Gallatin Co., Illinois
- m: 09 Aug 1849 in Shawneetown, Gallatin Co., Illinois
- d: 09 Jan 1923 in Junction, Gallatin Co., Illinois

Edward Leavell
- b: Abt. 1760 in Virginia
- m: Abt. 1789 in Prince William Co., Virginia
- d: 26 Dec 1846 in Gallatin Co., Illinois

Mary Fisher Leavell
- b: 28 Jan 1809 in Prince William Co., Virginia
- d: 29 Mar 1882 in Gallatin Co., Illinois

Rosamond Wiatt
- b: Abt. 1775 in Prince William Co., Virginia
- d: 17 Mar 1847 in Gallatin Co., Illinois

Martha Jane Baldwin
- b: 19 Jul 1856 in Marion Co., Illinois
- m: 15 Feb 1877 in Home of Mary Jones (Sister of Martha), Marion Co., Illinois
- d: 09 Nov 1946 in Jermyn, Jack Co., Texas

Valentine Tite
- b: Unknown in ?
- m: Unknown in ?
- d: Unknown in ?

Harriet Tite
- b: 11 Jun 1829 in Gallatin Co., Illinois
- d: 20 Nov 1863 in Gallatin Co., Illinois

Mary Buffington
- b: Unknown in ?
- d: Unknown in ?

Elmer Elisha Wilton (1881-1945)
[5th. Generation From Henry Wilton (1769-1820)]

&

Eula May Rhoades (1887-1966)
& Family

Elmer Elisha Wilton was the second child of Henry Franklin Wilton and Martha Jane Baldwin, born December 17, 1881 in Parker County, Texas. Henry and Martha had made Veal Station in Parker County their home shortly after their marriage in 1877. Then, in 1886, they moved to Jack County, Texas, first settling in the Bumble Bee Community, and then, in 1889, they settled permanently near the Winn Hill Community in Jack County. Elmer attended school at Winn Hill and helped on the farm during his early years.

February 1911, Elmer married Eula May Rhoades, daughter of Sylvester Jacob Rhoades and Martha Cathern Reeves. Eula's parents added the "May" to her name, because she was born on the 1st day of May, in 1887. Eula was also born and raised in Jack County, Texas, and she attended school at Pleasant Hill. Sometime between 1910 and 1920, Eula's parents moved to Childress in Childress County, Texas, but Elmer and Eula made their home on the Wilton farm, living next to Elmer's parents. In 1917, Elmer bought the East half of his father's land of 265 acres, where they farmed and raised some livestock.

The Wilton homeplace was located about 1 &1/2 miles from Winn Hill, and about 3 &1/2 miles away was the town of Jermyn. The next largest town was Jacksboro, which was located about 12 miles away. While Elmer did most of the heavy work of farming, Eula was also good at helping to manage the farm. She raised chickens and turkeys, sold cream, and she had a good garden. They also participated in community affairs and attended the Winn Hill Baptist Church.

Elmer and Eula had three sons, who were all raised on the Wilton homeplace. The oldest son, Luther Virgil Wilton, nicknamed "L.V." and "Bus," was born January 1912; the middle son, Charles Anthony Wilton, nicknamed "Ance," was born January 1914; and, the youngest son, Clyde Chalmer Wilton, was born November 1919. Clyde, being the youngest son, was always called by Eula, "my baby boy." Clyde recalled that he was always embarrassed by that name, until he was about 45 years old, and then he accepted the title with no problem. Another memory related by Clyde was that all the family members had chores to do, and one of his chores, which he disliked, was to pick up wood chips from the wood pile each evening to use for kindling in the cookstove. He also recalled that when there was a heavy rain, Eula had all of her sons out in the garden, pulling weeds, while the ground was still wet.

Tragically, Elmer died prematurely in January 1945, at the age of 64, as the result of being kicked by a horse. After his death, Eula moved to Jacksboro, Texas, where she purchased a lot on Thompson Street and had the house at the homeplace moved the 12 miles to Jacksboro. By that time, her children had moved away with their own families, and the home in Jacksboro became the place that was most remembered by her grandchildren and other relatives.

After moving to Jacksboro, Eula still kept her roots in farming, having a large garden on one side of the house. There was also a small rent house on the other side of the house. Although she no longer lived in the Winn Hill Community, Eula kept the land where the homeplace had been. Whenever family members visited from out of town, they often made the trip to the old Wilton homeplace, remembering the joys of former days, and some family members also kept cattle on the land. The discovery of oil on the land was a great help in supporting Eula and family members in later years.

Although Eula did not travel much, she did make one memorable trip to Hawaii in 1954, to visit her son Clyde and family, who were there as a result of Clyde's military assignment. Though she was apprehensive about air travel, she bravely made the plane flight by herself. By all accounts, she had fond memories of the occasion, but she did not want to make the flight ever again.

Eula was remembered by family as a good mother, a faithful wife, and a devout Christian. She died in 1966 at the age of 78, and she was buried at the Winn Hill Cemetery, beside her husband.

Family Group Sheet

Husband: Elmer Elisha Wilton

Born: 17 Dec 1881 in: Parker Co., Texas
Married: 26 Feb 1911 in: Jermyn, Jack Co., Texas
Died: 12 Jan 1945 in: Jacksboro, Jack Co., Texas
Father: Henry Franklin Wilton
Mother: Martha Jane Baldwin

Wife: Eula May Rhoades

Born: 01 May 1887 in: Jermyn, Jack Co., Texas
Died: 16 Jan 1966 in: Clay Co., Texas
Father: Sylvestor Jacob Rhoades
Mother: Martha Cathern Reeves

CHILDREN

1 M
Name: Luther Virgil Wilton
Born: 12 Jan 1912 in: Winn Hill, Jack Co., Texas
Died: 20 Sep 1992 in: Irving, Dallas Co., Texas
Married: 03 May 1940 in: Parker Co., Texas
Spouse: Verda Louise Bohannon
Married: 01 Dec 1985 in: Tarrant Co., Texas
Spouse: Jennie Esther Stephenson

2 M
Name: Charles Anthony Wilton
Born: 29 Jan 1914 in: Precinct #4, Jack Co., Texas
Died: 01 Mar 1996 in: Jacksboro, Jack Co., Texas
Married: 20 Dec 1939 in: Jacksboro, Jack Co., Texas
Spouse: Merle Modell Nall

3 M
Name: Clyde Chalmer Wilton
Born: 22 Nov 1919 in: Jermyn, Jack Co., Texas
Married: 17 Oct 1943 in: Winn Hill, Jack Co., Texas
Spouse: Larue Vivian Haley

ELMER ELISHA WILTON Standard Pedigree Tree

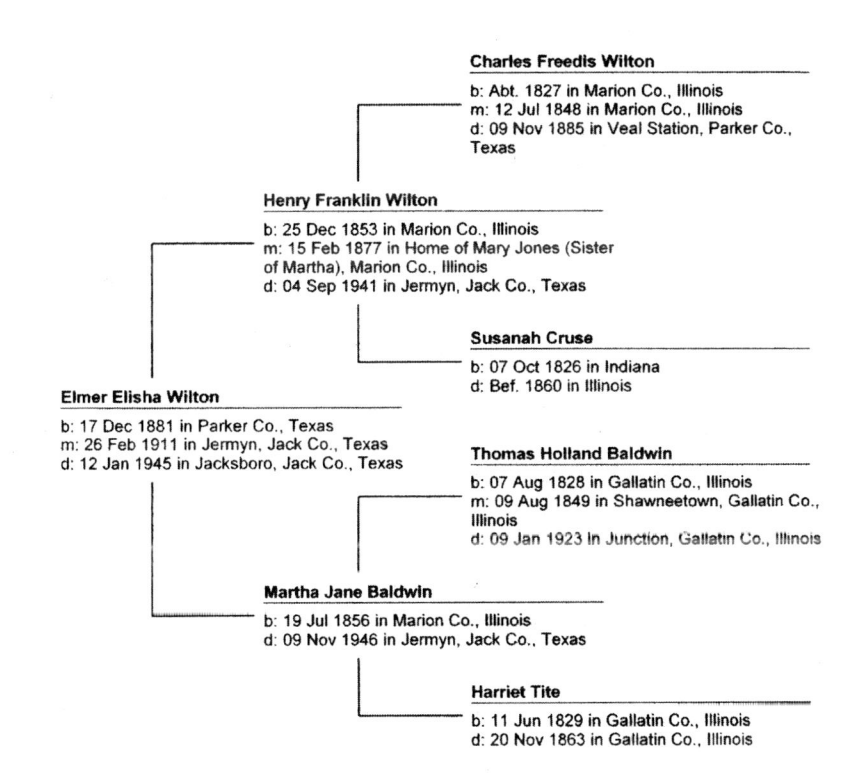

Elmer Elisha Wilton
b: 17 Dec 1881 in Parker Co., Texas
m: 26 Feb 1911 in Jermyn, Jack Co., Texas
d: 12 Jan 1945 in Jacksboro, Jack Co., Texas

- **Henry Franklin Wilton**
  b: 25 Dec 1853 in Marion Co., Illinois
  m: 15 Feb 1877 in Home of Mary Jones (Sister of Martha), Marion Co., Illinois
  d: 04 Sep 1941 in Jermyn, Jack Co., Texas

  - **Charles Freedis Wilton**
    b: Abt. 1827 in Marion Co., Illinois
    m: 12 Jul 1848 in Marion Co., Illinois
    d: 09 Nov 1885 in Veal Station, Parker Co., Texas

  - **Susanah Cruse**
    b: 07 Oct 1826 in Indiana
    d: Bef. 1860 in Illinois

- **Martha Jane Baldwin**
  b: 19 Jul 1856 in Marion Co., Illinois
  d: 09 Nov 1946 in Jermyn, Jack Co., Texas

  - **Thomas Holland Baldwin**
    b: 07 Aug 1828 in Gallatin Co., Illinois
    m: 09 Aug 1849 in Shawneetown, Gallatin Co., Illinois
    d: 09 Jan 1923 in Junction, Gallatin Co., Illinois

  - **Harriet Tite**
    b: 11 Jun 1829 in Gallatin Co., Illinois
    d: 20 Nov 1863 in Gallatin Co., Illinois

Notes: This Tree also applies to the other children of Henry Franklin Wilton & Martha Jane Baldwin: Virgil Wilton, Amy Rosalie Wilton, Holland Wilton, Charles Joseph Wilton, and Mary Alma Wilton.

EULA MAY RHOADES Standard Pedigree Tree

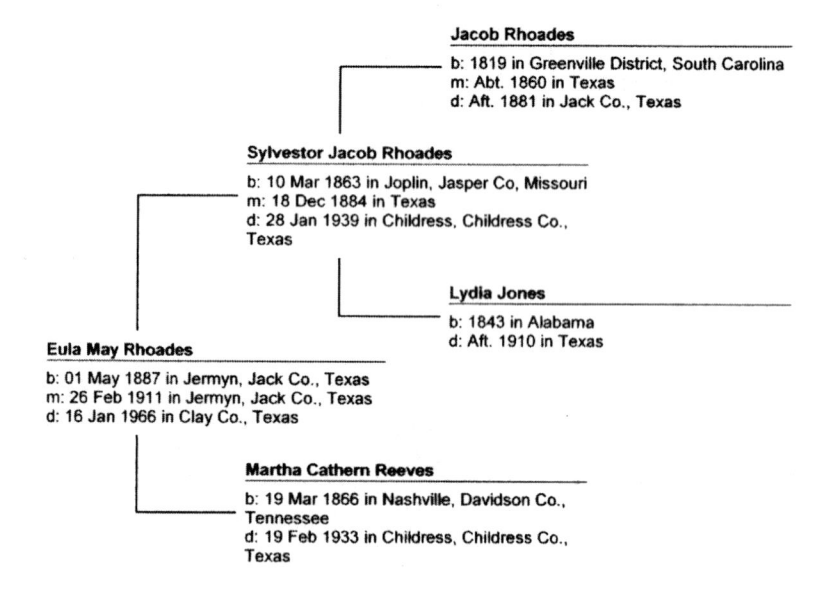

- **Jacob Rhoades**
  b: 1819 in Greenville District, South Carolina
  m: Abt. 1860 in Texas
  d: Aft. 1881 in Jack Co., Texas

- **Sylvestor Jacob Rhoades**
  b: 10 Mar 1863 in Joplin, Jasper Co, Missouri
  m: 18 Dec 1884 in Texas
  d: 28 Jan 1939 in Childress, Childress Co., Texas

- **Lydia Jones**
  b: 1843 in Alabama
  d: Aft. 1910 in Texas

- **Eula May Rhoades**
  b: 01 May 1887 in Jermyn, Jack Co., Texas
  m: 26 Feb 1911 in Jermyn, Jack Co., Texas
  d: 16 Jan 1966 in Clay Co., Texas

- **Martha Cathern Reeves**
  b: 19 Mar 1866 in Nashville, Davidson Co., Tennessee
  d: 19 Feb 1933 in Childress, Childress Co., Texas

Luther Virgil Wilton (1912-1992)
[6th. Generation from Henry Wilton (1769-1820)]

&

Verda Louise Bohannon (1918-1984)
& Family

&

Jennie Esther Stephenson (1917-2008)
& Family

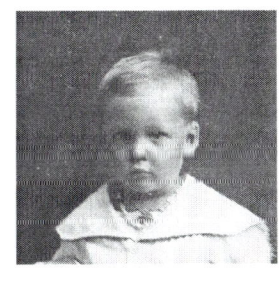

Luther Virgil (L.V.) Wilton was born Jan 1912 at the Wilton homeplace near Winn Hill, Texas, the oldest of three sons of Elmer & Eula Wilton. Spending his early years at the Wilton country home, there were numerous opportunities to get into mischief, and L.V.'s youngest brother, Clyde, remembered one such instance. Clyde remembered that his brothers L.V. and Anthony were one day playing football with friends using a tin can, since they didn't have access to a real football. In the process, the tin can hit L.V. in one of his teeth and put a chip in it. The result was a gold filling for the tooth, but also a reminder for the rest of his days of this youthful experience.

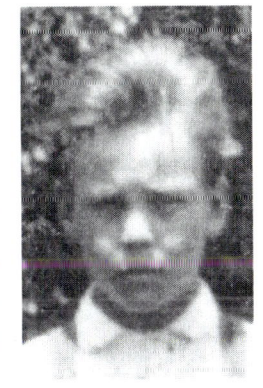

L.V. attended school at Winn Hill for his elementary education, and then he went to nearby Jermyn, Texas for high school. Since the school did not provide transportation at that time, L.V., along with his brother, Anthony, walked the seven mile round trip each day to Jermyn. Although discouraged about school near the time for graduation, he was inspired by one of the valedictory addresses he attended, and he stayed with his education. He graduated from Jermyn High School about 1931.

After finishing high school, L.V. lived at home for a while, trying the job of magazine salesman. Along with his friend and partner, Clifford Gregory, he made trips to the surrounding area plying his new trade. In those days, cash was a scarce commodity, so they bartered their magazines for things such as chickens and other staples. L.V. soon decided this occupation was not for him, so he quit that job after about six months. His friend, Clifford, who enjoyed that type of work, continued with the job and was a success as a salesman.

L.V. then moved to Ft. Worth to attend barber school. While still in barber school, he met his wife-to-be, Verda Louise Bohannon, and they were married May 3, 1940. However, he did not finish his barber training, deciding that this occupation was also not for him. While in Ft. Worth, he finally found a job that was to his liking when he was employed by the T.P. Coal & Oil Company as a bookkeeper. L.V. remained with the company for most of his adult life.

Toward the end of WWII, L.V. was drafted into the military service. Although he served briefly in Germany, he did not see action in combat, since the war came to an end. After his service in the military, L.V. and Verda had a son, named Luther Virgil Jr., born February 18, 1947, while the couple lived in Ft. Worth.

At one point, L.V.'s employer moved operations to Dallas, Texas, and L.V. moved with them. While working in Dallas, the family purchased a home in nearby Irving, Texas. After retiring from his job with the T.P. Coal & Oil Company, the family remained in their home in Irving. L.V.'s first wife, Verda, died December 1984, after succumbing to a bout with cancer.

L.V. married a second time to Jennie Stephenson in 1985, also retaining the home in Irving. One of L.V.'s favorite things to do, especially in his later years, was to play golf. He died in September 1992. Apparently, according to his own wishes, there was no funeral, and L.V. was buried in the Irving City Cemetery in an unmarked grave. After L.V.'s death, Jennie remarried, and she died May 2008.

Family Group Sheet

Husband: Luther Virgil Wilton

Born: 12 Jan 1912 — in: Winn Hill, Jack Co., Texas
Married: 03 May 1940 — in: Parker Co., Texas
Died: 20 Sep 1992 — in: Irving, Dallas Co., Texas
Father: Elmer Elisha Wilton
Mother: Eula May Rhoades
Other Spouses: Jennie Esther Stephenson

Wife: Verda Louise Bohannon

Born: 13 Oct 1918 — in: Clovis, New Mexico
Died: 27 Dec 1984 — in: Irving, Dallas Co., Texas
Father: David Pickens Bohannon
Mother: Harriet Elizabeth Creel

CHILDREN

1 M
Name: Luther Virgil Jr. Wilton
Born: 18 Feb 1947 — in: Ft. Worth, Tarrant Co., Texas
Married: 03 Mar 1972 — in: Dallas Co., Texas
Spouse: Mary L. Weinrich
Married: 03 Apr 1987 — in: Norman, Cleveland Co., Oklahoma
Spouse: Carol Marie Lavender

Family Group Sheet

Husband: Luther Virgil Wilton

Born: 12 Jan 1912 — in: Winn Hill, Jack Co., Texas
Married: 01 Dec 1985 — in: Tarrant Co., Texas
Died: 20 Sep 1992 — in: Irving, Dallas Co., Texas
Father: Elmer Elisha Wilton
Mother: Eula May Rhoades
Other Spouses: Verda Louise Bohannon

Wife: Jennie Esther Stephenson

Born: 07 Apr 1917 — in: St. Louis, St. Louis Co., Missouri
Died: 01 May 2008 — in: Irving, Dallas Co., Texas
Father: Harry S. Stephenson
Mother: Betty Nelson

LUTHER VIRGIL WILTON Standard Pedigree Tree

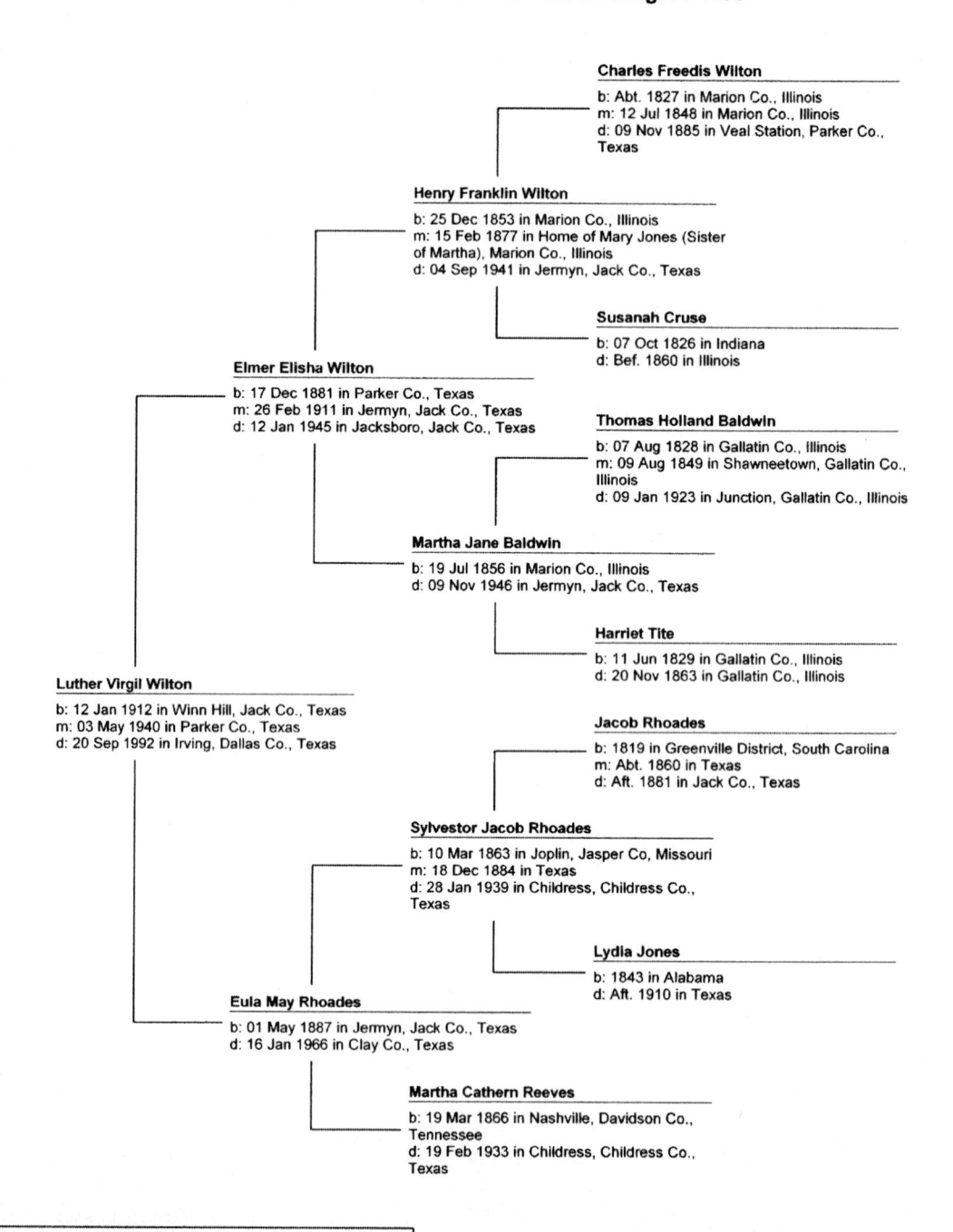

Luther Virgil Wilton
b: 12 Jan 1912 in Winn Hill, Jack Co., Texas
m: 03 May 1940 in Parker Co., Texas
d: 20 Sep 1992 in Irving, Dallas Co., Texas

- **Elmer Elisha Wilton**
  b: 17 Dec 1881 in Parker Co., Texas
  m: 26 Feb 1911 in Jermyn, Jack Co., Texas
  d: 12 Jan 1945 in Jacksboro, Jack Co., Texas

  - **Henry Franklin Wilton**
    b: 25 Dec 1853 in Marion Co., Illinois
    m: 15 Feb 1877 in Home of Mary Jones (Sister of Martha), Marion Co., Illinois
    d: 04 Sep 1941 in Jermyn, Jack Co., Texas

    - **Charles Freedis Wilton**
      b: Abt. 1827 in Marion Co., Illinois
      m: 12 Jul 1848 in Marion Co., Illinois
      d: 09 Nov 1885 in Veal Station, Parker Co., Texas

    - **Susanah Cruse**
      b: 07 Oct 1826 in Indiana
      d: Bef. 1860 in Illinois

  - **Martha Jane Baldwin**
    b: 19 Jul 1856 in Marion Co., Illinois
    d: 09 Nov 1946 in Jermyn, Jack Co., Texas

    - **Thomas Holland Baldwin**
      b: 07 Aug 1828 in Gallatin Co., Illinois
      m: 09 Aug 1849 in Shawneetown, Gallatin Co., Illinois
      d: 09 Jan 1923 in Junction, Gallatin Co., Illinois

    - **Harriet Tite**
      b: 11 Jun 1829 in Gallatin Co., Illinois
      d: 20 Nov 1863 in Gallatin Co., Illinois

- **Eula May Rhoades**
  b: 01 May 1887 in Jermyn, Jack Co., Texas
  d: 16 Jan 1966 in Clay Co., Texas

  - **Sylvestor Jacob Rhoades**
    b: 10 Mar 1863 in Joplin, Jasper Co, Missouri
    m: 18 Dec 1884 in Texas
    d: 28 Jan 1939 in Childress, Childress Co., Texas

    - **Jacob Rhoades**
      b: 1819 in Greenville District, South Carolina
      m: Abt. 1860 in Texas
      d: Aft. 1881 in Jack Co., Texas

    - **Lydia Jones**
      b: 1843 in Alabama
      d: Aft. 1910 in Texas

  - **Martha Cathern Reeves**
    b: 19 Mar 1866 in Nashville, Davidson Co., Tennessee
    d: 19 Feb 1933 in Childress, Childress Co., Texas

Notes: This Tree also applies to the other children of Elmer Elisha Wilton & Eula May Rhoades: Charles Anthony Wilton & Clyde Chalmer Wilton.

VERDA LOUISE BOHANNON Standard Pedigree Tree

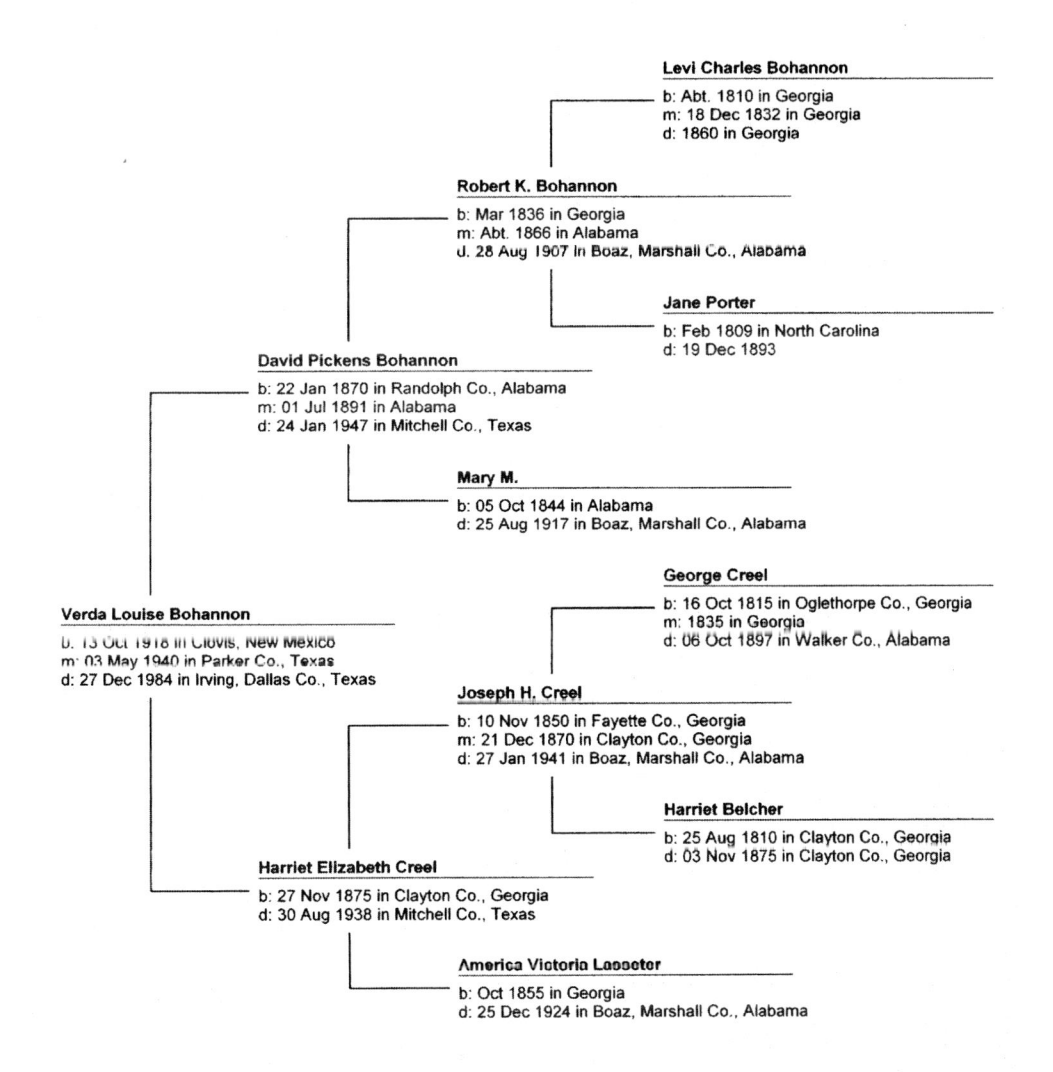

- **Verda Louise Bohannon**
  b: 13 Oct 1918 in Clovis, New Mexico
  m: 03 May 1940 in Parker Co., Texas
  d: 27 Dec 1984 in Irving, Dallas Co., Texas

  - **David Pickens Bohannon**
    b: 22 Jan 1870 in Randolph Co., Alabama
    m: 01 Jul 1891 in Alabama
    d: 24 Jan 1947 in Mitchell Co., Texas

    - **Robert K. Bohannon**
      b: Mar 1836 in Georgia
      m: Abt. 1866 in Alabama
      d: 28 Aug 1907 in Boaz, Marshall Co., Alabama

      - **Levi Charles Bohannon**
        b: Abt. 1810 in Georgia
        m: 18 Dec 1832 in Georgia
        d: 1860 in Georgia

      - **Jane Porter**
        b: Feb 1809 in North Carolina
        d: 19 Dec 1893

    - **Mary M.**
      b: 05 Oct 1844 in Alabama
      d: 25 Aug 1917 in Boaz, Marshall Co., Alabama

  - **Harriet Elizabeth Creel**
    b: 27 Nov 1875 in Clayton Co., Georgia
    d: 30 Aug 1938 in Mitchell Co., Texas

    - **Joseph H. Creel**
      b: 10 Nov 1850 in Fayette Co., Georgia
      m: 21 Dec 1870 in Clayton Co., Georgia
      d: 27 Jan 1941 in Boaz, Marshall Co., Alabama

      - **George Creel**
        b: 16 Oct 1815 in Oglethorpe Co., Georgia
        m: 1835 in Georgia
        d: 06 Oct 1897 in Walker Co., Alabama

      - **Harriet Belcher**
        b: 25 Aug 1810 in Clayton Co., Georgia
        d: 03 Nov 1875 in Clayton Co., Georgia

    - **America Victoria Lassseter**
      b: Oct 1855 in Georgia
      d: 25 Dec 1924 in Boaz, Marshall Co., Alabama

Luther Virgil Jr. Wilton (1947-   )
[7th. Generation from Henry Wilton (1769-1820)]

&

Mary L. Weinrich (1939-   )
& Family

&

Carol Marie Lavender (1943-1991)
& Family

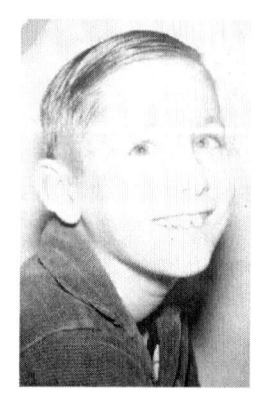

Luther Virgil Jr. (Spike) Wilton, the son of Luther Virgil (L.V.) Wilton and Verda Louise Bohannon, was born February 1947 in Ft. Worth in Tarrant County, Texas. L.V. and Verda had made Ft. Worth their home after their marriage in May 1940. Sometime later, L.V.'s job with the T.P Coal & Oil Company encouraged a move to Dallas, and the family settled permanently in nearby Irving, Texas. After completion of high school and college, Spike pursued a career as an engineer.

Spike first married Mary L. Weinrich in March 1972. Spike married again in 1987 to Carol Marie Lavender, and they settled in Oklahoma. Spike's second wife died in December 1991 in Norman, Oklahoma.

Family Group Sheet

Husband: Luther Virgil Jr. Wilton	
Born: 18 Feb 1947	in: Ft. Worth, Tarrant Co., Texas
Married: 03 Mar 1972	in: Dallas Co., Texas
Father: Luther Virgil Wilton	
Mother: Verda Louise Bohannon	
Other Spouses: Carol Marie Lavender	
Wife: Mary L. Weinrich	
Born: Abt. 1939	
Other Spouses: Ernest Edward Neading	

Family Group Sheet

Husband: Luther Virgil Jr. Wilton	
Born: 18 Feb 1947	in: Ft. Worth, Tarrant Co., Texas
Married: 03 Apr 1987	in: Norman, Cleveland Co., Oklahoma
Father: Luther Virgil Wilton	
Mother: Verda Louise Bohannon	
Other Spouses: Mary L. Weinrich	
Wife: Carol Marie Lavender	
Born: 07 Jan 1943	in: North Charleroi, Washington Co., Pennsylvania
Died: 21 Dec 1991	in: Norman, Cleveland Co., Oklahoma

LUTHER VIRGIL JR. WILTON Standard Pedigree Tree

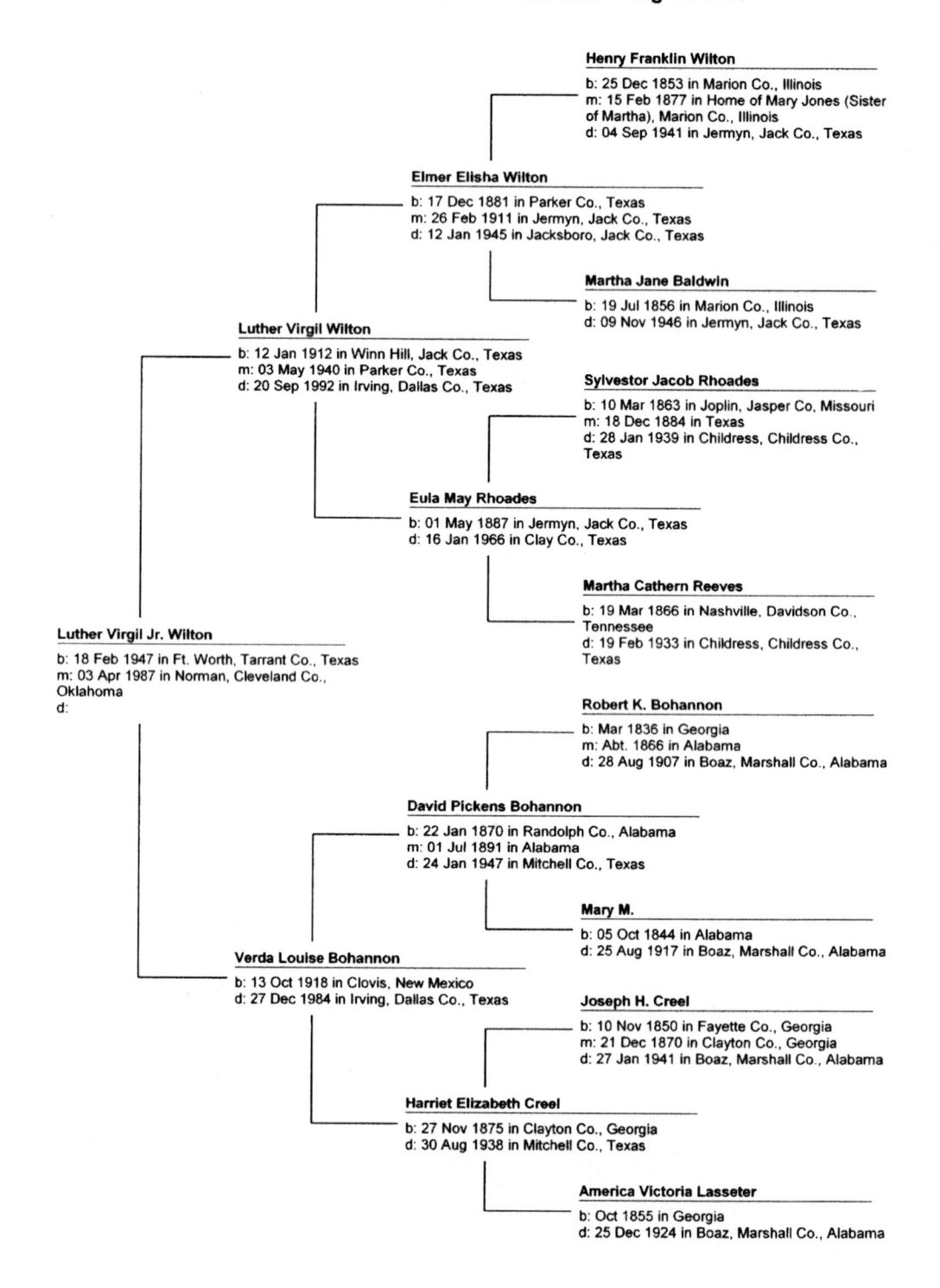

Luther Virgil Jr. Wilton
b: 18 Feb 1947 in Ft. Worth, Tarrant Co., Texas
m: 03 Apr 1987 in Norman, Cleveland Co., Oklahoma
d:

- **Luther Virgil Wilton**
  b: 12 Jan 1912 in Winn Hill, Jack Co., Texas
  m: 03 May 1940 in Parker Co., Texas
  d: 20 Sep 1992 in Irving, Dallas Co., Texas

  - **Elmer Elisha Wilton**
    b: 17 Dec 1881 in Parker Co., Texas
    m: 26 Feb 1911 in Jermyn, Jack Co., Texas
    d: 12 Jan 1945 in Jacksboro, Jack Co., Texas

    - **Henry Franklin Wilton**
      b: 25 Dec 1853 in Marion Co., Illinois
      m: 15 Feb 1877 in Home of Mary Jones (Sister of Martha), Marion Co., Illinois
      d: 04 Sep 1941 in Jermyn, Jack Co., Texas

    - **Martha Jane Baldwin**
      b: 19 Jul 1856 in Marion Co., Illinois
      d: 09 Nov 1946 in Jermyn, Jack Co., Texas

  - **Eula May Rhoades**
    b: 01 May 1887 in Jermyn, Jack Co., Texas
    d: 16 Jan 1966 in Clay Co., Texas

    - **Sylvestor Jacob Rhoades**
      b: 10 Mar 1863 in Joplin, Jasper Co, Missouri
      m: 18 Dec 1884 in Texas
      d: 28 Jan 1939 in Childress, Childress Co., Texas

    - **Martha Cathern Reeves**
      b: 19 Mar 1866 in Nashville, Davidson Co., Tennessee
      d: 19 Feb 1933 in Childress, Childress Co., Texas

- **Verda Louise Bohannon**
  b: 13 Oct 1918 in Clovis, New Mexico
  d: 27 Dec 1984 in Irving, Dallas Co., Texas

  - **David Pickens Bohannon**
    b: 22 Jan 1870 in Randolph Co., Alabama
    m: 01 Jul 1891 in Alabama
    d: 24 Jan 1947 in Mitchell Co., Texas

    - **Robert K. Bohannon**
      b: Mar 1836 in Georgia
      m: Abt. 1866 in Alabama
      d: 28 Aug 1907 in Boaz, Marshall Co., Alabama

    - **Mary M.**
      b: 05 Oct 1844 in Alabama
      d: 25 Aug 1917 in Boaz, Marshall Co., Alabama

  - **Harriet Elizabeth Creel**
    b: 27 Nov 1875 in Clayton Co., Georgia
    d: 30 Aug 1938 in Mitchell Co., Texas

    - **Joseph H. Creel**
      b: 10 Nov 1850 in Fayette Co., Georgia
      m: 21 Dec 1870 in Clayton Co., Georgia
      d: 27 Jan 1941 in Boaz, Marshall Co., Alabama

    - **America Victoria Lasseter**
      b: Oct 1855 in Georgia
      d: 25 Dec 1924 in Boaz, Marshall Co., Alabama

Charles Anthony Wilton (1914-1996)
[6th. Generation From Henry Wilton (1769-1820)]

&

Merle Modell Nall (1921-1994)
& Family

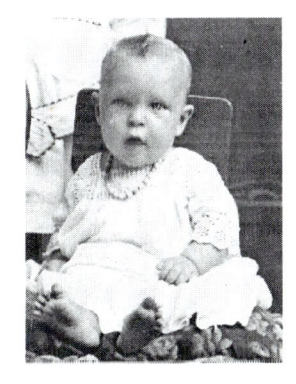

Charles Anthony Wilton ("Athany," or "Ance," as he was known to family) was born in 1914 in Jack County, Texas, the second of the three sons of Elmer Wilton and Eula (Rhoades) Wilton. Elmer and Eula had settled at the Wilton homeplace, located about 1 & 1/2 miles from the Winn Hill Community, 3 &1/2 miles from the town of Jermyn, Texas, and about 12 miles from Jacksboro, Texas, shortly after their marriage in 1911. Anthony attended elementary school at Winn Hill and high school at nearby Jermyn, Texas. Due to an unfortunate altercation with his math teacher, Anthony quit school before graduating from high school.

Anthony was remembered most for his adventurous spirit, and there were numerous examples that attested to why he got his reputation. One such instance occurred when he decided to test a theory he had heard that if one grabbed a flower while a bee was still in it, the bee wouldn't be able to sting you. He quickly learned the faulty reasoning behind that theory when he tried it and promptly got stung. Another theory he had heard was that if one grabbed a skunk and held it by the tail, the skunk would not be able to spray you with its scent. Well, he suffered dearly for a while when he learned that also did not work. Anthony also had a hobby of grabbing snakes by the tail and popping their heads off by whipping them in the air. He decided to give that hobby up finally one day, when the snake he was handling crawled down his arm instead of losing its head.

In 1939, Anthony married Modell Nall, daughter of John Mark Nall & Ora Sanders. For about three years, the couple remained in Jack County, Texas, where Anthony began working as a pumper in the oil field. This occupation became Anthony's life's work, and he worked for the G.E. Kadane and Sons Company for about thirty years, until his retirement. His work took him to Wichita and Archer counties for a number of years, before later returning again to Jack County.

A large part of Anthony's career with the oil company was spent near Dundee in Archer County, Texas, where he lived at an isolated outpost. This was the ideal set-up for Anthony, because he loved the outdoor life. His house was supplied by the oil company, and he was free to raise his own chickens and coon dogs. He was especially fond of taking his coon dogs on wolf hunts out in the surrounding countryside. Also, only a short distance away, there was a water tank, which was his major water source, but was also a good place to go fishing, if he so desired.

Anthony and Modell had four children, with the first two separated by a gap of about 18 years before the second two came along. The first child, Connie Charles Wilton, was born April 1943, and the second child, Treva Daphane Wilton, was born November 1945, both being born in Young County, Texas. The third child, Toni Dell Wilton, born June 1962, and the fourth child, Curtis Lee Wilton, born October 1966, were both born in Jacksboro in Jack County, Texas.

The Wilton home in Dundee brought fond memories to a number of nephews and nieces, who on occasion spent their summer months visiting with their favorite Uncle "Ance" and family. Aaron Wilton, a nephew of Anthony, recalled that it was particularly enjoyable to make the visit, since Anthony's two older children were about his same age. Aaron remembered the great times he had fishing at the pond, riding his cousin's motor scooter on the country roads, accompanying Anthony on his oil pumping rounds, sitting by the air cooler in the evenings, and playing dominos to pass the time.

In 1966, after the death of Anthony's mother, Eula (Rhoades) Wilton, and at Anthony's request, his work assignment was relocated to Jacksboro, Texas. The family lived in the Wilton home in Jacksboro, which had been given to Anthony by Eula as part of his inheritance. That was where Anthony and Modell lived for the remainder of their days. While living in Jacksboro, Anthony retired from his oil field work, but he continued to keep a large garden, along with grapevines and fruit trees, and he kept a small herd of cattle at the Wilton homeplace near Winn Hill.

Anthony and Modell both belonged to the Southwest Baptist Church, and they participated in school and community affairs. Their two younger children, both born in Jacksboro, spent much of their formative years while the family lived in Jacksboro. Sadly, their oldest son, Connie Wilton, died prematurely in March 1971 of a brain tumor, after serving in the U.S.A.F. during the Vietnam Conflict.

After long bouts with diabetes and kidney disease, Modell died in February 1994. Anthony died March 1, 1996. They were both buried at the Winn Hill Cemetery.

Family Group Sheet

Husband: Charles Anthony Wilton

Born: 29 Jan 1914 in: Precinct #4, Jack Co., Texas
Married: 20 Dec 1939 in: Jacksboro, Jack Co., Texas
Died: 01 Mar 1996 in: Jacksboro, Jack Co., Texas
Father: Elmer Elisha Wilton
Mother: Eula May Rhoades

Wife: Merle Modell Nall

Born: 11 May 1921 in: Loving, Young Co., Texas
Died: 20 Feb 1994 in: Jacksboro, Jack Co., Texas
Father: John Mark Nall
Mother: Ora Maggie Sanders

CHILDREN

1 M
Name: Connie Charles Wilton
Born: 07 Apr 1943 in: Young Co., Texas
Died: 17 Mar 1971 in: Jacksboro, Jack Co., Texas

2 F
Name: Treva Daphane Wilton
Born: 24 Nov 1945 in: Graham, Young Co., Texas
Died: 19 Jun 2008 in: Graham, Young Co., Texas
Married: 06 Jan 1967 in: Wichita Co., Texas
Spouse: Jerry Lavern Davis

3 F
Name: Toni Dell Wilton
Born: 20 Jun 1962 in: Jacksboro, Jack Co., Texas
Married: 30 Jan 1983 in: Tarrant Co., Texas
Spouse: Najib A. Talhouk

4 M
Name: Curtis Lee Wilton
Born: 13 Oct 1966 in: Jacksboro, Jack Co., Texas
Married: 28 Apr 1989 in: Jack Co, Texas
Spouse: Deloris Lorraine Walker

MERLE MODELL NALL Standard Pedigree Tree

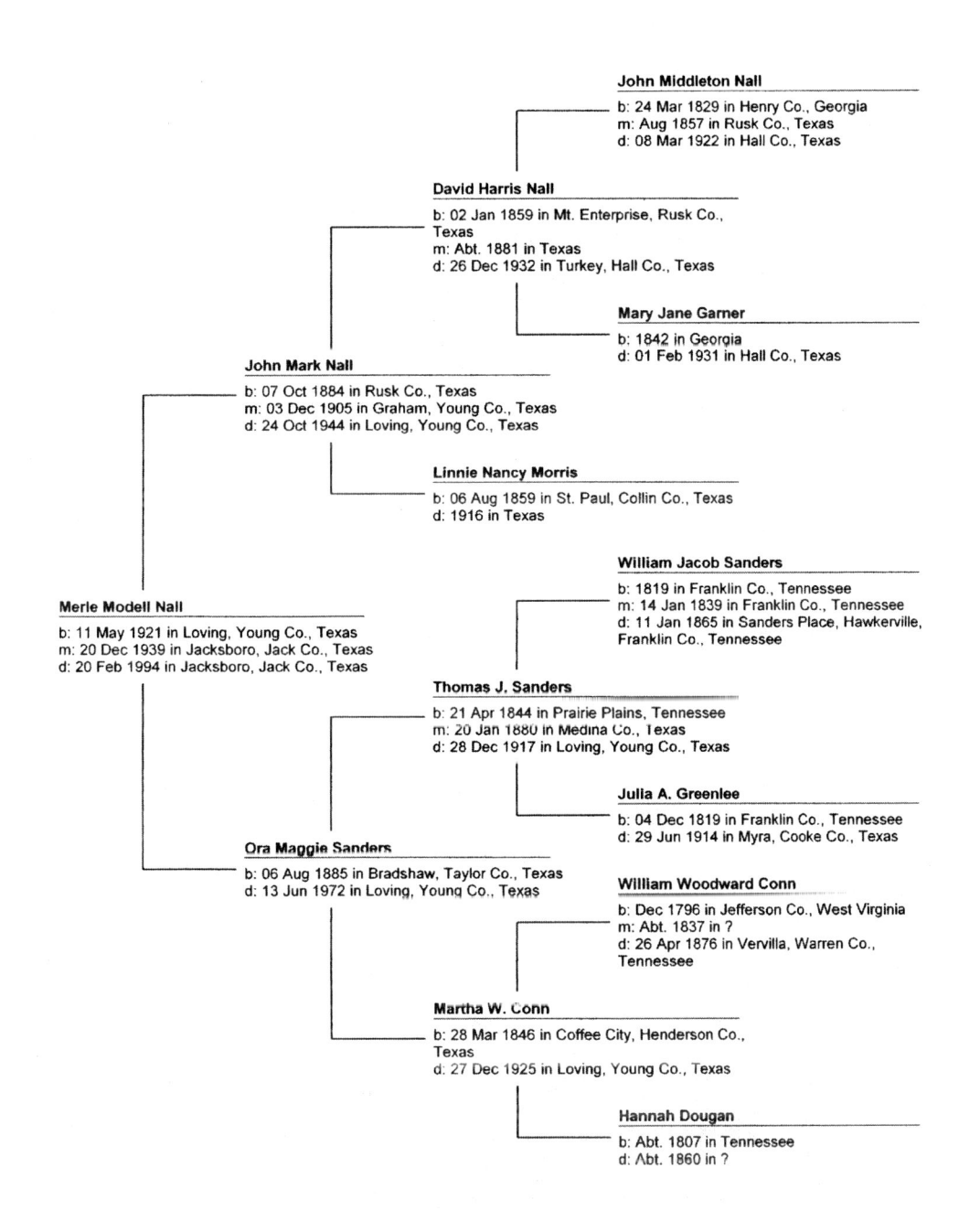

Merle Modell Nall
b: 11 May 1921 in Loving, Young Co., Texas
m: 20 Dec 1939 in Jacksboro, Jack Co., Texas
d: 20 Feb 1994 in Jacksboro, Jack Co., Texas

- **John Mark Nall**
  b: 07 Oct 1884 in Rusk Co., Texas
  m: 03 Dec 1905 in Graham, Young Co., Texas
  d: 24 Oct 1944 in Loving, Young Co., Texas

  - **David Harris Nall**
    b: 02 Jan 1859 in Mt. Enterprise, Rusk Co., Texas
    m: Abt. 1881 in Texas
    d: 26 Dec 1932 in Turkey, Hall Co., Texas

    - **John Middleton Nall**
      b: 24 Mar 1829 in Henry Co., Georgia
      m: Aug 1857 in Rusk Co., Texas
      d: 08 Mar 1922 in Hall Co., Texas

    - **Mary Jane Garner**
      b: 1842 in Georgia
      d: 01 Feb 1931 in Hall Co., Texas

  - **Linnie Nancy Morris**
    b: 06 Aug 1859 in St. Paul, Collin Co., Texas
    d: 1916 in Texas

- **Ora Maggie Sanders**
  b: 06 Aug 1885 in Bradshaw, Taylor Co., Texas
  d: 13 Jun 1972 in Loving, Young Co., Texas

  - **Thomas J. Sanders**
    b: 21 Apr 1844 in Prairie Plains, Tennessee
    m: 20 Jan 1880 in Medina Co., Texas
    d: 28 Dec 1917 in Loving, Young Co., Texas

    - **William Jacob Sanders**
      b: 1819 in Franklin Co., Tennessee
      m: 14 Jan 1839 in Franklin Co., Tennessee
      d: 11 Jan 1865 in Sanders Place, Hawkerville, Franklin Co., Tennessee

    - **Julia A. Greenlee**
      b: 04 Dec 1819 in Franklin Co., Tennessee
      d: 29 Jun 1914 in Myra, Cooke Co., Texas

  - **Martha W. Conn**
    b: 28 Mar 1846 in Coffee City, Henderson Co., Texas
    d: 27 Dec 1925 in Loving, Young Co., Texas

    - **William Woodward Conn**
      b: Dec 1796 in Jefferson Co., West Virginia
      m: Abt. 1837 in ?
      d: 26 Apr 1876 in Vervilla, Warren Co., Tennessee

    - **Hannah Dougan**
      b: Abt. 1807 in Tennessee
      d: Abt. 1860 in ?

Connie Charles Wilton (1943-1971)
[7th. Generation From Henry Wilton (1769-1820)]

Connie Charles Wilton, born April 1943 in Young County, Texas, was the oldest child of Charles Anthony Wilton and Merle Modell Nall. Connie's father was a pumper in the oil field, and the family made a number of moves in connection with his work. During Connie's high school years, the family lived in Dundee in Archer County, Texas, and Connie attended school at the Valley View High School in adjacent Wichita County, Texas, where he participated in school athletic activities and excelled in baseball and football. After graduating from high school about 1961, Connie attended college at the Midwestern University in Wichita Falls in Wichita County, Texas.

During the Vietnam Conflict, Connie served for three years with the U.S.A.F. He became ill with a brain tumor while serving in Okinawa, and after having surgery, he was released from the military with a medical discharge. He returned to Jacksboro in Jack County, Texas, where his parents were living at the time, remaining there until his death in 1971.

Connie's illness was a shock to all who knew him, but his short life always brought pleasant memories. He was a fine Christian young man, and for awhile he served as a deacon at the Southwest Baptist Church in Jacksboro, Texas. Connie was buried at the Winn Hill Cemetery in Jack County, Texas.

CONNIE CHARLES WILTON Standard Pedigree Tree

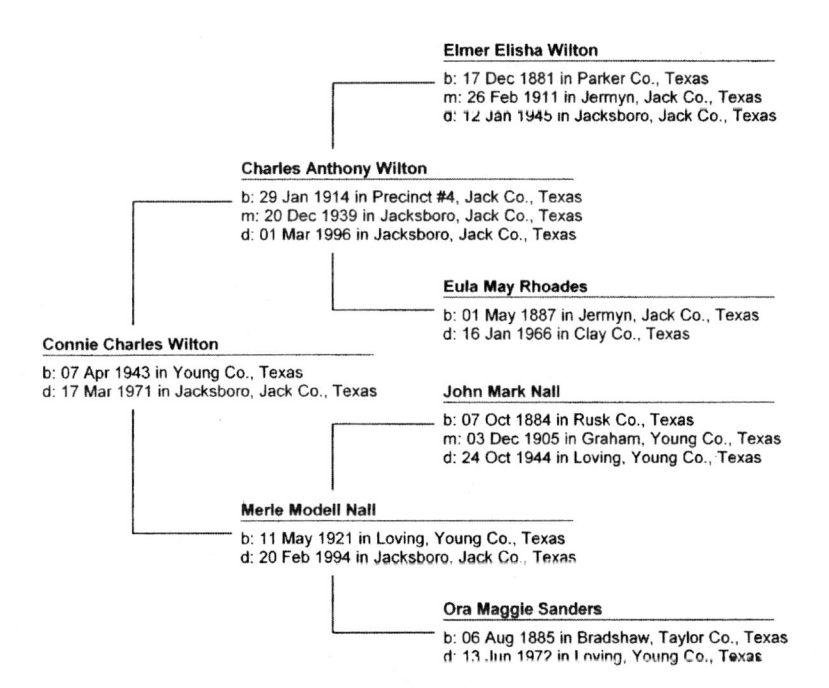

Charles Anthony Wilton
b: 29 Jan 1914 in Precinct #4, Jack Co., Texas
m: 20 Dec 1939 in Jacksboro, Jack Co., Texas
d: 01 Mar 1996 in Jacksboro, Jack Co., Texas

- **Elmer Elisha Wilton**
  b: 17 Dec 1881 in Parker Co., Texas
  m: 26 Feb 1911 in Jermyn, Jack Co., Texas
  d: 12 Jan 1945 in Jacksboro, Jack Co., Texas

- **Eula May Rhoades**
  b: 01 May 1887 in Jermyn, Jack Co., Texas
  d: 16 Jan 1966 in Clay Co., Texas

Connie Charles Wilton
b: 07 Apr 1943 in Young Co., Texas
d: 17 Mar 1971 in Jacksboro, Jack Co., Texas

Merle Modell Nall
b: 11 May 1921 in Loving, Young Co., Texas
d: 20 Feb 1994 in Jacksboro, Jack Co., Texas

- **John Mark Nall**
  b: 07 Oct 1884 in Rusk Co., Texas
  m: 03 Dec 1905 in Graham, Young Co., Texas
  d: 24 Oct 1944 in Loving, Young Co., Texas

- **Ora Maggie Sanders**
  b: 06 Aug 1885 in Bradshaw, Taylor Co., Texas
  d: 13 Jun 1972 in Loving, Young Co., Texas

Notes: This Tree also applies to the other children of Charles Anthony Wilton & Merle Modell Nall: Treva Daphane Wilton, Toni Dell Wilton, and Curtis Lee Wilton.

Treva Daphane Wilton (1945-2008)
[7th. Generation From Henry Wilton (1769-1820)]

&

Jerry Lavern Davis (1946-   )
& Family

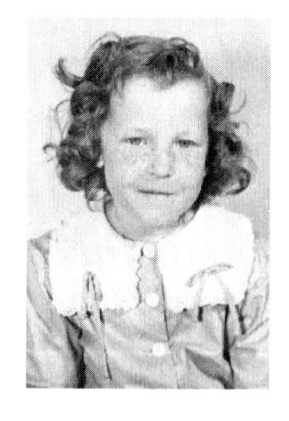

Treva Daphane Wilton was the second child of Charles Anthony Wilton & Merle Modell Wilton, born November 1945 in Graham, Texas. Much of her childhood was spent near Dundee, Texas, where her father worked as a pumper for an oil company. While the family lived at an isolated country outpost in a home provided by the oil company, Treva attend school in the adjacent Wichita County, Texas. Treva graduated from the Valley View High School in Wichita County about 1963.

Treva married Jerry Lavern Davis, who also lived in the Dundee area, in January 1967. Following the birth of their first child, Michelle Lynn Davis, in Harris Co., Texas, they moved to East Texas. While in East Texas, Treva went to college at the University of Texas at El Paso, Texas, where she received a teaching degree. Their second child, Shannon Lynn Davis, was born while they were in El Paso.

Sometime later, Treva and Jerry were separated, and Treva tried to continue with her teaching career, which took her to Raymondville in the Rio Grande Valley. After about a year, she returned home with her parents, who then were living in Jacksboro, Texas. In 1981, Treva had her third child, Tony Kelly Davis.

Due to a mental breakdown, Treva ended up living most of the rest of her years in an assisted living home. Treva died in June 2008 in Graham in Young County, Texas.

Family Group Sheet

Husband: Jerry Lavern Davis

Born: 15 Oct 1946 in: Wichita Falls, Wichita Co., Texas
Married: 06 Jan 1967 in: Wichita Co., Texas
Father: Lavern Meldon Davis
Mother: Ruth Marie Anderson

Wife: Treva Daphane Wilton

Born: 24 Nov 1945 in: Graham, Young Co., Texas
Died: 19 Jun 2008 in: Graham, Young Co., Texas
Father: Charles Anthony Wilton
Mother: Merle Modell Nall

CHILDREN

1 F
Name: Michelle Lynn Davis
Born: 09 Sep 1967 in: Harris Co., Texas

2 F
Name: Shannon Lynn Davis
Born: 14 Nov 1973 in: El Paso Co., Texas

3 M
Name: Tony Kelly Davis
Born: 21 Nov 1981 in: Mineral Wells, Palo Pinto Co., Texas
Married: 02 Dec 2006 in: Bryan, Brazos Co., Texas
Spouse: Bertha Fernandez

Toni Dell Wilton (1962-   )
[7th. Generation From Henry Wilton (1769-1820)]

&

Najib A. Talhouk (1958-   )
& Family

Toni Dell Wilton, born June 1962 in Jacksboro, Texas, was the third child of Charles Anthony Wilton and Merle Modell Nall. Anthony and Modell relocated permanently in Jacksboro, Texas about 1966, so Toni Dell spent most of her school years in Jacksboro, graduating from Jacksboro High School about 1980. She then attended the Bryan Institute at Arlington, Texas.

Toni Dell married Najib Talhouk, and they settled in Tarrant County, Texas. Toni and Najib had two children, Abbat Anthony Talhouk, born January 1984, and Nauib Jr. Talhouk, born February 1986, both being born in Tarrant County.

Family Group Sheet

Husband: Najib A. Talhouk		
Born: 15 Feb 1958	in: Beirut, Lebanon	
Married: 30 Jan 1983	in: Tarrant Co., Texas	
Father: A. M. Talhouk		
Mother: Elane Touma		
Wife: Toni Dell Wilton		
Born: 20 Jun 1962	in: Jacksboro, Jack Co., Texas	
Father: Charles Anthany Wilton		
Mother: Merle Modell Nall		

CHILDREN

1 M	Name: Abbat Anthony Talhouk		
	Born: 27 Jan 1984	in: Tarrant Co., Texas	
2 M	Name: Najib Jr. Talhouk		
	Born: 11 Feb 1986	in: Tarrant Co., Texas	

Curtis Lee Wilton (1966-   )
[7th. Generation From Henry Wilton (1769-1820)]

&

Deloris Lorraine Walker (1966-   )
& Family

Curtis Lee Wilton, born October 1966 in Jacksboro, Texas, was the fourth, and last, child of Charles Anthony Wilton and Merle Modell Nall. Anthony and Modell had just resettled in Jacksboro about the time Curtis was born, so Curtis spent his early years in Jacksboro. Curtis attended Jacksboro High School, where he was a member of the football team, and where he graduated about 1984. Following high school, Curtis enlisted with the U.S. Marine Corps, where he served 1986-1990.

In April 1989, Curtis married Deloris (Delo) Lorraine Walker, daughter of John Earl Walker and Charlene Rae Ingram. Following his military service, Curtis was employed in the oil field as a truck driver for the Halliburton Corporation. Curtis and Delo had two children, Baylor Christian Wilton, born November 1994 in Wichita Falls, Texas, and Ethan Coe Wilton, born June 1997 in Decatur, Texas. Beginning in 1998, the family moved to the Jacksboro area, making it their permanent home.

Family Group Sheet

Husband: Curtis Lee Wilton	
Born: 13 Oct 1966	in: Jacksboro, Jack Co., Texas
Married: 28 Apr 1989	in: Jack Co, Texas
Father: Charles Anthony Wilton	
Mother: Merle Modell Nall	
Wife: Deloris Lorraine Walker	
Born: 02 Nov 1966	in: Tuscaloosa, Tuscaloosa Co., Alabama
Father: John Earl Walker	
Mother: Charlene Rae Ingram	

	CHILDREN	
1 F	Name: Baylor Christian Wilton Born: 01 Nov 1994	in: Wichita Falls, Wichita Co., Texas
2 M	Name: Ethan Coe Wilton Born: 02 Jun 1997	in: Decatur, Wise Co., Texas

Clyde Chalmer Wilton (1919-)
[6th. Generation From Henry Wilton (1769-1820)]

&

Larue Vivian Haley (1923-2004)
& Family

Clyde Chalmer Wilton, born November 1919 in Jermyn, Texas, was the youngest son of Elmer Elisha Wilton and Eula May Rhoades. Since their marriage in February 1911, Elmer and Eula had made the Wilton homeplace their home, which was located about 3 &1/2 miles from Jermyn and about 12 miles from Jacksboro, Texas, in Jack County. Clyde grew up on the Wilton homeplace, where his father was a stock farmer and the family worked hard to make the farm a success.

Clyde's early education began at the nearby Winn Hill Community, where he attended elementary school. After completing his elementary education, Clyde then attended high school at Jermyn, Texas, where he graduated from the Jermyn High School in 1937. Then, in 1938, he continued his education at Weatherford Jr. College, followed by attending North Texas State Teacher's College (NTSTC) in Denton, Texas, from January 1939 to May 1940. It was while attending NTSTC that Clyde was "called" to the Christian ministry, and he began a career as a Baptist preacher and pastor.

After leaving NTSTC and surrendering his life to Jesus Christ, Clyde spent a year back on the Wilton farm, where he spent time studying the Bible and becoming the pastor of his home church at the Winn Hill Community, the Bethany Baptist Church.

Following this time of reflection and Christian service at home, Clyde then continued his formal education at Howard Payne College in Brownwood, Texas, where he graduated with a B.A. in Bible in May 1943.

It was while attending at Howard Payne College that Clyde met his wife-to-be, Larue Vivian Haley, the daughter of Abraham (Abe) Jefferson Haley and Marintha Evelyn Gilbert. Larue, the youngest child of Abe and Marintha (Gilbert) Haley, grew up in South Texas and graduated from the Edinburg High School in Edinburg, Texas. She was able to attend Howard Payne College with the help of her pastor, Raymond Drews, of the Hargill Baptist Church in Hargill, Texas. Clyde and Larue were married October 17, 1943 at the Winn Hill Bethany Baptist Church in Jack County, Texas.

For the two years following graduation from Howard Payne College, Clyde worked part-time and pastored several small churches. And, in August 1945, Clyde and Larue had their first child, named Aaron Zanoah Wilton, who was born in Jacksboro, Texas. Shortly afterward, beginning in September 1945, Clyde attended the Southwestern Baptist Theological Seminary in Fort Worth, Texas to complete his formal education. During his three years at the seminary, he also pastored churches in Salesville and Bomarton, Texas, and in May 1948, he graduated with a Th.M. degree. For a time after graduation from the seminary, Clyde pastored a church in Bellevue, Texas. It was during that time that Clyde and Larue had their second child, named Fawncyne Regina Wilton, born June 1950 in Bowie, Texas.

Beginning February 1951, Clyde entered the military as a chaplain in the USAF. After being inducted at Brooks AFB, Texas, he trained at the chaplain's school in Pennsylvania, and he began his first duty assignment at Chanute AFB, Illinois, in April 1952. For the next ten years, Clyde had assignments in Hawaii, Texas, and

Japan. During this time, two more children were added to the family. The third child, Kathy Ilene Wilton, was born June 1953 in Honolulu, Hawaii; and, the fourth child, Stanley Wilton, was born September 1958 in McAllen, Texas. In June 1962, Clyde left active duty with the military, at the rank of Captain, but he remained in the USAF Reserve until he formally retired from the military in November 1979, with the rank of Lt. Colonel.

After leaving active military duty, Clyde continued his civilian calling as a Baptist preacher and pastor. He next pastored the Skyline Baptist Church in Killen, Texas for five years between 1962 and 1967. Finally, starting in 1967, he became the pastor of Emmanuel Baptist Church in Bryan, Texas, where he pastored until retiring from the active ministry in December 2007, after serving at the same church for 40 years.

Clyde and Larue were blessed with celebrating their 50th. wedding anniversary in Bryan, Texas in 1993. Several years prior to that, in 1981, Larue was diagnosed with Parkinson's Disease, and she experienced a progressive decline in health over the next 23 years. Clyde's opinion of Larue was that she was "a special person of genuine character, being the ideal wife and a wonderful mother for her children, all of whom dearly loved her." Clyde also liked to quote Proverbs to describe Larue: "She takes good care of her family and is never lazy. Her children praise her, and with great pride her husband says, 'There are many good women, but you are the best!' " Larue was a devout Christian, and she worked in the church, taking on many responsibilities, including service as the church pianist. Larue died in June 2004, after almost 61 years of marriage, and she was buried at the Winn Hill Cemetery in Jack County, Texas.

After retiring as senior pastor of Emmanuel Baptist Church in 2007, Clyde continued being active in the spiritual activities of the community. His interests included attending the weekly men's prayer breakfast and the local Toastmasters Club. He also taught Greek and Hebrew to anyone interested in attending his weekly classes, and he published his own translation of the New Testament. Clyde continued being active with Emmanuel Baptist Church, where he served as "pastor emeritus," as a member of the Elder Board, and as a Council member of the Emmanuel Lighthouse Mission, a woman's shelter located at the church.

Among Clyde's other interests were a lifelong hobby of playing checkers, which he was very good at, and when young, up to his 70's, keeping honeybees. He was also very much involved with healthy eating and maintaining a regular exercise program.

Family Group Sheet

Husband: Clyde Chalmer Wilton	
Born: 22 Nov 1919	in: Jermyn, Jack Co., Texas
Married: 17 Oct 1943	in: Winn Hill, Jack Co., Texas
Father: Elmer Elisha Wilton	
Mother: Eula May Rhoades	

Wife: Larue Vivian Haley	
Born: 20 Mar 1923	in: Plymouth (Samnorwood), Collingsworth Co., Texas
Died: 21 Jun 2004	in: Bryan, Brazos County, Texas
Father: Abraham Jefferson Haley	
Mother: Marintha Evelyn Gilbert	

CHILDREN

#		
1 M	Name: Aaron Zanoah Wilton	
	Born: 07 Aug 1945	in: Jacksboro, Jack Co., Texas
	Married: 13 Aug 1988	in: College Station, Brazos Co., Texas
	Spouse: Ilda Kay Bradberry	
2 F	Name: Regina Fawncyne Wilton	
	Born: 08 Jun 1950	in: Bowie, Montague Co., Texas
	Married: 03 Aug 1973	in: Brazos Co., Texas
	Spouse: Douglas Ray Bolton	
	Married: 26 May 1984	in: College Station, Brazos Co., Texas
	Spouse: Brad Reese Phillips	
	Married: 28 Feb 1992	in: Bryan, Brazos Co., Texas
	Spouse: Robert Monroe Worley	
3 F	Name: Kathy Ilene Wilton	
	Born: 06 Jun 1953	in: Tripler Army Hospital, Honolulu, Hawaii
	Married: 14 Aug 1973	in: Bryan, Brazos Co., Texas
	Spouse: David Randall Wimpee	
	Married: 17 Jul 1998	in: Bryan, Brazos Co., Texas
	Spouse: Richard Michael Hartmann	
4 M	Name: Stanley Wilton	
	Born: 13 Sep 1958	in: McAllen, Hidalgo Co., Texas
	Married: 10 Jun 1978	in: Bryan, Brazos Co., Texas
	Spouse: Karen Gayle Sawyer	
	Married: 24 Jan 1998	in: College Station, Brazos Co., Texas
	Spouse: Marlo Jennifer James	

LARUE VIVIAN HALEY Standard Pedigree Tree

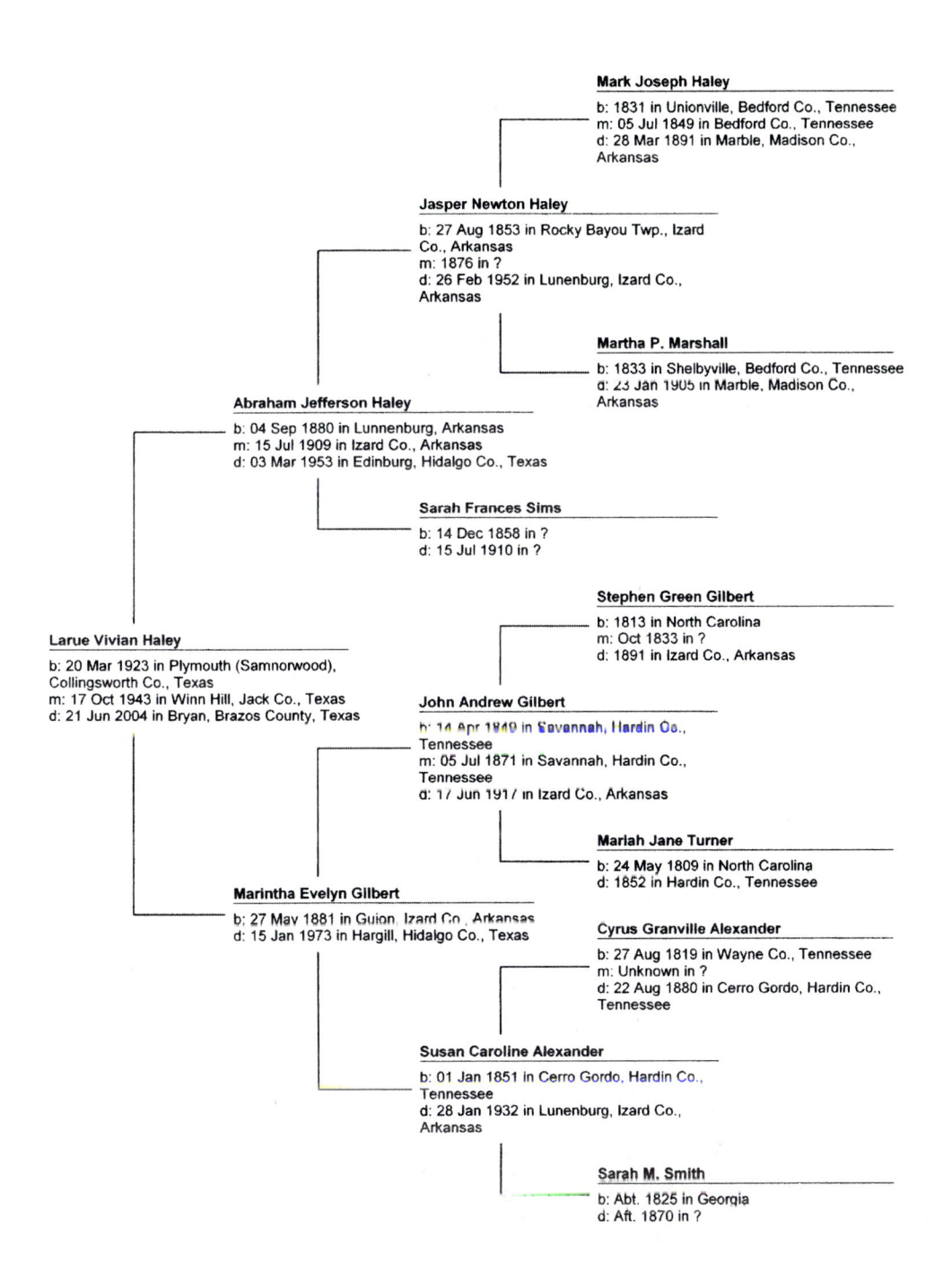

Larue Vivian Haley
b: 20 Mar 1923 in Plymouth (Samnorwood), Collingsworth Co., Texas
m: 17 Oct 1943 in Winn Hill, Jack Co., Texas
d: 21 Jun 2004 in Bryan, Brazos County, Texas

- **Abraham Jefferson Haley**
  b: 04 Sep 1880 in Lunnenburg, Arkansas
  m: 15 Jul 1909 in Izard Co., Arkansas
  d: 03 Mar 1953 in Edinburg, Hidalgo Co., Texas

  - **Jasper Newton Haley**
    b: 27 Aug 1853 in Rocky Bayou Twp., Izard Co., Arkansas
    m: 1876 in ?
    d: 26 Feb 1952 in Lunenburg, Izard Co., Arkansas

    - **Mark Joseph Haley**
      b: 1831 in Unionville, Bedford Co., Tennessee
      m: 05 Jul 1849 in Bedford Co., Tennessee
      d: 28 Mar 1891 in Marble, Madison Co., Arkansas

    - **Martha P. Marshall**
      b: 1833 in Shelbyville, Bedford Co., Tennessee
      d: 23 Jan 1905 in Marble, Madison Co., Arkansas

  - **Sarah Frances Sims**
    b: 14 Dec 1858 in ?
    d: 15 Jul 1910 in ?

- **Marintha Evelyn Gilbert**
  b: 27 May 1881 in Guion, Izard Co., Arkansas
  d: 15 Jan 1973 in Hargill, Hidalgo Co., Texas

  - **John Andrew Gilbert**
    b: 14 Apr 1849 in Savannah, Hardin Co., Tennessee
    m: 05 Jul 1871 in Savannah, Hardin Co., Tennessee
    d: 17 Jun 1917 in Izard Co., Arkansas

    - **Stephen Green Gilbert**
      b: 1813 in North Carolina
      m: Oct 1833 in ?
      d: 1891 in Izard Co., Arkansas

    - **Mariah Jane Turner**
      b: 24 May 1809 in North Carolina
      d: 1852 in Hardin Co., Tennessee

  - **Susan Caroline Alexander**
    b: 01 Jan 1851 in Cerro Gordo, Hardin Co., Tennessee
    d: 28 Jan 1932 in Lunenburg, Izard Co., Arkansas

    - **Cyrus Granville Alexander**
      b: 27 Aug 1819 in Wayne Co., Tennessee
      m: Unknown in ?
      d: 22 Aug 1880 in Cerro Gordo, Hardin Co., Tennessee

    - **Sarah M. Smith**
      b: Abt. 1825 in Georgia
      d: Aft. 1870 in ?

Aaron Zanoah Wilton (1945-   )
[7th. Generation From Henry Wilton (1769-1820)]

&

Ilda Kay Bradberry (1941-   )
& Family

Aaron Z. Wilton, born August 1945 in Jacksboro, Texas, was the oldest child of Clyde Chalmer Wilton and Larue Vivian Haley. Shortly after their marriage in October 1943, Clyde and Larue were living at the Wilton homeplace near Jacksboro. Clyde had just graduated from college at Howard Payne College and was continuing his career as a Baptist preacher and pastor. Beginning in September 1945, the family moved to Fort Worth, Texas, where Clyde attended the Southwestern Baptist Theological Seminary. After completing seminary in May 1948 and pastoring a church for awhile in Bellevue, Texas, in February 1951, Clyde embarked on a career as a chaplain in the USAF.

In 1952, Aaron attended part of the first grade in Jacksboro, Texas, which was where the family lived temporarily just before Clyde began his first military assignment in Hawaii. In that same year, Aaron finished his first school year at Wheeler AFB in Hawaii. From then on, through Aaron's high school years, following the transient nature of the military life, the family changed address some 17 times, and Aaron went to 9 different schools. During those military years, the family spent time in Illinois, Texas, Hawaii, and Japan.

After spending twelve years in military service, Aaron's dad left the active military in June 1962. At that time, the family briefly lived in Jacksboro, Texas near Clyde's mother, and Aaron began his senior year of high school at the Jacksboro High School. Before the year was over, Clyde took a job as pastor in Killeen, Texas, but Aaron was allowed to stay with his grandmother, Eula (Rhoades) Wilton, to finish his last year of high school in Jacksboro. So, Aaron attended part of first grade at Jacksboro, in 1952, and also finished high school at Jacksboro, in 1963, but the time between was spent between Texas and across the globe as far as Japan.

Following high school, Aaron first attended college at Mary Hardin-Baylor College in Belton, Texas, while living at home in Killeen, Texas. In September 1964, he transferred to Baylor University in Waco, Texas, where, in August 1967, he graduated with a B.A. degree. It wasn't until after graduating from Baylor University that Aaron made a decision to pursue a career as a pharmacist. In September 1967, he began studies at the University of Texas Pharmacy School in Austin, Texas.

In May 1969, Aaron was forced to take a detour from his pharmacy training, when he received a draft notice from the U.S. Army, since his school deferments had run out. That was the time of the Vietnam Conflict, and instead of being drafted into the U.S. Army, Aaron chose to enlist in the USAF. Fortunately, Aaron was allowed to serve as a pharmacy technician, and he served his enlistment at the Wright-Patterson AFB Hospital in Ohio. In July 1973, Aaron was honorably discharged from the military at the rank of Staff Sergeant.

After leaving the military, Aaron returned to the University of Texas Pharmacy School, where he graduated in May 1974 with a B.S. degree in Pharmacy and became registered to practice pharmacy in Texas. Aaron's first employment as a pharmacist was in

Beaumont, Texas, where he worked from June 1974 thru October 1976. At that time, his parents and siblings were living in Bryan/College Station, Texas, and Aaron chose to relocate to Bryan, Texas. Except for the period of 1990 to 1997, when he worked as a pharmacist at the Parkland Hospital in Dallas, Texas, Aaron worked in Bryan/College Station, considering that his real home, until he retired from pharmacy in December 2006.

In August 1988, Aaron married Ilda Kay Bradberry. Kay was the daughter of Lawrence Bradberry and Leverta (Ruffin) Bradberry and the widow of Larry Orsak. Kay, along with her three children from her previous marriage, had made their home in College Station since about 1972. After marriage, Aaron and Kay stayed briefly in Dallas, Texas, 1990-1997, and then they made Bryan/College Station their permanent home. They were both active in church life, being members of the Central Baptist Church in Bryan, Texas, where Kay sang in the church choir and Aaron played trumpet in the church orchestra. Aaron also served on the council of the Emmanuel Lighthouse Mission, a women's shelter located at the Emmanuel Baptist Church, where Aaron's dad served for 40 years as pastor.

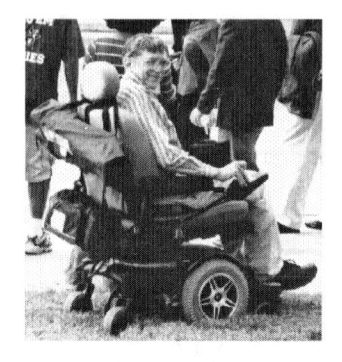

About 1995, Aaron was diagnosed with the condition of peripheral neuropathy. His illness made it increasingly difficult to function as a pharmacist, and he was forced to retire early from his pharmacy job in December 2006, at the age of 61. In retirement, he continued to be active in his church activities, and he was able to be partially mobile with physical aids and the help of his wife.

Family Group Sheet

Husband: Aaron Zanoah Wilton

    Born: 07 Aug 1945   in: Jacksboro, Jack Co., Texas
    Married: 13 Aug 1988   in: College Station, Brazos Co., Texas
    Father: Clyde Chalmer Wilton
    Mother: Larue Vivian Haley

Wife: Ilda Kay Bradberry

    Born: 09 May 1941   in: Bastrop, Morehouse Parish, Louisiana
    Father: Lawrence Bradberry
    Mother: Leverta Ruffin
        Other Spouses: Larry Simon Orsak

AARON ZANOAH WILTON Standard Pedigree Tree

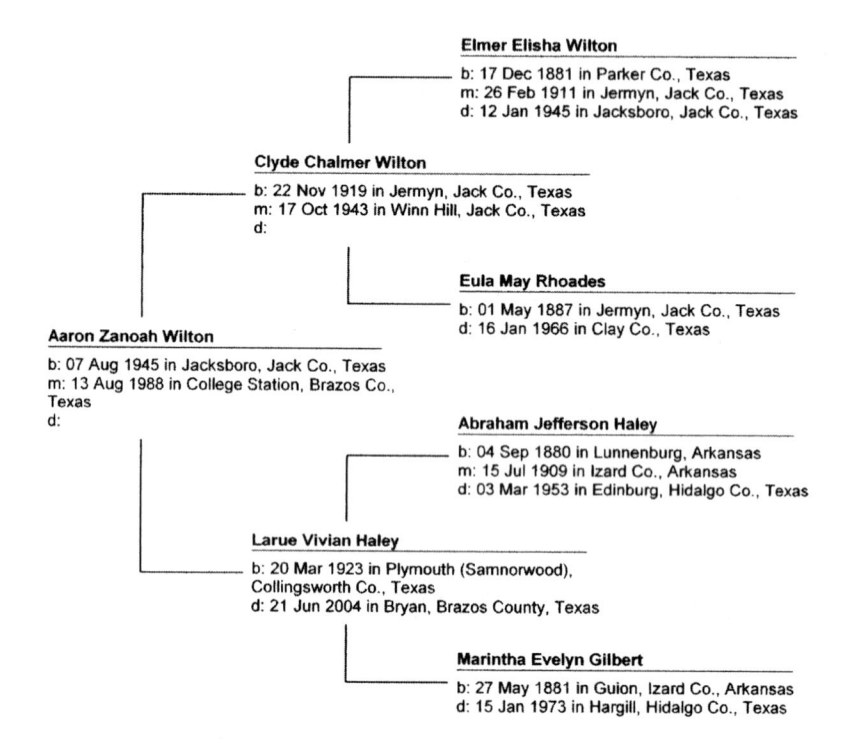

Elmer Elisha Wilton
b: 17 Dec 1881 in Parker Co., Texas
m: 26 Feb 1911 in Jermyn, Jack Co., Texas
d: 12 Jan 1945 in Jacksboro, Jack Co., Texas

Clyde Chalmer Wilton
b: 22 Nov 1919 in Jermyn, Jack Co., Texas
m: 17 Oct 1943 in Winn Hill, Jack Co., Texas
d:

Eula May Rhoades
b: 01 May 1887 in Jermyn, Jack Co., Texas
d: 16 Jan 1966 in Clay Co., Texas

Aaron Zanoah Wilton
b: 07 Aug 1945 in Jacksboro, Jack Co., Texas
m: 13 Aug 1988 in College Station, Brazos Co., Texas
d:

Abraham Jefferson Haley
b: 04 Sep 1880 in Lunnenburg, Arkansas
m: 15 Jul 1909 in Izard Co., Arkansas
d: 03 Mar 1953 in Edinburg, Hidalgo Co., Texas

Larue Vivian Haley
b: 20 Mar 1923 in Plymouth (Samnorwood), Collingsworth Co., Texas
d: 21 Jun 2004 in Bryan, Brazos County, Texas

Marintha Evelyn Gilbert
b: 27 May 1881 in Guion, Izard Co., Arkansas
d: 15 Jan 1973 in Hargill, Hidalgo Co., Texas

Notes: This Tree also applies to the other children of Clyde Chalmer Wilton & Larue Vivian Haley: Regina Fawncyne Wilton, Kathy Ilene Wilton, and Stanley Wilton.

ILDA KAY BRADBERRY Standard Pedigree Tree

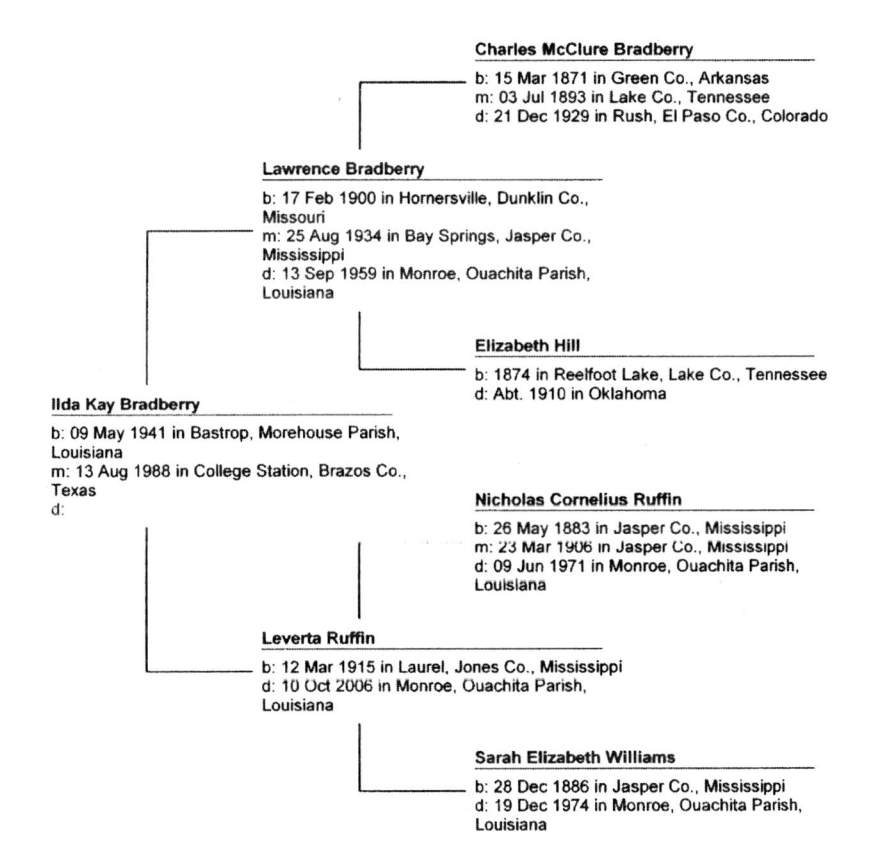

Ilda Kay Bradberry
b: 09 May 1941 in Bastrop, Morehouse Parish, Louisiana
m: 13 Aug 1988 in College Station, Brazos Co., Texas
d:

- **Lawrence Bradberry**
  b: 17 Feb 1900 in Hornersville, Dunklin Co., Missouri
  m: 25 Aug 1934 in Bay Springs, Jasper Co., Mississippi
  d: 13 Sep 1959 in Monroe, Ouachita Parish, Louisiana

  - **Charles McClure Bradberry**
    b: 15 Mar 1871 in Green Co., Arkansas
    m: 03 Jul 1893 in Lake Co., Tennessee
    d: 21 Dec 1929 in Rush, El Paso Co., Colorado

  - **Elizabeth Hill**
    b: 1874 in Reelfoot Lake, Lake Co., Tennessee
    d: Abt. 1910 in Oklahoma

- **Leverta Ruffin**
  b: 12 Mar 1915 in Laurel, Jones Co., Mississippi
  d: 10 Oct 2006 in Monroe, Ouachita Parish, Louisiana

  - **Nicholas Cornelius Ruffin**
    b: 26 May 1883 in Jasper Co., Mississippi
    m: 23 Mar 1906 in Jasper Co., Mississippi
    d: 09 Jun 1971 in Monroe, Ouachita Parish, Louisiana

  - **Sarah Elizabeth Williams**
    b: 28 Dec 1886 in Jasper Co., Mississippi
    d: 19 Dec 1974 in Monroe, Ouachita Parish, Louisiana

Regina Fawncyne Wilton (1950-   )
[7th. Generation From Henry Wilton (1769-1820)]

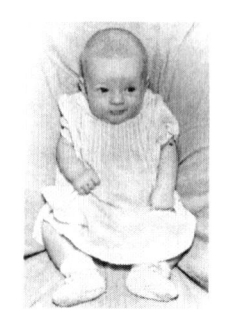

Regina Fawncyne Wilton was born June 8, 1950 at Bowie in Montague County, Texas, the daughter, and second child, of Clyde Chalmer Wilton and Larue Vivian Haley. Her father had just recently, in May 1948, graduated from the Southwestern Baptist Theological Seminary in Fort Worth, Texas, and he had taken a position as pastor of the Bellevue Baptist Church in Bellevue, Texas in Cooke County. Fawncyne was born just ten miles away in the adjacent Montague County.

In February 1951, Clyde, Fawncyne's father, left his civilian job and entered the military service to begin a career as a chaplain in the USAF. For the next twelve years, the family followed Clyde in his military assignments, which took them to Illinois, Texas, Hawaii, and Japan. Each assignment lasted no more than 3 years, with the family changing addresses many times, and the children attending many different schools. However, they also got to see a lot of the world that otherwise might not have been available to them.

After twelve years of military service, in June 1962, Clyde left the active military and again went into civilian service as a Baptist preacher and pastor. His first civilian opportunity after the military was in Killen, Texas, where he was the pastor of the Skyline Baptist Church from 1962 to 1967. In 1967, the family moved once again from Killeen to Bryan, Texas, where Clyde became the pastor of the Emmanuel Baptist Church. After many years of being transient, the family found a permanent place in Bryan, where Clyde remained for the next forty years, retiring as senior pastor in December 2007.

When the family moved to Bryan in 1967, Fawncyne was in the middle of her senior year of high school. She completed her senior year in Bryan, Texas at the Stephen F. Austin school, in 1968. Following high school, and until 1973, Fawncyne worked part of the time and attended college.

In August 1973, Fawncyne married Douglas Bolton, son of Otis Bolton and Esther Akin. At that time, Douglas was the assistant manager for the Kroger Food Store in Bryan. A short time later, the couple was transferred first to a store in Temple, Texas, and then to Conroe, Texas. It was in Conroe that Fawncyne and Douglas had a son, Jeremy Chad Bolton, who was born April 1975. Four years later, in 1979, the couple divorced, and Fawncyne moved back to Bryan, where she worked at the Ornamental Metal Fasting Industries (OMC). After five years at OMC, where she worked in customer service and inventory control, Fawncyne married a second time, in May 1984, to Brad Reese Phillips, son of Alvin Phillips and Bobbi Dragon. They divorced in November 1986.

Fawncyne remained active in community activities and in her church. Through her business activities, she met Robert Worley, who also began attending the same church. On February 29, 1992, Fawncyne married Robert Monroe Worley, son of Harold Leonard Worley and Mildred Louise Biddy. Robert worked for the Economic Development Corporation in Bryan, and Fawncyne continued working in marketing. Fawncyne also went back to college at Texas A&M University (TAMU) in College Station, where she graduated and received a bachelor's degree in sociology in 1994.

After graduating from TAMU, Fawncyne worked at the Crestview Retirement Community as a volunteer coordinator, and then she decided to continue working in long-term care and to advance her skills in that area. In 1996, after doing home studies and on-the-job training at Crestview Retirement Community, she earned her Texas Social Worker's License. She also continued her education at the McClennan Community College in Waco, Texas, where she studied Nursing Home Administration. In the same year, 1996, Fawncyne earned her Texas Nursing Home Administrator's License. Then, after two years she took a position at the Southwood Assisted Living Facility and received certification as a Texas Assisted Living Manager.

In 2002, Fawncyne and Robert moved to Dumas in Moore County, Texas, where Robert accepted a position with the Economic Development Corporation located there. During their first 2 years in Dumas, Fawncyne worked as a nursing home administrator. She then changed her career path into the mental health field.

In 2007, the couple moved again, this time to Brazoria County, Texas, where Robert became the Executive Director of the Brazoria County Alliance of Economic Development in Angleton, Texas. In addition to the new work opportunity, the couple was happily to again be moving closer to their family that was still living in Bryan/College Station. For awhile, Fawncyne worked in a partnership position in mental health and juvenile justice, and as a mentor for scheduled youths in Brazoria County. Later she became a nursing home administrator of a local nursing home.

After building a new home in Clute in Brazoria County, Texas, the couple hoped to settle permanently in the area. One of their great loves was to go salmon fishing in Alaska with Robert's relatives, who lived there. Looking toward retirement, their hope was to at least have a winter home in Alaska.

Family Group Sheet

Husband: Douglas Ray Bolton

Born: 06 Nov 1948 in: Bryan, Brazos County, Texas
Married: 03 Aug 1973 in: Brazos Co., Texas
Father: Otis Tastius Bolton
Mother: Esther Thelma Akin

Wife: Regina Fawncyne Wilton

Born: 08 Jun 1950 in: Bowie, Montague Co., Texas
Father: Clyde Chalmer Wilton
Mother: Larue Vivian Haley
Other Spouses: Brad Reese Phillips, Robert Monroe Worley

CHILDREN

1 M Name: Jeremy Chad Bolton
Born: 28 Apr 1975 in: Montgomery Co., Texas

Family Group Sheet

Husband: Brad Reese Phillips

Born: 14 Dec 1947 in: Hutchinson Co., Texas
Married: 26 May 1984 in: College Station, Brazos Co., Texas
Father: Alvin Phillips
Mother: Bobbi Dragon

Wife: Regina Fawncyne Wilton

Born: 08 Jun 1950 in: Bowie, Montague Co., Texas
Father: Clyde Chalmer Wilton
Mother: Larue Vivian Haley
Other Spouses: Douglas Ray Bolton, Robert Monroe Worley

Family Group Sheet

Husband: Robert Monroe Worley

Born: 12 Mar 1945 in: Lubbock, Lubbock Co., Texas
Married: 28 Feb 1992 in: Bryan, Brazos Co., Texas
Father: Harold Leonard Worley
Mother: Mildred Louise Biddy
Other Spouses: Sandy Frances Aldaco, Patricia Jean Mobberley

Wife: Regina Fawncyne Wilton

Born: 08 Jun 1950 in: Bowie, Montague Co., Texas
Father: Clyde Chalmer Wilton
Mother: Larue Vivian Haley
Other Spouses: Douglas Ray Bolton, Brad Reese Phillips

Kathy Ilene Wilton (1953-   )
[7th. Generation from Henry Wilton (1769-1820)]

&

David Randall Wimpee (1951-   )
& Family

&

Richard Michael Hartmann (1952-   )
& Family

Kathy Ilene Wilton, daughter of Clyde Chalmer Wilton and Larue Vivain Haley, was born June 6, 1953 at Tripler Army Hospital at Honolulu, Hawaii. At the time of Kathy's birth, the family was living at Wheeler A.B. in Hawaii, where Clyde Wilton was serving as a USAF chaplain. There were some tense moments during December 1953, when Kathy developed asthma, and for a short while, it was not certain whether she would survive. Although she continued to have problems with asthma for several years, the condition did not remain a crisis for her or the family.

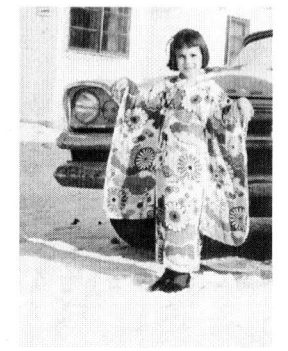

After leaving Hawaii in 1955, the family also spent time in Texas and Japan, following Clyde's assignments with the military. Kathy particularly remembered the years of 1959-1962 in Japan with fondness. She first began school while living at the Misawa Air Base in Japan, and she remembered loving to shop at the town of Misawa, located just outside of the air base, where she would buy chocolate umbrellas. During the winters, the weather was very cold, but she remembered playing in the snow and making snow angels.

In 1962, Kathy's dad left the active military service, and after first staying at Killeen, Texas from 1962 to 1967, the family settled permanently in Bryan, Texas, located in Brazos County. In Bryan, Kathy attended school at the Stephen F. Austin High School, where she graduated in May 1971. Following high school, she attended the Texas A&M University in the sister city of College Station, Texas, and she graduated in 1975 with a B.A. degree. Kathy then began a career in the Bryan/College Station area as an elementary school teacher.

While still in high school, Kathy began singing with a church singing group, called the Sounds of Salvation. On August 14, 1973, she married Randy Wimpee, who was also a member of the group. They continued to sing with the group until it disbanded a number of years later. Kathy and Randy made their home in Bryan, Texas, where Randy was employed as a salesman for a church construction company, and Kathy taught locally at the public school. They were both active in the Aldersgate Methodist Church, where Randy was also the music leader.

Kathy and Randy had three children. The first child, Sherah Rebecca Wimpee, was born March 1976; the second child, Cynthia (Cindy) Joy Wimpee, was born July 1977; and, the third child, Justin David Wimpee, was born March 1986. All three were active in tennis, and a lot of the family time outside of church activities was spent at tennis tournaments. Also, Cindy's first two years of college were aided with the help of a tennis scholarship, and Justin later went to Mercer University in Georgia on a tennis scholarship. On winter holidays, the family enjoyed snow skiing, taking trips to Crested Butte and Purgatory in

Colorado and to Red River in New Mexico. Kathy and Randy were divorced in October 1995.

Kathy married a second time to Richard (Mike) Hartmann, on July 17, 1998 in Bryan, Texas. Mike was a local building contractor, and the couple built a new home and settled in College Station, Texas. Mike and Kathy enjoyed fishing, hunting, and camping together.

Family Group Sheet

Husband: David Randall Wimpee

Born: 15 Apr 1951	in: Bryan, Brazos County, Texas
Married: 14 Aug 1973	in: Bryan, Brazos Co., Texas
Father: Robert Lee Wimpee	
Mother: Audrey Jean Halbrooks	

Wife: Kathy Ilene Wilton

Born: 06 Jun 1953	in: Tripler Army Hospital, Honolulu, Hawaii
Father: Clyde Chalmer Wilton	
Mother: Larue Vivian Haley	
Other Spouses: Richard Michael Hartmann	

CHILDREN

1 F
- Name: Sherah Rebecca Wimpee
- Born: 13 Mar 1976 in: Bryan, Brazos Co., Texas
- Married: 11 Jan 1997 in: Bryan, Brazos Co., Texas
- Spouse: Stephen Bennett Syptak

2 F
- Name: Cynthia Joy Wimpee
- Born: 25 Jul 1977 in: Bryan, Brazos Co., Texas
- Married: 21 Aug 1999 in: Brenham, Brazos Co., Texas
- Spouse: Brant Douglas Buche

3 M
- Name: Justin David Wimpee
- Born: 29 Mar 1986 in: Brazos Co., Texas

Family Group Sheet

Husband: Richard Michael Hartmann

Born: 04 Feb 1952	in: Houston, Harris Co., Texas
Married: 17 Jul 1998	in: Bryan, Brazos Co., Texas
Father: Richard Henry Hartmann	
Mother: Patricia Cimo	
Other Spouses: Noreen Gaye Klovance, Jane Bennett Rathbun	

Wife: Kathy Ilene Wilton

Born: 06 Jun 1953	in: Tripler Army Hospital, Honolulu, Hawaii
Father: Clyde Chalmer Wilton	
Mother: Larue Vivian Haley	
Other Spouses: David Randall Wimpee	

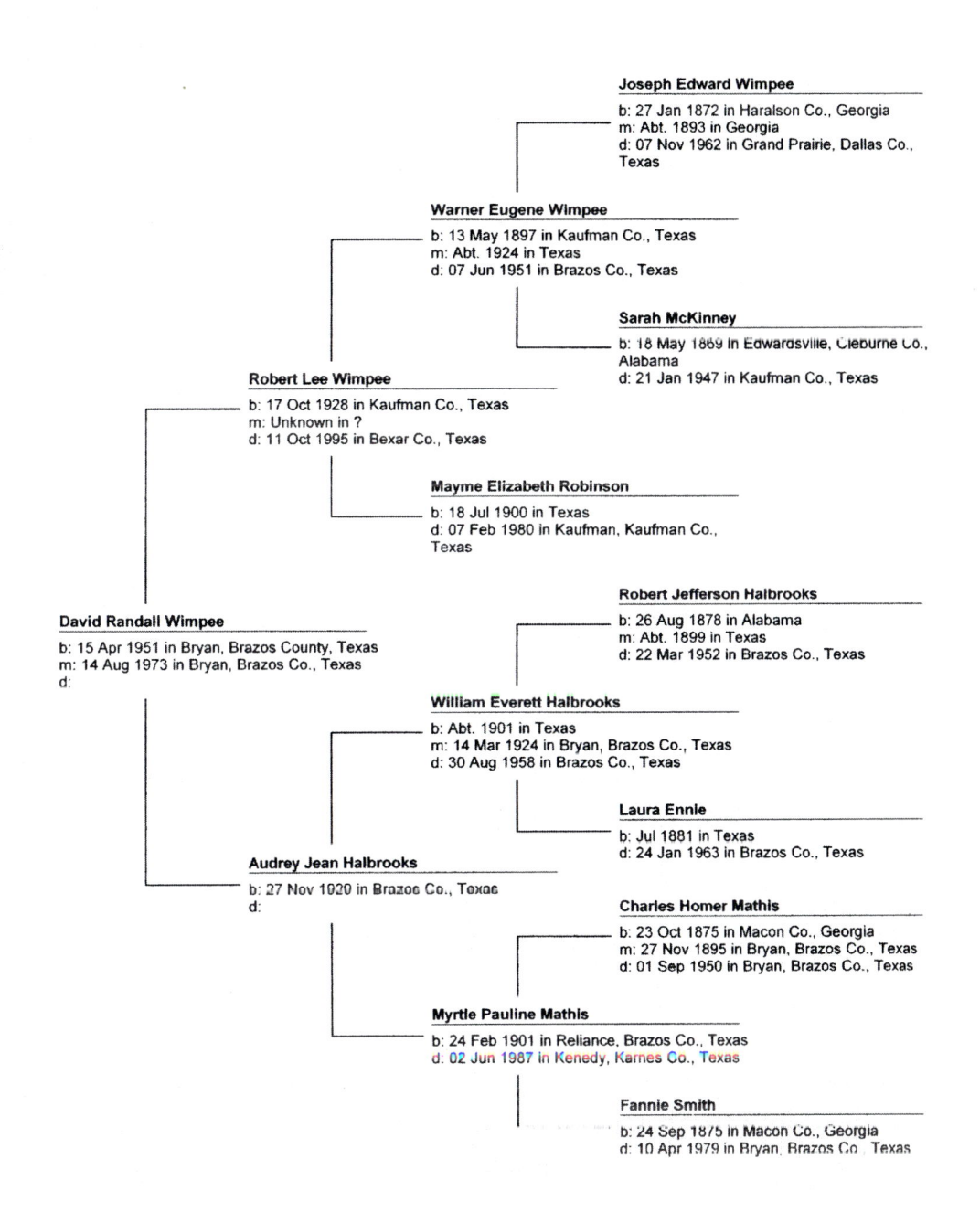

DAVID RANDALL WIMPEE Standard Pedigree Tree

David Randall Wimpee
b: 15 Apr 1951 in Bryan, Brazos County, Texas
m: 14 Aug 1973 in Bryan, Brazos Co., Texas
d:

- **Robert Lee Wimpee**
  b: 17 Oct 1928 in Kaufman Co., Texas
  m: Unknown in ?
  d: 11 Oct 1995 in Bexar Co., Texas

  - **Warner Eugene Wimpee**
    b: 13 May 1897 in Kaufman Co., Texas
    m: Abt. 1924 in Texas
    d: 07 Jun 1951 in Brazos Co., Texas

    - **Joseph Edward Wimpee**
      b: 27 Jan 1872 in Haralson Co., Georgia
      m: Abt. 1893 in Georgia
      d: 07 Nov 1962 in Grand Prairie, Dallas Co., Texas

    - **Sarah McKinney**
      b: 18 May 1869 in Edwardsville, Cleburne Co., Alabama
      d: 21 Jan 1947 in Kaufman Co., Texas

  - **Mayme Elizabeth Robinson**
    b: 18 Jul 1900 in Texas
    d: 07 Feb 1980 in Kaufman, Kaufman Co., Texas

- **Audrey Jean Halbrooks**
  b: 27 Nov 1929 in Brazos Co., Texas
  d:

  - **William Everett Halbrooks**
    b: Abt. 1901 in Texas
    m: 14 Mar 1924 in Bryan, Brazos Co., Texas
    d: 30 Aug 1958 in Brazos Co., Texas

    - **Robert Jefferson Halbrooks**
      b: 26 Aug 1878 in Alabama
      m: Abt. 1899 in Texas
      d: 22 Mar 1952 in Brazos Co., Texas

    - **Laura Ennie**
      b: Jul 1881 in Texas
      d: 24 Jan 1963 in Brazos Co., Texas

  - **Myrtle Pauline Mathis**
    b: 24 Feb 1901 in Reliance, Brazos Co., Texas
    d: 02 Jun 1987 in Kenedy, Karnes Co., Texas

    - **Charles Homer Mathis**
      b: 23 Oct 1875 in Macon Co., Georgia
      m: 27 Nov 1895 in Bryan, Brazos Co., Texas
      d: 01 Sep 1950 in Bryan, Brazos Co., Texas

    - **Fannie Smith**
      b: 24 Sep 1875 in Macon Co., Georgia
      d: 10 Apr 1979 in Bryan, Brazos Co., Texas

RICHARD MICHAEL HARTMANN Standard Pedigree Tree

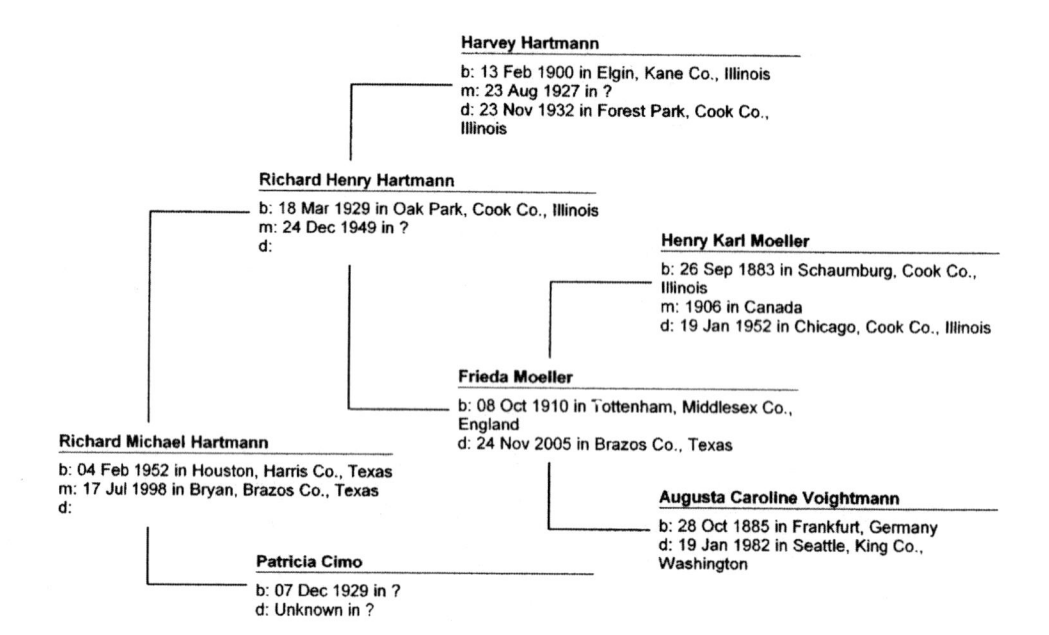

Richard Michael Hartmann
b: 04 Feb 1952 in Houston, Harris Co., Texas
m: 17 Jul 1998 in Bryan, Brazos Co., Texas
d:

- **Richard Henry Hartmann**
  b: 18 Mar 1929 in Oak Park, Cook Co., Illinois
  m: 24 Dec 1949 in ?
  d:

  - **Harvey Hartmann**
    b: 13 Feb 1900 in Elgin, Kane Co., Illinois
    m: 23 Aug 1927 in ?
    d: 23 Nov 1932 in Forest Park, Cook Co., Illinois

  - **Frieda Moeller**
    b: 08 Oct 1910 in Tottenham, Middlesex Co., England
    d: 24 Nov 2005 in Brazos Co., Texas

    - **Henry Karl Moeller**
      b: 26 Sep 1883 in Schaumburg, Cook Co., Illinois
      m: 1906 in Canada
      d: 19 Jan 1952 in Chicago, Cook Co., Illinois

    - **Augusta Caroline Voightmann**
      b: 28 Oct 1885 in Frankfurt, Germany
      d: 19 Jan 1982 in Seattle, King Co., Washington

- **Patricia Cimo**
  b: 07 Dec 1929 in ?
  d: Unknown in ?

Sherah Rebecca Wimpee (1976-)
[8th. Generation From Henry Wilton (1769-1820)]

&

Stephen Bennett Syptak (1974-)
& Family

Sherah Rebecca Wimpee, born March 13, 1976, was the first child of David Radall Wimpee and Kathy Ilene Wilton. Sherah grew up in Bryan, Texas and graduated from Bryan High School. On January 11, 1997, Sherah married her high school sweetheart, Stephen Bennett Syptak, son of Albert Benjamin Syptak and Sharon Ann Wehring. In addition to both graduating from bryan High School, Sherah and Stephen also graduated from Texas A&M University in College Station, Texas. After Stephen completed his formal training, the couple settled in Bryan, where Stephen worked as an attorney and Sherah worked as an aerobics instructor and personal fitness trainer.

Family Group Sheet

Husband: Stephen Bennett Syptak	
Born: 27 Jun 1974	in: Bryan, Brazos Co., Texas
Married: 11 Jan 1997	in: Bryan, Brazos Co., Texas
Father: Albert Benjamin Jr. Syptak	
Mother: Sharon Ann Wehring	

Wife: Sherah Rebecca Wimpee	
Born: 13 Mar 1976	in: Bryan, Brazos Co., Texas
Father: David Randall Wimpee	
Mother: Kathy Ilene Wilton	

CHILDREN

1 F	Name: Ashton Lee Syptak	
	Born: 08 May 2000	in: Houston, Harris Co., Texas
2 M	Name: Bennett Ryan Syptak	
	Born: 11 May 2004	in: Bryan, Brazos Co., Texas

SHERAH REBECCA WIMPEE Standard Pedigree Tree

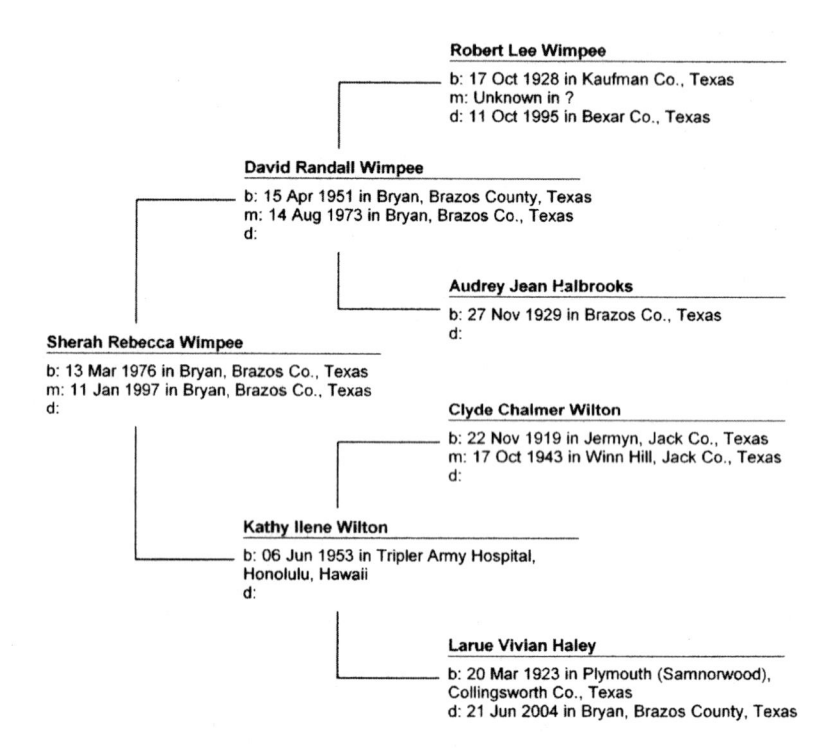

Robert Lee Wimpee
b: 17 Oct 1928 in Kaufman Co., Texas
m: Unknown in ?
d: 11 Oct 1995 in Bexar Co., Texas

David Randall Wimpee
b: 15 Apr 1951 in Bryan, Brazos County, Texas
m: 14 Aug 1973 in Bryan, Brazos Co., Texas
d:

Audrey Jean Halbrooks
b: 27 Nov 1929 in Brazos Co., Texas
d:

Sherah Rebecca Wimpee
b: 13 Mar 1976 in Bryan, Brazos Co., Texas
m: 11 Jan 1997 in Bryan, Brazos Co., Texas
d:

Clyde Chalmer Wilton
b: 22 Nov 1919 in Jermyn, Jack Co., Texas
m: 17 Oct 1943 in Winn Hill, Jack Co., Texas
d:

Kathy Ilene Wilton
b: 06 Jun 1953 in Tripler Army Hospital, Honolulu, Hawaii
d:

Larue Vivian Haley
b: 20 Mar 1923 in Plymouth (Samnorwood), Collingsworth Co., Texas
d: 21 Jun 2004 in Bryan, Brazos County, Texas

Notes: This Tree also applies to the other children of David Randall Wimpee & Kathy Ilene Wilton: Cynthia Joy Wimpee and Justin David Wimpee.

Cynthia Joy Wimpee (1977-   )
[8th. Generation From Henry Wilton (1769-1820)]
&
Brant Douglas Buche (1976-   )
& Family

Cynthia (Cindy) Joy Wimpee, the second child of Kathy Ilene Wilton and David Randall Wimpee, was born July 25, 1977 in Bryan, Texas. Cindy grew up in Bryan and graduated from Bryan High School, and following high school, she graduated from Texas A&M University with a degree in History. On August 21, 1999, Cindy married her high school sweetheart, Brant Douglas Buche. In addition to graduating from Bryan High School, Brant also attended Texas A&M University, where he graduated with both bachelor's and master's degrees in English, and where he taught for several years. Cindy later continued her education, obtaining a degree in nursing, and she worked as an oncology nurse at the St. Joseph Hospital in Bryan, Texas.

Family Group Sheet

Husband: Brant Douglas Buche	
Born: 09 Nov 1976	in: Ft. Scott, Bourbon Co., Kansas
Married: 21 Aug 1999	in: Brenham, Brazos Co., Texas
Father: Daniel Lee Buche	
Mother: Janice Susan Dennigan	

Wife: Cynthia Joy Wimpee	
Born: 25 Jul 1977	in: Bryan, Brazos Co., Texas
Father: David Randall Wimpee	
Mother: Kathy Ilene Wilton	

	CHILDREN	
1 M	Name: Braden Daniel Buche Born: 08 Dec 2000	in: Bryan, Brazos Co., Texas
2 M	Name: Connor Dylan Buche Born: 27 Mar 2003	in: Bryan, Brazos Co., Texas
3 M	Name: Ethan Luke Buche Born: 28 Sep 2004	in: Bryan, Brazos Co., Texas

Stanley Wilton (1958-   )
[7th. Generation from Henry Wilton (1769-1820)]

&

Karen Gayle Sawyer (1951-   )
& Family

&

Marlo Jennifer James (1969-   )
& Family

Stanley Wilton, the fourth and last child of Clyde Chalmer Wilton and Larue Vivian Wilton, was born September 1958 in McAllen in Hidalgo County, Texas. At the time of his birth, Stanley's dad was serving as a USAF chaplain at Moore AFB, Texas, which was located about 19 miles northwest of McAllen, Texas. Less than a year later, in June 1959, the family moved to Misawa AB, Japan, where Clyde Wilton was stationed until June 1962.

In 1962, Clyde Wilton left active service in the military, and the family moved again to Texas. After first staying in Killeen, Texas, from 1962 to 1967, the family settled permanently in Bryan in Brazos County, Texas. Stanley attended school in Bryan from the completion of 6th grade through high school.

After graduating in 1977 from Bryan High School, Stanley was employed, beginning 1978, with the Engineering Office Supply (E.O.S.) of College Station, Texas. After leaving E.O.S. from 1983 to 1986 for an engineering supply business venture in Lufkin, Texas, he returned to E.O.S. About 1994, in partnership with longtime friend and business associate, Lock Pachall, he bought out E.O.S., and he began his own business in Bryan, named Wilton's OfficeWorks.

In June 1978, Stanley married Gayle (Sawyer) Morsko. After living for a number of years in Bryan and Lufkin, Texas, the couple divorced in 1994.

Stanley married a second time in January 1998 to Marlo Jennifer James, daughter of Bela Michael James and Mary Betty Whitman. Marlo was also from the Bryan/College Station area, having graduated in May 1987 from A&M Consolidated High School in College Station, Texas. She also received a B.S. Degree in Social Work in December 1992 from Stephen F. Austin State University in Nacogdoches, Texas. Marlo became a licensed social worker, and for a while she worked at University Hills Nursing Home and Crestview Methodist Retirement Home in Bryan. More recently, she became a stay-at-home mom and helped with the Wilton's OfficeWorks accounting.

Stanley and Marlo had two daughters, Haley Nicole Wilton, born October 1999, and Macey Louise Wilton, born April 2002, both being born in Bryan, Texas. Stan and Marlo built a new home in College Station in 2006, where they hoped to settle permanently with their two daughters.

The family loved to engage in outdoor activities, such as camping, traveling, and kids' sports activities. Haley enjoyed soccer, basketball, ice-skating, and any other sport she was allowed to participate in. Macey, on the other hand, tried several sports but had trouble deciding what she liked. Stan also enjoyed hunting and fishing when he could find the time. In addition to the outdoors, Marlo was an avid scrapbooker, being a founding member of the local scrapbooking club called L.A.S.S.I.E.S. She also loved going on scrapbooking retreats and annual state conventions.

Family Group Sheet

Husband: Stanley Wilton

    Born: 13 Sep 1958   in: McAllen, Hidalgo Co., Texas
    Married: 24 Jan 1998   in: College Station, Brazos Co., Texas
    Father: Clyde Chalmer Wilton
    Mother: Larue Vivian Haley
        Other Spouses: Karen Gayle Sawyer

Wife: Marlo Jennifer James

    Born: 25 Aug 1969   in: Bryan, Brazos County, Texas
    Father: Bela Michael James
    Mother: Mary Betty Whitman

CHILDREN

1 F   Name: Haley Nicole Wilton
        Born: 07 Oct 1999   in: Bryan, Brazos County, Texas

2 F   Name: Macey Louise Wilton
        Born: 28 Apr 2002   in: Bryan, Brazos County, Texas

MARLO JENNIFER JAMES Standard Pedigree Tree

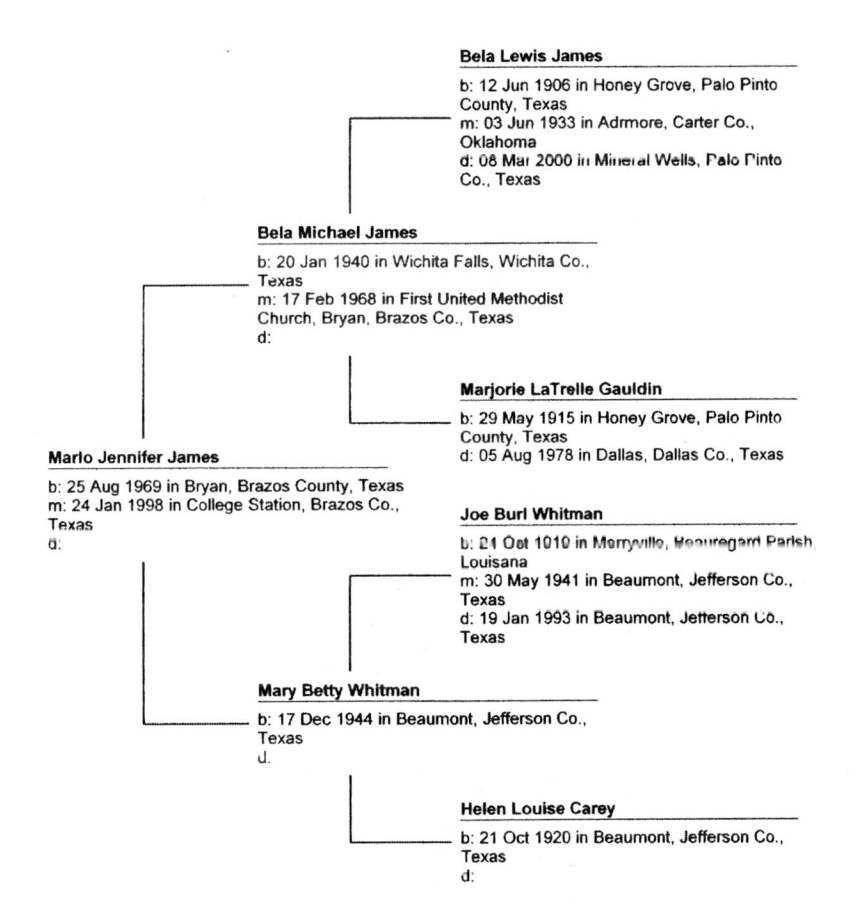

Marlo Jennifer James
b: 25 Aug 1969 in Bryan, Brazos County, Texas
m: 24 Jan 1998 in College Station, Brazos Co., Texas
d:

- **Bela Michael James**
  b: 20 Jan 1940 in Wichita Falls, Wichita Co., Texas
  m: 17 Feb 1968 in First United Methodist Church, Bryan, Brazos Co., Texas
  d:

  - **Bela Lewis James**
    b: 12 Jun 1906 in Honey Grove, Palo Pinto County, Texas
    m: 03 Jun 1933 in Adrmore, Carter Co., Oklahoma
    d: 08 Mar 2000 in Mineral Wells, Palo Pinto Co., Texas

  - **Marjorie LaTrelle Gauldin**
    b: 29 May 1915 in Honey Grove, Palo Pinto County, Texas
    d: 05 Aug 1978 in Dallas, Dallas Co., Texas

- **Mary Betty Whitman**
  b: 17 Dec 1944 in Beaumont, Jefferson Co., Texas
  d:

  - **Joe Burl Whitman**
    b: 21 Oct 1919 in Merryville, Beauregard Parish, Louisana
    m: 30 May 1941 in Beaumont, Jefferson Co., Texas
    d: 19 Jan 1993 in Beaumont, Jefferson Co., Texas

  - **Helen Louise Carey**
    b: 21 Oct 1920 in Beaumont, Jefferson Co., Texas
    d:

Amy Rosalie Wilton (1884-1958)
[5th. Generation From Henry Wilton (1769-1820)]

&

Jacob Newton Parrish (1873-1939)
& Family

Amy Rosalie Wilton, born September 1884 in Springtown in Parker County, Texas, was the third child of Henry Franklin Wilton and Martha Jane Baldwin. After Henry and Martha were married in 1877, the family first settled at Veal Station in Parker County, Texas, and their first three children were all born in Parker County. Shortly after Amy was born, about 1886, the family moved to Jack County, Texas to the Bumble Bee Prairie Community. Then, about 1889, the family settled permanently near the Winn Hill Community in Jack County, Texas.

Amy spent her formative years growing up on her father's farm, the Wilton homeplace, which was located about 3 &1/2 miles from Winn Hill. She rode on horseback to school at Winn Hill with her brothers, since it was too far to walk. She was good at riding sidesaddle, which she loved to do.

In February 1911, Amy married Jacob Newton (Jake) Parrish, son of John Buchanan Parrish and Susannah B. King. She was married in a double wedding, along with her brother, Elmer Elisha Wilton, who married Eula May Rhoades. Bro. Sampley married the two couples in a buggy, located in Jack County, somewhere in the vicinity of Berwick.

Amy and Jake settled in Berwick in Jack County, Texas, and they had three children. The first child, Herman Sterling Parish, was born November 1913 in Berwick, but he died January 1915. The second child, Hazel Evelyn Parrish, was born December 1915 in Berwick; and the third child, Herbert Charles Parrish, was born October 1919 in Jacksboro, Texas. In the 1920 Federal Census of Jack County, Texas, Jake Parrish, age 48, occupation farmer, was listed with Ama (Alma) Parrish, wife, age 36, and children Hazel Parrish, age 5, and Herbert Parrish, age 1. In the 1930 Federal Census of Jack County, Jake N. Parrish, age 57, occupation farmer, was listed with Amie R. Parrish, wife, age 45, and children Hazel E. Parrish, age 14, and Herbert C. Parrish, age 10.

Jacob was a successful farmer and rancher. He was also interested in government and community affairs, and he and Amy belonged to the Methodist Church. Jacob died in August 1939 and was buried in the Winn Hill Cemetery in Jack County.

About 1941, Amy moved to Jacksboro, Texas, where she was active in the First Baptist Church and a member of the Rebecca Lodge. She also worked as a practical nurse for several years. Amy died June 1958 in Jacksboro, and she was buried in the Winn Hill Cemetery.

Family Group Sheet

Husband: Jacob Newton Parrish

Born: 27 Sep 1873 — in: Lamar Co., Texas
Married: 26 Feb 1911 — in: Jermyn, Jack Co., Texas
Died: 28 Aug 1939 — in: Berwick, Jack Co., Texas
Father: John Buchanan Parrish
Mother: Susannah B. King

Wife: Amy Rosalie Wilton

Born: 12 Sep 1884 — in: Springtown, Parker Co., Texas
Died: 06 Jun 1958 — in: Jacksboro, Jack Co., Texas
Father: Henry Franklin Wilton
Mother: Martha Jane Baldwin

CHILDREN

1 M
Name: Herman Sterling Parrish
Born: 11 Nov 1913 — in: Berwick, Jack Co., Texas
Died: 14 Jan 1915 — in: Jack Co., Texas

2 F
Name: Hazel Evelyn Parrish
Born: 07 Dec 1915 — in: Berwick, Jack Co., Texas
Died: 11 Apr 2005 — in: Dallas Co., Texas
Married: 16 Dec 1936 — in: Jacksboro, Jack Co., Texas
Spouse: Robert Wade Marley

3 M
Name: Herbert Charles Parrish
Born: 08 Oct 1919 — in: Jacksboro, Jack Co., Texas
Died: 29 Jun 2000 — in: Denton, Denton Co., Texas
Married: 12 Aug 1941 — in: Denton, Denton Co., Texas
Spouse: Edrie Maurice Talley

JACOB NEWTON PARRISH Standard Pedigree Tree

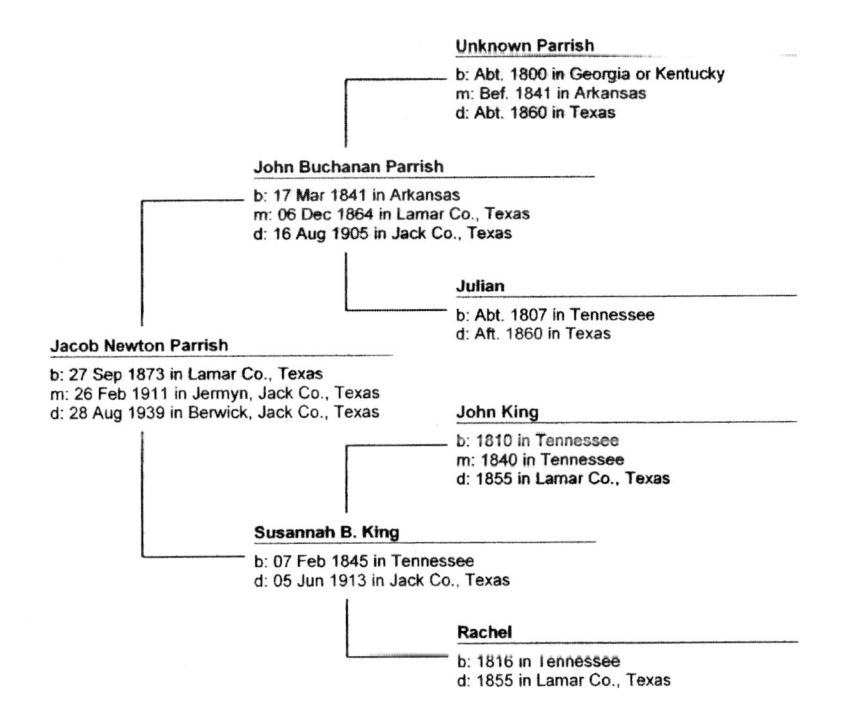

Jacob Newton Parrish
b: 27 Sep 1873 in Lamar Co., Texas
m: 26 Feb 1911 in Jermyn, Jack Co., Texas
d: 28 Aug 1939 in Berwick, Jack Co., Texas

- **John Buchanan Parrish**
  b: 17 Mar 1841 in Arkansas
  m: 06 Dec 1864 in Lamar Co., Texas
  d: 16 Aug 1905 in Jack Co., Texas
  - **Unknown Parrish**
    b: Abt. 1800 in Georgia or Kentucky
    m: Bef. 1841 in Arkansas
    d: Abt. 1860 in Texas
  - **Julian**
    b: Abt. 1807 in Tennessee
    d: Aft. 1860 in Texas

- **Susannah B. King**
  b: 07 Feb 1845 in Tennessee
  d: 05 Jun 1913 in Jack Co., Texas
  - **John King**
    b: 1810 in Tennessee
    m: 1840 in Tennessee
    d: 1855 in Lamar Co., Texas
  - **Rachel**
    b: 1816 in Tennessee
    d: 1855 in Lamar Co., Texas

Hazel Evelyn Parrish (1915-2005)
[6th. Generation From Henry Wilton (1769-1820)]

&

Robert Wade Marley (1910-1996)
& Family

Hazel Evelyn Parrish, the second child of Amy Rosalie Wilton and Jacob Newton (Jake) Parrish, was born December 1915 at Berwick in Jack County, Texas. Amy and Jake had made Berwick their home since their marriage in 1911. Hazel had two brothers, but her older brother, Herman Sterling Parrish, died in infancy.

Hazel remembered with fondness her early years, when she periodically went with her grandparents, Henry Franklin Wilton and Martha (Baldwin) Wilton, to buy groceries in nearby Jermyn, Texas. Jermyn was about 8 miles west of Berwick and about 4 miles west of the Wilton homeplace, where Henry and Martha lived. Since Henry and Martha did not have a car at that time, Hazel assisted them with the Parrish family car. She remembered trading at the Jones General Store, where she thought at the time that one "could buy almost anything," and at Nell's Drug Store in Jermyn. Her uncle, Charlie Wilton, and some of her cousins, also lived in Jermyn, and she enjoyed visiting with them, as well.

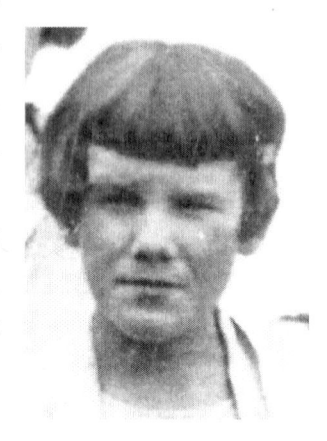

Hazel's formal education did not begin until the second grade, because her mother first taught her at home. For the second through the fifth grades, Hazel attended school at Winn Hill, which had only one teacher. Beginning with the sixth grade, she transferred to Center Point/Berwick, which had a two teacher school. While a junior in high school, Hazel transferred to Jacksboro; and then for her senior year of high school, she attended the Jermyn High School, where she graduated in 1932. Since she got a head start at home, Hazel graduated from high school at the age of 16, with only 10 years of formal schooling. There were only eleven in her graduating class at Jermyn, with the baccalaureate service being held at the Methodist Church, and the graduation ceremony at the school.

Following high school, Hazel attended Weatherford Junior College in Weatherford, Texas for two years. Then, she went to North Texas State Teachers College (NTSTC) in Denton, Texas, where she graduated with a bachelor's degree in 1936. She later returned to NTSTC, and in 1959 she received a master's degree. From 1957 to 1981, Hazel was a second grade teacher in the Jacksboro Elementary School.

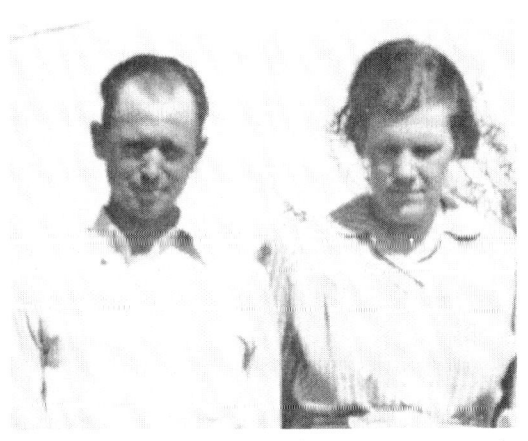

In 1936, Hazel married Robert Wade Marley, son of John Henry Marley and Telula Chaddick, who were also residents of Jack County. For awhile, they lived in the Berwick Community, and then, in 1956, they moved to Jacksboro, Texas. Robert raised registered Hereford cattle and quarter horses on the Parrish Ranch, and he also worked as a pumper in the oil field for a number of years. Between 1939 and 1950, Robert and Hazel had five children. After moving to Jacksboro, all five of their children graduated from Jacksboro High School.

Both Robert and Hazel had memories of growing up during the "Great Depression," a time when nothing came easily and one had to work hard for whatever he got. They recalled a time of reading by kerosene lamps, having no air-conditioning, no running water, and no electricity. Their parents did, however, own a Model-T Ford, and they both were fortunate to be able to come to Jacksboro on Saturdays and to attend church there on Sundays.

Robert and Hazel were also active in community activities. Robert was a member of the Masonic Lodge, and Hazel taught Sunday School at the First Baptist Church and participated in the Order of Eastern Star and the Order of Rainbow for Girls. Robert died June 1996 in Jack County, Texas, and Hazel died April 2005 in Dallas County, Texas.

Family Group Sheet

Husband: Robert Wade Marley

Born: 18 Aug 1910 — in: Senate, Jack Co., Texas
Married: 16 Dec 1936 — in: Jacksboro, Jack Co., Texas
Died: 16 Jun 1996 — in: Jack Co., Texas
Father: John Henry Marley
Mother: Telula Victoria Chaddick

Wife: Hazel Evelyn Parrish

Born: 07 Dec 1915 — in: Berwick, Jack Co., Texas
Died: 11 Apr 2005 — in: Dallas Co., Texas
Father: Jacob Newton Parrish
Mother: Amy Rosalie Wilton

CHILDREN

1. F
Name: Martha Laverne Marley
Born: 19 Mar 1939 — in: Jacksboro, Jack Co., Texas
Died: 26 Apr 1991 — in: Cleburne, Johnson Co., Texas
Married: 20 Aug 1969 — in: Germany
Spouse: Ernest Cardenas

2. F
Name: Patricia Ann Marley
Born: 03 Mar 1942 — in: Jacksboro, Jack Co., Texas
Married: 03 Jun 1961
Spouse: Frank Derrell Jackson
Married: 11 Sep 1986 — in: Dallas, Dallas Co., Texas
Spouse: James Liston

3. M
Name: Thomas Wayne Marley
Born: 11 Oct 1943 — in: Jacksboro, Jack Co., Texas
Married: 22 Dec 1962 — in: Texas
Spouse: Veda Vell Underwood
Married: 15 Feb 1997 — in: Denton Co., Texas
Spouse: Patricia J. Murdock

4. M
Name: Robert Wade Jr. Marley
Born: 10 Oct 1947 — in: Graham, Young Co., Texas
Married: 01 Nov 1968 — in: Jack Co., Texas
Spouse: Kathryn June Farris

5. M
Name: Charles Victor Marley
Born: 29 Nov 1950 — in: Graham, Young Co., Texas
Married: 05 Jul 1975 — in: Dallas Co., Texas
Spouse: Diane Lynette Hutson

HAZEL EVELYN PARRISH Standard Pedigree Tree

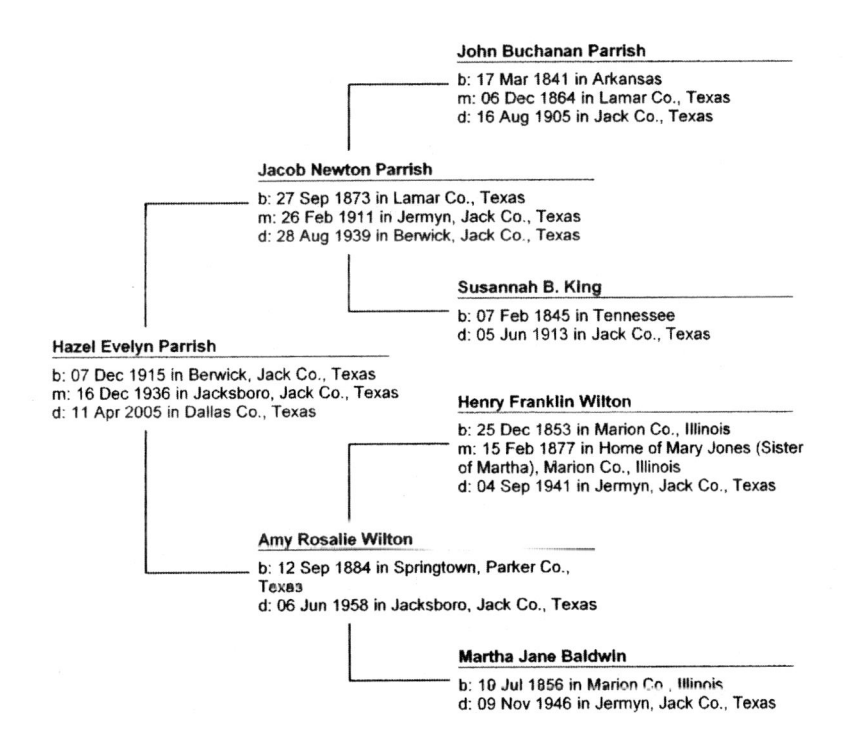

John Buchanan Parrish
b: 17 Mar 1841 in Arkansas
m: 06 Dec 1864 in Lamar Co., Texas
d: 16 Aug 1905 in Jack Co., Texas

Jacob Newton Parrish
b: 27 Sep 1873 in Lamar Co., Texas
m: 26 Feb 1911 in Jermyn, Jack Co., Texas
d: 28 Aug 1939 in Berwick, Jack Co., Texas

Susannah B. King
b: 07 Feb 1845 in Tennessee
d: 05 Jun 1913 in Jack Co., Texas

Hazel Evelyn Parrish
b: 07 Dec 1915 in Berwick, Jack Co., Texas
m: 16 Dec 1936 in Jacksboro, Jack Co., Texas
d: 11 Apr 2005 in Dallas Co., Texas

Henry Franklin Wilton
b: 25 Dec 1853 in Marion Co., Illinois
m: 15 Feb 1877 in Home of Mary Jones (Sister of Martha), Marion Co., Illinois
d: 04 Sep 1941 in Jermyn, Jack Co., Texas

Amy Rosalie Wilton
b: 12 Sep 1884 in Springtown, Parker Co., Texas
d: 06 Jun 1958 in Jacksboro, Jack Co., Texas

Martha Jane Baldwin
b: 10 Jul 1856 in Marion Co., Illinois
d: 09 Nov 1946 in Jermyn, Jack Co., Texas

Notes: This Tree also applies to the other children of Jacob Newton Parrish & Amy Rosalie Wilton: Herman Sterling Parrish and Herbert Charles Parrish.

ROBERT WADE MARLEY Standard Pedigree Tree

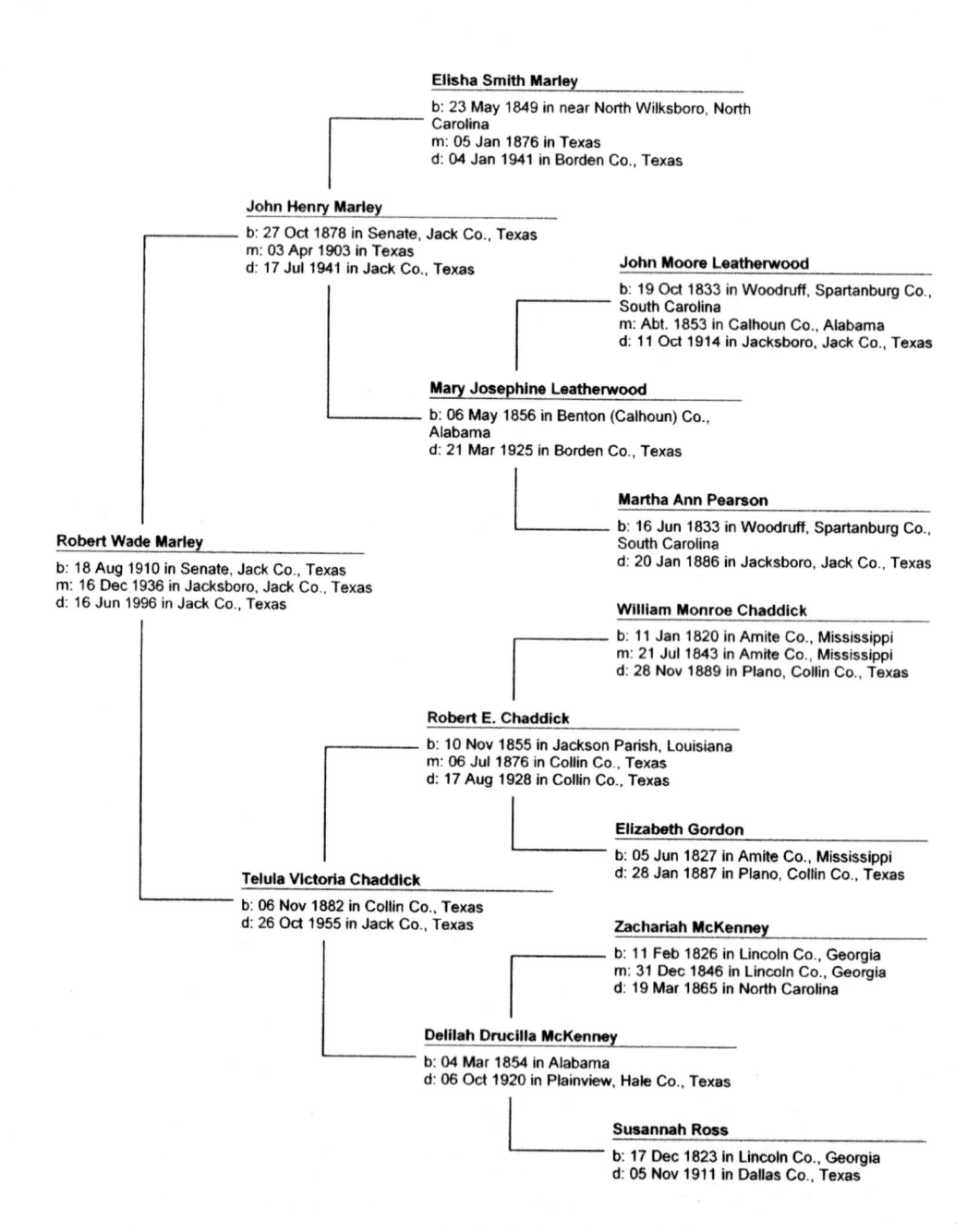

Robert Wade Marley
b: 18 Aug 1910 in Senate, Jack Co., Texas
m: 16 Dec 1936 in Jacksboro, Jack Co., Texas
d: 16 Jun 1996 in Jack Co., Texas

- **John Henry Marley**
  b: 27 Oct 1878 in Senate, Jack Co., Texas
  m: 03 Apr 1903 in Texas
  d: 17 Jul 1941 in Jack Co., Texas

  - **Elisha Smith Marley**
    b: 23 May 1849 in near North Wilksboro, North Carolina
    m: 05 Jan 1876 in Texas
    d: 04 Jan 1941 in Borden Co., Texas

  - **Mary Josephine Leatherwood**
    b: 06 May 1856 in Benton (Calhoun) Co., Alabama
    d: 21 Mar 1925 in Borden Co., Texas

    - **John Moore Leatherwood**
      b: 19 Oct 1833 in Woodruff, Spartanburg Co., South Carolina
      m: Abt. 1853 in Calhoun Co., Alabama
      d: 11 Oct 1914 in Jacksboro, Jack Co., Texas

    - **Martha Ann Pearson**
      b: 16 Jun 1833 in Woodruff, Spartanburg Co., South Carolina
      d: 20 Jan 1886 in Jacksboro, Jack Co., Texas

- **Telula Victoria Chaddick**
  b: 06 Nov 1882 in Collin Co., Texas
  d: 26 Oct 1955 in Jack Co., Texas

  - **Robert E. Chaddick**
    b: 10 Nov 1855 in Jackson Parish, Louisiana
    m: 06 Jul 1876 in Collin Co., Texas
    d: 17 Aug 1928 in Collin Co., Texas

    - **William Monroe Chaddick**
      b: 11 Jan 1820 in Amite Co., Mississippi
      m: 21 Jul 1843 in Amite Co., Mississippi
      d: 28 Nov 1889 in Plano, Collin Co., Texas

    - **Elizabeth Gordon**
      b: 05 Jun 1827 in Amite Co., Mississippi
      d: 28 Jan 1887 in Plano, Collin Co., Texas

  - **Delilah Drucilla McKenney**
    b: 04 Mar 1854 in Alabama
    d: 06 Oct 1920 in Plainview, Hale Co., Texas

    - **Zachariah McKenney**
      b: 11 Feb 1826 in Lincoln Co., Georgia
      m: 31 Dec 1846 in Lincoln Co., Georgia
      d: 19 Mar 1865 in North Carolina

    - **Susannah Ross**
      b: 17 Dec 1823 in Lincoln Co., Georgia
      d: 05 Nov 1911 in Dallas Co., Texas

Martha Laverne Marley (1939-1991)
[7th. Generation From Henry Wilton (1769-1820)]

&

Ernest Cardenas (1932-   )
& Family

Martha Laverne Marley, the first child of Robert Wade Marley and Hazel Evelyn Parrish, was born March 1939 in Jacksboro in Jack County, Texas. The family originally settled in the Berwick Community in Jack County, but they moved to Jacksboro in 1956. Martha finished high school at the Jacksboro High School in Jacksboro, Texas.

Following high school, Martha attended North Texas State University (NTSU) in Denton, Texas, where she received two college degrees. She then was employed with the U.S. Army in West Germany for four years as a librarian. She later settled in Cleburne, Texas, where she worked as a high school librarian.

In 1969, while still in Germany, Martha married Ernest Cardenas, who was from San Antonio, Texas. They had one daughter, Donna Faye Cardenas, who was born December 1970 at Fort Riley in Kansas. Martha and Ernest were divorced June 1984 in Johnson County, Texas. Martha died April 1991 in Cleburne in Johnson County, Texas.

Family Group Sheet

Husband: Ernest Cardenas	
Born: Mar 1932	in: Texas
Married: 20 Aug 1969	in: Germany

Wife: Martha Laverne Marley	
Born: 19 Mar 1939	in: Jacksboro, Jack Co., Texas
Died: 26 Apr 1991	in: Cleburne, Johnson Co., Texas
Father: Robert Wade Marley	
Mother: Hazel Evelyn Parrish	

CHILDREN		
1 F	Name: Donna Faye Cardenas Born: 01 Dec 1970	in: Fort Riley, Gary Co., Kansas

MARTHA LAVERNE MARLEY Standard Pedigree Tree

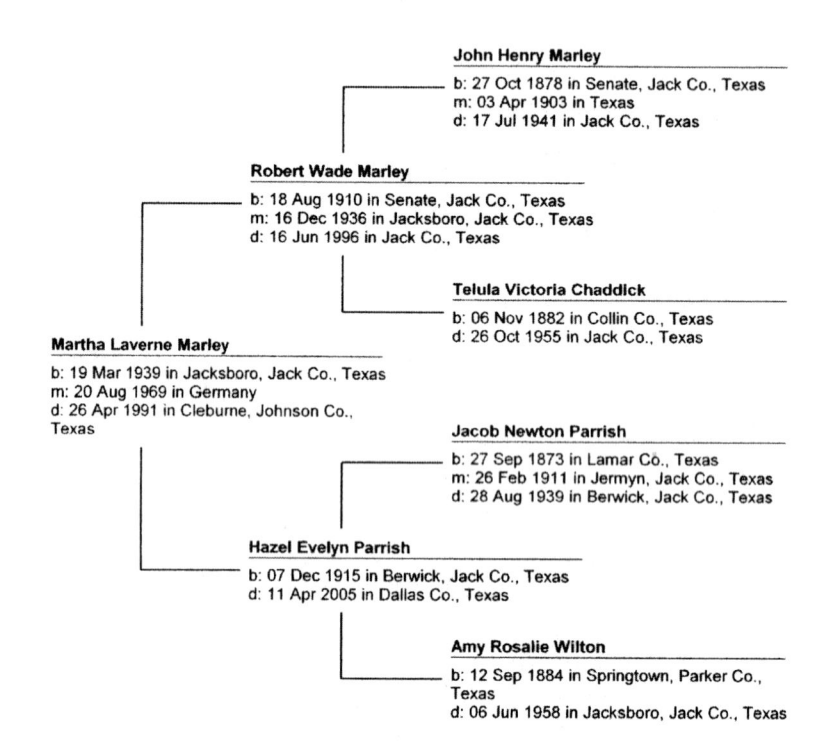

Martha Laverne Marley
b: 19 Mar 1939 in Jacksboro, Jack Co., Texas
m: 20 Aug 1969 in Germany
d: 26 Apr 1991 in Cleburne, Johnson Co., Texas

- **Robert Wade Marley**
  b: 18 Aug 1910 in Senate, Jack Co., Texas
  m: 16 Dec 1936 in Jacksboro, Jack Co., Texas
  d: 16 Jun 1996 in Jack Co., Texas
  - **John Henry Marley**
    b: 27 Oct 1878 in Senate, Jack Co., Texas
    m: 03 Apr 1903 in Texas
    d: 17 Jul 1941 in Jack Co., Texas
  - **Telula Victoria Chaddick**
    b: 06 Nov 1882 in Collin Co., Texas
    d: 26 Oct 1955 in Jack Co., Texas

- **Hazel Evelyn Parrish**
  b: 07 Dec 1915 in Berwick, Jack Co., Texas
  d: 11 Apr 2005 in Dallas Co., Texas
  - **Jacob Newton Parrish**
    b: 27 Sep 1873 in Lamar Co., Texas
    m: 26 Feb 1911 in Jermyn, Jack Co., Texas
    d: 28 Aug 1939 in Berwick, Jack Co., Texas
  - **Amy Rosalie Wilton**
    b: 12 Sep 1884 in Springtown, Parker Co., Texas
    d: 06 Jun 1958 in Jacksboro, Jack Co., Texas

Notes: This Tree also applies to the other children of Robert Wade Marley & Hazel Evelyn Parrish: Patricia Ann Marley, Thomas Wayne Marley, Robert Wade Jr. Marley, and Charles Victor Marley.

Patricia Ann Marley (1942-   )
[7th. Generation From Henry Wilton (1769-1820)]

&

Frank Derrell Jackson
& Family

&

James Liston
& Family

Patricia Ann Marley, the second of five children of Robert Wade Marley and Hazel Evelyn Parrish, was born March 1942 in Jacksboro, Texas. Beginning in 1956, the family made Jacksboro their home, and Patricia graduated from Jacksboro High School in Jacksboro, Texas.

Following high school, Patricia attended the Dallas Community College and for a time settled in Dallas, Texas, where she worked for the Kroger Company.

In June 1961, Patricia married Frank Derrell Jackson of Lipan, Texas. They had one daughter, Mary Ann Jackson, born September 1966 in Weatherford, Texas. Patricia married a second time to James Liston in September 1984 in Dallas, Texas.

Family Group Sheet

Husband: Frank Derrell Jackson	
Born: Unknown	in: Texas
Married: 03 Jun 1961	in: Texas

Wife: Patricia Ann Marley	
Born: 03 Mar 1942	in: Jacksboro, Jack Co., Texas
Father: Robert Wade Marley	
Mother: Hazel Evelyn Parrish	
Other Spouses: James Liston	

CHILDREN

1 F	Name: Mary Ann Jackson	
	Born: 28 Sep 1966	in: Weatherford, Parker Co., Texas

Family Group Sheet

Husband: James Liston	
Born: Unknown	
Married: 11 Sep 1986	in: Dallas, Dallas Co., Texas

Wife: Patricia Ann Marley	
Born: 03 Mar 1942	in: Jacksboro, Jack Co., Texas
Father: Robert Wade Marley	
Mother: Hazel Evelyn Parrish	
Other Spouses: Frank Derrell Jackson	

Thomas Wayne Marley (1943-   )
[7th. Generation From Henry Wilton (1769-1820)]

&

Veda Vell Underwood (1944-   )
& Family

&

Patricia J. Murdock (1940-   )
& Family

Thomas Wayne Marley, the third child of Robert Wade Marley and Hazel Evelyn Parrish, was born October 1943 in Jacksboro, Texas. After first settling in the Berwick Community of Jack County, Texas, Robert and Hazel moved the family, in 1956, to Jacksboro, where Thomas later graduated from the Jacksboro High School.

In 1962, Thomas married Veda Underwood of Jermyn, Texas. Their first child, Bryan Charles Marley, was born March 1967 at Wichita Falls, Texas. From 1967 to 1971, Thomas served in the USAF in Germany, and their second son, Steven Thomas Marley, was born March 1969 in Wiesbaden, Germany.

At one point, Thomas received a college degree from North Texas State University (NTSU) in Denton, Texas. He also settled in Denton, where he owned and operated a cabinet shop. Thomas married a second time in Denton, Texas, on February 15, 1997, to Patricia Murdock.

Family Group Sheet

Husband: Thomas Wayne Marley

Born: 11 Oct 1943 in: Jacksboro, Jack Co., Texas
Married: 22 Dec 1962 in: Texas
Father: Robert Wade Marley
Mother: Hazel Evelyn Parrish
Other Spouses: Patricia J. Murdock

Wife: Veda Vell Underwood

Born: 1944 in: Texas

CHILDREN

1 M	Name: Bryan Charles Marley	
	Born: 03 Mar 1967	in: Wichita Falls, Wichita Co., Texas
2 M	Name: Steven Thomas Marley	
	Born: 26 Mar 1969	in: Wiesbaden, Germany

Family Group Sheet

Husband: Thomas Wayne Marley

Born: 11 Oct 1943 in: Jacksboro, Jack Co., Texas
Married: 15 Feb 1997 in: Denton Co., Texas
Father: Robert Wade Marley
Mother: Hazel Evelyn Parrish
Other Spouses: Veda Vell Underwood

Wife: Patricia J. Murdock

Born: Abt. 1940

Robert Wade Jr. Marley (1947-   )
[7th. Generation From Henry Wilton (1769-1820)]

&

Kathryn June Farris (1949-   )
& Family

Robert Wade Jr. Marley, the fourth of five children of Robert Wade Marley and Hazel Evelyn Parrish, was born October 1947 in Graham in Young County, Texas. After the family settled in Jacksboro, Texas, in 1956, Robert later graduated from the Jacksboro High School. After high school, Robert attended the Ranger Junior College in Ranger, Texas.

In November 1968, Robert married Kathryn June Farris, of Jacksboro, Texas. Robert and Kathryn had two children, who were both born in Graham, Texas. Their first child, Kelly Wade Marley, was born April 1976; and, their second child, Lisa Kaye Marley, was born November 1979.

At one point, Robert moved to Fairbanks, Alaska, where he owned and operated a trucking business.

Family Group Sheet

Husband: Robert Wade Jr. Marley

Born: 10 Oct 1947	in: Graham, Young Co., Texas
Married: 01 Nov 1968	in: Jack Co., Texas
Father: Robert Wade Marley	
Mother: Hazel Evelyn Parrish	

Wife: Kathryn June Farris

Born: Abt. 1949	in: Texas

CHILDREN

1 M	Name: Kelly Wade Marley Born: 15 Apr 1976	in: Graham, Young Co., Texas
2 F	Name: Lisa Kaye Marley Born: 18 Nov 1979	in: Graham, Young Co., Texas

Charles Victor Marley (1950-   )
[7th. Generation From Henry Wilton (1769-1820)]

&

Diane Lynette Hutson (1950-   )
& Family

Charles Victor Marley, the fifth and last child of Robert Wade Marley and Hazel Evelyn Parrish, was born November 1950 in Graham, Texas. The family first settled in the Berwick Community of Jack County, Texas after the marriage of Robert and Hazel in 1936. In 1956, the family moved to Jacksboro, Texas, and that is where Charles attended school through high school.

After high school, Charles first attended the North Texas State University (NTSU) in Denton, Texas, where he received a bachelor's degree. He then went on to attend the East Texas State University (ETSU) in Commerce, Texas, where he received a master's degree. For several years he was a coach in Dallas schools, and then he moved to Mesquite, Texas, where he owned a financial service business, which specialized in retirement and tax planning.

In 1975, Charles married Diane Lynette Hutson, who was from Fort Worth, Texas. They had two children, Michael Ryan Marley, born July 1979 in Dallas, Texas, and Rachel Elizabeth Marley, born March 1986.

Family Group Sheet

Husband: Charles Victor Marley	
Born: 29 Nov 1950	in: Graham, Young Co., Texas
Married: 05 Jul 1975	in: Dallas Co., Texas
Father: Robert Wade Marley	
Mother: Hazel Evelyn Parrish	

Wife: Diane Lynette Hutson	
Born: Abt. 1950	in: Texas

	CHILDREN	
1 M	Name: Michael Ryan Marley	
	Born: 07 Jul 1979	in: Dallas, Dallas Co., Texas
2 F	Name: Rachel Elizabeth Marley	
	Born: 29 Mar 1986	

Herbert Charles Parrish (1919-2000)
[6th. Generation From Henry Wilton (1769-1820)]

&

Edrie Maurice Talley (1921-   )
& Family

Herbert Charles Parrish, the third and last child of Jacob Newton (Jake) Parrish and Amy Rosalie (Wilton) Parrish, was born October 1919 in Jacksboro, Texas. Jake and Amy had made their home in Berwick in Jack County, Texas since their marriage in 1911, and Herbert began his formal education in the school at nearby Winn Hill. After later transferring to the Center Point/Berwick school, then to the Jacksboro school, and finally to the school at Jermyn, Texas, Herbert graduated from Jermyn High School in 1936. Following high school, Herbert attended North Texas State Teachers College in Denton, Texas, where he received a bachelor's degree in 1939 and a master's degree in 1941.

In August 1941, Herbert married Edrie Maurice Talley, daughter of Robert Byron Talley and Mai Belle Wilkinson, in Denton, Texas. After the U.S. entered World War II in 1941, Herbert joined the U.S. Navy, enlisting as an ensign. Before leaving the active military, he advanced to the rank of Lieutenant Commander. After leaving the active military, he continued to serve in the U.S. Naval Reserve for twenty years.

At one point, Herbert attended Ohio State University, where he obtained a PhD in mathematics in 1955. While still in Ohio, Herbert and Edrie had their first son, Byron Newton Parrish, who was born October 1948 in Columbus, Ohio.

Beginning in 1949, Herbert became an assistant professor of mathematics at North Texas State University (later named University of North Texas, or UNT) in Denton, Texas. Then, from 1955 to 1958, he was an associate professor of mathematics, and from 1958 until his retirement in 1985, he was a professor and director of the mathematics department at UNT. Herbert was also a member of a number of prestigious mathematics organizations, and he was listed in "Who's Who of America."

Herbert and Edrie had two other children after they settled in Denton, Texas. Their second child, Norman Wilton Parrish, was born June 1951; and, their third and last child, Roberta Jean Parrish, was born May 1954, both being born in Denton. Herbert died June 2000 in Denton, Texas and was buried at the Restlawn Cemetery, also located in Denton.

Family Group Sheet

Husband: Herbert Charles Parrish

Born: 08 Oct 1919 — in: Jacksboro, Jack Co., Texas
Married: 12 Aug 1941 — in: Denton, Denton Co., Texas
Died: 28 Jun 2000 — in: Denton, Denton Co., Texas
Father: Jacob Newton Parrish
Mother: Amy Rosalie Wilton

Wife: Edrie Maurice Talley

Born: 20 Jul 1921 — in: Frisco, Collin Co., Texas
Father: Robert Byron Talley
Mother: Mai Belle Wilkinson

CHILDREN

1 M
Name: Byron Newton Parrish
Born: 01 Oct 1948 — in: Columbus, Franklin Co., Ohio
Married: 05 May 1970
Spouse: Kathlelen Mooney

2 M
Name: Norman Wilton Parrish
Born: 01 Jun 1951 — in: Denton, Denton Co., Texas
Married: 09 Jun 1973 — in: Denton Co., Texas
Spouse: Joyce Fay Buttrill

3 F
Name: Roberta Jean Parrish
Born: 14 May 1954 — in: Denton, Denton Co., Texas
Married: 15 Jul 1978 — in: Travis Co., Texas
Spouse: Michael Peter Starbird

Byron Newton Parrish (1948-   )
[7th. Generation From Henry Wilton (1769-1820)]

&

Kathlelen Mooney
& Family

Byron Newton Parrish, born October 1948 in Columbus, Ohio, was the first of three children of Herbert Charles Parrish and Edrie Maurice Talley. Most of his formative years were spent in Denton, Texas, but Byron was born while Herbert & Edrie were temporarily living in Ohio.

Byron married Kathlelen Mooney in May 1970 and the family settled near the Boston area of Massachusetts.

Family Group Sheet

Husband: Byron Newton Parrish	
Born: 01 Oct 1948	in: Columbus, Franklin Co., Ohio
Married: 05 May 1970	
Father: Herbert Charles Parrish	
Mother: Edrie Maurice Talley	
Wife: Kathlelen Mooney	
Born: Unknown	

	CHILDREN
1 M	Name: Kyle Parrish Born: 02 Apr 1975
2 F	Name: Amanda Parrish Born: 07 Jul 1981

BYRON NEWTON PARRISH Standard Pedigree Tree

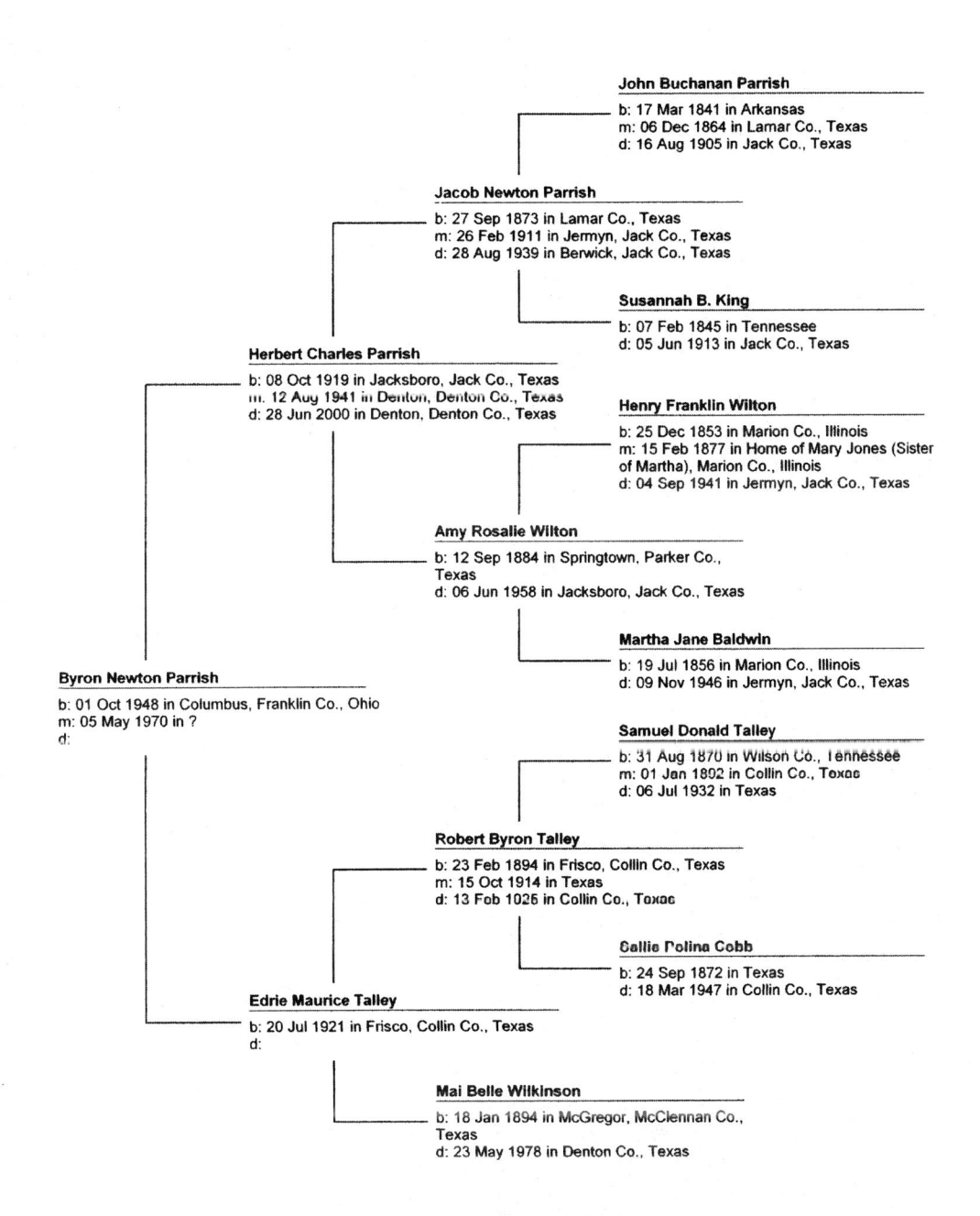

Byron Newton Parrish
b: 01 Oct 1948 in Columbus, Franklin Co., Ohio
m: 05 May 1970 in ?
d:

- **Herbert Charles Parrish**
  b: 08 Oct 1919 in Jacksboro, Jack Co., Texas
  m: 12 Aug 1941 in Denton, Denton Co., Texas
  d: 28 Jun 2000 in Denton, Denton Co., Texas

  - **Jacob Newton Parrish**
    b: 27 Sep 1873 in Lamar Co., Texas
    m: 26 Feb 1911 in Jermyn, Jack Co., Texas
    d: 28 Aug 1939 in Berwick, Jack Co., Texas

    - **John Buchanan Parrish**
      b: 17 Mar 1841 in Arkansas
      m: 06 Dec 1864 in Lamar Co., Texas
      d: 16 Aug 1905 in Jack Co., Texas

    - **Susannah B. King**
      b: 07 Feb 1845 in Tennessee
      d: 05 Jun 1913 in Jack Co., Texas

  - **Amy Rosalie Wilton**
    b: 12 Sep 1884 in Springtown, Parker Co., Texas
    d: 06 Jun 1958 in Jacksboro, Jack Co., Texas

    - **Henry Franklin Wilton**
      b: 25 Dec 1853 in Marion Co., Illinois
      m: 15 Feb 1877 in Home of Mary Jones (Sister of Martha), Marion Co., Illinois
      d: 04 Sep 1941 in Jermyn, Jack Co., Texas

    - **Martha Jane Baldwin**
      b: 19 Jul 1856 in Marion Co., Illinois
      d: 09 Nov 1946 in Jermyn, Jack Co., Texas

- **Edrie Maurice Talley**
  b: 20 Jul 1921 in Frisco, Collin Co., Texas
  d:

  - **Robert Byron Talley**
    b: 23 Feb 1894 in Frisco, Collin Co., Texas
    m: 15 Oct 1914 in Texas
    d: 13 Feb 1926 in Collin Co., Texas

    - **Samuel Donald Talley**
      b: 31 Aug 1870 in Wilson Co., Tennessee
      m: 01 Jan 1892 in Collin Co., Texas
      d: 06 Jul 1932 in Texas

    - **Sallie Polina Cobb**
      b: 24 Sep 1872 in Texas
      d: 18 Mar 1947 in Collin Co., Texas

  - **Mai Belle Wilkinson**
    b: 18 Jan 1894 in McGregor, McClennan Co., Texas
    d: 23 May 1978 in Denton Co., Texas

Notes: This Tree also applies to the other children of Herbert Charles Parrish & Edrie Maurice Talley: Norman Wilton Parrish and Roberta Jean Parrish.

Norman Wilton Parrish (1951-)
[7th. Generation From Henry Wilton (1769-1820)]

&

Joyce Fay Buttrill (1950-)
& Family

Norman Wilton Parrish, born June 1951 in Denton, Texas, was the second child of Herbert Charles Parrish and Edrie Maurice Talley. Following his active military service with the U.S. Navy and while pursuing a career as a mathematics professor, Herbert Parrish settled the family in Denton in Denton County, Texas. Norman was also born and raised in Denton, Texas.

In June 1973, in Denton, Texas, Norman married Joyce Fay Buttrill, the daughter of Wilbur D. Buttrill and Ruth Faught. Norman and Joyce had three children, all born in Texas. The first child, Emily Parrish, was born May 4, 1981; the second child, Rachel Sarah Parrish, was born March 4, 1983; and, the third child, Nathan Edward Parrish, was born October 3, 1985. At one point the family settled in the Houston area in Harris County, Texas.

Family Group Sheet

Husband: Norman Wilton Parrish
- Born: 01 Jun 1951 in: Denton, Denton Co., Texas
- Married: 09 Jun 1973 in: Denton Co., Texas
- Father: Herbert Charles Parrish
- Mother: Edrie Maurice Talley

Wife: Joyce Fay Buttrill
- Born: 19 Nov 1950 in: Denton Co., Texas
- Father: Wilbur D. Buttrill
- Mother: Ruth Faught

CHILDREN

1 F	Name: Emily Parrish	Born: 04 May 1981	in: Texas
2 F	Name: Rachel Sarah Parrish	Born: 04 Mar 1983	in: Harris Co., Texas
3 M	Name: Nathan Edward Parrish	Born: 03 Oct 1985	in: Montgomery Co., Texas

Roberta Jean Parrish (1954-)
[7th. Generation From Henry Wilton (1769-1820)]

&

Michael Peter Starbird (1948-)
& Family

Roberta Jean Parrish, the third and last child of Herbert Charles Parrish and Edrie Maurice Talley, was born May 1954 in Denton, Texas. The family had settled in Denton in Denton County, Texas in the early 1950's, when Herbert Parrish began a career as a mathematics professor at the University of North Texas in Denton.

In July 1978, Roberta married Michael Peter Starbird, in Travis County, Texas. Roberta and Michael had two children, both born in Travis County. The first child, Talley Kate Starbird, was born July 23, 1985; and, the second child, Bryn Ellen Starbird, was born August 28, 1987. At one point the family settled in Austin in Travis County, Texas.

Family Group Sheet

Husband: Michael Peter Starbird	
Born: 10 Jul 1948	in: Los Angeles Co., California
Married: 15 Jul 1978	in: Travis Co., Texas
Father: William Brinton Starbird	
Mother: Mary Ellen Hughes	

Wife: Roberta Jean Parrish	
Born: 14 May 1954	in: Denton, Denton Co., Texas
Father: Herbert Charles Parrish	
Mother: Edrie Maurice Talley	

CHILDREN

1 F	Name: Talley Kate Starbird Born: 23 Jul 1985	in: Travis Co., Texas
2 F	Name: Bryn Ellen Starbird Born: 28 Aug 1987	in: Travis Co., Texas

Charles Joseph Wilton (1891-1967)
[5th. Generation from Henry Wilton (1769-1820)]

&
Lona Blanche Parrish (1894-1926)
& Family

&
Lydia Ann Evans (1910-1958)
& Family

Charles Joseph Wilton, born March 12, 1891 in Jack County, Texas, was the fifth child of Henry Franklin Wilton and Martha Jane Baldwin. He was actually born halfway between Mt. Heckla in Bryson, Texas and Lost Valley in Jermyn, Texas. Henry and Martha had settled permanently near the Winn Hill Community in Jack County in about 1889, and that was where Charles Joseph (Charlie) grew up as a child. Early on, he was dubbed with the name, "Eppie Bro Titus Joseph Adolphus Charles Wilton," but that was shortened to "Charlie."

Until about 1913, Charlie lived on the Wilton homeplace, located about 3 &1/2 miles from Jermyn and about 1 &1/2 miles from Winn Hill, where he helped the family with the farming. In the 1900 Federal Census of Jack County, Texas, Charlie was listed at age 9, along with his parents and two brothers and two sisters. In the 1910 Federal Census of Jack County, Texas, Charlie was listed at age 19, along with his parents and one brother and two sisters. By that time, an older brother, Virgil Wilton, had died. One other brother, Holland Wilton, had died in infancy in 1890, shortly before Charlie was born.

In September 1913, Charlie married Lona Blanche Parrish, daughter of John Thomas Parrish and Neoma Demer Clark. They were married by Lona's grandfather, Elder D.J.E. Clark, who was a Primitive Baptist preacher. For awhile, the couple lived in their own one room home on the Wilton homeplace, located about 200 yards south of the Henry Franklin Wilton home.

In 1916, the family moved to Jermyn, Texas, where Charlie was employed with the Gulf, Texas, and Western (G.T.& W.) Railroad, which had concentrated considerable resources in Jermyn. In addition to a machine shop and roundhouse, there was a depot, a huge water tower, and a giant coil hoist; and, as long as the railroad remained in operation, the town of Jermyn was "booming." Charlie became an apprentice to become a boilermaker and acetylene welder.

Between 1914 and 1925, Charlie and Lona had six children, with five of them being born in Jermyn, Texas. In the 1920 Federal Census of Jack County, Charlie was listed at age 28, with an occupation of railroad shop machinist, along with his wife, Lona, age 25, and three of their children, Thomas Wilton, Emerson Wilton, and Lona, their oldest daughter. After the 1920 census, their three other children, Nola Oletha Wilton, Charles Vernon Wilton, and Verna Faye Wilton, were born. Charles Vernon Wilton died in infancy in August 1924.

After a bout with cancer, Charlie's first wife, Lona, died in 1926. There was a discrepancy about the exact date. The official state record of her date of death was listed as June 1926, but family records indicate the date was actually September 1926. Family records suggest that after Lona underwent surgery to remove a malignant tumor in Floydada, Texas, she recovered sufficiently in August 1926 to return to the Riddle home in Bryson in Jack County,

Texas, after braving the trip on dirt roads in their 1921 Model T Ford. According to those records, Lona died September 1926 in the Riddle home. She was buried at the Winn Hill Cemetery.

After Lona died in 1926, Charlie acted as father and mother to the children. In the 1930 Federal Census of Jack County, Texas, Charlie was listed at age 39, widowed, with an occupation of railroad boilermaker, along with four of his children. The youngest daughter, Verna Faye Wilton, born August 1925, was living with relatives at the time.

In 1935, Charlie was married a second time, to Lydia Ann Evans, daughter of Frank M. Evans and Rebecca Alma Birdsong. In the 1930 Federal Census of Jack County, Texas, Lydia Evans was living just 3 dwellings away from Charlie in Jermyn. While still living in Jermyn, Texas, between 1936 and 1946, Charlie and Lydia had five children. Although the G.T.&W. Railroad discontinued passenger service in 1936 and began a steady decline in its connection with Jermyn, Charlie continued with the railroad until retiring after 28 years of service.

About 1948, Charlie moved the family to Jacksboro, Texas. One additional child, Raymond Eugene Wilton, was born January 1949 in Jacksboro. Charlie was supported by railroad retirement and social security benefits until his death in September 1967. He was buried in the Winn Hill Cemetery in Jack County, Texas.

Family Group Sheet

Husband: Charles Joseph Wilton

Born: 12 Mar 1891 in: Bryson, Jack Co., Texas
Married: 17 Sep 1913 in: Jack Co., Texas
Died: 28 Sep 1967 in: Jacksboro, Jack Co., Texas
Father: Henry Franklin Wilton
Mother: Martha Jane Baldwin
Other Spouses: Lydia Ann Evans

Wife: Lona Blanche Parrish

Born: 07 Apr 1894 in: Jermyn, Jack Co., Texas
Died: Sep 1926 in: Jermyn, Jack Co., Texas
Father: John Thomas Parrish
Mother: Neoma Demer Clark

CHILDREN

1 M
Name: Thomas Vester Wilton
Born: 05 Oct 1914 in: Jack Co., Texas
Died: 15 May 2006 in: Jacksboro, Jack Co., Texas
Married: 01 May 1948 in: Texas
Spouse: Vera Norma Cox

2 M
Name: Emerson Van Wilton
Born: 23 Nov 1915 in: Jermyn, Jack Co., Texas
Died: 27 Feb 2008 in: Mobile, Alabama
Married: 19 May 1939 in: Mobile, Mobile Co., Alabama
Spouse: Catherine A. Duke

3 F
Name: Lona Oretha Wilton
Born: 08 Mar 1918 in: Jermyn, Jack Co., Texas

4 F
Name: Nola Oletha Wilton
Born: 22 Feb 1922 in: Jermyn, Jack Co., Texas
Died: 03 Aug 2002 in: Potter Co., Texas
Married: 19 May 1939 in: Texas
Spouse: Jethro Doyle Little

5 M
Name: Charles Vernon Wilton
Born: 27 Jul 1924 in: Jermyn, Jack Co., Texas
Died: 07 Aug 1924 in: Jermyn, Jack Co., Texas

6 F
Name: Verna Faye Wilton
Born: 02 Aug 1925 in: Jermyn, Jack Co., Texas
Married: 09 Jun 1946 in: Texas
Spouse: Thomas Sheridan Crabtree

Family Group Sheet

Husband: Charles Joseph Wilton

Born: 12 Mar 1891 in: Bryson, Jack Co., Texas
Married: 1935 in: Waurika, Jefferson Co., Oklahoma
Died: 28 Sep 1967 in: Jacksboro, Jack Co., Texas
Father: Henry Franklin Wilton
Mother: Martha Jane Baldwin
Other Spouses: Lona Blanche Parrish

Wife: Lydia Ann Evans

Born: 21 Apr 1910 in: Paris, Lamar Co., Texas
Died: 17 Nov 1958 in: Tarrant Co., Texas
Father: Frank M. Evans
Mother: Rebecca Alma Birdsong

CHILDREN

1 M
Name: Lee O'Norvell Wilton
Born: 10 Feb 1936 in: Jermyn, Jack Co., Texas
Married: 22 Jun 1957 in: Jacksboro, Jack Co., Texas
Spouse: Linda Fay Edwards

2 M
Name: Charles Joseph Jr. Wilton
Born: 21 Sep 1937 in: Jermyn, Jack Co., Texas
Married: 23 Sep 1957 in: Santa Ana, Orange Co., California
Spouse: Wilma Anita Yaw

3 F
Name: Charlene Lenoy Wilton
Born: 26 Oct 1940 in: Jacksboro, Jack Co., Texas
Married: 07 Aug 1956 in: Graham, Young Co., Texas
Spouse: A.J. Jackson

4 F
Name: Colleen Rebecca Wilton
Born: 24 Feb 1946 in: Jack Co., Texas
Married: 26 Sep 1963 in: Texas
Spouse: Alton J. Gary

5 M
Name: Raymond Eugene Wilton
Born: 12 Jan 1949 in: Jacksboro, Jack Co., Texas
Married: 28 Apr 1967 in: Jack Co, Texas
Spouse: Janice Carol McAnear

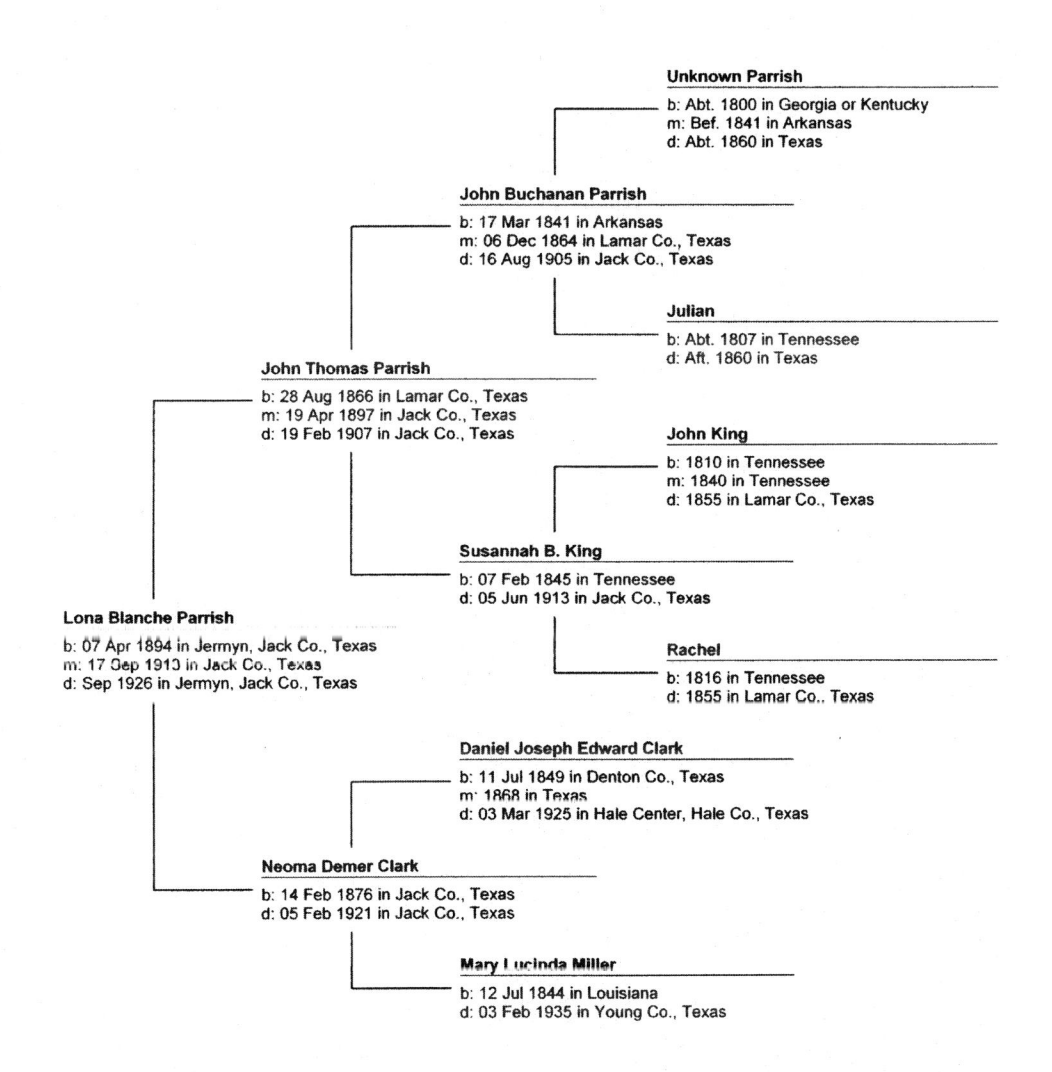

LONA BLANCHE PARRISH Standard Pedigree Tree

Lona Blanche Parrish
b: 07 Apr 1894 in Jermyn, Jack Co., Texas
m: 17 Sep 1913 in Jack Co., Texas
d: Sep 1926 in Jermyn, Jack Co., Texas

- **John Thomas Parrish**
  b: 28 Aug 1866 in Lamar Co., Texas
  m: 19 Apr 1897 in Jack Co., Texas
  d: 19 Feb 1907 in Jack Co., Texas

  - **John Buchanan Parrish**
    b: 17 Mar 1841 in Arkansas
    m: 06 Dec 1864 in Lamar Co., Texas
    d: 16 Aug 1905 in Jack Co., Texas

    - **Unknown Parrish**
      b: Abt. 1800 in Georgia or Kentucky
      m: Bef. 1841 in Arkansas
      d: Abt. 1860 in Texas

    - **Julian**
      b: Abt. 1807 in Tennessee
      d: Aft. 1860 in Texas

  - **Susannah B. King**
    b: 07 Feb 1845 in Tennessee
    d: 05 Jun 1913 in Jack Co., Texas

    - **John King**
      b: 1810 in Tennessee
      m: 1840 in Tennessee
      d: 1855 in Lamar Co., Texas

    - **Rachel**
      b: 1816 in Tennessee
      d: 1855 in Lamar Co., Texas

- **Neoma Demer Clark**
  b: 14 Feb 1876 in Jack Co., Texas
  d: 05 Feb 1921 in Jack Co., Texas

  - **Daniel Joseph Edward Clark**
    b: 11 Jul 1849 in Denton Co., Texas
    m: 1868 in Texas
    d: 03 Mar 1925 in Hale Center, Hale Co., Texas

  - **Mary Lucinda Miller**
    b: 12 Jul 1844 in Louisiana
    d: 03 Feb 1935 in Young Co., Texas

LYDIA ANN EVANS Standard Pedigree Tree

Frank M. Evans
b: 24 Feb 1842 in South Carolina
m: 31 Mar 1899 in Texas
d: 1924 in ?

Lydia Ann Evans
b: 21 Apr 1910 in Paris, Lamar Co., Texas
m: 1935 in Waurika, Jefferson Co., Oklahoma
d: 17 Nov 1958 in Tarrant Co., Texas

Francis M. Birdsong
b: Apr 1852 in Tennessee
m: 30 Oct 1873 in Giles Co., Tennessee
d: Bet. 1900 - 1910 in Texas

Rebecca Alma Birdsong
b: 19 Oct 1876 in Parker Co., Texas
d: 27 May 1951 in Jacksboro, Jack Co., Texas

Anderson Lowry
b: 1809 in Orange Co., Virginia
m: 29 Oct 1834 in Clark Co., Kentucky
d: 1876 in Elkton, Hickory Co., Missouri

Louisa Lowry
b: Jul 1852 in Clark Co., Kentucky
d: 19 Dec 1934 in Jack Co., Texas

Catherine Niblake
b: 1812 in Virginia
d: 1880 in Kentucky

Thomas Vester Wilton (1914-2006)
[6th. Generation From Henry Wilton (1769-1820)]

&

Vera Norma Cox (1916-   )
& Family

Thomas Vester Wilton, the oldest child of Charles Joseph Wilton and Lona Blanche Parrish, was born October 1914 in Jack County, Texas. It was recorded that Vester was born on a Monday morning, just as the sun was rising. The doctor, who helped Mrs. Rosie Winn in the delivery, arrived in a horse-drawn carriage, slightly inebriated. Vester, as he was known to his relatives and friends, was born while his parents were still living at the Wilton homeplace in a small one room house not far from the Henry Franklin Wilton home.

In 1916, the family moved to Jermyn, Texas, located about 3 &1/2 miles from the Wilton homeplace, where Charles Joseph (Charlie) Wilton began working for the G.T.&W. Railroad. For about the next 28 years, Jermyn became the family's home, and that was where Vester was raised. Attending school at Jermyn High School was a memorable time for Vester. One fond memory was of the time when he was a member of the Jermyn High School football team, which consisted of all Wilton brothers and cousins. It was sometimes confusing to the referees when the substitutions were always called, "Wilton for Wilton." Also, at one not so pleasant time, Vester broke his nose in one of those games. He recalled that the game was called off because the field became too bloody.

While still in high school, Vester recalled that he once secured the job of janitor. He enticed his brother, Van Wilton, to be his helper and paid him half of his $20 monthly salary. With their salary, they felt almost "rich."

In 1926, Vester's mother, Lona (Parrish) Wilton died of cancer, and his father took over the task of raising the family of then five children. Then, in 1935, Charlie remarried, to Lydia Ann Evans, and there were another 5 members eventually added to the family. After Charlie retired from his job with the railroad about 1948, the family relocated to Jacksboro, Texas.

After graduating from high school in 1936, Vester worked for a while in Bryson, Texas for his Uncle Lewis Riddle. Then, in 1940, he enlisted in the USAF, which became his lifetime career. Vester served in the military for 20 years, seeing action in WWII and the Korean War.

While still in the military, Vester met Vera Cox, while visiting his father in Jacksboro, who was then having medical problems. Vester later married Vera, the daughter of John Henry Cox and Hattie Stewart, in May 1948. After Vester retired from military service in 1960, they made their home in Jacksboro, Texas. On May 1, 2000, Vester and Vera celebrated their 50th wedding anniversary. Vester died May 15, 2006 and was buried in the Winn Hill Cemetery.

Family Group Sheet

Husband: Thomas Vester Wilton

    Born: 05 Oct 1914   in: Jack Co., Texas
  Married: 01 May 1948   in: Texas
    Died: 15 May 2006   in: Jacksboro, Jack Co., Texas
  Father: Charles Joseph Wilton
  Mother: Lona Blanche Parrish

Wife: Vera Norma Cox

    Born: 1916   in: Texas
  Father: John Henry Cox
  Mother: Hattie Estella Stewart
    Other Spouses: John Thurman Arms

THOMAS VESTER WILTON Standard Pedigree Tree

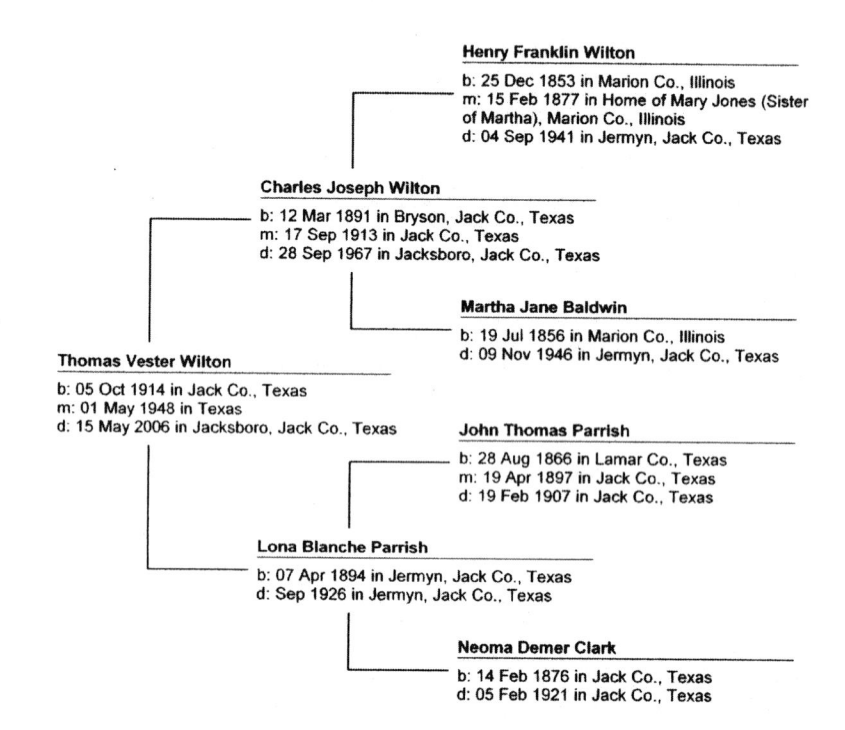

Henry Franklin Wilton
b: 25 Dec 1853 in Marion Co., Illinois
m: 15 Feb 1877 in Home of Mary Jones (Sister of Martha), Marion Co., Illinois
d: 04 Sep 1941 in Jermyn, Jack Co., Texas

Charles Joseph Wilton
b: 12 Mar 1891 in Bryson, Jack Co., Texas
m: 17 Sep 1913 in Jack Co., Texas
d: 28 Sep 1967 in Jacksboro, Jack Co., Texas

Martha Jane Baldwin
b: 19 Jul 1856 in Marion Co., Illinois
d: 09 Nov 1946 in Jermyn, Jack Co., Texas

Thomas Vester Wilton
b: 05 Oct 1914 in Jack Co., Texas
m: 01 May 1948 in Texas
d: 15 May 2006 in Jacksboro, Jack Co., Texas

John Thomas Parrish
b: 28 Aug 1866 in Lamar Co., Texas
m: 19 Apr 1897 in Jack Co., Texas
d: 19 Feb 1907 in Jack Co., Texas

Lona Blanche Parrish
b: 07 Apr 1894 in Jermyn, Jack Co., Texas
d: Sep 1926 in Jermyn, Jack Co., Texas

Neoma Demer Clark
b: 14 Feb 1876 in Jack Co., Texas
d: 05 Feb 1921 in Jack Co., Texas

Notes: This Tree also applies to the other children of Charles Joseph Wilton & Lona Blanche Wilton: Emerson Van Wilton, Lona Oretha Wilton, Nola Oletha Wilton, Charles Vernon Wilton, and Verna Faye Wilton.

VERA NORMA COX Standard Pedigree Tree

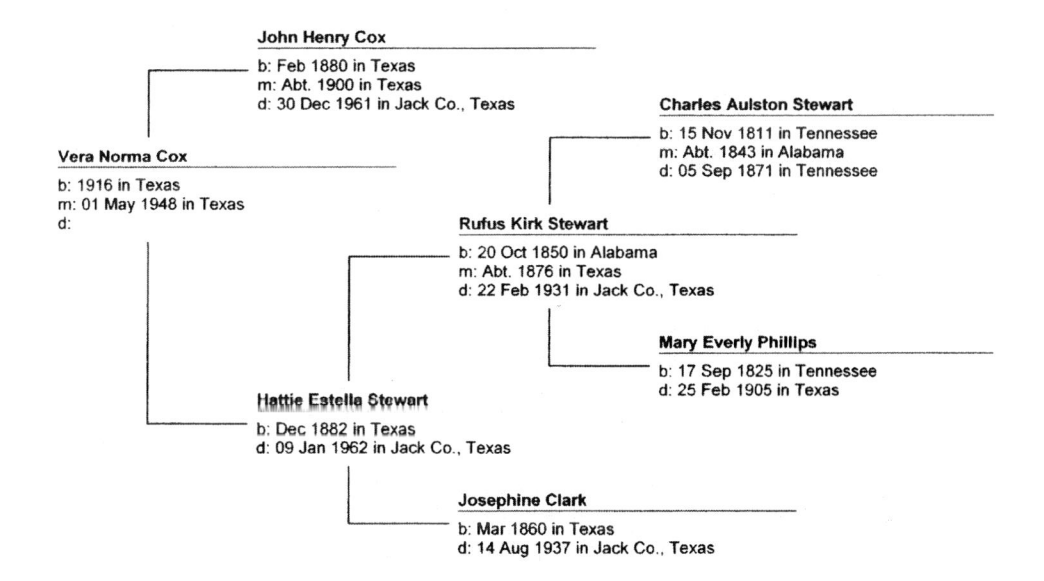

Vera Norma Cox
b: 1916 in Texas
m: 01 May 1948 in Texas
d:

- **John Henry Cox**
  b: Feb 1880 in Texas
  m: Abt. 1900 in Texas
  d: 30 Dec 1961 in Jack Co., Texas

- **Hattie Estella Stewart**
  b: Dec 1882 in Texas
  d: 09 Jan 1962 in Jack Co., Texas

  - **Rufus Kirk Stewart**
    b: 20 Oct 1850 in Alabama
    m: Abt. 1876 in Texas
    d: 22 Feb 1931 in Jack Co., Texas

    - **Charles Aulston Stewart**
      b: 15 Nov 1811 in Tennessee
      m: Abt. 1843 in Alabama
      d: 05 Sep 1871 in Tennessee

    - **Mary Everly Phillips**
      b: 17 Sep 1825 in Tennessee
      d: 25 Feb 1905 in Texas

  - **Josephine Clark**
    b: Mar 1860 in Texas
    d: 14 Aug 1937 in Jack Co., Texas

Emerson Van Wilton (1915-2008)
[6th. Generation From Henry Wilton (1769-1820)]

&

Catherine A. Duke (1914-   )
& Family

Emerson Van Wilton, born November 1915 in Jermyn in Jack County, Texas, was the second child of Charles Joseph Wilton and Lona Blanche Parrish. Van, as he was known by family and friends, had many fond memories of his early years growing up in Jermyn, which, along with Jacksboro, he rated among the best places in all of Jack County. During this time, 1915 thru 1936, Jermyn was in its heyday of reaping the benefits of having the G.T. &W Railroad depot and roundhouse in town. However, Jermyn was never able to support a movie house, so the young people often went to Jacksboro on Saturdays, where they would see movies at the Jacksboro Opera House Theater.

Van recalled that in the winter months, he and his brother, Vester Wilton, took turns starting a morning fire in the living room heater. To prepare for the day, they washed their face and hands, in water that had been drawn the night before, wet their hair and combed it properly, and then made a trip to the outhouse. By the time they got back to the house, their hair would be mixed with ice droplets. In 1929, their whole world changed, when gas lines were run to each house and houses were wired for electricity. He and Vester no longer wore long handles, since there was no longer a need to build a fire in the mornings.

One of Van's memories while attending Jermyn High School was of the time during the football season. The football team consisted of all Wilton brothers and cousins. The team members were L.V. Wilton and brother Anthony Wilton, Ted Wilton and brother Cecil Wilton, and Van Wilton and brother Vester Wilton. When the team was organized, there were not enough uniforms to go around, so they actually asked to borrow some uniforms from the opposing team. They were so unfamiliar with their equipment that when Ted Wilton put on his helmet, he did not realize that he had put the helmet on backwards, until he complained to Van of discomfort with the helmet during their first quarter of play. A blister on his nose was a result. Also, there was confusion with the referees when the substitutions were made, which were always "Wilton for Wilton." The referees did not immediately realize that all the team members were named Wilton.

Van recalled that Jermyn was surrounded by farms and ranches, and since slavery was a thing of the past, the young people of Jermyn were used for the work of chopping, picking, and baling cotton, and working with the threshing machines in the wheat fields. When he was about 17 years old, Van was in charge of a bundle wagon drawn by two large mules. Since he was only 5'6" tall, it was difficult to get a bridle on those old tall mules. He learned to dislike them very much by the time harvest season was completed.

When it came time to tear down the old Jermyn High School building, about 1935, in preparation for rebuilding a new high school, Van was on their payroll. It was at this time that many of his friends were beginning to leave Jermyn to pursue their livelihoods elsewhere, and Van was also working at the Wichita Falls State Hospital. One of his friends named "Zeke" wrote him a letter which stated, "Quit what you are doing. Uncle Jim Moreland will get you a job with U.S. Gypsum Co." It wasn't long after that, in 1936, than Van sadly left Jermyn for Mobile, Alabama, where he was eventually employed by the National Gypsum Co.

It was in Mobile, Alabama that Van spent most of the rest of his life. He became a foreman with the National Gypsum Co. and later retired in Mobile, Alabama, where his family settled. On May 19, 1939, he married Catherine A. Duke, daughter of John H. Duke and Josephine Schreiner. After 68 years of marriage, Van and Catherine had 5 children, 18 grandchildren, and 21 great-grandchildren. Van died in Mobile, Alabama on February 27, 2008.

Family Group Sheet

Husband: Emerson Van Wilton

Born: 23 Nov 1915 in: Jermyn, Jack Co., Texas
Married: 19 May 1939 in: Mobile, Mobile Co., Alabama
Died: 27 Feb 2008 in: Mobile, Alabama
Father: Charles Joseph Wilton
Mother: Lona Blanche Parrish

Wife: Catherine A. Duke

Born: 25 Nov 1914 in: Mobile, Mobile Co., Alabama
Father: John H. Duke
Mother: Josephine Schreiner

CHILDREN

1 M
Name: Charles Vernon Wilton
Born: 30 Mar 1940 in: Mobile, Mobile Co., Alabama
Married: Jan 1961 in: Mobile, Mobile Co., Alabama
Spouse: Carol L. Bardsley

2 F
Name: Mary Jo Wilton
Born: 25 Jun 1942 in: Mobile, Mobile Co., Alabama
Married: 13 Oct 1962 in: Mobile, Mobile Co., Alabama
Spouse: Michael Albert Adams

3 F
Name: Deborah Agnes Wilton
Born: 05 Aug 1949 in: Mobile, Mobile Co., Alabama
Married: 20 Nov 1971 in: Mobile, Mobile Co., Alabama
Spouse: Robert Louis Johnson

4 M
Name: David Van Wilton
Born: 30 Oct 1950 in: Mobile, Mobile Co., Alabama
Married: 02 Jul 1971 in: Mobile, Mobile Co., Alabama
Spouse: Linda Cannon

5 F
Name: Catherine Elizabeth Wilton
Born: 22 Dec 1955 in: Mobile, Mobile Co., Alabama
Married: 16 Apr 1977 in: Alabama
Spouse: Felix J. II Turner
Married: 22 Sep 1991 in: Alabama
Spouse: Leslie J. Strikmiller

CATHERINE A. DUKE Standard Pedigree Tree

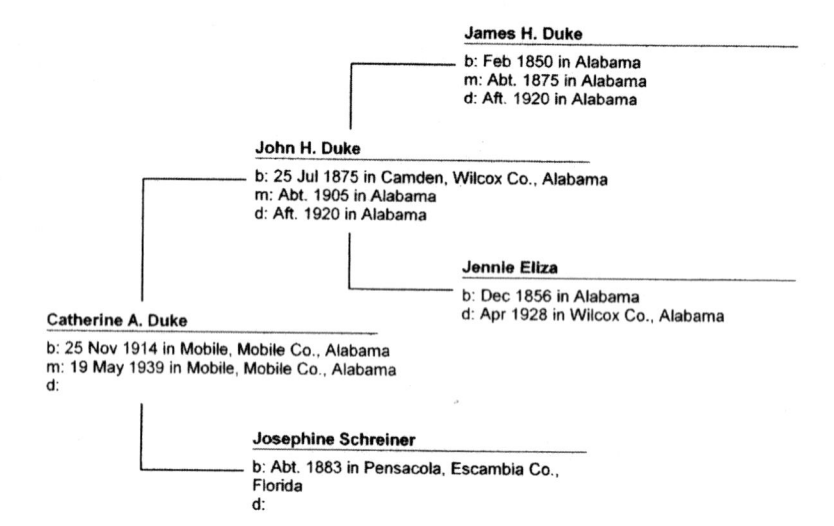

James H. Duke
b: Feb 1850 in Alabama
m: Abt. 1875 in Alabama
d: Aft. 1920 in Alabama

John H. Duke
b: 25 Jul 1875 in Camden, Wilcox Co., Alabama
m: Abt. 1905 in Alabama
d: Aft. 1920 in Alabama

Jennie Eliza
b: Dec 1856 in Alabama
d: Apr 1928 in Wilcox Co., Alabama

Catherine A. Duke
b: 25 Nov 1914 in Mobile, Mobile Co., Alabama
m: 19 May 1939 in Mobile, Mobile Co., Alabama
d:

Josephine Schreiner
b: Abt. 1883 in Pensacola, Escambia Co., Florida
d:

Charles Vernon Wilton (1940-)
[7th. Generation From Henry Wilton (1769-1820)]

&

Carol L. Bardsley (1941-)
& Family

Family Group Sheet

Husband: Charles Vernon Wilton

Born: 30 Mar 1940	in: Mobile, Mobile Co., Alabama
Married: Jan 1961	in: Mobile, Mobile Co., Alabama
Father: Emerson Van Wilton	
Mother: Catherine A. Duke	

Wife: Carol L. Bardsley

Born: 09 Nov 1941	in: Philadelphia, Montgomery Co., Pennsylvania

CHILDREN

1 M
Name: Charles Vernon Jr. Wilton
Born: 26 Aug 1961 in: Mobile, Mobile Co., Alabama
Married: Unknown
Spouse: Cindy

2 M
Name: Mark Terrance Wilton
Born: 27 Jun 1962 in: Mobile, Mobile Co., Alabama
Married: Unknown
Spouse: Cindy

3 M
Name: Christopher Dennis Wilton
Born: 17 Jun 1965 in: Mobile, Mobile Co., Alabama
Married: Unknown
Spouse: Carla

4 M
Name: Harold Emerson Wilton
Born: 27 Feb 1976 in: Mobile, Mobile Co., Alabama
Married: Unknown
Spouse: Staci Deanne Parnell

CHARLES VERNON WILTON Standard Pedigree Tree

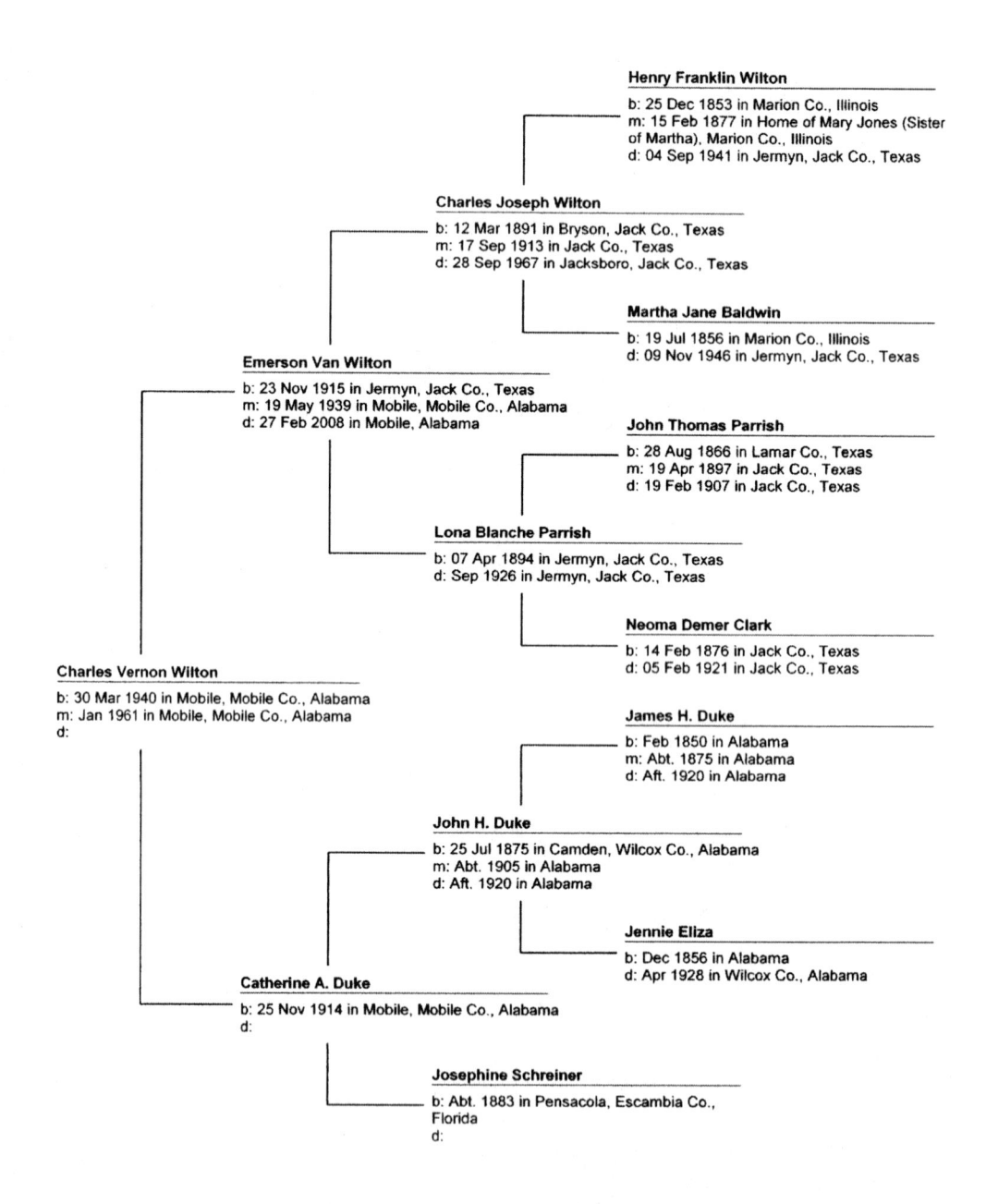

Charles Vernon Wilton
b: 30 Mar 1940 in Mobile, Mobile Co., Alabama
m: Jan 1961 in Mobile, Mobile Co., Alabama
d:

- **Emerson Van Wilton**
  b: 23 Nov 1915 in Jermyn, Jack Co., Texas
  m: 19 May 1939 in Mobile, Mobile Co., Alabama
  d: 27 Feb 2008 in Mobile, Alabama

  - **Charles Joseph Wilton**
    b: 12 Mar 1891 in Bryson, Jack Co., Texas
    m: 17 Sep 1913 in Jack Co., Texas
    d: 28 Sep 1967 in Jacksboro, Jack Co., Texas

    - **Henry Franklin Wilton**
      b: 25 Dec 1853 in Marion Co., Illinois
      m: 15 Feb 1877 in Home of Mary Jones (Sister of Martha), Marion Co., Illinois
      d: 04 Sep 1941 in Jermyn, Jack Co., Texas

    - **Martha Jane Baldwin**
      b: 19 Jul 1856 in Marion Co., Illinois
      d: 09 Nov 1946 in Jermyn, Jack Co., Texas

  - **Lona Blanche Parrish**
    b: 07 Apr 1894 in Jermyn, Jack Co., Texas
    d: Sep 1926 in Jermyn, Jack Co., Texas

    - **John Thomas Parrish**
      b: 28 Aug 1866 in Lamar Co., Texas
      m: 19 Apr 1897 in Jack Co., Texas
      d: 19 Feb 1907 in Jack Co., Texas

    - **Neoma Demer Clark**
      b: 14 Feb 1876 in Jack Co., Texas
      d: 05 Feb 1921 in Jack Co., Texas

- **Catherine A. Duke**
  b: 25 Nov 1914 in Mobile, Mobile Co., Alabama
  d:

  - **John H. Duke**
    b: 25 Jul 1875 in Camden, Wilcox Co., Alabama
    m: Abt. 1905 in Alabama
    d: Aft. 1920 in Alabama

    - **James H. Duke**
      b: Feb 1850 in Alabama
      m: Abt. 1875 in Alabama
      d: Aft. 1920 in Alabama

    - **Jennie Eliza**
      b: Dec 1856 in Alabama
      d: Apr 1928 in Wilcox Co., Alabama

  - **Josephine Schreiner**
    b: Abt. 1883 in Pensacola, Escambia Co., Florida
    d:

Notes: This Tree also applies to the other children of Emerson Van Wilton & Catherine A. Duke: Mary Jo Wilton, Deborah Jane Wilton, David Van Wilton, and Catherine Elizabeth Wilton.

Mary Jo Wilton (1942-   )
[7th. Generation From Henry Wilton (1769-1820)]

&

Michael Albert Adams (1942-   )
& Family

Mary Jo Wilton, the second child of Emerson Van Wilton & Catherine A. Duke, was born June 1942 in Mobile, Alabama. After they were married in 1939, Van and Catherine had made their home in Mobile in Mobile County, Alabama, and that is where Mary Jo was born and raised.

On October 13, 1962, Mary Jo married her high school sweetheart, Michael Albert Adams, the son of Jesse Woodrow Adams and Mary Earle Moncrief. They also settled in the Mobile, Alabama area, where they raised six children, the last, Timothy Mitchell Adams, being married on June 9, 2007. As of 2007, Mary Jo and Albert had 10 granddaughters and 6 grandsons, for a total of 16 grandchildren.

After working for nearly 45 years in sales, mostly in the insurance business, Michael retired in January 2007. Mary Jo was a stay at home wife and mother until all their children were raised, and then she started a career as secretary for the City of Mobile Electrical Department. She planned to retire from her job on March 31, 2008, after ten years of service.

Michael and Mary Jo had a strong faith in God, which was an influence from their parents while growing up, and which was a comfort throughout their lives before and after they were married. For more than 30 years, they were members of St. Dominic's Catholic Church in Mobile, Alabama.

Family Group Sheet

Husband: Michael Albert Adams

Born: 16 Apr 1942 in: Fairhope, Baldwin Co., Alabama
Married: 13 Oct 1962 in: Mobile, Mobile Co., Alabama
Father: Jesse Woodrow Adams
Mother: Mary Earle Moncrief

Wife: Mary Jo Wilton

Born: 25 Jun 1942 in: Mobile, Mobile Co., Alabama
Father: Emerson Van Wilton
Mother: Catherine A. Duke

CHILDREN

1 M
Name: Michael Albert Adams
Born: 29 Dec 1963 in: Mobile, Mobile Co., Alabama
Married: Unknown
Spouse: Sonia

2 F
Name: Melissa Adams
Born: 09 Jan 1965 in: Mobile, Mobile Co., Alabama
Married: Unknown
Spouse: Allen Ritchie

3 F
Name: Ann Michelle Adams
Born: 10 May 1967 in: Alabama
Married: 02 Jan 1993 in: St. Dominic Catholic Church, Mobile, Mobile Co., Alabama
Spouse: Walter Phillip Proctor

4 F
Name: Melanie Adams
Born: 20 Jul 1969 in: Alabama
Married: Unknown
Spouse: David Fromdahl

5 M
Name: Matthew Joseph Adams
Born: 18 Feb 1977 in: Wichita, Sedgwick Co., Kansas
Married: 04 May 2002 in: Mobile, Mobile Co., Alabama
Spouse: Elizabeth Cary Meztista

6 M
Name: Timothy Mitchell Adams
Born: 19 Apr 1984 in: Alabama
Married: 09 Jun 2007 in: Mobile, Alabama
Spouse: Gretchen Elizabeth Buschmann

MICHAEL ALBERT ADAMS Standard Pedigree Tree

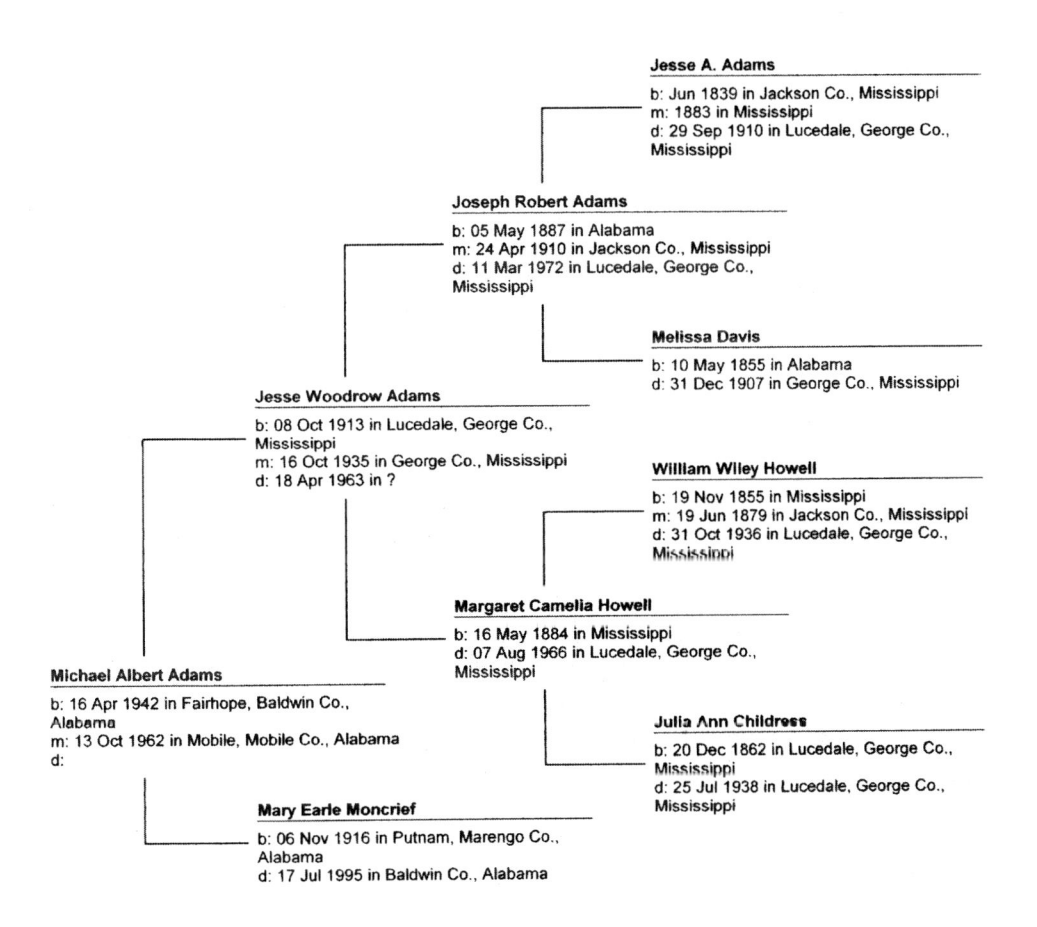

Michael Albert Adams
b: 16 Apr 1942 in Fairhope, Baldwin Co., Alabama
m: 13 Oct 1962 in Mobile, Mobile Co., Alabama
d:

- **Jesse Woodrow Adams**
  b: 08 Oct 1913 in Lucedale, George Co., Mississippi
  m: 16 Oct 1935 in George Co., Mississippi
  d: 18 Apr 1963 in ?

  - **Joseph Robert Adams**
    b: 05 May 1887 in Alabama
    m: 24 Apr 1910 in Jackson Co., Mississippi
    d: 11 Mar 1972 in Lucedale, George Co., Mississippi

    - **Jesse A. Adams**
      b: Jun 1839 in Jackson Co., Mississippi
      m: 1883 in Mississippi
      d: 29 Sep 1910 in Lucedale, George Co., Mississippi

    - **Melissa Davis**
      b: 10 May 1855 in Alabama
      d: 31 Dec 1907 in George Co., Mississippi

  - **Margaret Camelia Howell**
    b: 16 May 1884 in Mississippi
    d: 07 Aug 1966 in Lucedale, George Co., Mississippi

    - **William Wiley Howell**
      b: 19 Nov 1855 in Mississippi
      m: 19 Jun 1879 in Jackson Co., Mississippi
      d: 31 Oct 1936 in Lucedale, George Co., Mississippi

    - **Julia Ann Childress**
      b: 20 Dec 1862 in Lucedale, George Co., Mississippi
      d: 25 Jul 1938 in Lucedale, George Co., Mississippi

- **Mary Earle Moncrief**
  b: 06 Nov 1916 in Putnam, Marengo Co., Alabama
  d: 17 Jul 1995 in Baldwin Co., Alabama

Michael Albert Jr. Adams (1963-   )
[8th. Generation From Henry Wilton (1769-1820)]

&

Sonia
& Family

Family Group Sheet

Husband: Michael Albert Adams	
Born: 29 Dec 1963	in: Mobile, Mobile Co., Alabama
Married: Unknown	
Father: Michael Albert Adams	
Mother: Mary Jo Wilton	

Wife: Sonia
Born: Unknown

	CHILDREN
1 F	Name: Savannah Marie Adams Born: 25 Aug 1993
2 F	Name: Shannon Mae Adams Born: 05 May 1995
3 M	Name: John Michael Van Adams Born: 08 Jan 1997

MICHAEL ALBERT JR. ADAMS Standard Pedigree Tree

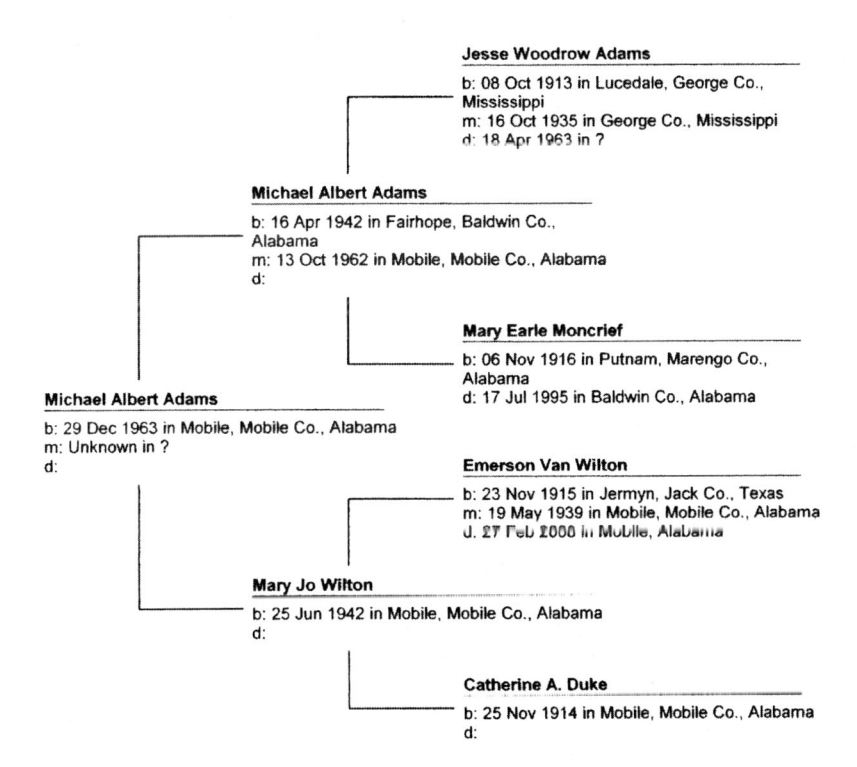

Michael Albert Adams
b: 29 Dec 1963 in Mobile, Mobile Co., Alabama
m: Unknown in ?
d:

- **Michael Albert Adams**
  b: 16 Apr 1942 in Fairhope, Baldwin Co., Alabama
  m: 13 Oct 1962 in Mobile, Mobile Co., Alabama
  d:

  - **Jesse Woodrow Adams**
    b: 08 Oct 1913 in Lucedale, George Co., Mississippi
    m: 16 Oct 1935 in George Co., Mississippi
    d: 18 Apr 1963 in ?

  - **Mary Earle Moncrief**
    b: 06 Nov 1916 in Putnam, Marengo Co., Alabama
    d: 17 Jul 1995 in Baldwin Co., Alabama

- **Mary Jo Wilton**
  b: 25 Jun 1942 in Mobile, Mobile Co., Alabama
  d:

  - **Emerson Van Wilton**
    b: 23 Nov 1915 in Jermyn, Jack Co., Texas
    m: 19 May 1939 in Mobile, Mobile Co., Alabama
    d: 27 Feb 2000 in Mobile, Alabama

  - **Catherine A. Duke**
    b: 25 Nov 1914 in Mobile, Mobile Co., Alabama
    d:

Notes: This Tree also applies to the other children of Michael Albert Adams & Mary Jo Wilton: Melissa Adams, Ann Michelle Adams, Melanie Adams, Matthew Joseph Adams, and Timothy Mitchell Adams.

Melissa Adams (1965-   )
[8th. Generation From Henry Wilton (1769-1820)]

&

Allen Ritchie
& Family

Family Group Sheet

Husband: Allen Ritchie	
Born: Unknown	
Married: Unknown	

Wife: Melissa Adams	
Born: 09 Jan 1965	in: Mobile, Mobile Co., Alabama
Father: Michael Albert Adams	
Mother: Mary Jo Wilton	

	CHILDREN
1 F	Name: Mary Catherine Ritchie Born: 22 Oct 1991
2 M	Name: Michael Wen Ritchie Born: 17 Jul 1995

Ann Michelle Adams (1967-)
[8th. Generation From Henry Wilton (1769-1820)]

&

Walter Philip Proctor (1960-)
& Family

Family Group Sheet

Husband: Walter Phillip Proctor	
Born: 22 May 1960	in: Huntsville, Madison Co., Alabama
Married: 02 Jan 1993	in: St. Dominic Catholic Church, Mobile, Mobile Co., Alabama
Father: Walter Franklin Proctor	
Mother: Myra Opal Bellomy	

Wife: Ann Michelle Adams	
Born: 10 May 1967	in: Alabama
Father: Michael Albert Adams	
Mother: Mary Jo Wilton	

CHILDREN

1 M	Name: Walter Jackson Proctor	
	Born: 17 May 1996	in: Mobile, Mobile Co., Alabama
2 M	Name: Samuel Joseph Proctor	
	Born: 17 May 1996	in: Mobile, Mobile Co., Alabama
3 F	Name: Myra Margaret Proctor	
	Born: 05 Dec 2002	in: Mobile, Mobile Co., Alabama

Melanie Adams (1969-   )
[8th. Generation From Henry Wilton (1769-1820)]

&

David Fromdahl
& Family

Family Group Sheet

Husband: David Fromdahl

Born: Unknown
Married: Unknown

Wife: Melanie Adams

Born: 20 Jul 1969   in: Alabama
Father: Michael Albert Adams
Mother: Mary Jo Wilton

CHILDREN

1 F   Name: Hannah Catherine Fromdahl
      Born: 13 Dec 1996

Matthew Joseph Adams (1977-   )
[8th. Generation From Henry Wilton (1769-1820)]

&

Elizabeth Cary Meztista (1977-   )
& Family

Matthew was born February 18, 1997 in Wichita, Kansas, the 5th. child of Michael Albert Adams and Mary Jo Wilton. Except for a short time of about 4 years when his dad was transferred to Kansas by his employer, Metropolitan Life Insurance Company, the family lived in the Mobile/Baldwin Counties area of Alabama.

Matthews's formative years were spent in Mobile, Alabama. At the age of 5, he began school at the Little Flower Catholic School, where he attended until 1984. Then, from 1984-1991, he attended the St. Dominic Catholic School; and, from 1991-1995, he attended high school at the McGill-Toolen Catholic High School, where he graduated in 1995.

After completing high school, Matthew attended the University of South Alabama in Mobile, Alabama from 1999-2001, where he graduated in December 2001 with a degree in Accounting. He then took a job in public accounting.

Matthew married Elizabeth Cary Meztista of Mobile, Alabama, on May 4, 2002. They had one child, William Emerson Adams, born April 2004, who was named after Matthew's grandfather, Emerson Van Wilton.

Family Group Sheet

Husband: Matthew Joseph Adams

Born: 18 Feb 1977 in: Wichita, Sedgwick Co., Kansas
Married: 04 May 2002 in: Mobile, Mobile Co., Alabama
Father: Michael Albert Adams
Mother: Mary Jo Wilton

Wife: Elizabeth Cary Meztista

Born: 21 May 1977 in: Mobile, Mobile Co., Alabama

CHILDREN

1 M
Name: William Emerson Adams
Born: 09 Apr 2004 in: Mobile, Mobile Co., Alabama

Timothy Mitchell Adams (1984-   )
[8th. Generation From Henry Wilton (1769-1820)]

&

Gretchen Elizabeth Buschmann
& Family

Family Group Sheet

Husband: Timothy Mitchell Adams	
Born: 19 Apr 1984	in: Alabama
Married: 09 Jun 2007	in: Mobile, Alabama
Father: Michael Albert Adams	
Mother: Mary Jo Wilton	

Wife: Gretchen Elizabeth Buschmann
Born: Unknown
Father: Bruce Oom Buschmann

Deborah Agnes Wilton (1949-   )
[7th. Generation From Henry Wilton (1769-1820)]

&

Robert Louis Johnson (1949-   )
& Family

Family Group Sheet

Husband: Robert Louis Johnson	
Born: 13 Jan 1949	in: Mobile, Mobile Co., Alabama
Married: 20 Nov 1971	in: Mobile, Mobile Co., Alabama
Father: Claude August Johnson	
Mother: Marion Theresa Wahl	

Wife: Deborah Agnes Wilton	
Born: 05 Aug 1949	in: Mobile, Mobile Co., Alabama
Father: Emerson Van Wilton	
Mother: Catherine A. Duke	

CHILDREN

1 M	Name: Jeremy Wahl Johnson	
	Born: 16 Dec 1974	in: Mobile, Mobile Co., Alabama
	Married: 25 Jul 1999	in: La Grange, Troup Co., Georgia
	Spouse: Amber Brooke Baker	
2 M	Name: Joshua Wilton Johnson	
	Born: 16 Dec 1974	in: Mobile, Mobile Co., Alabama
3 F	Name: Ann Marie Johnson	
	Born: 11 Apr 1979	in: Mobile, Mobile Co., Alabama
4 F	Name: Sarah Theresa Johnson	
	Born: 25 Jul 1983	in: Mobile, Mobile Co., Alabama

Jeremy Wahl Johnson (1974-   )
[8th. Generation From Henry Wilton (1769-1820)]

&

Amber Brooke Baker (1980-   )
& Family

Family Group Sheet

Husband: Jeremy Wahl Johnson	
Born: 16 Dec 1974	in: Mobile, Mobile Co., Alabama
Married: 25 Jul 1999	in: La Grange, Troup Co., Georgia
Father: Robert Louis Johnson	
Mother: Deborah Agnes Wilton	

Wife: Amber Brooke Baker	
Born: 28 Jan 1980	in: La Grange, Troup Co., Georgia

CHILDREN

1 M	Name: Bryan Gregory Johnson	
	Born: 12 Nov 1999	in: La Grange, Troup Co., Georgia
2 M	Name: Ethan Michael Johnson	
	Born: 20 Feb 2003	in: La Grange, Troup Co., Georgia
3 M	Name: Hayden Andrew Johnson	
	Born: 21 Feb 2006	in: La Grange, Troup Co., Georgia

JEREMY WAHL JOHNSON Standard Pedigree Tree

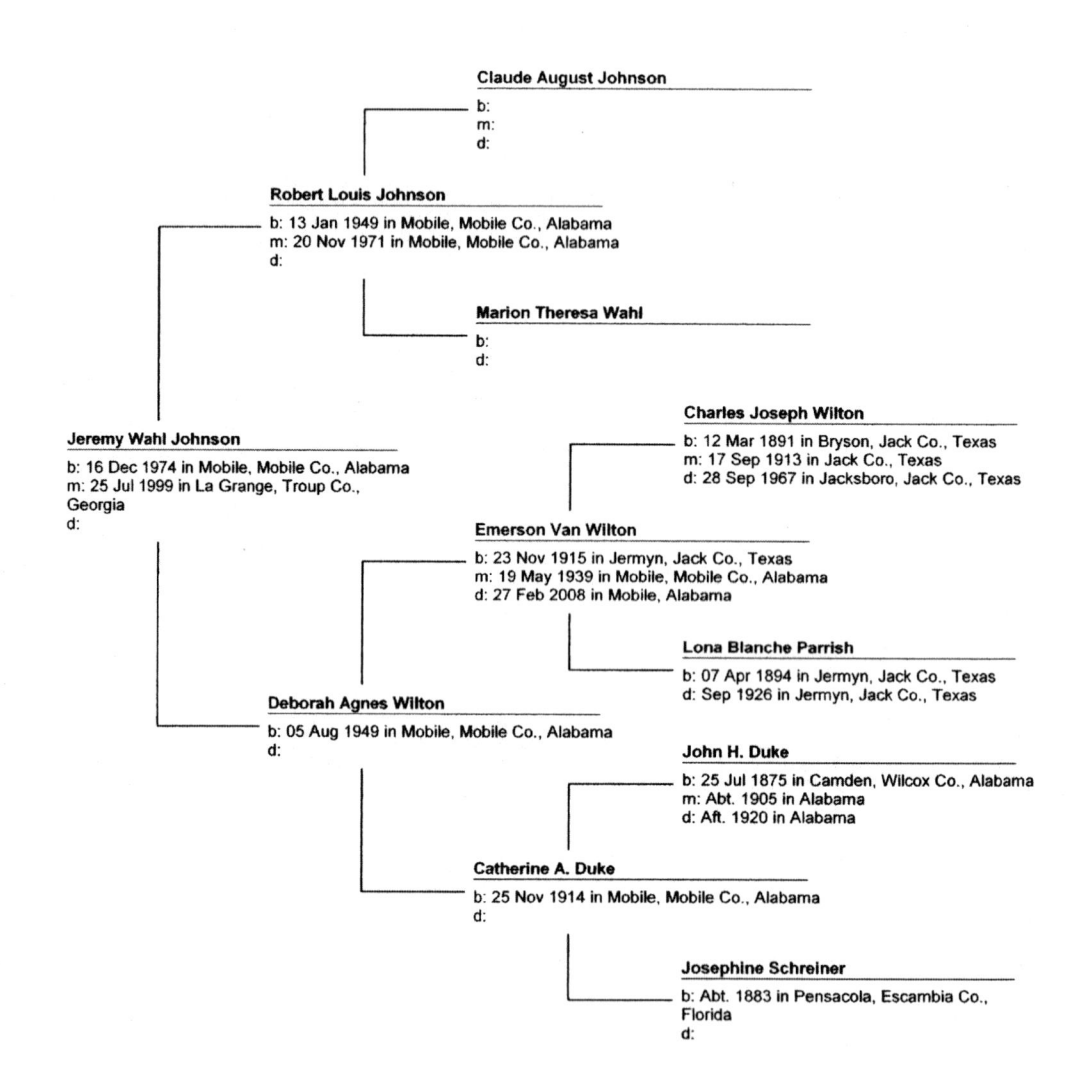

- **Claude August Johnson**
  - b:
  - m:
  - d:

- **Robert Louis Johnson**
  - b: 13 Jan 1949 in Mobile, Mobile Co., Alabama
  - m: 20 Nov 1971 in Mobile, Mobile Co., Alabama
  - d:

- **Marion Theresa Wahl**
  - b:
  - d:

- **Jeremy Wahl Johnson**
  - b: 16 Dec 1974 in Mobile, Mobile Co., Alabama
  - m: 25 Jul 1999 in La Grange, Troup Co., Georgia
  - d:

- **Charles Joseph Wilton**
  - b: 12 Mar 1891 in Bryson, Jack Co., Texas
  - m: 17 Sep 1913 in Jack Co., Texas
  - d: 28 Sep 1967 in Jacksboro, Jack Co., Texas

- **Emerson Van Wilton**
  - b: 23 Nov 1915 in Jermyn, Jack Co., Texas
  - m: 19 May 1939 in Mobile, Mobile Co., Alabama
  - d: 27 Feb 2008 in Mobile, Alabama

- **Lona Blanche Parrish**
  - b: 07 Apr 1894 in Jermyn, Jack Co., Texas
  - d: Sep 1926 in Jermyn, Jack Co., Texas

- **Deborah Agnes Wilton**
  - b: 05 Aug 1949 in Mobile, Mobile Co., Alabama
  - d:

- **John H. Duke**
  - b: 25 Jul 1875 in Camden, Wilcox Co., Alabama
  - m: Abt. 1905 in Alabama
  - d: Aft. 1920 in Alabama

- **Catherine A. Duke**
  - b: 25 Nov 1914 in Mobile, Mobile Co., Alabama
  - d:

- **Josephine Schreiner**
  - b: Abt. 1883 in Pensacola, Escambia Co., Florida
  - d:

Notes: This Tree also applies to the other children of Robert Louis Johnson & Deborah Agnes Wilton: Joshua Wilton Johnson, Ann Marie Johnson, and Sarah Theresa Johnson.

David Van Wilton (1950-   )
[7th. Generation From Henry Wilton (1769-1820)]

&

Linda Cannon
& Family

Family Group Sheet

Husband: David Van Wilton	
Born: 30 Oct 1950	in: Mobile, Mobile Co., Alabama
Married: 02 Jul 1971	in: Mobile, Mobile Co., Alabama
Father: Emerson Van Wilton	
Mother: Catherine A. Duke	

Wife: Linda Cannon
Born: Unknown

	CHILDREN
1 M	Name: David Patrick Wilton Born: Nov 1975
2 F	Name: Genevieve Wilton Born: 05 Apr 1980

Catherine Elizabeth Wilton (1955-   )
[7th. Generation from Henry Wilton (1769-1820)]

&
Felix J. II Turner
& Family

&
Leslie J. Strikmiller (1948-   )
& Family

Family Group Sheet

Husband: Felix J. II Turner

Born: Unknown
Married: 16 Apr 1977 in: Alabama

Wife: Catherine Elizabeth Wilton

Born: 22 Dec 1955 in: Mobile, Mobile Co., Alabama
Father: Emerson Van Wilton
Mother: Catherine A. Duke
Other Spouses: Leslie J. Strikmiller

CHILDREN

1 M Name: Felix Johnson Turner
Born: 21 Apr 1981 in: Alabama

2 F Name: Lauren Elizabeth Turner
Born: 08 May 1986 in: Alabama

Family Group Sheet

Husband: Leslie J. Strikmiller

Born: 15 May 1948 in: New Orleans, Orleans Parish, Louisana
Married: 22 Sep 1991 in: Alabama

Wife: Catherine Elizabeth Wilton

Born: 22 Dec 1955 in: Mobile, Mobile Co., Alabama
Father: Emerson Van Wilton
Mother: Catherine A. Duke
Other Spouses: Felix J. II Turner

Lona Oretha Wilton (1918-   )
[6th. Generation From Henry Wilton (1769-1820)]

Lona Oretha Wilton, the third child of Charles Joseph (Charlie) Wilton and Lona Blanche Parrish, was born March 8, 1918 in Jermyn, Texas. The family had made Jermyn their home in 1916 after Charlie Wilton began working for the G.T.&W. Railroad, which had major holdings in Jermyn at the time.

While growing up in Jermyn, Oretha recalled that one of her outstanding memories as a child was in the person of Dr. Winstead. To her, he was a giant of a man, because he was the one who assisted in delivering most of her mother's babies.

Another memory during her early years was of downtown Jermyn, where at the south end of the block was the Jones Store, and at the northward end was the Elbert Moore Store; and, in between was Mr. Pevehouse's drug store. She remembered that at about the age of 8 years, she would often run into Dr. Winstead along that street. He would always say, "Let me see your tongue," a habit which was common for doctors of those days. Of course, when she did as he said, he would then say, "Go tell Walter Pevehouse you need an ice cream cone." Oretha remembered that ice cream as being the best she had ever tasted.

In her adult years, Oretha's career work was with the Arco Oil Co. After retiring, she lived in Dallas, Texas.

341

Nola Oletha Wilton (1922-2002)
[6th. Generation From Henry Wilton (1769-1820)]

&

Jethro Doyle Little (1921-1988)
& Family

Nola Oletha Wilton, born February 22, 1922 in Jermyn, Texas, was the fourth child of Charles Joseph (Charlie) Wilton and Lona Blanche Parrish. The family had settled in Jermyn, Texas in 1916, when Charlie began work with the G.T.&W. Railroad, which had a machine shop and roundhouse located in Jermyn. Oletha's formative years were spent in Jermyn, where she grew up and went to school.

In May 1939, Oletha married Jethro Doyle Little, son of Johnie Burns Little and Arrie Missouri Slaughter. For awhile, the family lived in the Graham area in Young County. Their first two children, Marquita Carol Little, born December 1940, and Royce Wilton Little, born September 1942, were both born in Graham, Texas.

At one point, the family resettled in Amarillo in Potter County, Texas. Their third child, Charlotte Lynette Little, was born February 1954 in Amarillo. Oletha and Jethro were divorced in April 1970 in Potter County, Texas.

Jethro died August 1988 in Gray County, Texas, and Oletha died August 2002 in Potter County, Texas.

Family Group Sheet

Husband: Jethro Doyle Little	
Born: 14 Jan 1921	in: Donie, Freestone Co., Texas
Married: 19 May 1939	in: Texas
Died: 30 Aug 1988	in: Gray Co., Texas
Father: Johnie Burns Little	
Mother: Arrie Missouri Slaughter	

Wife: Nola Oletha Wilton	
Born: 22 Feb 1922	in: Jermyn, Jack Co., Texas
Died: 03 Aug 2002	in: Potter Co., Texas
Father: Charles Joseph Wilton	
Mother: Lona Blanche Parrish	

CHILDREN

1 F	Name: Marquita Carol Little Born: 01 Dec 1940 Married: 03 Mar 1965 Spouse: Byron Everett Lenerose	in: Graham, Young Co., Texas
2 M	Name: Royce Wilton Little Born: 28 Sep 1942 Married: Unknown Spouse: Marilyn Silva	in: Graham, Young Co., Texas
3 F	Name: Charlotte Lynette Little Born: 28 Feb 1954 Married: 24 Oct 1974 Spouse: Richard Bryan Ashford	in: Amarillo, Potter Co., Texas in: Potter Co., Texas

Marquite Carol Little (1940-   )
[7th. Generation From Henry Wilton (1769-1820)]

&

Byron Everett Lenerose (1941-   )
& Family

Family Group Sheet

Husband: Byron Everett Lenerose	
Born: 1941	
Married: 03 Mar 1965	
Wife: Marquita Carol Little	
Born: 01 Dec 1940	in: Graham, Young Co., Texas
Father: Jethro Doyle Little	
Mother: Nola Oletha Wilton	
CHILDREN	
1 M — Name: Tyson Craig Lenerose	
Born: 23 Mar 1976	in: Potter Co., Texas

MARQUITA CAROL LITTLE Standard Pedigree Tree

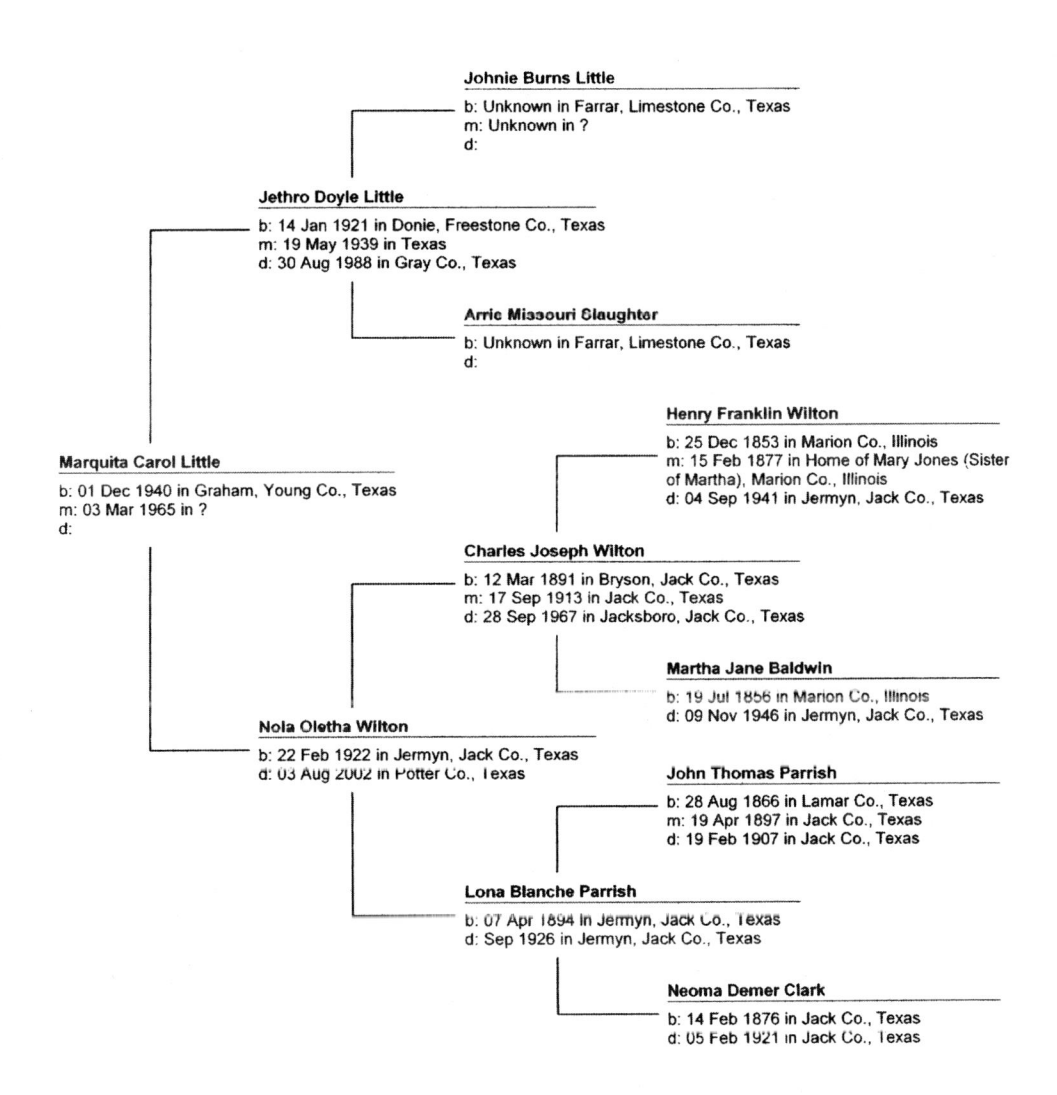

Marquita Carol Little
b: 01 Dec 1940 in Graham, Young Co., Texas
m: 03 Mar 1965 in ?
d:

- **Jethro Doyle Little**
  b: 14 Jan 1921 in Donie, Freestone Co., Texas
  m: 19 May 1939 in Texas
  d: 30 Aug 1988 in Gray Co., Texas

  - **Johnie Burns Little**
    b: Unknown in Farrar, Limestone Co., Texas
    m: Unknown in ?
    d:

  - **Arrie Missouri Slaughter**
    b: Unknown in Farrar, Limestone Co., Texas
    d:

- **Nola Oletha Wilton**
  b: 22 Feb 1922 in Jermyn, Jack Co., Texas
  d: 03 Aug 2002 in Potter Co., Texas

  - **Charles Joseph Wilton**
    b: 12 Mar 1891 in Bryson, Jack Co., Texas
    m: 17 Sep 1913 in Jack Co., Texas
    d: 28 Sep 1967 in Jacksboro, Jack Co., Texas

    - **Henry Franklin Wilton**
      b: 25 Dec 1853 in Marion Co., Illinois
      m: 15 Feb 1877 in Home of Mary Jones (Sister of Martha), Marion Co., Illinois
      d: 04 Sep 1941 in Jermyn, Jack Co., Texas

    - **Martha Jane Baldwin**
      b: 19 Jul 1856 in Marion Co., Illinois
      d: 09 Nov 1946 in Jermyn, Jack Co., Texas

  - **Lona Blanche Parrish**
    b: 07 Apr 1894 in Jermyn, Jack Co., Texas
    d: Sep 1926 in Jermyn, Jack Co., Texas

    - **John Thomas Parrish**
      b: 28 Aug 1866 in Lamar Co., Texas
      m: 19 Apr 1897 in Jack Co., Texas
      d: 19 Feb 1907 in Jack Co., Texas

    - **Neoma Demer Clark**
      b: 14 Feb 1876 in Jack Co., Texas
      d: 05 Feb 1921 in Jack Co., Texas

Notes: This Tree also applies to the other children of Jethro Doyle Little & Nola Oletha Wilton: Royce Wilton Little and Charlotte Lynette Little.

Verna Faye Wilton (1925-   )
[6th. Generation From Henry Wilton (1769-1820)]

&

Thomas Sheridan Crabtree (1921-1982)
& Family

Verna Faye Wilton, born August 2, 1925 in Jermyn, Texas, was the sixth and last child of Charles Joseph (Charlie) Wilton and Lona Blanche Parrish. The family had made Jermyn their home since 1916, when Charlie began working for the G.T.&W. Railroad, which had a machine shop, a roundhouse, and other assets located in Jermyn.

Shortly after Verna Faye was born, her mother, Lona Blanche Parrish, died of cancer, in 1926. Her father continued to live in Jermyn and to raise the family, and that was where Verna Faye spent her early years. She had many fond memories of Jermyn, and she described it as a "friendly place, a special place for growing up."

In June 1946, Verna Faye married Thomas Sheridan Crabtree, son of Sheridan Blair Crabtree and Helen Emily Martin. Sometime later, the family settled in Dallas, Texas. Verna Faye and Thomas Sheridan had two children, Carol Ann Crabtree, born September 1954, and Thomas Blair Crabtree, born May 1957, both born in Dallas, Texas. Thomas Sheridan Crabtree died May 1982 in Dallas County, Texas.

Family Group Sheet

Husband:	**Thomas Sheridan Crabtree**	
Born:	08 Nov 1924	in: West Palm Beach, Palm Beach Co., Florida
Married:	09 Jun 1946	in: Texas
Died:	19 May 1982	in: Dallas Co., Texas
Father:	Sheridan Blair Crabtree	
Mother:	Helen Emily Martin	
Wife:	**Verna Faye Wilton**	
Born:	02 Aug 1925	in: Jermyn, Jack Co., Texas
Father:	Charles Joseph Wilton	
Mother:	Lona Blanche Parrish	

CHILDREN

1 F	Name:	Carol Ann Crabtree	
	Born:	18 Sep 1954	in: Dallas, Dallas Co., Texas
2 M	Name:	Thomas Blair Crabtree	
	Born:	24 May 1957	in: Dallas, Dallas Co., Texas
	Married:	20 Aug 1983	in: Denton Co., Texas
	Spouse:	Kaprellan Agnes Ml Jualre	

THOMAS SHERIDAN CRABTREE Standard Pedigree Tree

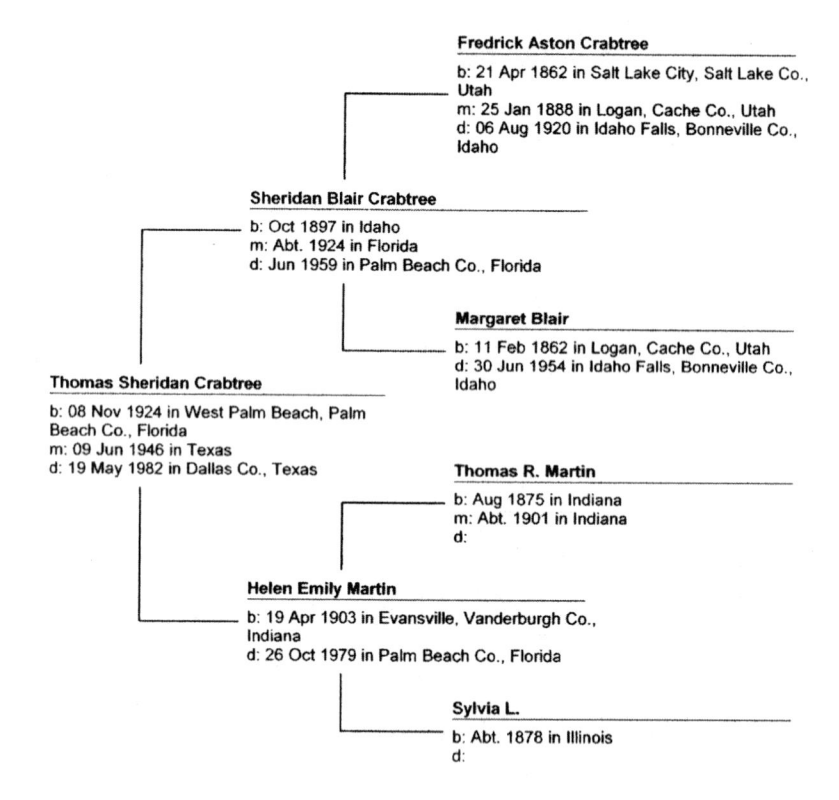

Fredrick Aston Crabtree
b: 21 Apr 1862 in Salt Lake City, Salt Lake Co., Utah
m: 25 Jan 1888 in Logan, Cache Co., Utah
d: 06 Aug 1920 in Idaho Falls, Bonneville Co., Idaho

Sheridan Blair Crabtree
b: Oct 1897 in Idaho
m: Abt. 1924 in Florida
d: Jun 1959 in Palm Beach Co., Florida

Margaret Blair
b: 11 Feb 1862 in Logan, Cache Co., Utah
d: 30 Jun 1954 in Idaho Falls, Bonneville Co., Idaho

Thomas Sheridan Crabtree
b: 08 Nov 1924 in West Palm Beach, Palm Beach Co., Florida
m: 09 Jun 1946 in Texas
d: 19 May 1982 in Dallas Co., Texas

Thomas R. Martin
b: Aug 1875 in Indiana
m: Abt. 1901 in Indiana
d:

Helen Emily Martin
b: 19 Apr 1903 in Evansville, Vanderburgh Co., Indiana
d: 26 Oct 1979 in Palm Beach Co., Florida

Sylvia L.
b: Abt. 1878 in Illinois
d:

Carol Ann Crabtree (1954-   )
[7th. Generation From Henry Wilton (1769-1820)]

Family Group Sheet

Carol Ann Crabtree

Born: 18 Sep 1954   in: Dallas, Dallas Co., Texas
Father: Thomas Sheridan Crabtree
Mother: Verna Faye Wilton

CAROL ANN CRABTREE Standard Pedigree Tree

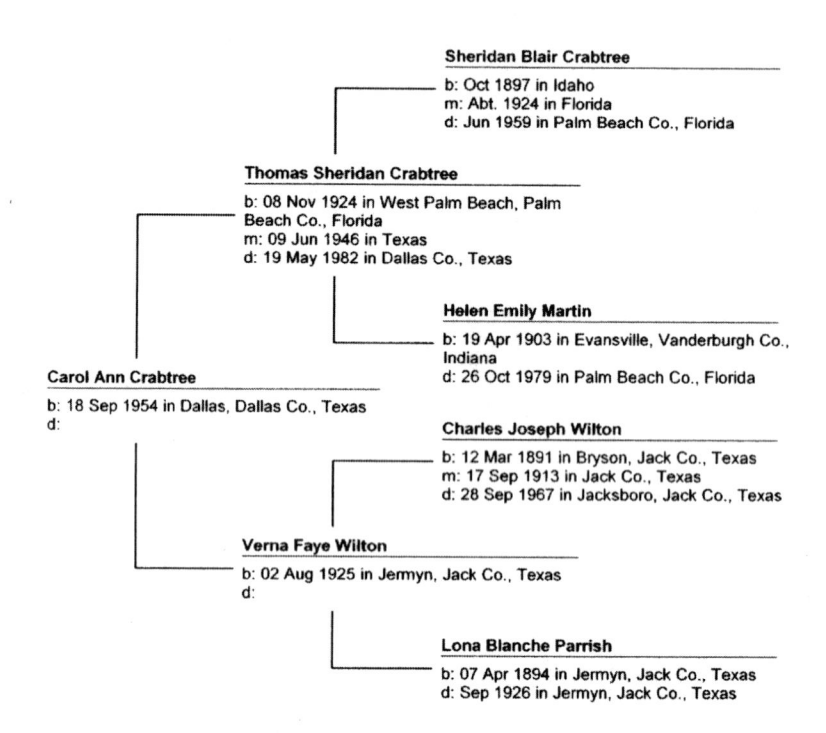

Carol Ann Crabtree
b: 18 Sep 1954 in Dallas, Dallas Co., Texas
d:

- **Thomas Sheridan Crabtree**
  b: 08 Nov 1924 in West Palm Beach, Palm Beach Co., Florida
  m: 09 Jun 1946 in Texas
  d: 19 May 1982 in Dallas Co., Texas
  - **Sheridan Blair Crabtree**
    b: Oct 1897 in Idaho
    m: Abt. 1924 in Florida
    d: Jun 1959 in Palm Beach Co., Florida
  - **Helen Emily Martin**
    b: 19 Apr 1903 in Evansville, Vanderburgh Co., Indiana
    d: 26 Oct 1979 in Palm Beach Co., Florida

- **Verna Faye Wilton**
  b: 02 Aug 1925 in Jermyn, Jack Co., Texas
  d:
  - **Charles Joseph Wilton**
    b: 12 Mar 1891 in Bryson, Jack Co., Texas
    m: 17 Sep 1913 in Jack Co., Texas
    d: 28 Sep 1967 in Jacksboro, Jack Co., Texas
  - **Lona Blanche Parrish**
    b: 07 Apr 1894 in Jermyn, Jack Co., Texas
    d: Sep 1926 in Jermyn, Jack Co., Texas

Notes: This Tree also applies to the other child of Thomas Sheridan Crabtree & Verna Faye Wilton: Thomas Blair Crabtree.

Thomas Blair Crabtree (1957-   )
[7th. Generation From Henry Wilton (1769-1820)]

&

Kaprelian Agnes Mi Juaire (1961-   )
& Family

Family Group Sheet

Husband: Thomas Blair Crabtree

Born: 24 May 1957   in: Dallas, Dallas Co., Texas
Married: 20 Aug 1980   in: Denton Co., Texas
Father: Thomas Sheridan Crabtree
Mother: Verna Faye Wilton

Wife: Kaprelian Agnes Mi Juaire

Born: Apr 1961

CHILDREN

1 M   Name: Michel Blair Crabtree
      Born: 19 Nov 1995   in: Dallas Co., Texas

Lee O'Norvell Wilton (1936-   )
[6th. Generation From Henry Wilton (1769-1820)]

&

Linda Fay Edwards
& Family

Lee O'Norvell Wilton, born February 10, 1936 in Jermyn, Texas, was the first child of Charles Joseph (Charlie) Wilton and Lydia Ann Evans. After Charlie's first wife, Lona Blanche Parrish, died in 1926, Charlie continued to raise his family of then five children and to work for the G.T.&W. Railroad located in Jermyn. Charlie remarried to Lydia Ann Evans in 1935. Together, they had five children while still living in Jermyn. After Charlie retired from his job with the railroad, about 1948, the family relocated to Jacksboro, Texas.

In June 1957, Lee married Linda Fay Edwards in Jacksboro, Texas. After first settling in Jacksboro, Lee and Linda had three children, Terri Lynn Wilton, born July 1959, Leland Norvell Wilton, born January 1962, and Letha Fay Wilton, born October 1963. At one point, the family resettled in Olney in Young County, Texas.

Family Group Sheet

Husband: Lee O'Norvell Wilton

Born: 10 Feb 1936 in: Jermyn, Jack Co., Texas
Married: 22 Jun 1957 in: Jacksboro, Jack Co., Texas
Father: Charles Joseph Wilton
Mother: Lydia Ann Evans

Wife: Linda Fay Edwards

Born: Unknown

CHILDREN

1 F
Name: Terri Lynn Wilton
Born: 07 Jul 1959 in: Jack Co., Texas
Married: 28 May 1977 in: Denton Co., Texas
Spouse: Johnny Ray Cruit

2 M
Name: Leland Norvell Wilton
Born: 30 Jan 1962 in: Jacksboro, Jack Co., Texas
Died: 01 Sep 2008 in: Olney, Young Co., Texas
Married: 11 Jul 1987 in: Young Co., Texas
Spouse: Claudine Marie Rockenbaugh

3 F
Name: Letha Fay Wilton
Born: 05 Oct 1963 in: Jacksboro, Jack Co., Texas
Married: 19 Dec 1980 in: Young Co., Texas
Spouse: Troy David Jr. Keathley
Married: 21 Aug 1990 in: Young Co., Texas
Spouse: Max L. Young

LEE O'NORVELL WILTON Standard Pedigree Tree

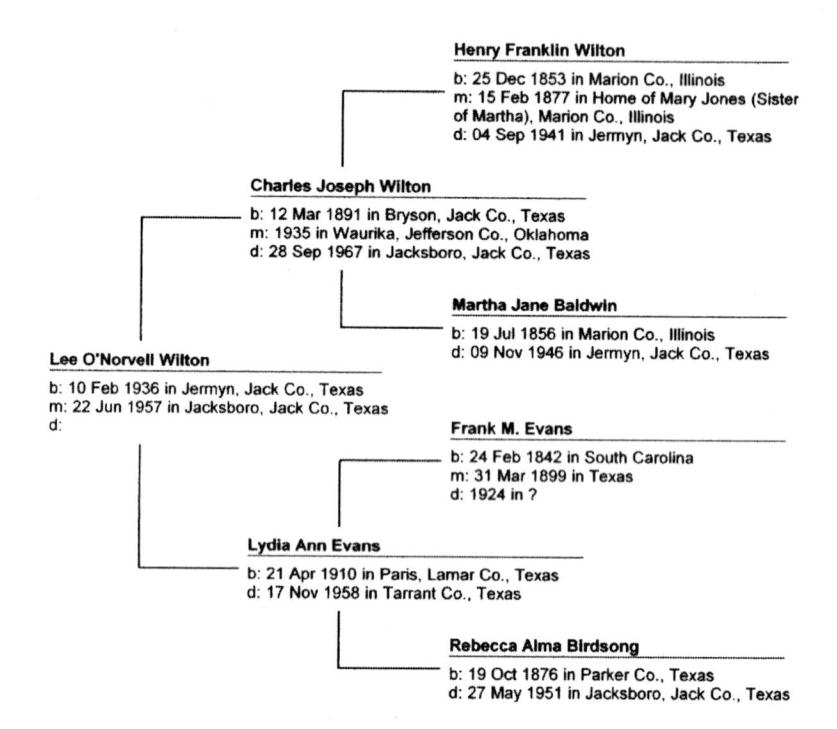

Lee O'Norvell Wilton
b: 10 Feb 1936 in Jermyn, Jack Co., Texas
m: 22 Jun 1957 in Jacksboro, Jack Co., Texas
d:

- **Charles Joseph Wilton**
  b: 12 Mar 1891 in Bryson, Jack Co., Texas
  m: 1935 in Waurika, Jefferson Co., Oklahoma
  d: 28 Sep 1967 in Jacksboro, Jack Co., Texas

  - **Henry Franklin Wilton**
    b: 25 Dec 1853 in Marion Co., Illinois
    m: 15 Feb 1877 in Home of Mary Jones (Sister of Martha), Marion Co., Illinois
    d: 04 Sep 1941 in Jermyn, Jack Co., Texas

  - **Martha Jane Baldwin**
    b: 19 Jul 1856 in Marion Co., Illinois
    d: 09 Nov 1946 in Jermyn, Jack Co., Texas

- **Lydia Ann Evans**
  b: 21 Apr 1910 in Paris, Lamar Co., Texas
  d: 17 Nov 1958 in Tarrant Co., Texas

  - **Frank M. Evans**
    b: 24 Feb 1842 in South Carolina
    m: 31 Mar 1899 in Texas
    d: 1924 in ?

  - **Rebecca Alma Birdsong**
    b: 19 Oct 1876 in Parker Co., Texas
    d: 27 May 1951 in Jacksboro, Jack Co., Texas

Notes: This Tree also applies to the other children of Charles Joseph Wilton & Lydia Ann Evans: Charles Joseph Jr. Wilton, Charlene Lenoy Wilton, Coleen Rebecca Wilton, and Raymond Eugene Wilton.

Terri Lynn Wilton (1959-   )
[7th. Generation From Henry Wilton (1769-1820)]

&

Johnny Ray Cruit (1956-   )
& Family

Family Group Sheet

Husband: Johnny Ray Cruit	
Born: 14 Nov 1956	in: Ector Co., Texas
Married: 28 May 1977	in: Denton Co., Texas

Wife: Terri Lynn Wilton	
Born: 07 Jul 1959	in: Jack Co., Texas
Father: Lee O'Norvell Wilton	
Mother: Linda Fay Edwards	

CHILDREN

1 M	Name: Jeremy Ray Cruit	
	Born: 30 Mar 1980	in: Denton Co., Texas
	Married: 24 Jul 1999	in: Titus Co., Texas
	Spouse: Michelle Elaine Whatley	
2 F	Name: Jaclyn Ruth Cruit	
	Born: 09 Feb 1985	in: Titus Co., Texas

TERRI LYNN WILTON Standard Pedigree Tree

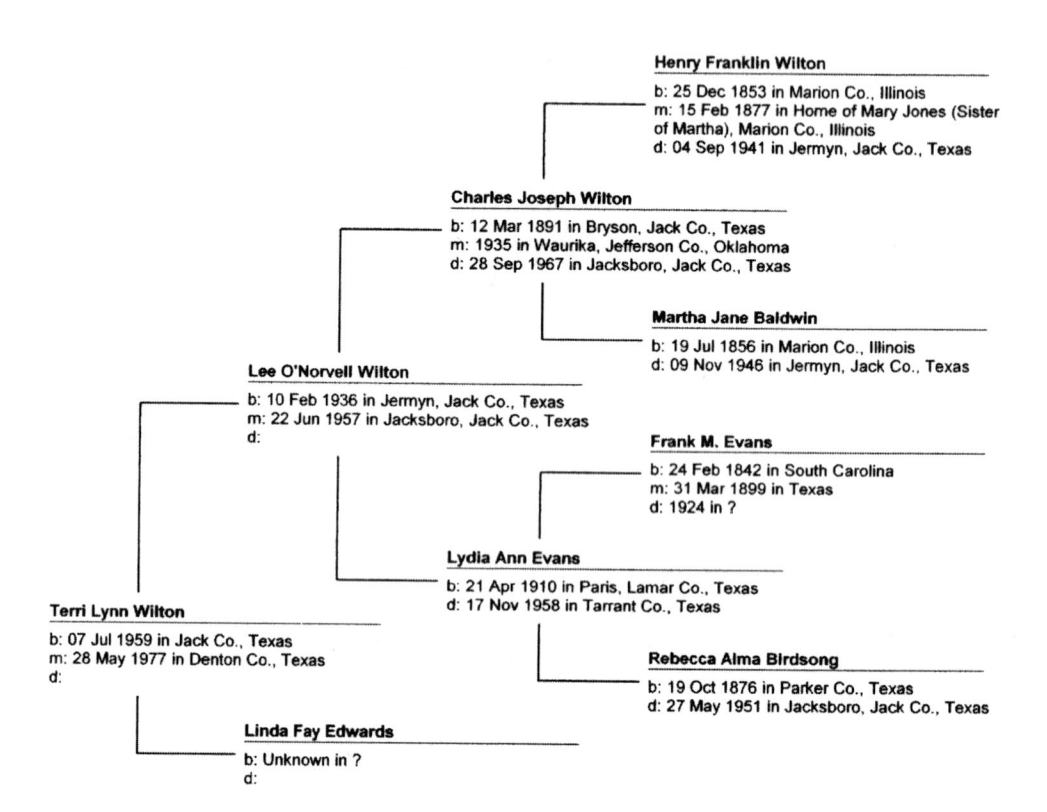

Henry Franklin Wilton
b: 25 Dec 1853 in Marion Co., Illinois
m: 15 Feb 1877 in Home of Mary Jones (Sister of Martha), Marion Co., Illinois
d: 04 Sep 1941 in Jermyn, Jack Co., Texas

Charles Joseph Wilton
b: 12 Mar 1891 in Bryson, Jack Co., Texas
m: 1935 in Waurika, Jefferson Co., Oklahoma
d: 28 Sep 1967 in Jacksboro, Jack Co., Texas

Martha Jane Baldwin
b: 19 Jul 1856 in Marion Co., Illinois
d: 09 Nov 1946 in Jermyn, Jack Co., Texas

Lee O'Norvell Wilton
b: 10 Feb 1936 in Jermyn, Jack Co., Texas
m: 22 Jun 1957 in Jacksboro, Jack Co., Texas
d:

Frank M. Evans
b: 24 Feb 1842 in South Carolina
m: 31 Mar 1899 in Texas
d: 1924 in ?

Lydia Ann Evans
b: 21 Apr 1910 in Paris, Lamar Co., Texas
d: 17 Nov 1958 in Tarrant Co., Texas

Terri Lynn Wilton
b: 07 Jul 1959 in Jack Co., Texas
m: 28 May 1977 in Denton Co., Texas
d:

Rebecca Alma Birdsong
b: 19 Oct 1876 in Parker Co., Texas
d: 27 May 1951 in Jacksboro, Jack Co., Texas

Linda Fay Edwards
b: Unknown in ?
d:

Notes: This Tree also applies to the other children of Lee O'Norvell Wilton & Linda Fay Edwards: Leland Norvell Wilton and Letha Fay Wilton.

Leland Norvell Wilton (1962-2008)
[7th. Generation From Henry Wilton (1769-1820)]

&

Claudine Marie Rockenbaugh (1959-   )
& Family

Family Group Sheet

Husband: Leland Norvell Wilton	
Born: 30 Jan 1962	in: Jacksboro, Jack Co., Texas
Married: 11 Jul 1987	in: Young Co., Texas
Died: 01 Sep 2008	in: Olney, Young Co., Texas
Father: Lee O'Norvell Wilton	
Mother: Linda Fay Edwards	

Wife: Claudine Marie Rockenbaugh	
Born: 20 Jun 1959	in: Alameda Co., California

#	CHILDREN	
1 M	Name: Christopher James Wilton	
	Born: 06 Apr 1987	In: Young Co., Texas
2 F	Name: Elena Loree Wilton	
	Born: 19 Jun 1988	in: Young Co., Texas
3 M	Name: Aaron Norvell Wilton	
	Born: 28 Feb 1995	In: Young Co., Texas

Letha Fay Wilton (1963-)
[7th. Generation From Henry Wilton (1769-1820)]

&

Troy David Jr. Keathley (1963-)
& Family

Family Group Sheet

Husband: Troy David Jr. Keathley	
Born: 29 Aug 1963	in: Young Co., Texas
Married: 19 Dec 1980	in: Young Co., Texas

Wife: Letha Fay Wilton	
Born: 05 Oct 1963	in: Jacksboro, Jack Co., Texas
Father: Lee O'Norvell Wilton	
Mother: Linda Fay Edwards	
Other Spouses: Max L. Young	

CHILDREN

1 M	Name: Keith Brent Keathley	
	Born: 26 Jun 1981	in: Archer Co., Texas
2 M	Name: Derek Scott Keathley	
	Born: 22 Mar 1983	in: Young Co., Texas

Charles Joseph Jr. Wilton (1937-   )
[6th. Generation From Henry Wilton (1769-1820)]

&

Wilma Anita Yaw (1936-   )
& Family

Family Group Sheet

Husband: Charles Joseph Jr. Wilton	
Born: 21 Sep 1937	in: Jermyn, Jack Co., Texas
Married: 23 Sep 1957	in: Santa Ana, Orange Co., California
Father: Charles Joseph Wilton	
Mother: Lydia Ann Evans	
Wife: Wilma Anita Yaw	
Born: 28 Feb 1936	in: Charlotte, Mecklenburg Co., North Carolina
Father: Sylis Aaron Yaw	
Mother: Pearl Catholine Blackman	

CHILDREN

1 M	Name: Charles Joseph III Wilton	
	Born: 08 Jul 1958	in: Santa Ana, Orange Co., California
2 F	Name: Vernie F. Wilton	
	Born: 21 Sep 1960	in: Santa Ana, Orange Co., California
3 F	Name: Veria F. Wilton	
	Born: 21 Sep 1960	in: Santa Ana, Orange Co., California

Charlene Lenoy Wilton (1940-   )
[6th. Generation From Henry Wilton (1769-1820)]

&

A.J. Jackson (1938-1998)
& Family

Family Group Sheet

Husband: A.J. Jackson

Born: 16 Mar 1938   in: near Shannon, Clay Co., Texas
Married: 07 Aug 1956   in: Graham, Young Co., Texas
Died: 25 Feb 1998   in: Jack Co., Texas
Father: Andrew Burlington Jackson
Mother: Bessie Irene Maxwell

Wife: Charlene Lenoy Wilton

Born: 26 Oct 1940   in: Jacksboro, Jack Co., Texas
Died: 20 Feb 2003   in: Texas
Father: Charles Joseph Wilton
Mother: Lydia Ann Evans

CHILDREN

1 F
Name: Sheila Darlene Jackson
Born: 12 Jul 1959   in: Jacksboro, Jack Co., Texas
Married: 11 Aug 1976   in: Jack Co, Texas
Spouse: Noble Montgomery Willmon

2 F
Name: Brenda Joyce Jackson
Born: 20 Aug 1963   in: Jacksboro, Jack Co., Texas
Married: 17 Sep 1982   in: Jack Co, Texas
Spouse: Kyle W. Willams

Sheila Darlene Jackson (1959-   )
[7th. Generation From Henry Wilton (1769-1820)]

&

Noble Montgomery Willmon (1955-   )
& Family

Family Group Sheet

Husband: Noble Montgomery Willmon		
Born: 28 Feb 1955	in: Parker Co., Texas	
Married: 11 Aug 1976	in: Jack Co., Texas	
Father: Noble Oran Willmon		
Mother: Charlotte Ilene Underwood		
Wife: Sheila Darlene Jackson		
Born: 12 Jul 1959	in: Jacksboro, Jack Co., Texas	
Father: A.J. Jackson		
Mother: Charlene Lenoy Wilton		

	CHILDREN	
1 M	Name: Shawn Christopher Willmon	
	Born: 20 Mar 1977	in: Graham, Young Co., Texas
	Married: 14 Aug 2001	in: Jack Co, Texas
	Spouse: Serena Kay Molhusen	
2 F	Name: Crystal Michelle Willmon	
	Born: 15 Jun 1978	in: Jacksboro, Jack Co., Texas
	Married: 23 Feb 2002	in: Jack Co, Texas
	Spouse: Eduardo E. Lucio	

SHEILA DARLENE JACKSON Standard Pedigree Tree

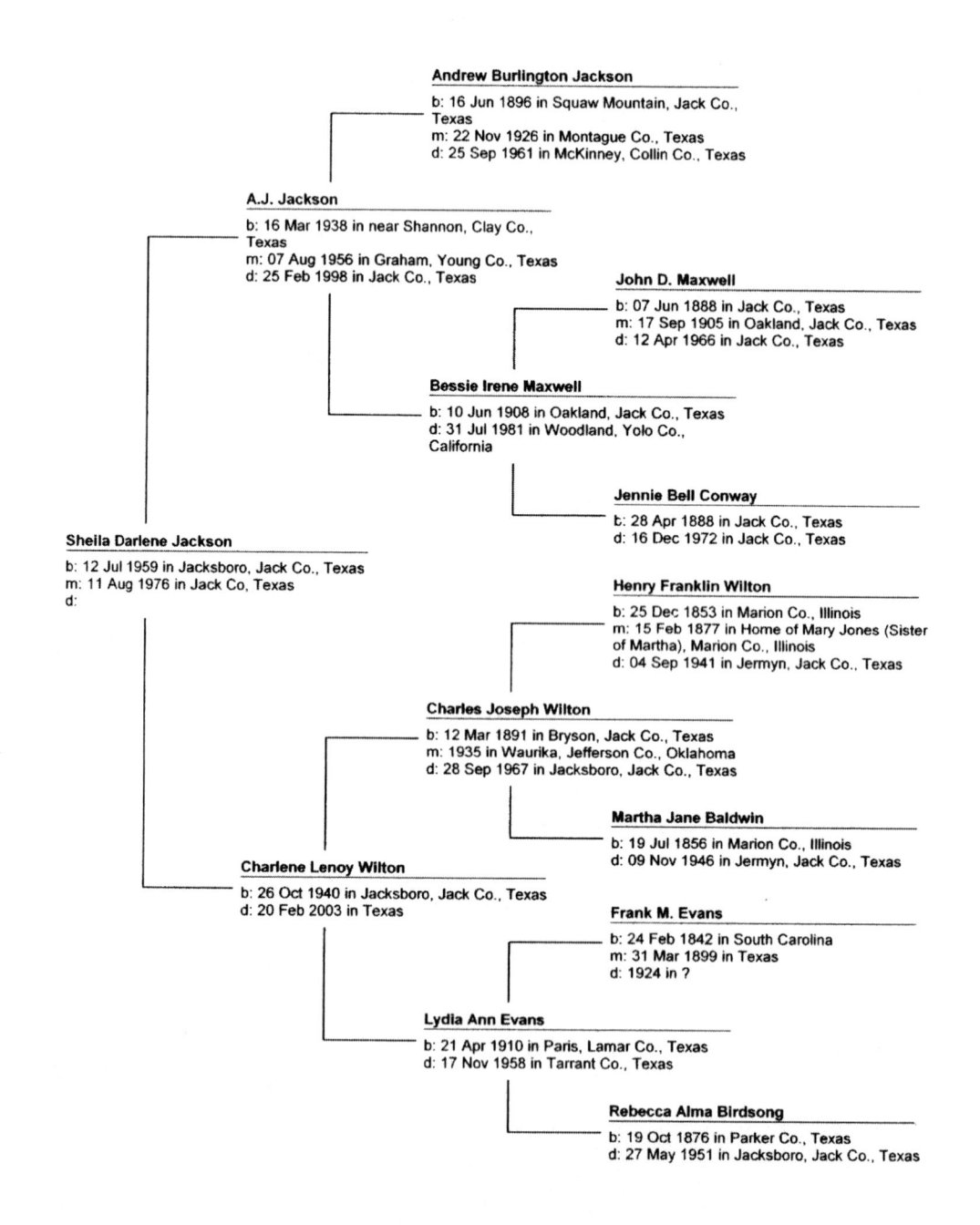

Sheila Darlene Jackson
b: 12 Jul 1959 in Jacksboro, Jack Co., Texas
m: 11 Aug 1976 in Jack Co, Texas
d:

A.J. Jackson
b: 16 Mar 1938 in near Shannon, Clay Co., Texas
m: 07 Aug 1956 in Graham, Young Co., Texas
d: 25 Feb 1998 in Jack Co., Texas

Andrew Burlington Jackson
b: 16 Jun 1896 in Squaw Mountain, Jack Co., Texas
m: 22 Nov 1926 in Montague Co., Texas
d: 25 Sep 1961 in McKinney, Collin Co., Texas

Bessie Irene Maxwell
b: 10 Jun 1908 in Oakland, Jack Co., Texas
d: 31 Jul 1981 in Woodland, Yolo Co., California

John D. Maxwell
b: 07 Jun 1888 in Jack Co., Texas
m: 17 Sep 1905 in Oakland, Jack Co., Texas
d: 12 Apr 1966 in Jack Co., Texas

Jennie Bell Conway
b: 28 Apr 1888 in Jack Co., Texas
d: 16 Dec 1972 in Jack Co., Texas

Charlene Lenoy Wilton
b: 26 Oct 1940 in Jacksboro, Jack Co., Texas
d: 20 Feb 2003 in Texas

Charles Joseph Wilton
b: 12 Mar 1891 in Bryson, Jack Co., Texas
m: 1935 in Waurika, Jefferson Co., Oklahoma
d: 28 Sep 1967 in Jacksboro, Jack Co., Texas

Henry Franklin Wilton
b: 25 Dec 1853 in Marion Co., Illinois
m: 15 Feb 1877 in Home of Mary Jones (Sister of Martha), Marion Co., Illinois
d: 04 Sep 1941 in Jermyn, Jack Co., Texas

Martha Jane Baldwin
b: 19 Jul 1856 in Marion Co., Illinois
d: 09 Nov 1946 in Jermyn, Jack Co., Texas

Lydia Ann Evans
b: 21 Apr 1910 in Paris, Lamar Co., Texas
d: 17 Nov 1958 in Tarrant Co., Texas

Frank M. Evans
b: 24 Feb 1842 in South Carolina
m: 31 Mar 1899 in Texas
d: 1924 in ?

Rebecca Alma Birdsong
b: 19 Oct 1876 in Parker Co., Texas
d: 27 May 1951 in Jacksboro, Jack Co., Texas

Notes: This Tree also applies to the other child of A.J. Jackson & Charlene Lenoy Wilton: Brenda Joyce Jackson.

Colleen Rebecca Wilton (1946-   )
[6th. Generation From Henry Wilton (1769-1820)]

&

Alton J. Gary (1941-   )
& Family

Family Group Sheet

Husband: Alton J. Gary

Born: 19 Jun 1941   in: Jacksboro, Jack Co., Texas
Married: 26 Sep 1963   in: Texas
Father: J.C. Nathaniel Gary
Mother: Ettie Mae Hart

Wife: Colleen Rebecca Wilton

Born: 24 Feb 1946   in: Jack Co., Texas
Father: Charles Joseph Wilton
Mother: Lydia Ann Evans

CHILDREN

1 F
Name: Debra Deann Gary
Born: 26 Sep 1964   in: Jack Co., Texas
Married: 14 Nov 1981   in: Jack Co, Texas
Spouse: Michael Leslie Jump

2 M
Name: John Alton Gary
Born: 02 Aug 1967   in: Jack Co., Texas
Married: 27 Feb 1988   in: Jack Co., Texas
Spouse: Jacquelyn Donnet Simpson

3 F
Name: Sherri Loraine Gary
Born: 21 Aug 1971   in: Jack Co., Texas
Married: 31 Aug 1990   in: Jack Co, Texas
Spouse: Heath Lee Trudgen

ALTON J. GARY Standard Pedigree Tree

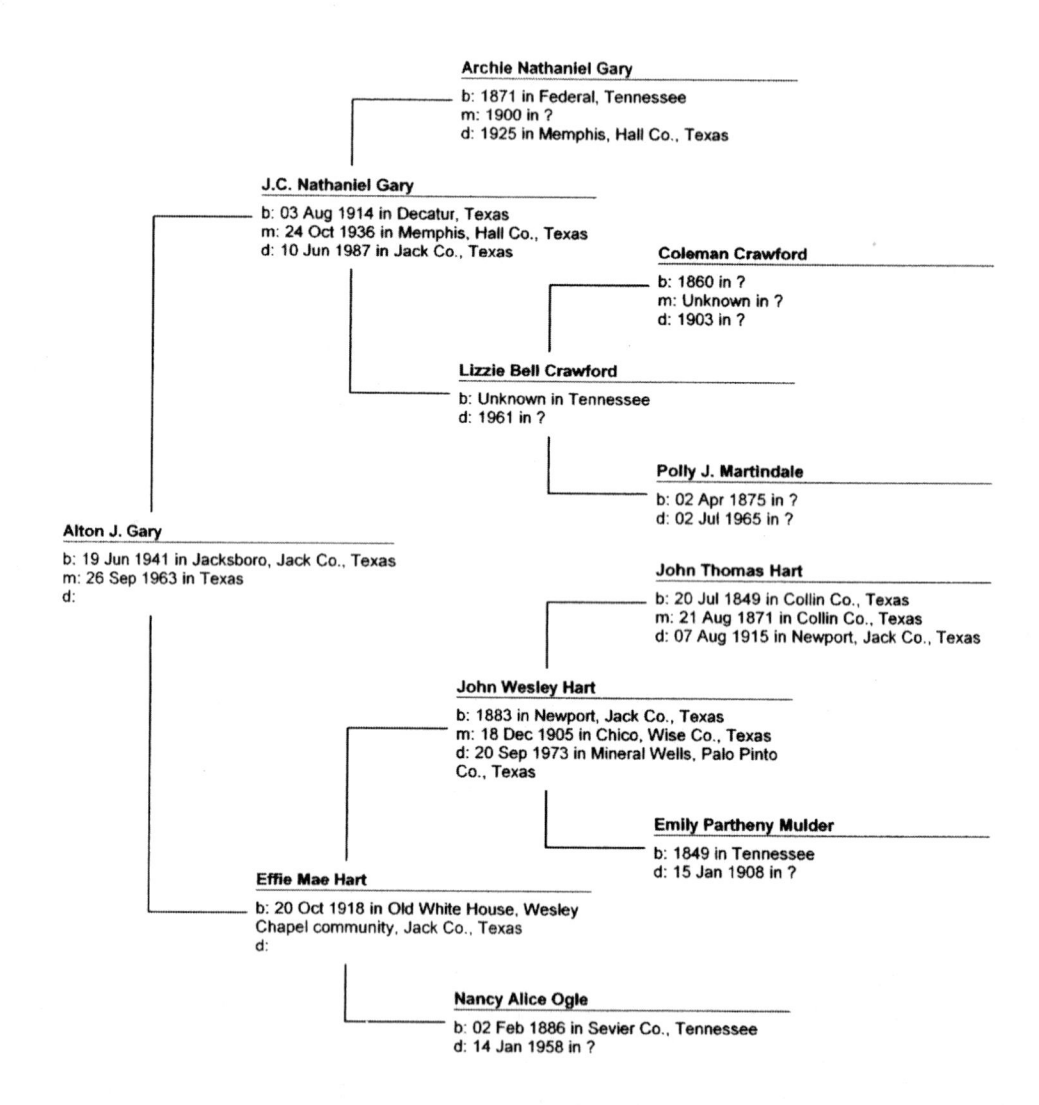

- **Archie Nathaniel Gary**
  b: 1871 in Federal, Tennessee
  m: 1900 in ?
  d: 1925 in Memphis, Hall Co., Texas

- **J.C. Nathaniel Gary**
  b: 03 Aug 1914 in Decatur, Texas
  m: 24 Oct 1936 in Memphis, Hall Co., Texas
  d: 10 Jun 1987 in Jack Co., Texas

- **Coleman Crawford**
  b: 1860 in ?
  m: Unknown in ?
  d: 1903 in ?

- **Lizzie Bell Crawford**
  b: Unknown in Tennessee
  d: 1961 in ?

- **Polly J. Martindale**
  b: 02 Apr 1875 in ?
  d: 02 Jul 1965 in ?

- **Alton J. Gary**
  b: 19 Jun 1941 in Jacksboro, Jack Co., Texas
  m: 26 Sep 1963 in Texas
  d:

- **John Thomas Hart**
  b: 20 Jul 1849 in Collin Co., Texas
  m: 21 Aug 1871 in Collin Co., Texas
  d: 07 Aug 1915 in Newport, Jack Co., Texas

- **John Wesley Hart**
  b: 1883 in Newport, Jack Co., Texas
  m: 18 Dec 1905 in Chico, Wise Co., Texas
  d: 20 Sep 1973 in Mineral Wells, Palo Pinto Co., Texas

- **Emily Partheny Mulder**
  b: 1849 in Tennessee
  d: 15 Jan 1908 in ?

- **Effie Mae Hart**
  b: 20 Oct 1918 in Old White House, Wesley Chapel community, Jack Co., Texas
  d:

- **Nancy Alice Ogle**
  b: 02 Feb 1886 in Sevier Co., Tennessee
  d: 14 Jan 1958 in ?

Debra Deann Gary (1964-   )
[7th. Generation From Henry Wilton (1769-1820)]

&

Michael Leslie Jump (1961-   )
& Family

Family Group Sheet

Husband: Michael Leslie Jump	
Born: 17 Apr 1961	
Married: 14 Nov 1981	in: Jack Co, Texas
Wife: Debra Deann Gary	
Born: 26 Sep 1964	in: Jack Co., Texas
Father: Alton J. Gary	
Mother: Colleen Rebecca Wilton	

	CHILDREN	
1 F	Name: Valeria Michelle Jump	
	Born: 08 Jun 1982	in: Palo Pinto Co., Texas
2 F	Name: Mandi Lynn Jump	
	Born: 14 Feb 1986	in: Young Co., Texas

John Alton Gary (1967-   )
[7th. Generation From Henry Wilton (1769-1820)]

&

Jacquelyn Donnet Simpson (1968-   )
& Family

Family Group Sheet

Husband: John Alton Gary	
Born: 02 Aug 1967	in: Jack Co., Texas
Married: 27 Feb 1988	in: Jack Co., Texas
Father: Alton J. Gary	
Mother: Colleen Rebecca Wilton	

Wife: Jacquelyn Donnet Simpson	
Born: Abt. 1968	

	CHILDREN	
1 F	Name: Brandi Mae Gary	
	Born: 01 Oct 1989	in: Young Co., Texas
2 M	Name: Alton Nathaniel Gary	
	Born: 17 Jun 1988	in: Young Co., Texas

Sherri Loraine Gary (1971-   )
[7th. Generation From Henry Wilton (1769-1820)]

&

Heath Lee Trudgen (1968-   )
& Family

Family Group Sheet

Husband: Heath Lee Trudgen

    Born: 28 Oct 1968   in: Tarrant Co., Texas
    Married: 31 Aug 1990   in: Jack Co, Texas
    Father: Kenneth Doyle Trudgen
    Mother: Sherry Sue Anderson
        Other Spouses: Brandie L. Harris

Wife: Sherri Loraine Gary

    Born: 21 Aug 1971   in: Jack Co., Texas
    Father: Alton J. Gary
    Mother: Colleen Rebecca Wilton

CHILDREN

1 M   Name: Justin Lee Trudgen
         Born: 06 Dec 1991   in: Young Co., Texas

Mary Alma Wilton (1895-1979)
[5th. Generation From Henry Wilton (1769-1820)]

&

James Roscoe Reynolds (1896-1974)
& Family

Mary Alma Wilton, the sixth and youngest child of Henry Franklin Wilton and Martha Jane Baldwin, was born November 23, 1895 in Jermyn in Jack County, Texas. Henry and Martha had settled permanently near the Winn Hill Community in Jack County about 1889. Mary attended school at Winn Hill, which was about 1 &1/2 miles away from the Wilton homeplace. She often rode a horse to school, along with her brother, Charles Joseph Wilton.

In August 1924, Mary married James Roscoe (Jim) Reynolds, the son of William Rufus Reynolds and Alma Lena Meadows. Jim had an additional connection with the Wilton family, because his father's second wife, Ida May Wilton, was Mary Alma's older cousin, the daughter of Thomas Abslum Wilton and Easter B. Clark. The Reynolds family was musically talented and loved to sing, and it was through attending gospel-singing conventions in surrounding counties with Mary Alma that their romance blossomed.

Jim was originally from Talladega, Alabama, but his father brought the family to Texas about 1912, after the death his first wife, Alma Lena Meadows. After the outbreak of World War I, Jim joined the Army, being inducted at Fort Worth, Texas. He served in France as a driver of a munitions truck, carrying ammunition to the soldiers in the trenches on the front lines. It was during this time that his father remarried. By the time of the 1920 Federal Census, Jim was living alone as a farm laborer in Archer County, Texas.

After their marriage in 1924, Mary and Jim settled first at Jean in Young County, Texas, where Jim rented a farm. Their first child was born November 1925 while they lived at Jean, but he died the same day he was born.

During the late 1920's, when the oil boom began in Young and Archer Counties, Jim got a job with the Sinclair Oil Company (later changed to Arco), which became his life's work. For several years, the family lived on various oil leases around Megargel in Archer County, Texas, and four of the couple's children, Margie Helen Reynolds, Herman Atwood Reynolds, James Weldon Reynolds, and Verna Evelyn Reynolds, were born in Olney in the adjacent Young County. In the 1930 Federal Census of Archer County, Texas, James R. Reynolds was listed at age 34, with an occupation of oil field pumper, along with his wife, Mary Reynolds, and two of his children, Margie Reynolds, age 3 &7/12, and Atwood Reynolds, age 11/12.

At one point, the Sinclair Oil Company sent Jim to East Texas to work, forcing him to leave the family back in Jack County, Texas with Mary's parents. After only a few months, Jim petitioned the company to send him to a suitable place where both he and his family could live together. Since the company valued him as an employee, they agreed and sent him and his family to Coahoma in Howard County, Texas. Their youngest son, Clarence Chalmer Reynolds, was born August 1935, while the family was living at Coahoma.

Jim was later transferred to Illinois for a time, and then, about 1941, to Kentucky, where he settled permanently. In Kentucky, the family first settled in Poole in Webster County. That was where all five of the children graduated from high school. After retiring from the Arco Oil Company, Jim and Mary moved to nearby Henderson in Henderson County, Kentucky, where they remained for the rest of their lives.

Mary and Jim participated in school and community affairs, and they loved to travel. Some of their travels brought them back to Jack County, Texas, where their two youngest children later settled. Jim died just three months before their 50th. wedding anniversary, which would have been on August 9, 1974. Mary died September 1979, and they were both buried in Henderson, Kentucky.

Family Group Sheet

Husband: James Roscoe Reynolds

Born: 08 May 1896 in: Oxford, Talladega Co., Alabama
Married: 09 Aug 1924 in: Bryson, Jack Co., Texas
Died: 01 May 1974 in: Henderson, Henderson C., Kentucky
Father: William Rufus Reynolds
Mother: Alma Lena Meadows

Wife: Mary Alma Wilton

Born: 23 Nov 1895 in: Jermyn, Jack Co., Texas
Died: 04 Sep 1979 in: Henderson, Henderson Co., Kentucky
Father: Henry Franklin Wilton
Mother: Martha Jane Baldwin

CHILDREN

1 F
Name: Unknown Reynolds
Born: 05 Jun 1925 in: Jean, Young Co., Texas
Died: 05 Jun 1925 in: Jean, Young Co., Texas

2 F
Name: Marjorie Helen Reynolds
Born: 05 Aug 1927 in: Olney, Young Co., Texas
Married: 05 Jun 1947 in: Poole, Webster Co., Kentucky
Spouse: James William Tapp

3 M
Name: Herman Atwood Reynolds
Born: 06 May 1929 in: Olney, Young Co., Texas
Married: 11 Feb 1950 in: Poole, Webster Co., Kentucky
Spouse: Betty Rose Lykins

4 M
Name: James Weldon Reynolds
Born: 22 Mar 1931 in: Olney, Young Co., Texas
Married: 09 Sep 1951 in: Poole, Webster Co., Kentucky
Spouse: Connie Ann Metz

5 F
Name: Verna Evelyn Reynolds
Born: 17 Sep 1934 in: Olney, Young Co., Texas
Died: 05 May 1983 in: Mineral Wells, Palo Pinto Co., Texas
Married: 04 Aug 1962 in: Henderson, Henderson Co., Kentucky
Spouse: Bert Wallace

6 M
Name: Clarence Chalmer Reynolds
Born: 21 Aug 1935 in: Olney, Young Co., Texas
Married: 01 Oct 1963 in: Baton Rouge, East Baton Rouge Parish, Louisiana
Spouse: Betty Claire Decker

JAMES ROSCOE REYNOLDS Standard Pedigree Tree

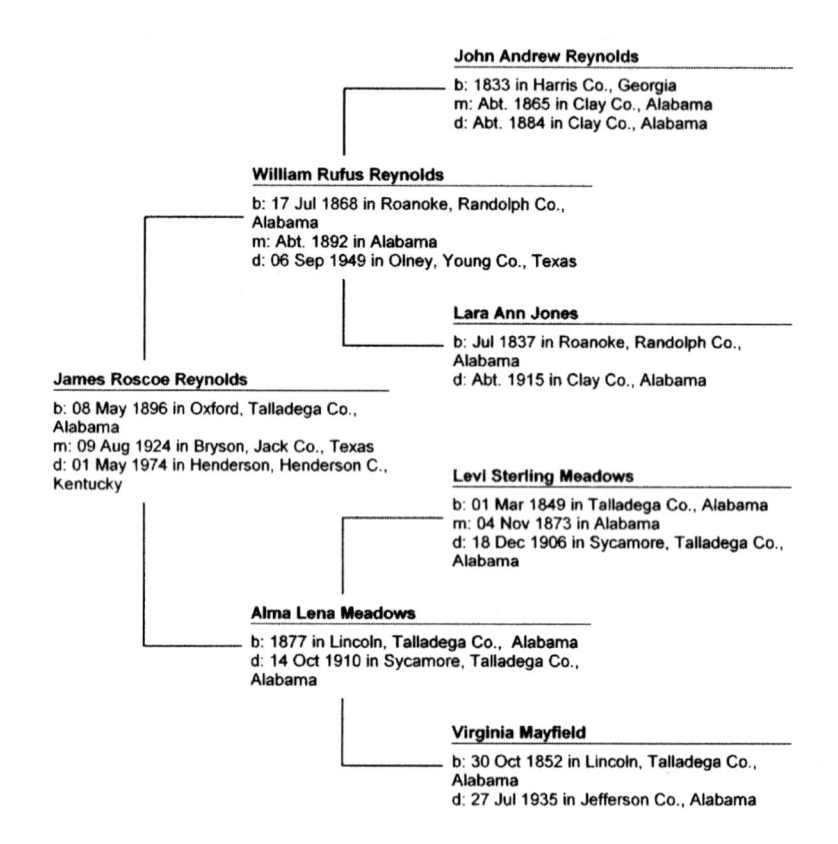

James Roscoe Reynolds
b: 08 May 1896 in Oxford, Talladega Co., Alabama
m: 09 Aug 1924 in Bryson, Jack Co., Texas
d: 01 May 1974 in Henderson, Henderson C., Kentucky

- **William Rufus Reynolds**
  b: 17 Jul 1868 in Roanoke, Randolph Co., Alabama
  m: Abt. 1892 in Alabama
  d: 06 Sep 1949 in Olney, Young Co., Texas
  - **John Andrew Reynolds**
    b: 1833 in Harris Co., Georgia
    m: Abt. 1865 in Clay Co., Alabama
    d: Abt. 1884 in Clay Co., Alabama
  - **Lara Ann Jones**
    b: Jul 1837 in Roanoke, Randolph Co., Alabama
    d: Abt. 1915 in Clay Co., Alabama

- **Alma Lena Meadows**
  b: 1877 in Lincoln, Talladega Co., Alabama
  d: 14 Oct 1910 in Sycamore, Talladega Co., Alabama
  - **Levi Sterling Meadows**
    b: 01 Mar 1849 in Talladega Co., Alabama
    m: 04 Nov 1873 in Alabama
    d: 18 Dec 1906 in Sycamore, Talladega Co., Alabama
  - **Virginia Mayfield**
    b: 30 Oct 1852 in Lincoln, Talladega Co., Alabama
    d: 27 Jul 1935 in Jefferson Co., Alabama

Marjorie Helen Reynolds (1927-   )
[6th. Generation From Henry Wilton (1769-1820)]

&

James William Tapp (1926-   )
& Family

Marjorie Helen (Margie) Reynolds, the first living child of James Roscoe (Jim) Reynolds and Mary Alma Wilton, was born August 5, 1927 in Olney in Young County, Texas. Beginning in the late 1920's, Jim Reynolds began working for the Sinclair Oil Company (later named Arco), and as a result the family made a number of moves, which were required by his job in the oil field. For several years, around the time of Margie's birth, the family lived in the Megargel area of Archer County, Texas.

Through the 3rd grade, Margie attended school at Megargel, and she remembered those years as being some of "the good old days." She recalled that her mother, being a housewife and homemaker, was very talented at sewing dresses. She was able to cut out a dress pattern after just seeing the dress. She was also a good cook, and Margie remembered having biscuits every day.

In addition to working in the oil field, her dad played on a local baseball team as a 3rd baseman. As were the other Reynolds in his family, Jim was also talented musically, and he sang with a group that met at the schoolhouse on Sundays, singing as long as from 10AM to 3PM. The family would eat lunch there, and the children would play on the swings and seesaws.

Another joy for Margie was visiting with her grandpa Henry Wilton and grandma Martha (Baldwin) Wilton who lived in nearby Jack County, Texas. Margie recalled that they usually had an early garden, with crops such as green peas and green onions, which would be ready for harvest before anyone else. In their house was a long table at one end of the entrance hall, and when Christmas came around, which was also grandpa's birthday, there would be a coconut cake at one end of the table and a chocolate cake decorated with pecans on the other end. The pecans were grown right at their home along their creek bank. When the time came for them to exchange Christmas gifts, they would move to the living room, where there was also an organ, and suddenly they would hear Santa's bells coming up the road. There would be packages for everyone, which were usually little boxes that grandma had gotten from ordering candy from Sears, which she filled with nuts, candy, and popcorn.

In the summers, when Marjorie often visited with her grandma Martha (Baldwin) Wilton, she would also visit with her Uncle Elmer Wilton and Aunt Eula (Rhoades) Wilton, who lived nearby. She would walk to their house, and when it was time to leave, they would give her a sack of fruit, containing such things as peaches and grapes. A favorite reminder from grandpa Wilton about those fruit sacks would always be, "don't swallow the seeds." She also remembered cousin Clyde Wilton, Elmer's son, and cousin Herbert Parrish, who made radios in school. The first ones they made required the use of earphones, but they later made better ones. Marjorie also remembered spending a night or two during those times with her Aunt Amy (Wilton) Parrish and Uncle Jacob Parrish. On Saturdays, they would take her to Jacksboro, Texas, where they would go to the dime store and grocery store.

On the Reynolds side of the family, Margie had her grandpa Reynolds, who lived in Archer County, Texas. He ran a grocery store in the oil field area at Olney, along with a lady named Miss Mae. Margie recalled that grandpa and grandma Reynolds lived in a two-story ranch house with a porch on two sides. Some of her aunts and uncles, who did not live far away, often came to the house to play cards or dominoes for entertainment. Her dad also had bought some land in Jacksboro, where he kept cows, sheep, goats, and a couple of horses.

About 1936, Jim was transferred to East Texas, and the family was briefly separated, with the family staying behind to live with relatives in Jack County, Texas. After Jim convinced his employer to find him a place where he could live together with his family, he was reassigned to Coahoma, located in Southwest Texas. Some of Margie's memories while living at Coahoma were playing croquet and baseball on the grounds at their home, and for the first time taking piano lessons. On Sundays, the family went to the local Baptist church, and sometimes they met nearby for gospel singing. Margie's neighbors, the McGee's and the Clanton's, were highly regarded and left with her a lasting impression.

Due to the transient nature of her dad's job, the family moved again about 1940 to McLeansboro, Illinois. While there, Margie went to the city school for the 8th grade. She remembered that the 8th graders were separated into two classes of 30 students each. By contrast, at the same time, her brother and sister went to a one-room schoolhouse.

Finally, about 1941, the family made its last move, this time to Poole, Kentucky. This was where Margie and her brothers and sister eventually graduated from high school, also enjoying taking part in many school activities. This was the time during WWII, and good houses were scarce, but the oil company built a house for them that had running water and bathrooms, which was then a luxury. Margie remembered that during this time there were soldiers in the area that did their marching at night, and she could hear their gear clanking. Her mom was noted as saying, "don't be afraid, they are friendly."

Following high school, Margie worked for a time with her friend Lucille Pruitt in a nearby hosiery mill. Lucille's boyfriend, who was a farmer, would come to get them at their work when it was rainy. It was through them that Margie met her husband-to-be, James William Tapp, son of Jesse Lee Tapp and Willie Lorene Callis. After dating for about a year, Margie and James were married on June 5, 1947 at Poole, Kentucky. They were married by a high school teacher at his home, with her brother, Atwood Reynolds, and her friend, Ruth Bradley, standing up for them.

Margie's first home after marriage was an apartment in Henderson, Kentucky. By 1953, Margie and James had their own house built on Oak Street, and their first child, Terri Tapp, was born there on March 8, 1956. Their second child, Tammy Tapp, was born June 19, 1959, the same month and day as James' birthday. In fact, when Tammy was born, there had been a birthday party planned for James on that day, but the "stork" postponed the party, when they instead drove through the snow to the hospital for Tammy's birth.

In 1969, Margie and family moved to McClure Ave. in Henderson, Kentucky. James worked at a number of jobs, some of which included the Double Cola Bottling Company, pumping oil wells for awhile in the oil field, and at Ken's Pump & Supply. He worked hard and did extra work, since he preferred that Margie not have to work. Margie commented that "God has been awfully good to us." They were active in their local church, Hyland Baptist Church, for most of their years in Henderson, where they attended Sunday school and sang in the choir. In 1997 they celebrated their 50th wedding anniversary, and in 2007 they also had their 60th year of marriage.

Family Group Sheet

Husband: James William Tapp

Born: 19 Jun 1926 in: Webster Co., Kentucky
Married: 05 Jun 1947 in: Poole, Webster Co., Kentucky
Father: Jesse Lee Tapp
Mother: Willie Lorene Callis

Wife: Marjorie Helen Reynolds

Born: 05 Aug 1927 in: Olney, Young Co., Texas
Father: James Roscoe Reynolds
Mother: Mary Alma Wilton

CHILDREN

1 F
Name: Terri Lynn Tapp
Born: 08 Mar 1956 in: Henderson, Henderson Co., Kentucky
Married: 27 Sep 1980 in: Henderson, Henderson Co., Kentucky
Spouse: Ricky Allen Brown

2 F
Name: Tammy Jo Tapp
Born: 19 Jun 1959 in: Henderson, Henderson Co., Kentucky
Married: 26 Jun 1982 in: Henderson Co., Kentucky
Spouse: Kirk Gregory Storey

MARJORIE HELEN REYNOLDS Standard Pedigree Tree

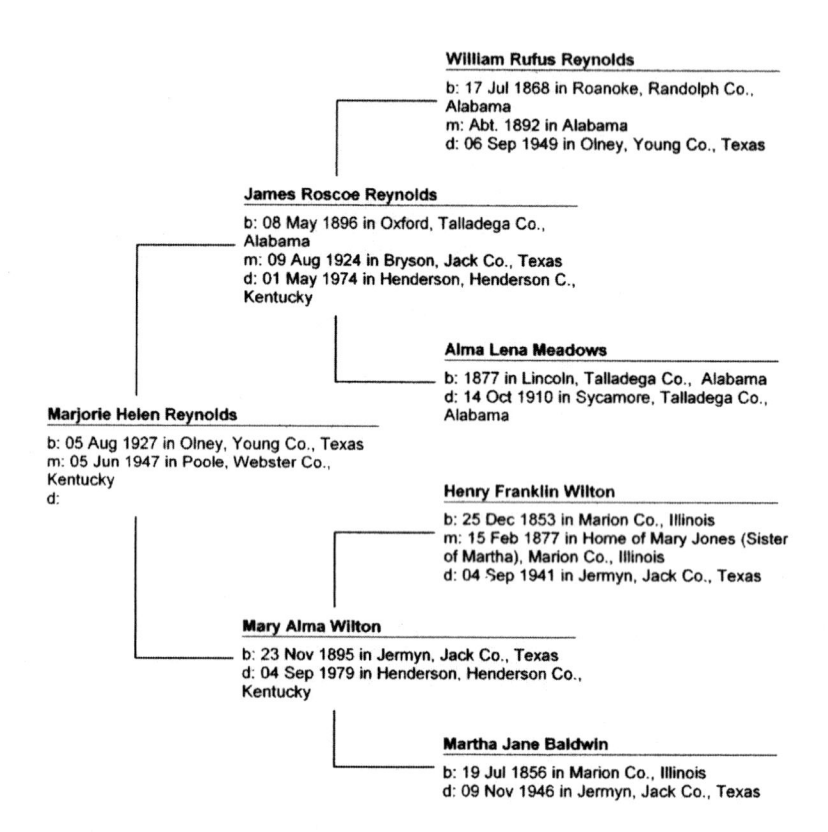

Marjorie Helen Reynolds
b: 05 Aug 1927 in Olney, Young Co., Texas
m: 05 Jun 1947 in Poole, Webster Co., Kentucky
d:

- **James Roscoe Reynolds**
  b: 08 May 1896 in Oxford, Talladega Co., Alabama
  m: 09 Aug 1924 in Bryson, Jack Co., Texas
  d: 01 May 1974 in Henderson, Henderson C., Kentucky
  - **William Rufus Reynolds**
    b: 17 Jul 1868 in Roanoke, Randolph Co., Alabama
    m: Abt. 1892 in Alabama
    d: 06 Sep 1949 in Olney, Young Co., Texas
  - **Alma Lena Meadows**
    b: 1877 in Lincoln, Talladega Co., Alabama
    d: 14 Oct 1910 in Sycamore, Talladega Co., Alabama

- **Mary Alma Wilton**
  b: 23 Nov 1895 in Jermyn, Jack Co., Texas
  d: 04 Sep 1979 in Henderson, Henderson Co., Kentucky
  - **Henry Franklin Wilton**
    b: 25 Dec 1853 in Marion Co., Illinois
    m: 15 Feb 1877 in Home of Mary Jones (Sister of Martha), Marion Co., Illinois
    d: 04 Sep 1941 in Jermyn, Jack Co., Texas
  - **Martha Jane Baldwin**
    b: 19 Jul 1856 in Marion Co., Illinois
    d: 09 Nov 1946 in Jermyn, Jack Co., Texas

Notes: This Tree also applies to the other children of James Roscoe Reynolds & Mary Alma Wilton: Herman Atwood Reynolds, James Weldon Reynolds, Verna Evelyn Reynolds, and Clarence Chalmer Reynolds.

JAMES WILLIAM TAPP Standard Pedigree Tree

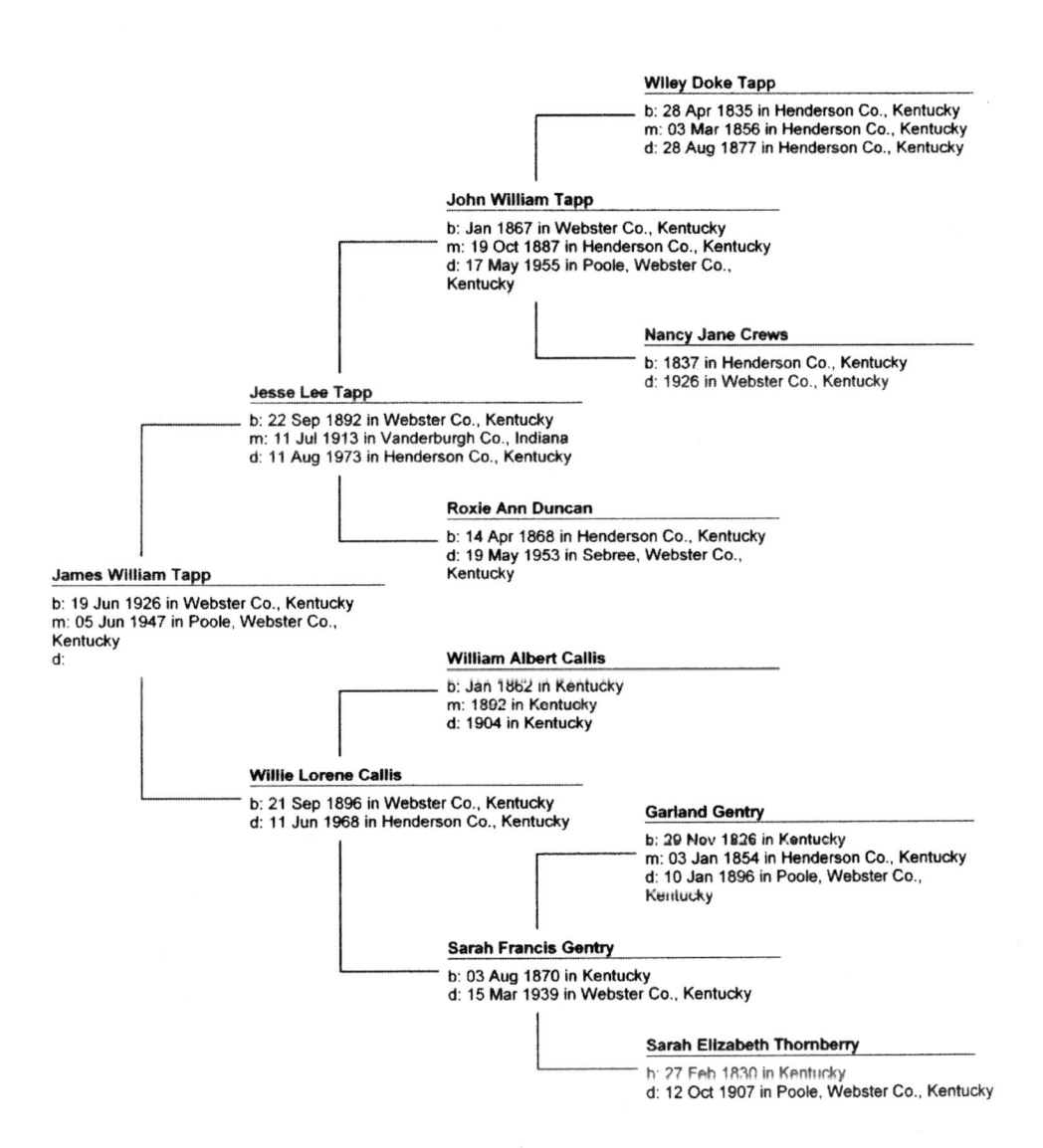

James William Tapp
b: 19 Jun 1926 in Webster Co., Kentucky
m: 05 Jun 1947 in Poole, Webster Co., Kentucky
d:

- **Jesse Lee Tapp**
  b: 22 Sep 1892 in Webster Co., Kentucky
  m: 11 Jul 1913 in Vanderburgh Co., Indiana
  d: 11 Aug 1973 in Henderson Co., Kentucky

  - **John William Tapp**
    b: Jan 1867 in Webster Co., Kentucky
    m: 19 Oct 1887 in Henderson Co., Kentucky
    d: 17 May 1955 in Poole, Webster Co., Kentucky

    - **Wiley Doke Tapp**
      b: 28 Apr 1835 in Henderson Co., Kentucky
      m: 03 Mar 1856 in Henderson Co., Kentucky
      d: 28 Aug 1877 in Henderson Co., Kentucky

    - **Nancy Jane Crews**
      b: 1837 in Henderson Co., Kentucky
      d: 1926 in Webster Co., Kentucky

  - **Roxie Ann Duncan**
    b: 14 Apr 1868 in Henderson Co., Kentucky
    d: 19 May 1953 in Sebree, Webster Co., Kentucky

- **Willie Lorene Callis**
  b: 21 Sep 1896 in Webster Co., Kentucky
  d: 11 Jun 1968 in Henderson Co., Kentucky

  - **William Albert Callis**
    b: Jan 1862 in Kentucky
    m: 1892 in Kentucky
    d: 1904 in Kentucky

  - **Sarah Francis Gentry**
    b: 03 Aug 1870 in Kentucky
    d: 15 Mar 1939 in Webster Co., Kentucky

    - **Garland Gentry**
      b: 29 Nov 1826 in Kentucky
      m: 03 Jan 1854 in Henderson Co., Kentucky
      d: 10 Jan 1896 in Poole, Webster Co., Kentucky

    - **Sarah Elizabeth Thornberry**
      b: 27 Feb 1830 in Kentucky
      d: 12 Oct 1907 in Poole, Webster Co., Kentucky

Terri Lynn Tapp (1956-   )
[7th. Generation From Henry Wilton (1769-1820)]

&

Ricky Allen Brown (1954-   )
& Family

Terri Lynn Tapp, daughter of James William Tapp and Marjorie Helen (Margie) Reynolds, was born March 8, 1956 at the Methodist Hospital in Henderson in Henderson County, Kentucky. Margie and James lived in Henderson for all of their adult lives, and that was where Terri was also raised. Until the 3rd grade, Terri lived at 1518 Oak St., and then the family moved just two miles away to a new, larger house. While growing up in Henderson, Terri attended Miss D's Kindergarten, South Heights Grade School, Barrett Middle School, and Henderson City High School. She completed her formal education by graduating in 1980 from Western Kentucky University in Bowling Green, Kentucky, with a B.S. Degree in Marketing and Distributive Education.

Terri met her husband-to-be, Ricky Allen Brown, son of William Lester Brown and Wilma Jean Duncan, at her home church, the Hyland Baptist Church, located in Henderson, Kentucky. After dating for about ten years, they were married on September 27, 1980 at the Hyland Baptist Church.

Ricky, born September 1954 in Henderson, Kentucky, was also raised in the Henderson area. Growing up, he attended the Webster County school system, the Holy Name Catholic School, and Henderson City High School. He later attended trade school to become an Iron Worker and Carpenter.

After their marriage, Terri and Ricky lived in a country home in Henderson County that Ricky built, the first one that he built as a builder and contractor. The couple had one child, a daughter named Heather Nicole Brown, who was born June 12, 1984 in Henderson.

For awhile, Rickey worked through the Iron Workers Local #103, and Terri taught marketing at a vocational school in Owensboro, Kentucky. As of 2007, Ricky worked as a builder, contractor, and developer, and Terri worked for the University of Evansville in a grant program to promote healthier living in Southern Indiana. Their daughter graduated from the University of Southern Indiana in May 2007, and she then married her high school sweetheart on September 29, 2007.

Family Group Sheet

Husband: Ricky Allen Brown	
Born: 18 Sep 1954	in: Henderson, Henderson Co., Kentucky
Married: 27 Sep 1980	in: Henderson, Henderson Co., Kentucky
Father: William Lester Brown	
Mother: Wilma Jean Duncan	

Wife: Terri Lynn Tapp	
Born: 08 Mar 1956	in: Henderson, Henderson Co., Kentucky
Father: James William Tapp	
Mother: Marjorie Helen Reynolds	

	CHILDREN	
1 F	Name: Heather Nicole Brown	
	Born: 12 Jun 1984	in: Henderson, Henderson Co., Kentucky
	Married: 29 Sep 2007	in: Gatlinburg, Sevier Co., Tennessee
	Spouse: Jacob Christopher Husk	

TERRI LYNN TAPP Standard Pedigree Tree

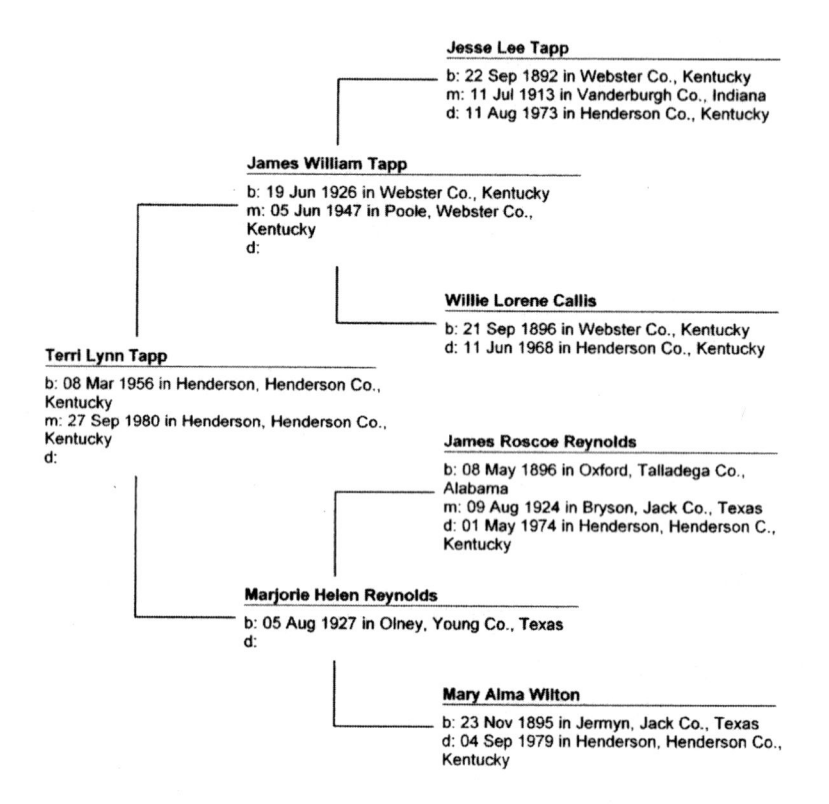

Jesse Lee Tapp
b: 22 Sep 1892 in Webster Co., Kentucky
m: 11 Jul 1913 in Vanderburgh Co., Indiana
d: 11 Aug 1973 in Henderson Co., Kentucky

James William Tapp
b: 19 Jun 1926 in Webster Co., Kentucky
m: 05 Jun 1947 in Poole, Webster Co., Kentucky
d:

Willie Lorene Callis
b: 21 Sep 1896 in Webster Co., Kentucky
d: 11 Jun 1968 in Henderson Co., Kentucky

Terri Lynn Tapp
b: 08 Mar 1956 in Henderson, Henderson Co., Kentucky
m: 27 Sep 1980 in Henderson, Henderson Co., Kentucky
d:

James Roscoe Reynolds
b: 08 May 1896 in Oxford, Talladega Co., Alabama
m: 09 Aug 1924 in Bryson, Jack Co., Texas
d: 01 May 1974 in Henderson, Henderson C., Kentucky

Marjorie Helen Reynolds
b: 05 Aug 1927 in Olney, Young Co., Texas
d:

Mary Alma Wilton
b: 23 Nov 1895 in Jermyn, Jack Co., Texas
d: 04 Sep 1979 in Henderson, Henderson Co., Kentucky

Notes: This Tree also applies to the other child of James William Tapp & Marjorie Helen Reynolds: Tammy Jo Tapp.

RICKY ALLEN BROWN Standard Pedigree Tree

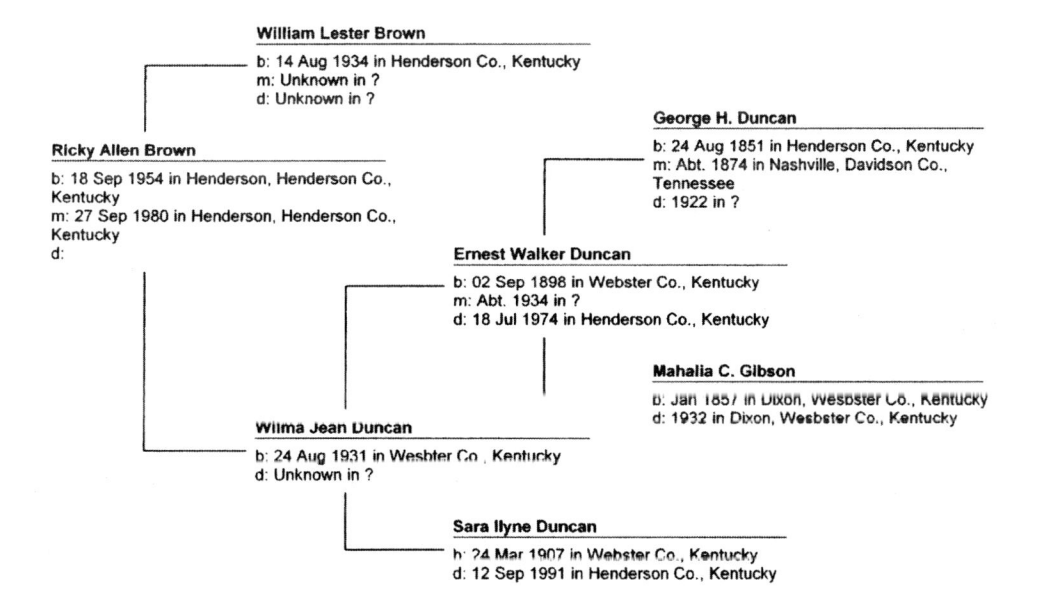

William Lester Brown
b: 14 Aug 1934 in Henderson Co., Kentucky
m: Unknown in ?
d: Unknown in ?

Ricky Allen Brown
b: 18 Sep 1954 in Henderson, Henderson Co., Kentucky
m: 27 Sep 1980 in Henderson, Henderson Co., Kentucky
d:

George H. Duncan
b: 24 Aug 1851 in Henderson Co., Kentucky
m: Abt. 1874 in Nashville, Davidson Co., Tennessee
d: 1922 in ?

Ernest Walker Duncan
b: 02 Sep 1898 in Webster Co., Kentucky
m: Abt. 1934 in ?
d: 18 Jul 1974 in Henderson Co., Kentucky

Mahalia C. Gibson
b: Jan 1857 in Dixon, Wesbster Co., Kentucky
d: 1932 in Dixon, Wesbster Co., Kentucky

Wilma Jean Duncan
b: 24 Aug 1931 in Wesbter Co., Kentucky
d: Unknown in ?

Sara Ilyne Duncan
b: 24 Mar 1907 in Webster Co., Kentucky
d: 12 Sep 1991 in Henderson Co., Kentucky

Heather Nicole Brown (1984-   )
[8th. Generation From Henry Wilton (1769-1820)]

&

Jacob Christopher Husk (1985-   )
& Family

Heather Nicole Brown, daughter of Ricky Allen Brown and Terri Lynn Tapp, was born June 12, 1984 in Henderson in Henderson County, Kentucky. As was typical of her Reynolds side of the family, Heather was born with copper red hair, which was thick and about an inch long at birth. Heather was raised in Henderson, where she began her formal education by attending the Immanuel Baptist Temple Kindergarten and the Bend Gate Grade School. For the fourth grade, she transferred to the Henderson Christian School, and then she attended the Henderson South Jr. High School. She later graduated from the Henderson County High School.

After completing high school, Heather attended the University of Southern Indiana in Evansville, Indiana, located just across the Indiana and Kentucky border from Henderson. Heather graduated from the University of Southern Indiana in May 2007 with a degree in Health Services. As of 2007, she intended to continue her education by pursuing a nursing degree.

On September 29, 2007, Heather married her high school sweetheart, Jacob Christopher Husk, son of Jacob L. Husk and Teresia S. Watson. The marriage was performed on a mountain top in the Great Smokey Mountains in Gatlinburg, Tennessee. They were married by Nicole's church youth pastor, Eric Allen.

After marriage, the couple moved to Young Street in Henderson, Kentucky, which was on the same street as Christopher's parents. Christopher worked on weekends as a welder, and he customized cars and trucks for shows in the evenings. He was also a youth pastor for his church on weekends and Wednesday nights. Heather worked at St. Mary's Medical Center in the rehab department, while also working toward her nursing degree.

Family Group Sheet

Husband: Jacob Christopher Husk

Born: 23 Jun 1985 in: Henderson Co., Kentucky
Married: 29 Sep 2007 in: Gatlinburg, Sevier Co., Tennessee
Father: Jacob L. Husk
Mother: Teresia S. Watson

Wife: Heather Nicole Brown

Born: 12 Jun 1984 in: Henderson, Henderson Co., Kentucky
Father: Ricky Allen Brown
Mother: Terri Lynn Tapp

HEATHER NICOLE BROWN Standard Pedigree Tree

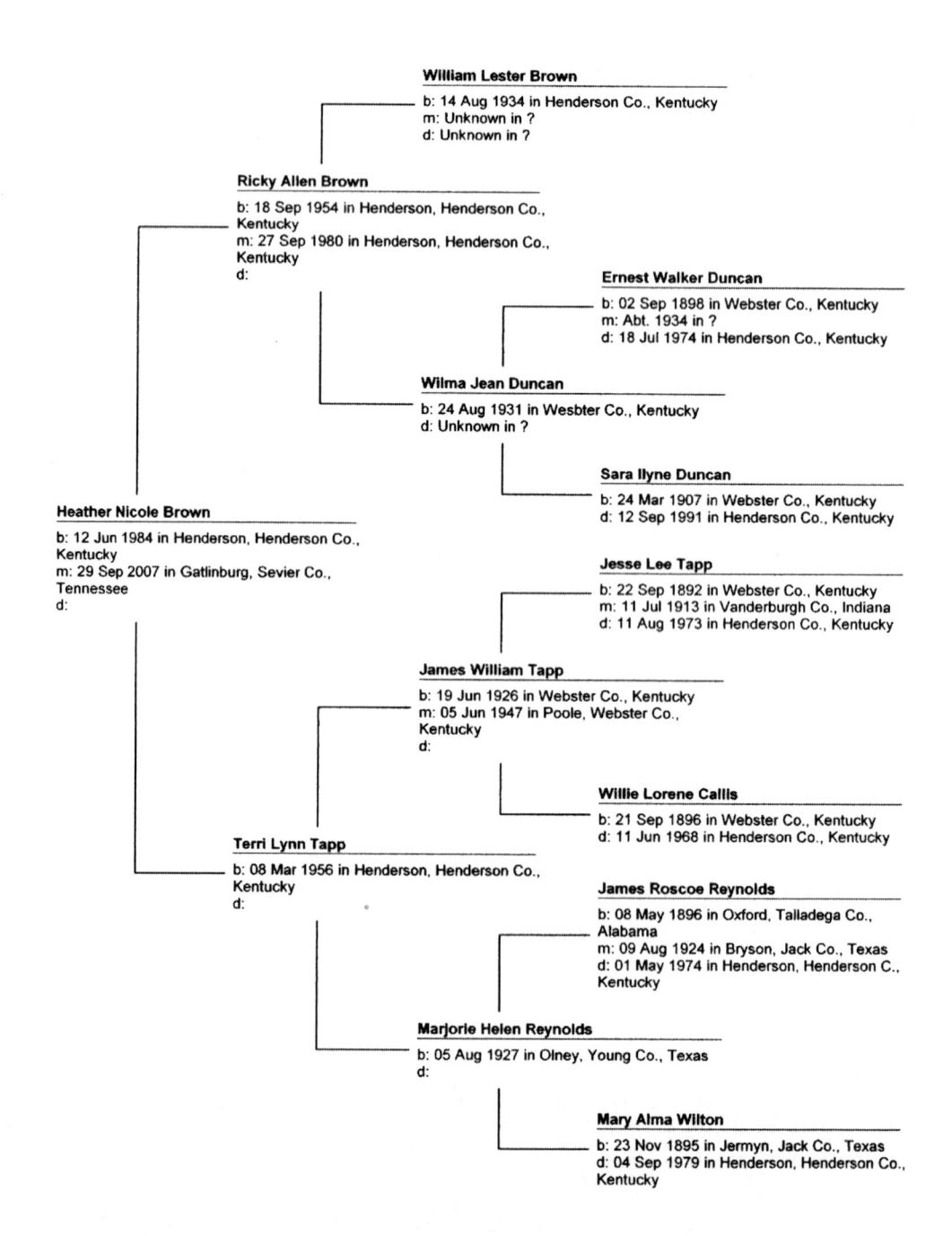

Heather Nicole Brown
b: 12 Jun 1984 in Henderson, Henderson Co., Kentucky
m: 29 Sep 2007 in Gatlinburg, Sevier Co., Tennessee
d:

- **Ricky Allen Brown**
  b: 18 Sep 1954 in Henderson, Henderson Co., Kentucky
  m: 27 Sep 1980 in Henderson, Henderson Co., Kentucky
  d:
  - **William Lester Brown**
    b: 14 Aug 1934 in Henderson Co., Kentucky
    m: Unknown in ?
    d: Unknown in ?
  - **Wilma Jean Duncan**
    b: 24 Aug 1931 in Wesbter Co., Kentucky
    d: Unknown in ?
    - **Ernest Walker Duncan**
      b: 02 Sep 1898 in Webster Co., Kentucky
      m: Abt. 1934 in ?
      d: 18 Jul 1974 in Henderson Co., Kentucky
    - **Sara Ilyne Duncan**
      b: 24 Mar 1907 in Webster Co., Kentucky
      d: 12 Sep 1991 in Henderson Co., Kentucky

- **Terri Lynn Tapp**
  b: 08 Mar 1956 in Henderson, Henderson Co., Kentucky
  d:
  - **James William Tapp**
    b: 19 Jun 1926 in Webster Co., Kentucky
    m: 05 Jun 1947 in Poole, Webster Co., Kentucky
    d:
    - **Jesse Lee Tapp**
      b: 22 Sep 1892 in Webster Co., Kentucky
      m: 11 Jul 1913 in Vanderburgh Co., Indiana
      d: 11 Aug 1973 in Henderson Co., Kentucky
    - **Willie Lorene Callis**
      b: 21 Sep 1896 in Webster Co., Kentucky
      d: 11 Jun 1968 in Henderson Co., Kentucky
  - **Marjorie Helen Reynolds**
    b: 05 Aug 1927 in Olney, Young Co., Texas
    d:
    - **James Roscoe Reynolds**
      b: 08 May 1896 in Oxford, Talladega Co., Alabama
      m: 09 Aug 1924 in Bryson, Jack Co., Texas
      d: 01 May 1974 in Henderson, Henderson C., Kentucky
    - **Mary Alma Wilton**
      b: 23 Nov 1895 in Jermyn, Jack Co., Texas
      d: 04 Sep 1979 in Henderson, Henderson Co., Kentucky

Tammy Jo Tapp (1959-   )
[7th. Generation From Henry Wilton (1769-1820)]

&

Kirk Gregory Storey (1958-   )
& Family

Tammy Jo Tapp, the younger daughter of James William Tapp and Marjorie Helen Reynolds, was born June 19, 1959 in Henderson in Henderson County, Kentucky. Tammy was raised in Henderson, first attending school at South Heights Elementary Scool, which was not far from the Tapp home at the time. She later attended Henderson City High School, which in 1977, merged with the Henderson County School system. It was during that time that Tammy met her husband-to-be, Kirk Gregory Storey, son of Melvin Leonard Storey and Barbara Jo Kennedy. Tammy's school locker was located next to Kirk's.

Following high school, Tammy and Kirk both attended Murray State University in Murray, Kentucky. The couple were married June 26, 1982 in Henderson County, Kentucky. Tammy continued her education, graduating with a B.A. Degree in Biology from Murray State University. She then attended St. Mary's School of Medical Technology, where she received a B.A. Degree in Medical Technology. While attending at St. Mary's School, Tammy was hired by St. Mary's Hospital, where she continued to work for more than 26 years.

Shortly after their marriage in 1982, Tammy and Kirk first moved to Evansville, Indiana, located directly across the Ohio River from Henderson, Kentucky. A year later, on October 30, 1983, they had their first child, named Joseph Gregory Storey, born in Vanderburgh County, Indiana. The family later relocated to Newburgh, Indiana, which was located just 5 miles east of

Evansville on the Ohio River. On May 20, 1988, the couple had a second child, named Jami Kristine Storey, also born in Vanderburgh County, Indiana.

In the early 1990's, the family decided to move back to Kentucky, settling in Poole in Webster County, Kentucky, which was the childhood home of both of Tammy's parents. Their home was also located just 8 miles away from where Tammy's grandparents, Mary Alma (Wilton) Reynolds and James Roscoe Reynolds, once lived and are now buried.

Family Group Sheet

Husband: Kirk Gregory Storey

Born: 19 Sep 1958 in: Evansville, Vanderburgh Co., Indiana
Married: 26 Jun 1982 in: Henderson Co., Kentucky
Father: Melvin Leonard Storey
Mother: Barbara Jo Kennedy

Wife: Tammy Jo Tapp

Born: 19 Jun 1959 in: Henderson, Henderson Co., Kentucky
Father: James William Tapp
Mother: Marjorie Helen Reynolds

CHILDREN

1 M Name: Joseph Gregory Storey
     Born: 30 Oct 1983 in: Vanderburgh Co., Indiana

2 F Name: Jami Kristine Storey
     Born: 20 May 1988 in: Vanderburgh Co., Indiana

Herman Atwood Reynolds (1929-   )
[6th. Generation From Henry Wilton (1769-1820)]

&

Betty Rose Lykins (1933-   )
& Family

Family Group Sheet

Husband: Herman Atwood Reynolds	
Born: 06 May 1929	in: Olney, Young Co., Texas
Married: 11 Feb 1950	in: Poole, Webster Co., Kentucky
Father: James Roscoe Reynolds	
Mother: Mary Alma Wilton	

Wife: Betty Rose Lykins	
Born: 31 May 1933	in: Salyersville, Magoffin Co., Kentucky
Father: Darlie Raymond Lykins	
Mother: Grace Howard	

CHILDREN

1 F	Name: Debra Jean Reynolds	
	Born: 27 Nov 1951	in: Madisonville, Hopkins Co., Kentucky
	Married: 18 Dec 1971	in: Dixon, Webster Co., Kentucky
	Spouse: Perry Wayne Melton	
	Married: 25 Nov 1984	in: Henderson, Henderson Co., Kentucky
	Spouse: John Elliott Knight	
2 F	Name: Linda Kay Reynolds	
	Born: 02 Mar 1953	in: Madisonville, Hopkins Co., Kentucky
	Married: 25 Apr 1992	in: Henderson, Henderson Co., Kentucky
	Spouse: James Franklin Farris	
3 M	Name: Monty Duane Reynolds	
	Born: 13 Apr 1964	in: Henderson, Henderson Co., Kentucky
	Married: 25 May 1986	in: Henderson, Henderson Co., Kentucky
	Spouse: Catherine Elaine Pruitt	

BETTY ROSE LYKINS Standard Pedigree Tree

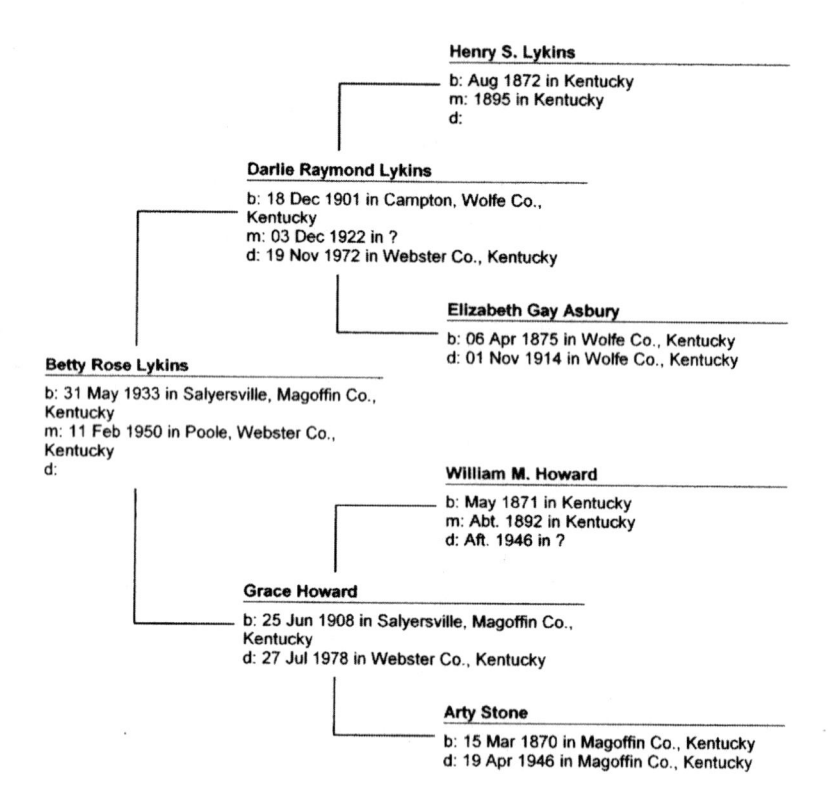

Betty Rose Lykins
b: 31 May 1933 in Salyersville, Magoffin Co., Kentucky
m: 11 Feb 1950 in Poole, Webster Co., Kentucky
d:

- **Darlie Raymond Lykins**
  b: 18 Dec 1901 in Campton, Wolfe Co., Kentucky
  m: 03 Dec 1922 in ?
  d: 19 Nov 1972 in Webster Co., Kentucky
  - **Henry S. Lykins**
    b: Aug 1872 in Kentucky
    m: 1895 in Kentucky
    d:
  - **Elizabeth Gay Asbury**
    b: 06 Apr 1875 in Wolfe Co., Kentucky
    d: 01 Nov 1914 in Wolfe Co., Kentucky

- **Grace Howard**
  b: 25 Jun 1908 in Salyersville, Magoffin Co., Kentucky
  d: 27 Jul 1978 in Webster Co., Kentucky
  - **William M. Howard**
    b: May 1871 in Kentucky
    m: Abt. 1892 in Kentucky
    d: Aft. 1946 in ?
  - **Arty Stone**
    b: 15 Mar 1870 in Magoffin Co., Kentucky
    d: 19 Apr 1946 in Magoffin Co., Kentucky

Debra Jean Reynolds (1951-   )
[7th. Generation from Henry Wilton (1769-1820)]

&
Perry Wayne Melton (1951-2007)
& Family

&
John Elliott Knight (1951-   )
& Family

Family Group Sheet

Husband: Perry Wayne Melton

Born: 11 Mar 1951 — in: Henderson, Henderson Co., Kentucky
Married: 18 Dec 1971 — in: Dixon, Webster Co., Kentucky
Died: 18 Mar 2007 — in: Henderson, Henderson Co., Kentucky
Father: Albert D. Melton
Mother: Oleda May Calvert

Wife: Debra Jean Reynolds

Born: 27 Nov 1951 — in: Madisonville, Hopkins Co., Kentucky
Father: Herman Atwood Reynolds
Mother: Betty Rose Lykins
Other Spouses: John Elliott Knight

CHILDREN

1 M Name: Brandon Wayne Melton
     Born: 02 Mar 1981 — in: Henderson, Henderson Co., Kentucky

Family Group Sheet

Husband: John Elliott Knight

Born: 12 Mar 1951 — in: Evansville, Vanderburgh Co., Indiana
Married: 25 Nov 1984 — in: Henderson, Henderson Co., Kentucky
Father: Edgar Warren Knight
Mother: Martha Virginia Brandt

Wife: Debra Jean Reynolds

Born: 27 Nov 1951 — in: Madisonville, Hopkins Co., Kentucky
Father: Herman Atwood Reynolds
Mother: Betty Rose Lykins
Other Spouses: Perry Wayne Melton

DEBRA JEAN REYNOLDS Standard Pedigree Tree

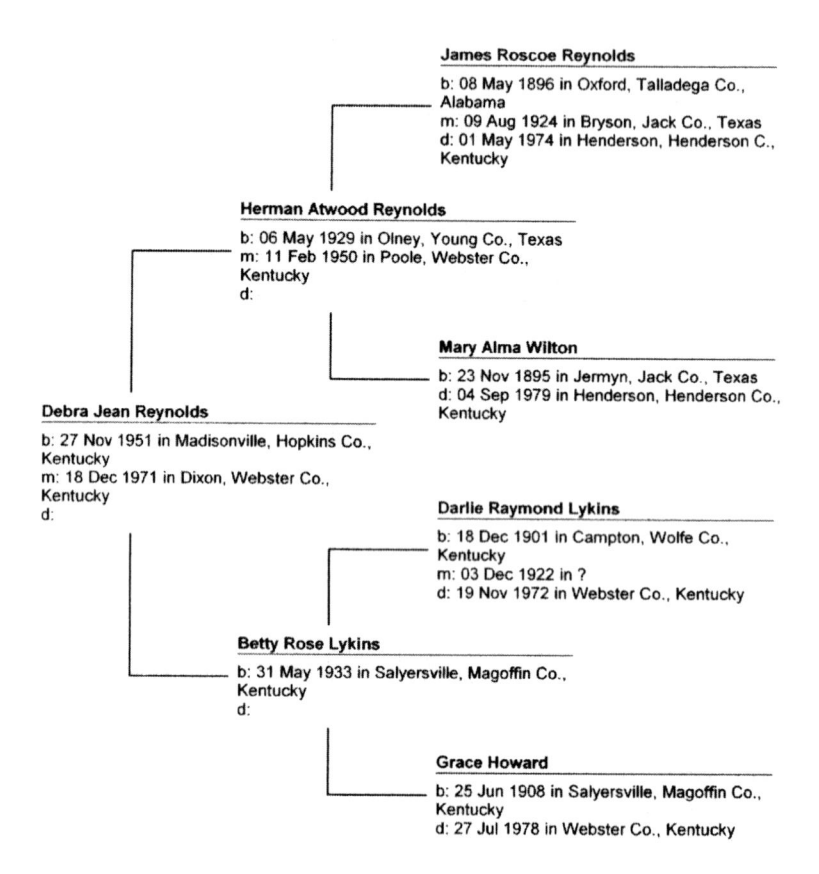

James Roscoe Reynolds
b: 08 May 1896 in Oxford, Talladega Co., Alabama
m: 09 Aug 1924 in Bryson, Jack Co., Texas
d: 01 May 1974 in Henderson, Henderson C., Kentucky

Herman Atwood Reynolds
b: 06 May 1929 in Olney, Young Co., Texas
m: 11 Feb 1950 in Poole, Webster Co., Kentucky
d:

Mary Alma Wilton
b: 23 Nov 1895 in Jermyn, Jack Co., Texas
d: 04 Sep 1979 in Henderson, Henderson Co., Kentucky

Debra Jean Reynolds
b: 27 Nov 1951 in Madisonville, Hopkins Co., Kentucky
m: 18 Dec 1971 in Dixon, Webster Co., Kentucky
d:

Darlie Raymond Lykins
b: 18 Dec 1901 in Campton, Wolfe Co., Kentucky
m: 03 Dec 1922 in ?
d: 19 Nov 1972 in Webster Co., Kentucky

Betty Rose Lykins
b: 31 May 1933 in Salyersville, Magoffin Co., Kentucky
d:

Grace Howard
b: 25 Jun 1908 in Salyersville, Magoffin Co., Kentucky
d: 27 Jul 1978 in Webster Co., Kentucky

Notes: This Tree also applies to the other children of Herman Atwood Reynolds & Betty Rose Lykins: Linda Kay Reynolds, and Monty Duane Reynolds.

Linda Kay Reynolds (1953-)
[7th. Generation From Henry Wilton (1769-1820)]

&

James Franklin Farris (1954-)
& Family

Family Group Sheet

Husband: James Franklin Farris

    Born: 26 May 1954   in: Henderson, Henderson Co., Kentucky
    Married: 23 Apr 1992   In: Henderson, Henderson Co., Kentucky
    Father: Charles William Farris
    Mother: Marinetta Reed

Wife: Linda Kay Reynolds

    Born: 02 Mar 1953   in: Madisonville, Hopkins Co., Kentucky
    Father: Herman Atwood Reynolds
    Mother: Betty Rose Lykins

Monty Duane Reynolds (1964-   )
[7th. Generation From Henry Wilton (1769-1820)]

&

Catherine Elaine Pruitt (1964-   )
& Family

Family Group Sheet

Husband: Monty Duane Reynolds	
Born: 13 Apr 1964	in: Henderson, Henderson Co., Kentucky
Married: 25 May 1986	in: Henderson, Henderson Co., Kentucky
Father: Herman Atwood Reynolds	
Mother: Betty Rose Lykins	

Wife: Catherine Elaine Pruitt	
Born: 15 Nov 1964	in: Henderson, Henderson Co., Kentucky
Father: Donald R. Pruitt	
Mother: Marilyn E.	

CHILDREN

1 M	Name: Joshua Duane Reynolds	
	Born: 20 May 1988	in: Henderson, Henderson Co., Kentucky
2 M	Name: Justin Duane Reynolds	
	Born: 30 Jan 1997	in: Henderson, Henderson Co., Kentucky

James Weldon Reynolds (1931-   )
[6th. Generation From Henry Wilton (1769-1820)]

&

Connie Ann Metz (1933-   )
& Family

James Weldon (Red) Reynolds was born March 23, 1931 in Olney, Texas, the son of James Roscoe Reynolds and Mary Alma Wilton. He was the middle of six children, the oldest having died at birth, with an older sister and brother, and also with a younger sister and brother. The family was transient during his early years, since his father worked in the oil field for the Sinclair Oil Company. After living in Archer County, Texas for a number of years, the family moved to Coahoma in Southwest Texas, then to Hamilton County, Illinois, and finally to Poole in Webster County, Kentucky. It was in Kentucky that the family finally set down roots, finding a permanent place they could call home.

By the time the family resettled in Poole, Kentucky, Red was in the third grade. He continued his formal education in Poole, and he graduated from Poole High School in 1951. In that same year, his high school sweetheart, Connie Ann Metz, daughter of Charles Metz and Naomi Lee Pinkston, also graduated. After Red got a job in a nearby factory, he and Connie were married in Poole, Kentucky on September 9, 1951.

Shortly after their marriage in 1951, the couple moved to Henderson in Henderson County, Kentucky, where their first son,

Gary Wayne Reynolds, was born on September 2, 1952. Red loved the outdoors, and he soon decided that he did not really like working in a factory. He then began working at different jobs in the oil field.

As a result of Red's working in the oil field, the family made several moves during the years that followed. However, while still living in Henderson, Red and Connie had two more sons, Kenneth Wade Reynolds, born March 17, 1956, and David Allan Reynolds, born June 26, 1959. A short time later, the family moved to Evansville in Vanderburgh, Indiana, followed by moves to Madisonville in Hopkins County, Kentucky, and to Owensville in Gibson County, Indiana. In May 1966, Red changed jobs to the Ashland Oil Company, with the new job of carrying fuel as a tanker driver.

Sometime later, Red moved to Elizabeth in Allegheny County, Pennsylvania, where he bought a house and where the family settled permanently. While living in Pennsylvania, Red and Connie had a fourth son, Michael Bruce Reynolds, who was born March 31, 1971.

In 1991, Red retired, and together with Connie, continued to maintain their home in Elizabeth, Pennsylvania, where their interests included working in the yard, participating in church activities, and traveling.

Family Group Sheet

Husband: James Weldon Reynolds

Born: 22 Mar 1931 — in: Olney, Young Co., Texas
Married: 09 Sep 1951 — in: Poole, Webster Co., Kentucky
Father: James Roscoe Reynolds
Mother: Mary Alma Wilton

Wife: Connie Ann Metz

Born: 22 May 1933 — in: Christian Co., Kentucky
Father: Charles Metz
Mother: Naomi Lee Tapp Pinkston

CHILDREN

1 M
Name: Gary Wayne Reynolds
Born: 02 Sep 1952 — in: Henderson, Henderson Co., Kentucky
Married: 21 Sep 1973 — in: Elizabeth, Allegheny Co., Pennsylvania
Spouse: Denise Louise Perisich

2 M
Name: Kenneth Wade Reynolds
Born: 17 Mar 1956 — in: Henderson, Henderson Co., Kentucky
Married: 12 Jun 1976 — in: Pennsylvania
Spouse: Sophia Ann Hayden
Married: 02 Jan 2000 — in: Washington, Washington Co., Pennsylvania
Spouse: Debra Bruss

3 M
Name: David Alan Reynolds
Born: 26 Jun 1959 — in: Henderson, Henderson Co., Kentucky
Married: 11 Aug 1984 — in: Pennsylvania
Spouse: Janet Louise Behanna

4 M
Name: Michael Bruce Reynolds
Born: 31 Mar 1971 — in: McKeesport, Allegheny Co., Pennsylvania
Married: 07 Sep 1996 — in: West Elizabeth, Allegheny Co., Pennsylvania
Spouse: Bonnie Dodds

Gary Wayne Reynolds (1952-)
[7th. Generation From Henry Wilton (1769-1820)]

&

Denise Louise Perisich (1954-)
& Family

Family Group Sheet

Husband: Gary Wayne Reynolds

Born: 02 Sep 1952   in: Henderson, Henderson Co., Kentucky
Married: 21 Sep 1973   in: Elizabeth, Allegheny Co., Pennsylvania
Father: James Weldon Reynolds
Mother: Connie Ann Metz

Wife: Denise Louise Perisich

Born: 13 Oct 1954

GARY WAYNE REYNOLDS Standard Pedigree Tree

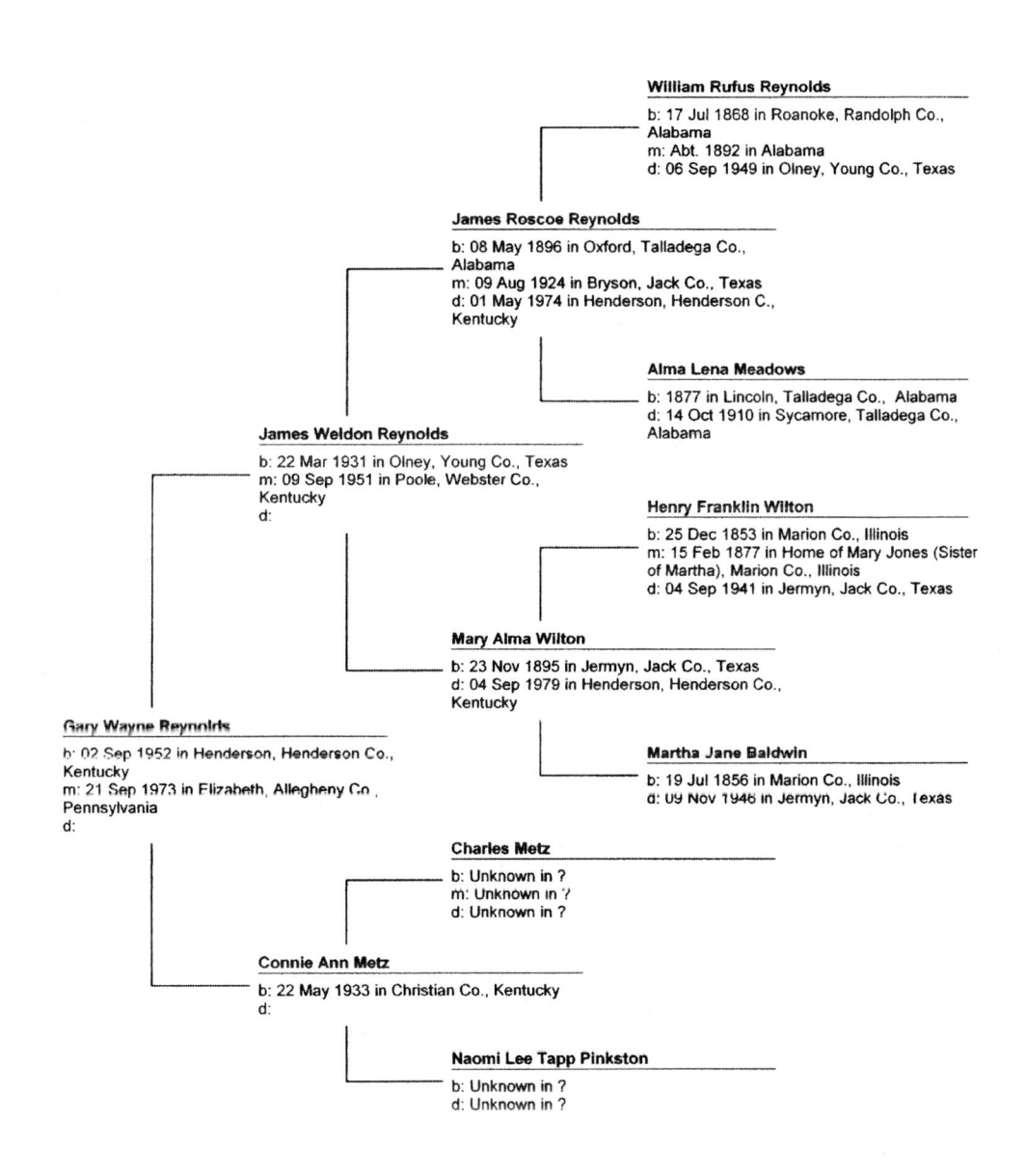

Gary Wayne Reynolds
b: 02 Sep 1952 in Henderson, Henderson Co., Kentucky
m: 21 Sep 1973 in Elizabeth, Allegheny Co., Pennsylvania
d:

- **James Weldon Reynolds**
  b: 22 Mar 1931 in Olney, Young Co., Texas
  m: 09 Sep 1951 in Poole, Webster Co., Kentucky
  d:

  - **James Roscoe Reynolds**
    b: 08 May 1896 in Oxford, Talladega Co., Alabama
    m: 09 Aug 1924 in Bryson, Jack Co., Texas
    d: 01 May 1974 in Henderson, Henderson C., Kentucky

    - **William Rufus Reynolds**
      b: 17 Jul 1868 in Roanoke, Randolph Co., Alabama
      m: Abt. 1892 in Alabama
      d: 06 Sep 1949 in Olney, Young Co., Texas

    - **Alma Lena Meadows**
      b: 1877 in Lincoln, Talladega Co., Alabama
      d: 14 Oct 1910 in Sycamore, Talladega Co., Alabama

  - **Mary Alma Wilton**
    b: 23 Nov 1895 in Jermyn, Jack Co., Texas
    d: 04 Sep 1979 in Henderson, Henderson Co., Kentucky

    - **Henry Franklin Wilton**
      b: 25 Dec 1853 in Marion Co., Illinois
      m: 15 Feb 1877 in Home of Mary Jones (Sister of Martha), Marion Co., Illinois
      d: 04 Sep 1941 in Jermyn, Jack Co., Texas

    - **Martha Jane Baldwin**
      b: 19 Jul 1856 in Marion Co., Illinois
      d: 09 Nov 1946 in Jermyn, Jack Co., Texas

- **Connie Ann Metz**
  b: 22 May 1933 in Christian Co., Kentucky
  d:

  - **Charles Metz**
    b: Unknown in ?
    m: Unknown in ?
    d: Unknown in ?

  - **Naomi Lee Tapp Pinkston**
    b: Unknown in ?
    d: Unknown in ?

Notes: This Tree also applies to the other children of James Weldon Reynolds & Connie Ann Metz: Kenneth Wade Reynolds, David Alan Reynolds, and Michael Bruce Reynolds.

Kenneth Wade Reynolds (1956-)
[7th. Generation From Henry Wilton (1769-1820)]

&

Sophia Ann Hayden (1957-)
& Family

&

Debra Bruss (1958-)
& Family

Family Group Sheet

Husband: Kenneth Wade Reynolds	
Born: 17 Mar 1956	in: Henderson, Henderson Co., Kentucky
Married: 12 Jun 1976	in: Pennsylvania
Father: James Weldon Reynolds	
Mother: Connie Ann Metz	
Other Spouses: Debra Bruss	
Wife: Sophia Ann Hayden	
Born: 24 Jul 1957	

	CHILDREN
1 F	Name: Renee Christian Reynolds Born: 26 Mar 1978
2 M	Name: Kenneth Lee Reynolds Born: 30 Jan 1983
3 F	Name: Shanta Susan Reynolds Born: 30 Jan 1983

Family Group Sheet

Husband: Kenneth Wade Reynolds

    Born: 17 Mar 1956   in: Henderson, Henderson Co., Kentucky
  Married: 02 Jan 2000   in: Washington, Washington Co., Pennsylvania
   Father: James Weldon Reynolds
  Mother: Connie Ann Metz
    Other Spouses: Sophia Ann Hayden

Wife: Debra Bruss

    Born: 08 Jun 1958

David Alan Reynolds (1959-   )
[7th. Generation From Henry Wilton (1769-1820)]

&

Janet Louise Behanna (1963-   )
& Family

Family Group Sheet

	Husband: David Alan Reynolds	
	Born: 26 Jun 1959	in: Henderson, Henderson Co., Kentucky
	Married: 11 Aug 1984	in: Pennsylvania
	Father: James Weldon Reynolds	
	Mother: Connie Ann Metz	
	Wife: Janet Louise Behanna	
	Born: 26 Jul 1963	
	CHILDREN	
1 M	Name: Stephen James Reynolds	
	Born: 14 Mar 1993	
2 M	Name: Aaron John Reynolds	
	Born: 18 Feb 1996	
3 M	Name: Jordan Andrew Reynolds	
	Born: 12 Jul 1999	

Michael Bruce Reynolds (1971-)
[7th. Generation From Henry Wilton (1769-1820)]

&

Bonnie Dodds (1976-)
& Family

Family Group Sheet

Husband: Michael Bruce Reynolds

Born: 31 Mar 1971   in: McKeesport, Allegheny Co., Pennsylvania
Married: 07 Sep 1996   in: West Elizabeth, Allegheny Co., Pennsylvania
Father: James Weldon Reynolds
Mother: Connie Ann Metz

Wife: Bonnie Dodds

Born: 10 Jun 1976

CHILDREN

1 F	Name: Briana Nicole Reynolds Born: 22 Jul 1993	
2 F	Name: Miranda Lynn Reynolds Born: 19 Sep 1995	
3 F	Name: Hunter Faye Reynolds Born: 27 Jul 2000	

Verna Evelyn Reynolds (1934-   )
[6th. Generation From Henry Wilton (1769-1820)]

&

Bert Wallace (1933-   )
& Family

Verna Evelyn Reynolds, born September 17, 1933 in Olney in Young County, Texas, was the daughter of James Roscoe (Jim) Reynolds and Mary Alma Wilton. After the family settled permanently in Kentucky about 1941, Evelyn spent most of her school years in Poole in Webster County, Kentucky, where she later graduated from high school.

In August 1962, Evelyn married Bert Wallace in Henderson, Kentucky. Bert was originally from Indiana, graduating from high school in Wheatland, Indiana and later graduating from Indiana University. After their marriage, the couple first lived in Kentucky, where their two children were born. Their first child, Diana Grace Wallace, was born May 30, 1964 in Henderson County, Kentucky; and their second child, Timothy Reynolds Wallace, was born June 12, 1965 in Henderson County, Kentucky.

The family lived for awhile in Indiana, and then about 1971, they moved to Mineral Wells in Palo Pinto County, Texas. Evelyn died May 5, 1983 in Mineral Wells, Texas.

Family Group Sheet

Husband: Bert Wallace	
Born: 07 Dec 1933	in: Washington, Daviess Co, Indiana
Married: 04 Aug 1962	in: Henderson, Henderson Co., Kentucky

Wife: Verna Evelyn Reynolds	
Born: 17 Sep 1934	in: Olney, Young Co., Texas
Died: 05 May 1983	in: Mineral Wells, Palo Pinto Co., Texas
Father: James Roscoe Reynolds	
Mother: Mary Alma Wilton	

CHILDREN

1 F	Name: Diana Grace Wallace	
	Born: 30 May 1964	in: Henderson Co., Kentucky
2 M	Name: Timothy Reynolds Wallace	
	Born: 12 Jun 1965	in: Henderson Co., Kentucky

Clarence Chalmer Reynolds (1935-   )
[6th. Generation From Henry Wilton (1769-1820)]

&

Betty Claire Decker (1938-   )
& Family

Clarence Chalmer (Straw) Reynolds, born August 21, 1935, was the sixth and last child of James Roscoe Reynolds (Jim) and Mary Alma Wilton. Since Jim worked in the oil field for Sinclair Oil Company, the family was forced to make frequent moves. After first living in Texas for a number of years, by the time of his 2nd grade, Straw attended school in Carmi, Illinois. By about 1941, the family finally settled permanently in Poole in Webster County, Kentucky, where Straw graduated from high school.

Following high school, Straw attended Western Kentucky State Teachers College, where he graduated with a degree in Industrial Arts, and he then received a commission in the U.S.A.F. as a second lieutenant. What followed was a distinguished career in the U.S. military, which took him to many parts of the world. During the Viet Nam Conflict, Straw flew 230 combat missions in the Republic of Vietnam. One hundred and twenty of those missions were in the 01 Birddog as a forward air controller, followed with 115 missions in the F100 Super Saber. He served nearly twenty-eight years in the Air Force, earning the Distinguished Flying Cross and the Air Medal with twenty Oak Leaf Clusters. After he was promoted to Lieutenant Colonel, he served as squadron commander of the 182 Tactical Fighter Squadron with the Texas Air National Guard in San Antonio, Texas.

On one of his early overseas assignments with the RAF at Lakenheath, England, where he served with a nuclear weapons alert crew flying the F100, he met a school teacher by the name of Betty Claire Decker, from Baton Rouge, Louisiana. He married Betty the following year, and they had two children while stationed at Luke AFB in Phoenix, Arizona. The first child, James Randall Reynolds, was born in 1965; and the second child, Anne Elizabeth Reynolds, was born in 1968. As of 2007, both children lived in Texas, with Anne starting her own family, having a daughter, named Brianna Grace Fortini.

After retiring from the U.S.A.F., Straw became a flight director for Loral Aviation, flying a 235-foot helium balloon with a 24-foot radar dish, with the mission of searching for illegal aircraft entering the continental U.S.

Straw's other interests included painting with acrylics and taking art courses. As of 2007, Straw and Betty lived in San Antonio in Bexar County, Texas.

Family Group Sheet

Husband: Clarence Chalmer Reynolds

Born: 21 Aug 1935	in: Olney, Young Co., Texas
Married: 01 Oct 1963	in: Baton Rouge, East Baton Rouge Parish, Louisiana
Father: James Roscoe Reynolds	
Mother: Mary Alma Wilton	

Wife: Betty Claire Decker

Born: 1938	in: Zachary, East Baton Rouge Parish, Louisiana
Father: William James Decker	
Mother: Vivian Claire Patrick	

CHILDREN

1 M	Name: James Randall Reynolds	
	Born: 1965	in: Luke AFB, Phoenix, Arizona
2 F	Name: Anne Elizabeth Reynolds	
	Born: 1968	in: Luke AFB, Phoenix, Arizona
	Married: 2002	in: Padre Island, Texas
	Spouse: Mark Fortini	

Anne Elizabeth Reynolds (1968-   )
[7th. Generation From Henry Wilton (1769-1820)]

&

Mark A. Fortini (1962-   )
& Family

Family Group Sheet

Husband: Mark A. Fortini	
Born: 1962	in: Galveston Co., Texas
Married: 13 Sep 2002	in: Galveston Co., Texas
Father: Anthony Fortini	
Mother: Mildred Louise Jordan	
Wife: Anne Elizabeth Reynolds	
Born: 1968	in: Luke AFB, Phoenix, Arizona
Father: Clarence Chalmer Reynolds	
Mother: Betty Claire Decker	

CHILDREN

1 F — Name: Brianna Grace Fortini
       Born: Jun 2007

Joseph C. Wilton (1834-1900)
[3rd. Generation from Henry Wilton (1769-1820)]

&

Mary Annis Prewitt (1835~1871)
& Family

&

Sarah Elizabeth Baldwin (1852-1930)
& Family

Joseph C. Wilton, the third child of Thomas Wilton and Mary Alma Maddux, was born August 16, 1834 in Illinois. About the time of his birth, the family was living in Clinton County, Illinois. Sometime after 1840, the family relocated to the adjacent Marion County, Illinois. By the 1850 Federal Census of Marion County, Illinois, Joseph was listed at age 16, living at home with his parents and two brothers and and two sisters.

In February 1858, Joseph married Mary Annis Prewitt in Marion County, Illinois. Mary was the daughter of Elisha Prewitt and Elizabeth Russell. In the 1860 Federal Census of Marion County, Illinois, Joseph was listed at age 24, with an occupation of farmer, along with his wife, Mary A., age 21, and one son, Erastus, age 1. Just two dwellings away from Joseph, his father, Thomas Wilton, was living with his wife and three of their children.

Available evidence suggests that Joseph had three other children about this time, Rosa Wilton, born about 1863, Thomas Wilton, born 1869, and John Wilton, born 1871. There is evidence of a Joseph C. Wilton who married a Mrs. Martha Headly in Marion County, Illinois on November 29, 1866. If this was our ancestor,

Joseph C. Wilton, that would suggest that Joseph and Mary (Prewitt) Wilton were the parents of Erastus Wilton and Rosa Wilton, but that Joseph and Martha were the parents of Thomas Wilton and John Wilton. There were also records of land transactions in Marion County, Illinois in 1867 involving a Joseph C. Wilton and wife, Martha Wilton. An additional bit of information was found in the 1870 Federal Census of Marion County, Illinois of the family of a John C. Wilton (possibly our Joseph C. Wilton), age 36, and Martha Wilton, age 25, along with children, Erastus Wilton, Rosa Wilton, Thomas Wilton, and John Wilton. This family lived just two dwellings away from the family of Thomas Baldwin, whose daughter, Sarah Baldwin, was later married to Joseph C. Wilton. In any case, whether there was just one wife or two wives during this time, they were both out of the picture by 1871.

During the Civil War, Joseph served on the side of the Union as a corporal with the 111 Illinois Infantry. Joseph enlisted as a private on August 4, 1862, with an address listed as Patoka, Illinois. He was mustered out on July 27, 1865, with the rank of corporal, after serving two years and eleven months.

On February 19, 1871, in Marion County, Illinois, Joseph C. married again, to Sarah Elizabeth Baldwin, the daughter of Thomas Holland Baldwin and Harriet Tite. There was an additional connection of this Baldwin family with the Wilton family, since Sarah's younger sister, Martha Jane Baldwin, married Henry Franklin Wilton, a nephew of Joseph C. Wilton. While still living in Illinois, Joseph and Sarah had four children, Sarah Frances Wilton, born March 1872, Harriett Carrie Wilton, born June 1874, Martha Wilton, born December 1876, and Mary Wilton, born August 1879.

About 1880, the family relocated to Parker County, Texas. In the 1880 Federal Census of Parker County, Texas, Joseph (J.C.) Wilton was listed at age 45, with an occupation of farmer, along with his wife, Sarah E. Wilton, age 27, three children by his first wife, and four children by his second wife. The youngest child, Mary Wilton, was listed at age 9 months, having been born in August 1879 while the family was still in Illinois. Available records indicate that for awhile Joseph had a store in Dido in Tarrant County, Texas. The town later became a "ghost town," after a railroad bypassed it, going instead through the nearby town of Saginaw.

For a time, Joseph and family lived in an area between Springtown, Texas, located in Parker County, and Azle, Texas, which straddles both Parker and Tarrant Counties. He later moved to a farm near the Old Jefferson Crossing, which is now a part of Eagle Mountain Lake in Tarrant County, Texas. The family lived there until about 1929, when they were forced to moved when the area became Eagle Mountain Lake.

Another record of the time indicates that Joseph C. and family were of the Methodist faith and members of the Peden Church. The record of a quarterly conference held in 1896 showed them on the register of the Weatherford District, Springtown Circuit. The church eventually merged with the First United Methodist Church of Azle, Texas.

After the family settled in Texas, Joseph and Sarah had four other children, Nona Wilton, born November 1881, Joseph S. Wilton, born October 1884, Vanzant V. Wilton, born June 1893, and Maude Wilton, born before 1900. The youngest child, Maude, died in infancy. In the 1900 Federal Census of Tarrant County, Texas, Joseph was listed at age 65, with an occupation of farmer, along with his wife, Sarah, age 47, and five of their children. Joseph died November 9, 1900 in Tarrant County and was buried at the Nelson Cemetery in Azle, Texas.

After Joseph died in 1900, Sarah applied for and received pension benefits for the time that Joseph had been in the Civil War. At the time of the 1910 Federal Census of Tarrant County, Texas, Sarah was listed at age 56, along with two of her sons, J.S. (Joseph S.) Wilton, age 28, and V.V. (Vanzant V.) Wilton, age 19. Beginning with the 1920 Federal Census of Tarrant County, Texas, Sarah was listed, at age 67, with the family of her son, Jodie (Joseph) S. Wilton, and his family. In the 1930 Federal Census of Tarrant County, Texas, Sarah was listed at age 77, again with her son Jodie (Joseph) S. Wilton and his family. Sarah died April 28, 1930 in Tarrant County, Texas, and she was buried with her husband at the Nelson Cemetery in Azle, Texas.

Family Group Sheet

Husband: Joseph C. Wilton

Born: 16 Aug 1834 in: Illinois
Married: 24 Feb 1858 in: Marion Co., Illinois
Died: 09 Nov 1900 in: Tarrant Co., Texas
Father: Thomas Wilton
Mother: Mary Alma Maddux
Other Spouses: Sarah Elizabeth Baldwin

Wife: Mary Annis Prewitt

Born: 1835 in: Illinois
Died: Abt. 1871 in: Illinois
Father: Elisha Prewett
Mother: Elizabeth Russell

CHILDREN

1 M
Name: Erastus Wilton
Born: 1859 in: Illinois
Died: 06 Jul 1933 in: Wichita Co., Texas

2 F
Name: Rosa Wilton
Born: Abt. 1863 in: Illinois
Died: Unknown

3 M
Name: Thomas Wilton
Born: 1869 in: Illinois
Died: Unknown

4 M
Name: John Wilton
Born: 1871 in: Illinois
Died: Unknown

Family Group Sheet

Husband: Joseph C. Wilton

Born: 16 Aug 1834 in: Illinois
Married: 19 Feb 1871 in: Marion Co., Illinois
Died: 09 Nov 1900 in: Tarrant Co., Texas
Father: Thomas Wilton
Mother: Mary Alma Maddux
Other Spouses: Mary Annis Prewitt

Wife: Sarah Elizabeth Baldwin

Born: 02 Aug 1852 in: Illinois
Died: 28 Apr 1930 in: Tarrant Co., Texas
Father: Thomas Holland Baldwin
Mother: Harriet Tite

CHILDREN

1 F	Name: Sarah Frances Wilton Born: 06 Mar 1872 Died: 09 Dec 1956 Married: 02 Sep 1891 Spouse: John Keeton Gibson	in: Marion Co., Illinois in: Memphis, Hall Co., Texas in: Parker Co., Texas
2 F	Name: Harriett Carrie Wilton Born: 30 Jun 1874 Died: 19 Aug 1957 Married: Abt. 1893 Spouse: David W. Cherry	in: Illinois in: Tarrant Co., Texas in: Texas
3 F	Name: Martha Wilton Born: Dec 1876 Died: Aft. 1920 Married: 21 Oct 1900 Spouse: Temple Worth Howard	in: Illinois in: Texas in: Tarrant Co., Texas
4 F	Name: Mary Wilton Born: 17 Aug 1879 Died: 01 Jan 1961 Married: Abt. 1906 Spouse: Isaac W. Cole	in: Illinois in: Tarrant Co., Texas in: Texas
5 F	Name: Nona Wilton Born: 22 Nov 1881 Died: 26 Mar 1959 Married: Abt. 1902 Spouse: William Walter Wiley	in: Texas in: Tarrant Co., Texas in: Texas
6 M	Name: Joseph S. Wilton Born: 17 Oct 1884 Died: 04 Jun 1982 Married: Abt. 1910 Spouse: Bessie Smith	in: Texas in: Harris Co., Texas in: Texas
7 M	Name: Vanzant V. Wilton Born: 06 Jun 1893 Died: 04 Jan 1915	in: Texas in: Eagle Mountain, Tarrant Co., Texas
8 F	Name: Maude Wilton Born: Bef. 1900 Died: Bef. 1900	in: Texas in: Texas

SARAH ELIZABETH BALDWIN Standard Pedigree Tree

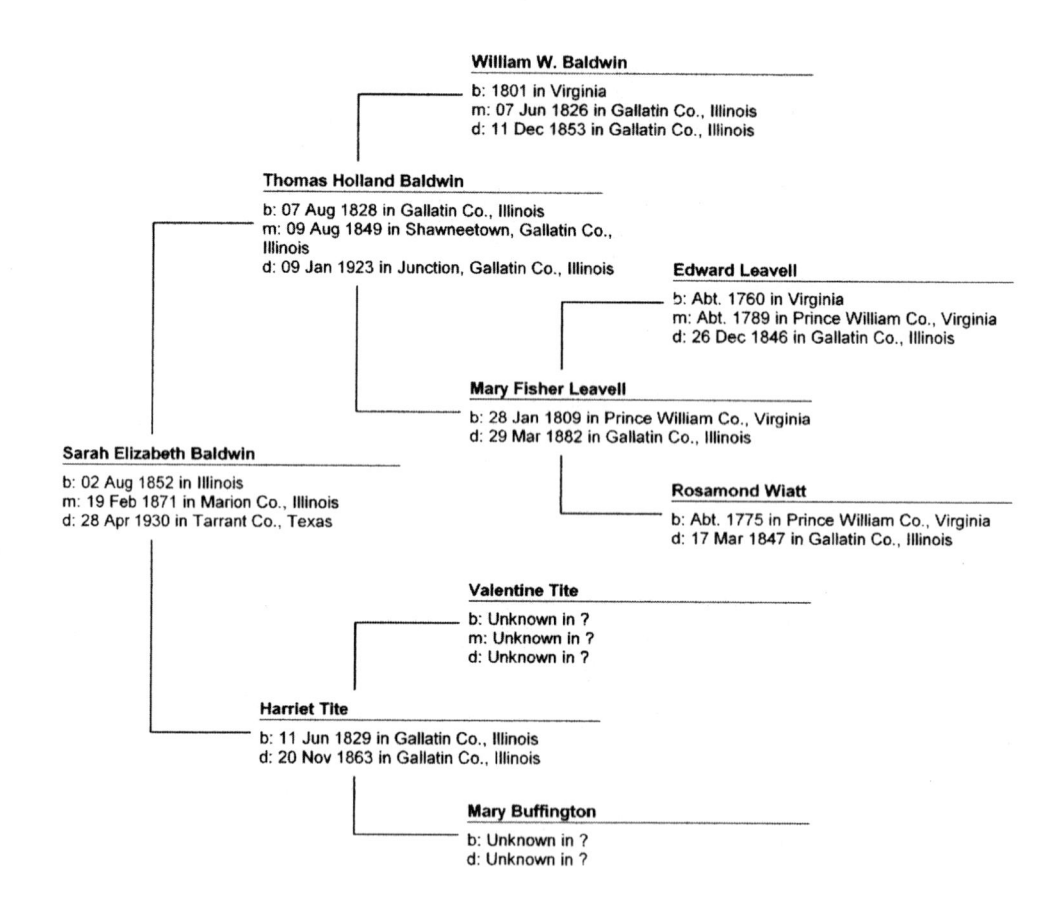

Sarah Elizabeth Baldwin
b: 02 Aug 1852 in Illinois
m: 19 Feb 1871 in Marion Co., Illinois
d: 28 Apr 1930 in Tarrant Co., Texas

- **Thomas Holland Baldwin**
  b: 07 Aug 1828 in Gallatin Co., Illinois
  m: 09 Aug 1849 in Shawneetown, Gallatin Co., Illinois
  d: 09 Jan 1923 in Junction, Gallatin Co., Illinois
  - **William W. Baldwin**
    b: 1801 in Virginia
    m: 07 Jun 1826 in Gallatin Co., Illinois
    d: 11 Dec 1853 in Gallatin Co., Illinois
  - **Mary Fisher Leavell**
    b: 28 Jan 1809 in Prince William Co., Virginia
    d: 29 Mar 1882 in Gallatin Co., Illinois
    - **Edward Leavell**
      b: Abt. 1760 in Virginia
      m: Abt. 1789 in Prince William Co., Virginia
      d: 26 Dec 1846 in Gallatin Co., Illinois
    - **Rosamond Wiatt**
      b: Abt. 1775 in Prince William Co., Virginia
      d: 17 Mar 1847 in Gallatin Co., Illinois
- **Harriet Tite**
  b: 11 Jun 1829 in Gallatin Co., Illinois
  d: 20 Nov 1863 in Gallatin Co., Illinois
  - **Valentine Tite**
    b: Unknown in ?
    m: Unknown in ?
    d: Unknown in ?
  - **Mary Buffington**
    b: Unknown in ?
    d: Unknown in ?

Sarah Frances Wilton (1872-1956)
[4th. Generation From Henry Wilton (1769-1820)]
&
John Keeton Gibson (1871-1944)
& Family

Family Group Sheet

Husband: John Keeton Gibson

Born:	02 Jun 1871	in: Marion Co., Arkansas
Married:	02 Sep 1891	in: Parker Co., Texas
Died:	17 May 1944	in: Memphis, Hall Co., Texas
Father:	William I. Gibson	
Mother:	Nuk Messick	

Wife: Sarah Frances Wilton

Born:	06 Mar 1872	in: Marion Co., Illinois
Died:	09 Dec 1956	in: Memphis, Hall Co., Texas
Father:	Joseph C. Wilton	
Mother:	Sarah Elizabeth Baldwin	

CHILDREN

1 M Name: Jesse Ivan Gibson
- Born: 07 Jul 1892 in: Reno, Parker Co., Texas
- Died: 18 Oct 1973 in: Bell, Los Angeles Co., California

2 M Name: John Otis Gibson
- Born: 12 Jan 1895 in: Reno, Parker Co., Texas
- Died: Jul 1975 in: Memphis, Hall Co., Texas

3 F Name: Myrl Martha Gibson
- Born: 27 Sep 1896 in: Ft. Worth, Tarrant Co., Texas
- Died: 12 May 1988 in: Shamrock, Wheeler Co., Texas
- Married: 1916 in: Texas
- Spouse: Howard Felton Leake

4 F Name: Ireneous Crumble Gibson
- Born: 22 Dec 1898 in: Ft. Worth, Tarrant Co., Texas
- Died: 21 May 1969 in: Bell, Los Angeles Co., California
- Married: Bef. 1935 in: California
- Spouse: Mary Allen

5 F Name: Marzella Clovene Gibson
- Born: 12 Sep 1901 in: Texas
- Died: 04 Jan 1991 in: Placerville, El Dorado Co., California
- Married: Abt. 1923 in: California
- Spouse: Duval Elbert Brumley

6 M Name: James Vanzant Gibson
- Born: 06 Apr 1905 in: Texas
- Died: 19 Mar 1979 in: Los Angeles Co., California

7 M Name: Earl Gibson
- Born: 03 Jul 1907 in: Texas
- Died: Unknown in: Bell, California

8 F Name: Martella Gibson
- Born: 15 Sep 1909 in: Texas
- Died: 1910 in: Texas

9 F Name: Marietta Gibson
- Born: 04 Jul 1912 in: Texas
- Died: Aug 1975 in: Downey, California

SARAH FRANCES WILTON Standard Pedigree Tree

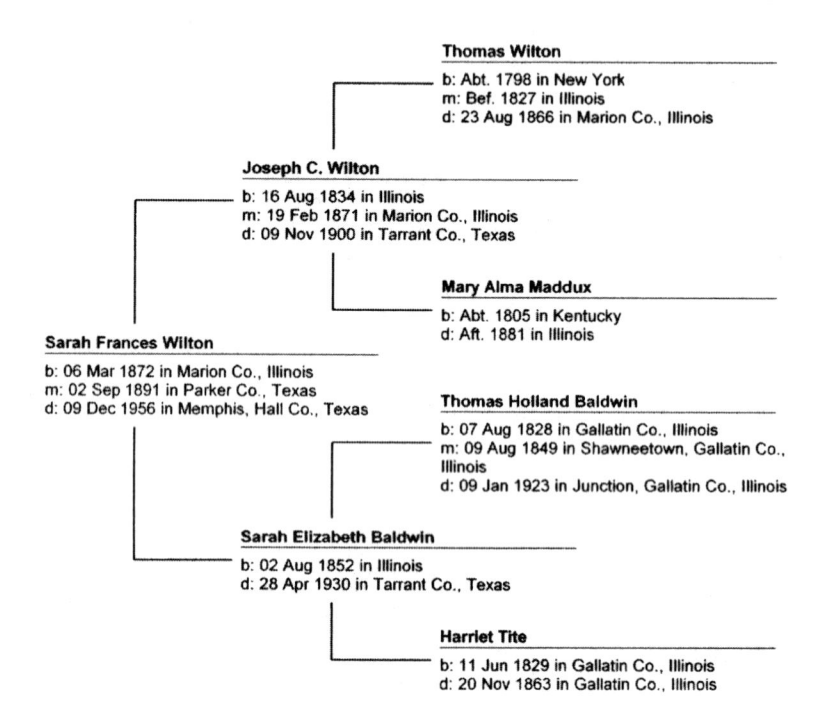

Sarah Frances Wilton
b: 06 Mar 1872 in Marion Co., Illinois
m: 02 Sep 1891 in Parker Co., Texas
d: 09 Dec 1956 in Memphis, Hall Co., Texas

- **Joseph C. Wilton**
  b: 16 Aug 1834 in Illinois
  m: 19 Feb 1871 in Marion Co., Illinois
  d: 09 Nov 1900 in Tarrant Co., Texas
  - **Thomas Wilton**
    b: Abt. 1798 in New York
    m: Bef. 1827 in Illinois
    d: 23 Aug 1866 in Marion Co., Illinois
  - **Mary Alma Maddux**
    b: Abt. 1805 in Kentucky
    d: Aft. 1881 in Illinois

- **Sarah Elizabeth Baldwin**
  b: 02 Aug 1852 in Illinois
  d: 28 Apr 1930 in Tarrant Co., Texas
  - **Thomas Holland Baldwin**
    b: 07 Aug 1828 in Gallatin Co., Illinois
    m: 09 Aug 1849 in Shawneetown, Gallatin Co., Illinois
    d: 09 Jan 1923 in Junction, Gallatin Co., Illinois
  - **Harriet Tite**
    b: 11 Jun 1829 in Gallatin Co., Illinois
    d: 20 Nov 1863 in Gallatin Co., Illinois

Notes: This Tree also applies to the other children of Joseph C. Wilton & Sarah Elizabeth Baldwin: Harriet Carrie Wilton, Martha Wilton, Mary Wilton, Nona Wilton, Joseph S. Wilton, Vanzant V. Wilton, and Maude Wilton.

Harriett Carrie Wilton (1874-1957)
[4th. Generation From Henry Wilton (1769-1820)]

&

David W. Cherry (1869-1930)
& Family

Family Group Sheet

Husband: David W. Cherry	
Born: 22 Mar 1869	in: Henderson Co., Tennessee
Married: Abt. 1893	in: Texas
Died: 29 Apr 1930	in: Tarrant Co., Texas
Father: Marcus Lafayette Cherry	
Mother: Louisa Carolina Stanfield	

Wife: Harriett Carrie Wilton	
Born: 30 Jun 1874	in: Illinois
Died: 19 Aug 1957	in: Tarrant Co., Texas
Father: Joseph C. Wilton	
Mother: Sarah Elizabeth Baldwin	

	CHILDREN	
1 M	Name: Arthur Raymond Cherry	
	Born: 24 Oct 1895	in: Reno, Parker Co., Texas
	Died: 06 Oct 1946	in: Wise Co., Texas
2 M	Name: Oscar A. Cherry	
	Born: Abt. 1902	in: Texas

DAVID W. CHERRY Standard Pedigree Tree

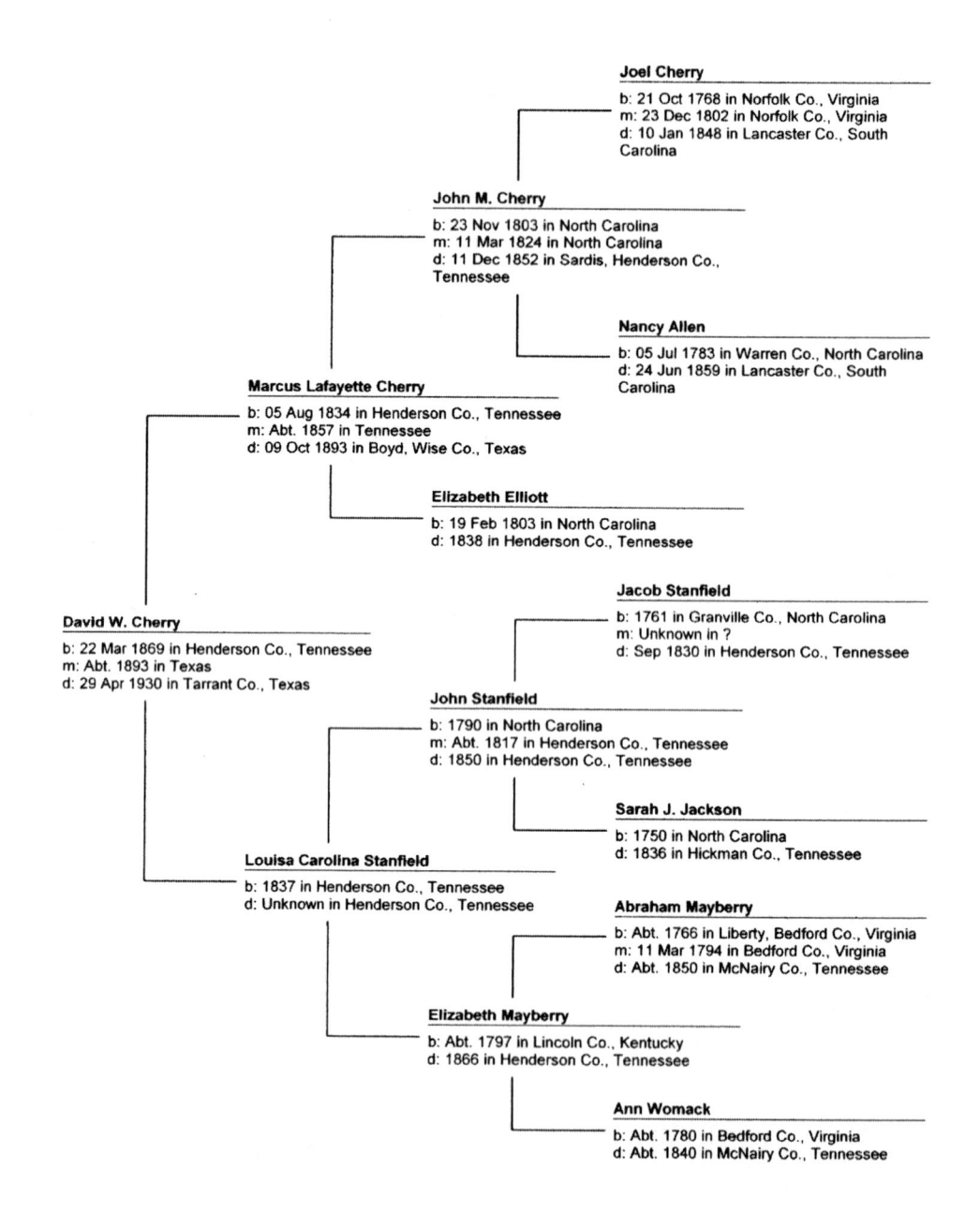

- **David W. Cherry**
  - b: 22 Mar 1869 in Henderson Co., Tennessee
  - m: Abt. 1893 in Texas
  - d: 29 Apr 1930 in Tarrant Co., Texas
  - **Marcus Lafayette Cherry**
    - b: 05 Aug 1834 in Henderson Co., Tennessee
    - m: Abt. 1857 in Tennessee
    - d: 09 Oct 1893 in Boyd, Wise Co., Texas
    - **John M. Cherry**
      - b: 23 Nov 1803 in North Carolina
      - m: 11 Mar 1824 in North Carolina
      - d: 11 Dec 1852 in Sardis, Henderson Co., Tennessee
      - **Joel Cherry**
        - b: 21 Oct 1768 in Norfolk Co., Virginia
        - m: 23 Dec 1802 in Norfolk Co., Virginia
        - d: 10 Jan 1848 in Lancaster Co., South Carolina
      - **Nancy Allen**
        - b: 05 Jul 1783 in Warren Co., North Carolina
        - d: 24 Jun 1859 in Lancaster Co., South Carolina
    - **Elizabeth Elliott**
      - b: 19 Feb 1803 in North Carolina
      - d: 1838 in Henderson Co., Tennessee
  - **Louisa Carolina Stanfield**
    - b: 1837 in Henderson Co., Tennessee
    - d: Unknown in Henderson Co., Tennessee
    - **John Stanfield**
      - b: 1790 in North Carolina
      - m: Abt. 1817 in Henderson Co., Tennessee
      - d: 1850 in Henderson Co., Tennessee
      - **Jacob Stanfield**
        - b: 1761 in Granville Co., North Carolina
        - m: Unknown in ?
        - d: Sep 1830 in Henderson Co., Tennessee
      - **Sarah J. Jackson**
        - b: 1750 in North Carolina
        - d: 1836 in Hickman Co., Tennessee
    - **Elizabeth Mayberry**
      - b: Abt. 1797 in Lincoln Co., Kentucky
      - d: 1866 in Henderson Co., Tennessee
      - **Abraham Mayberry**
        - b: Abt. 1766 in Liberty, Bedford Co., Virginia
        - m: 11 Mar 1794 in Bedford Co., Virginia
        - d: Abt. 1850 in McNairy Co., Tennessee
      - **Ann Womack**
        - b: Abt. 1780 in Bedford Co., Virginia
        - d: Abt. 1840 in McNairy Co., Tennessee

Martha Wilton (1876~1920)
[4th. Generation From Henry Wilton (1769-1820)]

&

Temple Worth Howard (1878-1932)
& Family

Family Group Sheet

Husband: Temple Worth Howard

Born: 12 Nov 1878 in: Shelby Co., Illinois
Married: 21 Oct 1900 in: Tarrant Co., Texas
Died: 25 Feb 1932 in: Hall Co., Texas
Father: William W. Howard
Mother: Helen

Wife: Martha Wilton

Born: Dec 1876 in: Illinois
Died: Aft. 1920 in: Texas
Father: Joseph C. Wilton
Mother: Sarah Elizabeth Baldwin

CHILDREN

1. F — Name: Vertia Howard, Born: 1903 in: Texas
2. F — Name: Vertie Howard, Born: 1903 in: Texas
3. F — Name: Mable Howard, Born: 1905 in: Texas
4. M — Name: Roy Howard, Born: 1909 in: Texas
5. F — Name: Ruth Howard, Born: 1909 in: Texas
6. M — Name: Worth Howard, Born: 1911 in: Texas
7. F — Name: Mary Howard, Born: 1914 in: Texas

TEMPLE WORTH HOWARD Standard Pedigree Tree

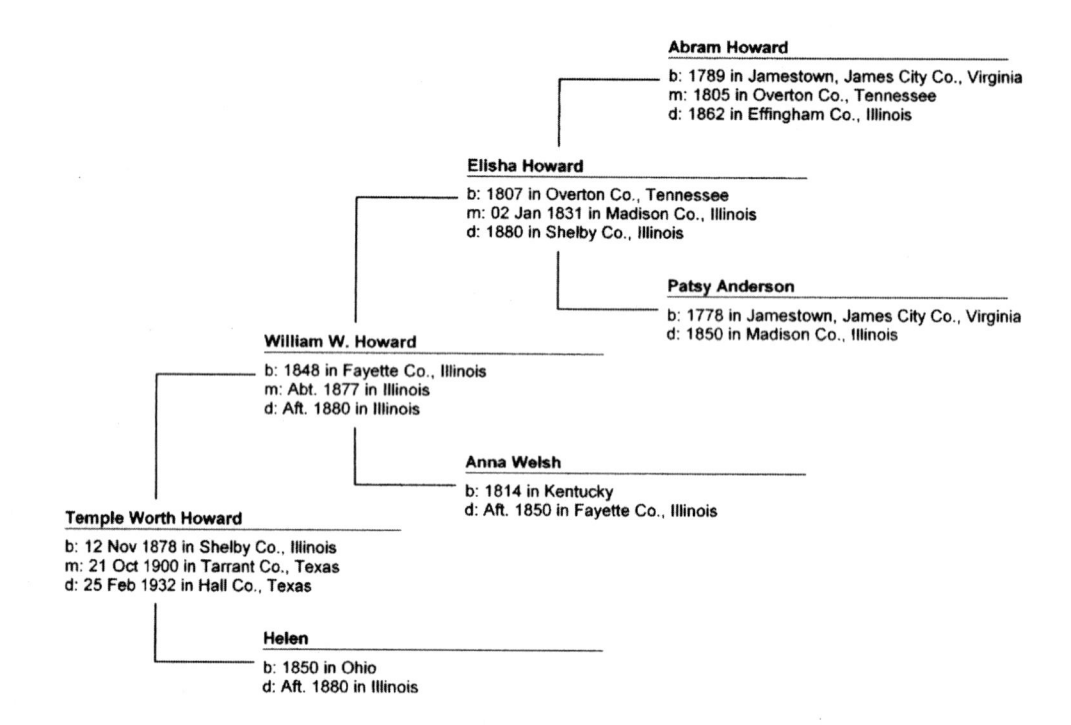

```
                                                            Abram Howard
                                                            b: 1789 in Jamestown, James City Co., Virginia
                                                            m: 1805 in Overton Co., Tennessee
                                                            d: 1862 in Effingham Co., Illinois

                                    Elisha Howard
                                    b: 1807 in Overton Co., Tennessee
                                    m: 02 Jan 1831 in Madison Co., Illinois
                                    d: 1880 in Shelby Co., Illinois

                                                            Patsy Anderson
                                                            b: 1778 in Jamestown, James City Co., Virginia
                                                            d: 1850 in Madison Co., Illinois

            William W. Howard
            b: 1848 in Fayette Co., Illinois
            m: Abt. 1877 in Illinois
            d: Aft. 1880 in Illinois

                                    Anna Welsh
                                    b: 1814 in Kentucky
                                    d: Aft. 1850 in Fayette Co., Illinois

Temple Worth Howard
b: 12 Nov 1878 in Shelby Co., Illinois
m: 21 Oct 1900 in Tarrant Co., Texas
d: 25 Feb 1932 in Hall Co., Texas

            Helen
            b: 1850 in Ohio
            d: Aft. 1880 in Illinois
```

Mary Wilton (1879-1961)
[4th. Generation From Henry Wilton (1769-1820)]

&

Isaac W. Cole (1876-1931)
& Family

Family Group Sheet

Husband: Isaac W. Cole

Born: 01 Apr 1876	in: Tennessee
Married: Abt. 1906	in: Texas
Died: 22 Oct 1931	in: Tarrant Co., Texas

Wife: Mary Wilton

Born: 17 Aug 1879	in: Illinois
Died: 01 Jan 1961	in: Tarrant Co., Texas
Father: Joseph C. Wilton	
Mother: Sarah Elizabeth Baldwin	

CHILDREN

1 M	Name: Herman Cole Born: Abt. 1907	in: Texas
2 F	Name: Hazle Cole Born: Abt. 1916	in: Texas

Nona Wilton (1881-1959)
[4th. Generation From Henry Wilton (1769-1820)]

&

William Walter Wiley (1880-1957)
& Family

Family Group Sheet

Husband: William Walter Wiley	
Born: 12 Aug 1880	in: Texas
Married: Abt. 1902	in: Texas
Died: 14 Aug 1957	in: Tarrant Co., Texas
Father: William Warren Wiley	
Mother: Mary A. Hinkle	
Wife: Nona Wilton	
Born: 22 Nov 1881	in: Texas
Died: 26 Mar 1959	in: Tarrant Co., Texas
Father: Joseph C. Wilton	
Mother: Sarah Elizabeth Baldwin	

CHILDREN

1. M — Name: William Melvin Wiley
   - Born: 18 Sep 1903 in: Texas
   - Died: 20 Mar 1972 in: Tarrant Co., Texas

2. M — Name: Joe Wiley
   - Born: 25 Nov 1905 in: Texas
   - Died: Oct 1984 in: Grapevine, Tarrant Co., Texas

3. M — Name: Wilton English Wiley
   - Born: 22 Jul 1915 in: Texas
   - Died: 08 Jul 1969 in: Fort Worth, Tarrant Co., Texas
   - Married: 28 Mar 1939 in: Texas
   - Spouse: Evelyn Irene Morrow

WILLIAM WALTER WILEY Standard Pedigree Tree

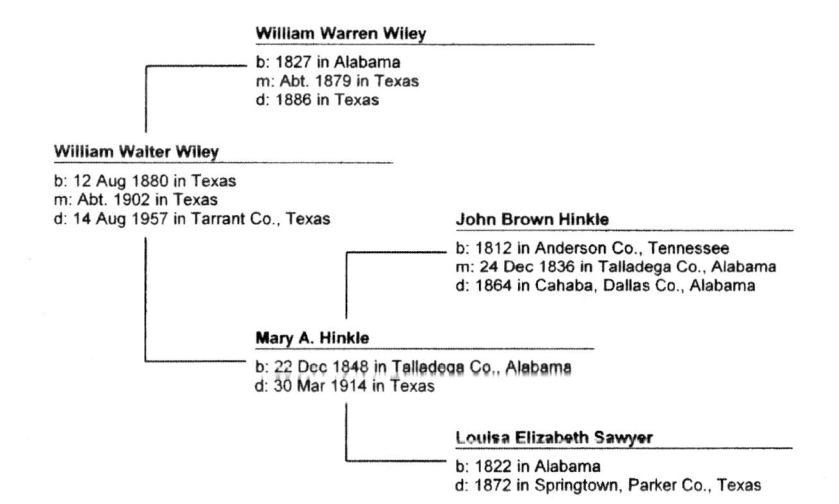

William Walter Wiley
b: 12 Aug 1880 in Texas
m: Abt. 1902 in Texas
d: 14 Aug 1957 in Tarrant Co., Texas

William Warren Wiley
b: 1827 in Alabama
m: Abt. 1879 in Texas
d: 1886 in Texas

Mary A. Hinkle
b: 22 Dec 1848 in Talladega Co., Alabama
d: 30 Mar 1914 in Texas

John Brown Hinkle
b: 1812 in Anderson Co., Tennessee
m: 24 Dec 1836 in Talladega Co., Alabama
d: 1864 in Cahaba, Dallas Co., Alabama

Louisa Elizabeth Sawyer
b: 1822 in Alabama
d: 1872 in Springtown, Parker Co., Texas

Wilton English Wiley (1915-1969)
[5th. Generation From Henry Wilton (1769-1820)]

&

Evelyn Irene Morrow (1919-1995)
& Family

Family Group Sheet

Husband: Wilton English Wiley

Born: 22 Jul 1915	in: Texas
Married: 28 Mar 1939	in: Texas
Died: 08 Jul 1969	in: Fort Worth, Tarrant Co., Texas
Father: William Walter Wiley	
Mother: Nona Wilton	

Wife: Evelyn Irene Morrow

Born: 18 Nov 1919	in: Fort Worth, Tarrant Co., Texas
Died: 06 Apr 1995	in: Azle, Tarrant Co., Texas
Father: Thomas Vernon Morrow	
Mother: Gladys Greta Younger	

CHILDREN

1 M
- Name: Wilton Madison Wiley
- Born: 29 Sep 1942 — in: Tarrant Co., Texas
- Married: 28 May 1969 — in: Tarrant Co., Texas
- Spouse: Glenda G. Gann

2 M
- Name: Larry Glen Wiley
- Born: 04 Aug 1953 — in: Tarrant Co., Texas
- Married: 01 Sep 1984 — in: Tarrant Co., Texas
- Spouse: Janet Arlene Compton

WILLIAM ENGLISH WILEY Standard Pedigree Tree

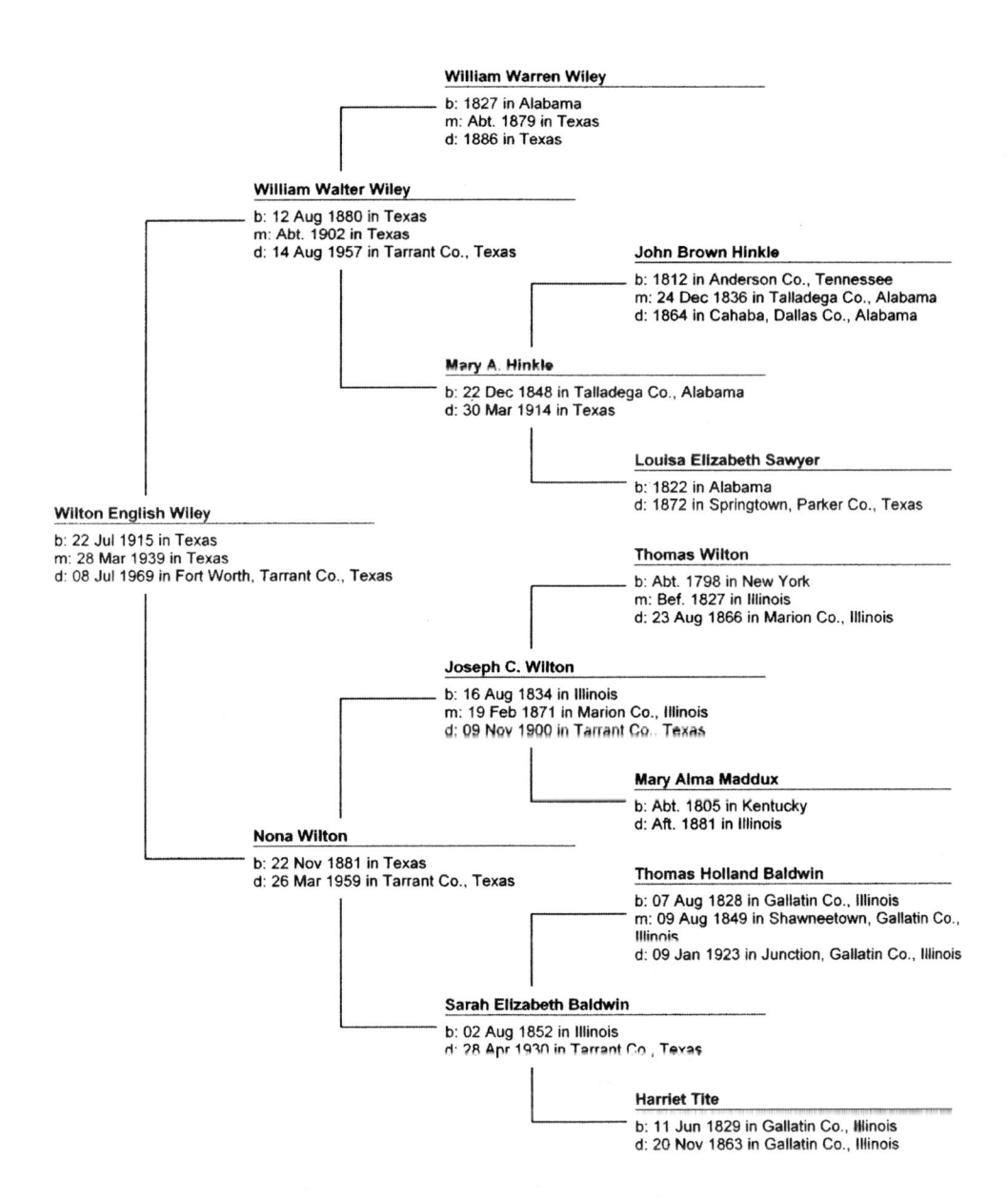

Wilton English Wiley
b: 22 Jul 1915 in Texas
m: 28 Mar 1939 in Texas
d: 08 Jul 1969 in Fort Worth, Tarrant Co., Texas

William Walter Wiley
b: 12 Aug 1880 in Texas
m: Abt. 1902 in Texas
d: 14 Aug 1957 in Tarrant Co., Texas

William Warren Wiley
b: 1827 in Alabama
m: Abt. 1879 in Texas
d: 1886 in Texas

Mary A. Hinkle
b: 22 Dec 1848 in Talladega Co., Alabama
d: 30 Mar 1914 in Texas

John Brown Hinkle
b: 1812 in Anderson Co., Tennessee
m: 24 Dec 1836 in Talladega Co., Alabama
d: 1864 in Cahaba, Dallas Co., Alabama

Louisa Elizabeth Sawyer
b: 1822 in Alabama
d: 1872 in Springtown, Parker Co., Texas

Nona Wilton
b: 22 Nov 1881 in Texas
d: 26 Mar 1959 in Tarrant Co., Texas

Joseph C. Wilton
b: 16 Aug 1834 in Illinois
m: 19 Feb 1871 in Marion Co., Illinois
d: 09 Nov 1900 in Tarrant Co., Texas

Thomas Wilton
b: Abt. 1798 in New York
m: Bef. 1827 in Illinois
d: 23 Aug 1866 in Marion Co., Illinois

Mary Alma Maddux
b: Abt. 1805 in Kentucky
d: Aft. 1881 in Illinois

Sarah Elizabeth Baldwin
b: 02 Aug 1852 in Illinois
d: 28 Apr 1930 in Tarrant Co., Texas

Thomas Holland Baldwin
b: 07 Aug 1828 in Gallatin Co., Illinois
m: 09 Aug 1849 in Shawneetown, Gallatin Co., Illinois
d: 09 Jan 1923 in Junction, Gallatin Co., Illinois

Harriet Tite
b: 11 Jun 1829 in Gallatin Co., Illinois
d: 20 Nov 1863 in Gallatin Co., Illinois

Notes: This Tree also applies to the other children of William Walter Wiley & Nona Wilton: William Melvin Wiley and Joe Wiley.

EVELYN IRENE MORROW Standard Pedigree Tree

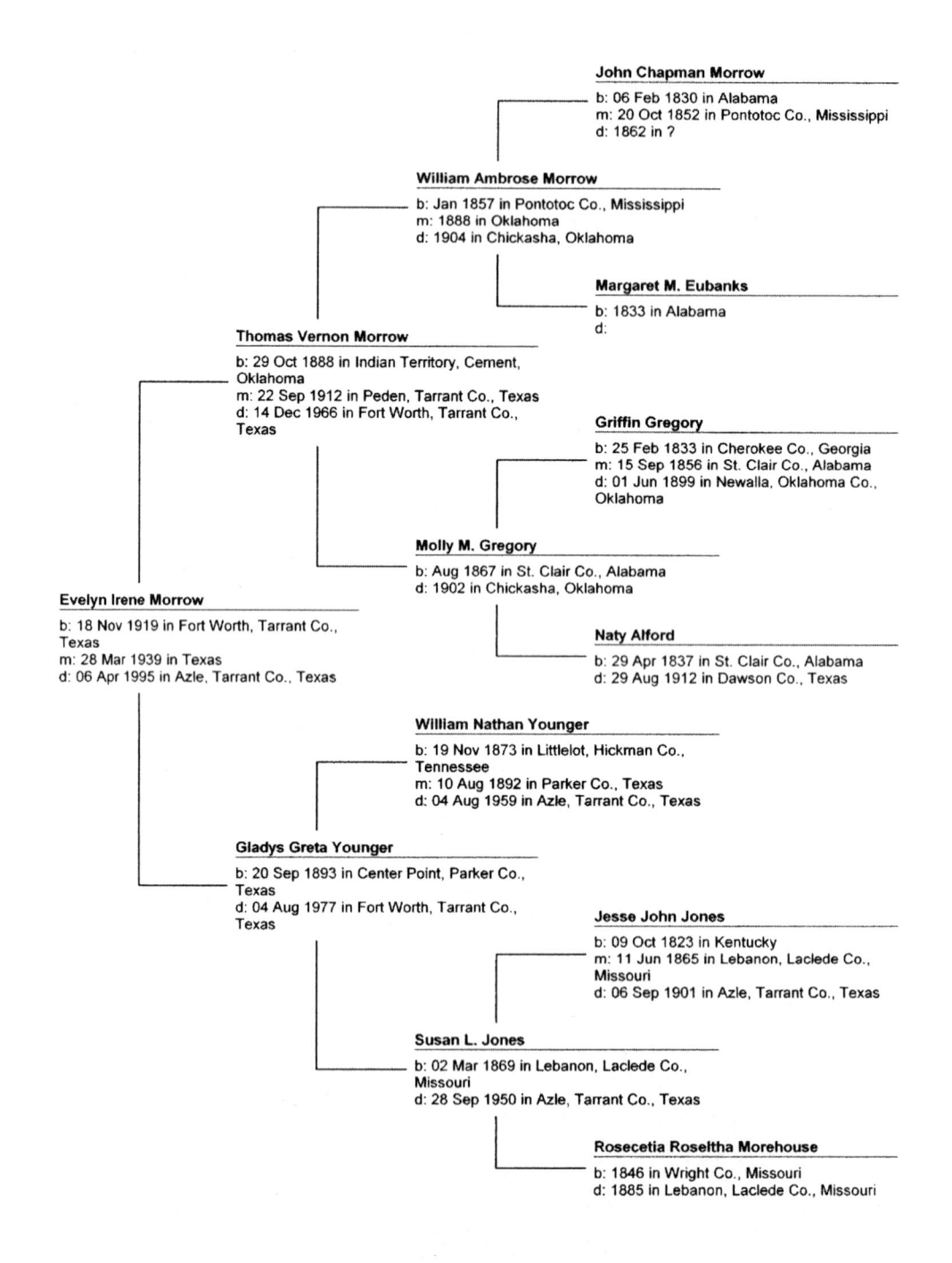

Evelyn Irene Morrow
b: 18 Nov 1919 in Fort Worth, Tarrant Co., Texas
m: 28 Mar 1939 in Texas
d: 06 Apr 1995 in Azle, Tarrant Co., Texas

- **Thomas Vernon Morrow**
  b: 29 Oct 1888 in Indian Territory, Cement, Oklahoma
  m: 22 Sep 1912 in Peden, Tarrant Co., Texas
  d: 14 Dec 1966 in Fort Worth, Tarrant Co., Texas

  - **William Ambrose Morrow**
    b: Jan 1857 in Pontotoc Co., Mississippi
    m: 1888 in Oklahoma
    d: 1904 in Chickasha, Oklahoma

    - **John Chapman Morrow**
      b: 06 Feb 1830 in Alabama
      m: 20 Oct 1852 in Pontotoc Co., Mississippi
      d: 1862 in ?

    - **Margaret M. Eubanks**
      b: 1833 in Alabama
      d:

  - **Molly M. Gregory**
    b: Aug 1867 in St. Clair Co., Alabama
    d: 1902 in Chickasha, Oklahoma

    - **Griffin Gregory**
      b: 25 Feb 1833 in Cherokee Co., Georgia
      m: 15 Sep 1856 in St. Clair Co., Alabama
      d: 01 Jun 1899 in Newalla, Oklahoma Co., Oklahoma

    - **Naty Alford**
      b: 29 Apr 1837 in St. Clair Co., Alabama
      d: 29 Aug 1912 in Dawson Co., Texas

- **Gladys Greta Younger**
  b: 20 Sep 1893 in Center Point, Parker Co., Texas
  d: 04 Aug 1977 in Fort Worth, Tarrant Co., Texas

  - **William Nathan Younger**
    b: 19 Nov 1873 in Littlelot, Hickman Co., Tennessee
    m: 10 Aug 1892 in Parker Co., Texas
    d: 04 Aug 1959 in Azle, Tarrant Co., Texas

  - **Susan L. Jones**
    b: 02 Mar 1869 in Lebanon, Laclede Co., Missouri
    d: 28 Sep 1950 in Azle, Tarrant Co., Texas

    - **Jesse John Jones**
      b: 09 Oct 1823 in Kentucky
      m: 11 Jun 1865 in Lebanon, Laclede Co., Missouri
      d: 06 Sep 1901 in Azle, Tarrant Co., Texas

    - **Rosecetia Roseltha Morehouse**
      b: 1846 in Wright Co., Missouri
      d: 1885 in Lebanon, Laclede Co., Missouri

Joseph S. Wilton (1884-1982)
[4th. Generation From Henry Wilton (1769-1820)]

&

Bessie Smith (1893-1998)
& Family

Joseph S. Wilton, born October 1884 in Texas, was the son of Joseph C. Wilton and Sarah Elizabeth Baldwin. The family had resettled in Parker County, Texas about 1880 after leaving Illinois. By 1900, the family had moved to the adjacent Tarrant County. In November 1900, Joseph's father died, and his mother took over the responsibility of raising the five children still living at home.

In the 1910 Federal Census of Tarrant County, Texas, J.S. (Joseph S.) Wilton was listed at age 28, with an occupation of farm laborer, living with his mother, Mrs. S.E. Wilton, then age 56, and younger brother, V.V. (Vanzant V.) Wilton. Also, in the 1910 Census, in the same Texas county and precinct, Joseph's wife-to-be, Bessie M. Smith, was also living with her parents and brother. It was about the same year of 1910 that Joseph S. Wilton married Bessie Smith, daughter of John Calvin Smith and Annie Rebecca Robertson.

For a number of years, Joseph S. and Bessie continued to live in Tarrant County, Texas. In the 1920 Federal Census of Tarrant County, Jodie S. (Joseph S.) Wilton was listed at age 36, with an occupation of farmer, along with his wife, Bessie Wilton, and mother and two daughters. Joseph S. and Bessie had a total of four children, Nona Fay Wilton, born August 30, 1913, Virgie Vivian Wilton, born December 23, 1916, Margaret Wilton, born 1921, and Joseph Drexel Wilton, born January 17, 1930. In the 1930 Federal Census of Tarrant County, Jodie S. (Joseph S.) was listed at age 45, along with his wife, Bessie W. Wilton, and four children and mother, Sarah E. Wilton.

Joseph S. died June 1982, and Bessie died April 1989 in Tarrant County, Texas.

Family Group Sheet

Husband: Joseph S. Wilton

Born: 17 Oct 1884 — in: Texas
Married: Abt. 1910 — in: Texas
Died: 04 Jun 1982 — in: Harris Co., Texas
Father: Joseph C. Wilton
Mother: Sarah Elizabeth Baldwin

Wife: Bessie Smith

Born: 30 Dec 1893 — in: Texas
Died: 25 Apr 1989 — in: Tarrant Co., Texas
Father: John Calvin Smith
Mother: Annie Rebecca Robertson

CHILDREN

1. F
   Name: Nona Fay Wilton
   Born: 30 Aug 1913 — in: Texas
   Died: 14 Mar 2007 — in: Tarrant Co., Texas
   Married: Abt. 1933 — in: Texas
   Spouse: James Roger Sullivan

2. F
   Name: Virgie Vivian Wilton
   Born: 23 Dec 1916 — in: Texas
   Died: 01 Jul 1975 — in: Harris Co., Texas
   Married: Abt. 1935 — in: Texas
   Spouse: Truman Combest Stubbs

3. F
   Name: Margaret Wilton
   Born: 1921 — in: Texas
   Married: Unknown
   Spouse: Leland Hall

4. M
   Name: Joseph Drexel Wilton
   Born: 17 Jan 1930 — in: Tarrant Co., Texas
   Married: Abt. 1958 — in: Texas
   Spouse: Frances Virginia Champ

BESSIE SMITH Standard Pedigree Tree

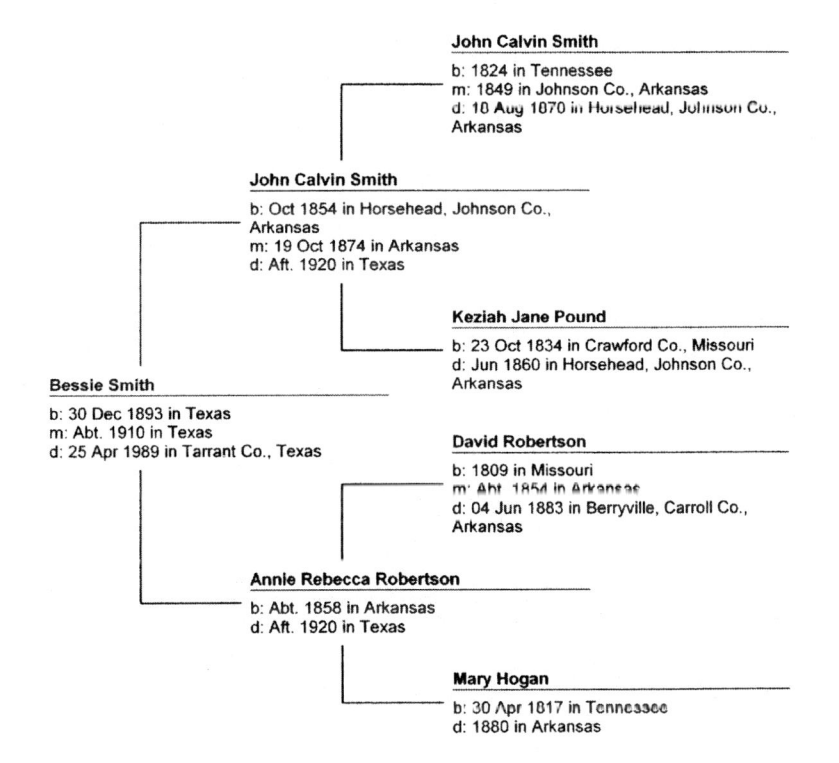

Bessie Smith
b: 30 Dec 1893 in Texas
m: Abt. 1910 in Texas
d: 25 Apr 1989 in Tarrant Co., Texas

- **John Calvin Smith**
  b: Oct 1854 in Horsehead, Johnson Co., Arkansas
  m: 19 Oct 1874 in Arkansas
  d: Aft. 1920 in Texas
  - **John Calvin Smith**
    b: 1824 in Tennessee
    m: 1849 in Johnson Co., Arkansas
    d: 10 Aug 1870 in Horsehead, Johnson Co., Arkansas
  - **Keziah Jane Pound**
    b: 23 Oct 1834 in Crawford Co., Missouri
    d: Jun 1860 in Horsehead, Johnson Co., Arkansas

- **Annie Rebecca Robertson**
  b: Abt. 1858 in Arkansas
  d: Aft. 1920 in Texas
  - **David Robertson**
    b: 1809 in Missouri
    m: Abt. 1854 in Arkansas
    d: 04 Jun 1883 in Berryville, Carroll Co., Arkansas
  - **Mary Hogan**
    b: 30 Apr 1817 in Tennessee
    d: 1880 in Arkansas

Nona Fay Wilton (1913-2007)
[5th. Generation From Henry Wilton (1769-1820)]

&

James Roger Sullivan
& Family

Family Group Sheet

Husband: James Roger Sullivan	
Born: Unknown	in: Texas
Married: Abt. 1933	in: Texas

Wife: Nona Fay Wilton	
Born: 30 Aug 1913	in: Texas
Died: 14 Mar 2007	in: Tarrant Co., Texas
Father: Joseph S. Wilton	
Mother: Bessie Smith	

CHILDREN

1 M	Name: Charles Roger Sullivan	
	Born: 29 Mar 1934	in: Tarrant Co., Texas
2 F	Name: Rodera Fay Sullivan	
	Born: 20 Nov 1938	in: Tarrant Co., Texas
3 M	Name: Jimmy Dwayne Sullivan	
	Born: 11 May 1943	in: Tarrant Co., Texas
	Died: 23 May 2007	in: Tarrant Co., Texas

NONA FAY WILTON Standard Pedigree Tree

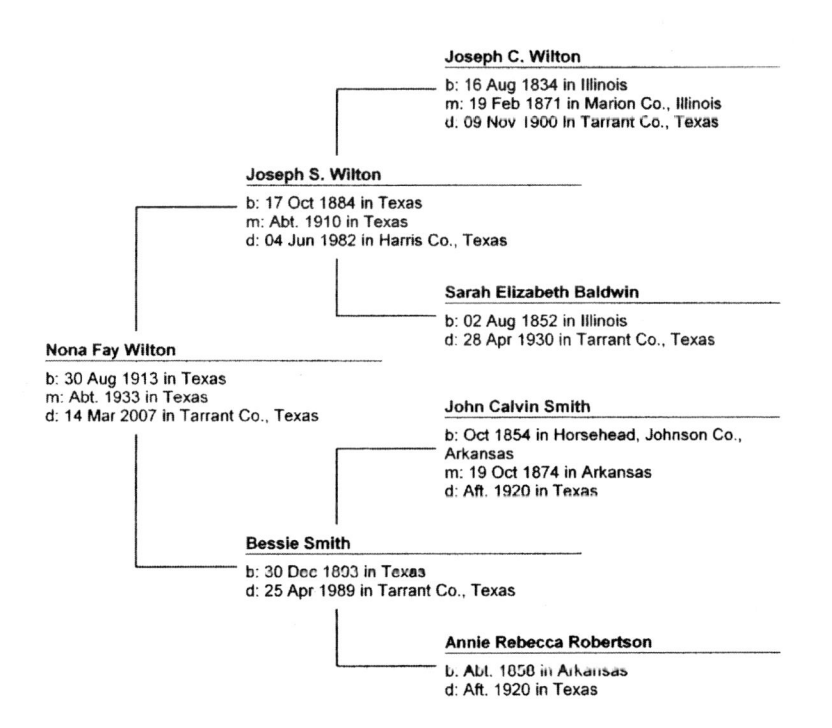

- **Joseph S. Wilton**
  - b: 17 Oct 1884 in Texas
  - m: Abt. 1910 in Texas
  - d: 04 Jun 1982 in Harris Co., Texas
    - **Joseph C. Wilton**
      - b: 16 Aug 1834 in Illinois
      - m: 19 Feb 1871 in Marion Co., Illinois
      - d: 09 Nov 1900 in Tarrant Co., Texas
    - **Sarah Elizabeth Baldwin**
      - b: 02 Aug 1852 in Illinois
      - d: 28 Apr 1930 in Tarrant Co., Texas

Nona Fay Wilton
- b: 30 Aug 1913 in Texas
- m: Abt. 1933 in Texas
- d: 14 Mar 2007 in Tarrant Co., Texas

- **Bessie Smith**
  - b: 30 Dec 1893 in Texas
  - d: 25 Apr 1989 in Tarrant Co., Texas
    - **John Calvin Smith**
      - b: Oct 1854 in Horsehead, Johnson Co., Arkansas
      - m: 19 Oct 1874 in Arkansas
      - d: Aft. 1920 in Texas
    - **Annie Rebecca Robertson**
      - b: Abt. 1858 in Arkansas
      - d: Aft. 1920 in Texas

Notes: This Tree also applies to the other children of Joseph S. Wilton & Bessie Smith: Virgie Vivian Wilton, Margaret Wilton, and Joseph Drexel Wilton.

Virgie Vivian Wilton (1916-1975)
[5th. Generation From Henry Wilton (1769-1820)]

&

Truman Combest Stubbs (1910-2000)
& Family

Family Group Sheet

Husband: Truman Combest Stubbs	
Born: 18 Jun 1910	in: Texas
Married: Abt. 1935	in: Texas
Died: 29 Oct 2000	in: Tarrant Co., Texas

Wife: Virgie Vivian Wilton	
Born: 23 Dec 1916	in: Texas
Died: 01 Jul 1975	in: Harris Co., Texas
Father: Joseph S. Wilton	
Mother: Bessie Smith	

CHILDREN

1 F	Name: Wanda Vonciel Stubbs	
	Born: 01 May 1936	in: Tarrant Co., Texas
	Married: 16 Aug 1958	in: Texas
	Spouse: Billy Ray Caldwell	
	Married: 30 Jan 1978	in: Tarrant Co., Texas
	Spouse: Merle Losson Gulick	

2 M	Name: Truman Kenneth Stubbs	
	Born: 03 Dec 1937	in: Tarrant Co., Texas
	Married: 19 Mar 1966	in: Tarrant Co., Texas
	Spouse: Paula Jean Bass	

3 M	Name: Jerry Lynn Stubbs	
	Born: 06 Jan 1941	in: Tarrant Co., Texas

Wanda Vonciel Stubbs (1936-)
[6th. Generation from Henry Wilton (1769-1820)]

&
Billy Ray Caldwell (1932-)
& Family

&
Merle Losson Gulick (1939-)
& Family

Family Group Sheet

Husband: Billy Ray Caldwell

Born: 1932
Married: 16 Aug 1958 in: Texas

Wife: Wanda Vonciel Stubbs

Born: 01 May 1936 in: Tarrant Co., Texas
Father: Truman Combest Stubbs
Mother: Virgie Vivian Wilton
Other Spouses: Merle Losson Gulick

CHILDREN

1 F	Name: Caryn Denise Caldwell Born: 22 Sep 1961 Married: 28 Aug 1982 Spouse: Steven Vern Weaver	in: Tarrant Co., Texas in: Collin Co., Texas
2 F	Name: Jeana Lynette Caldwell Born: 03 Mar 1965 Married: 02 Jul 1983 Spouse: Tracy Lynn Braley	in: Tarrant Co., Texas in: Collin Co., Texas
3 M	Name: Craig Randall Caldwell Born: 17 Nov 1966 Married: 10 Jun 1995 Spouse: Lisa R. Lawson	in: Tarrant Co., Texas in: Collin Co., Texas

Family Group Sheet

Husband: Merle Losson Gulick

Born: 14 Apr 1939 in: Los Angeles Co., California
Married: 30 Jan 1978 in: Tarrant Co., Texas
Other Spouses: Dannie Jean Price

Wife: Wanda Vonciel Stubbs

Born: 01 May 1936 in: Tarrant Co., Texas
Father: Truman Combest Stubbs
Mother: Virgie Vivian Wilton
Other Spouses: Billy Ray Caldwell

WANDA VONCIEL STUBBS Standard Pedigree Tree

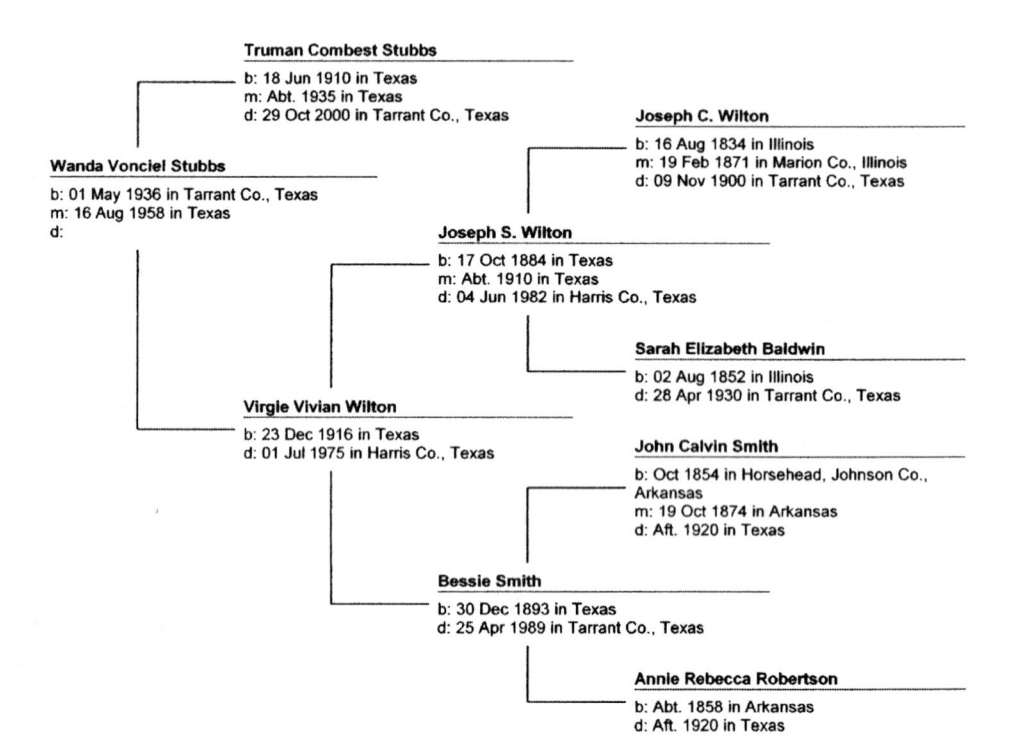

Wanda Vonciel Stubbs
b: 01 May 1936 in Tarrant Co., Texas
m: 16 Aug 1958 in Texas
d:

Truman Combest Stubbs
b: 18 Jun 1910 in Texas
m: Abt. 1935 in Texas
d: 29 Oct 2000 in Tarrant Co., Texas

Joseph S. Wilton
b: 17 Oct 1884 in Texas
m: Abt. 1910 in Texas
d: 04 Jun 1982 in Harris Co., Texas

Joseph C. Wilton
b: 16 Aug 1834 in Illinois
m: 19 Feb 1871 in Marion Co., Illinois
d: 09 Nov 1900 in Tarrant Co., Texas

Sarah Elizabeth Baldwin
b: 02 Aug 1852 in Illinois
d: 28 Apr 1930 in Tarrant Co., Texas

Virgie Vivian Wilton
b: 23 Dec 1916 in Texas
d: 01 Jul 1975 in Harris Co., Texas

Bessie Smith
b: 30 Dec 1893 in Texas
d: 25 Apr 1989 in Tarrant Co., Texas

John Calvin Smith
b: Oct 1854 in Horsehead, Johnson Co., Arkansas
m: 19 Oct 1874 in Arkansas
d: Aft. 1920 in Texas

Annie Rebecca Robertson
b: Abt. 1858 in Arkansas
d: Aft. 1920 in Texas

Notes: This Tree also applies to the other children of Truman Combest Stubbs & Virgie Vivian Wilton: Truman Kenneth Stubbs and Jerry Lynn Stubbs.

Truman Kenneth Stubbs (1937-   )
[6th. Generation From Henry Wilton (1769-1820)]

&

Paula Jean Bass (1945-   )
& Family

Family Group Sheet

Husband: Truman Kenneth Stubbs		
Born: 03 Dec 1937	in: Tarrant Co., Texas	
Married: 19 Mar 1966	in: Tarrant Co., Texas	
Father: Truman Combest Stubbs		
Mother: Virgie Vivian Wilton		
Wife: Paula Jean Bass		
Born: 31 Oct 1945	in: Tarrant Co., Texas	

CHILDREN

1 M
- Name: Sid Richard Stubbs
- Born: 04 Sep 1966 in: Tarrant Co., Texas
- Married: 22 Dec 1990 in: Tarrant Co., Texas
- Spouse: Tammy Renee Honeycutt

2 F
- Name: Sheila Renee Stubbs
- Born: 23 Sep 1969 in: Tarrant Co., Texas

Joseph Drexel Wilton (1930-   )
[5th. Generation From Henry Wilton (1769-1820)]

&

Frances Virginia Champ
& Family

Family Group Sheet

Husband: Joseph Drexel Wilton	
Born: 17 Jan 1930	in: Tarrant Co., Texas
Married: Abt. 1958	in: Texas
Father: Joseph S. Wilton	
Mother: Bessie Smith	

Wife: Frances Virginia Champ	
Born: Unknown	

CHILDREN

#		
1 F	Name: Mary Frances Wilton	
	Born: 20 Oct 1958	in: Tarrant Co., Texas
	Married: 28 Nov 1975	in: Morris Co., Texas
	Spouse: Walter Lee Robertson	
2 F	Name: Cathy Ann Wilton	
	Born: 08 Nov 1960	in: Tarrant Co., Texas
	Married: 21 Nov 1981	in: Harris Co., Texas
	Spouse: Mikael Dewayne Price	
3 M	Name: Gilbert Douglas Wilton	
	Born: 01 Jul 1963	in: Fannin Co., Texas

Vazant V. Wilton (1893-1915)
[5th. Generation From Henry Wilton (1769-1820)]

Vanzant V. (Van) Wilton, the last living child of Joseph C. Wilton and Sarah Elizabeth Baldwin, was born June 6, 1893. At the time Van was born, the family had resettled in the Parker and Tarrant counties area of Texas. Van's father died in November 1900, and his mother then took over the task of raising the children who were still living at home.

Van died prematurely on January 4, 1915, at the age of 21, at Eagle Mountain in Tarrant County, Texas. According to family recollection, Van died from a rattlesnake bite, possibly occurring while hunting. Thinking that chicken's blood could draw out the snake poison, the family took Van to a neighbor to get a chicken for that purpose. The neighbor refused to give them the chicken, and when Van died, the family partially blamed the neighbor for Van's dying.

Rudolph Wilton (1839-1929)
[3rd. Generation from Henry Wilton (1769-1820)]

&

Nancy A. Wall (1837~1870)
& Family

&

Ellen Jane Pauley (1844-1925)
& Family

Rudolph Wilton, the fourth child of Thomas Wilton and Mary Alma Maddux, was born September 3, 1839 in Illinois. The family was then living in Clinton County, Illinois, and sometime after 1940, the family moved to the adjacent Marion County, where Rudolph was raised and spent most of his early years. In the 1860 Federal Census of Marion County Illinois, Rudolph was listed at age 21, living with his father and mother and two younger sisters.

In August of 1861, Rudolph enlisted as a Private with Company M, 3rd Cavalry of the Union Army for service in the Civil War. At that time, his residence was listed as Fayette County, Illinois, which was the adjacent county north of Marion County. After serving for four years, Rudolph was mustered out of the army on October 10, 1865 at Springfield, Illinois.

Evidence suggests that Rudolph had a first marriage sometime before 1862 to a Nancy A. Wall. According to a deed record in Marion Co., Illinois (Deed Record Book 12, Marion Co., Illinois, p.401), dated September 6, 1867, Rudolph was married to Nancy A. Wilton. The record was of land sold to his brother, Charles F. Wilton. Also, in the 1870 Federal Census of St. Clair

County, Illinois, there was a Rudolph Wilden (or Wilton), listed at age 31, with an occupation of farmer, along with his wife, Nancy, age 33, and son, Isaac, age 11/12. Living just one dwelling away in the same census was the family of Isaac Nichols, whose wife, Nancy, was later shown in the 1880 Federal Census of St. Clair County to have a son by a previous marriage named James I. Wall, and a grandson by the name of Isaac H. Wilton.

On November 20, 1879, in Marion County, Illinois, Rudolph married a second time to Ellen Jane Pauley, daughter of Lewis Pauley and Rebecca Thorpe. This was also Ellen's second marriage, and she had five children from her previous marriage to Henry Carter. In the 1880 Federal Census of Fayette County, Illinois, Rudolph was listed at age 40, with an occupation of farmer, along with his wife, Ellen J., age 36, and four Carter children.

Sometime after 1880, the family settled again in Marion County, Illinois, where Rudolph and Ellen had two children of their own. Their first child, Bertha Pauline Wilton, was born May 1884, and their second child, Blanche Mae Wilton, was born March 1886. In the 1900 Federal Census of Marion County, Illinois, Rudolph Wilton was listed at age 61, along with his wife, Ellen J. Wilton, and daughters Polly B. Wilton and Blanch M. Wilton, both in their mid teens. In both the 1910 and 1920 Federal Censuses of Marion County, Illinois, Rudolph and Ellen were living alone at home. Ellen died January 10, 1925 in Patoka in Marion County, Illinois, and, Rudolph died November 5, 1928, also in Patoka, Illinois. They were both buried in the Patoka Cemetery in Patoka, Illinois.

Family Group Sheet

Husband: Rudolph Wilton

Born: 03 Sep 1839 in: Illinois
Married: Bef. 1862 in: Illinois
Died: 05 Nov 1928 in: Patoka, Marion Co., Illinois
Father: Thomas Wilton
Mother: Mary Alma Maddux
Other Spouses: Ellen Jane Pauley

Wife: Nancy A. Wall

Born: Abt. 1837 in: Illinois
Died: Bet. 1870 - 1880 in: Illinois

CHILDREN

1 M
Name: Isaac H. Wilton
Born: 15 Sep 1868 in: Illinois
Died: 04 Dec 1949 in: Los Angeles Co., California
Married: Abt. 1888 in: Illinois
Spouse: Maye Toole

Family Group Sheet

Husband: Rudolph Wilton

Born: 03 Sep 1839 in: Illinois
Married: 20 Nov 1879 in: Marion Co., Illinois
Died: 05 Nov 1928 in: Patoka, Marion Co., Illinois
Father: Thomas Wilton
Mother: Mary Alma Maddux
Other Spouses: Nancy A. Wall

Wife: Ellen Jane Pauley

Born: 12 Jun 1844 in: Illinois
Died: 10 Jan 1925 in: Patoka, Marion Co., Illinois
Father: Lewis Pauley
Mother: Rebecca Thorpe
Other Spouses: Henry Carter

CHILDREN

1 F
Name: Bertha Pauline Wilton
Born: 18 May 1884 in: Marion Co., Illinois
Died: Jan 1973 in: Marion Co., Illinois
Married: 02 Sep 1901 in: Marion Co., Illinois
Spouse: Ellis Madison Outhouse

2 F
Name: Blanche Mae Wilton
Born: Mar 1886 in: Patoka, Marion Co., Illinois
Died: Aft. 1930 in: Illinois
Married: 28 May 1908 in: Patoka, Marion Co., Illinois
Spouse: Joseph Henry Humes

Bertha Pauline Wilton (1884-1973)
[4th. Generation From Henry Wilton (1769-1820)]

&

Ellis Madison Outhouse (1880-1951)
& Family

Family Group Sheet

Husband: Ellis Madison Outhouse

Born: 12 May 1880 — in: Pope, Fayette Co., Illinois
Married: 02 Sep 1901 — in: Marion Co., Illinois
Died: 1951 — in: Illinois
Father: Joseph Martin Outhouse
Mother: Betty Ann Booher

Wife: Bertha Pauline Wilton

Born: 18 May 1884 — in: Marion Co., Illinois
Died: Jan 1973 — in: Marion Co., Illinois
Father: Rudolph Wilton
Mother: Ellen Jane Pauley

CHILDREN

1. M — Name: Carl B. Outhouse
   Born: 1903 — in: Illinois

2. M — Name: Joseph O. Outhouse
   Born: 1906 — in: Illinois

3. F — Name: Loretta Outhouse
   Born: 1908 — in: Illinois

4. M — Name: Talmadge Edwin Outhouse
   Born: 10 Nov 1912 — in: Illinois
   Died: 29 Jan 1998 — in: Aviston, Clinton Co., Illinois
   Married: Unknown — in: Illinois
   Spouse: Mildred Gertrude Ainscough

5. M — Name: Marion W. Outhouse
   Born: 31 Dec 1914 — in: Illinois
   Died: 05 Jun 1998 — in: Boone Co., Iowa

BERTHA PAULINE WILTON Standard Pedigree Tree

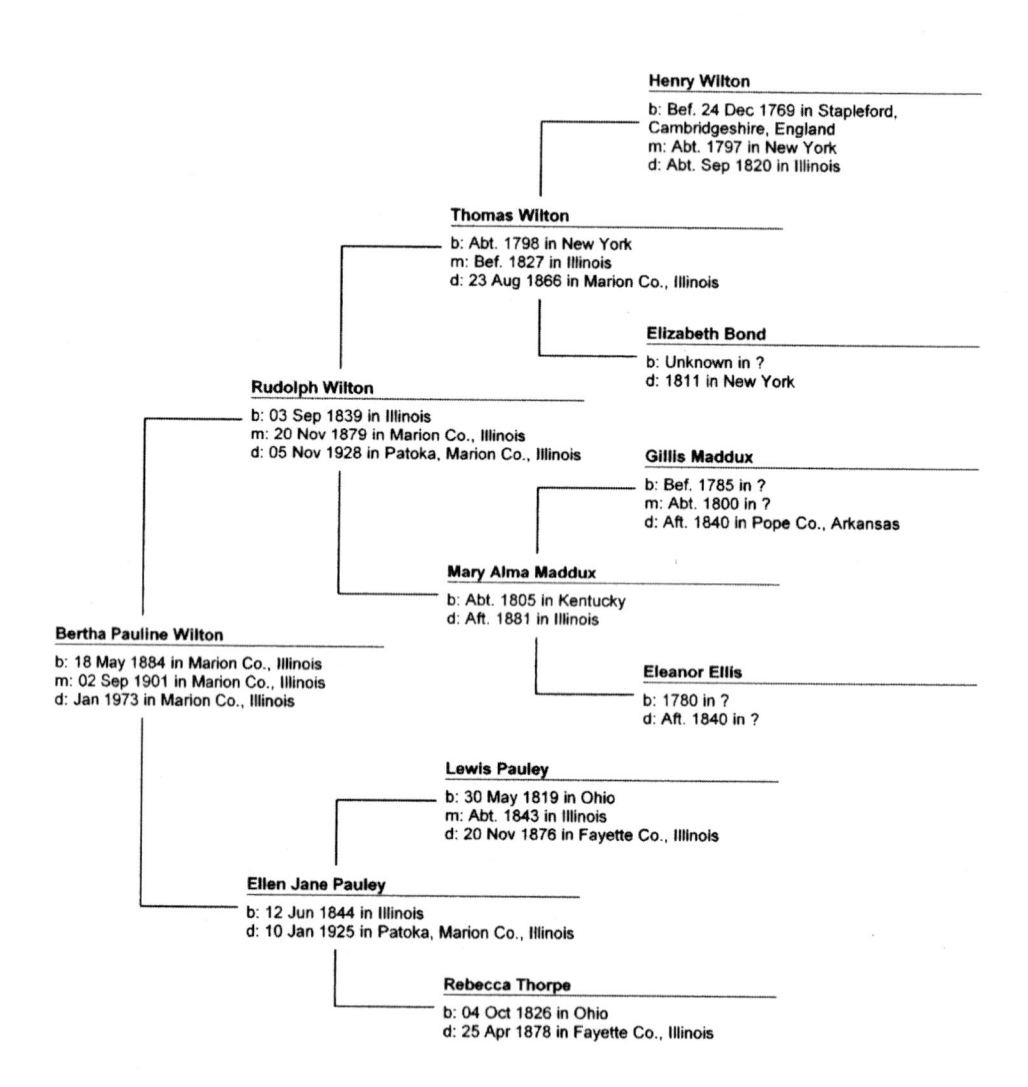

Henry Wilton
b: Bef. 24 Dec 1769 in Stapleford, Cambridgeshire, England
m: Abt. 1797 in New York
d: Abt. Sep 1820 in Illinois

Thomas Wilton
b: Abt. 1798 in New York
m: Bef. 1827 in Illinois
d: 23 Aug 1866 in Marion Co., Illinois

Elizabeth Bond
b: Unknown in ?
d: 1811 in New York

Rudolph Wilton
b: 03 Sep 1839 in Illinois
m: 20 Nov 1879 in Marion Co., Illinois
d: 05 Nov 1928 in Patoka, Marion Co., Illinois

Gillis Maddux
b: Bef. 1785 in ?
m: Abt. 1800 in ?
d: Aft. 1840 in Pope Co., Arkansas

Mary Alma Maddux
b: Abt. 1805 in Kentucky
d: Aft. 1881 in Illinois

Eleanor Ellis
b: 1780 in ?
d: Aft. 1840 in ?

Bertha Pauline Wilton
b: 18 May 1884 in Marion Co., Illinois
m: 02 Sep 1901 in Marion Co., Illinois
d: Jan 1973 in Marion Co., Illinois

Lewis Pauley
b: 30 May 1819 in Ohio
m: Abt. 1843 in Illinois
d: 20 Nov 1876 in Fayette Co., Illinois

Ellen Jane Pauley
b: 12 Jun 1844 in Illinois
d: 10 Jan 1925 in Patoka, Marion Co., Illinois

Rebecca Thorpe
b: 04 Oct 1826 in Ohio
d: 25 Apr 1878 in Fayette Co., Illinois

Notes: This Tree also applies to the other child of Rudolph Wilton & Ellen Jane Pauley: Blanche Mae Wilton.

ELLIS MADISON OUTHOUSE Standard Pedigree Tree

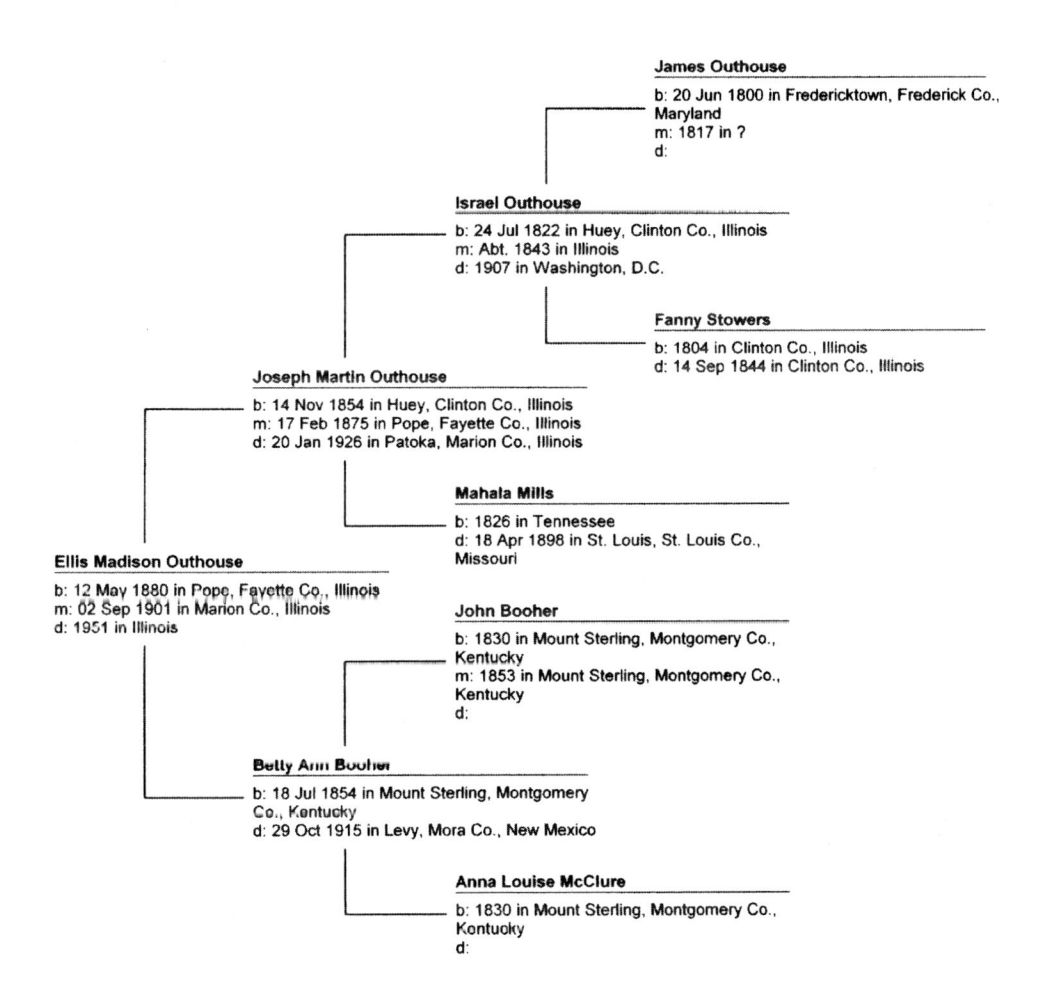

James Outhouse
b: 20 Jun 1800 in Fredericktown, Frederick Co., Maryland
m: 1817 in ?
d:

Israel Outhouse
b: 24 Jul 1822 in Huey, Clinton Co., Illinois
m: Abt. 1843 in Illinois
d: 1907 in Washington, D.C.

Fanny Stowers
b: 1804 in Clinton Co., Illinois
d: 14 Sep 1844 in Clinton Co., Illinois

Joseph Martin Outhouse
b: 14 Nov 1854 in Huey, Clinton Co., Illinois
m: 17 Feb 1875 in Pope, Fayette Co., Illinois
d: 20 Jan 1926 in Patoka, Marion Co., Illinois

Mahala Mills
b: 1826 in Tennessee
d: 18 Apr 1898 in St. Louis, St. Louis Co., Missouri

Ellis Madison Outhouse
b: 12 May 1880 in Pope, Fayette Co., Illinois
m: 02 Sep 1901 in Marion Co., Illinois
d: 1951 in Illinois

John Booher
b: 1830 in Mount Sterling, Montgomery Co., Kentucky
m: 1853 in Mount Sterling, Montgomery Co., Kentucky
d:

Betty Ann Booher
b: 18 Jul 1854 in Mount Sterling, Montgomery Co., Kentucky
d: 29 Oct 1915 in Levy, Mora Co., New Mexico

Anna Louise McClure
b: 1830 in Mount Sterling, Montgomery Co., Kentucky
d:

Blanche Mae Wilton (1886~1930)
[4th. Generation From Henry Wilton (1769-1820)]

&

Joseph Henry Humes (1881-1954)
& Family

Family Group Sheet

Husband: Joseph Henry Humes	
Born: 25 Sep 1881	in: Patoka, Marion Co., Illinois
Married: 28 May 1908	in: Patoka, Marion Co., Illinois
Died: Jan 1954	in: Bloomington, McLean Co., Illinois
Father: Peter Humes	
Mother: Mary Schmering	
Wife: Blanche Mae Wilton	
Born: Mar 1886	in: Patoka, Marion Co., Illinois
Died: Aft. 1930	in: Illinois
Father: Rudolph Wilton	
Mother: Ellen Jane Pauley	

Mary Elizabeth Wilton (1842-1898)
[3rd. Generation from Henry Wilton (1769-1820)]

&

James Martin Burkett (1841-1903)
& Family

Mary Elizabeth Wilton, born 1842 in Salem in Marion County, Illinois, was the fifth child of Thomas Wilton and Mary Alma Maddux. The family had made Marion County their permanent home shortly after 1840, following a move from the adjacent Clinton County, Illinois.

On August 7, 1861, Mary Elizabeth married James (John) Martin Burkett, son of Needham Burkett and Annis Pruett. Shortly after their marriage, in September 1861, John enlisted as a Private in the Union Army in Co. E of the 11th Infantry for service in the Civil War. After his first three months of service, he re-enlisted in Co. D of the US Veterans Volunteer Infantry and served until September 1865, when he was honorably discharged.

After John's military service, the family lived in Marion County, Illinois for awhile, where Mary and John had three children. The first child, William Franklin Burkett, was born 1865; the second child, Mary Annise Burkett, was born 1869; and, the third child, John Freedis Burkett, was born 1877. After Mary's father, Thomas Wilton, died in November 1867, Mary E. Burkett and John Burkett, her husband, were listed as heirs to the estate of Thomas Wilton, when a petition to sell land from the estate was filed in April 1868. Mary's brother, Joseph C. Wilton, was listed as the administrator of the estate.

In the 1880 Federal Census of Marion County, Illinois, J.M. Burkett was listed at age 38, with an occupation of farmer, along with his wife, Mary E. Burkett, age 38, and children, William Burkett, age 15, Mary A. Burkett, age 9, and John F. Burkett, age 3. About 1882, the family moved to Butler County, Missouri.

According to the Burkett Family Bible, Mary E. Burkett died 1898 at the Pike Slough Road, located in Butler County, Missouri, and Martin Burkett died January 14, 1903 in Poplar Bluff in Butler County, Missouri.

Family Group Sheet

Husband: James Martin Burkett

Born: 1841	in: Fayette Co., Illinois
Married: 07 Aug 1861	in: Edgewood, Effingham Co., Illinois
Died: 14 Jan 1903	in: Poplar Bluff, Butler Co., Missouri
Father: Needham Burkett	
Mother: Annis Prewett	

Wife: Mary Elizabeth Wilton

Born: Abt. 1842	in: Salem, Marion Co., Illinois
Died: 13 Aug 1898	in: Poplar Bluff, Butler Co., Missouri
Father: Thomas Wilton	
Mother: Mary Alma Maddux	

CHILDREN

1. M — Name: William Franklin Burkett
   - Born: 1865 — in: Foster Twp, Marion Co., Illinois
   - Died: 1896 — in: Poplar Bluff, Butler Co., Missouri
   - Married: 13 Oct 1887 — in: Poplar Bluff, Butler Co., Missouri
   - Spouse: Louisa Lydia Lyda Jane Humphries

2. F — Name: Mary Annise Burkett
   - Born: 27 Oct 1869 — in: Salem, Marion Co., Illinois
   - Died: 30 Apr 1912 — in: Poplar Bluff, Butler Co., Missouri
   - Married: 28 Sep 1887 — in: Poplar Bluff, Butler Co., Missouri
   - Spouse: Reuben Isaac Fletcher Humphries

3. M — Name: John Freedis Burkett
   - Born: 1877 — in: Salem, Marion Co., Illinois
   - Died: Bef. 1898 — in: Illinois

William Franklin Burkett (1865-1896)
[4th. Generation From Henry Wilton (1769-1820)]

&

Louisa Jane Humphries (1871-1936)
& Family

William Franklin Burkett, born 1865 in Marion County, Illinois, was the oldest child of James (John) Martin Burkett and Mary Elizabeth Wilton. William's early years were spent in Marion County, where his dad was a farmer. About 1882, the family moved to Butler County, Missouri.

On October 13, 1887, in Poplar Bluff in Butler County, Missouri, William married Louisa Jane Humphries, daughter of Reuben Aaron Humphries and Lucy O'Briant. The couple had two children, both born in Poplar Bluff. The first child, Dorothea Edith Burket, was born 1888; and, the second child, Elmer Franklin Burkett, was born September 22, 1890.

William Franklin Burkett died 1896 in Poplar Bluff, Missouri, and after William's death, Louisa (Lydia) remarried. Available records suggest that she was married about 7 more times after her first marriage to William. Louisa died April 9, 1936 in Poplar Bluff, Missouri.

Family Group Sheet

Husband: William Franklin Burkett	
Born: 1865	in: Foster Twp, Marion Co., Illinois
Married: 13 Oct 1887	in: Poplar Bluff, Butler Co., Missouri
Died: 1896	in: Poplar Bluff, Butler Co., Missouri
Father: James Martin Burkett	
Mother: Mary Elizabeth Wilton	

Wife: Louisa Jane Humphries	
Born: 09 May 1871	in: Salem, Marion Co., Illinois
Died: 09 Apr 1936	in: Poplar Bluff, Butler Co., Missouri
Father: Reuben Aaron Humphries	
Mother: Lucy O'Briant	

CHILDREN

1. F
   - Name: Dorothea Edith Burkett
   - Born: 1888 — in: Poplar Bluff, Butler Co., Missouri
   - Died: 1934 — in: Sacramento, California
   - Married: Unknown
   - Spouse: George Crowell
   - Married: Unknown
   - Spouse: Thomas S. Cordona

2. M
   - Name: Elmer Franklin Burkett
   - Born: 22 Sep 1890 — in: Poplar Bluff, Butler Co., Missouri
   - Died: 11 Jun 1969 — in: St. Louis Co., Missouri
   - Married: 24 Apr 1912 — in: Woodward Co., Oklahoma
   - Spouse: Elsie Marie Hall
   - Married: 01 Jul 1939 — in: Butler Co., Missouri
   - Spouse: Lucy Collins

WILLIAM FRANKILIN BURKETT Standard Pedigree Tree

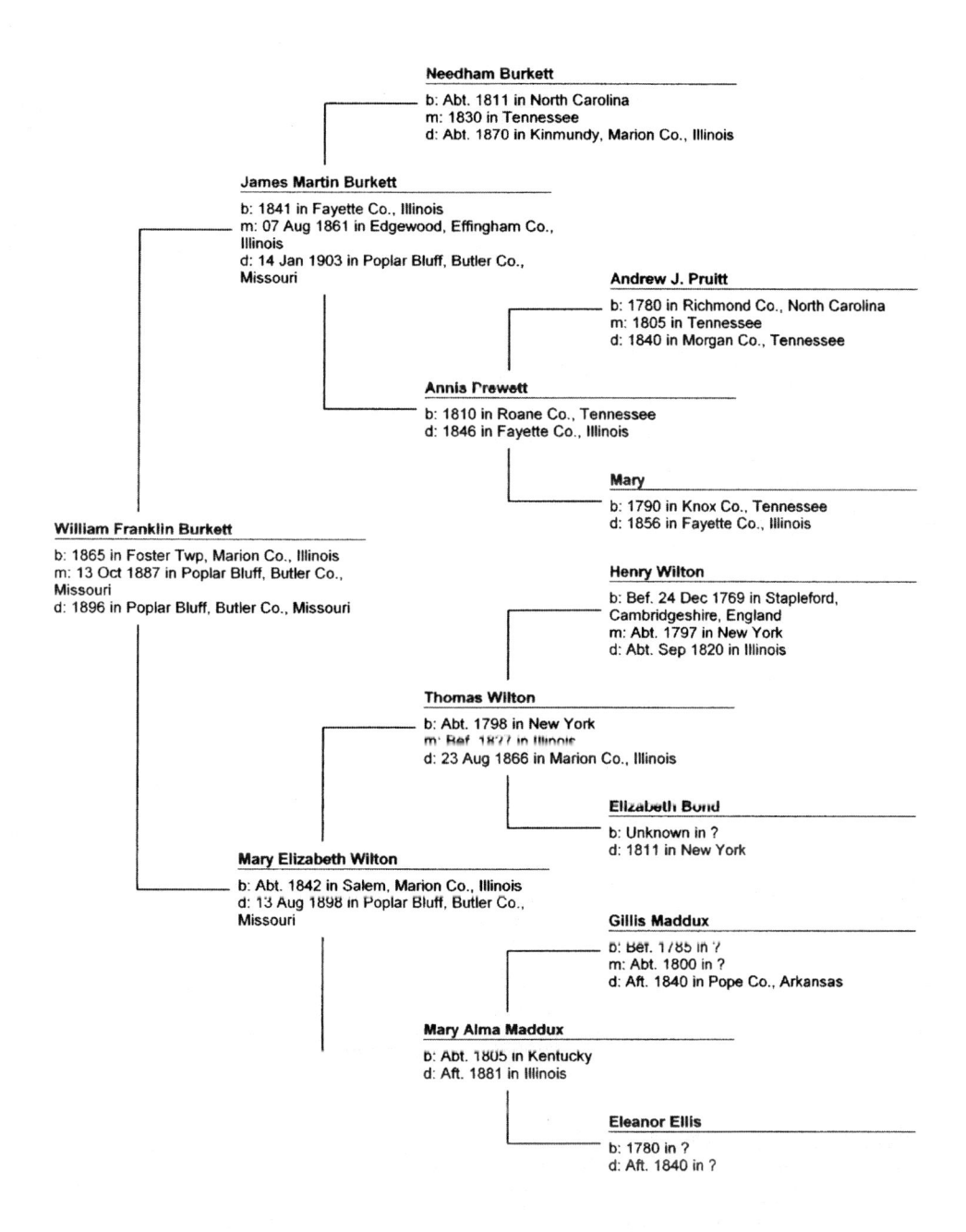

Needham Burkett
b: Abt. 1811 in North Carolina
m: 1830 in Tennessee
d: Abt. 1870 in Kinmundy, Marion Co., Illinois

James Martin Burkett
b: 1841 in Fayette Co., Illinois
m: 07 Aug 1861 in Edgewood, Effingham Co., Illinois
d: 14 Jan 1903 in Poplar Bluff, Butler Co., Missouri

Andrew J. Pruitt
b: 1780 in Richmond Co., North Carolina
m: 1805 in Tennessee
d: 1840 in Morgan Co., Tennessee

Annis Prewett
b: 1810 in Roane Co., Tennessee
d: 1846 in Fayette Co., Illinois

Mary
b: 1790 in Knox Co., Tennessee
d: 1856 in Fayette Co., Illinois

William Franklin Burkett
b: 1865 in Foster Twp, Marion Co., Illinois
m: 13 Oct 1887 in Poplar Bluff, Butler Co., Missouri
d: 1896 in Poplar Bluff, Butler Co., Missouri

Henry Wilton
b: Bef. 24 Dec 1769 in Stapleford, Cambridgeshire, England
m: Abt. 1797 in New York
d: Abt. Sep 1820 in Illinois

Thomas Wilton
b: Abt. 1798 in New York
m: Bef. 1822 in Illinois
d: 23 Aug 1866 in Marion Co., Illinois

Elizabeth Bond
b: Unknown in ?
d: 1811 in New York

Mary Elizabeth Wilton
b: Abt. 1842 in Salem, Marion Co., Illinois
d: 13 Aug 1898 in Poplar Bluff, Butler Co., Missouri

Gillis Maddux
b: Bef. 1785 in ?
m: Abt. 1800 in ?
d: Aft. 1840 in Pope Co., Arkansas

Mary Alma Maddux
b: Abt. 1805 in Kentucky
d: Aft. 1881 in Illinois

Eleanor Ellis
b: 1780 in ?
d: Aft. 1840 in ?

Notes: This Tree also applies to the other children of James Martin Burkett & Mary Elizabeth Wilton: Mary Annise Burkett and John Freedis Burkett.

LOUISA JANE HUMPHRIES Standard Pedigree Tree

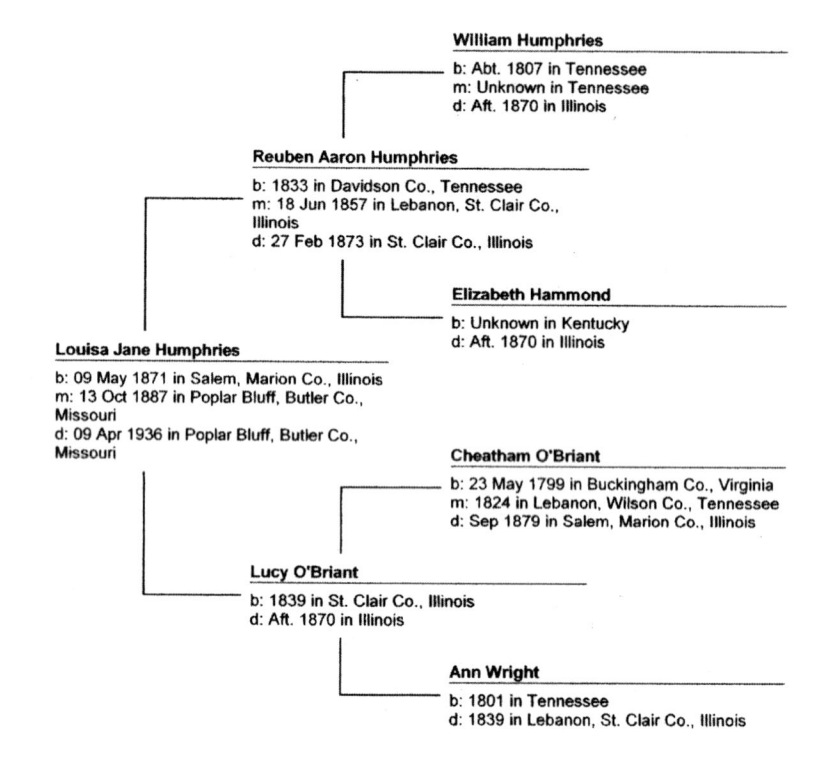

Louisa Jane Humphries
b: 09 May 1871 in Salem, Marion Co., Illinois
m: 13 Oct 1887 in Poplar Bluff, Butler Co., Missouri
d: 09 Apr 1936 in Poplar Bluff, Butler Co., Missouri

- **Reuben Aaron Humphries**
  b: 1833 in Davidson Co., Tennessee
  m: 18 Jun 1857 in Lebanon, St. Clair Co., Illinois
  d: 27 Feb 1873 in St. Clair Co., Illinois

  - **William Humphries**
    b: Abt. 1807 in Tennessee
    m: Unknown in Tennessee
    d: Aft. 1870 in Illinois

  - **Elizabeth Hammond**
    b: Unknown in Kentucky
    d: Aft. 1870 in Illinois

- **Lucy O'Briant**
  b: 1839 in St. Clair Co., Illinois
  d: Aft. 1870 in Illinois

  - **Cheatham O'Briant**
    b: 23 May 1799 in Buckingham Co., Virginia
    m: 1824 in Lebanon, Wilson Co., Tennessee
    d: Sep 1879 in Salem, Marion Co., Illinois

  - **Ann Wright**
    b: 1801 in Tennessee
    d: 1839 in Lebanon, St. Clair Co., Illinois

Dorothea Edith Burkett (1888-1934)
[5th. Generation from Henry Wilton (1769-1820)]

&

George Crowell
& Family

&

Thomas S. Cordona
& Family

Family Group Sheet

Husband: George Crowell

Born: Unknown
Married: Unknown
Died: 1914

Wife: Dorothea Edith Burkett

Born: 1888   in: Poplar Bluff, Butler Co., Missouri
Died: 1934   in: Sacramento, California
Father: William Franklin Burkett
Mother: Louisa Jane Humphries
Other Spouses: Thomas S. Cordona

Family Group Sheet

Husband: Thomas S. Cordona

Born: Abt. 1880   in: Italy
Married: Unknown

Wife: Dorothea Edith Burkett

Born: 1888   in: Poplar Bluff, Butler Co., Missouri
Died: 1934   in: Sacramento, California
Father: William Franklin Burkett
Mother: Louisa Jane Humphries
Other Spouses: George Crowell

CHILDREN

1 F   Name: Jeroma Cordona
       Born: Unknown

2 M   Name: Thomas S. Jr. Cordona
       Born: Unknown

DOROTHEA EDITH BURKETT Standard Pedigree Tree

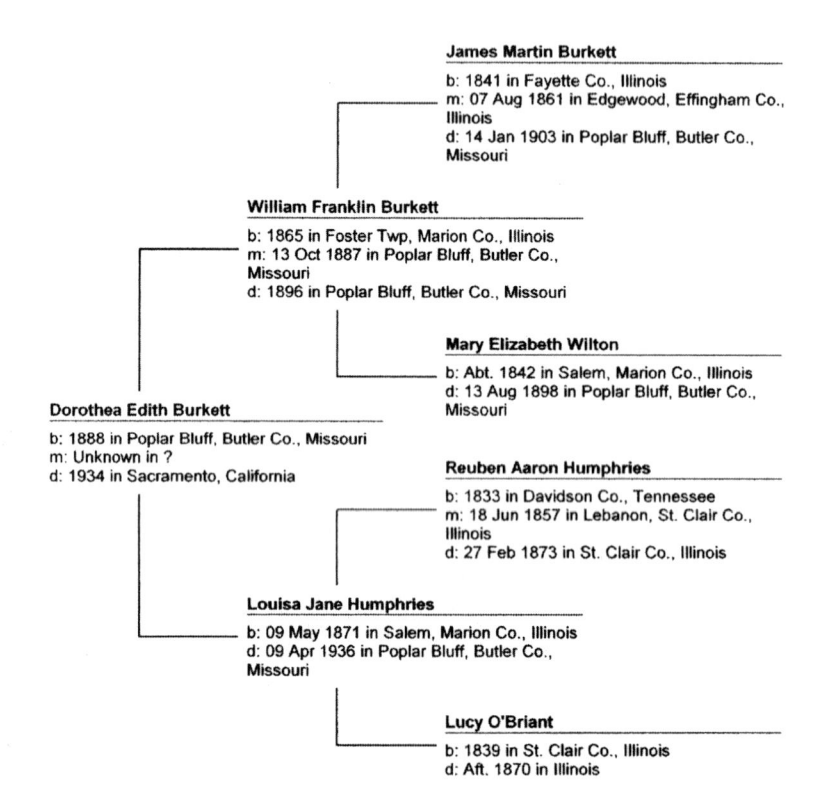

James Martin Burkett
b: 1841 in Fayette Co., Illinois
m: 07 Aug 1861 in Edgewood, Effingham Co., Illinois
d: 14 Jan 1903 in Poplar Bluff, Butler Co., Missouri

William Franklin Burkett
b: 1865 in Foster Twp, Marion Co., Illinois
m: 13 Oct 1887 in Poplar Bluff, Butler Co., Missouri
d: 1896 in Poplar Bluff, Butler Co., Missouri

Mary Elizabeth Wilton
b: Abt. 1842 in Salem, Marion Co., Illinois
d: 13 Aug 1898 in Poplar Bluff, Butler Co., Missouri

Dorothea Edith Burkett
b: 1888 in Poplar Bluff, Butler Co., Missouri
m: Unknown in ?
d: 1934 in Sacramento, California

Reuben Aaron Humphries
b: 1833 in Davidson Co., Tennessee
m: 18 Jun 1857 in Lebanon, St. Clair Co., Illinois
d: 27 Feb 1873 in St. Clair Co., Illinois

Louisa Jane Humphries
b: 09 May 1871 in Salem, Marion Co., Illinois
d: 09 Apr 1936 in Poplar Bluff, Butler Co., Missouri

Lucy O'Briant
b: 1839 in St. Clair Co., Illinois
d: Aft. 1870 in Illinois

Notes: This Tree also applies to the other child of William Franklin Burkett & Louise Jane Humphries: Elmer Franklin Burkett.

Elmer Franklin Burkett (1890-1969)
[5th. Generation from Henry Wilton (1769-1820)]

&

Elsie Marie Hall (1895-1937)
& Family

&

Lucy Collins (1911-1968)
& Family

Elmer Franklin Burkett was the second and last child of William Franklin Burkett and Louisa Jane Humphries. He was born September 22, 1890 in Poplar Bluff in Butler County, Missouri, where he spent his formative years.

After his father died in 1896, his mother remarried several times, and his whereabouts was sketchy until about 1912, when he was located in Oklahoma. On April 24, 1912, in Woodward County, Oklahoma, Elmer married Elsie Marie Hall, the daughter of Eli Thomas Hall and Isa Dora Hollcroft. Elmer and Elsie had their first three children while living in Oklahoma. Their first child, Amos Franklin Burkett, was born March 31, 1913; their second child, Mildred Irene Burkett, was born January 10, 1915; and, their third child, Dorothea Edith Burkett, who was given the same name as Elmer's sister, was born 1917.

Sometime shortly after 1917, the family relocated to Missouri. In the 1920 Federal Census of Ripley County, Missouri, Elmer Burkett was listed at age 28, with an occupation of saw mill laborer, along with his wife, Elsie Burkett, age 24, and their first three children. By June 1921, the family was located near Neelyville in Butler County, Missouri, where their fourth child, Helen Anna

Burkett, was born. From 1921 thru 1935, Elmer and Elsie had 7 children, all born in Neelyville, Missouri. Together with the three children born in Oklahoma, the couple had a total of 10 children. Elmer's first wife, Elsie, died on February 17, 1937 in Neelyville, Missouri, and she was buried at the Hvam Cemetery in Poplar Bluff, Missouri.

On July 1, 1939, Elmer remarried, to Lucy Collins, a widow Anderson, and daughter of Frank and Lula Collins, also residents of Missouri. Apparently, Elmer and Lucy did not have any additional children, and Lucy died July 1968 in Butler County, Missouri. Elmer Franklin Burkett died June 11, 1969 in St. Louis County, Missouri and was buried at the Hvam Cemetery in Poplar Bluff, Missouri.

Family Group Sheet

Husband: Elmer Franklin Burkett

Born: 22 Sep 1890 in: Poplar Bluff, Butler Co., Missouri
Married: 24 Apr 1912 in: Woodward Co., Oklahoma
Died: 11 Jun 1969 in: St. Louis Co., Missouri
Father: William Franklin Burkett
Mother: Louisa Jane Humphries
Other Spouses: Lucy Collins

Wife: Elsie Marie Hall

Born: 14 Dec 1895 in: Adair Co., Missouri
Died: 17 Feb 1937 in: Neelyville, Butler Co., Missouri
Father: Eli Thomas Hall
Mother: Isa Dora Hollcroft

CHILDREN

1 M
Name: Amos Franklin Burkett
Born: 31 Mar 1913 in: Oklahoma
Died: 13 Apr 1959 in: Missouri
Married: 01 Jul 1933 in: Butler Co., Missouri
Spouse: Allie Caroline Sanders

2 F
Name: Mildred Irene Burkett
Born: 10 Jan 1915 in: Oklahoma
Died: 03 May 1982 in: St. Louis Co., Missouri
Married: 17 Nov 1931 in: Butler Co., Missouri
Spouse: Roy Morgan

3 F
Name: Dorothea Edith Burkett
Born: 1917 in: Oklahoma
Married: Unknown
Spouse: Ira Johnson

4 F
Name: Helen Anna Burkett
Born: 02 Jun 1921 in: Neelyville, Butler Co., Missouri
Died: 09 Feb 1987 in: Butler Co., Missouri
Married: 26 Dec 1939 in: Poplar Bluff, Butler Co., Missouri
Spouse: Thomas Benjamin Gowen

5 M
Name: Raymond Isaac Burkett
Born: 02 Aug 1923 in: Neelyville, Butler Co., Missouri
Died: 10 Nov 1997 in: Jefferson Co., Missouri
Married: Unknown
Spouse: Alice Miller

6 F
Name: Mary Eileen Burkett
Born: 09 Oct 1925 in: Neelyville, Butler Co., Missouri
Died: 08 Jul 1996 in: Missouri
Married: Unknown
Spouse: Claud Howard Stogsdill

7 F
Name: Jeroma Lee Burkett
Born: 22 Feb 1928 in: Neelyville, Butler Co., Missouri
Died: 13 Jun 2004 in: St. Louis Co., Missouri
Married: Aft. 1942
Spouse: Wendell B. Herr

8 F
Name: Jane Lucille Burkett
Born: 13 Jan 1930 in: Neelyville, Butler Co., Missouri
Died: 24 May 1976 in: Belleville, St. Clair Co., Illinois
Married: 01 Mar 1947
Spouse: Odis Stogsdill

9 F
Name: Ione Maxine Burkett
Born: 1934 in: Neelyville, Butler Co., Missouri
Married: Unknown
Spouse: Herbert Lee Chattam

10 M
Name: Elmer Leroy Burkett
Born: 21 Aug 1935 in: Neelyville, Butler Co., Missouri
Died: 16 Aug 1999 in: Missouri
Married: Unknown
Spouse: Kathy
Married: Unknown
Spouse: Ardith Easton

ELSIE MARIE HALL Standard Pedigree Tree

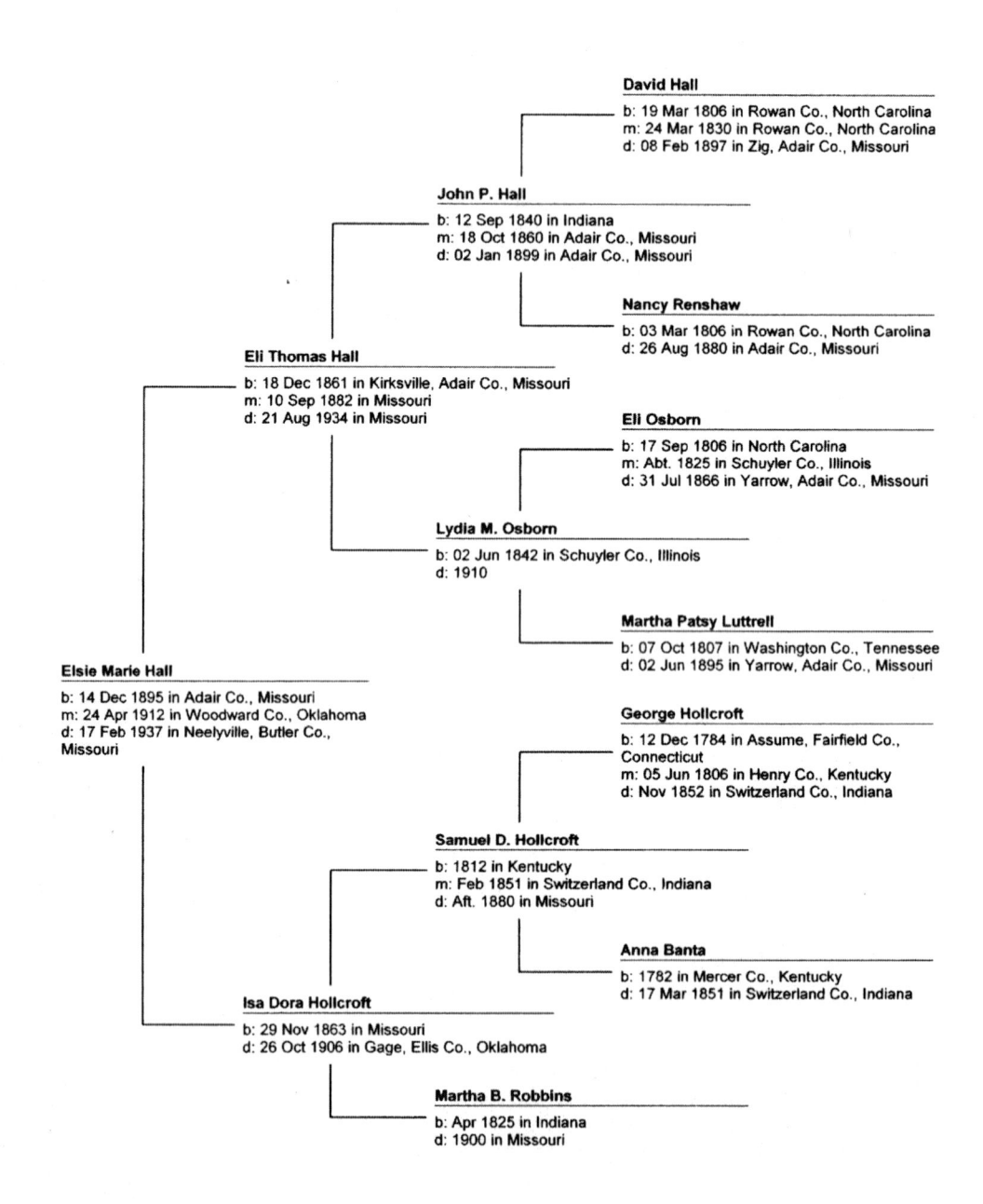

Elsie Marie Hall
b: 14 Dec 1895 in Adair Co., Missouri
m: 24 Apr 1912 in Woodward Co., Oklahoma
d: 17 Feb 1937 in Neelyville, Butler Co., Missouri

- **Eli Thomas Hall**
  b: 18 Dec 1861 in Kirksville, Adair Co., Missouri
  m: 10 Sep 1882 in Missouri
  d: 21 Aug 1934 in Missouri

  - **John P. Hall**
    b: 12 Sep 1840 in Indiana
    m: 18 Oct 1860 in Adair Co., Missouri
    d: 02 Jan 1899 in Adair Co., Missouri

    - **David Hall**
      b: 19 Mar 1806 in Rowan Co., North Carolina
      m: 24 Mar 1830 in Rowan Co., North Carolina
      d: 08 Feb 1897 in Zig, Adair Co., Missouri

    - **Nancy Renshaw**
      b: 03 Mar 1806 in Rowan Co., North Carolina
      d: 26 Aug 1880 in Adair Co., Missouri

  - **Lydia M. Osborn**
    b: 02 Jun 1842 in Schuyler Co., Illinois
    d: 1910

    - **Eli Osborn**
      b: 17 Sep 1806 in North Carolina
      m: Abt. 1825 in Schuyler Co., Illinois
      d: 31 Jul 1866 in Yarrow, Adair Co., Missouri

    - **Martha Patsy Luttrell**
      b: 07 Oct 1807 in Washington Co., Tennessee
      d: 02 Jun 1895 in Yarrow, Adair Co., Missouri

- **Isa Dora Hollcroft**
  b: 29 Nov 1863 in Missouri
  d: 26 Oct 1906 in Gage, Ellis Co., Oklahoma

  - **Samuel D. Hollcroft**
    b: 1812 in Kentucky
    m: Feb 1851 in Switzerland Co., Indiana
    d: Aft. 1880 in Missouri

    - **George Hollcroft**
      b: 12 Dec 1784 in Assume, Fairfield Co., Connecticut
      m: 05 Jun 1806 in Henry Co., Kentucky
      d: Nov 1852 in Switzerland Co., Indiana

    - **Anna Banta**
      b: 1782 in Mercer Co., Kentucky
      d: 17 Mar 1851 in Switzerland Co., Indiana

  - **Martha B. Robbins**
    b: Apr 1825 in Indiana
    d: 1900 in Missouri

Amos Franklin Burkett (1913-1959)
[6th. Generation From Henry Wilton (1769-1820)]

&

Allie Caroline Sanders (1917-1998)
& Family

Family Group Sheet

Husband: Amos Franklin Burkett

Born: 31 Mar 1913	in: Oklahoma
Married: 01 Jul 1933	in: Butler Co., Missouri
Died: 13 Apr 1959	in: Missouri
Father: Elmer Franklin Burkett	
Mother: Elsie Marie Hall	

Wife: Allie Caroline Sanders

Born: 1917	in: Missouri
Died: 1998	
Father: Samuel J. Sanders	
Mother: Mary	

CHILDREN

1. M
   - Name: Billy Gene Burkett
   - Born: 07 Oct 1934 — in: Butler Co., Missouri
   - Died: 27 May 1998 — in: St. Louis Co., Missouri
   - Married: 28 Jul 1952 — in: Berkeley, St. Louis Co., Missouri
   - Spouse: Darlene Joy Lewis

2. M
   - Name: Arthur Franklin Burkett
   - Born: Dec 1941 — in: Missouri
   - Married: Abt. 1962 — in: Missouri
   - Spouse: Jo Ann Sparks

AMOS FRANKLIN BURKETT Standard Pedigree Tree

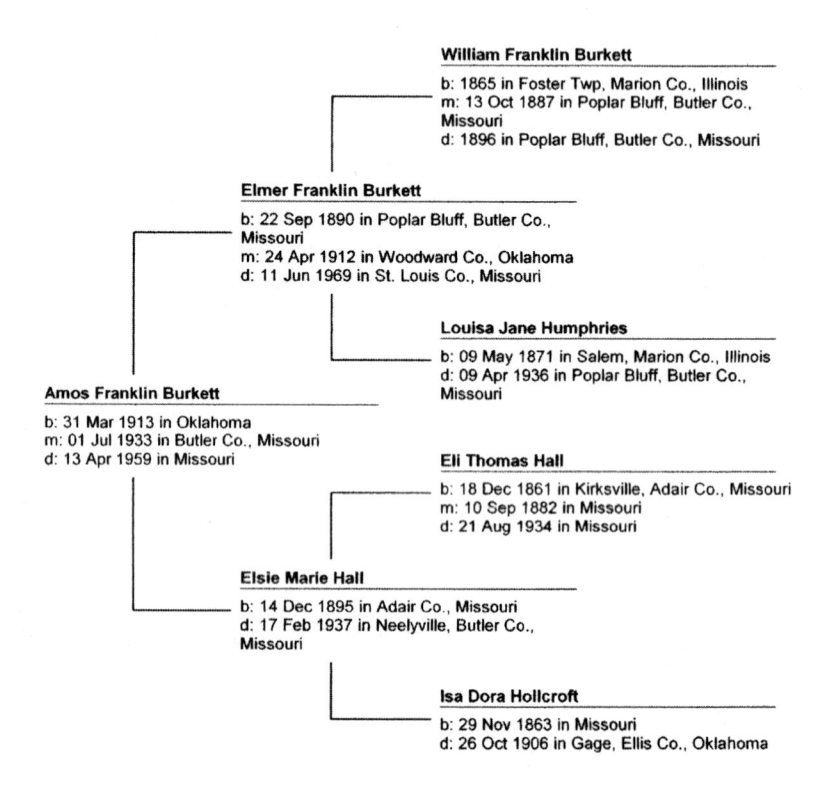

Amos Franklin Burkett
b: 31 Mar 1913 in Oklahoma
m: 01 Jul 1933 in Butler Co., Missouri
d: 13 Apr 1959 in Missouri

- **Elmer Franklin Burkett**
  b: 22 Sep 1890 in Poplar Bluff, Butler Co., Missouri
  m: 24 Apr 1912 in Woodward Co., Oklahoma
  d: 11 Jun 1969 in St. Louis Co., Missouri
  - **William Franklin Burkett**
    b: 1865 in Foster Twp, Marion Co., Illinois
    m: 13 Oct 1887 in Poplar Bluff, Butler Co., Missouri
    d: 1896 in Poplar Bluff, Butler Co., Missouri
  - **Louisa Jane Humphries**
    b: 09 May 1871 in Salem, Marion Co., Illinois
    d: 09 Apr 1936 in Poplar Bluff, Butler Co., Missouri

- **Elsie Marie Hall**
  b: 14 Dec 1895 in Adair Co., Missouri
  d: 17 Feb 1937 in Neelyville, Butler Co., Missouri
  - **Eli Thomas Hall**
    b: 18 Dec 1861 in Kirksville, Adair Co., Missouri
    m: 10 Sep 1882 in Missouri
    d: 21 Aug 1934 in Missouri
  - **Isa Dora Hollcroft**
    b: 29 Nov 1863 in Missouri
    d: 26 Oct 1906 in Gage, Ellis Co., Oklahoma

Notes: This Tree also applies to the other children of Elmer F. Burkett & Elsie M. Hall: Mildred I. Burkett, Dorothea E. Burkett, Helen A. Burkett, Raymond I. Burkett, Mary E. Burkett, Jeroma Burkett, Jane Burkett, Ione Burkett, and Elmer L. Burkett.

Mildred Irene Burkett (1915-1982)
[6th. Generation From Henry Wilton (1769-1820)]

&

Roy Morgan (1910~1997)
& Family

Family Group Sheet

Husband: Roy Morgan	
Born: Abt. 1910	
Married: 17 Nov 1931	in: Butler Co., Missouri
Died: Abt. 1997	

Wife: Mildred Irene Burkett	
Born: 10 Jan 1915	in: Oklahoma
Died: 03 May 1982	in: St. Louis Co., Missouri
Father: Elmer Franklin Burkett	
Mother: Elsie Marie Hall	

CHILDREN

1. M
   - Name: Kelly Dale Morgan
   - Born: Unknown
   - Married: Unknown
   - Spouse: Edith Hanley

2. F
   - Name: Ruby Irene Morgan
   - Born: Unknown
   - Married: Unknown
   - Spouse: Richard Ebersahl

3. F
   - Name: Margaret Elsie Morgan
   - Born: Unknown
   - Married: Unknown
   - Spouse: Delbert Lee Woods

4. F
   - Name: Agnes Rosemary Morgan
   - Born: Unknown
   - Married: Unknown
   - Spouse: Charles Brimm

Dorothea Edith Burkett (1917-   )
[6th. Generation From Henry Wilton (1769-1820)]

&

Ira Johnson (1915-1995)
& Family

Family Group Sheet

Husband: Ira Johnson
Born: 1915 Married: Unknown Died: 1995

Wife: Dorothea Edith Burkett
Born: 1917   in: Oklahoma Father: Elmer Franklin Burkett Mother: Elsie Marie Hall

	CHILDREN
1 M	Name: Jimmy Johnson Born: Unknown Married: Unknown Spouse: Sandra Bennett
2 M	Name: Robert Gene Johnson Born: Unknown Married: Unknown Spouse: Darlene Downs
3 F	Name: Maryanne Johnson Born: Unknown Married: Unknown Spouse: Larry Cowan

Helen Anna Burkett (1921-1987)
[6th. Generation From Henry Wilton (1769-1820)]

&

Thomas Benjamin Gowen (1916-2001)
& Family

Family Group Sheet

Husband: Thomas Benjamin Gowen	
Born: 13 Aug 1916	in: Butler Co., Missouri
Married: 26 Dec 1939	in: Poplar Bluff, Butler Co., Missouri
Died: 13 Oct 2001	in: Butler Co., Missouri
Father: James Burton Gowen	
Mother: Ethel Ryan	

Wife: Helen Anna Burkett	
Born: 02 Jun 1921	in: Neelyville, Butler Co., Missouri
Died: 09 Feb 1987	in: Butler Co., Missouri
Father: Elmer Franklin Burkett	
Mother: Elsie Marie Hall	

CHILDREN

1. M
   - Name: Vernon Dean Gowen
   - Born: 17 Dec 1940   in: Missouri
   - Died: 18 Feb 1977   in: Butler Co., Missouri
   - Married: Unknown
   - Spouse: Carlene

THOMAS BENJAMIN GOWEN Standard Pedigree Tree

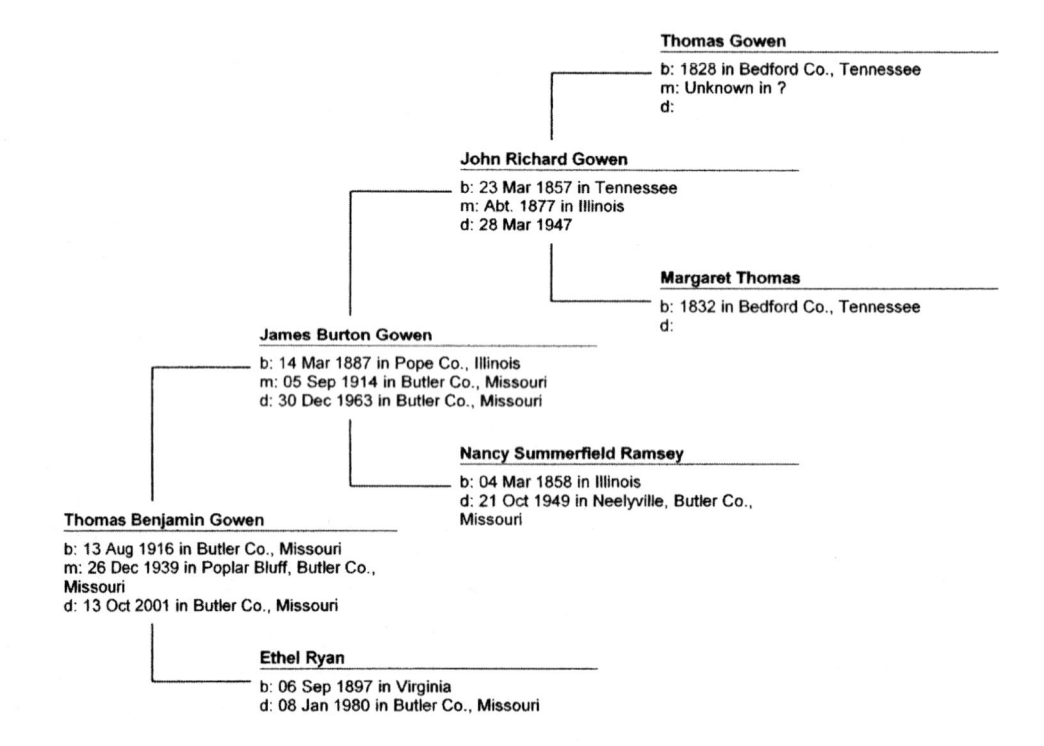

Thomas Gowen
b: 1828 in Bedford Co., Tennessee
m: Unknown in ?
d:

John Richard Gowen
b: 23 Mar 1857 in Tennessee
m: Abt. 1877 in Illinois
d: 28 Mar 1947

Margaret Thomas
b: 1832 in Bedford Co., Tennessee
d:

James Burton Gowen
b: 14 Mar 1887 in Pope Co., Illinois
m: 05 Sep 1914 in Butler Co., Missouri
d: 30 Dec 1963 in Butler Co., Missouri

Nancy Summerfield Ramsey
b: 04 Mar 1858 in Illinois
d: 21 Oct 1949 in Neelyville, Butler Co., Missouri

Thomas Benjamin Gowen
b: 13 Aug 1916 in Butler Co., Missouri
m: 26 Dec 1939 in Poplar Bluff, Butler Co., Missouri
d: 13 Oct 2001 in Butler Co., Missouri

Ethel Ryan
b: 06 Sep 1897 in Virginia
d: 08 Jan 1980 in Butler Co., Missouri

Raymond Isaac Burkett (1923-1997)
[6th. Generation From Henry Wilton (1769-1820)]

&

Alice Miller
& Family

Family Group Sheet

Husband: Raymond Isaac Burkett

Born: 02 Aug 1923 in: Neelyville, Butler Co., Missouri
Married: Unknown
Died: 10 Nov 1997 in: Jefferson Co., Missouri
Father: Elmer Franklin Burkett
Mother: Elsie Marie Hall

Wife: Alice Miller

Born: 1925
Died: 1998

CHILDREN

1 M
Name: Johny Burkett
Born: Unknown
Married: Unknown
Spouse: Leah

2 M
Name: Gary Burkett
Born: 1954
Died: 1977
Married: Unknown
Spouse: Mrs. G. Burkett

3 M
Name: Curtis Burkett
Born: 1959
Died: 1978

Mary Eileen Burkett (1925-1996)
[6th. Generation From Henry Wilton (1769-1820)]

&

Claud Howard Stogsdill (1923-1992)
& Family

Family Group Sheet

Husband: Claud Howard Stogsdill	
Born: 21 Sep 1923	
Married: Unknown	
Died: 08 Mar 1992	

Wife: Mary Eileen Burkett	
Born: 09 Oct 1925	in: Neelyville, Butler Co., Missouri
Died: 08 Jul 1996	in: Missouri
Father: Elmer Franklin Burkett	
Mother: Elsie Marie Hall	

	CHILDREN
1 M	Name: Larry Dale Stogsdill Born: Unknown Married: Unknown Spouse: Peggy Mollencamp
2 F	Name: Terry Marie Stogsdill Born: Unknown Married: Unknown Spouse: Stan Steen Married: Unknown Spouse: Terry Nelson Married: Unknown Spouse: Byron Allen
3 F	Name: Claudia Stogsdill Born: Unknown Married: Unknown Spouse: Larry Sharp

Jeroma Lee Burkett (1928-2004)
[6th. Generation From Henry Wilton (1769-1820)]

&

Wendell B. Herr (1918-1995)
& Family

Family Group Sheet

Husband: Wendell B. Herr	
Born: 10 Apr 1918	in: Illinois
Married: Aft. 1942	
Died: 11 May 1995	in: Missouri
Wife: Jeroma Lee Burkett	
Born: 22 Feb 1928	in: Neelyville, Butler Co., Missouri
Died: 13 Jun 2004	in: St. Louis Co., Missouri
Father: Elmer Franklin Burkett	
Mother: Elsie Marie Hall	

Jane Lucille Burkett (1930-1976)
[6th. Generation From Henry Wilton (1769-1820)]

&

Odis Stogsdill (1925-1973)
& Family

Family Group Sheet

Husband: Odis Stogsdill	
Born: 09 Oct 1925	in: Powhatan, Lawrence Co., Arkansas
Married: 01 Mar 1947	
Died: 22 Oct 1973	in: Harrisonville, Monroe Co., Illinois
Other Spouses: Betty Ellis Call, Wilma Hines Motes	

Wife: Jane Lucille Burkett	
Born: 13 Jan 1930	in: Neelyville, Butler Co., Missouri
Died: 24 May 1976	in: Belleville, St. Clair Co., Illinois
Father: Elmer Franklin Burkett	
Mother: Elsie Marie Hall	

CHILDREN

1 M
- Name: Leonard Dale Stogsdill
- Born: 1948
- Married: 1968 in: Nebraska
- Spouse: Sandra Lund

2 M
- Name: Michael James Stogsdill
- Born: 1950
- Married: 1968 in: St. Clair Co., Illinois
- Spouse: Judy A. Melton
- Married: 17 Nov 1995
- Spouse: Donna Hufendick

3 F
- Name: Brenda Jane Stogsdill
- Born: 28 Jun 1952 in: St. Louis, Missouri
- Married: 19 Mar 1970 in: St. Clair Co., Illinois
- Spouse: Joe William Starwalt
- Married: Unknown
- Spouse: Gary Michael Sr. Rodgers

Ione Maxine Burkett (1934-   )
[6th. Generation From Henry Wilton (1769-1820)]

&

Herbert Lee Chattam
& Family

Family Group Sheet

Husband: Herbert Lee Chattam

Born: Unknown
Married: Unknown

Wife: Ione Maxine Burkett

Born: 1934   in: Neelyville, Butler Co., Missouri
Father: Elmer Franklin Burkett
Mother: Elsie Marie Hall

CHILDREN

#		
1 M	Name: Ronald Duane Chattam	Born: Unknown
2 M	Name: Garry Lee Chattam	Born: Unknown
3 F	Name: Linda Kathleen Chattam	Born: Unknown

Elmer Leroy Burkett (1935-1999)
[6th. Generation From Henry Wilton (1769-1820)]

&

Ardith Easton
& Family

&

Kathy
& Family

Family Group Sheet

Husband: Elmer Leroy Burkett

Born: 21 Aug 1935   in: Neelyville, Butler Co., Missouri
Married: Unknown
Died: 16 Aug 1999   in: Missouri
Father: Elmer Franklin Burkett
Mother: Elsie Marie Hall
    Other Spouses: Kathy

Wife: Ardith Easton

Born: Unknown

CHILDREN

1 M   Name: John Franklin Burkett
       Born: Unknown

2 M   Name: Robert Gene Burkett
       Born: Unknown

Family Group Sheet

Husband: Elmer Leroy Burkett

Born: 21 Aug 1935   in: Neelyville, Butler Co., Missouri
Married: Unknown
Died: 16 Aug 1999   in: Missouri
Father: Elmer Franklin Burkett
Mother: Elsie Marie Hall
    Other Spouses: Ardith Easton

Wife: Kathy

Born: Unknown

CHILDREN

1 M   Name: Marc Burkett
       Born: Unknown

Mary Annise Burkett (1869-1912)
[4th. Generation from Henry Wilton (1769-1820)]

&

Reuben Isaac Fletcher Humphries (1866-1940)
& Family

Mary Annise (Mollie) Burkett was born October 27, 1869 in Salem in Marion County, Illinois. She was the second child of James (John) Martin Burkett and Mary Elizabeth Wilton. After his discharge from the Civil War in 1865, John had settled the family in Marion County, Illinois. About 1882, the family relocated to Butler County, Missouri.

On September 28, 1887, in Poplar Bluff in Butler County, Missouri, Mollie married Reuben Isaac Fletcher Humphries, son of Reuben Aaron Humphries and Lucy O'Briant. Mollie and Reuben had an additional family connection, in that Mollie's brother, William Franklin Burkett, married Reuben's sister, Louisa Jane Humphries. Between 1889 and 1908, while living in Poplar Bluff, Missouri, Mollie and Reuben had at least seven children.

Mollie died April 30, 1912 in Poplar Bluff, Missouri, and she was buried at the Black River Cemetery in Poplar Bluff. Reuben continued to raise the family and remarried in July 1913 to Polena (Kellogg) Haney. Reuben and Lena remained in the area and had one daughter of their own, Mary Edith Humphries, born February 19, 1917 in Poplar Bluff.

Evidence suggests that Reuben and Lena were separated sometime about 1925. Reuben was married a third time, to Mary Russell, who was quite a number of years younger, on September 5, 1925 in Butler County, Missouri. Available information also suggests that Reuben and Lena were later remarried, and in the 1930

Federal Census of Butler County, Missouri, Isaac Humphries was again listed at age 63, along with wife, Lena Humphries, age 48, and daughter, Mary E. Humphries, age 13. In the 1930 Federal Census of Butler County, living nearby were the families of Reuben's sons, Jesse Humphries, Charles Humphries, and Otto Humphries.

Reuben died February 9, 1940 in Poplar Bluff, Missouri, and he was buried in the Black River Cemetery in Poplar Bluff.

Family Group Sheet

Husband: Reuben Isaac Fletcher Humphries

- Born: 14 Oct 1866 in: Salem, Marion Co., Illinois
- Married: 28 Sep 1887 in: Poplar Bluff, Butler Co., Missouri
- Died: 09 Feb 1940 in: Poplar Bluff, Butler Co., Missouri
- Father: Reuben Aaron Humphries
- Mother: Lucy O'Briant
- Other Spouses: Polena G. Kellogg, Mary Russell

Wife: Mary Annise Burkett

- Born: 27 Oct 1869 in: Salem, Marion Co., Illinois
- Died: 30 Apr 1912 in: Poplar Bluff, Butler Co., Missouri
- Father: James Martin Burkett
- Mother: Mary Elizabeth Wilton

CHILDREN

1 M
- Name: Jesse Martin Humphries
- Born: 18 Jun 1889 in: Poplar Bluff, Butler Co., Missouri
- Died: Jul 1968 in: Poplar Bluff, Butler Co., Missouri
- Married: 26 Jun 1919 in: Poplar Bluff, Butler Co., Missouri
- Spouse: Edith Lynn

2 M
- Name: Charles William Humphries
- Born: 04 Jun 1891 in: Poplar Bluff, Butler Co., Missouri
- Died: 18 Apr 1973 in: Poplar Bluff, Butler Co., Missouri
- Married: 02 Sep 1916 in: Poplar Bluff, Butler Co., Missouri
- Spouse: Josephine Deckard
- Married: 04 Mar 1921 in: Doniphan, Ripley Co., Missouri
- Spouse: Frances Anna Bescheinen

3 M
- Name: Ben Humphries
- Born: 1895 in: Poplar Bluff, Butler Co., Missouri
- Died: 1941 in: Sikeston, Missouri
- Married: 10 Jan 1918 in: Butler Co., Missouri
- Spouse: Jennie May Hicks

4 M
- Name: James Humphries
- Born: 1901 in: Poplar Bluff, Butler Co., Missouri
- Died: 1970
- Married: 18 Oct 1930 in: Poplar Bluff, Butler Co., Missouri
- Spouse: Edith Reed

5 M
- Name: Otto Franklin Humphries
- Born: 27 Mar 1902 in: Poplar Bluff, Butler Co., Missouri
- Died: 16 Jun 1965 in: Camden, Kent Co., Delaware
- Married: 12 Jun 1929 in: Poplar Bluff, Butler Co., Missouri
- Spouse: Mary Amstutz

6 M
- Name: Issac F. Humphries
- Born: 28 Apr 1905 in: Poplar Bluff, Butler Co., Missouri
- Died: 26 Apr 1970 in: Baker Co., Oregon
- Married: 07 Feb 1925 in: Butler Co., Missouri
- Spouse: Ruby May Fuller

7 M
- Name: Raymond Humphries
- Born: 05 Jun 1908 in: Poplar Bluff, Butler Co., Missouri
- Died: Feb 1975 in: St. Louis Co., Missouri
- Married: 26 Jan 1929 in: Butler Co., Missouri
- Spouse: LaNelle Sanders

REUBEN ISAAC FLETCHER HUMPHRIES Standard Pedigree Tree

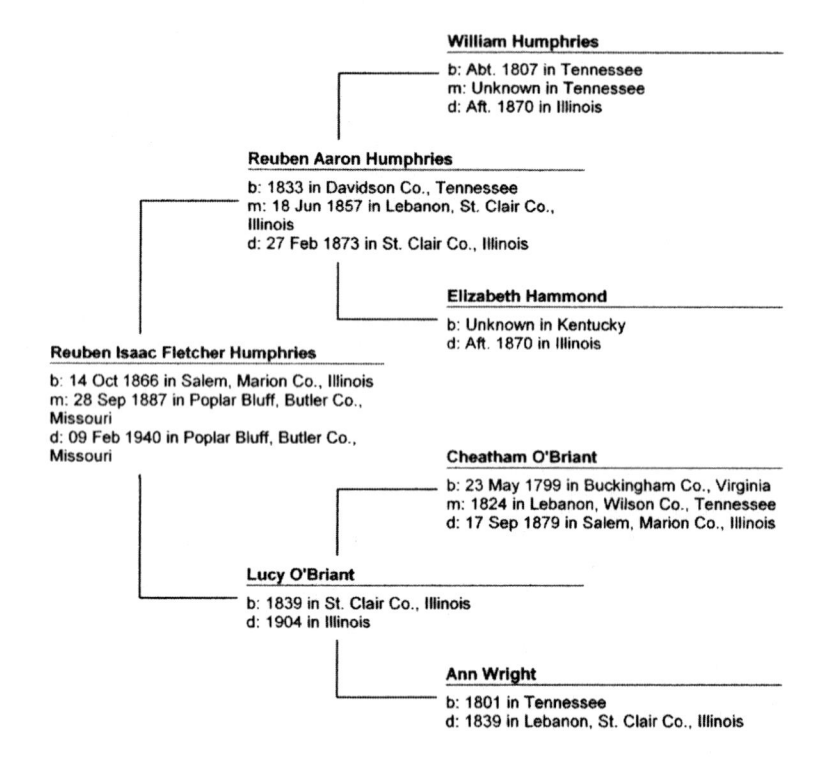

Reuben Isaac Fletcher Humphries
b: 14 Oct 1866 in Salem, Marion Co., Illinois
m: 28 Sep 1887 in Poplar Bluff, Butler Co., Missouri
d: 09 Feb 1940 in Poplar Bluff, Butler Co., Missouri

- **Reuben Aaron Humphries**
  b: 1833 in Davidson Co., Tennessee
  m: 18 Jun 1857 in Lebanon, St. Clair Co., Illinois
  d: 27 Feb 1873 in St. Clair Co., Illinois
  - **William Humphries**
    b: Abt. 1807 in Tennessee
    m: Unknown in Tennessee
    d: Aft. 1870 in Illinois
  - **Elizabeth Hammond**
    b: Unknown in Kentucky
    d: Aft. 1870 in Illinois

- **Lucy O'Briant**
  b: 1839 in St. Clair Co., Illinois
  d: 1904 in Illinois
  - **Cheatham O'Briant**
    b: 23 May 1799 in Buckingham Co., Virginia
    m: 1824 in Lebanon, Wilson Co., Tennessee
    d: 17 Sep 1879 in Salem, Marion Co., Illinois
  - **Ann Wright**
    b: 1801 in Tennessee
    d: 1839 in Lebanon, St. Clair Co., Illinois

Charles William Humphries (1891-1973)
[5th. Generation from Henry Wilton (1769-1820)]

&

Josephine Deckard (1899-1921)
& Family

&

Frances Anna Bescheinen (1903-1990)
& Family

Family Group Sheet

Husband: Charles William Humphries

- Born: 04 Jun 1891 — in: Poplar Bluff, Butler Co., Missouri
- Married: 02 Sep 1916 — in: Poplar Bluff, Butler Co., Missouri
- Died: 18 Apr 1973 — in: Poplar Bluff, Butler Co., Missouri
- Father: Reuben Isaac Fletcher Humphries
- Mother: Mary Annise Burkett
- Other Spouses: Frances Anna Bescheinen

Wife: Josephine Deckard

- Born: Feb 1899 — in: Poplar Bluff, Butler Co., Missouri
- Died: 27 Mar 1921 — in: Poplar Bluff, Butler Co., Missouri

CHILDREN

1. F — Name: Vada Fay Humphries
   - Born: 05 Aug 1917 — in: Butler Co., Missouri
   - Died: 28 Apr 1994 — in: Ottawa Co., Oklahoma
   - Married: 13 Dec 1934 — in: Harviell, Butler Co., Missouri
   - Spouse: Raleigh McGowen

2. M — Name: Charles Eugene Humphries
   - Born: 02 Dec 1918 — in: Poplar Bluff, Butler Co., Missouri
   - Died: 15 Jun 1965 — in: Poplar Bluff, Butler Co., Missouri
   - Married: 19 Oct 1941 — in: Kirksville, Adair Co., Missouri
   - Spouse: Doloris Iola Davis

Family Group Sheet

Husband: Charles William Humphries

Born: 04 Jun 1891 in: Poplar Bluff, Butler Co., Missouri
Married: 04 Mar 1921 in: Doniphan, Ripley Co., Missouri
Died: 18 Apr 1973 in: Poplar Bluff, Butler Co., Missouri
Father: Reuben Isaac Fletcher Humphries
Mother: Mary Annise Burkett
Other Spouses: Josephine Deckard

Wife: Frances Anna Bescheinen

Born: 01 Dec 1903 in: Loose Creek, Osage Co., Missouri
Died: 05 May 1990 in: Poplar Bluff, Butler Co., Missouri
Father: Henry Joseph Bescheinen
Mother: Mary Josepha Lock

CHILDREN

1 F
Name: Clara Mae Humphries
Born: Abt. 1922 in: Missouri

2 M
Name: Johnnie Humphries
Born: Abt. 1925 in: Missouri

3 M
Name: James Henry Humphries
Born: 17 Jun 1926 in: Poplar Bluff, Butler Co., Missouri
Died: 03 Jul 1970 in: Poplar Bluff, Butler Co., Missouri
Married: Unknown
Spouse: Ann

4 M
Name: Junior Humphries
Born: Aug 1928 in: Missouri
Married: Unknown
Spouse: Louise Shelton

5 M
Name: Orville Lee Humphries
Born: 20 Feb 1933 in: Poplar Bluff, Butler Co., Missouri
Died: 18 Jul 1958 in: Poplar Bluff, Butler Co., Missouri

6 M
Name: Franklin Humphries
Born: Unknown in: Missouri

7 F
Name: Shirley Ann Humphries
Born: Oct 1939 in: Missouri
Married: Unknown
Spouse: Russell Birdsong

8 F
Name: Delores Fay Humphries
Born: Unknown
Married: Unknown
Spouse: Alton Durwood Ryals

9 F
Name: Betty Jo Humphries
Born: Unknown
Married: Unknown
Spouse: William Lankfords

CHARLES WILLIAM HUMPHRIES Standard Pedigree Tree

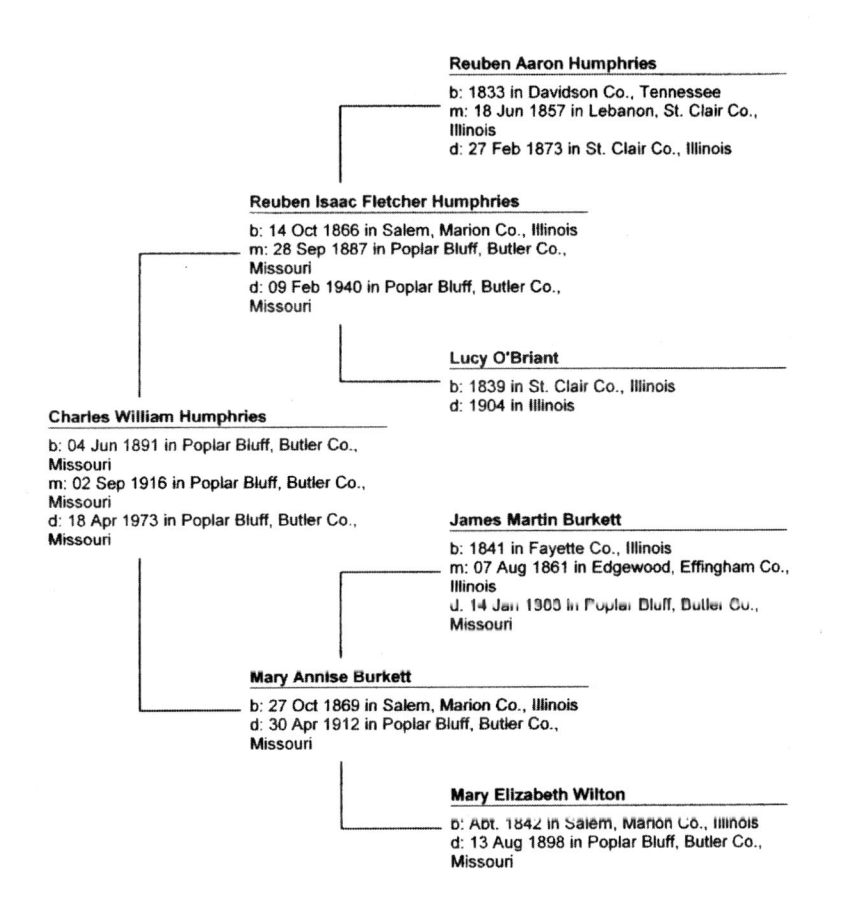

Reuben Aaron Humphries
b: 1833 in Davidson Co., Tennessee
m: 18 Jun 1857 in Lebanon, St. Clair Co., Illinois
d: 27 Feb 1873 in St. Clair Co., Illinois

Reuben Isaac Fletcher Humphries
b: 14 Oct 1866 in Salem, Marion Co., Illinois
m: 28 Sep 1887 in Poplar Bluff, Butler Co., Missouri
d: 09 Feb 1940 in Poplar Bluff, Butler Co., Missouri

Lucy O'Briant
b: 1839 in St. Clair Co., Illinois
d: 1904 in Illinois

Charles William Humphries
b: 04 Jun 1891 in Poplar Bluff, Butler Co., Missouri
m: 02 Sep 1916 in Poplar Bluff, Butler Co., Missouri
d: 18 Apr 1973 in Poplar Bluff, Butler Co., Missouri

James Martin Burkett
b: 1841 in Fayette Co., Illinois
m: 07 Aug 1861 in Edgewood, Effingham Co., Illinois
d: 14 Jan 1903 in Poplar Bluff, Butler Co., Missouri

Mary Annise Burkett
b: 27 Oct 1869 in Salem, Marion Co., Illinois
d: 30 Apr 1912 in Poplar Bluff, Butler Co., Missouri

Mary Elizabeth Wilton
b: Abt. 1842 in Salem, Marion Co., Illinois
d: 13 Aug 1898 in Poplar Bluff, Butler Co., Missouri

Notes: This Tree also applies to the other children of Reuben I.F. Humphries & Mary Annise Burkett: Jesse Martin Humphries, Ben Humphries, James Humphries, Otto F. Humphries, Isaac F. Humphries, and Raymond Humphries.

FRANCES ANNA BESCHEINEN Standard Pedigree Tree

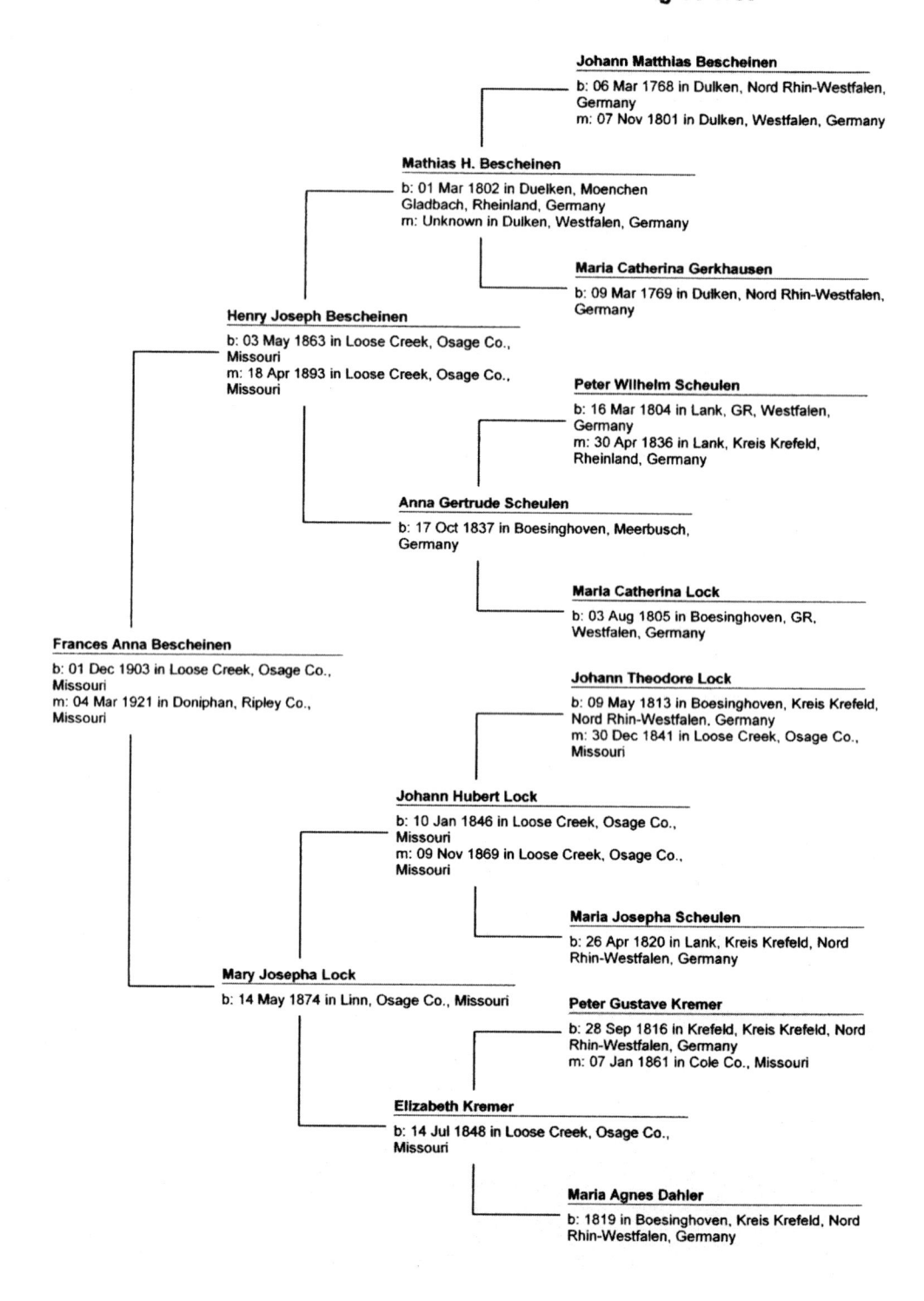

- **Frances Anna Bescheinen**
  b: 01 Dec 1903 in Loose Creek, Osage Co., Missouri
  m: 04 Mar 1921 in Doniphan, Ripley Co., Missouri
  - **Henry Joseph Bescheinen**
    b: 03 May 1863 in Loose Creek, Osage Co., Missouri
    m: 18 Apr 1893 in Loose Creek, Osage Co., Missouri
    - **Mathias H. Bescheinen**
      b: 01 Mar 1802 in Duelken, Moenchen Gladbach, Rheinland, Germany
      m: Unknown in Dulken, Westfalen, Germany
      - **Johann Matthias Bescheinen**
        b: 06 Mar 1768 in Dulken, Nord Rhin-Westfalen, Germany
        m: 07 Nov 1801 in Dulken, Westfalen, Germany
      - **Maria Catherina Gerkhausen**
        b: 09 Mar 1769 in Dulken, Nord Rhin-Westfalen, Germany
    - **Anna Gertrude Scheulen**
      b: 17 Oct 1837 in Boesinghoven, Meerbusch, Germany
      - **Peter Wilhelm Scheulen**
        b: 16 Mar 1804 in Lank, GR, Westfalen, Germany
        m: 30 Apr 1836 in Lank, Kreis Krefeld, Rheinland, Germany
      - **Maria Catherina Lock**
        b: 03 Aug 1805 in Boesinghoven, GR, Westfalen, Germany
  - **Mary Josepha Lock**
    b: 14 May 1874 in Linn, Osage Co., Missouri
    - **Johann Hubert Lock**
      b: 10 Jan 1846 in Loose Creek, Osage Co., Missouri
      m: 09 Nov 1869 in Loose Creek, Osage Co., Missouri
      - **Johann Theodore Lock**
        b: 09 May 1813 in Boesinghoven, Kreis Krefeld, Nord Rhin-Westfalen, Germany
        m: 30 Dec 1841 in Loose Creek, Osage Co., Missouri
      - **Maria Josepha Scheulen**
        b: 26 Apr 1820 in Lank, Kreis Krefeld, Nord Rhin-Westfalen, Germany
    - **Elizabeth Kremer**
      b: 14 Jul 1848 in Loose Creek, Osage Co., Missouri
      - **Peter Gustave Kremer**
        b: 28 Sep 1816 in Krefeld, Kreis Krefeld, Nord Rhin-Westfalen, Germany
        m: 07 Jan 1861 in Cole Co., Missouri
      - **Maria Agnes Dahler**
        b: 1819 in Boesinghoven, Kreis Krefeld, Nord Rhin-Westfalen, Germany

Vada Fay Humphries (1917-1994)
[6th. Generation From Henry Wilton (1769-1820)]

&

Raleigh McGowen (1908-1971)
& Family

Family Group Sheet

Husband: Raleigh McGowen

Born: 27 Apr 1908 in: Missouri
Married: 13 Dec 1934 in: Harviell, Butler Co., Missouri
Died: Jul 1971 in: Ottawa Co., Oklahoma
Father: William S. McGowen
Mother: Sarah Cagle

Wife: Vada Fay Humphries

Born: 05 Aug 1917 in: Butler Co., Missouri
Died: 28 Apr 1994 in: Ottawa Co., Oklahoma
Father: Charles William Humphries
Mother: Josephine Deckard

CHILDREN

1 M	Name: Robert McGowen Born: 1935	in: Missouri
2 M	Name: Elvis McGowen Born: 12 May 1938 Died: 20 Jan 2007 Married: 29 Jun 2002 Spouse: Bonnie McCoy	in: Poplar Bluff, Butler Co., Missouri in: Ottawa, Franklin Co., Kansas in: Ottawa, Franklin Co., Kansas
3 M	Name: Charles Wesley McGowen Born: Sep 1942	in: Missouri
4 F	Name: Barbara McGowen Born: Unknown	in: Missouri
5 M	Name: Richard McGowen Born: Unknown	in: Missouri

VADA FAY HUMPHRIES Standard Pedigree Tree

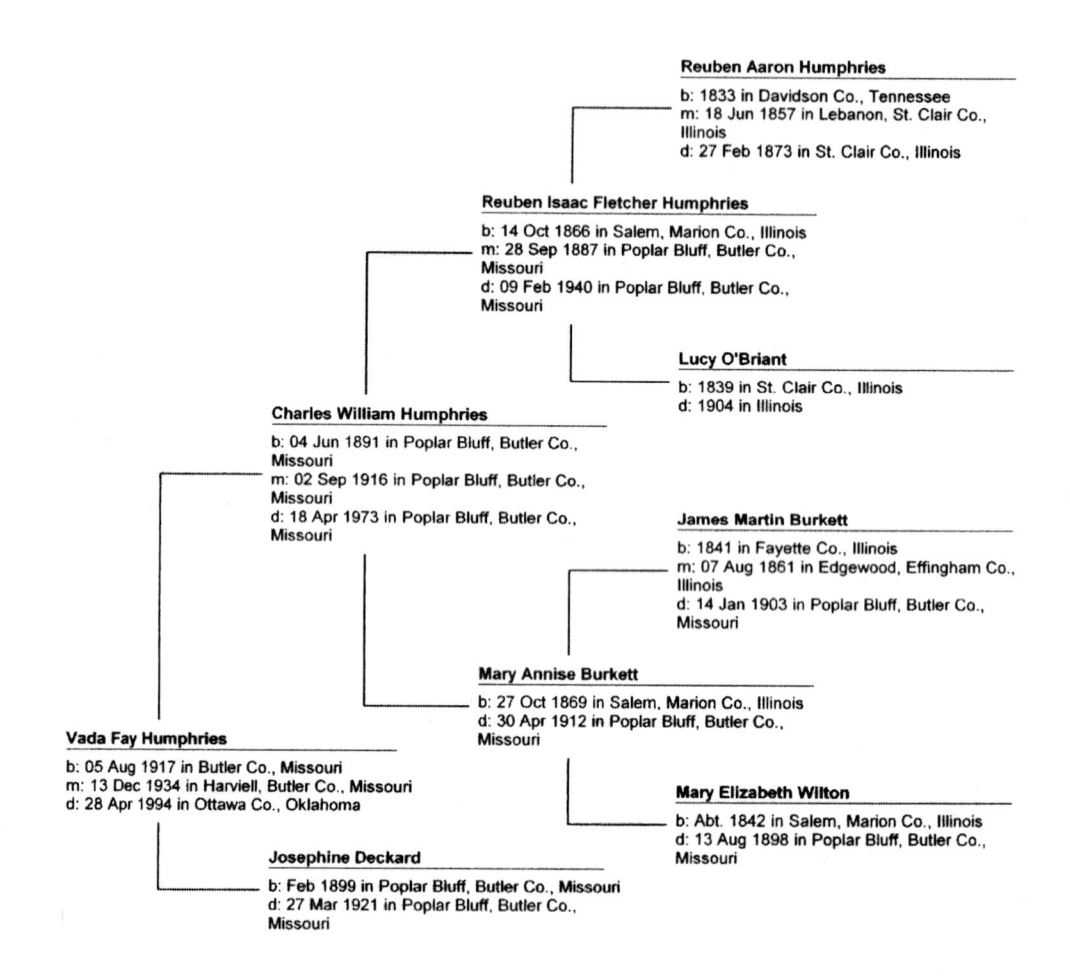

Reuben Aaron Humphries
b: 1833 in Davidson Co., Tennessee
m: 18 Jun 1857 in Lebanon, St. Clair Co., Illinois
d: 27 Feb 1873 in St. Clair Co., Illinois

Reuben Isaac Fletcher Humphries
b: 14 Oct 1866 in Salem, Marion Co., Illinois
m: 28 Sep 1887 in Poplar Bluff, Butler Co., Missouri
d: 09 Feb 1940 in Poplar Bluff, Butler Co., Missouri

Lucy O'Briant
b: 1839 in St. Clair Co., Illinois
d: 1904 in Illinois

Charles William Humphries
b: 04 Jun 1891 in Poplar Bluff, Butler Co., Missouri
m: 02 Sep 1916 in Poplar Bluff, Butler Co., Missouri
d: 18 Apr 1973 in Poplar Bluff, Butler Co., Missouri

James Martin Burkett
b: 1841 in Fayette Co., Illinois
m: 07 Aug 1861 in Edgewood, Effingham Co., Illinois
d: 14 Jan 1903 in Poplar Bluff, Butler Co., Missouri

Mary Annise Burkett
b: 27 Oct 1869 in Salem, Marion Co., Illinois
d: 30 Apr 1912 in Poplar Bluff, Butler Co., Missouri

Vada Fay Humphries
b: 05 Aug 1917 in Butler Co., Missouri
m: 13 Dec 1934 in Harviell, Butler Co., Missouri
d: 28 Apr 1994 in Ottawa Co., Oklahoma

Mary Elizabeth Wilton
b: Abt. 1842 in Salem, Marion Co., Illinois
d: 13 Aug 1898 in Poplar Bluff, Butler Co., Missouri

Josephine Deckard
b: Feb 1899 in Poplar Bluff, Butler Co., Missouri
d: 27 Mar 1921 in Poplar Bluff, Butler Co., Missouri

Notes: The Tree also applies to the other child of Charles William Humphries & Josephine Deckard: Charles Eugene Humphries.

RALEIGH MCGOWEN Standard Pedigree Tree

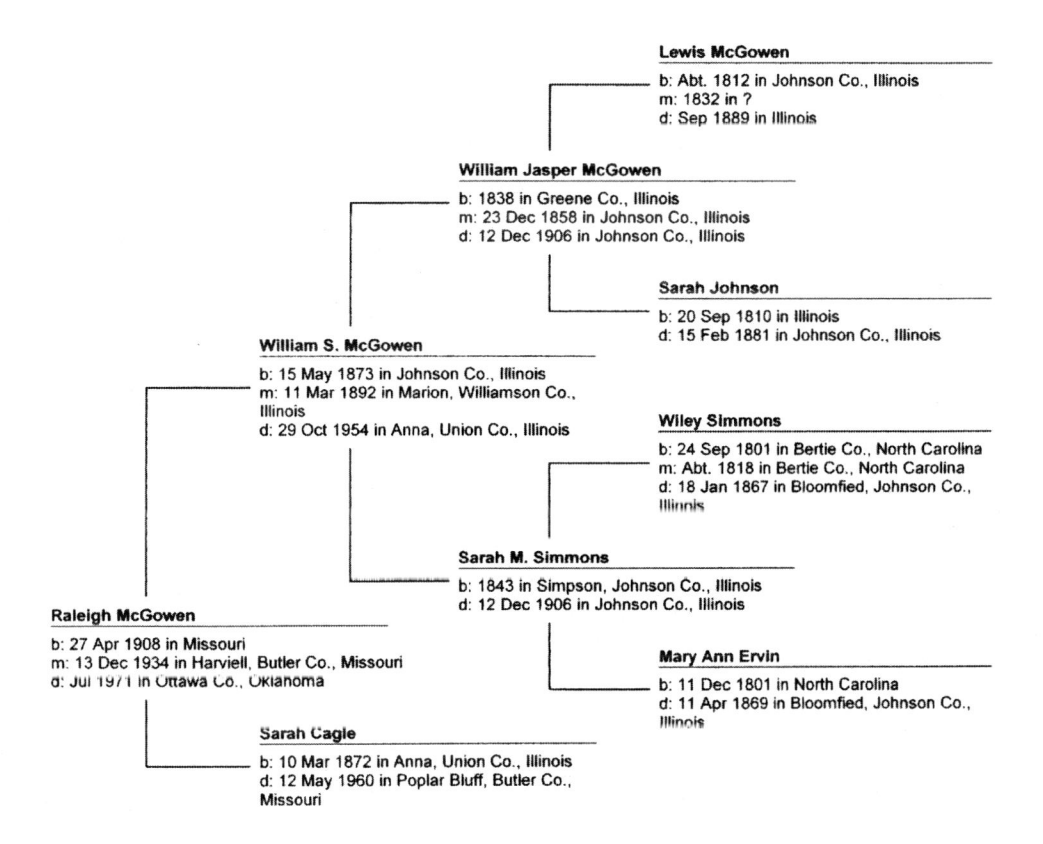

Lewis McGowen
b: Abt. 1812 in Johnson Co., Illinois
m: 1832 in ?
d: Sep 1889 in Illinois

William Jasper McGowen
b: 1838 in Greene Co., Illinois
m: 23 Dec 1858 in Johnson Co., Illinois
d: 12 Dec 1906 in Johnson Co., Illinois

Sarah Johnson
b: 20 Sep 1810 in Illinois
d: 15 Feb 1881 in Johnson Co., Illinois

William S. McGowen
b: 15 May 1873 in Johnson Co., Illinois
m: 11 Mar 1892 in Marion, Williamson Co., Illinois
d: 29 Oct 1954 in Anna, Union Co., Illinois

Wiley Simmons
b: 24 Sep 1801 in Bertie Co., North Carolina
m: Abt. 1818 in Bertie Co., North Carolina
d: 18 Jan 1867 in Bloomfied, Johnson Co., Illinois

Sarah M. Simmons
b: 1843 in Simpson, Johnson Co., Illinois
d: 12 Dec 1906 in Johnson Co., Illinois

Mary Ann Ervin
b: 11 Dec 1801 in North Carolina
d: 11 Apr 1869 in Bloomfied, Johnson Co., Illinois

Raleigh McGowen
b: 27 Apr 1908 in Missouri
m: 13 Dec 1934 in Harviell, Butler Co., Missouri
d: Jul 1971 in Ottawa Co., Oklahoma

Sarah Cagle
b: 10 Mar 1872 in Anna, Union Co., Illinois
d: 12 May 1960 in Poplar Bluff, Butler Co., Missouri

Ben Humphries (1895-1941)
[5th. Generation from Henry Wilton (1769-1820)]

&

Jennie May Hicks (1896-   )
& Family

Family Group Sheet

Husband: Ben Humphries

Born: 1895 — in: Poplar Bluff, Butler Co., Missouri
Married: 10 Jan 1918 — in: Butler Co., Missouri
Died: 1941 — in: Sikeston, Missouri
Father: Reuben Isaac Fletcher Humphries
Mother: Mary Annise Burkett

Wife: Jennie May Hicks

Born: Nov 1896 — in: Missouri

CHILDREN

1. M
   Name: George Isaac Humphries
   Born: 30 May 1918 — in: Butler Co., Missouri
   Died: 11 Nov 1972 — in: Missouri
   Married: 23 May 1940 — in: Butler Co., Missouri
   Spouse: Mary Pearl Johnson

2. F
   Name: Mary Elizabeth Humphries
   Born: 1920 — in: Butler Co., Missouri
   Died: Oct 1973 — in: Memphis, Shelby Co., Tennessee
   Married: 09 Mar 1937 — in: Poplar Bluff, Butler Co., Missouri
   Spouse: Emmett Jr. West
   Married: 12 Nov 1941 — in: Poplar Bluff, Butler Co., Missouri
   Spouse: Ethmer C. Rhodes

3. M
   Name: Lee Warren Humphries
   Born: 03 Nov 1922 — in: Missouri
   Died: 19 Jun 1976 — in: Tennessee
   Married: Unknown
   Spouse: Laura Pearl Ferrell

James Humphries (1901-1970)
[5th. Generation from Henry Wilton (1769-1820)]

&

Edith Reed (1896-1945)
& Family

Family Group Sheet

Husband: James Humphries

Born: 1901 in: Poplar Bluff, Butler Co., Missouri
Married: 18 Oct 1930 in: Poplar Bluff, Butler Co., Missouri
Died: 1970
Father: Reuben Isaac Fletcher Humphries
Mother: Mary Annise Burkett

Wife: Edith Reed

Born: 1896 in: Missouri
Died: 1945

CHILDREN

1 M Name: Billy Humphries
     Born: Unknown

2 F Name: Mollie Humphries
     Born: Unknown

Otto Franklin Humphries (1902-1965)
[5th. Generation from Henry Wilton (1769-1820)]

&

Mary Amstutz (1911-1972)
& Family

Family Group Sheet

Husband: Otto Franklin Humphries	
Born: 27 Mar 1902	in: Poplar Bluff, Butler Co., Missouri
Married: 12 Jun 1929	in: Poplar Bluff, Butler Co., Missouri
Died: 16 Jun 1965	in: Camden, Kent Co., Delaware
Father: Reuben Isaac Fletcher Humphries	
Mother: Mary Annise Burkett	

Wife: Mary Amstutz	
Born: 22 Jan 1911	in: Michigan
Died: Aug 1972	in: Kent Co., Delaware
Father: Christian C. Amstutz	
Mother: Mary D. Hershberger	

CHILDREN

1. M — Name: J.L. Humphries
   - Born: Unknown in: Delaware
   - Married: Unknown
   - Spouse: Anna Stoltzfus

2. M — Name: Andrew Allen Humphries
   - Born: Unknown in: Delaware

3. M — Name: Ray Humphries
   - Born: Unknown in: Delaware

4. M — Name: Isaac Humphries
   - Born: 14 Apr 1940 in: Delaware
   - Died: Jul 1966 in: Delaware
   - Married: Unknown
   - Spouse: Beverly Ellen Jobe

5. M — Name: Robert Humphries
   - Born: 18 May 1944 in: Dover, Kent Co., Delaware
   - Died: 12 Jan 2005 in: Dover, Kent Co., Delaware

6. F — Name: Betty Humphries
   - Born: Unknown in: Delaware

7. M — Name: John William Humphries
   - Born: Jun 1947 in: Delaware

MARY AMSTUTZ Standard Pedigree Tree

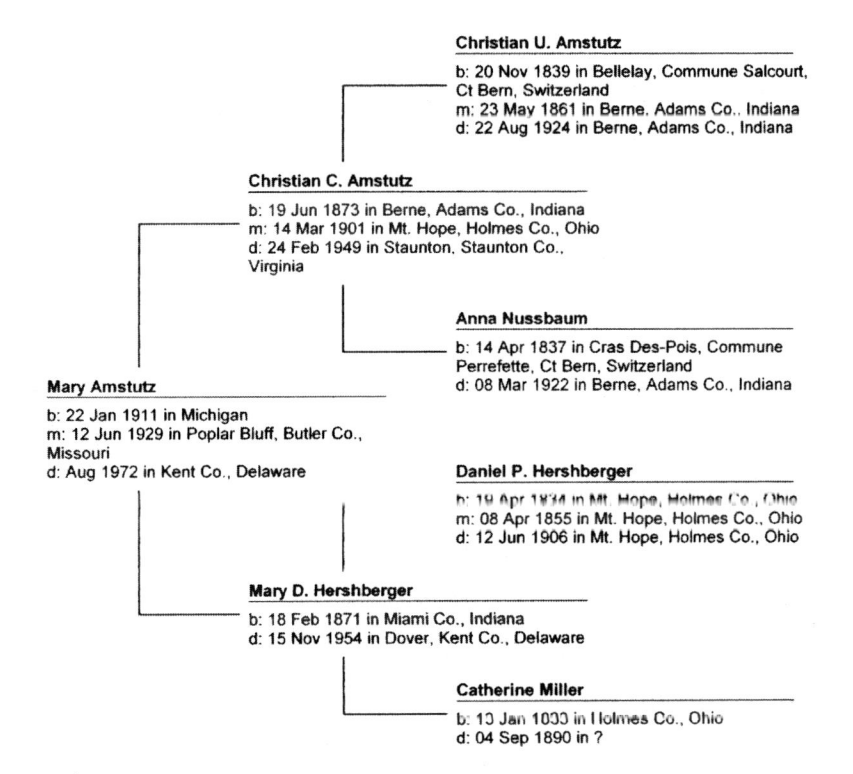

Christian U. Amstutz
b: 20 Nov 1839 in Bellelay, Commune Salcourt, Ct Bern, Switzerland
m: 23 May 1861 in Berne, Adams Co., Indiana
d: 22 Aug 1924 in Berne, Adams Co., Indiana

Christian C. Amstutz
b: 19 Jun 1873 in Berne, Adams Co., Indiana
m: 14 Mar 1901 in Mt. Hope, Holmes Co., Ohio
d: 24 Feb 1949 in Staunton, Staunton Co., Virginia

Anna Nussbaum
b: 14 Apr 1837 in Cras Des-Pois, Commune Perrefette, Ct Bern, Switzerland
d: 08 Mar 1922 in Berne, Adams Co., Indiana

Mary Amstutz
b: 22 Jan 1911 in Michigan
m: 12 Jun 1929 in Poplar Bluff, Butler Co., Missouri
d: Aug 1972 in Kent Co., Delaware

Daniel P. Hershberger
b: 19 Apr 1834 in Mt. Hope, Holmes Co., Ohio
m: 08 Apr 1855 in Mt. Hope, Holmes Co., Ohio
d: 12 Jun 1906 in Mt. Hope, Holmes Co., Ohio

Mary D. Hershberger
b: 18 Feb 1871 in Miami Co., Indiana
d: 15 Nov 1954 in Dover, Kent Co., Delaware

Catherine Miller
b: 13 Jan 1833 in Holmes Co., Ohio
d: 04 Sep 1890 in ?

Raymond Humphries (1908-1975)
[5th. Generation from Henry Wilton (1769-1820)]

&

LaNelle Sanders (1912-1995)
& Family

Family Group Sheet

Husband: Raymond Humphries

    Born: 05 Jun 1908   in: Poplar Bluff, Butler Co., Missouri
Married: 26 Jan 1929   in: Butler Co., Missouri
    Died: Feb 1975   in: St. Louis Co., Missouri
    Father: Reuben Isaac Fletcher Humphries
    Mother: Mary Annise Burkett

Wife: LaNelle Sanders

    Born: 16 Jul 1912   in: Missouri
    Died: 11 Jan 1995   in: St. Louis Co., Missouri

CHILDREN

1 M
    Name: James Ralph Humphries
    Born: Dec 1929   in: Missouri
    Married: Unknown
    Spouse: Shirley Ann Bathon

Ellen Wilton (1845-1919)
[3rd. Generation from Henry Wilton (1769-1820)]

&

Felix Monroe Marshall (1844-1924)
& Family

Family Group Sheet

Husband: Felix Monroe Marshall	
Born: Oct 1844	in: Tennessee
Married: 11 Apr 1867	in: Marion Co., Illinois
Died: 05 Oct 1924	in: Urbana, Champaign Co., Illinois

Wife: Ellen Wilton	
Born: May 1845	in: Illinois
Died: 29 Sep 1919	in: Urbana, Champaign Co., Illinois
Father: Thomas Wilton	
Mother: Mary Alma Maddux	

CHILDREN

#		
1 F	Name: Larah Marshall Born: 1868	in: Illinois
2 M	Name: Oliver Marshall Born: 1870	in: Illinois
3 F	Name: Mary E. Marshall Born: 1872	in: Illinois
4 M	Name: Charles M. Marshall Born: Dec 1875	in: Illinois
5 F	Name: Ella B. Marshall Born: Jul 1879	in: Illinois
6 M	Name: Rollo Marshall Born: Aug 1881	in: Illinois
7 F	Name: Carrie H. Marshall Born: May 1883	in: Illinois
8 F	Name: Mabel G. Marshall Born: Aug 1886	in: Illinois
9 F	Name: Temperance L. Marshall Born: Mar 1888	in: Illinois

Charles Wilton (1805-1866)
[2nd. Generation From Henry Wilton (1768-1820)]

&

Mary Harbison (1811-1855)
& Family

Charles Wilton, born about 1805 in New York, was the second child by Henry Wilton's second marriage. Henry's second wife, Elizabeth Bond, died in 1811 in New York while the family was making plans to relocate to Illinois. By the Fall of 1811, Henry Wilton had married a third time, and the family was located in Shawneetown in Gallatin County, Illinois. Sometime after Henry Wilton died in 1820, Charles Wilton moved from Gallatin County to Clinton County, Illinois.

On September 27, 1832, Charles married Mary Harbison in Clinton County, Illinois. Beginning with the 1840 Federal Census, Charles Wilton was listed in Clinton County, and he was also listed in the 1850 and 1860 Federal Census' of Clinton County, where his occupation was listed as "farmer." Between 1827 and 1851, Charles and Mary had eight children.

Mary (Harbison) Wilton died November 9, 1855, presumably in Illinois. By the 1860 Federal Census of Clinton County, Illinois, Charles was listed at age 52, along with four of his youngest living children. One child, Martha Jane Wilton, had died while in infancy. Charles Wilton died April 2, 1866 in Clinton County, Illinois.

Family Group Sheet

Husband: Charles Wilton

Born: 1805 in: New York
Married: 27 Sep 1832 in: Clinton Co., Illinois
Died: 02 Apr 1866 in: Clinton Co., Illinois
Father: Henry Wilton
Mother: Elizabeth Bond

Wife: Mary Harbison

Born: 19 Dec 1811 in: Kentucky
Died: 09 Nov 1855 in: Illinois

CHILDREN

1 F
Name: Elizabeth Emeline Wilton
Born: 1827 in: Illinois
Died: 06 Dec 1851 in: Illinois

2 F
Name: Sarah Agnes Wilton
Born: 04 May 1833 in: Clinton Co., Illinois
Died: 21 Sep 1915 in: Carlyle, Clinton Co., Illinois
Married: 21 Apr 1859 in: Clinton Co., Illinois
Spouse: John Foster
Married: 29 Mar 1870 in: Clinton Co., Illinois
Spouse: Edward Allen

3 F
Name: Harriet Caroline Wilton
Born: 04 Oct 1834 in: Illinois
Died: Bef. 1866
Married: 05 Nov 1857 in: Clinton Co., Illinois
Spouse: Nathan Moore

4 M
Name: William Henry Wilton
Born: 08 Aug 1836 in: Illinois
Died: Bef. 1866

5 M
Name: Joseph Franklin Wilton
Born: 23 Mar 1838 in: Clinton Co., Illinois
Died: 31 Dec 1924 in: Carlyle, Clinton Co., Illinois
Married: Abt. 1865 in: Illinois
Spouse: Celia Anne Nichols

6 F
Name: Laura Ann Wilton
Born: 28 Jan 1840 in: Illinois
Married: 09 Sep 1863 in: Clinton Co., Illinois
Spouse: Hiram Allen

7 F
Name: Martha Jane Wilton
Born: 08 Dec 1845 in: Illinois
Died: 08 May 1846 in: Illinois

8 M
Name: Charles Shadrach Wilton
Born: 20 Jul 1851 in: Illinois
Died: 12 Nov 1877 in: Huey, Clinton Co., Illinois

Sarah Agnes Wilton (1833-1915)
[3rd. Generation from Henry Wilton (1769-1820)]

&
John Foster (1830~1867)
& Family

&
Edward Allen (1837~1915)
& Family

Family Group Sheet

Husband: John Foster

Born: Abt. 1830	in: Illinois
Married: 21 Apr 1859	in: Clinton Co., Illinois
Died: Bet. Apr 1866 - Mar 1867	in: Illinois

Wife: Sarah Agnes Wilton

Born: 04 May 1833	in: Clinton Co., Illinois
Died: 21 Sep 1915	in: Carlyle, Clinton Co., Illinois
Father: Charles Wilton	
Mother: Mary Harbison	
Other Spouses: Edward Allen	

CHILDREN

1. M — Name: Charles Henry Foster
   - Born: Mar 1860 — in: Illinois
   - Died: Aft. 1930 — in: Illinois

2. F — Name: Laura Sophia Foster
   - Born: Nov 1867 — in: Illinois
   - Died: Aft. 1930 — in: Illinois
   - Married: 19 May 1891 — in: Clinton Co., Illinois
   - Spouse: Pat Flanagan

Family Group Sheet

Husband: Edward Allen

Born: Abt. 1837 in: Montgomery Co., Illinois
Married: 29 Mar 1870 in: Clinton Co., Illinois
Died: Bef. 1915

Wife: Sarah Agnes Wilton

Born: 04 May 1833 in: Clinton Co., Illinois
Died: 21 Sep 1915 in: Carlyle, Clinton Co., Illinois
Father: Charles Wilton
Mother: Mary Harbison
Other Spouses: John Foster

CHILDREN

1 F
Name: Mary Allen
Born: 1871 in: Illinois
Died: Aft. 1939
Married: 04 Sep 1895 in: Clinton Co., Illinois
Spouse: W.W. Youngblood

2 M
Name: Harry Allen
Born: 1873 in: Illinois

3 F
Name: Clara L. Allen
Born: 1878 in: Illinois

SARAH AGNES WILTON Standard Pedigree Tree

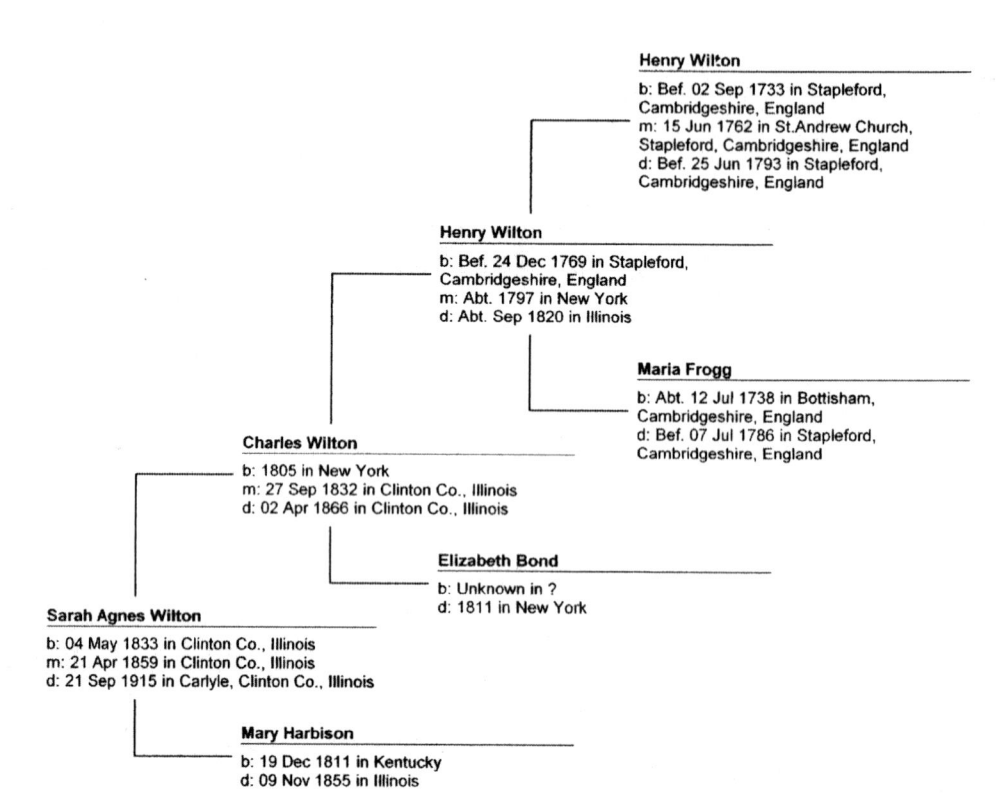

Henry Wilton
b: Bef. 02 Sep 1733 in Stapleford, Cambridgeshire, England
m: 15 Jun 1762 in St.Andrew Church, Stapleford, Cambridgeshire, England
d: Bef. 25 Jun 1793 in Stapleford, Cambridgeshire, England

Henry Wilton
b: Bef. 24 Dec 1769 in Stapleford, Cambridgeshire, England
m: Abt. 1797 in New York
d: Abt. Sep 1820 in Illinois

Maria Frogg
b: Abt. 12 Jul 1738 in Bottisham, Cambridgeshire, England
d: Bef. 07 Jul 1786 in Stapleford, Cambridgeshire, England

Charles Wilton
b: 1805 in New York
m: 27 Sep 1832 in Clinton Co., Illinois
d: 02 Apr 1866 in Clinton Co., Illinois

Elizabeth Bond
b: Unknown in ?
d: 1811 in New York

Sarah Agnes Wilton
b: 04 May 1833 in Clinton Co., Illinois
m: 21 Apr 1859 in Clinton Co., Illinois
d: 21 Sep 1915 in Carlyle, Clinton Co., Illinois

Mary Harbison
b: 19 Dec 1811 in Kentucky
d: 09 Nov 1855 in Illinois

Notes: This Tree also applies to the other children of Charles Wilton & Mary Harbison: Elizabeth Emeline Wilton, Harriet Caroline Wilton, William Henry Wilton, Joseph Franklin Wilton, Laura Ann Wilton, and Charles Shadrach Wilton.

Laura Sophia Foster (1867~1930)
[4th. Generation from Henry Wilton (1769-1820)]

&

Pat Flanagan (1861~1920)
& Family

Family Group Sheet

Husband: Pat Flanagan	
Born: May 1861	in: Canada
Married: 19 May 1891	in: Clinton Co., Illinois
Died: Aft. 1920	in: Illinois

Wife: Laura Sophia Foster	
Born: Nov 1867	in: Illinois
Died: Aft. 1930	in: Illinois
Father: John Foster	
Mother: Sarah Agnes Wilton	

	CHILDREN	
1 F	Name: Edith Flanagan Born: Mar 1892	in: Missouri
2 M	Name: Charles Flanagan Born: Sep 1893	in: Missouri

LAURA SOPHIA FOSTER Standard Pedigree Tree

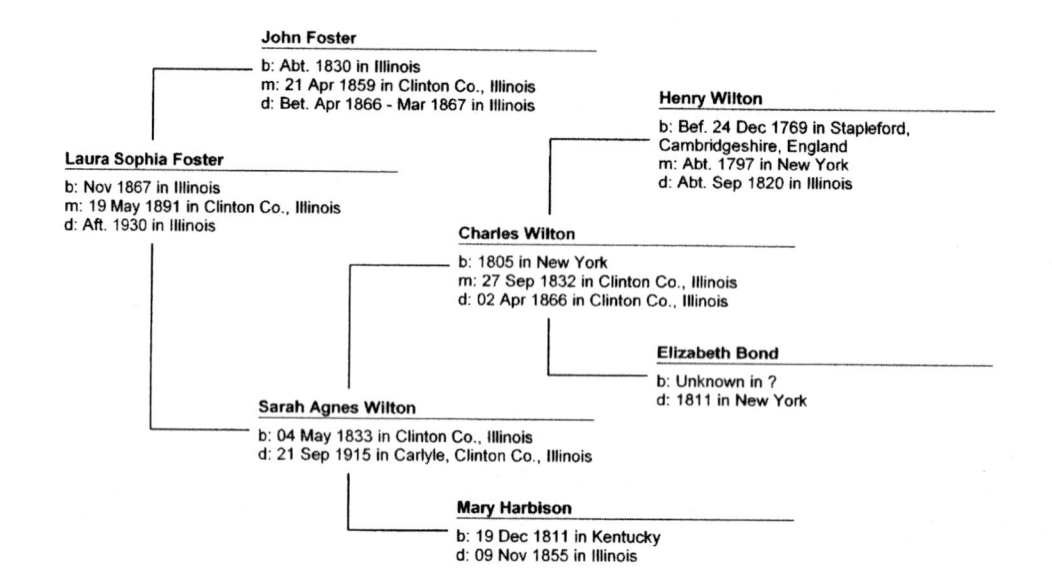

Laura Sophia Foster
b: Nov 1867 in Illinois
m: 19 May 1891 in Clinton Co., Illinois
d: Aft. 1930 in Illinois

John Foster
b: Abt. 1830 in Illinois
m: 21 Apr 1859 in Clinton Co., Illinois
d: Bet. Apr 1866 - Mar 1867 in Illinois

Charles Wilton
b: 1805 in New York
m: 27 Sep 1832 in Clinton Co., Illinois
d: 02 Apr 1866 in Clinton Co., Illinois

Henry Wilton
b: Bef. 24 Dec 1769 in Stapleford, Cambridgeshire, England
m: Abt. 1797 in New York
d: Abt. Sep 1820 in Illinois

Elizabeth Bond
b: Unknown in ?
d: 1811 in New York

Sarah Agnes Wilton
b: 04 May 1833 in Clinton Co., Illinois
d: 21 Sep 1915 in Carlyle, Clinton Co., Illinois

Mary Harbison
b: 19 Dec 1811 in Kentucky
d: 09 Nov 1855 in Illinois

Notes: This Tree also applies to the other child of Sarah Agnes Wilton & John Foster: Charles Henry Foster.

Harriet Caroline Wilton (1834~1866)
[3rd. Generation from Henry Wilton (1769-1820)]

&
Nathan Moore
& Family

Family Group Sheet

Husband: Nathan Moore	
Born: Unknown	
Married: 05 Nov 1857	in: Clinton Co., Illinois
Wife: Harriet Caroline Wilton	
Born: 04 Oct 1834	in: Illinois
Died: Bef. 1866	
Father: Charles Wilton	
Mother: Mary Harbison	

	CHILDREN	
1 M	Name: Charles Thomas Moore	
	Born: Bet. 1857 - 1866	in: Clinton Co., Illinois

Joseph Franklin Wilton (1838-1924)
[3rd. Generation from Henry Wilton (1769-1820)]

&

Celia Anne Nichols (1847-1929)
& Family

Joseph Franklin Wilton, the 5th child of Charles Wilton and Mary Harbison, was born March 23, 1838 in Clinton County, Illinois. The family had made Clinton County their home in the early 1830's, and that was where Joseph Franklin spent his early years.

About 1865, Joseph Franklin married Celia Anne Nichols, daughter of David Nichols and Mary Jane Foster. By the 1870 Federal Census of Clinton County, Illinois, Joseph Wilton was listed at age 32, with an occupation of farmer, along with Celia Wilton, age 22, and two children, Ida Wilton, age 4, and Mary Wilton, age 2. The post office location in the 1870 census was Carlyle, Illinois, and for the Federal Censuses of 1880, 1900, 1910, and 1920, their address was also Carlyle in Clinton County, Illinois. Joseph and Celia had a total of eight children, all born in Illinois. Two of the children, Josie Celia Wilton and Laura Caroline Wilton, died before the age of three.

Records indicate that at least in 1890, Joseph was a member of the board of education, and in 1904, he was one of the highway commissioners of Carlyle. In a Carlyle newspaper article of July 22, 1904, it was recorded that Joseph Wilton was the first one to cross over a new iron bridge that had just been constructed over the local levee. The article also stated that he had the distinction of being the first to drive across a suspension bridge erected in 1854 and first to cross over an iron bridge constructed on the levee east of the town in 1893. He was therefore "the first to cross over the bridges...erected on the eastern approach to this city in the past forty-five years."

In the 1910 Federal Census of Clinton County, Illinois, Joseph Wilton was listed at age 72, as head of household, along with Celia Wilton, age 62, and Sarah Wilton, daughter, age 24, with occupation of public school teacher. Also living in the household was Ella Rinesmith, widowed daughter, age 42, with occupation of public school teacher, and Harold Rinesmith, grandson, age 10. By the 1920 Federal Census of Clinton County, Illinois, Joseph Wilton, age 82, and Celia Wilton, age 72, were still living with Ella Rinesmith, then age 57, with an occupation of school teacher, but their roles were reversed, since by that time Ella Rinesmith was the head of household.

Joseph Franklin Wilton died December 31, 1924 in Carlyle, Illinois, and he was buried in the Carlyle Cemetery. Celia (Nichols) Wilton died about five years later on March 24, 1929, and she was also buried in the Carlyle Cemetery.

Family Group Sheet

Husband: Joseph Franklin Wilton

Born: 23 Mar 1838 — in: Clinton Co., Illinois
Married: Abt. 1865 — in: Illinois
Died: 31 Dec 1924 — in: Carlyle, Clinton Co., Illinois
Father: Charles Wilton
Mother: Mary Harbison

Wife: Celia Anne Nichols

Born: 06 Dec 1847 — in: Foster twp, Marion Co., Illinois
Died: 24 Mar 1929 — in: Carlyle, Clinton Co., Illinois
Father: David Nichols
Mother: Mary Jane Foster

CHILDREN

1 F
Name: Ida May Wilton
Born: 25 Feb 1866 — in: Carlyle, Clinton Co., Illinois
Died: 15 Feb 1960 — in: Odin, Marion Co., Illinois
Married: 05 Jun 1889 — in: Carlyle, Clinton Co., Illinois
Spouse: Charles Henry Scott

2 F
Name: Mary Ella Wilton
Born: 16 Feb 1868 — in: Carlyle, Clinton Co., Illinois
Died: 05 Jun 1942 — in: Illinois
Married: 11 Nov 1896 — in: Clinton Co., Illinois
Spouse: Walter C. Rinesmith

3 F
Name: Laura Caroline Wilton
Born: Apr 1873 — in: Illinois
Died: 31 Jan 1876 — in: Carlyle, Clinton Co., Illinois

4 F
Name: Josie Celia Wilton
Born: 01 Nov 1875 — in: Carlyle, Clinton Co., Illinois
Died: 19 Jan 1878 — in: Carlyle, Clinton Co., Illinois

5 M
Name: Joseph Charles Wilton
Born: 16 Jun 1878 — in: Carlyle, Clinton Co., Illinois
Died: 24 Feb 1950 — in: St. Louis, St. Louis Co., Missouri
Married: 16 Aug 1899 — in: Clinton Co., Illinois
Spouse: Nettie M. Miller

6 M
Name: Nichols Wilton
Born: 11 Sep 1880 — in: Illinois
Died: 15 Jun 1965 — in: Carlyle, Clinton Co., Illinois
Married: 16 Mar 1904 — in: Clinton Co., Illinois
Spouse: Anna A. Pepperkorn

7 M
Name: Walter W. Wilton
Born: 27 Jan 1883 — in: Macoupin Co., Illinois
Died: 14 Nov 1954 — in: Breese, Clinton Co., Illinois
Married: 29 Oct 1906 — in: Marion Co., Illinois
Spouse: Jennie Louise Baxter

8 F
Name: Sarah L. Wilton
Born: 25 Jul 1885 — in: Illinois
Died: 1946 — in: Illinois
Married: Unknown
Spouse: Francis C. Ballew

CELIA ANNE NICHOLS Standard Pedigree Tree

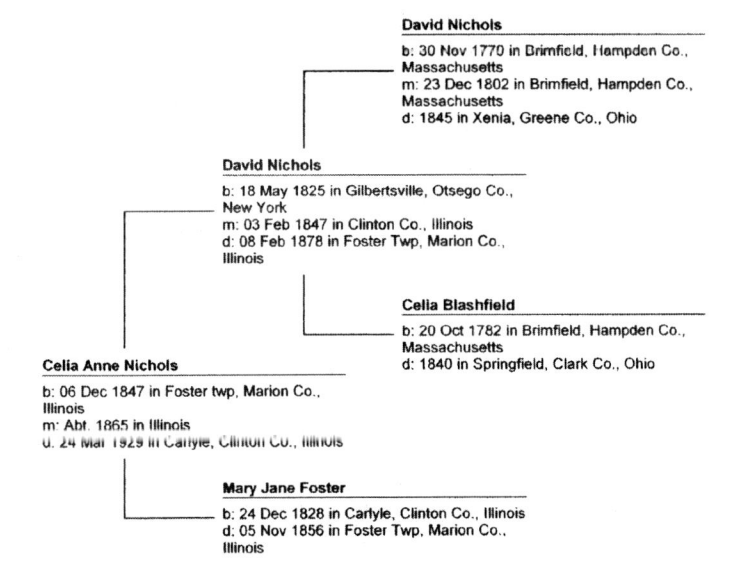

David Nichols
b: 30 Nov 1770 in Brimfield, Hampden Co., Massachusetts
m: 23 Dec 1802 in Brimfield, Hampden Co., Massachusetts
d: 1845 in Xenia, Greene Co., Ohio

David Nichols
b: 18 May 1825 in Gilbertsville, Otsego Co., New York
m: 03 Feb 1847 in Clinton Co., Illinois
d: 08 Feb 1878 in Foster Twp, Marion Co., Illinois

Celia Blashfield
b: 20 Oct 1782 in Brimfield, Hampden Co., Massachusetts
d: 1840 in Springfield, Clark Co., Ohio

Celia Anne Nichols
b: 06 Dec 1847 in Foster twp, Marion Co., Illinois
m: Abt. 1865 in Illinois
d: 24 Mar 1929 in Carlyle, Clinton Co., Illinois

Mary Jane Foster
b: 24 Dec 1828 in Carlyle, Clinton Co., Illinois
d: 05 Nov 1856 in Foster Twp, Marion Co., Illinois

Ida May Wilton (1866-1960)
[4th. Generation from Henry Wilton (1769-1820)]

&

Charles Henry Scott (1862-1925)
& Family

Family Group Sheet

Husband: Charles Henry Scott

Born: 01 Mar 1862	in: Irvington, Washington Co., Illinois
Married: 05 Jun 1889	in: Carlyle, Clinton Co., Illinois
Died: 10 Jan 1925	in: Beckemeyer, Clinton Co., Illinois
Father: John T. Scott	
Mother: Lucinda T. Cottems	

Wife: Ida May Wilton

Born: 25 Feb 1866	in: Carlyle, Clinton Co., Illinois
Died: 15 Feb 1960	in: Odin, Marion Co., Illinois
Father: Joseph Franklin Wilton	
Mother: Celia Anne Nichols	

CHILDREN

1 F
- Name: Ella Mae Scott
- Born: Dec 1891 — in: Beckemeyer, Clinton Co., Illinois
- Died: 1970
- Married: Abt. 1916 — in: Illinois
- Spouse: Lee Collignon

2 M
- Name: Rolla Walter Scott
- Born: 30 Jun 1894 — in: Carlyle, Clinton Co., Illinois
- Died: 31 Mar 1985 — in: Beckemeyer, Clinton Co., Illinois
- Married: 14 May 1919 — in: Beckemeyer, Clinton Co., Illinois
- Spouse: Clara Ackmann

3 M
- Name: Joseph H. Scott
- Born: 10 Feb 1897 — in: Beckemeyer, Clinton Co., Illinois
- Died: 12 Jun 1964 — in: Illinois
- Married: 30 Mar 1918 — in: Beckemeyer, Clinton Co., Illinois
- Spouse: Marrie Gouy

4 M
- Name: Charles Glen Scott
- Born: 14 May 1900 — in: Beckemeyer, Clinton Co., Illinois
- Died: 06 Mar 1966 — in: Beckemeyer, Clinton Co., Illinois
- Married: 17 Nov 1923 — in: Beckemeyer, Clinton Co., Illinois
- Spouse: Sophia Anna Kuczka

5 F
- Name: Lois Scott
- Born: 18 Jan 1903 — in: Beckemeyer, Clinton Co., Illinois
- Died: 12 Jul 2001 — in: Carlyle, Clinton Co., Illinois
- Married: 02 Jun 1925 — in: Illinois
- Spouse: Arthur Christ Beckemeyer

6 M
- Name: Floyd Scott
- Born: 26 Sep 1904 — in: Beckemeyer, Clinton Co., Illinois
- Died: 05 May 1994 — in: Okeechobee Co., Florida
- Married: 1924
- Spouse: Mary Osterkamp

IDA MAY WILTON Standard Pedigree Tree

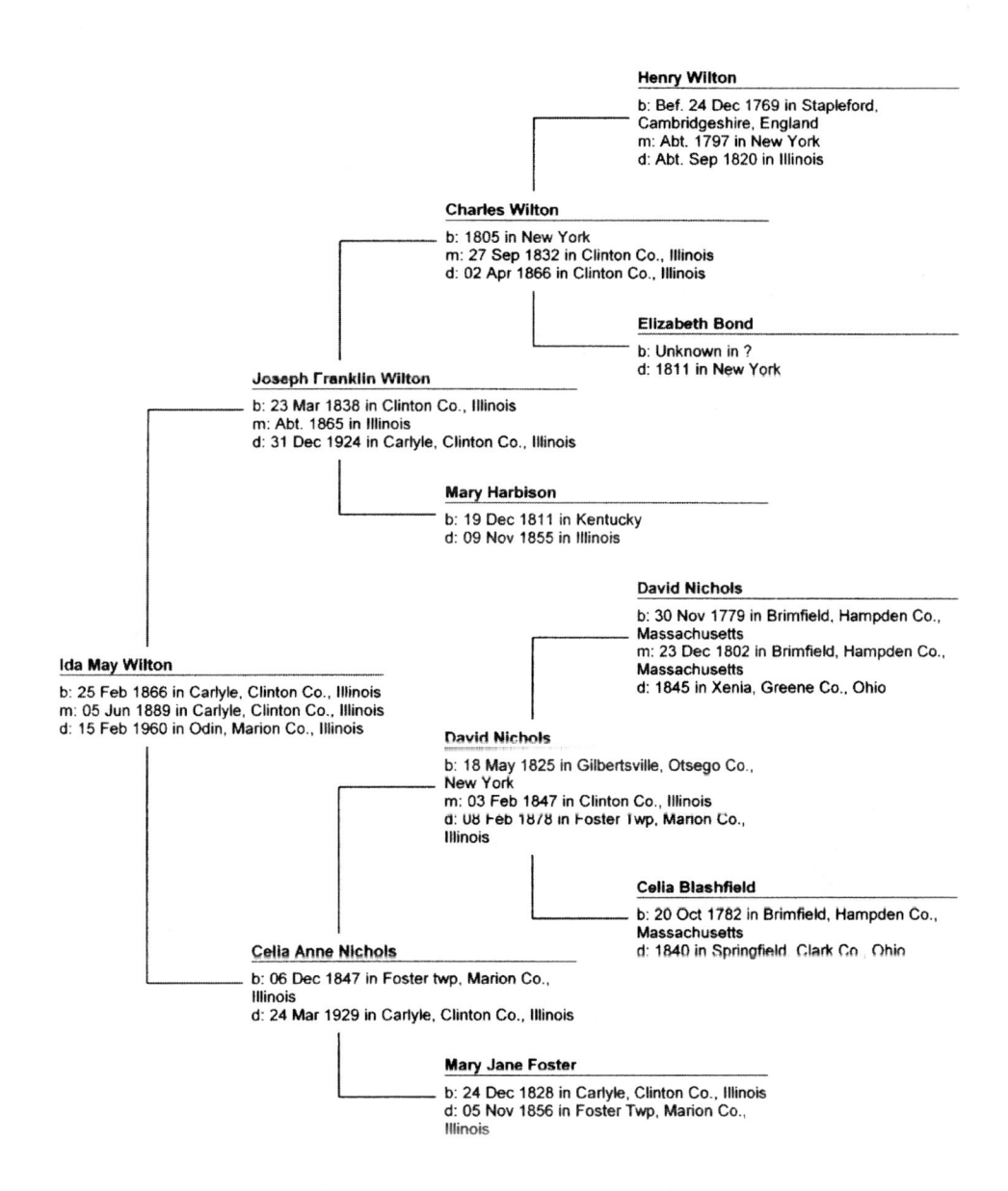

- **Ida May Wilton**
  - b: 25 Feb 1866 in Carlyle, Clinton Co., Illinois
  - m: 05 Jun 1889 in Carlyle, Clinton Co., Illinois
  - d: 15 Feb 1960 in Odin, Marion Co., Illinois

  - **Joseph Franklin Wilton**
    - b: 23 Mar 1838 in Clinton Co., Illinois
    - m: Abt. 1865 in Illinois
    - d: 31 Dec 1924 in Carlyle, Clinton Co., Illinois

    - **Charles Wilton**
      - b: 1805 in New York
      - m: 27 Sep 1832 in Clinton Co., Illinois
      - d: 02 Apr 1866 in Clinton Co., Illinois

      - **Henry Wilton**
        - b: Bef. 24 Dec 1769 in Stapleford, Cambridgeshire, England
        - m: Abt. 1797 in New York
        - d: Abt. Sep 1820 in Illinois

      - **Elizabeth Bond**
        - b: Unknown in ?
        - d: 1811 in New York

    - **Mary Harbison**
      - b: 19 Dec 1811 in Kentucky
      - d: 09 Nov 1855 in Illinois

  - **Celia Anne Nichols**
    - b: 06 Dec 1847 in Foster twp, Marion Co., Illinois
    - d: 24 Mar 1929 in Carlyle, Clinton Co., Illinois

    - **David Nichols**
      - b: 18 May 1825 in Gilbertsville, Otsego Co., New York
      - m: 03 Feb 1847 in Clinton Co., Illinois
      - d: 08 Feb 1878 in Foster Twp, Marion Co., Illinois

      - **David Nichols**
        - b: 30 Nov 1779 in Brimfield, Hampden Co., Massachusetts
        - m: 23 Dec 1802 in Brimfield, Hampden Co., Massachusetts
        - d: 1845 in Xenia, Greene Co., Ohio

      - **Celia Blashfield**
        - b: 20 Oct 1782 in Brimfield, Hampden Co., Massachusetts
        - d: 1840 in Springfield, Clark Co., Ohio

    - **Mary Jane Foster**
      - b: 24 Dec 1828 in Carlyle, Clinton Co., Illinois
      - d: 05 Nov 1856 in Foster Twp, Marion Co., Illinois

Notes: This Tree also applies to the other children of Joseph Franklin Wilton & Celia Anne Nichols: Mary Ella Wilton, Laura Caroline Wilton, Josie Celia Wilton, Joseph Charles Wilton, Nichols Wilton, Walter W. Wilton, and Sarah L. Wilton.

Ella Mae Scott (1891-1970)
[5th. Generation from Henry Wilton (1769-1820)]

&

Lee Collignon (1890-1956)
& Family

Family Group Sheet

Husband: Lee Collignon

Born: 29 Mar 1890   in: Trenton, Clinton Co., Illinois
Married: Abt. 1916   in: Illinois
Died: 08 Oct 1956
Father: John Martin Collignon
Mother: Anna Mary Emig

Wife: Ella Mae Scott

Born: Dec 1891   in: Beckemeyer, Clinton Co., Illinois
Died: 1970
Father: Charles Henry Scott
Mother: Ida May Wilton

ELLA MAE SCOTT Standard Pedigree Tree

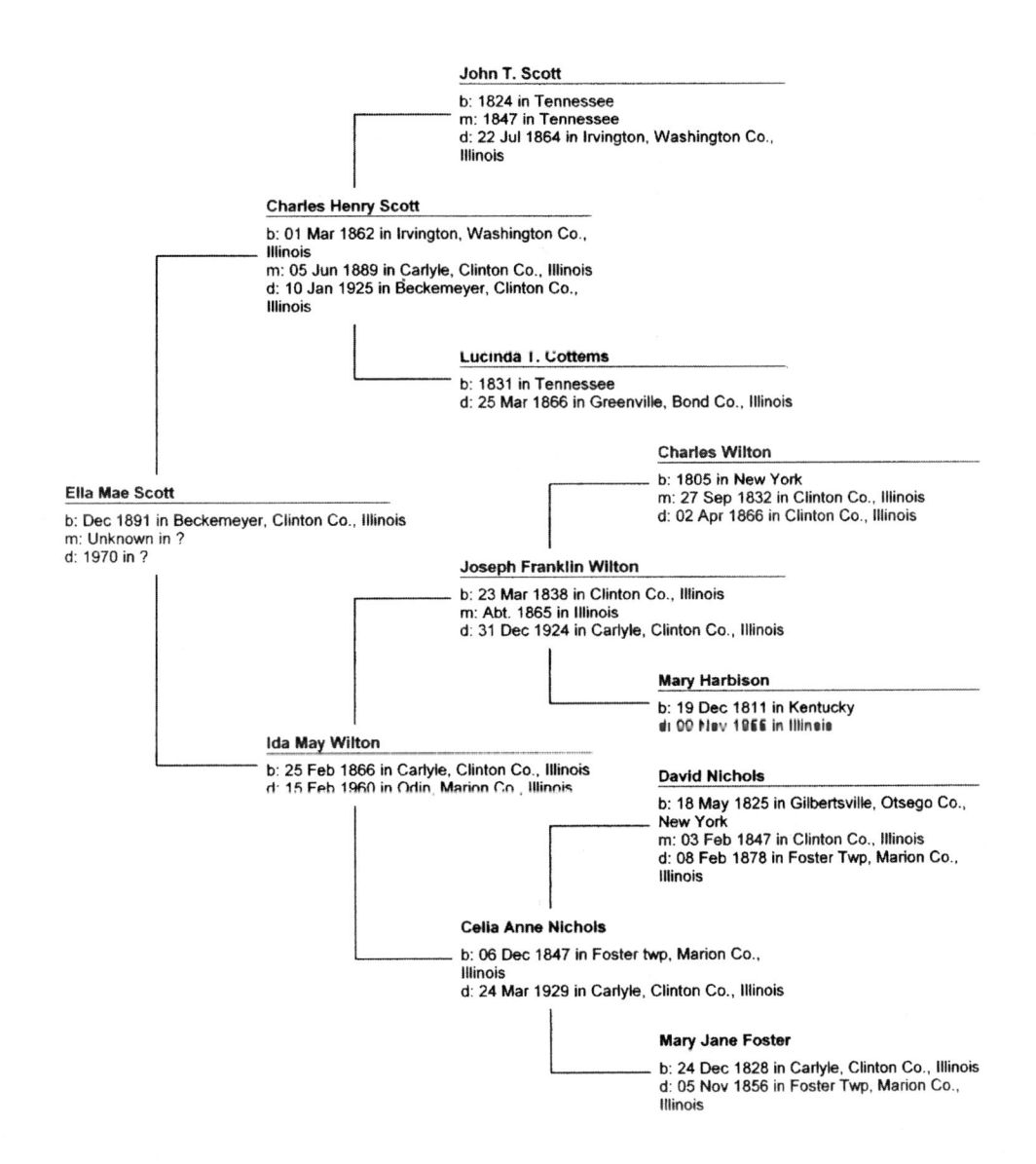

Ella Mae Scott
b: Dec 1891 in Beckemeyer, Clinton Co., Illinois
m: Unknown in ?
d: 1970 in ?

Charles Henry Scott
b: 01 Mar 1862 in Irvington, Washington Co., Illinois
m: 05 Jun 1889 in Carlyle, Clinton Co., Illinois
d: 10 Jan 1925 in Beckemeyer, Clinton Co., Illinois

John T. Scott
b: 1824 in Tennessee
m: 1847 in Tennessee
d: 22 Jul 1864 in Irvington, Washington Co., Illinois

Lucinda I. Cottems
b: 1831 in Tennessee
d: 25 Mar 1866 in Greenville, Bond Co., Illinois

Ida May Wilton
b: 25 Feb 1866 in Carlyle, Clinton Co., Illinois
d: 15 Feb 1960 in Odin, Marion Co., Illinois

Joseph Franklin Wilton
b: 23 Mar 1838 in Clinton Co., Illinois
m: Abt. 1865 in Illinois
d: 31 Dec 1924 in Carlyle, Clinton Co., Illinois

Charles Wilton
b: 1805 in New York
m: 27 Sep 1832 in Clinton Co., Illinois
d: 02 Apr 1866 in Clinton Co., Illinois

Mary Harbison
b: 19 Dec 1811 in Kentucky
d: 00 Nov 1866 in Illinois

Celia Anne Nichols
b: 06 Dec 1847 in Foster twp, Marion Co., Illinois
d: 24 Mar 1929 in Carlyle, Clinton Co., Illinois

David Nichols
b: 18 May 1825 in Gilbertsville, Otsego Co., New York
m: 03 Feb 1847 in Clinton Co., Illinois
d: 08 Feb 1878 in Foster Twp, Marion Co., Illinois

Mary Jane Foster
b: 24 Dec 1828 in Carlyle, Clinton Co., Illinois
d: 05 Nov 1856 in Foster Twp, Marion Co., Illinois

Notes: This Tree also applies to the other children of Ida May Wilton & Charles Henry Scott: Rolla Walter Scott, Joseph H. Scott, Charles Glen Scott, Lois Scott, and Floyd Scott.

Rolla Walter Scott (1894-1985)
[5th. Generation from Henry Wilton (1769-1820)]

&

Clara Ackmann (1895-1978)
& Family

Family Group Sheet

Husband: Rolla Walter Scott		
Born: 30 Jun 1894	in: Carlyle, Clinton Co., Illinois	
Married: 14 May 1919	in: Beckemeyer, Clinton Co., Illinois	
Died: 31 Mar 1985	in: Beckemeyer, Clinton Co., Illinois	
Father: Charles Henry Scott		
Mother: Ida May Wilton		
Wife: Clara Ackmann		
Born: 15 Sep 1895	in: Clinton Co., Illinois	
Died: 12 Mar 1978	in: Beckemeyer, Clinton Co., Illinois	

CHILDREN

1. F
   - Name: Genevia A. Scott
   - Born: 28 Feb 1920 — in: Beckemeyer, Clinton Co., Illinois
   - Died: 15 Sep 1968 — in: Carlyle, Clinton Co., Illinois
   - Married: 30 Nov 1940 — in: Illinois
   - Spouse: Herbert Edward Beckemeyer

2. M
   - Name: Wilton R. Scott
   - Born: 19 Aug 1921 — in: Beckemeyer, Clinton Co., Illinois
   - Married: 1942 — in: Illinois
   - Spouse: Mary L. Hanlon

Joseph H. Scott (1897-1964)
[5th. Generation from Henry Wilton (1769-1820)]

&

Marrie Gouy (1896-1985)
& Family

Family Group Sheet

Husband: Joseph H. Scott	
Born: 10 Feb 1897	in: Beckemeyer, Clinton Co., Illinois
Married: 30 Mar 1918	in: Beckemeyer, Clinton Co., Illinois
Died: 12 Jun 1964	in: Illinois
Father: Charles Henry Scott	
Mother: Ida May Wilton	
Wife: Marrie Gouy	
Born: 08 Oct 1896	in: Illinois
Died: 30 Sep 1985	in: Beckemeyer, Clinton Co., Illinois

Charles Glen Scott (1900-1966)
[5th. Generation from Henry Wilton (1769-1820)]

&

Sophia Anna Kuczka (1903-1991)
& Family

Family Group Sheet

Husband: Charles Glen Scott

Born: 14 May 1900 — in: Beckemeyer, Clinton Co., Illinois
Married: 17 Nov 1923 — in: Beckemeyer, Clinton Co., Illinois
Died: 06 Mar 1966 — in: Beckemeyer, Clinton Co., Illinois
Father: Charles Henry Scott
Mother: Ida May Wilton

Wife: Sophia Anna Kuczka

Born: 06 Feb 1903 — in: Germany
Died: 01 Feb 1991 — in: Beckemeyer, Clinton Co., Illinois
Father: Joseph Kuczka
Mother: Maria Przyblla

Lois Scott (1903-2001)
[5th. Generation from Henry Wilton (1769-1820)]

&

Arthur Christ Beckemeyer (1897-1991)
& Family

Family Group Sheet

Husband: Arthur Christ Beckemeyer

Born: 16 Oct 1897	in: Wade, Clinton Co., Illinois
Married: 02 Jun 1925	in: Illinois
Died: 11 Apr 1991	in: Breese, Clinton Co., Illinois
Father: William H. J. Beckemeyer	
Mother: Mary H.	

Wife: Lois Scott

Born: 18 Jan 1903	in: Beckemeyer, Clinton Co., Illinois
Died: 12 Jul 2001	in: Carlyle, Clinton Co., Illinois
Father: Charles Henry Scott	
Mother: Ida May Wilton	

CHILDREN

1 F
- Name: Lois Beckemeyer
- Born: 19 Sep 1926 — in: Illinois
- Died: 19 Sep 1926 — in: Illinois

2 F
- Name: Joyce May Beckemeyer
- Born: 11 Aug 1927 — in: Deckemeyer, Clinton Co., Illinois
- Died: 13 Jul 2000 — in: Belleville, St. Clair Co., Illinois
- Married: 19 Sep 1948 — in: Illinois
- Spouse: Elmer Beckmann
- Married: 13 Feb 1958 — in: Illinois
- Spouse: Rudolph Jesenick
- Married: 18 Jan 1966 — in: Illinois
- Spouse: Jesse E. Ripple

3 F
- Name: Mildred Beckemeyer
- Born: Aft. 1930 — in: Illinois
- Died: Bef. 2002

4 M
- Name: William Beckemeyer
- Born: Aft. 1930 — in: Illinois

Floyd Scott (1904-1994)
[5th. Generation from Henry Wilton (1769-1820)]

&

Mary Osterkamp (1908-1972)
& Family

Family Group Sheet

Husband: Floyd Scott

Born: 26 Sep 1904   in: Beckemeyer, Clinton Co., Illinois
Married: 1924
Died: 05 May 1994   in: Okeechobee Co., Florida
Father: Charles Henry Scott
Mother: Ida May Wilton

Wife: Mary Osterkamp

Born: 06 Jan 1908   in: Illinois
Died: 01 Jan 1972   in: Detroit, Wayne Co., Michigan
Father: Frank Osterkamp
Mother: Mary Dewart

Mary Ella Wilton (1868-1942)
[4th. Generation from Henry Wilton (1769-1820)]

&

Walter C. Rinesmith (1866-1902)
& Family

Family Group Sheet

Husband: Walter C. Rinesmith	
Born: 01 Sep 1866	in: Landsburg, Perry Co., Pennsylvania
Married: 11 Nov 1896	in: Clinton Co., Illinois
Died: 26 Oct 1902	in: Carlyle, Clinton Co., Illinois
Father: William Rinesmith	
Mother: Eliza Jane Rhoades	

Wife: Mary Ella Wilton	
Born: 16 Feb 1868	in: Carlyle, Clinton Co., Illinois
Died: 05 Jun 1942	in: Illinois
Father: Joseph Franklin Wilton	
Mother: Celia Anne Nichols	

CHILDREN		
1 M	Name: Harold Walter Rinesmith	
	Born: 08 Apr 1900	in: Carlyle, Clinton Co., Illinois
	Died: May 1969	in: St. Louis City Co., Missouri

WALTER C. RINESMITH Standard Pedigree Tree

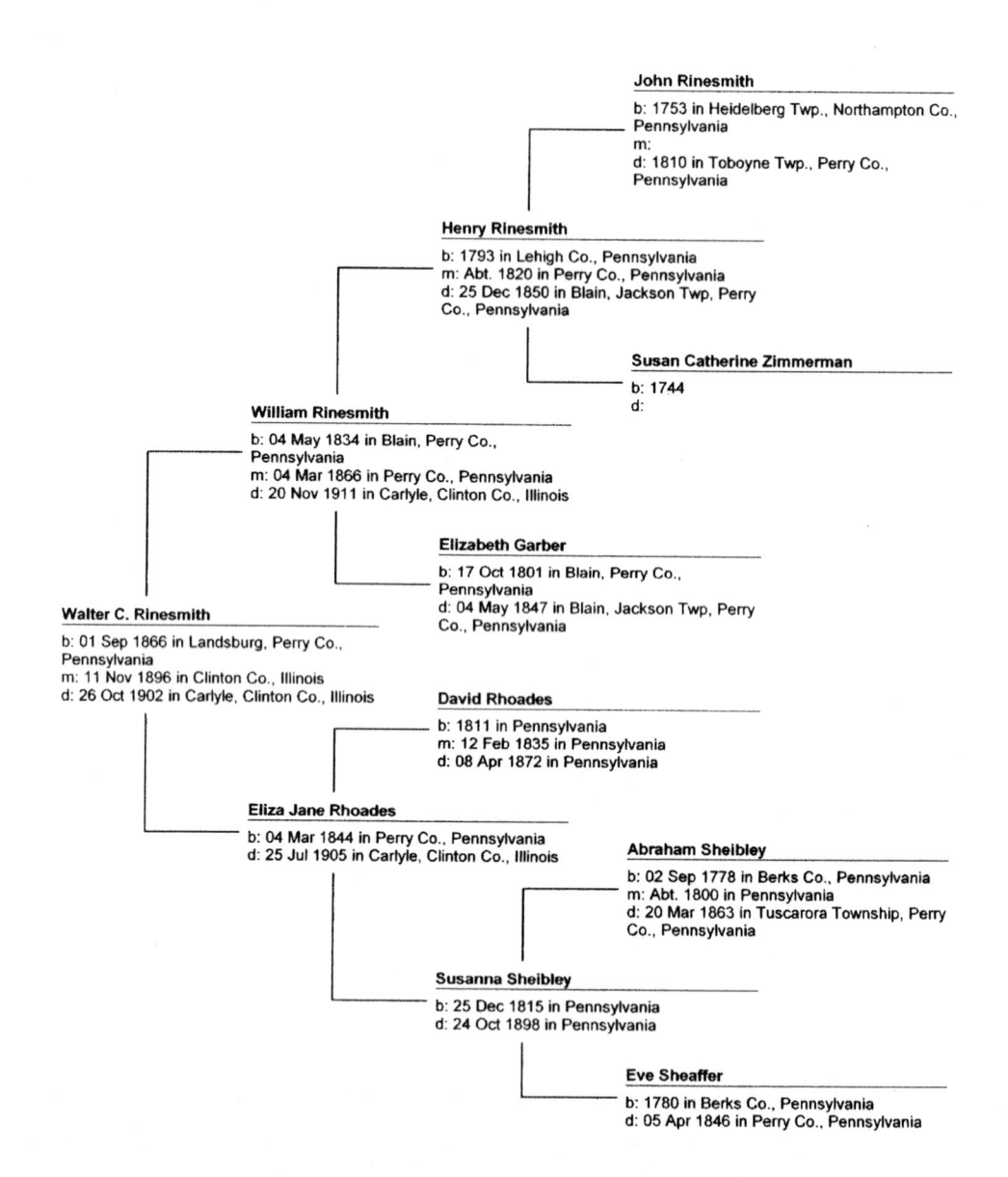

Walter C. Rinesmith
b: 01 Sep 1866 in Landsburg, Perry Co., Pennsylvania
m: 11 Nov 1896 in Clinton Co., Illinois
d: 26 Oct 1902 in Carlyle, Clinton Co., Illinois

- **William Rinesmith**
  b: 04 May 1834 in Blain, Perry Co., Pennsylvania
  m: 04 Mar 1866 in Perry Co., Pennsylvania
  d: 20 Nov 1911 in Carlyle, Clinton Co., Illinois

  - **Henry Rinesmith**
    b: 1793 in Lehigh Co., Pennsylvania
    m: Abt. 1820 in Perry Co., Pennsylvania
    d: 25 Dec 1850 in Blain, Jackson Twp, Perry Co., Pennsylvania

    - **John Rinesmith**
      b: 1753 in Heidelberg Twp., Northampton Co., Pennsylvania
      m:
      d: 1810 in Toboyne Twp., Perry Co., Pennsylvania

    - **Susan Catherine Zimmerman**
      b: 1744
      d:

  - **Elizabeth Garber**
    b: 17 Oct 1801 in Blain, Perry Co., Pennsylvania
    d: 04 May 1847 in Blain, Jackson Twp, Perry Co., Pennsylvania

- **Eliza Jane Rhoades**
  b: 04 Mar 1844 in Perry Co., Pennsylvania
  d: 25 Jul 1905 in Carlyle, Clinton Co., Illinois

  - **David Rhoades**
    b: 1811 in Pennsylvania
    m: 12 Feb 1835 in Pennsylvania
    d: 08 Apr 1872 in Pennsylvania

  - **Susanna Sheibley**
    b: 25 Dec 1815 in Pennsylvania
    d: 24 Oct 1898 in Pennsylvania

    - **Abraham Sheibley**
      b: 02 Sep 1778 in Berks Co., Pennsylvania
      m: Abt. 1800 in Pennsylvania
      d: 20 Mar 1863 in Tuscarora Township, Perry Co., Pennsylvania

    - **Eve Sheaffer**
      b: 1780 in Berks Co., Pennsylvania
      d: 05 Apr 1846 in Perry Co., Pennsylvania

Joseph Charles Wilton (1878-1950)
[4th. Generation from Henry Wilton (1769-1820)]

&

Nettie M. Miller (1876-1959)
& Family

Family Group Sheet

Husband: Joseph Charles Wilton	
Born: 16 Jun 1878	in: Carlyle, Clinton Co., Illinois
Married: 16 Aug 1899	in: Clinton Co., Illinois
Died: 24 Feb 1950	in: St. Louis, St. Louis Co., Missouri
Father: Joseph Franklin Wilton	
Mother: Celia Anne Nichols	
Wife: Nettie M. Miller	
Born: 01 May 1876	in: Illinois
Died: 02 Jan 1959	in: Missouri

CHILDREN

1 F
- Name: Celia E. Wilton
- Born: 03 Feb 1902 — in: Illinois
- Died: 30 Nov 1983 — in: St. Louis City Co., Missouri

2 F
- Name: Edna I. Wilton
- Born: 06 Jun 1903 — in: Illinois
- Died: 24 Dec 1993 — in: Clinton Co., Illinois

Nichols Wilton (1880-1965)
[4th. Generation from Henry Wilton (1769-1820)]

&

Anna A. Pepperkorn (1885-1977)
& Family

Family Group Sheet

Husband: Nichols Wilton

Born: 11 Sep 1880 — in: Illinois
Married: 16 Mar 1904 — in: Clinton Co., Illinois
Died: 15 Jun 1965 — in: Carlyle, Clinton Co., Illinois
Father: Joseph Franklin Wilton
Mother: Celia Anne Nichols

Wife: Anna A. Pepperkorn

Born: 03 Jul 1885 — in: Illinois
Died: 05 Jan 1977 — in: St. Louis Co., Missouri
Father: Frederick William Pepperkorn
Mother: Matilda Burger

CHILDREN

1 M
Name: Paul L. Wilton
Born: 29 May 1905 — in: Illinois
Died: 10 Aug 1997 — in: St. Louis Co., Missouri

2 M
Name: Joseph Clifford Wilton
Born: 30 Jan 1908 — in: Carlyle, Clinton Co., Illinois
Died: Apr 1970 — in: Kansas
Married: 11 Feb 1950 — in: Kansas City, Jackson Co., Missouri
Spouse: Eleanor Elizabeth Ibach
Married: 30 Apr 1966 — in: Kansas City, Jackson Co., Missouri
Spouse: Thilmoan M. Renne

3 M
Name: David Nichols Wilton
Born: 13 Aug 1918 — in: Illinois
Died: 16 Apr 1963 — in: Rheinstrasse, Germany

ANNA A. PEPPERKORN Standard Pedigree Tree

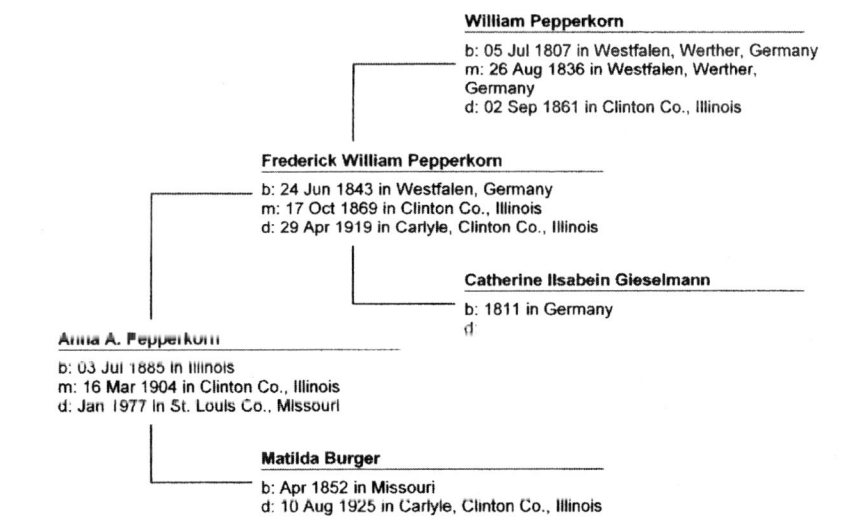

William Pepperkorn
b: 05 Jul 1807 in Westfalen, Werther, Germany
m: 26 Aug 1836 in Westfalen, Werther, Germany
d: 02 Sep 1861 in Clinton Co., Illinois

Frederick William Pepperkorn
b: 24 Jun 1843 in Westfalen, Germany
m: 17 Oct 1869 in Clinton Co., Illinois
d: 29 Apr 1919 in Carlyle, Clinton Co., Illinois

Catherine Ilsabein Gieselmann
b: 1811 in Germany
d:

Anna A. Pepperkorn
b: 03 Jul 1885 in Illinois
m: 16 Mar 1904 in Clinton Co., Illinois
d: Jan 1977 in St. Louis Co., Missouri

Matilda Burger
b: Apr 1852 in Missouri
d: 10 Aug 1925 in Carlyle, Clinton Co., Illinois

Walter W. Wilton (1883-1954)
[4th. Generation from Henry Wilton (1769-1820)]

&

Jennie Louise Baxter (1884-1969)
& Family

Family Group Sheet

Husband: Walter W. Wilton

Born: 27 Jan 1883 — in: Macoupin Co., Illinois
Married: 29 Oct 1906 — in: Marion Co., Illinois
Died: 14 Nov 1954 — in: Breese, Clinton Co., Illinois
Father: Joseph Franklin Wilton
Mother: Celia Anne Nichols

Wife: Jennie Louise Baxter

Born: Jun 1884 — in: Illinois
Died: 1969 — in: Carlyle, Clinton Co., Illinois

CHILDREN

1 M
Name: Walter Ralph Wilton
Born: 1917 — in: Illinois
Died: 14 Apr 1920 — in: Carlyle, Clinton Co., Illinois

2 M
Name: Robert Harry Wilton
Born: 24 Feb 1923 — in: Carlyle, Clinton Co., Illinois
Married: 22 Oct 1945 — in: Doncaster, Yorkshire, England
Spouse: Olive Linda Steggall

Robert Harry Wilton (1923-)
[5th. Generation from Henry Wilton (1769-1820)]

&

Olive Linda Steggall (1920-2003)
& Family

Family Group Sheet

Husband: Robert Harry Wilton	
Born: 24 Feb 1923	in: Carlyle, Clinton Co., Illinois
Married: 22 Oct 1945	in: Doncaster, Yorkshire, England
Father: Walter W. Wilton	
Mother: Jennie Louise Baxter	

Wife: Olive Linda Steggall	
Born: 28 May 1920	in: Bedford, England
Died: 26 Feb 2003	in: Breese, Clinton Co., Illoinois
Father: Oliver Steggall	
Mother: Linda Collins	

	CHILDREN	
1 M	Name: Robert E. Wilton	
	Born: Jan 1947	in: Illinois
2 M	Name: Michael Wilton	
	Born: Aft. 1949	in: Illinois

ROBERT HARRY WILTON Standard Pedigree Tree

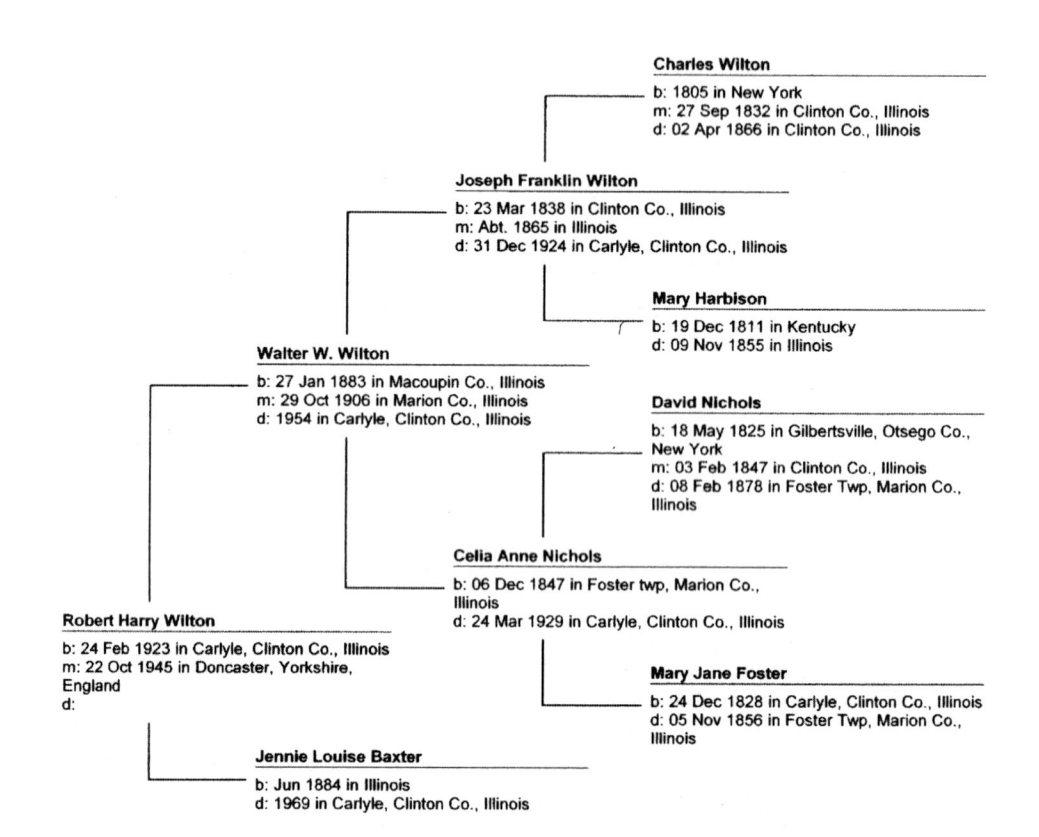

- **Robert Harry Wilton**
  - b: 24 Feb 1923 in Carlyle, Clinton Co., Illinois
  - m: 22 Oct 1945 in Doncaster, Yorkshire, England
  - d:

  - Father: **Walter W. Wilton**
    - b: 27 Jan 1883 in Macoupin Co., Illinois
    - m: 29 Oct 1906 in Marion Co., Illinois
    - d: 1954 in Carlyle, Clinton Co., Illinois

    - Father: **Joseph Franklin Wilton**
      - b: 23 Mar 1838 in Clinton Co., Illinois
      - m: Abt. 1865 in Illinois
      - d: 31 Dec 1924 in Carlyle, Clinton Co., Illinois

      - Father: **Charles Wilton**
        - b: 1805 in New York
        - m: 27 Sep 1832 in Clinton Co., Illinois
        - d: 02 Apr 1866 in Clinton Co., Illinois

      - Mother: **Mary Harbison**
        - b: 19 Dec 1811 in Kentucky
        - d: 09 Nov 1855 in Illinois

    - Mother: **Celia Anne Nichols**
      - b: 06 Dec 1847 in Foster twp, Marion Co., Illinois
      - d: 24 Mar 1929 in Carlyle, Clinton Co., Illinois

      - Father: **David Nichols**
        - b: 18 May 1825 in Gilbertsville, Otsego Co., New York
        - m: 03 Feb 1847 in Clinton Co., Illinois
        - d: 08 Feb 1878 in Foster Twp, Marion Co., Illinois

      - Mother: **Mary Jane Foster**
        - b: 24 Dec 1828 in Carlyle, Clinton Co., Illinois
        - d: 05 Nov 1856 in Foster Twp, Marion Co., Illinois

  - Mother: **Jennie Louise Baxter**
    - b: Jun 1884 in Illinois
    - d: 1969 in Carlyle, Clinton Co., Illinois

Notes: This Tree also applies to the other child of Walter W. Wilton & Jennie Louise Baxter: Walter Ralph Wilton

Sarah L. Wilton (1885-1946)
[4th. Generation from Henry Wilton (1769-1820)]

&

Francis C. Ballew (1885-1962)
& Family

Family Group Sheet

Husband: Francis C. Ballew	
Born: 1885	
Married: Unknown	
Died: 1962	
Wife: Sarah L. Wilton	
Born: 25 Jul 1885	in: Illinois
Died: 1946	in: Illinois
Father: Joseph Franklin Wilton	
Mother: Celia Anne Nichols	

Sophia Wilton (1808-1875)
[2nd. Generation From Henry Wilton (1768-1820)]

Sophia Wilton, born about 1808 in New York, was the third and last child of Henry Wilton and Elizabeth Bond. Henry Wilton had moved the family from New York to Shawneetown in Gallatin County, Illinois in 1811. Sometime after Henry died in 1820, the family began to migrate to other counties in Illinois, and by 1840, two of Sophia's brothers by Henry's second marriage, Thomas Wilton and Charles Wilton, were listed in the federal census of Clinton County, Illinois.

In the 1850 Federal Census of Clinton County, Illinois, Sophia Wilton was listed along with Britanna Wilton, Sophia's half sister by Henry's third marriage. In the 1860 Federal Census of Clinton County, Illinois, under the Post Office of Carlyle, Sophia Wilton was listed at age 55, by herself. In the same census, but a number of dwellings apart, Britanna Wilton was also listed.

Apparently, Sophia was rather eccentric, because she stated her age differently on various occasions. Perhaps under certain situations she preferred for people to think she was older than was the case. As was mentioned in the Union Banner newspaper of Carlyle, Illinois on August 5, 1875, Sophia was reported as being the half sister of Harry Wilton, son of Henry Wilton and his first wife, who was born in 1794. That would conform to the estimated birth date of about 1808.

Sophia died August 1875 in Clinton County, Illinois, and she was buried in the Wilton cemetery in Clement Township in Clinton County. Concerning Sophia's estate, there was a mention in the Carlyle Constitution and Union newspaper of July 5, 1877 about a lot she had owned in Carlyle, Illinois. It was reported that the executor of the estate, a Sheriff Allen, sold the land at auction for a purchase price of $2,900, a substantial sum for that time, for a lot that was described as "one of the best, if not the best, business location in Carlyle...."

Acknowledgments

As mentioned earlier, this book is the culmination of many years of accumulating family information, and it has come from a variety of sources. The story would not be complete without giving credit to some of those who have provided inspiration and shared resources along the journey.

After interest was first inspired within the immediate family, feelers went out to many family members, with the hope of enlisting others in our quest for information. There were always mixed results, with some responding favorably, but most were not encouraging. After a number of years passed of searching through archives and census reports, we at long last began to correspond with other descendants of similar interests, which increasingly made our job easier.

Some of the first to respond favorably were Brenda Rogers and Nick and Linda Griffin, who shared information that helped to extend our knowledge and to inspire research into other areas. Sometime later, we were fortunate to correspond with B.J. Lawrence, who had worked extensively on another family line. He also had valuable Wilton information he was willing to share. Also deserving mention was input by Robert St. John Wilton and an Englishman by the name of Alan Bullwinkle.

A special "thanks" goes to Mary Shackelton, a descendant of Henry Wilton and his third wife, Mary Cook. She also did work on our Henry Wilton and Elizabeth Bond branch of the tree, and she was helpful in filling holes in our information and providing leads to follow up and to verify.

Although not specifically recognized, over more recent years, a lot of valuable information has become available by searching the internet, which has allowed a fair amount of research from the comfort of home and the family computer.

Index of Individuals

Ackmann -
  Clara: 502
Adams -
  Ann Michelle: 326, 331
  Jesse A.: 327
  Jesse Woodrow: 326, 327, 329
  John Michael Van: 328
  Joseph Robert: 327
  Matthew Joseph: 326, 333-334
  Melanie: 326, 332
  Melissa: 326, 330
  Michael Albert: 321, 325-327, 328, 329, 330, 331, 332, 334, 335
  Michael Albert Jr.: 326, 328-329
  Savannah Marie: 328
  Shannon Mae: 328
  Timothy Mitchell: 326, 335
  William Emerson: 334
Adcock -
  Mary: 127
Admire -
  Ida Bell: 21, 84-86
  Livey Leslie: 85, 86
  William K.: 86
Ainscough -
  Mildred Gertrude: 441
Akin -
  Esther Thelma: 269
Alexander -
  Cyrus Granville: 259
  Louisa Emily: 188
  Susan Caroline: 259

Alford -
  Naty: 426
Allen -
  Clara L.: 489
  Daisy Retta: 196, 198, 201, 207
  Edward: 487, 488-489
  Gary Lynn: 215, 219
  Harry: 489
  Hiram: 487
  Mary: 489
  Nancy: 418
  Tabitha: 194
Amstutz -
  Christian C.: 482, 483
  Christian U.: 483
  Mary: 471, 482-483
Anderson -
  Bobbye Gail: 34
  Lisa Christine: 34
  Lucy Collins: 448
  Patsy: 420
  Patsy Jean: 34
  Ruth Marie: 249
  Travis Dewayne: 34
  Travis Leon: 34
Asbury -
  Elizabeth Gay: 390
Ashford -
  Richard Bryan: 343
Bailey -
  Dorothy Jean: 83
  Russell: 74, 83
  Russell Nolan: 83

Baker -
- Amber Brooke: 337

Baldwin -
- Martha Jane: 16, 222-226, 230, 231, 236, 240, 284, 289, 303, 309, 310, 316, 324, 345, 354, 356, 362, 371, 378, 399
- Sarah Elizabeth: 409-411, 413, 414, 416, 417, 419, 421, 422, 425, 428, 431, 434
- Thomas Holland: 225, 226, 231, 236, 413, 414, 416, 425
- William W.: 226, 414

Bales -
- Tana Lynn: 65, 70

Ballew -
- Francis C.: 496, 515

Banta -
- Anna: 456

Bardsley -
- Carol L.: 321, 323

Barron -
- Emily Aramantha: 136

Bass -
- Paula Jean: 432, 435

Baxter -
- Jennie Louise: 496, 512, 513, 514

Beckemeyer -
- Arthur Christ: 505
- Lois: 505
- Joyce Mae: 505
- Mildred: 505
- William: 505

Behanna -
- Janet Louise: 397, 402

Belcher -
- Harriet: 237

Bescheinen -
- Frances Anna: 471, 474, 476
- Henry Joseph: 474, 476
- Johann Matthias: 476
- Mathias H.: 476

Bevers -
- Brenda: 179
- Gwendolyn Inez: 179, 180-181
- Lee Roy: 161, 178-179, 180, 181
- Roy Duane: 179

Biddy -
- Mildred Louise: 269

Birdsong -
- Francis M.: 312
- Rebecca Alma: 310, 312, 354, 356, 362
- Russell: 474

Blackmore -
- Harriet Eliza: 105
- William N.: 105

Blair -
- Florence: 81
- Margaret: 348

Blashfield -
- Celia: 497, 499

Bohannon -
- David Pickens: 235, 237, 240
- Levi Charles: 237
- Robert K.: 237, 240
- Verda Louise: 230, 233-235, 237, 240

Bolton -
    Douglas Ray: 258, 266-269
    Jeremy Chad: 269
    Otis Tastius: 269
Bond -
    Elizabeth: 5, 10, 11, 17, 23, 442,
        449, 487, 490, 492, 499
Booher -
    Betty Ann: 441, 443
    John: 443
Boucher -
    Timi Lyn: 38, 42
Bowen -
    Cori Denise: 71
    Gary Donald: 71
    Jeffery Heath: 71
Boyd -
    Bernice Evelyn: 204, 207
Bradberry -
    Charles McClure: 265
    Ilda Kay: 258, 260-265
    Lawrence: 263, 265
Brill -
    Laura Ann: 150
Britton -
    Del Duane: 215
Brock -
    Asalee: 174, 176
    George Washington: 174
    Stephen P. Bradham Jacob: 174
Brown -
    Brian Jeffrey: 120
    Donnie Jay: 117, 118-119
    Eric Joseph: 118
    George Andrew: 97
    Georgia Mabel: 95, 97, 99
    Gregory John: 118

    Heather Nicole: 381, 384-386
    Israel: 118
    John William: 89, 117, 118-119
    Nathan Leland: 120
    Rhonda Ellen: 120
    Ricky Allen: 377, 380-381,
        383, 386
    Travis Ray: 117, 120
    William Lester: 381, 383, 386
Bruss -
    Debra: 397, 400 401
Bryan -
    Charles C.: 170
    John: 164, 170
    Phillip Hale: 170
Bryant -
    Lula Sarah: 53
Buche -
    Braden Daniel: 277
    Brant Douglas: 272, 277
    Connor Dylan: 277
    Daniel Lee: 277
    Ethan Luke: 277
Buckley -
    Maria: 81
Buffington -
    Mary: 226, 414
Burch -
    Edwinona: 26, 46
Burger -
    Matilda: 510, 511
Burkett -
    Amos Franklin: 455, 457-458
    Arthur Franklin: 457
    Billy Gene: 457
    Curtis: 463
    Dorothea Edith: 448, 451-452,

Burkett - (Con't)
455, 460
Elmer Franklin: 448, 453-455,
457, 458, 459, 460, 461,
463, 464, 465, 466, 467,
468
Elmer Leroy: 455, 468
Helen Anna: 455, 461
Gary: 463
Ione Maxine: 455, 467
James Martin: 446, 448, 449,
452, 471, 475, 478
Jane Lucille: 455, 466
Jeroma Lee: 455, 465
John Franklin: 468
John Freedis: 446
Johnny: 463
Marc: 468
Robert Gene: 468
Mary Annise: 446, 469-471,
473, 474, 475, 478, 480,
481, 482, 484
Mary Eileen: 455, 464
Mildred Irene: 455, 459
Needham: 446, 449
Raymond Isaac: 455, 463
William Franklin: 446, 447-449,
451, 452, 455, 458

Burrage -
Lori Ann: 65, 68
Buschmann -
Gretchen Elizabeth: 326, 335
Buttrill -
Joyce Fay: 301, 304
Cagle -
Sarah: 477, 479

Caldwell -
Billy Ray: 432, 433
Caryn Denise: 433
Craig Randall: 433
Jeana Lynette: 433
Callis -
William Albert: 379
Willie Lorene: 377, 379, 382,
386
Campbell -
Dorsey Marion: 74, 82
Cannon -
Linda: 321, 339
Cardenas -
Donna Faye: 291
Ernest: 288, 291
Carey -
Helen Louise: 281
Carroll -
Kenneth Ray: 113, 115
Kennie Sue: 115
Nancy Lynn: 115
Carter -
John Raford: 114
Mary Francis: 114
Chaddick -
Robert E.: 290
Telula Victoria: 288, 290, 292
William Monroe: 290
Champ -
Frances Virginia: 428, 436
Chattam -
Herbert Lee: 455, 467
Cherry -
Arthur Raymond: 417
David W.: 413, 417, 418
Joel: 418

John M.: 418
Marcus Lafayette: 417, 418
Oscar A.: 417
Childress -
  Julia Ann: 327
Cimo -
  Patricia: 272, 274
Clark -
  Daniel Joseph Edward: 311
  Easter Britania: 16, 19, 21, 24, 26, 27, 30, 39, 52, 74, 77, 85, 89, 93, 109, 119, 124, 126, 129, 135, 157, 161, 165, 185, 193, 197, 201
  Ezra: 21, 24, 27, 30, 77
  John: 24
  Josephine: 317
  Neoma Demer: 309, 311, 316, 324, 345
Clifton -
  John Calvin: 188
  Stacy Pauline: 188
Cobb -
  Sallie Polina: 303
Cole -
  David Stanford: 221
  Herman: 421
  Hazle: 421
  Isaac W.: 413, 421
  Leland Stanford: 193, 221
Collignon -
  Lee: 500
Collins -
  Lucy: 453-455
Conn -
  Martha W.: 245
  William Woodward: 245

Conway -
  Jennie Bell: 362
  Ollie Louise: 173
Coon -
  Sophie E.: 95
Cooper -
  Martha Elizabeth: 155
Cordona -
  Thomas S.: 448, 451
Cottems -
  Lucinda T.: 498, 501
Couch -
  Cerro Gorda: 114
Cox -
  John Henry: 315, 317
  Vera Norma: 309, 313-315, 317
Crabtree -
  Carol Ann: 347, 349-350
  Frederick Aston: 348
  Michael Blair: 351
  Sheridan Blair: 347, 348, 350
  Thomas Blair: 347, 351
  Thomas Sheridan: 309, 346-347, 348, 349, 350, 351
Crawford -
  Coleman: 364
  Lizzie Bell: 364
Creel -
  George: 237
  Harriet Elizabeth: 235, 237, 240
  Joseph H.: 237, 240
Cress -
  Johann Nicholous Henrich: 18
  Susanna: 18, 23
Crews -
  Nancy Jane: 379

Criswell -
    Charles Edger: 148, 150, 152
    Charlotte Gail: 148, 151-152
    Everett Lynn: 148
    Jeremiah George: 150
    William Merton: 146, 148, 150, 151, 152

Crosier -
    Curtis Eugene: 107, 110
    Jason Todd: 110

Crowell -
    George: 448, 451

Cruit -
    Jaclyn Ruth: 355
    Jeremy Ray: 355
    Johnny Ray: 353, 355

Cruse -
    Absalom B.: 16, 18, 23
    Henry C.: 18, 23
    Johann Philip: 18
    Susanah: 10, 16, 18, 21, 23, 27, 30, 77, 225, 231, 236

Cumpton -
    Jo Evelyn: 161, 186-188, 189
    Joseph Herman: 187, 188

Dahler -
    Maria Agnes: 476

Daniels -
    Teresa Ann: 38, 43

Davis -
    Jerry Lavern: 244, 248-249
    Lavern Meldon: 249
    Melissa: 327
    Michelle Lynn: 249
    Shannon Lynn: 249
    Tony Kelly: 249

Deckard -
    Josephine: 471, 473, 477, 478

Decker -
    Betty Clair: 371, 406-407, 408
    William James: 407

Dennigan -
    Janice Susan: 277

Deroy -
    Patricia Lee: 120

Dewoody -
    Benjamin Tendol: 62, 63, 66
    George Clifton: 63
    Linda Lou: 62, 64-66, 68, 69
    Spencer Pinckney: 48, 62-63, 65, 66, 69, 71
    Terri Lynn: 62, 71
    Thomas Valintine: 63

Dipprey -
    Clyde Ernest: 190
    Edna Lorene: 189, 190
    George Barnes: 190

Dixon -
    Amelia Jane: 21, 25, 26, 29, 30, 33, 35, 39, 41
    E.P.: 26, 30, 39

Dixson -
    Alexander: 53
    Hazel Ann: 48, 51, 53, 54, 55, 56, 58
    Joseph: 53
    Robert Pyles: 51, 53, 55, 58

Dodds -
    Bonnie: 397, 403

Dodson -
    Bertha Evelyn: 187, 188
    Otha Thomas: 188
    Robert Bolin: 188

Dougan -
   Hannah: 245
Douse -
   Martha: 6, 11
Dragon -
   Bobbi: 269
Drake -
   Esther Elizabeth: 24
   Jacob: 24
Duke -
   Catherine A.: 309, 318-322, 323, 324, 326, 329, 336, 338, 339, 340
   James H.: 322, 324
   John H.: 321, 322, 324, 338
Duncan -
   Ernest Walker: 383, 386
   George H.: 383
   Roxie Ann: 379
   Sara Ilyne: 383, 386
   Wilma Jean: 381, 383, 386
Dunlap -
   Leslie C.: 38, 42
Dunn -
   Ambrose Wade: 53
   Lola Ella: 51, 53, 55, 58
   William Augusta: 53
Easton -
   Ardith: 455, 468
Eaton -
   Twilla Dawn: 95, 101
Eberhardt -
   Catherine: 18
Edwards -
   Linda Fay: 310, 352-353, 355, 356, 357, 358

Eldridge -
   Sarah Ann: 63
Eliza -
   Jennie: 322, 324
Elliott -
   Elizabeth: 418
   Mary: 81
Ellis -
   Eleanor: 10, 12, 17, 23, 442, 449
   Sally: 12, 17
Ennie -
   Laura: 273
Epperson -
   Meredith Rachelle: 184
   Ronald Dewayne: 183, 184
Ervin -
   Mary Ann: 479
Eubanks -
   Margaret M.: 426
Evans -
   Frank M.: 310, 312, 354, 356, 362
   Lydia Ann: 225, 306, 310, 312, 353, 354, 356, 359, 360, 362, 363
Farris -
   Kathryn June: 288, 297
Ferguson -
   Benjamin Sheppard IV: 215
Fernandez -
   Bertha: 249
Fite -
   Margaret: 78
Flanagan -
   Pat: 491

Forcum -
- Elizabeth: 158

Fortini -
- Brianna Grace: 408
- Mark Anthony: 408

Foshee -
- Cristal Dawn: 151
- Riley Eugene: 148, 151

Foster -
- Charles Henry: 488
- John: 487, 488, 491, 492
- Laura Sophia: 488, 491-492
- Mary Jane: 497, 499, 501, 514

Francis -
- John: 132
- Nancy: 132

Franklin -
- Mary Ann: 134

Freeman -
- Martha P.: 31

Fritz -
- Vicki Cheryl: 122, 123

Frogg -
- Maria: 6, 11, 17, 490
- Thomas: 6, 11

Fromdahl -
- David: 326, 332
- Hannah Catherine: 332

Frost -
- Nina G.: 154, 155
- Samuel Bacon: 155

Fry -
- Calyn Grace: 217
- David Evander: 215, 216, 218
- David Michael: 215, 217-218
- Jack Franklin: 193, 214-216, 217, 218, 219
- Jesse Franklin: 216
- Kathryn Michelle: 217
- Lewis M.: 216
- Marsha Karen: 215, 219-220
- Mary Helen: 215
- Molly Daire: 215

Fulcher -
- Ada Pearl: 148, 150, 152
- Nathaniel Peter: 150

Fuller -
- Ruby May: 471

Gaither -
- Basil: 158
- Elzy Florence: 22, 156-158
- Ivory: 158
- Joseph R.: 157, 158
- Sarah Francis: 156-157

Garber -
- Elizabeth: 508

Garner -
- Holly Karen: 219
- Mary Jane: 245
- Randall Lee: 215, 219
- Zachery Franklin: 219

Gary -
- Alton J.: 310, 363-364, 365, 366, 367
- Alton Nathaniel: 366
- Archie Nathaniel: 364
- Brandi Mae: 366
- Debra Deann: 363, 365
- J.C. Nathaniel: 363, 364
- John Alton: 363, 366
- Sherri Loraine: 363, 367

Gatton -
- Augerena: 158

Gauldin -
   Marjorie LaTrelle: 281
Gentry -
   Garland: 379
   Sarah Francis: 379
Gerkhausen -
   Maria Catherina: 476
Gibson -
   Earl: 415
   Ireneous Crumble: 415
   James Vanzant: 415
   John Keeton: 413, 415
   John Otis: 415
   Jesse Ivan: 415
   Mahalia C.: 383
   Marietta: 415
   Martella: 415
   Marzella Clovene: 415
   Myrl Martha: 415
Gieselmann -
   Catherine Ilsabein: 511
Gilbert -
   John Andrew: 259
   Marintha Evelyn: 258, 259, 264
   Stephen Green: 259
Gonzalez -
   Christy Darleen: 100
   Michael A.: 95, 100
Gooch -
   Kimberly Dawnette: 180
   Johnny Augustus: 179, 180
   Johnny Wade: 180
Gordon -
   Elizabeth: 290
Goucher -
   Clara Cleo: 92, 96

Gouy -
   Marrie: 503
Gowen -
   James Burton: 461, 462
   John Richard: 462
   Thomas: 462
   Thomas Benjamin: 455, 461-462
   Vernon Dean: 461
Grant -
   Rebecca Francis: 147
Gray -
   Douglas Edward: 154
   George Edwin: 154, 155
   Harlan Roy: 154
   Ira Dayley: 155
   Orvil Wade: 131, 153-155
Greenlee -
   Julia A.: 245
Gregory -
   Griffin: 426
   Molly M.: 426
Griffin -
   Bert Lee: 67
   Casey Lynn: 70
   Clay Randal: 70
   David Allan: 65, 68-69
   Garret Allan: 68
   Gregg Randal: 65, 70
   Haley Ann: 68
   Nikki Lynn: 62, 65, 67, 68, 69, 70
   Warren Lee: 65, 67, 69
Halbrooks -
   Audrey Jean: 272, 273, 276
   Robert Jefferson: 273

William Everett: 273
Haley -
　Abraham Jefferson: 258, 259, 264
　Jasper Newton: 259
　Larue Vivian: 230, 254-259, 263, 264, 269, 272, 276, 280
　Mark Joseph: 259
Hall -
　Carmen Denise: 100
　Dana Darleen: 95, 98-99
　David: 456
　Eli Thomas: 455, 456, 458
　Elsie Marie: 448, 453-456, 457, 458, 459, 460, 461, 463, 464, 465, 466, 467, 468
　Emily: 174
　Esther Ann: 141, 144
　Guy Kay: 213
　Iris Wynona: 193, 213
　John P.: 456
　Leland: 428
　Norma Dee: 95, 100
　Norman Russell: 92, 94-95, 97, 98, 99, 100, 101
　Roy Wells: 95, 97, 99
　Walter Preston: 97
Hamilton -
　Samuel Troy: 98
　Timothy Russell: 98
　Troy Duane: 95, 98
Hammond -
　Elizabeth: 450, 472
Hannah -
　Anita Marie: 183, 184-185
　Ashley Renee: 189
　Brian Kurt: 189
　Crystal Lynn: 189
　Derrell Lynn: 183
　Dolores Lee: 173, 175-176
　Eldon Ray: 187, 189
　Ester Elzada: 161, 163-165, 167, 168, 169, 170
　Francis Marion: 48, 49, 52, 161, 162, 165, 185
　Jackie Kathleen: 173, 177
　James Eldon: 161, 186-187, 189
　James Franklin: 22, 159-162, 164, 165, 168, 173, 176, 179, 181, 183, 185, 187
　James Wade: 49, 162, 174, 194
　John D.: 174, 194
　John Wade: 173, 174, 176
　Leonard Key: 161, 171-174, 175, 176, 177
　Leslie Jean: 183
　Leuticia: 21, 48, 49, 51, 52, 55, 58, 60, 66
　Mary: 193, 194, 197, 201
　Mary Lois: 161
　Olan Odessa: 161, 171-173, 175, 176, 177
　Ora Mae Inez: 161, 178-179, 180, 181
　Raymond Derrell: 161, 182-183, 184, 185
Harbison -
　Mary: 5, 487, 488, 489, 490, 492, 493, 496, 499, 501, 514
Harbour -
　Clarence A.: 200

Lomand Britt: 200
Ronald Dale: 196, 199-200
Harris -
Jeffie Suzanne: 213
Lonnie: 179, 181
Hart -
Effie Mae: 363, 364
John Thomas: 364
John Wesley: 364
Hartmann -
Harvey: 274
Richard Henry: 272, 274
Richard Michael: 258, 270-272, 274
Hash -
Alvin: 24
John: 24
Livonia: 21, 24, 27, 30, 77
Haskew -
Billy Clay: 134
Billy Joe: 137
Clarence Darkin: 131, 133-134, 136, 137, 138
Clayton D. Jr.: 137
Clayton Dee: 134, 137 138
Clinton: 134
Connie: 137
Connie Joe: 134
Helen: 137
Joseph Birdwell: 136
Josephine: 134
Nancy: 137
Ollie Bell: 137
Samuel Brown: 134, 136, 138
Sylvia Roberta: 134
Haskin -
Richard W.: 34

Haws -
Margaret C.: 147
Hayden -
Sophia Ann: 397, 400
Hearne -
Neal Chadwick: 40
Neal Fletcher: 40
Helvey -
Betty Imogene: 173
Prince Collins: 161, 171-173
Hemphill -
Elizabeth Irene: 80, 81
John: 81
Henderson -
Larry Dean: 213
Herr -
Wendell B.: 455, 465
Hershberger -
Daniel P.: 483
Mary D.: 482, 483
Hicks -
Jennie May: 471, 480
Hiett -
Respha Ellen: 90
Hill -
Elizabeth: 265
Hinkle -
John Brown: 423, 425
Mary A.: 422, 423, 425
Hoak -
George William: 37, 39, 41
Gladys Gertrude: 26, 37, 39, 41, 44
Hoffman -
Albert H.: 114
Mary Lucille: 89, 112-114, 115, 116

Ulie Albert: 113, 114, 116
Hogan -
  Mary: 429
Hollcroft -
  George: 456
  Isa Dora: 455, 456, 458
  Samuel D.: 456
Holley -
  Darla G.: 54
Hoot -
  Christopher Key: 175
  John Kevin: 175
  John Morgan: 173, 175
Hooten -
  Nancy Evaline: 198, 201
Hoskins -
  Mary: 193
Howard -
  Abram: 420
  Elisha: 420
  Grace: 389, 390, 392
  Mable: 419
  Mary: 419
  Roy: 419
  Ruth: 419
  Temple Worth: 413, 419-420
  Vertia: 419
  Vertie: 419
  William M.: 390
  William W.: 419, 420
  Worth: 419
Howell -
  Margaret Camelia: 327
  William Wiley: 327
Howlett -
  Carmen Roela: 89, 91-92, 95, 96, 99, 102
  John L.: 92, 96
Humes -
  Joseph Henry: 440, 444
  Nancy: 24
  Samuel: 24
Humphries -
  Ben: 471, 480
  Betty Jo: 474
  Charles Eugene: 473
  Charles William: 471, 473-475, 477, 478
  Clara Mae: 474
  Delores Fay: 474
  Franklin: 474
  George Isaac: 480
  Isaac F.: 471
  James: 471, 481
  James Henry: 474
  Jesse Martin: 471
  Johnnie: 474
  Junior: 474
  Lee Warren: 480
  Louisa Jane: 446, 447-448, 450, 451, 452, 455, 458
  Mary Elizabeth: 480
  Orville Lee: 474
  Otto Franklin: 471, 482
  Raymond: 471, 484
  Reuben Aaron: 448, 450, 452 471, 472, 475, 478
  Reuben Isaac Fletcher: 446, 469-472, 473, 474, 475, 478, 480, 481, 482, 484
  Shirley Ann: 474
  Vada Fay: 473, 477-478
  William: 450, 472

Husk -
- Jacob Christopher: 381, 384-385
- Jacob L.: 385

Huskey -
- Eula Mae: 48, 60, 61
- John R.: 60

Hutcheson -
- Sarah: 141, 144

Hutson -
- Diane Lynette: 288, 298

Ice -
- Rebecca May: 213

Inge -
- Bobby Wayne: 146
- Everett James: 131, 145-147, 148, 149, 152
- Francis Marion: 147
- Josephine: 146, 148-149, 151, 152
- Richard: 146, 147, 149

Ingram -
- Charlene Rae: 253

Jackson -
- A.J.: 310, 360, 361, 362
- Andrew Burlington: 360, 362
- Brenda Joyce: 360
- Frank Derrell: 288, 293-294
- Mary Ann: 294
- Sarah J.: 418
- Sheila Darlene: 360, 361-362

James -
- Bela Lewis: 281
- Bela Michael: 280, 281
- Marlo Jennifer: 258, 278-281

Johnson -
- Ann Marie: 336
- Byron Gregory: 337
- Claude August: 336, 338
- Ethan Michael: 337
- Hayden Andrew: 337
- Ira: 455, 460
- Jeremy Wahl: 336, 337-338
- Jimmy: 460
- Joshua Wilton: 336
- Maryanne: 460
- Robert Gene: 460
- Robert Louis: 321, 336, 337, 338
- Sarah: 479
- Sarah E.: 53
- Sarah Theresa: 336

Jones -
- James B.: 127
- Jesse John: 426
- Lara Ann: 126, 127, 129, 372
- Lydia: 232, 236
- Susan L.: 426

Juaire -
- Kaprelian Agnes Mi: 347, 351

Jump -
- Mandi Lynn: 365
- Michael Leslie: 365
- Valeria Michelle: 365

Kanutsen -
- Ura: 132

Kay -
- Betty Jo: 107
- Bobby Louis: 107, 111
- Linda Frances: 107, 108-109
- Nicholas Jordan: 111
- Paula Nell: 107, 110
- Robert Leonard: 89, 106-107, 108, 109, 110, 111

Zachary Adam: 111
Keathley -
- Derek Scott: 358
- Keith Brent: 358
- Troy David Jr.: 353, 358

Kennedy -
- Barbara Jo: 388

Kidwell -
- Malinda California: 155

King -
- John: 285, 311
- John Ted: 107, 110
- Joshua Tanner: 110
- Susannah B.: 284, 285, 289, 303, 311

Knight -
- John Elliott: 391
- Sarah Ward: 174

Kremer -
- Elizabeth: 476
- Peter Gustave: 476

Kuczka -
- Sophia Anna: 504

Lackland -
- Minerva: 63

Langston -
- Elizabeth: 53

Lankfords -
- William: 474

Lasseter -
- America Victoria: 237, 240

Lauton -
- Nancy Rebecca: 146, 147, 149

Lavender -
- Carol Marie: 235, 238-239

Leatherwood -
- John Moore: 290
- Mary Josephine: 290

Leavell -
- Edward: 226, 414
- Mary Fisher: 226, 414

Lebow -
- Jesse T.: 193, 221

Ledbetter -
- Reuben Bondurant: 31
- Vera Verta: 26, 28-29, 31, 32, 33, 35
- William Rice: 29, 31, 33, 35

Lee -
- Sophia: 127

Lemmon -
- Louisa: 49, 162
- Thomas: 49, 162

Lenerose -
- Byron Everett: 343, 344
- Tyson Craig: 344

Lewing -
- Peggy L.: 137

Ligon -
- Adrian Ray: 40
- Dennis Ray: 40
- Morgan Brittney: 40

Liston -
- James: 293-294

Little -
- Charlotte Lynette: 343
- Jethro Doyle: 309, 342-343, 344, 345
- Johnie Burns: 343, 345
- Marquita Carol: 343, 344-345
- Royce Wilton: 343

Lock -
- Johann Hubert: 476

Johann Theodore: 476
Maria Catherina: 476
Mary Josepha: 474, 476

Lohmann -
Matilda Mae: 190

Louton -
Louis Henry: 147
Nancy Rebecca: 146, 147

Loving -
Elizabeth Jane: 63
William D.: 63

Lowe -
Sandy D.: 54

Lowry -
Anderson: 312
Louisa: 312

Lucio -
Eduardo E.: 361

Lusby -
John Frederick: 53
Nora Ella: 53

Luttrell -
Martha Patsy: 456

Lybrand -
Don Bruce: 164, 169
Richard Don: 169
Vickie Renae: 169

Lykins -
Betty Rose: 371, 389-390, 391, 392, 393
Darlie Raymond: 389, 390, 392
Henry S.: 390

Lynn -
Edith: 471

Mabry -
Elizabeth: 63

MacIver -
Alison Ann: 61
Ian Richardson: 60, 61

Maddux -
Alexander: 12
Gillis: 10, 12, 17, 23, 442, 449
Mary Alma: 5, 7-10, 12, 16, 17, 23, 412, 416, 425, 440, 442, 446, 449, 485
Zepheniah: 12, 17

Maney -
Elizabeth D.: 86

Manning -
Sallie Louise: 174

Marley -
Bryan Charles: 296
Charles Victor: 288, 298
Elisha Smith: 290
John Henry: 288, 290, 292
Kelly Wade: 297
Lisa Kaye: 297
Martha Laverne: 288, 291-292
Michael Ryan: 298
Patricia Ann: 288, 293-294
Rachel Elizabeth: 298
Robert Wade: 284, 286-288, 290, 291, 292, 294, 296, 297, 298
Robert Wade Jr.: 288, 297
Steven Thomas: 296
Thomas Wayne: 288, 295-296

Marshall -
Carrie H.: 485
Charles M.: 485
Ella B.: 485
Felix Monroe: 10, 485

Larah: 485
Mabel G.: 485
Martha P.: 259
Mary E.: 485
Oliver: 485
Rollo: 485
Temperance L.: 485
Martin -
   Helen Emily: 347, 348, 350
   Thomas R.: 348
Martindale -
   Polly J.: 364
Martinez -
   Esther: 134, 137
   Zulema: 118
Mathis -
   Charles Homer: 273
   Myrtle Pauline: 273
Matranga -
   Joseph Anthony: 173, 177
   Lisa Deann: 177
   Michael Anthony: 177
Maxwell -
   Bessie Irene: 360, 362
   John D.: 362
Mayberry -
   Abraham: 418
   Elizabeth: 418
Mayfield -
   Virginia: 372
McAnear -
   Janice Carol: 310
McCasland -
   Andrew: 132
   Carrie Esther: 131, 145-146, 148, 149, 152
   Dora Elsie: 131, 153-154
   Hettie Jewel: 131, 139-140
   James: 132
   James Alexander: 131, 132, 135
   Jefferson Francis Asberry: 21, 130-132, 134, 135, 138, 140, 143, 146, 149, 154
   Ollie Belgium: 131, 133-135, 137, 138
   Verdia Ellen: 131, 142-143
McClure -
   Anna Louise: 443
McConnell -
   Vivian Maxine: 37, 38, 40, 41
McCormick -
   George: 216
   Jemima: 216
McCoy -
   Martin: 18, 23
   Rebecca: 16, 18, 23
McElroy -
   Sally Lucinda: 140, 141, 143, 144
McGehee -
   Rosa Lena: 183, 185
McGowen -
   Barbara: 477
   Charles Wesley: 477
   Elvis: 477
   Lewis: 479
   Raleigh: 477, 479
   Richard: 477
   Robert: 477
   William Jasper: 479
   William S.: 477, 479
McKenney -
   Delilah Drucilla: 290
   Zachariah: 290

McKinney -
  Sarah: 273
Meador -
  Sarah: 49, 162
Meadows -
  Alma Lena: 126, 371, 372, 378, 399
  Levi Sterling: 372
Melton -
  Brandon Wayne: 391
  John C.P.: 49, 162
  Louisa Jane: 49, 162
  Mary Adeline: 49, 52, 161, 162, 165
  Perry Wayne: 391
  William: 49, 162
Metz -
  Charles: 397, 399
  Connie Ann: 371, 395-397, 398, 399, 401, 403
Meztista -
  Elizabeth Cary: 326, 334
Michael -
  Willie Virginia: 37, 39, 41
Miller -
  Alice: 455, 463
  Catherine: 483
  Daniel Emory: 105
  John H.: 105
  Lana Ellen: 104, 105
  Mary Lucinda: 311
  Nettie M.: 496, 509
Mills -
  Mahala: 443
Milton -
  Mary E.: 174, 194

Moeller -
  Frieda: 274
  Henry Karl: 274
Molhusen -
  Serena Kay: 361
Moncrief -
  Mary Earle: 326, 327, 329
Mooney -
  Kathlelen: 301, 302
Moore -
  Nathan: 487, 493
Morehouse -
  Rosecetia Roseltha: 426
Morgan -
  Agnes Rosemary: 459
  Elizabeth: 53
  Kelly Dale: 459
  Margaret Elsie: 459
  Mary: 105
  Roy: 455, 459
  Ruby Irene: 459
Morris -
  Linnie Nancy: 245
Morrow -
  Evelyn Irene: 424, 426
  John Chapman: 426
  Thomas Vernon: 424, 426
  William Ambrose: 426
Mounts -
  Nancy Ann: 132
Mulder -
  Emily Partheny: 364
Murdock -
  Patricia J.: 288, 295-296
Nall -
  David Harris: 245

John Mark: 244, 245, 247
John Middleton: 245
Merle Modell: 230, 241-245, 247, 249, 251, 253
Neatherlin -
  Essie Lea: 62, 63, 66
  Franklin Ward: 63
  Louis Solomon: 63
Nelson -
  Betty: 235
Newkirk -
  Martha Carolina: 188
Newman -
  Jessie Earl: 22, 191-194, 196, 197, 201, 207, 213, 215, 218
  Sam Sr.: 193, 194, 197, 201
Niblake -
  Catherine: 312
Nichols -
  Celia Ann: 487, 494-497, 498, 499, 501, 507, 509, 510, 512, 514, 515
  David: 497, 499, 501, 514
Nigh -
  Abraham: 105
  Faye Beth: 104
  Iris Ann: 104
  John Warner: 105
  Marion Franklin: 104, 105
  Martha Sue: 104
  Thomas Jefferson: 89, 103-105
  Tommy Wayne: 104
  Wanda Lucille: 104
Nisle -
  Martha Carolyn: 37, 44

Nixdorf -
  Katharina: 89, 121-122, 123
Nolen -
  Mary Esther: 24
Nussbaum -
  Anna: 483
O'Briant -
  Cheatham: 450, 472
  Lucy: 448, 450, 452, 471, 472, 475, 478
Ogle -
  Nancy Alice: 364
Opsomer -
  Leo Gilbert: 74, 79
Osborn -
  Eli: 456
  Lydia M.: 456
Osterkamp -
  Mary: 506
Outhouse -
  Carl B.: 441
  Ellis Madison: 440, 441, 443
  Israel: 443
  James: 443
  Joseph Martin: 441, 443
  Joseph O.: 441
  Loretta: 441
  Marion W.: 441
  Talmadge Edwin: 441
Owen -
  Samuel Tine: 174
  Sarah Emmanitus: 174
Parrish -
  Amanda: 302
  Byron Newton: 301, 302-303
  Emily: 304

Hazel Evelyn: 284, 286-289, 291, 292, 294, 296, 297, 298
Herbert Charles: 284, 299-305
Herman Sterling: 284
Jacob Newton: 225, 282-285, 288, 289, 292, 301, 303
John Buchanan: 284, 285, 289, 303, 311
John Thomas: 309, 311, 316, 324, 345
Kyle: 302
Lona Blanche: 225, 306-311, 315, 316, 321, 324, 338, 343, 345, 347, 350
Nathan Edward: 304
Norman Wilton: 301, 304
Rachel Sarah: 304
Roberta Jean: 301, 305

Patrick -
Vivian Claire: 407

Patterson -
Sarah Elizabeth: 150

Pauley -
Ellen Jane: 10, 438-440, 441, 442, 444
Lewis: 440, 442

Payne -
Washington: 166

Payson -
Gary Leroy: 92, 94, 95
Norman Stephen: 95

Pearson -
Martha Ann: 290
Rosa Emmaline: 67

Pepperkorn -
Anna A.: 496, 510-511

Frederick William: 510, 511
William: 511

Perisich -
Denise Louise: 397, 398

Perry -
James Cecil: 164, 167
James Travis: 167
Keith Allen: 167
Mike W.: 167
Ronny: 167

Perryman -
Shirley: 113

Phillips -
Alvin: 269
Brad Reese: 258, 266-269
Mary Everly: 317

Pierce -
Leola Mae: 190

Pinkston -
Naomi Lee Tapp: 397, 399

Pitts -
Michael Wayne: 213

Porter -
Jane: 237

Post -
John Sidney: 136
Winney Josephine: 134, 136, 138

Potter -
Emily Anne: 211
Henry: 81
Jody Anson: 204, 210-211
Martha: 81

Pound -
Keziah Jane: 429

Powell -
Elizabeth: 12

Prewett -
 Annis: 446, 449
Proctor -
 Myra Margaret: 331
 Samuel Joseph: 331
 Walter Jackson: 331
 Walter Phillip: 326, 331
Pruett -
 Mary A.: 409-412
Pruitt -
 Andrew J.: 449
 Catherine Elaine: 394
 Patience: 90
Pyles -
 James: 53
 Tommie Eliza: 53
Rainwater -
 Darla Denise: 151
 Harve Mark: 148, 151
Ramsey -
 Nancy Summerfield: 462
Read -
 Elizabeth: 26, 30, 39
Redder -
 Hannah Elizabeth: 220
 Joseph Albert: 220
 Vincent Paul: 215, 219-220
Reed -
 Edith: 471, 481
Reeves -
 Martha Cathern: 230, 232, 236, 240
Reid -
 Lavonne: 65, 70
 Mary: 81
Renegar -
 Mary W.: 78

Renshaw -
 Nancy: 456
Reynolds -
 Aaron John: 402
 Anne Elizabeth: 407, 408
 Briana Nicole: 403
 Clarence Chalmer: 371, 406-407
 David Alan: 397, 402
 Debra Jean: 389, 391, 392
 Gary Wayne: 397, 398, 399
 Herman Atwood: 371, 389, 391, 392, 393, 394
 Hunter Faye: 403
 James Randall: 407
 James Roscoe: 225, 368-372, 378, 382, 386, 389, 392, 397, 399
 James Weldon: 371, 395-397, 398, 399, 400, 401, 402, 403
 John Andrew: 126, 127, 129, 372
 Jordan Andrew: 402
 Joshua Duane: 394
 Justin Duane: 394
 Kenneth Lee: 400
 Kenneth Wade: 397, 400-401
 Lennie: 54
 Linda Kay: 389, 393
 Marjorie Helen: 371, 373-378, 381, 382, 386, 388
 Michael Bruce: 397, 403
 Miranda Lynn: 403
 Monty Duane: 389, 394
 Norris Truett: 126, 128-129

Renee Christian: 400
Shanta Susan: 400
Spencer: 127
Stephen James: 402
Verna Evelyn: 371, 404-405
William Rufus: 21, 125-127, 129, 371, 372, 378, 399

Rhoades -
David: 508
Eliza Jane: 507, 508
Eula May: 225, 227-230, 232, 235, 236, 240, 244, 247, 258, 264
Jacob: 232, 236
Sylvester Jacob: 230, 232, 236, 240

Rhodes -
Rose Ann: 204, 205-206

Richardson -
Mary Ann: 10, 16

Richey -
Mary: 132

Rinesmith -
Harold Walter: 507
Henry: 508
John: 508
Walter C.: 496, 507-508
William: 507, 508

Ritchie -
Allen: 326, 330
Mary Catherine: 330
Michael Weir: 330

Robbins -
Martha B.: 456

Roberson -
Byno Lou: 131, 139-141
Donald Ralph: 143
Doris Dean: 140
Herold Wade: 143
Hezekiah Charles: 141, 144
Jackie Junior: 143
James: 141, 144
James Lafayette: 140, 141, 143, 144
Loretta Faye: 143
Mary Rebecca: 136
Maurice Errol: 131, 142-144
Maurice Ray: 143
Myrtle Marie: 140
Walter Gene: 140

Roberts -
Bama Loine: 32, 34, 35
Jim Bob: 32
Jimmy Edward: 29, 32, 35
Terry Edward: 32
Trena Nell: 32

Robertson -
Annie Rebecca: 428, 429, 431, 434
David: 429

Robinson -
Dicy E.: 105
Mayme Elizabeth: 273

Rockenbaugh -
Claudine Marie: 353, 357

Ross -
Susannah: 290

Ruffin -
Leverta: 263, 265
Nicholas Cornelius: 265

Russell -
Elizabeth: 412

Ryals -
Alton Durwood: 474

Ryan -
  Ethel: 461, 462
Ryland -
  Hannah M.: 105
Sanchez -
  Rodolpho David: 95, 101
Sanders -
  Allie Caroline: 455, 457
  LaNelle: 471, 484
  Ora Maggie: 244, 245, 247
  Samuel J.: 457
  Thomas J.: 245
  William Jacob: 245
Sansom -
  Mary Elizabeth: 78
  Thomas Lackey: 78
Sawyer -
  Karen Gayle: 258, 278, 280
  Louisa Elizabeth: 423, 425
Scheulen -
  Anna Gertrude: 476
  Maria Josepha: 476
  Peter Wilhelm: 476
Scholfield -
  Florence Martha: 74, 80, 81
  Frank Edgar: 80, 81
  James S.: 81
  James W.: 81
Schreiner -
  Josephine: 321, 322, 324, 338
Scott -
  Burton: 54
  Charles Glen: 498, 504
  Charles Henry: 496, 498, 500, 501, 502, 503, 504, 505, 506
  Ella Mae: 498, 500-501
  Floyd: 498, 506
  Genevia A.: 502
  John T.: 498, 501
  Joseph H.: 498, 503
  Lois: 498, 505
  Marleen: 51, 54
  Rolla Walter: 498, 502
  Wilton R.: 502
Sharp -
  Fernanda Columbus: 31
  Rose Lee: 29, 31, 33, 35
Shaw -
  Mary Elizabeth: 114
  Samuel Crawford: 114
Sheaffer -
  Eve: 508
Sheibley -
  Abraham: 508
  Susanna: 508
Shelton -
  Bruce Glenn: 56
  Harriett: 31
  Jimmy Earl: 51, 56, 57, 58
  Karen Larue: 56, 57-58
  Laura Lynn: 56
  Louise: 474
  William Maurice: 56, 58
Sheppard -
  Lawrence Bartlett: 198, 201
  Ozro Sr.: 196, 198, 201, 207
  Thelma Mae: 193, 195-196, 198, 200, 201, 204, 207
Shewmake -
  Buster: 217

Sherry Annette: 215, 217
Silva -
   Marilyn: 343
Simmons -
   Sarah M.: 479
   Wiley: 479
Sims -
   Sarah Frances: 259
Slaughter -
   Arric Missouri: 343, 345
Smith -
   Bessie: 413, 427-428, 429, 430, 431, 432, 434, 436
   Bobbie June: 179
   Fannie: 273
   John Calvin: 428, 429, 431, 434
   Sarah M.: 259
Souther -
   Barbara Lynn: 196, 202-204, 206, 207, 209, 211
   Melvin Herman: 204, 207
Spangler -
   Donna Jo: 215, 217
Spears -
   Betha Mahala: 215, 216, 218
   John Rufus: 216
Spradlin -
   Elizabeth Frances: 164, 166, 168
   Thomas Edward: 166
Stanfield -
   Jacob: 418
   John: 418
   Louisa Carolina: 417, 418
Starbird -
   Bryn Ellen: 305

Michael Peter: 301, 305
Talley Kate: 305
William Brinton: 305
Steggall -
   Olive Linda: 513
Stephens -
   Janice Darlene: 164, 169
   Sherry Jo: 164, 170
   Wanda Joy: 164, 167-168
   Wilburn Elton: 161, 163-164, 166, 167, 168, 169, 170
   Wiley Emmanuel: 164, 166, 168
Stephenson -
   Harry S.: 235
   Jennie Esther: 230, 233-235
Stewart -
   Charles Aulston: 317
   Hattie Estella: 315, 317
   Rufus Kirk: 317
Stogsdill -
   Brenda Jane: 466
   Claud Howard: 455, 464
   Claudia: 464
   Larry Dale: 464
   Leonard Dale: 466
   Michael James: 466
   Odis: 455, 466
   Terry Marie: 464
Stone -
   Arty: 390
Storey -
   Jami Kristine: 388
   Joseph Gregory: 388
   Kirk Gregory: 377, 387-388
   Melvin Leonard: 388

Stowers -
  Fanny: 443
Strahan -
  Edward Oscar: 114
  Winifred Pearl: 113, 114, 116
Strikmiller -
  Leslie J.: 321, 340
Stubbs -
  Jerry Lynn: 432
  Sheila Renee: 435
  Sid Richard: 435
  Truman Combest: 428, 432, 433, 434, 435
  Truman Kenneth: 432, 435
  Wanda Vonciel: 432, 433-434
Stumpf -
  Anna Catherina: 18
Sturgill -
  Theodocia: 24
Sullivan -
  Charles Roger: 430
  James Roger: 428, 430
  Jimmy Dwayne: 430
  Rodera Fay: 430
Syptak -
  Albert Benjamin Jr.: 275
  Ashton Lee: 275
  Bennett Ryan: 275
  Stephen Bennett: 272, 275
Talhouk -
  A.M.: 251
  Abbat Anthony: 251
  Najib A.: 244, 250-251
  Najib Jr.: 251
Talley -
  Edrie Maurice: 284, 299-301, 302, 303, 304, 305
  Robert Byron: 301, 303
  Samuel Donald: 303
Tapp -
  James William: 371, 373-377, 379, 381, 382, 386, 388
  Jesse Lee: 377, 379, 382, 386
  John William: 379
  Tammy Jo: 377, 387-388
  Terri Lynn: 377, 380-382, 385, 386
  Wiley Doke: 379
Teal -
  Rebecca Adaline: 166
Terrill -
  Virginia: 216
Thomas -
  Jacinda Lynn: 57
  Margaret: 462
  Robert William Jr.: 57
  Rowdy Wayne: 57
Thompson -
  Edith Jane: 166
  Mary: 24
  Rosita Tuerecta: 56, 58
  Sarah Celesten: 114
Thornberry -
  Sarah Elizabeth: 379
Thorpe -
  Rebecca: 440, 442
Tipton -
  Mary Ann: 90
Tite -
  Harriet: 225, 226, 231, 236, 413, 414, 416, 425
  Valentine: 226, 414
Toole -
  Maye: 440

Touma -
  Elane: 251
Townsend -
  Floyd Eugene: 107, 108
  Nancy Ann: 90
  Robert Bolling: 90
  Shelly Lynn: 108
Trudgen -
  Heath Lee: 367
  Justin Lee: 367
Turner -
  Felix J. II: 321, 340
  Felix Johnson: 340
  Lauren Elizabeth: 340
  Mariah Jane: 259
Underwood -
  Charlotte Ilene: 361
  Mary Elizabeth: 21, 74, 76, 77, 79, 80, 82, 83
  Veda Vell: 288, 295-296
Van Hoose -
  James MacDonald: 157
Vanderford -
  Darrel Ray: 173
Vanderkaay -
  David William: 57
  Shelbi Nicole: 57
Vawter -
  Cathy Lynn: 107, 111
Voightmann -
  Augusta Caroline: 274
Vondell -
  Nanalee: 92, 102
Wahl -
  Marion Theresa: 336, 338
Walker -
  Deloris Loraine: 244, 252-253
  James Fred: 183, 185
  John Earl: 253
  Lena Marie: 161, 182-183, 184, 185
Wall -
  Nancy A.: 10, 438-440
Wallace -
  Bert: 371, 404-405
  Diana Grace: 405
  Timothy Reynolds: 405
Walsh -
  Oscar Leonard: 67
  Rosa lee: 67, 69
Ward -
  Hattie Alma: 76, 78
  Hugh Thomas: 78
  Margaret Maria: 63
  William C.: 78
Watson -
  Teresia S.: 385
Wear -
  Hamilton Bradford: 90
  Mary Ann: 89, 90, 93, 109, 119, 124
Webster -
  Gayle: 118
Weinrich -
  Mary L.: 235, 238-239
Weir -
  William: 90
Wells -
  Julia Maude: 97
Welsh -
  Anna: 420
Welty -
  Bertha Lee: 74, 76, 78
  Christian: 78

Henry: 78
John Henry: 76, 78
Westmoreland -
　Rebecca: 216
Whatley -
　Michelle Elaine: 355
Whitman -
　Joe Burl: 281
　Mary Betty: 280, 281
Whitson -
　Horace Edwin: 189, 190
　Judy Marie: 189-190
Wiatt -
　Rosamond: 226, 414
Wiley -
　Joe: 422
　Larry Glen: 424
　William Melvin: 422
　William Walter: 413, 422-423, 424, 425
　William Warren: 422, 423, 425
　Wilton English: 422, 424-425
　Wilton Madison: 424
Wilkinson -
　Mai Belle: 301, 303
Williams -
　Annie Mable: 97
　Ester Lavonia: 67
　Jasper Newton: 90
　Joseph Soloman: 89, 90, 93, 109, 119, 124
　Nancy Ann: 21, 89, 90, 92, 93, 96, 104, 107, 109, 113, 116, 117, 119, 122, 124
　Sarah Elizabeth: 265
Williamson -
　Linda May: 204, 208-209

Willmon -
　Crystal Michelle: 361
　Noble Montgomery: 360, 361
　Noble Oran: 361
　Shawn Christopher: 361
Wilson -
　Hamilton Benjamin: 86
　Martha Ann: 85, 86
　Sarah Elizabeth: 157, 158
Wilton -
　Aaron Norvell: 357
　Aaron Zanoah: 258, 260-264
　Alva Eulene: 113, 115-116
　Alvin Henry: 21, 47-48, 51, 52, 55, 58, 60, 66, 89, 112-113, 115, 116
　Amy Rosalie: 225, 282-284, 288, 289, 292, 301, 303
　Angela Kay: 54
　Baily May: 209
　Baylor Christian: 253
　Benjamin Harrison: 22, 156-157
　Bertha Pauline: 440, 441-442
　Betty Lou: 46
　Billy Duane: 89, 121-122, 123, 124
　Blake Joseph: 209
　Blanche Mae: 440, 444
　Bobbye Loine: 29, 32, 33, 35
　Brady Don: 209
　Carless Carl: 74, 75-77
　Catherine Elizabeth: 321, 340
　Cathy Ann: 436
　Celia E.: 509
　Cecil Don: 196, 202-204, 206, 207, 209, 211

Wilton - (Con't)
- Cecil Winfred: 193
- Charlene Lenoy: 310, 360, 361, 362
- Charles: 5, 486-487, 488, 489, 490, 492, 493, 496, 499, 501, 514
- Charles Anthony: 230, 241-244, 247, 249, 251, 253
- Charles Freedis: 10, 13-17, 21, 23, 27, 30, 77, 225, 231, 236
- Charles Joseph: 225, 306-310, 315, 316, 321, 324, 338, 343, 345, 347, 350, 353, 354, 356, 359, 360, 362, 363
- Charles Joseph Jr.: 310, 359
- Charles Joseph III: 359
- Charles Shadrach: 487
- Charles Vernon: 309, 321, 323-324
- Charles Vernon Jr.: 323
- Charles Virgil: 46
- Christopher Dennis: 323
- Christopher James: 357
- Cindy Ranee: 43
- Clyde Chalmer: 230, 254-258, 263, 264, 269, 272, 276, 280
- Colleen Rebecca: 310, 363, 365, 366, 367
- Connie Charles: 244, 246-247
- Cora Belle: 74, 79
- Cory Wayne: 204, 209
- Curtis Lee: 244, 252-253
- Cyrus: 21, 84-85

David Alan: 44
David Nichols: 510
David Van: 321, 339
David Patrick: 339
Deborah Agnes: 321, 336, 338
Eater Virgil: 26, 45-46
Edna I.: 509
Effa Belle: 22, 159-161, 165, 168, 173, 176, 179, 181, 183, 185, 187
Elbert Claud: 193
Elena Loree: 357
Elizabeth Emeline: 487
Ellen: 10, 485
Elmer Elisha: 225, 227-231, 235, 236, 240, 244, 247, 258, 264
Emerson Van: 309, 318-321, 323, 324, 326, 329, 336, 338, 339, 340
Emma Livona: 21, 130-131, 134, 135, 138, 140, 143, 146, 149, 154
Erastus: 412
Ethan Coe: 253
Everett Waylin: 51, 54-55
Frank Edward: 37, 44
Franklin: 10
Freedus Ezra: 21, 25-27, 29, 30, 33, 35, 37, 39, 41
Genevieve: 339
George Keith: 37, 38-39, 40, 41
George Keith Jr.: 38, 42-43
Gerald Ray: 122, 123-124
Gerald Ray Jr.: 123
Gilbert Douglas: 436
Gladys Nell: 89, 106-107, 108,

Wilton - (Con't)
109, 111
- Haley Nicole: 280
- Harold Emerson: 323
- Harriet Caroline: 487, 493
- Harriett Carrie: 413, 417
- Helen Ruth: 89, 117, 118, 119
- Henry: 1-6, 11, 17, 23, 442, 449, 487, 490, 492, 499
- Henry Franklin: 16, 222-225, 230, 231, 236, 240, 284, 289, 303, 309, 310, 316, 324, 345, 354, 356, 362, 371, 378, 399
- Holland: 225
- Ida May: 21, 76, 125-126, 129
- Ida May: 496, 498-499, 500, 501, 502, 503, 504, 505, 506
- Ira Gayle: 113
- Ira John: 21, 87-89, 92, 93, 96, 102, 104, 107, 109, 113, 116, 117, 119, 122, 124
- Isaac H.: 440
- James Everett: 48, 50-52, 54, 55, 56, 58
- Janice Darlene: 92, 94-96, 98, 99, 100, 101
- Jeffrey Scott: 123
- Jesse Ruell: 26, 28-30, 32, 33, 35
- Jessica Lynn: 206
- Jimmy Dale: 113
- John: 412
- John M.: 193
- John Richard: 213
- Johnie Melvin: 22, 191-193, 196, 197, 201, 207, 213, 215, 218
- Jonna Kay: 42
- Joseph C.: 10, 409-413, 415, 416, 417, 419, 421, 422, 425, 428, 431, 434
- Joseph Charles: 496, 509
- Joseph Clifford: 510
- Joseph Drexel: 428, 436
- Joseph Franklin: 487, 494-496, 498, 499, 501, 507, 509, 510, 512, 514, 515
- Joseph S.: 413, 427-428, 430, 431, 432, 434, 436
- Josie Celia: 496
- Judy Inez: 60, 61
- Kathy Ilene: 258, 270-272, 275, 276, 277
- Kimberly Faye: 38, 40-41
- Larry Mac: 43
- Laura Ann: 487
- Laura Caroline: 496
- Lee Anne: 204, 210-211
- Lee O'Norvell: 310, 352-354, 355, 356, 357, 358
- Leland Norvell: 353, 357
- Letha Fay: 353, 358
- Lloyd Orville: 193, 212-213
- Lois: 85
- Lona Oretha: 309, 341
- Loretta Lynn: 213
- Lou D.: 89, 91-93, 95, 96, 99, 102
- Luther Eppie: 26, 36-37, 39, 41, 44
- Luther Virgil: 230, 233-236, 240

Wilton - (Con't)
- Luther Virgil Jr.: 235, 238-240
- Macey Louise: 280
- Margaret: 428
- Margie: 85
- Margie Nell: 196, 199-201
- Marion Grady: 21
- Mark Edward: 44
- Mark Terrance: 323
- Marlin Don: 204, 205-207
- Martha: 413, 419
- Martha Jane: 487
- Mary: 413, 421
- Mary Alma: 225, 368-371, 377, 378, 382, 386, 389, 392, 397, 399, 405, 407
- Mary Elizabeth: 10, 445-446, 448, 449, 452, 471, 475, 478
- Mary Ella: 38, 496, 507
- Mary Francis: 436
- Mary Jo: 321, 325-326, 328, 329, 330, 331, 332, 334, 335
- Mary Lucille: 89, 103-104
- Maude: 413
- Melba Louise: 193, 221
- Melvin Cleo: 48, 59-60, 61
- Melvin Wayman: 193, 195-197, 200, 201, 204, 207
- Michael: 513
- Michael Don: 206
- Michell Lynn: 43
- Monty Eugene: 102
- Neal Dwayne: 54
- Nichols: 496, 510
- Nola E.: 74, 82
- Nola Oletha: 309, 342-343, 344, 345
- Nona: 413, 422, 424, 425
- Nona Fay: 428, 430-431
- Ora Izora: 48, 62, 65, 66, 69, 71
- Ora Lenora: 51, 56, 58
- Paul L.: 510
- Raymond Eugene: 310
- Regina Fawncyne: 258, 266-269
- Robert E.: 513
- Robert Harry: 512, 513-514
- Roland Wayne: 102
- Ronnie Mack: 60
- Rosa: 412
- Rudolph: 10, 438-440, 441, 442, 444
- Ruel Calvin: 74, 80
- Samuel Harris: 85
- Sarah Agnes: 487, 488-490, 491, 492
- Sarah Frances: 413, 415-416
- Sarah L.: 496, 515
- Sharon: 60
- Silas: 21, 72-74, 76, 77, 79, 80, 82, 83
- Sophia: 5, 516
- Stanley: 258, 278-280
- Sylvia Leora: 74
- Terri Lynn: 353, 355-356
- Thomas: 5, 7-11, 16, 17, 23, 412, 413, 416, 425, 440, 442, 446, 449, 485
- Thomas Abslum: 16, 19-23, 26, 27, 30, 39, 52, 74, 77, 85, 89, 93, 109, 119, 124, 126, 129, 135, 157,

Wilton - (Con't)
    161, 165, 185, 193, 197, 201
  Thomas Erastus: 21
  Thomas Vester: 309, 313-316
  Timmy: 102
  Toni Dell: 244, 250-251
  Treva Daphane: 244, 248-249
  Vanessa Rhae: 43
  Vanzant V.: 413, 437
  Velma Lucile: 74, 83
  Veria F.: 359
  Verna Faye: 309, 346-347, 350, 351
  Vernie F.: 359
  Virgie Vivian: 428, 432, 433, 434, 435
  Virgil: 225
  Walter Ralph: 512
  Walter W.: 496, 512, 513, 514
  Warren: 46
  William Henry: 487
  Wilma Fasline: 193, 214-215, 217, 218, 219

Wimpee -
  Cynthia Joy: 272, 277
  David Randall: 258, 270-273, 275, 276, 277
  Joseph Edward: 273
  Justin David: 272
  Robert Lee: 272, 273, 276
  Sherah Rebecca: 272, 275-276
  Warner Eugene: 273

Womack -
  Ann: 418

Woodburn -
  Mary Spray: 105

Woods -
  Georgia Alice: 216

Worley -
  Harold Leonard: 269
  Robert Monroe: 258, 266-269

Wright -
  Ann: 450, 472

Yaw -
  Wilma Anita: 310, 359

Young -
  Mary Ellen: 86
  Max L.: 353

Youngblood -
  W.W.: 489

Younger -
  Gladys Greta: 424, 426
  William Nathan: 426

Zimmerman -
  Susan Catherine: 508